COMPARATIVE POLITICS

Nations and Theories in a Changing World

Second Edition

Lawrence C. Mayer

Texas Tech University

John H. Burnett

Texas Tech University

Suzanne Ogden

Northeastern University

Prentice Hall, Upper Saddle River, New Jersey   07458

Library of Congress Cataloging-in-Publication Data

Mayer, Lawrence C.
    Comparative politics : nations and theories in a changing world /
Lawrence C. Mayer, John H. Burnett, Suzanne Ogden. — 2nd ed.
        p.   cm.
    Includes bibliographical references and index.
    ISBN 0–13-373325–4
    1. Comparative government.   I. Burnett, John H.   II. Ogden,
Suzanne.   III. Title.
JF51.M44235   1996
320.3—dc20   95–34433
                                                         CIP

For Judy
and for Gabrielle, Arthur, Scotty, Joshua, and Etta

Acquisitions editor: Michael Bickerstaff
Editorial assistant: Anita Castro
Editorial/production supervision
  and interior design: Darrin Kiessling
Copy editor: Sherry Babbitt
Cover director: Jane Conte
Buyer: Bob Anderson

 © 1996, 1993 by Prentice-Hall, Inc.
Simon & Schuster/A Viacom Company
Upper Saddle River, New Jersey 07458

Printed in the United States of America
10 9 8 7 6 5 4 3 2

ISBN 0-13-373325-4

Prentice-Hall International (UK) Limited, *London*
Prentice-Hall of Australia Pty. Limited, *Sydney*
Prentice-Hall Canada Inc., *Toronto*
Prentice-Hall Hispanoamericana, S.A., *Mexico*
Prentice-Hall of India Private Limited, *New Delhi*
Prentice-Hall of Japan, Inc., *Tokyo*
Simon & Schuster Asia Pte. Ltd., *Singapore*
Editora Prentice-Hall do Brasil, Ltda., *Rio de Janeiro*

Contents

Chapter 8   The Nature of Political Development in the People's Republic of China   296

PART THREE   POLITICS IN LESS DEVELOPED COUNTRIES

Chapter 9   The Third World and Political Development   321

Preface

Faced with the plethora of new and established textbooks for a course called "Comparative Politics," the prospective author of an addition to this literature is faced with the formidable task of justifying the book. The mere claim that it is the most up-to-date contribution is inadequate justification, although being up-to-date is a considerable accomplishment in context of the rapid changes that constitute a theme of this book. A new book will quickly lose the glitter of being up-to-date. The unfolding of events soon overtakes that claim, and a more up-to-date book will soon be off the presses. Rather, the decision to write another textbook for an already crowded market should be based upon the intention to produce a work that is somehow unique in what it attempts to do.

It seems to us that a textbook should seek to carve out a distinctive place for itself, to go beyond the presentation of descriptive information about a series of governments, although the presentation of such information is needed. The contribution we hope to make with this volume is not only to present both theoretical and country studies, but to link the two kinds of material to provide coherent perspectives on the bewildering onslaught of changes that beset the world of politics.

Change itself is a vague theme, unless the content of that change is specified. Several patterns have emerged in the late 1980s and early 1990s on which we focus in the second edition of this volume. The most predominant change in the world of this period is the widespread transformation from authoritarian to democratic political formats, which includes the collapse of the Soviet Empire. The collapse of that empire allowed the emergence of a second major pattern—the rise to preeminence of the politics of ethnic or cultural defense, or the politics of irredentism. This phenomenon, which the present authors identified in 1977 as a growing force, has changed the face of cleavages in particular and politics in general in the democratic West as well as the less developed nations of Latin America, Africa, and Asia. The consequent loss of a sense of community, or "nationhood," among many of the states of the world and the consequences of this explosion of the crisis of community for the structures and processes of nation-states are explored throughout the book. We have also continued to explore the growing importance of the technocracy throughout the world, manifested through such phenomena as the growth of public bureaucracy and corporatism, which lead to a convergence of the nature of political processes in much of the industrialized world, a convergence that may spread to the less industrialized systems as they advance their state of technology.

The very phenomenon of rapid and fundamental change both challenges and renders the task of finding patterns in that change more crucial than ever. It is through the discernment of such patterns that the events of the contemporary world acquire meaning. We work from the assumption that unless raw information about politics is incorporated in some theoretic framework, it is meaningless.

Yet, theory constructed independently of data degenerates into an exercise in metaphysics. Theory should be applied to actual political structures and events. We therefore present the theory chapters as the introduction to a section on a category of nations, and then make a serious effort to construct the following country chapters to utilize and liberally refer to the theory chapters. The book is written without assuming that the student has any prior familiarity with either the theoretical literature or the politics and societies of the foreign systems that are covered. It is presented with the hope and expectation that students want more than information about other governments. A theoretical and explanatory perspective will allow the students both to enjoy the acquisition of this material and to retain it more effectively. Isolated data are quickly forgotten, while an understanding of structures, processes, and trends often stays with students after the course is over.

We wish to stress that we have written and organized this text to accommodate diverse perspectives on what comparative politics ought to encompass. Therefore, while we have striven for a measure of coherence among the diverse parts of this text, we have written and organized it so that each chapter can stand on its own, if desired. This will give instructors flexibility in the order and content of their courses. Some instructors may choose to skip the theoretically organized chapters (1, 2, 6, and 9) and move directly to the country chapters. The country chapters may be read in this way on their own. In particular, some instructors will undoubtedly feel that a consideration of the methodological issues raised in Chapter 1 does not belong in any undergraduate text. However, given the fact that modern comparative analysis is defined as a method, many instructors will think that the logic of comparison should be part of a core course in comparative politics. The feedback we have received takes both sides of this question. Hence, we feel that this unique contribution of our book should remain available to those who wish to use it.

The principal authors of this text, Lawrence C. Mayer and John H. Burnett, are grateful to Suzanne Ogden for the skill and professional manner with which she has contributed and now updated the chapter on China. China is too important a system to ignore, and the book clearly would be less complete without it. The principal authors have made the remaining chapters a cooperative effort from the outset. It can be fairly said that we jointly stand behind each of the interpretations made and conclusions drawn throughout the work.

In this second edition, in addition to a new chapter on Latin America, every chapter was substantially rewritten and updated in an effort to keep the book abreast of the unfolding of events and to reconsider the conclusions and inferences we have drawn. While many changes are dealt with and incorporated into the text, the main conclusions and generalizations of the first edition have been, we feel, reinforced rather than undermined by subsequent world events.

We are grateful to the anonymous reviewers of this text for their serious, constructive analyses. We have carefully considered each of their suggestions and incorporated many of them into the manuscript. We are especially grateful to Gary Elbow of Texas Tech University, whose expertise on Latin America and guidance helped immeasurably in preparing the new chapter on that area, and to Mr. Kalu Kalu, III, also of Texas Tech University, who shared his expert knowledge on his native country of Nigeria. Naturally, we assume full responsibility for any errors of fact and judgment that remain.

The authors are grateful to Prentice Hall for the encouragement and faith in this project that made a second edition possible. We are especially grateful for the skillful assistance of Nicole Signoretti, who helped guide the effort through editorial changes, and to the new editor, Michael Bickerstaff.

Lawrence C. Mayer
John H. Burnett
Suzanne Ogden

1

Introduction

"Books must follow sciences, and not sciences books."

Francis Bacon

Science is a concept that brings a positive image and a measure of legitimacy to an academic enterprise carrying that label. On the one hand, social scientists have long suffered a certain loss of respect because of the widespread perception that their work is not science. On the other hand, natural scientists are frequently regarded with a certain amount of awe because of the widespread identification of their efforts with science. Hence, in the 1950s many political scientists, along with other social scientists, began an effort to transform their field into one that enjoyed the many benefits of scientific respectability. Comparative politics, until that time always regarded as a subfield of political science, played a leading role in this effort.[1] In so doing, many of the leading scholars in comparative politics attempted to transform fundamentally their subfield into an integral part of "scientific" political science. This effort was only incompletely successful, and left the field of comparative politics internally divided and without a widely accepted sense of its own identity.

As any textbook that presumes to function as a core source for the field must do, this volume takes account of this internal disagreement. As such, it will present the materials studied in comparative politics from more than one perspective. The basic disagreement among scholars of comparative politics is whether the field should be defined by its goal—to make political science scientifically respectable—or by its subject—nations other than the United States. These two perspectives are summarized in Table 1-1.

Scholars who take the former position emphasize the process of generalizing across national and cultural boundaries—the process of being comparative. They are less interested in given nations as such than in how patterns of political phenomena appear across nations. Scholars who take the latter position are more interested in investigating the arrangement of factors within a given nation. By emphasizing the uniqueness of each such arrangement, and by stressing that the meaning of any social or political phenomenon is affected by the national setting in which it occurs, this latter group of scholars in effect deny the feasibility of generalizing about such phenomena across national borders. One cannot generalize about labor-based parties, for instance, because the very nature of each such party is a product of the unique arrangement of historical, geographical, cultural, and technological factors that

TABLE 1-1   Two Perspectives on Comparative Politics

The Traditional Perspective	*The Explanatory Perspective*
Defines the field geographically as the study of foreign governments	Defines the field as a method of applying explanatory generalizations in a variety of national settings or of generalizing about the impact of the attributes of whole systems on such generalizations
Assumes that since political phenomena are unique, it is meaningless to generalize about them because they are inseparable from the pattern of other factors in that context	Assumes one can meaningfully generalize about political phenomena independently of their context
Purpose of political analysis is essentially descriptive. The scientific method is inappropriate for the study of human behavior	Purpose of political analysis is explanatory. The structure of scientific explanation applies to the study of politics with some modifications
Focuses attention on constitutionally designated structures of major Western powers	Focuses on contextual factors weakening boundaries between political science and other social sciences
Presents analyses on a country-by-country basis	Presents material topically, generalizing across national and cultural boundaries
Relies on impressionistic understanding of political phenomena	Seeks to gather sensory data to test propositions that could be falsified by such data

make up the context in which each occurs. The position of these scholars is that nations should be studied one at a time as a unique arrangement of phenomena.

Hence, the field of comparative politics is internally divided as to its very nature. Those scholars who seek to transform the field into one with scientific respectability stress the effort at generalizing across national and cultural boundaries as the core of what comparative politics has to contribute to political science. For them, the reason for the existence of comparative politics is its role in developing cross-nationally valid explanations of political phenomena. The second group stresses the in-depth description and impressionistic understanding of various nations considered one at a time. This group rejects the explanatory purpose of comparative politics as unfeasible at this time. Moreover, it argues that students of comparative politics are so lacking in the basic information about the structures and processes of foreign govern-

ments that any attempt to speak theoretically about patterns in such countries would be meaningless. One must know how these different governments operate before generalizing about them. Hence, even if the development of cross-nationally valid explanatory theory is ultimately feasible, the acquisition of basic information about other countries must precede this lofty goal at the undergraduate level.

This textbook, in attempting to present the field of comparative politics in its diverse aspects accurately, will alternate between the comparative, generalizing, and theoretical material on the one hand and the country-by-country description of political phenomena on the other. The combination of these two approaches between the covers of the same book affords the authors the opportunity to bridge in some small measure the gap between what has heretofore been two distinct enterprises. Hence, the country studies will note the relevance of material in the theory chapters and the theory chapters will make liberal references to data in the country chapters. Theory, after all, should be about data, and data become meaningless unless incorporated into some kind of theoretic framework.

Despite this attempt to present and in some measure accommodate both of these different and in some respects incompatible views of comparative politics, the authors are sympathetic to the presumption that goals of generalizing across nations and explaining political phenomena are both feasible and desirable. In this view, and for the purposes of this text, the very definition of comparative politics is the construction of such cross-nationally applicable generalizations. When these generalizations logically imply facts or events, these facts or events are "explained." By this definition, explanatory generalizations may draw data from any relevant setting, and the United States is thus no longer off-limits to students of comparative politics. Studies drawn from single countries or geographic regions may be part of the enterprise of comparative political analysis if they are framed in such theoretic terms that their findings are potentially applicable to diverse national or cultural settings. Hence, the country or regional studies presented in this volume, while hopefully meeting the criteria of those who prefer a country-by-country perspective, are not necessarily inconsistent with a comparative perspective.

In seeking to support the explanatory rather than merely descriptive purpose of political science to which lip service has been widely given in the post–World War II era, comparative politics has become the only subfield of political science that defines itself methodologically rather than by the subject matter studied. Supporters of this view argue that comparative political analysis is a method, one that plays an invaluable role in the enterprise of building scientifically re-

spectable explanatory theory of political phenomena. It is important to understand the logic of this argument in order to understand the underlying purpose of much of what goes in comparative politics.

THE LOGIC OF COMPARATIVE ANALYSIS

The argument presented here is that comparative analysis is one of three methods used to overcome the overriding problem in formulating scientific explanations in social science research: the fact that social and political phenomena are the product of more factors than can be analyzed in any given study.[2] For example, if one wanted a complete explanation of the prevalence of political violence in a particular setting, one would have to account not only for the impact of such factors as all the relevant aspects of the history, culture, social and political structures, demography, and geography, but also for the behaviors and interactions of every significant participant in the events to be explained. Such a task would be beyond the life's work of any scholar. Hence, in social science, only some of the potential causal factors are analyzed, and all explanations are incomplete, while in the natural or physical sciences, explanations are more nearly complete.

However, the structure of any scientifically respectable explanation is the same regardless of the subject. The phenomenon to be explained is shown to be a particular case of a general statement of a relationship between concepts or categories of phenomena. For example, assume the fact to be explained is the Labour Party vote of an Indian émigré in Great Britain, a person whose socioeconomic status is clearly lower class. One may "understand" such a vote as a particular case of the proposition that lower-class members of frequently oppressed ethnic or racial minorities tend to vote for parties of the left. Since this individual is such a minority in this context, and since the Labour Party is the viable alternative on the political left, the case is scientifically "explained" by this general proposition. The individual case can be logically derived from the general proposition such that if the proposition were true, this case is what one should logically find in these circumstances. Such an explanatory proposition gives us the basis to predict the behavior of other cases not yet observed. Given the truth of the foregoing proposition, for example, it would be logical to expect that lower-class Hispanics and blacks in the United States would vote for the Democratic Party.

Implicitly, a proposition such as this infers causation. *Inference* is the mental process of moving from what is directly observed to a conclusion with some interpretation. The inference in this case is that there is something about the essential properties of being an oppressed minority and of voting for a party of the left such that the former properties cause the latter. In this way, the construction of explanatory theory allows us to draw inferences from the necessarily limited body of directly observed phenomena to an infinite class of expectations in given circumstances.

The ability to predict based on an explanation is one way of distinguishing an explanation that is scientific from one that is spurious, or not due to actual causation. An explanation that generates precise predictions is testable. We tentatively accept an explanation to the extent that predictions logically generated from it conform to observed reality. We can never prove a proposition or theory true because, since scientific theories refer to an infinite future, we can never view all the relevant evidence.[3] We can, however, set up the criteria for finding any proposition or theory false on the basis of not finding the phenomena that one expected to be logically generated from the theory. Thus, the biblical

account of creation, apart from any judgment about its ultimate truth, is not generally regarded by scholars as scientific because as a one-shot event, it does not logically generate any predictions about future findings; therefore, in principle it is not susceptible to falsification. There are no conceivable data to refute it.

The lack of correspondence between this classic model of scientific explanation and what is possible in the study of political phenomena should be immediately apparent. Political science is devoid of any general, theoretic propositions from which one can deduce the necessary occurrence of a reasonably significant and hence complex political event. The reason for this, as noted, is that such events or behaviors are the product of far more factors than could reasonably be encompassed in any given proposition or study. The action of even a single individual is the product of any number and combination of the almost infinite number and variety of experiences and stimuli in that person's life. The causes of events that are the product of the interaction of many individuals are increased exponentially.

Hence, any proposition about the causes of political behavior or events can only isolate some of the major causes of those events and would only be necessarily true assuming all other relevant but unanalyzed factors cancel one another out. In other words, the claims to truth in political science are true, other things being equal. Thus, the explanations of complex political phenomena that political science can offer are always incomplete, and the predictions that are generated from such explanations are what we call *probabilistic*. This means that they predict what will probably occur in certain circumstances (with a probability significantly greater than random chance) rather than what must necessarily occur in those circumstances. The essential structure of explanation remains the same as in the classic model: one deduces the prediction of the phenomenon to be explained from the general proposition. It is with regard to the accuracy of the prediction and the completeness of the explanation that political science differs from the natural sciences and the classic model of explanation.[4]

The incompleteness of our explanations is due to the aforementioned unavoidable presence of unanalyzed factors that affect the outcomes we wish to explain. Cases often do not conform to the predictions or expectations derived from an explanatory principle due to the influence of such unanalyzed variables. The next step in the analysis is to find patterns in these deviant cases and thereby to isolate the impact of one or more previously unanalyzed variable.

For example, one may find that there is a relationship between education and some kinds of political attitudes, such as a disposition toward tolerance of people with whom one disagrees. One may, however, find that among the educated people who show intolerance, contrary to the expectation such people are more tolerant, another trait may be common among these deviant cases and in fact may produce this deviance. For example, the active practice of a certain religion may produce intolerance even among the educated. One would then say that education produces tolerance in the presence of some religious orientations but not in the presence of others. By taking account of religion, we have made the explanation at once more complex and more accurate.

This difference between explanations in the natural sciences and in the social or behavioral sciences is reflected in the ability of the explanations in those respective classes of academic enterprise to generate predictions. Since the phenomena in the natural sciences can be isolated from other variables, predictions in those enterprises can be made *deterministically*. That is, if the explanatory theory is presumed true, scientists can say in these circumstances that certain result *must* follow. In the social sciences, however, scholars can only predict with a known probability of being wrong that, given the truth of their theory, certain results are more likely to appear than not. These are called probabilistic predictions. We can measure the explanatory power of our theories by the extent to which we increase the probability of a correct prediction over a random guess. Explanations are sometimes proposed for complex events that provide an answer as to why the event occurred but that do not increase one's power to predict other, not yet encountered instances of that kind of event. For example, the Nazis in Weimar Germany explained the economic and political troubles of their society in terms of too much Jewish influence. Yet that explanation would not increase one's ability to predict similar difficulties in other societies with a certain percentage of Jews in their population or elites. While the explanation was psychologically satisfying to Germans and thereby had *explanatory appeal*, it had no *explanatory power.*

Thus, we return to the assertion made at the beginning of this section that the task of accounting for the impact of previously unanalyzed variables is one of the most crucial contributions to the overall goal of building a body of explanatory theory in political science. Three basic research methods are utilized in this task. One is experimental research. Although the closest of the three to the natural science model, experimental research, involving as it does the deliberate application of the independent variable to an experimental group and the withholding of this variable from a control group, frequently raises serious questions of feasibility and/or practicality for political research. The second method, which is perhaps the most widely utilized by modern political science, is the use of statistics, especially inferential statistics. Inferential statistics may be viewed as a system for estimating the probability of error when drawing inferences about parameters (the attributes of the population to which one is referring) from the attributes of an observed sample or when inferring causation from an observed relationship among two or more variables. In social science, one almost always works from a sample of an infinite universe, a universe that the researcher never directly observes. Any given sample, randomly drawn, may be more or less representative of the universe as a whole. This notion of *sampling error* refers to the reality that the given samples will be more or less representative of the whole universe and does not imply mistake. Among the sources of error in causal inferences from a statistical relationship is the fact that the researcher is here again working from a sample and the unavoidable presence of unanalyzed variables.

Comparative analysis may be viewed as the third method for accounting for the unanalyzed variables that make the "other things being equal" qualifier an inescapable part of explanatory propositions in social research. Comparative analysis as a method in this sense may be defined as the construction of explanatory generalizations that are logically applicable to different national and hence different cultural settings. Comparative analysis becomes the appropriate method when the characteristics of the political systems themselves, if not the dependent or independent variables, are the previously unanalyzed factors for which one wants to account. Comparative analysis becomes the appropriate method for generalizing about political or social systems as whole units and thereby for taking account of the attributes of the context in which political behaviors and events occur. Among such contextual factors are a nation's historical experiences, geographical setting, social structure, and culture. These are factors for which the proper-

noun name of the system may constitute an adjective, such as the French attitude toward authority, the British insular geographical setting, or the Belgian cultural segmentation. Such factors may be presumed to have an impact on the response of individuals to any particular stimulus or experience such that an individual in one setting may react differently to a particular experience than an individual in another setting. Comparative analysis seeks to generalize about the impact of the settings or contexts in which political behavior and events occur.

For example, formal religious observance tends to promote a conservative orientation, and women up until recently have tended to be more religious; hence women have tended to be more conservative than men. Therefore, it was possible to offer the following causal model: gender $\rightarrow$ religiosity $\rightarrow$ political orientation. However, these relationships hold true in some nations and not in others. Specifically, the causal model seems to apply in those nations with a relatively higher degree of religiosity and not in those nations that are highly secularized. Among the latter group of nations, in England, for example, with only 2.5 percent of the population going to church at least once a month, the gender difference in religiosity disappears, as of course does the gender-based difference in political orientation. It will not do, however, to say that women are more conservative than men except in England, because England, being a proper noun, refers to a unique entity. Since the term *England* does not logically imply anything about any other nation, the explanation would stop at that point. Yet, explanatory principles must refer to infinite classes of cases to enable one to extrapolate from direct observation to prediction and thus to move beyond mere description. In the preceding example, therefore, one must be able to say what there is about England that causes it to be an exception to the principle or to generalize about the factors in the English context that makes that system an exception to the foregoing rule. In the words of Adam Przeworski and Henry Teune, one must translate the proper-noun names of systems into common-noun variables.[5] In our example, this would mean translating the term *England* into the concept of highly secularized nations. This task may be viewed as another way of defining the essence of the comparative method.

In this way, knowledge is actually advanced when a proposition that had held true in some contexts does not hold true in other contexts. When the proposition is falsified in a particular context, the impact of that context can now be assessed and added to a now increasingly complex theory. Thus, the comparative method seeks to build knowledge incrementally over time and numerous studies.

It can be seen from the foregoing that the comparative method is the appropriate method to use when a generalization appears to hold true in some settings but not in others. Comparison in such cases enables one to formulate a principle that delineates the distinction between the two classes of settings. Yet, one cannot even find out whether contextual factors are relevant in determining whether a generalization will hold true unless one first applies a generalization cross-nationally or cross-culturally. In this way, political analysis may in the end be inescapably comparative, and comparative analysis defined as a method may be indistinguishable from the attempt to construct political explanations.

This becomes obvious when the comparative method is viewed more broadly as the process of generalizing across contexts, whether they be time, space within a nation, or national boundaries. One may compare behavior within a given nation at different points in time, thus holding factors other than those associated with the modernization process more or less constant. One also may compare regions within a nation. Thus, the comparative method is appropriate for generalizing among the states in the United States. In this sense and in the sense that explanation is, as we have seen, inherently a generalizing activity, comparative analysis may be synonymous with the scientific study of politics. The critics of the comparative method are not so much addressing the appropriateness of the method for the scientific study of politics as they are generally skeptical about the potential usefulness of the scientific study of politics itself.

While the comparative method may be understood in the broad sense of cross-contextual generalization, the field of comparative politics for the purposes of this text encompasses the building of cross-national explanatory generalizations about political phenomena as well as the identification and delineation of data about various nations and social systems that are cross-nationally applicable and hence can contribute to the aforementioned theory-building enterprise. In other words, this text views the discipline of comparative politics as being concerned with generalizing about different types of nation-states and their settings.

THE POSITION THAT NATIONS AND EVENTS ARE UNIQUE

We have acknowledged that the logic of the foregoing arguments for a comparative orientation and the assumption that one may meaningfully generalize across national and cultural lines is not accepted by all scholars in our discipline. In fact, one school of thought argues that nations and events constitute a unique pattern of factors that can never be duplicated and that constitute the very essence of these nations and events. Hence, there can never be another France with its unique combination of historical, cultural, geographical, and demographic factors, not to mention the unique personalities that made up its unique history. Nor could there ever be another French Revolution occurring as it did at a particular point in history with a particular state of technology and particular persons present to influence its course.

Hence, it can never be meaningful, according to the extreme position of this school, to attempt to generalize about such unique phenomena. The meaning of phenomena is culturally specific, derived from the pattern of all of the contextual factors that comprise a given system. A social democratic party in Germany will thus necessarily connote something quite distinct from a social democratic party in Sweden or Great Britain. Therefore, one cannot meaningfully generalize about such parties across national or cultural boundaries.

Of course, scholars do not generally take extreme positions. The distinction between those who are optimistic about the possibilities of meaningfully generalizing across systems and those who, emphasizing the unique nature of such systems, are rather more pessimistic about the possibilities of such comparison is a difference of degree. Yet, there are scholars of this latter school who do tend to teach their courses and conduct their research on a country-by-country basis with little real attempt at comparison.[6] Many other scholars who are in principle sympathetic to the concept of the comparative method are skeptical of its utility for specific instances of teaching and research. The claimed revolution that changed comparative politics from an essentially descriptive enterprise to a generalizing and explanatory one is clearly a very incomplete revolution.[7]

The claim that persons and political events are unique is undeniable; yet, admission of that fact does not necessarily deny the possibility of meaningfully generalizing about them. The process of generalization and comparison in fact presumes that the objects of the comparison are in most respects unique. The process implies an inquiry into what common patterns may be found among objects that are in other respects different. A substantial body of research into the nature and causes of violence and revolution does denote a number of factors that such events have in common, despite the aforementioned uniqueness of the French and other revolutions. Moreover, the admission that political phenomena are affected by and thus cannot be studied in isolation from the context in which they occur does not mean that cross-contextual generalizations are futile. As observed, the essence of the comparative method involves generalizing about such contexts and their impact.

THE PLAN OF THIS BOOK: THEORY AND COUNTRY STUDIES

The authors of this text appreciate the value of the comparative method in building a body of increasingly complete explanatory theory as outlined above. Yet, we are also aware of the limits to what has been and can be achieved by this enterprise. In addition, we believe that there is merit in the skepticism many teachers express about attempting to teach cross-national theory to students who lack basic information and understanding about the structures and processes of types of political systems other than their own. It may be difficult to generalize about the preconditions of successful parliamentary democracy, for example, if students know little or nothing about how that type of system operates in general and in its numerous variations.

Thus, while we remain optimistic about

the value of discussing and analyzing the state of explanatory theory in comparative politics, we believe that it is important to include descriptions and analyses of the operation of political systems that represent major types of political systems in the world. Students frequently enter courses in comparative politics unfamiliar with the most basic structures and processes of political systems outside of their own. For example, American students frequently do not understand how the parliamentary forms of democracy operate, even though some version of parliamentary democracy is utilized by the vast majority of democratic governments in the world. However, students also frequently do not understand why they should care how parliamentary governments operate, given that most students will never spend much time abroad. Hence, it is important that these students understand how explanatory theory applicable to other countries is essential to explain and thus to some measure to control our own political environment in the United States. Theory is therefore important in giving students a reason to familiarize themselves with the variety of political systems in the world. Political facts by themselves have no intrinsic value other than their role in helping us to understand (in the sense of explaining) political phenomena.

By including both country studies and theory chapters in this book, we hope to help bridge the gap between the country-by-country advocates and the comparative theory advocates. With liberal references in the theory chapters to the factual material in the country chapters and with many efforts to show the theoretic relevance of the factual material in the country chapters, we hope to show that both approaches can contribute to what ought to be a common goal: increasing the body of knowledge about political phenomena throughout the world.

CONCEPTUAL FRAMEWORKS: SOME COMMONLY APPLICABLE CONCEPTS

The goal of cross-national generalization presumes that one can ask the same question in a variety of settings and the concepts and that terms used in that inquiry maintain a constant meaning in each of the several contexts in which they are or might be applied. The delineation of common concepts, common questions for inquiry (such as the causes of political stability or of political violence), and a common organizational scheme to be applicable in each of the political systems under scrutiny is what is meant by a *conceptual framework*. The development of various conceptual frameworks for analysis was a goal that consumed a large share of the time and energies of those scholars who advocated and sought to advance the theory-building, comparativist vision of the field. Similarly, many of the textbooks that apparently sought to represent that view included a long and elaborate introduction that purported to offer such a conceptual framework, a framework that provided the organizational and conceptual guide to render the goal of generalizing from the information in one political system to the information in others.

The search for these commonly applicable conceptual frameworks led to a preoccupation among students of comparative politics with the socioeconomic settings in which political systems are found. It was thought that the institutional or actual governmental makeup of political systems would vary so greatly as to render the development of widely applicable conceptual frameworks based upon such government factors a highly dubious prospect. Especially with the discovery and growing concern with Third World settings in the postwar era, the comparability of the traditional concepts and terms of political science became a serious problem.

However, it was argued, societies universally have certain attributes and perform in certain ways. Accordingly, political scientists in general and comparative politics specialists in Third World systems in particular began to coopt the concepts and theories of sociology and cultural anthropology as the basis of their conceptual frameworks. Gabriel Almond's now classic introduction to his *The Politics of Developing Areas* epitomizes the development of a conceptual framework emphasizing such sociological and anthropological conceptualization.[8] Some of these theoretical approaches, such as Almond's functionalism and the preoccupation with the input side of political analysis to the neglect of the nation-state itself, have subsequently come under serious criticism on both methodological and substantive grounds. The goal of identifying the functions performed by all societies and of giving the concepts of such functions empirical content has proved elusive. The neglect of the state has been recently addressed by a number of scholars as ignoring the focus that ultimately constitutes the essence and raison d'être of our discipline.[9] Nevertheless, these early ground-breaking efforts remain impressive attempts to build theory across widely disparate settings.

While this textbook does not pretend to offer anything as rigorous as a coherent conceptual framework, it does attempt to organize the country studies into common topics and to use some common concepts in order to facilitate comparison. Thus, in Table 1–2 we suggest some commonly used concepts (ideas), terms, and questions to apply to the diversity of political systems that will be examined in this book or that may be examined in the future so as to facilitate the goal of formulating meaningful generalizations about these systems. Since we are interested in what makes some political systems more effective than others, we summarize some of the most important factors that promote effective government, factors that we will be considering as we analyze the diversity of political systems in this book. We seek to orient students toward seeking patterns and generalizing about the political facts they encounter.

REQUIREMENTS FOR EFFECTIVE GOVERNMENT

Scholars such as Almond who have boldly tried to formulate universally applicable conceptual frameworks have generally based their work on the idea of listing processes, structures, or states of affairs that are needed for the effective functioning of a political system regardless of its type, factors that some scholars, such as David Apter, have called the "requisites" of a political system. The most important of these factors are summarized in Table 1-3.

The term *political system* itself may be unfamiliar to students used to traditional terms such as *nation* and *state*. A political system has been defined by the famous political scientist David Easton as those structures and processes that are engaged in "the authoritative allocation of values." This basic political function of determining with authority who gets how much of what may be done by a nation-state but is still done even when the nation-state as such does not exist, as in the premodern world. For example, organized interest groupings play an increasingly important although frequently unofficial role in the political process; hence, they are part of the political system but not part of the nation-state. The term *political system* is thus a more broadly applicable term than *nation-state* in that the latter is confined to those legal, sovereign entities that appeared first in the Western world. *Nation* may be distinguished from *state* in that the latter is a legal and sovereign entity, while the former is de-

TABLE 1-2   Important Concepts for Comparison

Political system: Those structures and processes that determine with accepted authority who gets how much of the things people value. The parts of the nation-state are part of the political system but so are structures and processes not part of the nation-state.

Nation: A large group of people sharing a common sense of belonging, a common peoplehood. This may include a sense of community (defined below).

State: The legal entity that exercises sovereign power over a given territory. The state may or may not coincide with the nation.

Context: The setting in which politics occurs. It consists of the culture, social structure, demographic factors, and historical experiences of a nation.

Political culture: The psychological dispositions or mental orientations that predispose individuals to react in certain ways to political objects.

Social structure or stratification system: The criteria by which people are grouped and divided (such as class, religion, or ethnicity) and the question of whether these groupings overlap or are mutually isolated.

Segmented society: A society in which the sub-groups mutually preclude personal interaction among individuals of different groupings.

Community: A set of individuals, usually a nation as defined above, who share, in addition to a sense of common peoplehood, a set of basic values.

Constitutional format: The fundamental rules that define the processes of deciding policy, choosing decision makers, and, if applicable, holding them accountable.

Legitimacy: Authority which is widely accepted as rightful. This acceptance is above and beyond whether there is approval of the performance of the system with regard to particular issues.

Sovereignty: An essential property of a state that refers to the final or ultimate legitimate power to make and enforce rules for the society.

Political development: A complex term variously defined. Here it includes industrialization, urbanization, the politicization (or mobilization) of the population, increasing complexity of social roles, and greater capabilities of the political system.

Political effectiveness: The ability of a political system to resolve important issues to the satisfaction of the dominant parts of the population so as to minimize challenges to the system itself. Political systems may be effective without necessarily being either democratic or just.

---

fined by a sense of peoplehood. Hence, we will see in the chapters that follow that German nationhood preceded the German state and that Nigeria may be a state but is still seeking its soul as a nation.

Each of our country studies will begin with a consideration of what we have called *contextual factors,* which are those factors that comprise the context of setting in which political events occur and in which a political system operates. Contextual factors have an impact on political systems but are not, strictly speaking, an integral part of them. Among such

contextual factors are a nation's historical background and experiences in the process of nation-building, its political culture and style, and its social stratification system and demographics. These factors are the essential source of the disagreements about public policy and the national interest, disagreements that constitute the issues that political processes must resolve. Constitutionally designated policy-making structures and processes do not operate in a vacuum but rather are so much a function of these contextual factors that one cannot possibly explain differences

TABLE 1-3   Factors Promoting Effective Government*

1. Resolution of the question of what kind of regime preceded the generation of divisive and substantive issues.
2. A widespread sense of community based upon the coincidence of the boundaries of the nation and the state. Ethnic and other population diversities detract from effective government only to the extent that they detract from this sense of community.
3. Legitimacy of the political system and especially of the constitutional format. Legitimacy is related to acceptance of the processes by which leaders are chosen and of some regularized processes for succession of leadership.
4. A substantial degree of pragmatism in the political culture—a willingness to modify principles to accommodate an ever changing world.

* This list does not claim to be exhaustive. Rather, these items are judged to be particularly important and thus provide some common avenues of inquiry for the systems examined in this volume.

among political systems without reference to them. These factors each require some elaboration and specification.

Nation-states are not natural phenomena. They are a form of political organization that appeared in the modern Western world centuries after the fall of the Roman Empire and only spread to the non-Western world in the twentieth century. For much of what we call the Third World, the nation-state is to a large extent a post–World War II phenomenon. Nation-building refers to the conscious or accidental processes and experiences that culminate in the various respective nation-states. Certain patterns in these experiences and accordingly in the nation-building process may be discerned, thus making it possible to generalize about the impact of a nation's history on its contemporary nature and attributes. While we are not interested in the history of these countries under scrutiny for its own sake, knowledge of their history is essential to an understanding of their present situation. Each country chapter will therefore begin with a consideration of such historical patterns.

The history of any nation may be viewed as the attempt to solve a series of problems that all nations must ultimately resolve if they are to operate effectively. These attempts have sometimes been referred to in the literature as "crises of political development."[10] We will see that while nations in the industrialized, or "developed," nations have resolved more of these so-called crises, or by definition have resolved them more completely than nations in the Third World, or "less developed," nations, the industrialized democracies have also had a highly imperfect record in resolving them. Moreover, the record of nations in all parts of the world in resolving these crises is positively related to their success as a stable, effective, and legitimate political system in the present modern era.

Among the historical facts that we will be considering in the country studies is the timing, sequence, and success in resolving these crises of development. The identification of these crises varies from one scholar to another; however, the essential meaning of the process is generally recognized by all scholars.

The first problem or crisis to be resolved is a combination of what Raymond Grew called the "identity crisis" and what Lucien Pye called the "crisis of penetration."[11] The elites of would-be nations must somehow establish legitimate control over the territory they aspire to govern. This involves the dissemination of the idea of nationhood among the population of the territory in question. Nationalism, as Rupert Emerson, perhaps the most notable of the authorities on the topic, has taught us, is basically an idea, a sense of common belonging, a consciousness, if you will.[12] Individuals living within the territory that will comprise the new nation must begin to identify themselves intellectually and emotionally as citizens of that nation (e.g., as British or French subjects rather than, say, Scottish or Norman). Frequently this involves breaking down earlier, more parochial loyalties.

The establishment of these emotional loyalties to the emerging national government facilitates the widespread acceptance, or legitimation, of that government. A legitimate government more easily establishes effective control over its subjects, thus solving the crisis of penetration. While the idea of nationhood may facilitate the establishment of legitimate control, the two problems are clearly separate. The Soviet Union maintained effective control over its constituent republics as well as de facto control over the Warsaw Pact nations for decades, but the idea of separate nationhood was never extinguished in these systems, and the legitimacy of Soviet control was eroded by this discrepancy between the persisting emotional ties to the idea of nationalism at the more parochial republic level and the actual control by the broader Soviet empire. The consequent collapse of the Soviet Empire in 1990 was unpredictable because scholars were unaware of the discrepancy.

Nation states may establish their legitimate control over their territory without resolving the question of regime, or the issue of what kind of constitutional format they will adopt. This involves not only the very general questions of whether the system will be democratic. The independent republics emerging from the collapse of the Soviet Empire in 1990 have established the idea of their na-

tionhood, and their governments have the administrative apparatus in place to establish effective control over their territory, but at this writing they are generally unclear and undecided about what kind of regime they want to set up except for a vague desire to be democratic in some unspecified way. It is unclear whether a presidential or parliamentary form of government shall emerge, and, if the latter, whether it shall be one with a strong cabinet domination of the legislature, as in Britain and most postwar industrial democracies, or one in which the constitution favors a weak executive dominated by the legislature. Will the systems be centralized with a strong national government, or will they be decentralized into some form of federation or confederation? Clearly, such questions must be answered if the regime format—the rules by which substantive issues are processed and resolved—can succeed in resolving difficult and controversial issues.

THE SEQUENTIAL RESOLUTION OF CRISES

Thus, one of the most important questions about the historical context involves the sequence in which crises have been resolved. A nation must first establish its identity and legitimacy before it can solve the question of regime. The question of regime must be resolved and the constitutional format must be established as legitimate for the effective resolution of subsequent substantive and divisive issues such as the expansion of effective participation in the politics of the system to a wider and wider segment of the population, the amelioration of the socioeconomic dislocations of industrialization, or the specification of the relationship between church and state. When the rules of the game are not legitimate, the divisive substantive issues will tend to be defined in terms of the constitutional format. One side of the substantive issue will favor one type of constitutional format, while the advocates of the other side will favor another. We will later see how the French have suffered the malady of arguing each emerging substantive issue in constitutional terms after the question of regime was placed on the table after the Revolution.

THE POLITICAL CULTURE

Among the aspects of a modern political system that are influenced by the experiences of a nation's past, perhaps the system's political culture is most affected. The concept of *political culture* is quite popular among those students of comparative politics who understand the boundaries of the field as encompassing more than the formal, constitutionally designated structures of government that defined its prewar focus.[13] The postwar era of comparative politics has been characterized by a concentration on contextual factors to such an extent that those on the cutting edge of the field are now complaining that the nation-state itself is being neglected. This rediscovery of the state is discussed below. While the contextual factors that generate inputs into the political system cannot be ignored in seeking to understand the political system itself, we have been reminded that the political system is that which we ultimately seek to understand; hence, our concern with contexts or inputs should not become an end in itself.

The concept of political culture refers to dispositional attributes, the internal state of individuals that predisposes them to respond in certain ways to certain stimuli, which pre-scientific terminology would simply dismiss as subjective. These attributes become part of the political culture when they refer to political objects and when they are so widely held among a population that they might be called typical. In such cases they are treated

as attributes of the system itself. Thus, when one speaks of the French attitude toward something, one means that this attitude is typical or modal among Frenchmen.

A nation's political culture includes the following attributes: attitudes toward authority; beliefs or conceptions of what is true; an ideological or pragmatic approach to decision making; feelings of attachment, alienation, rejection, trust, or distrust; knowledge and information; and basic values. (The dimensions of political culture are summarized in Table 1-4.) Attitudes toward authority may be classified as submissive, deferential, or egalitarian. A submissive attitude connotes unquestioned obedience. A deferential attitude implies an acceptance of authority and a disposition to grant those in authority discretion and leeway in day-to-day decision making. While accepting that some are more able to exercise authority than others, a deferential attitude differs from a submissive one in insisting that authority be ultimately accountable for the results of its decision making and for ruling in the public interest. An egalitarian attitude implies that people are equally qualified to make political and social judgments. Accordingly, egalitarians are less willing to grant great discretion to those in authority. Rather they tend to insist on close popular control of and limits in the exercise of authority.

Research in political socialization, the process by which political orientations are acquired and disseminated, finds that such political attitudes are acquired with a high degree of permanence rather early in life. Once acquired, they tend to be applied to a person's various roles—family, social, educational, occupational, and political. Therefore, it has been plausibly hypothesized that effective government requires that the orientation toward authority that the constitutional format demands should be more or less "congruent" to the corresponding orien-

TABLE 1-4   Dimensions of the Concept of Political Culture

Attitudes—a psychological orientation toward political objects, frequently involving normative conceptions of how things ought to be.

  Attitudes toward authority:

  egalitarian—people are relatively equal in their capacity to assume political roles and to make political judgments.

  authoritarian—some people are clearly more qualified to rule than others. The duty of the rest is unquestioned obedience.

  deferential—some people are more qualified to occupy leadership roles, but these people have an obligation to rule in the general interest and should be held accountable for the results of their rule.

Beliefs—conceptions of how things are, which may or may not be accurate.

  ideologies—a comprehensive system of beliefs that is relatively closed to being adjusted on the basis of new information.

    ideologism—a disposition to make political decisions on the basis of their consistency with a set of principles.

    pragmatism—a trial and error basis of reaching political decisions on the basis of results without regard to principles.

  assumptions that underlie social theories (as in the belief in the self-regulating market).

Feelings

  affect—a sense of belonging to the political system, that one has an interest in the well-being and success of the system, marked by a tendency to regard the system as "us" rather than "them."

  alienation—a sense of detachment from the system, that the interests of the system are distinct from one's own interests, marked by a tendency to regard the system as "them."

  an emotional attachment to various political symbols.

Cognition: knowledge and information.

Values—priorities and goals (when framed in terms of particular objects, values become attitudes).

  religion and *religiosity*

  fundamental values that may define the nature of the system (such as freedom or equality).

---

tation in that nation's culture.[14] Therefore, in those parts of the world in which unquestioned obedience to authority is a social norm, it may be difficult for people to adjust to the idea that they should hold government accountable for its political actions. It will be interesting to see, for example, whether the socialization process that has been going on in Eastern Europe during the more than forty years of Soviet domination will prove to be dysfunctional for the transition to democracy now that Soviet control in those societies has apparently been removed.

The distinction between a pragmatic and ideological political style is another cultural factor that may have an important effect on the operations of a political system. The former style implies that in choosing among alternative courses of public policy, decision makers are guided solely by whatever works in terms of the immediate objective on an essentially trial-and-error basis. Such an orientation involves small, step-by-step adjustments to the status quo on the basis of need and without regard to principle or internal consistency. Because it is characterized by such small, incremental changes, this style has been called *incrementalism*.[15] This style implies that decision makers are primarily guided by the need for consistency with some overriding principle or set of principles, with little regard for actual outcome. By being relatively insensitive to outcomes, ideologism does lend itself to adjustments to changing circumstances. Ideologies by definition are not sensitive to new information; hence, an ideological political style is dysfunctional for the adaptability that is thought to be important for the long-term effectiveness of a political system. Moreover, ideologism tends to perpetuate old issues and controversies long after the problems that generated them have ceased to exist, creating a situation that Herbert Spiro has called "recriminatory politics."[16] We will see, for example, how the cleavages generated by the French Revolution of 1789 remained politically salient for two centuries thereafter.

A critical factor in the ability of a system to function effectively and even persist over time with the necessity of resolving issues in ways that create both winners and losers is the feeling of identification with or alienation from the regime. We are speaking here of the question of whether the population tends to regard the regime as "us" or "them." When people identify with the regime, they perceive themselves having a personal stake in its well-being; therefore, they tend to accept and support the regime even when particular policy choices go against their perceived interests or preferences. This tendency to identify with a regime is related to

but goes beyond granting the regime legitimacy. It connotes positive support beyond the passive acceptance implied in the concept of legitimacy and is manifested in displays of patriotism. This identification with and sense of belonging to the regime is what sociologists call *system affect*. The converse feeling, *system alienation*, is manifested by widespread feelings of distrust of the government and public officials. Italians, for example, are widely reported to assume that most political and administrative officials merely want to line their pockets without regard for the public interest. Accordingly, they express little pride in their regime and would presumably be unwilling to take great risks, pay substantial costs, or endure serious deprivations to defend it. Such regimes are under constant pressure to substantively satisfy most of their populations to maintain popular acceptance, a requirement no regime can satisfy over time and a range of issues.

Third World countries, we will see, face a momentous task in establishing this type of feeling in light of traditional loyalties to more parochial groupings such as tribes, villages, or regions. We will see how Nigeria has struggled to create a sense of pride and trust in a national government in the face of more traditional, deep-seated loyalties to subcultures. This problem is not unknown in the Western world. For example, Canada has had a difficult time establishing a sense of national identity with its essentially Anglo-dominated regime among its French-speaking population.

A widespread sense of affect toward the system is usually based upon broadly shared basic values among the population that create a sense of community. The idea of community implies that the system is an organic reality that transcends the individuals who comprise it, based upon values that define its essence. A nation-state, the legal and political entity, may comprise more than one community, as in the case of the Anglo- and French-Canadian communities in Canada, the Flemish and Walloonian communities in Belgium, and the Ibo, Yoruba, Hausa, Tiv, and Fulani communities, among others, in Nigeria.

This sense of community is difficult to instill or socialize into a population that has developed a tradition of competing loyalties. Insofar as the concept of imperialism entails the imposition of political control on preexisting communities, empires face a difficult task in overriding the loyalties to these communities and establishing their own legitimacy. The collapse of the Soviet Union revealed that its suppression of ethnic and national loyalties even over a period of decades was not very successful. The Muslems in Azerbaijan, a constituent republic of the former USSR next to Iran, apparently felt more loyalty to their republic and to Islam than to the broader concept of the Soviet Union. Similarly, the feelings of loyalty of their people to Lithuania, Latvia, and Estonia were obviously not displaced by a system affect toward the Soviet Union. It may accordingly be suspected that primal political loyalties are quite persistent and that systems that establish the feelings of loyalties in their subjects before these people are mobilized by competing loyalties are able to establish their legitimacy much more firmly.

Legitimacy and the feelings of loyalty and belonging that underlie legitimacy are acquired over time. Mobilized populations generate demands and expectations that place considerable stress on a system. The expectations of immediate performance on substantive issues generated by a mobilized population does not afford a political system the time needed to acquire the deep-seated legitimacy that might enable it to weather a period of poor performance or highly controversial allocative decisions without losing substantial support from its citizens. Third World and Soviet-bloc systems were faced

with the monumental task of building legitimacy and affect within already mobilized and demanding populations with loyalties to previously established systems.

A third set of contextual factors may be discerned in the structure of social cleavages, or *social stratification*. This term refers to the criteria by which people are grouped or divided in a society. Such criteria may include socioeconomic class, religion, ethnicity, region, or language. Given the fact that in a reasonably complex society, the reality of specialization and division of labor generates unavoidable differences in interests and perspectives on the public interest, cleavages based upon material or economic interests—in other words, class-based cleavages—are always objectively present. The saliency of such cleavages in the consciousness of the citizenry, however, tends to be overriden by the saliency of other criteria of cleavage, especially noneconomic or symbolic criteria such as ethnicity, language, or culture. Class, therefore, may be viewed as a residual basis of cleavage, one that objectively exists but that becomes politically relevant only when symbolic criteria are not politically salient. We will see, for example, that Great Britain has been widely perceived as a quintessential example of a society based upon class largely because regionalism, ethnicity, and the like have not generally been regarded as politically important.

Class conflict has acquired a bad popular image in the United States. One reason is that it conflicts with the widespread American belief in the ultimate universal harmony of interests, a belief that is grounded in the classic liberal tradition noted by such scholarly observers of the American scene as Louis Hart. Second, class conflict is widely associated with Marxism, which is anathema to the dominant opinion leaders in the United States. However, given that some form of cleavage and some form of conflict based on those cleavages are inevitable, class conflict has been identified as considerably more manageable than other forms of conflict based on other forms of cleavage. Robert Alford argued as much in his comparison of politics in the four major Anglo-American democracies: the United States, Canada, Great Britain, and Australia.[17] The latter two systems had been predominantly based on class cleavages, while the former two are based upon other criteria of cleavage. Alford argues that the class politics of Britain and Australia have been a force for stable and successful politics in those two nations because class-based issues, revolving as they do around questions of allocation (who gets how much of what), suggest compromise solutions. By contrast, when the cleavages are based upon considerations of language, religion, or ethnicity, as in Canada, the issues revolve around questions of good and evil, right and wrong, true and false, which present no logical middle ground. Since compromise is the only alternative to the use of compulsion in resolving issues, the politics of class has more effectively encouraged the successful resolution of issues than have the politics of region, religion, ethnicity, or language.

As will be discussed in Part Two, which focuses on industrial democracies, Ronald Inglehart has produced an extensive body of research that documents a shift in basic values among the publics of Western democracies away from a predominant concern with class-related material values to a concern with nonclass-related "postmaterialist" values such as ecology, human rights, and war and peace.[18] This latter class of values generate precisely the kind of nonquantifiable issues that are not conducive to compromise solutions. Therefore, it may reasonably be expected that, with the growing predominance of postmaterialist values, the intensity of political conflict may increase.

The cleavages of society may take the form of *cross-cutting cleavages,* by which those individuals who are grouped according to one criterion, such as socioeconomic class, are not necessarily grouped on other criteria, such as ethnicity, language, or religion. Thus, in such a situation some of the poor will be Protestant while others will be Catholic, and the middle and upper classes will be similarly divided among the available religious denominations.

Because a system of cross-cutting cleavages will cause the people who are opposed on one issue or even on a set of issues to be allied on other issues and to share other interests, that cleavage system will tend to mitigate the intensity of any partisan animosity that may result from differences of perspective on particular issues. It has therefore been impressionistically assumed that cross-cutting cleavages will promote a lower intensity of partisanship and a more stable and successful democratic politics, an assumption about which some empirical research raises tentative questions.

Cleavages, rather than cross-cutting, may be *cumulative* or *mutually reinforcing,* such that the people grouped on one criterion will be grouped on others. In such a system, the population does not experience the mitigating effect of having those who are opponents on one issue working together on other matters. Conventional wisdom has been that such a society encourages intense, uncompromising political conflict and has a good probability of experiencing instability and violence. Northern Ireland is a society with cumulative cleavages, as the economically better-off tend to be Protestants who favor their political ties to the United Kingdom, while the less well-off tend to be Catholics who deeply resent their ties to Britain and instead favor joining the Republic of Ireland. People may grow up and live their lives in one of these two subcultures without ever getting to know those who live in the other. The intense level of partisanship and of politically motivated violence in Northern Ireland is well known, an apparent product of the intense hatreds that are allowed to fester among these two populations that live in such isolation from one another.

Cumulative cleavages, as we have defined them, constitute a special case of what are called *segmented societies,* in which there is very little personal interaction between individuals in different subcultural segments. For example, a typical person in rural Quebec would likely live out his or her entire life without developing any genuine friendship with a person who was not a *Québeçois.* Similarly, in Belgium, the Flemish and the Walloonians would seldom have any close interaction with the other subculture. Given their linguistic differences, which buttress their cultural differences, the members of these two subcultures depend on different sources of ideas and information, feel attachment to different symbols, and adhere to distinct sets of values.

Much impressionistic scholarship has identified the effective integration of such subcultural segments into the broader national culture as an attribute of modernization. Yet, as the foregoing examples clearly indicate, segmented societies are clearly a fact of life in what is generally regarded as the Western world. In addition to the examples of Canada and Belgium, Austria, Switzerland, and the Netherlands have clearly been identified as segmented societies.

Nevertheless, it remains true that segmentation is relatively more common among the less developed parts of the world. The residual effect of tribalism with tribal boundaries that are not congruent with the artificial national boundaries imposed by the colonial powers constitutes one powerful cause of such segmentation. In some instances, as we will see in the chapter on Nigeria (Chapter 10), several geographically defined tribal homelands may exist within a nation-state. Nigeria contains numerous ethnic groups with deep tribal roots, including the Hausa, Fulani, Kanuri, Yoruba, Ibo, and Tiv. Exacerbating Nigeria's lack of sociocultural integration is its enormous linguistic diversity, with almost four hundred distinct languages. Clearly this inability to communicate with one another is an important factor encouraging cultural segmentation, which in turn renders it more difficult to mobilize stable majorities to govern the country democratically. The failure of several attempts at civilian rule—let alone democratic government—is to a large extent a product of this difficulty.

The conventional wisdom that segmented societies are dysfunctional for stable democracy will be examined more closely in the chapter on industrial democracies (Chapter 2). To the extent that segmentation presents a problem to be overcome in the overall process of nation building, it may be that social segmentation has more widespread and serious consequences among Third World systems than among western industrial democracies. Among Second World Communist-bloc nations, the expression of subcultural autonomy was suppressed for decades by the dictatorial state's effort to impose cultural uniformity—monism rather than pluralism. The relaxation of these efforts under President Gorbachev's policies of *perestroika* in the former Soviet Union permitted the assertion of the autonomy of these heretofore suppressed subcultural loyalties. This assertion is what the present authors called "cultural defense" in an earlier work, in which we identified subcultural defense as an issue that would continue to be salient in Western societies and argued that it constituted a potentially important nonclass basis of cleavage in the Soviet Union.[19] Our judgment about the probable latency of the nationalities problem in the USSR was based on the fact that no one foresaw the weakening of government control in that system under the impact of *glasnost*. The experience of the former Soviet Union of being overwhelmed by the centrifugal forces of a segmented social system may be compared to the experience that Western and Third World nations have had in integrating and governing their segmented societies.

DECISION-MAKING STRUCTURES AND POSTINDUSTRIAL SOCIETY

Political scientists are not interested in contextual factors for their own sake but rather because they have a causal impact on political systems. Political systems constitute the ultimate focus of our inquiry. Political scientists have in fact been recently criticized for their overemphasis of the contextual or input factors to the neglect of the nation-state, and the rediscovery of the nation-state as a valid unit of analysis has become an *au courant* topic in political science lately. Despite the valid claims about the neglect of the nation-state and the scholarly importance of the concept, an idea that certainly has a traditional place in political science, the concerns about the limitations for comparative purposes of a concept that is essentially a formal legal one that developed out of Western political history remain valid. These concerns encouraged political scientists to develop and substitute the concept of a political system for the concept of a nation-state.

The term *political system* refers to those institutions and processes that are integrally involved in making authoritative decisions for a society. David Easton's now classic definition of a political system as that which is involved in "the authoritative allocation of values" may have said it as well as is possible.[20] The concept of a political system is thus broader than the concept of a nation-state in that it

refers to structures that are not normally regarded as part of the nation-state itself. The constitutionally designated decision-making structures and the designated pattern of interaction among them may be called the *constitutional format*. The presidential system with the separation of powers as practiced in the United States and the cabinet system as practiced in Great Britain are alternative constitutional formats. While the constitutional format may be the core of a political system, it is hardly its total extent. One may in fact distinguish among systems with respect to the degree to which informal institutions process and account for the actual decision-making processes.

For example, the present authors argued above that the imperatives of a modern industrial society impose certain patterns on the decision-making processes of political systems. Thus, systems at a given state of technology may exhibit certain patterns in the processes and structures through which decisions are reached, regardless of the differences in the constitutionally designated format of such systems. The finding of such patterns, we suspect, applies to the structures and processes of the actual format and not to the substantive content of the decisions themselves or the values they imply. To what extent, for example, can the Chinese maintain an ideological adherence to the antimodernist imperatives of the Maoist version of Leninist theory in the face of the conflicting imperatives of a modernizing society? This is a qualified application of what has been called *convergence theory*. We will reexamine the validity of qualified convergence in Chapter 12.

Specifically, a growing role of bureaucratic organizational forms—often in the administrative sector of the government—in the policy-making process has been identified by many scholars as an inevitable concomitant of an advanced state of technology. The cooptation of technologically trained experts by the policy-making process, whether or not these experts have an official or constitutionally designated role, seems to be inescapable in such advanced societies regardless of the variations in their constitutional format.[21] To the extent that the decision-making process is dominated by functionally specific experts in narrow aspects of advanced technology, the system is known as a *technocracy*—one ruled by the technocrats, people possessing the specialized knowledge and expertise required by the issues of an advanced industrial society.

Furthermore, the constitutional format in reasonably complex political systems is compromised by the role of organized interests in the decision-making process. Possessed of specialized knowledge and expertise as well as a stake in policy outcomes that greatly exceeds that of the general public, the number and influence of such groups have been growing in all systems but in modern systems in particular. The formalization of the interaction of between such groups and the political process in such institutions as corporatism (see in Chapter 2) is indicative of the importance and scope of this influence. Therefore, much of the actual decision making is controlled by technocrats. In a technocracy bureaucrats and their organized interests make the de facto decisions, and whatever political accountability may be built into the constitutional format is in effect bypassed. Thus, knowledge of the constitutional format is not the equivalent of knowledge of the actual political process.

The constitutional format may either be by-passed by informal processes, take on very different meanings or roles than its nominal counterpart in the industrialized world, or even be virtually nonexistent in Third World nations. Control of a movement such as antiimperialist forces, of a political party, or of military forces may enable an individual to effectively assume the role of head of government without holding any formal political office. Libya's Colonel Muammar al-Qaddafi is a well-known example of this phenomenon.

Despite the foregoing reservations about the universality of the role of constitutionally designated structures as we understand that role, a trend toward the importance of such structures may be discerned in both scholarship as well as in world affairs, which may be part of a trend toward democracy itself.[22] Democracy, which has certainly achieved renewed visibility as an attainable aspiration if not quite as a current reality in Eastern Europe, logically implies the importance of institutionalized procedures—the rules of the game—overriding that of substantive outcomes. This point is fully elaborated in Chapter 2. Certainly while one may identify the existence of a move toward democratization among formerly authoritarian systems in terms of such clues as greater tolerance of political and social dissent, it is the question of the emergence of certain structures and processes identified with the Western concept of democracy that provides the ultimate criterion of whether political democracy as it is understood in the West is in fact coming into being in Eastern Europe and elsewhere.

A CLASSIFICATION OF POLITICAL SYSTEMS

The universe of political formats is so varied and complex that it seems to cry out for classification, that basic tool for systematically sorting, organizing, and ultimately simplifying a complex array of phenomena by treating groups of otherwise unique factors on the basis of common properties. This is far from the first attempt to classify this universe; hence, we approach the task aware of its difficulties and pitfalls.[23] We are here attempting to classify political formats, the processes and structures by which decision making actually occurs rather than the format that is formally constitutionally designated. The classification of political formats appears in Table 1-5.

This classification of political systems by political format is not the same as classification by constitutional format. Instead it is based upon the actual processes for making authoritative decisions, insofar as these can be discerned, rather than those that are constitutionally designated. Actual and constitutionally designated formats may be more or less congruent with one another.

Systems may also be classified by other dimensions, most particularly by the level of socioeconomic development, as that concept is analyzed in Chapter 6. Two dimensions such

as these may then be cross-tabulated, with any given political system classified on both dimensions. Hence Nazi Germany may have been a populist dictatorship that was industrially or economically developed, while some charismatic Third World leaders identified with an anti-imperialist crusade, such as Libya's Qaddafi, may be classified as a populist dictator in an economically undeveloped system. This distinguishing of dimensions avoids the problem encountered by Almond's ground-breaking classification of political systems of mixing political, economic, and geographical criteria in the same scheme so that some systems belong in more than one cell.

This scheme also avoids the troublesome concept of totalitarianism and the ongoing

TABLE 1-5   The Classification of Political Systems by Decision-Making Format

I. Democratic systems (Legitimate opposition is offered in regular, competitive elections.)
  A. Presidential systems (The same directly elected individual is the head of both government and state.)
  B. Parliamentary system (The head of government is named by the separate head of state to be accountable to the representative assembly in the sense that the assembly can force the resignation of the head of government on a simple majority vote of no confidence.)
    1. Assembly-dominated system (The outcome of the election for the assembly does not normally determine the head of government, and governments will lose votes of no confidence several times in any decade.)
    2. Cabinet system (The government is normally determined by the parliamentary elections and is rarely threatened with the loss of a vote of confidence.)
II. Authoritarian systems (Either elections are not present, the opposition is suppressed by the use or threat of force by the government, or the government otherwise makes the elections not competitive with the use of fraud, intimidation, etc.)
  A. Dictatorships (One person is able to dictate policy unrestrained by considerations external to his or her own will.)
    1. Ordinary dictatorship (Political power is exercised for its own sake based on monopoly control of the means of coercion.)
    2. Populist dictatorship (The dictator creates a popular legitimacy based upon the widely held belief that the person embodies the will and values of the population, which are generally defined by an official millenaristic ideology, a closed set of ideas that posit a millennium that will presumably reshape the socioeconomic order. To the extent that a populist dictatorship attempts to reshape the fundamental structures and values of a society, it approaches the model that has been called totalitarian, which was once quite important in the literature but now is regarded with a great degree of skepticism.)
  B. Bureaucratic authoritarianism (The discretion of the political leader is constrained by the development of an autonomous public bureaucracy and/or military forces.)

debate over whether such systems ever really existed, as well as the difficulty presented by some less developed dictatorships, such as Khomeini's Iran, that may seem to resemble certain modern regimes, such as Nazi Germany, in important ways; yet Iran, for example, could never have been called totalitarian as that term is commonly understood to define a political system that obliterates the distinction between the public and private sector and transforms the basic structure and values of a society. This concept implies a level of effectiveness and control over society that is not present in less developed systems. Millenaristic dictatorships that seek to transform the socioeconomic order may be distinguished from one another by the extent to which they seemed to have penetrated and assumed actual control over that order. Thus, Iran under Khomeini and the various mullahs bears some resemblance to Nazi Germany in the sense of trying to run a state according to and make aspects of normally private life conform to the dictates of a millenaristic ideology, but Iran differs from Germany of that period in being unable to control all aspects of its society to the same extent that Nazis could. It apparently takes the technological capacities of a modern state to effectively penetrate and control society as implied by the concept of totalitarianism, and doubt remains as to whether any state can actually attain that degree of penetration and control. Nevertheless, less modern societies can base their legitimacy on populist support emanating from a millenaristic ideology.

Figure 1-1 graphically represents the relationship between the political format dimension and the socioeconomic development dimension. It is based upon the literature that say not only that a certain amount of economic and social modernization is essential for the level of control associated with the totalitarian model but that democracy as we know it may require a level of such modernization that brings about the emergence of a middle class and a minimal level of material well-being.[24] Other more recent scholars emphasize the working class role in bringing democracy into being.[25] These different perspectives agree that the structure of an industrialized society is more conducive to democratic formats than society dominated by owners of large landholdings supressing a large peasantry (as we will see had been the case until recently in much of Latin America).[26] The relationship between economic development and the emergence of democracy will be considered in Chapter 2 and in

	Presidential democracy	Parliamentary democracy	Ordinary dictatorship	Populist dictatorship	Praetorian or bureaucratic authoritarian
Industrial	USA, France (5th Republic) Israel	Great Britain, Germany	Kenya, Central African Republic	Nazi Germany	USSR after Stalin
Less industrial	Argentina, Philippines	Malaysia, India	Nicaragua under Somoza, Iraq	Iran, North Korea	Nigeria, Egypt

FIGURE 1-1 Cross-classification of systems by regime type and level of economic development.

the discussion of democratization in Latin America.

The utility of classifying political formats depends on two factors: one, whether each nation-state can be unambiguously placed in one and only one cell or category; and two, whether a nation's categorization on this scheme relates systematically to another variable or dimension. We believe that a justification can be made for placing any given nation within one category, although the justification in some cases may not be as self evident. France, for example, has been characterized as a mixture of the presidential and parliamentary formats. This ambiguity rests on a lack of consensus in identifying the actual head of the French government. Although a premier (prime minister) accountable to the National Assembly exists, we argue that the holder of this office does not function as the head of government as we understand that role. The transformation of political systems in Eastern Europe and in the Soviet Union itself will generate more debate as to the precise type of format existing in those political systems at a given point in time. While such dissensus may be unavoidable, these issues can be resolved by clarifying the criteria by which nations are assigned to one category or another.

With respect to the second factor, it would not matter whether a nation were classified as a parliamentary or cabinet democracy unless it could be shown that these types of systems perform differently from one another with respect to a conceptually distinct variable such as political stability. The type of political system may have utility as both an independent variable (putative cause of another factor) and a dependent variable, whereby the system type is explained by other variables, such as contextual ones. In any event, the ultimate utility of a typology of political formats is presumed by the move to bring the consideration of the nation-state back to the forefront of analysis.

Policy and Performance

The systematic study of political life was dominated by and almost identified with a paradigm (a conceptual framework or way of organizing and interpreting data) known as *systems analysis.* This framework views politics as the maintenance of an equilibrium between inputs (the contextual factors discussed above that generate demands and supports) and outputs (the decisions reached by the system with respect to the allocation of scarce resources and the values that define the system). In this scheme, the political system consists of the institutions and processes for converting the inputs into those outputs that can react to and relieve the stress placed upon the system by the inputs. We have discussed the contextual factors that we will examine in each nation under consideration as well as the variable of the political format or the political system itself. Until recent years, political scientists in general and comparativists in particular focused on the inputs from the contextual factors or the conversion processes of the political system itself. The study of the output side, known as public policy, has only come into vogue in recent decades.[27]

Yet, public policy is the way in which government affects our lives. The contextual factors and the conversion processes are of interest primarily with respect to how they influence public policy. Policy, after all, is what government does. Distinguishing again the formal legal aspects of government from the broader process of governing, public policy may be defined as the decisions government makes toward the achievement of some goal. Thus, while the passage of laws may constitute one aspect of the policy-making process, decisions by bureaucrats, executive orders by the head of government, the interpretation of laws by courts, and the selective enforcement of laws by police or administrative officials are all among the tools available to make policy. A single act of a government is not normally thought of as constituting public policy. Rather, public policy constitutes a series of actions defined in terms of some goal. The anti-inflationary policy favored by Anglo-American governments over the past decade, for example, may include fiscal activities (taxing and spending decisions) and monetarist activities involving various actions of the central banking system to restrict the supply of money. A foreign or defense policy may include decisions on various weapon systems, on the recruitment and deployment of military forces, and on the formation of alliances with other nations to promote a goal such as containment or deterrence.

The actions of government should be distinguished from the format of government. The choice between presidential democracy, British cabinet government, or a parliamentary system with a multitude of parties is a political variable, while the choice between market capitalism, welfare state capitalism, and state socialism is an economic variable. In nonacademic discourse, there has been a tendency to ignore the distinction between these political and economic dimensions and to equate certain political formats with certain

economic ones and vice versa. Specifically, there has been a tendency in the United States to equate democracy with market capitalism and to equate centrally planned economies with dictatorship. We will leave open the question of whether certain economic formats may encourage or impede certain political formats, a question susceptible to empirical inquiry. We are saying, however, that the two dimensions should not be equated by definition. Capitalism may or may not be conducive to democracy, but the two terms are definitionally distinct, and it is theoretically possible for any given political format to coexist with any given economic format. The types of political system have been categorized above. The major types of economic systems and the criteria for distinguishing them are delineated in Table 1-6.

The outline of economic systems presented in Table 1-6 describes three ideal or pure types. In practice, however, most nations adopt some modification or combination of these types. For example, the United States is closer to a free-enterprise market system than most other industrialized nations, yet it has gone a long way toward adopting policies of guaranteed well-being associated

TABLE 1-6   Major Types of Economic Systems

I. Capitalism (The major means of production, distribution, and exchange are owned by private [non-governmental] actors and run for profit.)
   A. Free-enterprise market capitalism (Decisions about what, where, and how much to produce or supply are left to the individual supplier or producer of the goods or services, and decisions about the allocation of who gets how much of what are left to the impersonal forces of supply and demand. Goods and services are competitively allocated, and material well-being is not guaranteed.)
   B. Welfare state capitalism (While the major means of production, distribution, and exchange are still in private hands and run for profit, many aspects of material well-being are regarded as rights to be guaranteed by public policy rather than competitively allocated. The greatest attainable level of material well-being is regarded as a value to be engineered by public policy. Values are allocated by rational decision making by designated actors rather than by impersonal forces; hence, this system entails a planned economy.)
II. Socialism (The major means of production, distribution, and exchange are owned and operated by the public sector, presumably in the public interest rather than for profit. The allocation of goods and services is rationally planned rather than left to market forces. Equality of material well-being is regarded as a value to be pursued by public policy.)

with the welfare state. It even contains a not insignificant amount of public ownership of the means of production, distribution, or exchange. It is theoretically possible for a system that has regular, genuine competitive elections to choose to adopt any of these three economic options or any combination thereof. Conversely, dictators could adopt either a planned, or command, economy or a market economy. A survey of patterns in the real world may or may not reveal that some kinds of economic and political formats tend to be associated with one another. These relationships can be tested empirically and justified logically. The preservation of a distinction between political and economic formats prevents these questions from being prematurely settled by definition and thereby permits their examination by systematic inquiry.

It may be that the combination of the foregoing pure types of economic formats is a product more of the state of technology and level of industrialization than of normative choice or value. The absence of real world manifestations of the pure types of any of these economic systems may suggest that they have proven unsatisfactory in actual performance. Particular economic arrangements may ultimately evolve and adapt to needs and circumstances, as do political formats in response to unfolding needs in each society. Of course, in a system with a pragmatic culture, this evolution will take place more quickly and painlessly than in an ideological system. Ultimately, however, an ideological style might inexorably succumb to the imperatives of advancing modernization and a shrinking world system.

We have discussed the idea of qualified convergence, the idea that an evolving state of technology inexorably associated with modernization forces patterns and similarities among the institutions and decision-making processes, regardless of differences in constitutional format, but that differences with respect to values and policy remain. The

events in Eastern Europe in 1990-1991 suggest that the idea of convergence may have applicability in the realm of economic format. As the events of the 1920s and 1930s convinced many that the pure market economics is unworkable in the real world, many in Eastern Europe, the Soviet Union, and elsewhere have become convinced that socialism and a purely planned economy are similarly unworkable. Formerly Marxist systems seem to be evolving to an as yet undetermined economic format partly in response to their former economic systems' inability to provide the minimal levels of expected prosperity. This evolution does appear to be moving in the direction of the welfare state capitalism predominant in Western Europe and even to a lesser extent in North America. Meanwhile, Great Britain, with the heaviest dose of public ownership in the West, is moving toward a degree of *privatization,* the transfer of the ownership of the means of production, distribution, and exchange from the public sector to the private sector. Yet, although for the past decade the British government has been in the hands of a prime minister more ideologically committed to the private sector than any other, this movement toward privatization and the undoing of welfare state guarantees has been limited. Thus while a degree of welfare state benefits has been institutionalized in the West, a trend toward increasing the private sector and introducing some market mechanisms may be discerned in the former Soviet bloc.

Policy results in the economic sector are measurable in terms of such standard economic indicators as gross national product (GNP), gross domestic product (GDP), per capita income, real spending power, unemployment rate, inflation rate, and balance-of-trade figures. One can thus draw conclusions about the success or failure of economic policies with a certain amount of empirical support. While some people regard the choice between a command economy, with its guaranteed levels of material equality, and a market economy as a choice with normative implications, the results of that choice become, to some extent, intersubjectively demonstrable. A certain economic format, unlike a political format, is not inherently good or bad but instead can be evaluated in terms of its results in a particular context.

CONCLUSIONS

By combining theoretic material on classes of political systems with chapters on particular national manifestations of those theories, we hope to show how patterns of contextual factors, decision-making structures and processes, and policy outcomes interact with one another in particular systems and how such specific knowledge can be integrated into theories that can fulfill the functions of any enterprise of academic inquiry with a degree of explanatory power. We are especially interested in identifying the factors that promote effective government, the ability to process and resolve the major issues confronting that society. In so doing, we attempt to identify patterns and trends in the political systems under consideration and the contexts in which those systems operate. This should allow one to extrapolate from the patterns and trends described in this volume to an expectation of what one would find in systems not examined here. We believe that it is important for students to understand both the politics of various countries for their own sake and the process of building explanations through the comparative method. Without the latter understanding, the question of why students should be expected to know anything about Great Britain and Western Europe, let alone Nigeria or China, is difficult to answer persuasively.

The inclusion of the theory chapters attests to the value that the authors place on drawing generalizations across systems. The ability to draw such generalizations from the analysis of individual nations depends on the organization of those analyses in comparable ways and with equivalent concepts. Accordingly, we have attempted to set forth an organizational scheme containing broadly applicable concepts, units of analysis, and questions that will permit comparison across national and cultural boundaries. If the chapters that follow not only enlighten students as to the variety of political structures in the world but also enable some of them to look for and perceive cross-national patterns in and relationships among social and political phenomena, this text will have succeeded as much as the authors have dared to hope.

NOTES

1. Among the many early calls for the transformation of the field from its traditional orientation to one that is putatively more scientific, perhaps the most famous is Roy Macridis, *The Study of Comparative Government* (New York: Random House, 1955). See also Harry Eckstein, "A Perspective on Comparative Politics, Past and Present," in Harry Eckstein and David Apter, eds., *Comparative Politics: A Reader* (New York: The Free Press, 1963).

2. This argument was developed in Arend Lijphart, "Comparative Politics and the Comparative Method," *American Political Science Review,* vol. 65, no. 3 (September 1971), pp. 682–693.

3. Karl Popper, *The Logic of Scientific Discovery* (New York: Harper Torchbooks, 1954), p. 27, referred to this inability to prove a scientific proposition true as "the problem of induction," the idea that one can never conclusively infer that any observed pattern will hold up for all time. For Popper, "the criterion of demarcation," that which distinguishes a proposition that is scientific from one that is not, is falsifiability.

4. See May Brodbeck, "Explanation, Prediction, and Imperfect Knowledge," in May Brodbeck, ed., *Readings in the Philosophy of Social Science* (New York: The Macmillan Co., 1968), pp. 363 ff., for the best exposition of the argument that the difference between natural and social science explanations lies not in their structure but in their completeness and in the accuracy of the predictions they generate.

5. Adam Przeworski and Henry Teune, *The Logic of Comparative Social Inquiry* (New York: John Wiley, 1970), pp. 26–30.

6. For an example of this school of thought, see Robert Wesson, *Modern Governments* (Englewood Cliffs, NJ: Prentice Hall, 1981), esp. p. 10.

7. For data on how incomplete the revolution is, see Lee Sigelman and George Gadbois, "Contemporary Comparative Politics: An Inventory and Assessment," *Comparative Political Studies*, vol. 16, no. 3 (October 1983), pp. 275–307; and Lawrence Mayer, "Practicing What We Preach: Comparative Politics in the 1980s," *Comparative Political Studies*, vol. 16, no. 2 (July 1983), pp. 173–94.

8. Gabriel Almond, "A Functional Approach to Comparative Politics," in Gabriel Almond and James Coleman, eds., *The Politics of the Developing Areas* (Princeton: Princeton University Press, 1960), pp. 1–63.

9. David Easton, *The Political System* (New York: Alfred A. Knopf, 1951), p. 129.

10. See, e.g., Lucien Pye, *Aspects of Political Development* (Boston: Little Brown, 1966), pp. 62–67; and Raymond Grew, ed., *Crises of Political Development in Europe and the United States* (Princeton: Princeton University Press, 1978).

11. Ibid.

12. Rupert Emerson, *From Empire to Nation* (Cambridge: Harvard University Press, 1960).

13. The literature on political culture is voluminous. Among the more recent contributions is John R. Gibbons, ed., *Contemporary Political Culture* (Newbury Park, CA: Sage Publications, 1989). Among the classic expositions of the dimensions and utility of the concept are Gabriel Almond and G. Bingham Powell, *Comparative Politics: A Developmental Approach* (Boston: Little Brown, 1966), pp. 50–72; and Gabriel Almond and Sidney Verba, *The Civic Culture* (Boston: Little Brown, 1965).

14. Harry Eckstein, "A Theory of Stable Democracy," in *Division and Cohesion in Democracy: A Study of Norway* (Princeton: Princeton University Press, 1966); and Harry Eckstein, "Authority Relations and Government Performance: A Theoretical Framework," *Comparative Political Studies*, vol. 2, no. 3 (October 1969), pp. 269–326.

15. This concept is developed with respect to Great Britain in Charles A. Lindblom, "The Science of Muddling Through," *Public Administration Review*, vol. 29, no. 2 (Spring 1959), pp. 79–88.

16. Herbert Spiro, *Government by Constitution* (New York: Random House, 1959), pp. 180–181. Spiro's book, dated as it is, still contains the best exposition of the concept of political style in Chapters 13 and 14.

17. Robert Alford, *Party and Society* (Chicago: Rand McNally, 1963).

18. Among the notable items in this sizable corpus of research, see Ronald Inglehart's *The Silent Revolution: Changing Values and Political Styles Among Western Publics* (Princeton: Princeton University Press, 1977); *Culture Shift in Advanced Industrial Society* (Princeton: Princeton University Press, 1989); "New Perspectives on Value Change," *Comparative Political Studies*, vol. 17, no. 4 (January 1985), pp. 485–535; and "The Changing Structure of Political Cleavages in Western Society," in Russell Dalton, Scott Flanagan, and Paul Beck, eds., *Electoral Change in Advanced Industrial Democracies* (Princeton: Princeton University Press, 1984), pp. 25–69. See also his debate with Scott Flanagan on this theory: "Value Change in Industrial Societies," *American Political Science Review*, vol. 81, no. 4 (December 1987), pp. 1289–1319.

19. Lawrence Mayer with John Burnett, *Politics in Industrial Societies: A Comparative Perspective* (New York: John Wiley: 1977), pp. 115 ff., 136–37.

20. Easton, *The Political System*, p. 129.

21. See Daniel Bell, *The Coming of Post Industrial Society* (New York: Basic Books, 1973).

22. See e.g., Seymour Lipset, "Some Social Requisites of Democracy," *The American Political Science Review*, vol. 53, no. 1 (March 1959), pp. 69–105; and Samuel Huntington, *The Third Wave* (Norman: University of Oklahoma Press, 1991), pp. 311–16.

23. Perhaps the most famous early effort to classify the universe of political systems is Gabriel Almond, "Comparative Political Systems," *Journal of Politics*, vol. 18, no. 3 (August 1956), pp. 391–409. For a critique of this scheme, see Lawrence Mayer, *Comparative Political Inquiry* (Homewood, IL: The Dorsey Press, 1972), pp. 17–19.

24. The classic statement of the critical role of the middle class in democratic development—"No bourgeois, no democracy"—is in Barrington Moore, *The Social Origins of Democracy and Dictatorship* (Boston: The Beacon Press, 1966), p. 418.

25. See e.g., Dietrich Rueschemeyer, Evelyne Huber Stephens, and John D. Stephens, *Capitalist Development and Democracy* (Chicago: University of Chicago Press, 1992). These authors, however, acknowledge that the variable position of middle-class elements in conjunction with the working-class elements is critical in determining the type of political system.

26. E.g., Howard Wiarda and Harvey Kline, eds., *Latin American Politics and Development*, 3rd ed. (Boulder, CO: Westview Press, 1990), pp. 27, 66–67, and passim.

27. Among the significant volumes in this burgeoning area are Arnold Heidenheimer, Hugh Heclo, and Carolyn Teich Adams, *Comparative Public Policy: The Politics of Social Choice in Europe and America*, 2nd ed., (New York: St. Martin's Press, 1983); and Hans Keman, "Politics, Policies, and Consequences," in Franz Lehner and Manfred Schmidt, eds., *The Political Management of Mixed Economies*.

2

Industrial Democracies: Ideals and Reality

"Democracy . . . is a charming form of government, full of variety and disorder, and dispensing a sort of equality to equals and unequals alike."

Plato, The Republic, *Book VIII*

Of the approximately 185 nations now holding United Nations membership, only some 20 or so may reasonably qualify for that class of systems generally identified as industrial democracies. The category of democracy itself is somewhat broader, as that format or a facsimile thereof has been increasingly adopted by some 30 nations over the past 20 years, especially among less industrialized nations, in what Sam Huntington has called the "third wave" of democratization.[1] Indeed, Huntington identifies some 72 nations that have at some point experimented with a democratic format since the first wave in the mid-nineteenth century.

This imprecision with respect to numbers is not accidental. While there may be a widespread consensus with respect to the inclusion of some nations in this category, no such consensus exists with a number of other nations, nations whose industrial or democratic status might be considered marginal. For example, the democratic status of Japan, a nation in which one party has controlled the government throughout the history of the current regime and is likely to do so for

the foreseeable future, may be questioned by some. The industrialized status of some of the Mediterranean democracies and some of the smaller European democracies is also open to question.

Yet it is important to establish the criteria for inclusion in the category of industrial democracies with sufficient precision to remove any ambiguity as to whether a given nation should be included. Without such precision, it will be impossible to ascertain with confidence whether any statement about the requisites, operation, or impact of industrial democracies holds true for all such nations. One could always explain away any apparent exception to such an assertion by declaring that the particular case is not really an industrial democracy.

CONCEPTUALIZING INDUSTRIAL DEMOCRACY

There are two difficult concepts to be specified here: an industrial society and a democratic political format. The former presents the fewest definitional problems in that it entails measurable *indicators* (observable phenomena that determine whether and to what extent a concept is presumed to be present). We use such indicators in political science because we use concepts or ideas that are "soft" in that they do not directly refer to the observable world.

An industrial society is generally "indicated" when over 50 percent of its work force is engaged in industrial pursuits or in the productive or secondary sector of society. When a level of productive efficiency is reached at an advanced state of technology so that fewer people can produce the goods of society, more of the work force moves into the service, or tertiary, sector. Such societies have been given the highly popular label, *postindustrial societies.*[2] They are characterized by a high degree of specialization and division of labor and a predominant role for technically trained experts, or *technocrats,* in the power structure and decision-making process of the societies. In the United States, one of the first systems to reach postindustrial status, over half of the work force is now engaged in one way or another in the processing of information. Later in this chapter, we shall discuss how the attributes of postindustrial societies modify the model of democracies and affect the attainment of democratic values.

The democracies of Western Europe and the Anglo-American world have either reached postindustrial status or approximate that status more closely than they do the early stages of industrialization. The present authors have argued elsewhere that this fact makes it useful to conceptualize the development of modern industrial societies as a continuous variable rather than as a dichotomous typology, or in other words to regard the nations under consideration as more or less mature industrial democracies as opposed to either industrial or postindustrial

democracies.[3] Simply to dichotomize the range of systems under consideration allows too great a variation within each category to be useful. The key attribute of postindustrial societies, we will see, is their advanced state of technology, a variable that is in principle a continuous one (that is, a "more or less" rather than an "either/or" condition).

The question of its scientific utility aside, the tripartite classification of societies as either preindustrial, industrial, or postindustrial has become well established in the political science literature, and the concept of postindustrial society has become particularly fashionable among scholars who seem to coin new terms faster than they create new ideas. As discussed at length by Daniel Bell and others,[4] the concept entails a society characterized by a highly advanced state of technology that in turn requires a high degree of specialization and division of labor. As issues such as arms control, protection of the environment, and management of an increasingly complex economy become more complicated, only technically trained specialists can fully grasp them. More and more decisions that once would have been made by the politically accountable legislatures and heads of government, for example, are made by these experts, or technocrats. Political systems whose decision-making process is dominated by technocrats are sometimes referred to as *technocracies,* irrespective of their formal or constitutionally designated political structure.

The importance of understanding the concept of a postindustrial (or mature industrial) society should become clear below when it is shown that the advanced technological complexity of such societies necessarily modifies the manner in which political democracies operate. In fact, there is a growing literature on trends in these societies such as the growing political role of the higher civil service or public bureaucracy and what scholars are calling *neocorporatism* (a concept that is fully discussed below).

The second major concept that must be more precisely defined and understood is political democracy itself. While the term *democracy* is a familiar one, its empirical content is imprecise and has been applied to a wide variety of political forms. Its widespread popularity is a function of the highly positive normative content that the term has acquired; many political leaders and political systems choose to call themselves democracies in order to transfer the positive image associated with the word to whatever political format they have adopted. For example, Kwame Nrumah of Ghana said that he was practicing "guided democracy," while Sekou Toure of Guinea claimed to be practicing "tutelary democracy." Even the former Soviet Union claimed to have established "democratic centralism" and to be following a truer form of democracy than exists in the West. More recently, many of the newly independent states of the former Soviet Union and the former Warsaw Pact nations aspire to a democratic form of government without a clear sense of the precise attributes of that format or of the prerequisites that enable democracy to emerge and be sustained.

Clearly, the term *democracy* has been defined in various ways, even when one ignores its misapplication to regimes that we in the West consensually regard as autocratic systems. A definition of the term must possess the following attributes if it is to be useful in analyzing the world that we know through our senses. First, it must unambiguously apply to the range of nations that we agree should be so classified and differentiate those nations from those that we agree should not be so classified. A definition that sets up criteria that no Western nation can meet is not useful, nor is one that could apply not only to Western nations but also to nations characterized by unrestrained one-party or one-elite rule.

As applied to Western systems, one may distinguish two types of conceptualizations of democracy: a minimal definition and more elaborate definitions. The minimal definition begins with the recognition that all modern and reasonably complex nations are ruled by elites. A large body of cross-national empirical research has established that the effective participation in the making of policy decisions is actually confined to a rather narrow segment of the population and that a small fraction of the citizens of modern political systems possess the knowledge, basic information, and interest required for effective political participation.[5] In that sense, a criterion of government by the people would eliminate all modern nations from the democratic category.

Responsiveness: A Core Democratic Value

Alternatively, democracy may be conceptualized in terms of the responsiveness of the elite that inevitably attends to the needs and demands of the citizens. Arend Lijphart, for example, argues that a nation is democratic to the extent that it acts "in accord with the people's preferences."[6] If democracy does not entail government actually by the people, it seems reasonable to argue that the concept at the very least entails government that readily responds to the needs and demands of the population. One criterion that is often cited in evaluating the degree of democracy attributed to a political format is the accuracy and speed with which the government responds to shifts in public opinion.

Yet the aforementioned lack of information and inclination on the part of the citizens means that all governments act with a good deal of autonomy from the societal preferences, as Eric Nordlinger has persuasively argued.[7] Public opinion, from which societal preferences are presumably determined, is generally inchoate and the product of opinion leaders, as Walter Lippman told us as early as 1922 and reemphasized by his concept of the "phantom public" in 1930.[8]

Accordingly, it is clear that the democratic model of a government retaining its legitimacy to govern as a function of its responsiveness to the spontaneously generated demands of the rational, informed, and active citizenry does not fully describe those advanced industrial states that we classify as democratic. It is therefore prudent not to rely exclusively on such criteria in a definition meant to apply to the variety of Western nations so classified.

The Minimal Criterion of Democracy

The criterion that does apply to that range of nations that we in the West normally regard as democracies, while excluding those nations that we commonly regard as autocracies (i.e., nondemocracies), is the one offered by Joseph Schumpeter in his classic work, *Capitalism, Socialism, and Democracy,* which defines democracy by competition for political leadership.[9] That is, in practical, procedural terms, democratic societies are defined as those that choose their governments with more or less regularly scheduled, competitive elections. A competitive election is one in which the opposition is not suppressed but rather is accepted as legitimate by the incumbent elites; it does not imply any particular rate of turnover or alternation of power among elites. This is an important fact, because some of the nations that are widely accepted as democracies experience long periods of control or a hegemony of power by one party or one set of elites.

Defining democracy in the Schumpeterian sense of competition among elites for political office has several major advantages. The first, which has already been discussed, is the fact that it best fits the reality of industrial nations by providing a criterion that actually distinguishes those nations that we normally consider to be democratic from those nations that are not usually regarded as in the democratic category. Some people may ascribe to nondemocratic nations on what is inevitably a judgmental basis a degree of political or socioeconomic equality, or even a degree of responsiveness to societal needs or preferences, that meets or even exceeds the degree of those attributes found in nations we regard as democratic. But the legitimacy of formal electoral competition is a criterion that is less likely to provoke disagreement as to whether it describes a particular nation.

Second, this criterion leaves the question of the relationship between democracy and values such as widespread participation, governmental responsiveness to societal demands, and the amount of political and socioeconomic equality open for inquiry or investigation, instead of being settled by definition. It is especially important to distinguish the variable of the type of political system from the question of that system's socioeconomic policies. It will become clear throughout this book, especially in the section on public policy, that the world's democracies pursue socioeconomic policies and systems that differ significantly in degree if not in kind from those found in the United States; hence, it would be misleading to imply any necessary connection between the economic policies and system used in the United States and political democracy. One may conceptualize these policies in the United States as tending toward what is commonly referred to as *market capitalism.* Capitalism is an economic system in which the major means of production, distribution, and exchange are owned by private (i.e., nongovernmental) actors (people or institutions) and run for profit. Such a system is logically compatible with either the presence or absence of competitive elections. The ideal type of a market system is one in which the values of society are allocated by the impersonal forces of supply and demand and the actors acquire these values on the basis of the ability to pay, which is acquired by a competitive process. Most other industrialized nations lean more in the direction of what is called *welfare state capitalism.* The ideal type of this system is still one in which the major means of production, distribution, and exchange are in nongovernmental hands and run for profit. However, in this type of system, a substantial amount of the major values of the society are guaranteed to individuals as a matter of right, regardless of the presence or absence of the ability to pay. A third type of economic system that is found to some extent among the world's democracies is called *state socialism,* in which the major means of production, distribution, and exchange are owned and operated by the state and ostensibly run in the public interest rather than by the profit motive. The rationale of this system and an analysis of its success will be discussed at length in the section on policy. For now, it should be noted that some industrial democracies, most notably Great Britain and France, have adopted far more public ownership than would be tolerated in the United States, although even those economic systems are a mixture of public and private ownership.

Varying claims have been advanced with regard to the relationship between a system's economic policies and its capacity to establish and sustain successful democracy, claims that will be discussed at length in the appropriate context. These claims should not be settled by definition; hence, it is important to keep the political variable analytically distinct from the question of the type of economic system. The autonomy of these variables was indicated in Tables 1-5 and 1-6. It should be noted that various combinations of economic and political attributes are possible; in other words, there is no *necessary* connection between one type of economic system and a certain type of political system.

Although the example of the Soviet bloc has caused a widespread association in American minds between socialism and dictatorships, it must be remembered that democratic socialism is not only a theoretic possibility but has approached reality in Great Britain, among other places. While Americans may view market capitalism as inexorably associated with democracy because of our own experience, our market economy is highly qualified by a substantial degree of the autonomy of producers from market forces and of governmental control. Moreover, the private ownership of the major means of production run for profit characterized the economic system of Nazi Germany; hence, while capitalism may promote democracy, it certainly does not guarantee it. Not only the planes, tanks, and munitions to run the Nazi war effort but even the crematoriums and gases used in the infamous death camps were developed and sold to the government for profit.

Third, as implied above, the Schumpeterian definition of democracy presents relatively fewer problems of measurement than do alternative standards such as equality or responsiveness. Reasonable people with equal access to the relevant information can therefore agree as to the democratic status of a given nation, which facilitates consensus as to whether propositions about democracies in general are consistent with the evidence.

Two political criteria have frequently been added to qualify the simple Schumpeterian standard of regular competitive elections: one, that in order to be meaningful, the competition must result in the more or less regular alternation of elites in and out of office; and two, that the choices presented in these competitive elections must reflect clear and meaningful alternatives of public policies. The question of whether these two criteria should be part of the definition of democracy is analyzed below in the section on accountability as another core democratic value. The first criterion would disqualify a number of systems commonly placed in the democratic category, systems in which one party controls the government for such long periods that the opposition does not have a realistic chance of winning any given election. Such a party would be said to exercise a *hegemony* of power, and the system would be called a *hegemonic* one. Sweden is a case in point. The Social Democrats were in power in the nation from 1935 to 1976. In India, the Congress Party has controlled the government since independence, except for one eight-month hiatus, and the Liberal Democratic Party of Japan did not lose control of its government during the entire history of its postwar democracy until 1993. In fact, in most Western democracies, rather long periods of control by one party with only brief interludes out of power seem to be the rule.

Western democracies have also generally seemed to fall short on the second criterion of providing clear and meaningful choices of public policy. As Anthony Downs pointed out decades ago, in a case of relatively aggregated party systems (a concept explored below and a situation that some view as increasingly characteristic of Western democracies), the programmatic and ideological positions of the competing parties tend to converge toward the amorphous center.[10] Thus, with the voter frequently faced with a "Tweedledum-Tweedledee" choice between two very similar and very vague programmatic or ideological choices, the question is raised as to whether they have a meaningful choice at all.

Accountability: Another Core Democratic Value

The question comes down to whether competitive elections are valued for their own sake (an absolute or consummatory value) or for what they can facilitate or bring about (an instrumental value). In other words, does the fact of legitimate opposition promote a value that is associated with democracy in that it distinguishes the class of systems commonly found in the democratic category from those that are not? It was noted that criteria such as the widespread participation of the citizenry in political roles, greater equality of socio-economic well-being or of political impact, and even the extent to which the government is responsive to or in some unspecified way represents or embodies the needs and interests of society may apply to or be plausibly claimed by all the systems that are consensually placed outside the democratic category.

However, one key attribute that seems to distinguish nations in the democratic category from other nations is that democratic elites operate under relatively narrower constraints or bounds of discretion than do elites of autocracies. Clearly, it will require a great deal more dissatisfaction with the performance of the government to generate a revolution to unseat an elite in an autocracy than it would take to cause the electorate to vote for an available legitimate opposition. In other words, democratic elites are relatively more *accountable* than elites in autocracies. *Accountability* here refers to a structure that creates a perception on the part of elites that their political well-being requires them to justify the results of how they have governed in terms of some conception of the public interest.

While all elites are accountable to some extent, those in democracies, as that term is conceptualized herein, are significantly more accountable than those in autocracies. Even in the case of hegemonic party systems such as Sweden's or Japan's, the presence of a legitimate opposition still pressures the elites to justify their policies to a much greater extent than would be the case if resort to armed insurrection constituted the only alternative to public dissatisfaction with governmental performance. The hegemony of the afore-mentioned party systems in fact appears to be attributable to the across-the-board success of their national policies. Sweden has one of the world's highest per capita incomes and an absence of significant pockets of abject poverty. There is widespread consensus on the legitimacy of its welfare state and no significant racial or ethnic minorities among the population. Its relatively low international profile means that Sweden is not operating under the perception of direct short-term threats to its security or other vital interests. In short, Swedish politics seems to lack any issue around which to mobilize a viable challenge to the incumbents. Japan has similarly not been faced with any significant problems with the major issues of economic prosperity, direct threats to security or other vital interests, or the integration of minority populations. However, the ruling party in Japan has been racked by a succession of corruption scandals that resulted in several changes of leadership. The party itself, however, managed to hold onto power until July, 1993. In other words, the ruling parties in these two systems maintained hegemony for so long because their respective populations are basically satisfied with their political performance.

Numerous scholars have suggested that for competitive elections to be meaningful, the major competing parties must offer distinct alternatives on the salient issues of public policy. The outcome of these issues must be resolved by the outcome of the party competition. The cleavages that define society should correspond to the cleavages that define the party system. Yet, there are significant attributes and trends in the party systems of Western democracies that raise serious questions about their ability to offer such meaningful and distinct choices on public policy.

The first such attribute is the oft-cited propensity of parties in highly aggregated, or two-party, systems to converge toward the same centrist majority. This tendency, perhaps most clearly articulated by Downs, is a function of the fact that rationality dictates that all parties compete for the majority in so far as that majority position can be ascertained.[11] Parties will not articulate a minority position merely to be different and present a choice. The result of this phenomenon is that the choice presented to the voter is six of one and half a dozen of the other. It is not clear, however, that this conventional wisdom is always consistent with the facts. Numerous instances may be cited of the polarization or the triumph of extremist or antidemocratic political forces in recent decades. In fact, the rise of parties of the populist right in western democracies—parties such as France's National Front, Germany's *Die Republikaner,* Belgium's *Vlaams Blok,* and Canada's Reform Party and *Bloc Québeçois,* has become an important topic drawing the attention of a growing group of scholars such as Hans-Georg Betz and Micheal Minkenberg. We will see in the following chapter that from the late 1970s to the early 1990s the two major parties in Great Britain were each captured by their respective militant wings—the Tories by the Thatcherite right and Labour by the socialist and pacifist left. More recently, over four decades of nearly unbroken centrist Christian Democratic rule in Italy was ended by the triumph of a coalition of right-wing parties, including Gianfranco Fini's National Alliance (formerly the Italian Social Movement, an unabashedly neofascist party) and the Northern League, whose main principle is separation from the southern part of the nation. The 1994 Canadian election results, discussed below, are another instance of the triumph of noncentrist forces in Western democracies, as is the ascension of leaders of the Republican right such as Newt Gingrich, Jesse Helms, and Alfonse D'Amato to control of the American Congress in 1994.

The second attribute or trend is articulated by Otto Kirchheimer in his now landmark article that describes the evolution of European party systems from fragmented systems articulating clearly distinct programmatic or ideological positions to what he calls "catch-all parties"[12] that attempt to appeal to the widest possible variety of voters and interests by avoiding the espousal of specific programs or principles. To the extent that a party can avoid taking clear stands on points of controversy, it will alienate fewer groups and interests and thus be able to appeal to a greater range of such groups. The aggregation of the previously fragmented French party system, whose fragmentation had almost become institutionalized during the Third and Fourth Republics, into the two political forces that one finds in the Fifth Republic is a classic case in point. The aggregation of the party system of the Federal Republic of Germany after its early fragmentation and after the extreme party fragmentation of the Weimar Republic is another classic manifestation of the Kirchheimer thesis. This perceived trend toward "catch-all parties" is epitomized by the deideologization of the Social Democratic Party of Germany from a Marxist party to a middle-class, bourgeois party with their famous 1959 Bad Godesburg Basic Program. Clearly, if Western parties no longer stand for anything very specific in terms of program or principle, they cannot fulfill the function of offering voters meaningful choices on public policy. As noted, the recent evidence is mixed as to whether the major parties of the West are so devoid of principle as to be appropriately labeled "catch-all" especially in light of the rise of a number of parties with clearly defined principles or programs such as the Greens, the National Alliance of Italy, and the various separatist parties of Italy, Belgium, and Canada discussed below.

THE RISE OF POSTMATERIALIST CLEAVAGES AND PARTY CONFLICT

A third trend that interferes with parties offering such policy alternatives to voters is the fact that the cleavages on which parties are based reflect values and issues that were salient to Western societies a generation ago but are less salient now. An important thesis in the comparative analysis of Western societies, which will be discussed in some detail in other contexts, is that such societies have undergone a reorientation in their basic values that is so fundamental as to be labeled a "silent revolution."[13] Parties were formed and achieved their identity in an era of comparative scarcity, when the main concerns were those of the distribution of material well-being. The parties of that era were identified with positions emanating from the perspective of class conflict, such as labor or modified Marxism. However, the generation raised since World War II in a period of prosperity is chiefly concerned with what the progenitor of this theory, Ronald Inglehart, calls "postmaterialist" values, which emanate from concerns over life style.[14] (Examples include issues involving ecology, civil liberties, feminism, or sexual morality.) Thus although the parties are not only traditionally identified with but almost emotionally attached to the rhetoric and symbols of class conflict, party conflict is not congruent with the actual issues that divide society.

This lack of salience of party cleavages and positions to the concerns of contemporary Western societies has led in some nations to a sharp decline in the extent to which individuals profess a basic attachment to a particular political party, a process called *dealignment*.[15] While party identification independent of actual votes has never had the degree of reality in Europe that it seems to have had in the United States, such identification was formerly much greater than it is now. This may be taken as further evidence of the growing irrelevance of the Western party systems to the resolution of actual political issues and the consequent failure of parties to present choices to the voter on the issues that matter.

Party Competition and Democracy

The aforementioned trends in party systems together lead inevitably to the conclusion that political parties in Western democracies do not offer real and meaningful choices to the voters on the salient issues of public policy. This conclusion begs the question of whether the mere fact of electoral competition between parties, even if they may not offer meaningful policy choices, still furthers the values inherent in the concept of democracy, especially the ideals of structured accountability.

The conclusion offered here is that the fact that competitive elections exist imposes a degree of accountability that is significantly greater than the accountability of dictatorships, irrespective of the extent to which dictators may claim to represent or embody the true interests of the society or of the degree of economic or political equality they claim to engineer. In a competitive system each of the major parties will tend to converge on the majority position because they believe that if they do not, the opposition will. Parties that want to control the government will not espouse a minority position merely to give the voters a choice. When it becomes clear to major party leaders, either through group or small party activity, that a new position either has or may potentially have majority support, the major parties will normally compete to accommodate that position, given the presence of a viable opposition. As discussed in the next chapter, there was speculation that the control of the British Labour Party by its

militant left in the late 1970s allowed Margaret Thatcher to pursue her agenda of the more ideological right. Without the presence of a legitimate opposition, parties are under no structured or imminent pressure to care what a majority of the population think or want.

THE CULTURAL REQUISITES OF DEMOCRACY

As comparative politics was transformed from an essentially descriptive to an explanatory enterprise, attention quickly turned to the context in which politics occurred. The constitutionally designated structures of government do not, after all, operate in a vacuum but rather in a context of social and cultural factors that affect the manner in which those formal political structures function. If one is going to explain something, one must analyze those phenomena that substantially affect that thing. Hence, political scientists were compelled to analyze those social and cultural factors that affect the operation of political systems, which previously had been left to the realm of sociologists and other social scientists. *Political culture* is a term that refers to those dispositional orientations toward political objects that have become so widely held among the members of a political system that they are used to characterize the political system itself. *Dispositional orientations* are those aspects of the internal state of an individual that dispose that person to react in certain ways to certain stimuli. Specifically, political culture refers to the attitudes, beliefs, and feelings about the political system or one's fellow human beings, as well as knowledge and information about political objects.

A literature has developed regarding the cultural properties necessary or at least supportive of the institutions of political democracy. The growth of this literature has been hampered until very recently by the logistical difficulties and expense involved in gathering data about the dispositional attributes of individuals. Until the late 1950s, most assertions about political culture were impressionistic, and many such propositions based on conventional wisdom proved vulnerable to the ultimate realities of hard data.

The first major cross-national and empirical study of the cultural attributes of successful democracy was Gabriel Almond and Sidney Verba's "Five Nation Study," reported in their book *The Civic Culture*.[16] The point of attack of this study was the dominant conventional wisdom model of the democratic political culture—what the authors called "the rational-activist model." This model held that successful democracies are built upon a citizenry that is well informed of the issues and alternatives of public policy, that takes an active role and interest in public affairs, and that will therefore threaten the tenure in office of any elites who do not govern in the rational interest of the majority of the public. The data from this study as well as those from a growing body of cross-national election and survey research belie the assumptions of the rational-activist model, and instead indicate that the citizens of Western democracies—including those well-established role models of the Anglo-American democracies—are neither politically active nor reasonably well informed about political issues. The figures vary from one study to another, but the most optimistic estimates of the American electorate—apparently the most active and best informed in the west—indicate that less than a quarter of the population could be classified as active and that from a quarter to a third of the population engage in no measurable political activity whatsoever.[17]

Therefore, according to Almond and Verba, an alternative to the rational-activist

model will have to distinguish the cultures of the "successful" democracies from those of the less successful ones. The model they offer—the "civic culture"—stresses a sense of an obligation to keep informed about and to participate in public affairs so competently and so effectively as to hold the elites accountable. In other words, although the rational-activist model is a myth, it is widely accepted by elites and citizens alike. Hence, the elites, believing in the myth and being aware of the citizens' potential involvement, act as if the citizens will be pounding on their door if they cannot justify how they govern in terms of the public interest.

Almond and Verba suggest that the ideal culture would not be the rational-activist model, even if it could be made a reality, for such an aroused citizenry continually holding the elites in close check would not afford the government the discretion inherent in the role of governing. Hence, they argue that the civic culture model provides an example of what they call "balanced disparities," in which the actually passive and uninformed citizenry allows government the discretion it needs while the myth of a potentially informed and aroused citizenry provides the necessary constraint on elite discretion. Since even democracies must be able to govern or they will fail, it has been suggested that successful democracies need "a healthy dose of authoritarianism."[18]

This raises an important variable in the consideration of the democratic culture—the dominant conceptions of authority. One may conveniently consider three alternative conceptions of authority: egalitarian, submissive, or deferential.

An egalitarian attitude toward authority entails a belief that people are relatively equal in their capacity to make political judgments and to assume major roles in the formation of public policy. The ordinary citizens know best what is in their own interests;

hence, the role of elites is to carry out the wishes of the electorate. Mechanisms such as referendums, recall provisions, and highly fragmented party systems should exist for keeping such elites under close control, with as little independent discretion as possible, by giving voice to every shadow of opinion in the society. Such a conception of authority resists giving elites the authority to govern, an authority that is also necessary to reconcile the claims of the many competing interests in any complex society. Hence, some theorists argued that a highly egalitarian conception of authority may contribute to the failure to resolve important issues and ultimately to political instability.

A submissive orientation toward authority, on the other hand, is inclined to grant more discretion to and impose fewer constraints upon the judgments of elites than are compatible with the democratic value of holding those elites structurally accountable. Based upon the assumption that some people or even, to a large extent, some classes of people are more fit to rule than others, the submissive orientation values the unquestioning obedience of subordinates to their respective superordinates.

Because the third conception of authority—deference—also entails the presumption that some people are more qualified to rule than others, it is harder to distinguish from submission than it is from egalitarianism. While deferential citizens are disposed to grant the elites wide discretion in the day-to-day business of governing, in their view the elites are responsible for governing in the public interest and are owed obedience only in so far as the overall impact of the policies of the government are justifiable in terms of some conception of that public interest. The deferential view therefore combines acceptance of the insulation from the daily passions of public opinion inherent in the function of governing with the democratic value

of the structured accountability of the elites to the public interest. Some scholars therefore suggest that while egalitarianism may seem like the most democratic conception of authority in that it emphasizes the maximum public control of elites, the deferential conception of authority best combines the ultimate democratic value of structured accountability with the imperatives of reasonably effective government.

Effective government, after all, must be legitimate. That is, the regime must be widely accepted and must have at least the passive loyalty of the predominant portion of its citizens, irrespective of its specific performance in the short run. (There is a growing body of evidence, however, that dissatisfaction with governmental performance over the long run may erode that diffuse acceptance or support.)[19] No government can expect always to satisfy most of its citizens. Unless the sense of an obligation to obey the laws and exhibit loyalty to the system overrides the question of satisfaction with the current outcome of political issues, regimes cannot survive. Deference is therefore an integral part of effective government in which elites are insulated from the day-to-day passions of public opinion by the citizens' disposition to assume they are acting in the public interest.

The criterion of competitive elections entails cultural as well as structural attributes. Specifically, elections cannot be genuinely competitive unless there is a high degree of tolerance of those with whom one disagrees on political or politically relevant issues. Without such tolerance, opposition will not be legitimate. In a democracy, the rules of the political game—the procedures by which decision makers are chosen and decisions are made—must be more important than the outcome. Otherwise, those in power will tend to use that power to suppress rather than tolerate their opposition. The tolerance about which we are speaking implies that those in power should be able to accept their defeat from the privileges of office by a mere vote. For this kind of tolerance to exist, the substance of the issues at stake should not be perceived as fundamental. What has been called the "ideological distance between parties,"[20] a measurable concept referring to the extent to which the principles on which each of the parties stands fundamentally differ, must not be too great. If the outcome of the election matters too much to the electorate, the acceptance of the process will not be more important than the outcome.

This kind of tolerance flourishes best when politics is predominantly thought of as conflicts of interest rather than conflicts between right and wrong or good and evil. Politics based upon considerations of class and the distribution of material well-being leads to greater tolerance of opposition and the propensity to compromise with one's opponents than does the politics of symbols emanating from such divisions as linguistic, religious, ethnic, or cultural cleavages.[21]

Democracy thus seems to require a cultural context in which the democratic format itself has acquired a deep-seated legitimacy that exceeds one's commitment to any given set of political outcomes. This legitimacy is acquired by institutions that have simply been around a long time and performing at a level that is at least passively satisfactory to the citizenry. Of course, this longevity is in turn acquired by satisfactory performance over a long enough period that the institutions in question can become accepted for their own sake. In effect, a kind of vicious circle is in operation here. Institutions can gain widespread acceptance or legitimacy by lasting over time, yet in order to last, surviving numerous inevitable crises in the process, institutions must be legitimate.

In Western nations, the acquisition of legitimacy for the democratic political format seems to be tied to the sequential resolution of issues, or crises.[22] Nations that have been able to resolve their major issues one by one, beginning with the decisions of what kind of regime or political format to adopt, have fared better than those nations that have been forced to resolve numerous divisive and substantive issues at the same time that they were resolving the question of regime. The regime can then acquire the longevity necessary for legitimacy before it alienates large segments of the society by trying to resolve other controversial issues. These issues, such as those arising out of the social dislocations of the early stages of industrialization or the relationship between church and state, tend to be argued in terms of alternatives of constitutional system or regime format, unless these constitutional or format questions are first removed from the political agenda by a cloak of legitimacy. The key to resolving the question of regime before the other divisive issues of politics arise seems to be to settle the question of regime before the mobilization of the masses.[23] The expansion of the politically relevant segments of the population will inevitably escalate the level of expectations and hence the pressure placed upon the regime, according to Samuel Huntington and other major theorists concerned with the less developed or emerging nations.[24] The nations of the Western world that have most successfully established legitimacy for a democratic format seem to be those that settled their question of regime before the onset of the modern era, especially before the *levée en masse* (mobilization of the masses), a hallmark of the French Revolution of 1789 and an idea that permeated Europe with the Napoleonic Wars. By the early nineteenth century, those nations that had not yet legitimized their political format would no longer have the option of following Huntington's prescription for political order in changing societies—building strong and legitimate institutions before mass mobilization is allowed

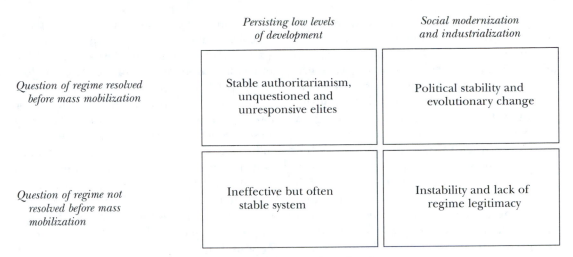

FIGURE 2-1   The impact of early resolution of the question of regime in system performance.

to take place. Latecomers to the nation-building process among Western industrial societies have had a relatively greater problem with constitutional stability than those that essentially completed that process before mass mobilization became an inexorable reality (see Figure 2-1). To the extent that this explanation of constitutional stability and the legitimacy of democratic institutions has validity, it is not encouraging for the prospects for stable democracy among the newly emerging nations that must resolve a range of desperately pressing problems while trying to build a stable political format.

SEGMENTED SOCIETIES AND THE PROBLEM OF COMMUNITY

Students of comparative politics have identified two types of cleavage structure: the criteria that both group and divide the individuals in a society. It is inevitable that individuals will develop loyalties other than those to the political system based on socioeconomic class, language, ethnicity, religion, geographic region, and the like. Individuals who are divided by one criterion, such as class, may be grouped by one or more other criteria, such as religion. In this kind of cleavage structure, called *cross-cutting cleavages,* individuals from any one grouping will be closely interacting and cooperating with those from several other groupings, a situation that would be expected to lower the intensity of partisan animosity and thereby help support a stable and successful political process.

The other type of cleavage structure, known as a *segmented society,* is one in which the lines of division are such that the subsections, or segments, of society are largely isolated from one another, so that individuals in one subgroup are unlikely to have personal interaction with individuals in others. Conventional wisdom says that segmented societies, given the absence of personal interaction to mitigate the formation of stereotyping and the building of intolerance, will tend to exacerbate the intensity of partisan animosity and make the process of negotiation and compromise, so essential to the democratic political process, much more difficult.

There are numerous examples of such relatively isolated subcultures among Western democracies, including the French Canadians in Canada, the Flemish and Walloons in Belgium, the four major ethnic groupings in the Netherlands, the Catholic Republicans and the Protestant Unionists in Northern Ireland, and the Catholic and the relatively secularized *lager* in Austria. When these subcultures are geographically defined, as with the French Canadian concentration in and around the province of Quebec, they will be represented by their own leadership, whose interest is in stressing and perpetuating the distinct interests of their segment. In such a case, the conflicts that grew out of class, linguistic, cultural, religious, or other diversities become intensified and hardened, and the independent power of their leaders is thereby enhanced. This is what Martin Heisler calls the "administrative regionalization" of these "culturally sensitive" policy areas.[25] These segmented groups become psychologically concerned about being culturally absorbed by a more numerous group in whose midst the minority resides, which Heisler calls the problem of "minorization."[26]

This raises the question of the legitimation of cultural diversities and the conflict between them and the concept of community. A *community* is an aggregation of interacting individuals defined by a set of shared values. This does not mean that all differences are eradicated, but there is agreement at some level on a set of fundamental values. Scholars are uncertain about the degree of consensus on fundamentals that is necessary for a political system to survive as a coherent entity. It does appear, however, that there is a point beyond which the promotion of multicultural distinctiveness can threaten the ability of a system to survive.

This has apparently been the case in Bel-

gium, where the fissiparous forces of three subcultures resulted in the transformation of that once-unitary nation that began in 1970 and culminated in a confederation in July 1993, with the approval of a constitutional change that took the ultimate authority, or sovereignty, with respect to issues salient to these respective subcultures (e.g., education, cultural affairs, regional planning, etc.) away from the central government and gave it to subcultural councils. (The Belgians call the new system a federation; however, with final authority clearly residing with regional governments, it has all the attributes of a confederation.)

Belgium's subcultures consist of the French-speaking, relatively more urbanized, and more secularized Walloons; the Flemish-speaking, historically more bucolic (nonurban in a pejorative or demeaning sense), and more religious Flemish; and the French-speaking Brusselites, who share the cultural attributes of the Walloons while comprising 80 percent of the inhabitants of the largest city within the geographical region of Flanders. One can, in fact, geographically locate the boundaries of Belgium's cultural linguistic groupings, which facilitates their political representation by their own leaders. These groupings, without a common linguistic, religious, or cultural orientation, do not share common sets of information and ideas. The 1993 state visits of Guy Spitaels, minister president of the Walloon government, to Paris, and of his Flemish counterpart, Luc Van den Brande, to The Hague, underscored the growing sense of Flanders and Wallonia as autonomous political systems. A new constitution in 1995 has shifted much additional power to the four regional assemblies: Flemish, Walloonian, French speaking Brusselites, and a small German speaking community in the East. These assemblies will oversee housing, environment, energy, transportation, employment, and agriculture. In this context, the Belgium party system has been transformed from the stable, three-party system that had existed for over a half-century, consisting of a Belgian Social Christian Party, a Belgian Socialist Party, and a Belgian Liberal Party, to a multiparty system first dominated by three parties of cultural defense (the Unified People's Party, the Walloon Assembly, and the Democratic Front of French-Speaking Brusselites) and now a fractionalized twelve-party system with no party drawing support evenly across the regions. For example, there is now a Flemish Social Christian Party and a Wallonian Social Christian Party, a Flemish Socialist Party and a Wallonian Socialist Party, and a Flemish Liberal Party and a Wallonian Liberal Party. Even the parties that are not duplicated in the major subcultures draw their support from one or the other subculture, just as the environmentalist party is almost exclusively Wallonian and the extremist anti-immigrant party is almost exclusively Flemish. The older parties of cultural defense have been losing ground to the

more specialized Flemish and Wallonian parties. The Walloonian Assembly has given way to more specialized Wallonian parties. The party line-up in Beligium as of the most recent general election (May, 1995) is presented in Table 2-1.

Canada, another clearly segmented society, has similarly been moving toward the transformation of its political system to accommodate the demands of its minority segments and fears of "minorisation," or cultural absorption. Its French Canadian subculture is largely found within the province of Quebec, rendering the elites of that province spokespersons for the group's separatist ambitions. The French Canadians, or *Québeçois,* are French speaking, Catholic, religious, extremely conservative, and alienated from the British Commonwealth connections of English-speaking Canada. They have a sense of being a superior but conquered people. Their motto is *Je me souviens*—"I remember." Their resentment against English-speaking Canada is so deep that the AWOL and deser-

TABLE 2-1   Party Strength in Belgium as of the May, 1995 Election

Party Seats	Percent of Votes	
	1995*	1991**
PSC, *Parti Social Chrétien,* Social Christian Wallonian	7.7	7.8
CVP, *Christelijke Volkspartij,* Social Christian Flemish	17.1	16.7
PS, *Parti Socialiste,* Wallonian Socialist	12.0	13.5
SP, *Socialistiche Partij,* Flemish Socialist	12.6	12.0
PVV, *Partij Voor Vrijhekd en Vooruitgang,* Flemish Liberal	13.1	11.9
PRL, *Parti Reforateur Libéral,* Wallonian Liberal	10.3	9.6
VB, *Vlaams Blok,* Flemish Right Wing Populist	7.8	6.6
Volksunie, Unified Peoples Flemish Regional Defense	4.7	5.9
Ecolo, Wallonian Environmentalist	4.1	5.1
Agalev, Flemish Environmentalist	4.4	4.9
FDF, *Frontdemocratique des Francophones Bruxellois,* Democratic Front of French-Speaking Brusselites	2.3	1.2

* 150 Seat Legislature of which Premier Deahane's center-left coalition retains 81 seats.

** 212 Seat Legislature.

Source: adopted from Keesing's *Record of World Events* (London: Longman's, 1993, 1995), vols. 37, 39.

tion rate among conscripted French Canadians in World War II—the last war in which the rest of the Western world was in agreement as to which side was evil—was over 50 percent. Legislation in Quebec forbids the public display of signs written in English, although the *Québeçois* insist on bilingualism throughout English-speaking Canada.

The *Bloc Québeçois,* the French Canadian party that commanded 54 of the 297 seats in the Canadian House of Commons, making it the second strongest party in that house and thereby the official opposition, is committed by its *raison d'être* to secession from the Canadian federation and the disintegration of Canada as we know it. Meanwhile, the Reform Party, a populist party of the far right bordering on fascism that won 52 seats in the 1994 elections, draws its constituency from the western prairie provinces, principally Alberta and eastern British Columbia, from which it won 46 of its 52 seats. The Liberals are the only Canadian party with anything close to a national constituency. The results of the 1994 election are displayed in Table 2-2.

The extent to which a sense of community—a set of shared values that define the nature of a system—is a precondition of a viable nation is unclear. Certainly, the fostering of multiculturalism, the defense and preser-vation of the distinct character of subcultures, and a resistance to the process of assimilation must come at the expense of the sense of community that gives a nation coherence. The experience of Belgium and Canada might give pause to the defenders of subcultural autonomy to the extent that such autonomy comes at the expense of the broader national culture.

Italy, as well, has suffered the fissiparous force of a regionally defined cultural defense. The southern half of the nation has remained less urbanized, more religious, more subject to political and social corruption, and generally less modernized than the industrialized north. The north, meanwhile, resents the domination of the southern-controlled bureaucracy and ineffective government. Secessionist sentiment in the north fueled the growth of the Northern League, which, allied with media magnate Silvio Berlusconi's Forza Italia and the National Alliance, heirs to the neofascist Italian Social Movement, formed a government without the Italian Popular Party, which was formerly the Catholic-backed Christian Democrats that had controlled all but one of Italy's 53 post–World War II governments. This event was significant in that it transformed the face of Italian politics, which, despite the numerous votes of no-confidence

TABLE 2-2   Party Strength in Canada as of the 1994 Election

Party	Seats in 1994	Seats Previously	Percent of Votes in 1994	Percent of Votes in 1988
PCP	2	154	16.1	43
Liberals	177	79	41.6	32
NDP	9	43	6.6	20
Bloc Québeçois	54	8	13.9	—
Reform Party	52	1	18.1	—
Others	1	2	3.7	—
Vacant	0	8	—	—
Total	295		100	

Source: Keesing's *Record of World Events,* vol. 39 (London: Longman's, 1994), p. 39679.

and low level of political legitimacy, had remained rather stable under the virtual hegemonc control of one political force for nearly half a century. Berlusconi's coalition, in turn, collapsed in late 1994 in the face of widespread corruption charges, thus leaving Italy without a credible alternative. Berlusconi's successor, appointed by Italian president and head of state, Oscar Luigi Scarfalo, is a technocrat banker, Lamberto Dini. Dini intended to serve as an interim premier, but has lasted longer than Berlusconi. Dini depends on support for center-right parties such as the PDS and the Popular Party, and has achieved much of his domestic legislative agenda. It is obvious, however, that Italy's new cleavage structure, fueled in part by regionally based cultural segmentation, has permanently fragmented the country's once stable, hegemonic, multiparty system. This is clearly shown by the fractionalized results of the 1993 elections (see Table 2-3), which are reminiscent of the fractionalization of Belgium's party system in the face of that country's unresolved cultural segmentation.

Other segmented societies seem to function relatively effectively. For example, one may identify four distinct cultural segments in the Netherlands: Catholic, orthodox Protestant (Calvinist and Dutch Reformed Church), liberal (secular, noncollectivist middle classes), and working class collectivist. These cleavages have been complicated by other issues that resulted in ten parties gaining seats in the May 1994 elections. Austria has also been characterized as segmented, with its two *lager,* or subcultural groups, the Catholics and the secular left, being relatively independent of one another; Austria, however, has suffered neither instability nor strong secessionist sentiments.

Arend Lijphart, using the Netherlands as a data base, developed his *consociational* model of how segmented societies may be able to function effectively.[27] Although most individuals from different segments do not ordinarily interact with one another, elites from the various segments may develop and even institutionalize patterns of cooperation that transcend the hostility and alienation felt by the

TABLE 2-3 Party Strength in Italy as of the 1993 Elections

Party	Percent of P.R. Votes	P.R. Seats	Direct Vote Seats
Freedom Alliance (right)	42.9	64	302
Forza Italia	21.0	30	
National Alliance	13.5	23	
Northern League	8.4	11	
Progressive Alliance (left)	34.4	49	164
Democratic Party of the Left	20.4	38	
Communists Refounded	6.0	11	
Greens	2.7	0	
Socialists	2.2	0	
Network	1.9	0	
Democratic Alliance	1.2	0	
Pact for Italy (centrist)	15.7	46	4
Italian Popular Party	11.1	29	
Segni Pact	4.6	13	
Others	8.0	5	

Source: Keesing's *Record of World Events,* vol. 40 (London: Longman's, 1993), p. 39920.

other members of each segment. The alternative to such overarching elite cooperation seems to be the devolution of power and authority to the subcultural elites, or, in other words, political decentralization that imperils the sovereignty of the central government, which has occurred in Belgium and threatens to occur in Canada.

THE STRUCTURE AND FORMAT OF DEMOCRACY AND THE PROBLEM OF POWER

Nations that are categorized as industrial democracies share the attribute of competition for political office. Within this category, however, is a considerable variation in the constitutionally designated structures. One finds presidential systems that vary in the strength and independence of the president, and parliamentary systems that vary in the comparative strength of the cabinet in relation to the legislature and the structure of the confidence mechanism that is fundamental to the parliamentary model. These various political formats, all of which are consistent with the broad conceptualization of political democracy arrived at above, are different responses to the basic problem of modern democracy—power.

The essence of the problem is as follows: since power involves the discretion to act in or contrary to the public interest, how does one grant the power to govern while at the same time guarding against the abuse of that power? There are two basic types of responses to this problem. The first is to fragment the power so that the exercise of power to make and implement significant public policy choices requires the spontaneous consent of a number of independent actors. The rationale is that while it is entirely possible that a single actor may choose to abuse his or her power, it is unlikely that a number of independent actors will agree to such an abuse. While such an arrangement may effectively guard against the misuse of power, it also makes it more difficult for the system to use power to make appropriate responses to pressing public needs or crises. The American political system, for example, is characterized by the existence of numerous veto groups, any one of whom can effectively negate a policy proposal. The chairs of the relevant congressional committees can refuse to hold hearings, the committee itself can vote an effective death sentence to a bill or even refuse to let it out of committee, a group of senators can conduct a filibuster, the rules committee can deny a bill the opportunity to be considered, the president can veto a bill, the courts can block its implementation, and so forth. However, no single actor has the power to enact a given policy. Hence, when decisive action is needed, the American national government appears to be immobilized. The inability of the Reagan administration and Congress to reach anything resembling a mutually acceptable plan of action in response to the stock market crash of 1987 or even to agree that an action was required is a case in point. The ability of various veto groups in 1994 to prevent the passage of either health care or welfare reform despite the Clinton administration's commitment to both projects is another example.

This exemplifies a perspective on democratic theory that views democracy as primarily concerned with constraining the potential abuse of power. Democratic government accordingly almost becomes identified with weak or immobilized government. The basic democratic value in this perspective is liberty defined as the absence of governmental restraints on individuals. With the rise of various critiques of classical liberalism, which emphasized individual freedom from governmental repression, writers such as Thomas Hill Green and the "Oxford Idealists" have pointed out that government is not the only source of coercion and restrictions on individual realization of one's human potential. Freedom to such critics means not only the absence of governmentally imposed coercion but also the ability to maximize one's life choices free from barriers external to oneself (i.e., barriers *not* including such factors as human talent, intelligence, or motivation). As industrial society began to mature in the twentieth century, it became increasingly apparent that social and economic circumstances that are not part of or directly created by government can also impose such barriers on the ability to maximize life choices or realize one's potential. Since it was beyond the capacity of isolated individuals to control these nongovernmental barriers, people looked to government to create the conditions needed to realize human freedom as defined in these more modern terms. In this view, the values of human freedom and the ability of people to achieve their human potential were not incompatible with a positive role for government.

Those who take this position that government has a positive role to play are inclined to seek to resolve the problem of power not by fragmenting it but rather by concentrating it, thereby clarifying the lines of responsibility and then holding it structurally accountable. We will see in the chapter on Great Britain (Chapter 3) the details of the classical model of how this may occur in the parliamentary format for democracy. For now, the broad outlines of this system as it relates to the structure of accountability will be noted and compared with the American presidential model. A third variant, the fragmented parliamentary model, will be discussed as well. However, although this model was common among European democracies in the earlier part of this century, it is becoming increasingly rare and is virtually extinct among major Western powers.

Cabinet, Presidential, and Parliamentary Formats Compared

The two broad categories of democratic format have conventionally been labeled *parliamentary* and *presidential*. The essential distinction between the two lies in the manner of choosing the head of government—that person primarily responsible for leadership in the formulation of public policy. Public policy is not really made by the legislature, for the policy-making function cannot effectively be coordinated among several hundred individuals. Rather, the principal role of the legislature in modern democracy is to impose constraints on the policy-making options of the head of government, primarily through the legislative control of the power of the purse. (We will see below how these roles evolved in the British experience.)

Another notable distinction is that in the parliamentary system the role of the head of government is distinct from the role of head of state, while in the presidential system the two roles are combined in the same individual. The head of state, as distinct from the head of government, is the role that symbolically embodies the unity of the nation as a whole. The occupant of this role performs many of the ceremonial functions that must be performed by someone who can effectively represent the state, such as entertaining foreign dignitaries in nonsubstantive meetings, honoring the nation's heroes, attending state funerals, and the like. In constitutional monarchies (such as the United Kingdom, Sweden, Denmark, Norway, the Netherlands, and Belgium among major Western nations), the monarch is the head of state. In republics with the parliamentary format, the president of the republic occupies this role. This president is a figure who has managed to rise above or stay aloof from the most controversial issues of partisan politics. Someone who may be called an "elder statesman" frequently occupies this role. It is important to understand that the head of state in a parliamentary system generally has no significant political power; this role is symbolic and ceremonial. However, the occupants of this role are not completely without actual or potential political functions. In 1994, for example, Italian President Scarfalo apparently played an active role in the discussions surrounding whether to call new elections in the wake of Prime Minister Berlusconi's resignation or to find a new coalition to form a cabinet able to maintain the confidence of the existing legislature. As will be discussed in Chapter 3, the royal prerogative remains legally available to Britain's queen but is probably only usable as an ultimate check on the gross abuse of power by the government or in the unforeseen case of a "hung" Parliament, in which no party has a clear plurality. Even this power is currently being challenged by the opposition Labour Party. Meanwhile, in Scandinavia Denmark's Queen Margrethe II can only rubber-stamp parliamentary legislation, and Sweden's King Carl XVI does not participate in the government at all. King Harald V of Norway, however, retains limited power to veto legislation and is the nominal commander in chief of the armed forces. These monarchs' ceremonial role is not insignificant, however. Queen Elizabeth II of Britain participated in 550 royal engagements in 1994, with a total of 2,878 such functions attended by the ten most active members of the royal family.[28] Were the burden of all of these appearances to fall upon the government, it would be onerous.

In a presidential system such as that in the United States, the roles of head of state and head of government are combined in one office, that of the president. Clearly, the burdens of the role of head of state constitute an excessive distraction from the critical and demanding tasks of the role of head of govern-

ment. Moreover, inasmuch as the president of the United States is inherently a partisan figure, he may, on the one hand, be less effective in embodying the nation as a whole. On the other hand, a politically astute president may be able to transfer the general support he derives from personifying the idea of the nation to partisan political goals. Most political scientists see value in the separation of these roles in two distinct offices. This separation may facilitate the distinction between loyalty to the idea of the nation or even to the constitutional regime and support for or opposition to the current administration or cabinet. In such a system, one may attack the position of the prime minister while still declaring loyalty to the monarch and the regime he or she represents.

In the basic parliamentary model, the legislature and the executive are chosen by the same process. The leaders of the parties or parliamentary groups assess the relative distribution of power among them and the current issues at stake, and, in consultation with the head of state, determine who can gather enough support to form a government and maintain at least for the time being the passive support of a majority of the legislature. This support is crucial, because in a parliamentary system, the *government*—which refers collectively to the prime minister and the cabinet—stays in office at the sufferance of such a majority. Specifically, the legislature may, at any time or for any reason or lack thereof, choose to vote on a motion of *no confidence* (sometimes called *censure*). The passage of such a measure by simple majority vote constitutionally compels the government to resign. In some systems the refusal of the legislature to pass a major legislative proposal of the government would be interpreted as a vote of no confidence and compel the government's resignation. In other systems, such as in the Netherlands, it would take a pattern of such rejections to be interpreted as a vote of no confidence. Thus, a government that cannot secure the enactment of its legislative program and is therefore unable to govern would not be allowed to remain in office, for that would leave the system in a state of stalemated stagnation. In most parliamentary systems, the power to vote no confidence is vested in the lower house; however, in a few, such as Italy, both houses participate in the process. Where the power is exclusively in the lower house, the upper house tends to become a powerless appendage to the system outside the logic of the political process.

A vote of no confidence or censure may be understood to apply to the entire cabinet collectively, as in Great Britain, or only to the prime minister or head of government, as in Italy. When cabinets or prime ministers are voted out of office on votes of no confidence or censure at relatively frequent intervals, this is called *cabinet instability*. This is a variable that may range from the high stability of Great Britain or older Commonwealth nations, which have experienced one or two such votes in the past hundred years, to nations such as Italy, which has had nearly 50 governments in the 40 or so years of the postwar republic, or the Netherlands, which has had fewer such votes but where it may take a year or so to resolve a cabinet crisis (the time between a successful vote of no confidence and the reconstitution of the government). Since cabinet instability is clearly dysfunctional for the ability of the government to govern and has characterized some of the less successful European democracies throughout the twentieth century, scholars have devoted considerable attention to explanations for the extent to which this phenomenon characterizes a parliamentary democracy, explanations that will be examined in some greater detail below.

When a vote of no confidence is passed, one of two things will happen. In some European democracies, most notably in Great Britain, the government has the power to request that the monarch dissolve Parliament and call new elections, a request that the monarch is normally not free to refuse. When the British prime minister declared a vote on financing the European Community in 1994 to be a question of confidence, there was some speculation that the queen would not have to call elections if the government lost. The government won that vote, however, rendering the question moot for the moment. Meanwhile, some commentators did think that the royal prerogative on the question of dissolution was alive and well. Labour, however, ahead at the end of 1994 by nearly 40 points in the opinion polls, promised to end that prerogative when they next won the election.

While this power of dissolution may be exercised whenever the government believes that it would have a strategic advantage in doing so (for example, if the polls indicate that an election at that time would increase the government's majority of seats in the House of Commons), the power of dissolution would certainly be used in the event of a vote of no confidence. It is sometimes argued that this ability to threaten legislators with having to stand for reelection and thus possibly losing their seat deters them from frivolously voting governments out of office for trivial reasons.

In other systems, the power of dissolution either does not exist or is so circumscribed by legal or cultural impediments that it cannot be used. In the event of a no-confidence vote in such systems, parliamentary and party leaders would have to consult with one another—usually with the head of state moderating the negotiations—in order to form another government without recourse to the electorate. The power of dissolution was abused by the French president, the monarchist Marshall MacMahon, to destroy the ability of the Third Republic to govern. Accordingly, the dissolution of the legislature became identified with right-wing opposition to the republic itself and thus was politically unusable. Because of this, during the Fourth Republic the power was constitutionally circumscribed by the provision that it could only be exercised after a vote of censure by an absolute majority of the Assembly. Governments, however, repeatedly fell by relative majorities in the Third and Fourth Republics and were reconstituted without consulting the electorate. Because of the frequency with which these governments fell without the power of dissolution being available to counter the power of the legislature to vote censure, many scholars concluded that the presence or absence of the power of dissolution explained a significant portion of the cabinet instability in parliamentary systems. However, this conclusion overlooks the fact that other systems—Norway, for instance—maintain cabinet stability without the availability of the power of dissolution.

To Americans or others used to a presidential system in which the head of government has a fixed tenure of office, the idea of a system in which the head of government can be removed by a simple majority of the legislature without any requirement for justifying that removal (as contrasted with the American impeachment proceedings that require a finding of "high crimes or misdemeanors") seems to invite the abuse of that removal power and the resulting cabinet instability. In fact, most European governments based upon a version of the parliamentary model are quite stable; the actual removal of a government on a vote of no confidence or censure is quite rare. While other systems have experienced a fair amount of cabinet instability (notably, the Third and Fourth French Republics, Weimar Germany, prewar Austria, Italy, and, in the sense of prolonged cabinet crises, the Netherlands), such insta-

bility is obviously not inherent in the nature of the parliamentary format.

Some of the causes of the variations in cabinet instability have been linked to attributes of party systems; hence, the discussion of such causes must wait until party systems are discussed. Meanwhile, the ability of governments to avoid frequent votes of no confidence in the face of unrestricted legislative power to pass such votes is not difficult to understand. The government in a parliamentary system is aware of the legislative power to vote it out of office. A prudent government will therefore ascertain the limits of legislative tolerance before pressing ahead with policy proposals that a majority of the legislature might find unacceptable. Unlike the situation in the United States, where the president may choose to disregard the opposition of Congress to his policies without fear that he will be driven from office, the British prime minister, for example, regularly consults with the rank-and-file members of his or her parliamentary party on policy proposals and will effect compromises on such proposals before bills are proposed or certainly before votes are taken. It may be argued that President Richard Nixon's confrontational tactics with Congress were based in part on his assumption that impeachment was not a realistic threat and that he was therefore insulated from the need to concern himself with congressional opposition.

Americans who tend to prefer the presidential format to the parliamentary one fear that the parliamentary model detracts from the democratic value of the accountability of the head of government to the society he or she governs because the electorate never directly votes on who will occupy that role. This is a valid concern in those systems with a party system that is so fragmented that the elections to the legislature do *not* produce a party with either a clear majority of seats or a strong enough plurality of such seats. In such systems, the question of who can form a government is *not* determined by the outcome of the election but in fact is left to postelection bargaining among legislative and party leaders. The outcome of such bargaining may not reflect the relative strength of the parties in the legislature. For example, several weaker parties may unite to form a government that does not include the strongest party. Something close to this has regularly occurred in Italy, where the bargaining process has kept the Communist Party out of the government even though it was the second strongest party overall and far stronger than some of the junior coalition partners of the dominant Christian Democrats. Moreover, in some parliamentary systems, as noted above, the power of dissolution is not in effect, and governments are regularly created without elections being held. In those systems in which the electoral outcome does not effectively determine who will form a government, and/or in those systems in which the vote of no confidence does not necessarily produce a dissolution and new elections, the causal nexus between the outcome of elections and the identity of the elites and the policies they pursue is lost. To the extent that democratic theory entails regular competitive elections that determine who the elites are and what range of policies they may pursue, this format of parliamentary democracy would in fact detract from the core democratic value of structured accountability. Such a format of legislative dominance and executive impotence, moreover, further detracts from accountability, because someone must first have power before being held accountable for its use.

The British model, shared increasingly by the parliamentary systems in major Western powers, involves a highly aggregated party with a strong plurality if not a majority of the seats in the legislature. Because Western European parties tend to a greater or lesser extent—but to a much greater extent than in the United States—to control the parliamentary votes of their own members of parliament (a fact discussed at greater length in the appropriate country studies), the governments in such systems have a far wider range of discretion in the formulation and implementation of policy compared to the American presidency or the French Third and Fourth Republics. As long as the government operates within these rather broad bounds of discretion, members of the parliamentary party vote as they are directed by their party leadership, a phenomenon known as *party discipline*. This enables the majority or strong plurality party to govern according to the principles and programs on which they ran without any real danger that their legislative agenda will be thwarted or diluted by legislative opposition. The winning party can, in fact, govern the nation, a phenomenon known as *responsible party government*. Because the winning party can govern according to its principles and programs, it can be held responsible for the consequences of how it has governed. Thus, by concentrating power, the cabinet system clarifies the lines of accountability. This concentration of political power, far from being incompatible with democratic values, as the widespread American perception would have it, may actually promote the core democratic value of structured accountability.

The question of the concentration of power is not merely a matter of constitutional format, as the preceding discussion of segmented societies makes clear. When cultural cleavages are geographically defined, federalism may institutionalize the independence of these subunits. Federalism is a system in which a national government and constituent governments rule over the same territory, with sovereign or final power resting with the national government (thus distinguishing a federation from a confederation);

however, the authority of the constituent governments to act in ways that do not conflict with a valid exercise of power by the national government does not depend on a grant of power from the national government (as provided by the Tenth Amendment to the U.S. Constitution). When the boundaries of the political subunits of a federation (states in the United States and Australia, provinces in Canada, _länder_ in Germany) coincide with the boundaries of the cultural diversities, parochial elites become spokespersons for these diversities with an interest in perpetuating and exacerbating the intensity of the divisions. For example, the leaders of French Canadian Quebec become advocates of French Canadian separatism rather than of their assimilation into the broader Canadian culture. Such a decentralization of power logically conflicts with the structure of accountability in the cabinet model of democracy with its presumed concentration of power. Thus, the announced plans by the British Labour Party in 1994 for the serious devolution of power by establishing Scottish and Welsh parliaments would, if carried out, alter the structure of accountability in that nation in important ways.

One of the problems that many Americans have with either parliamentary model is the fact that the voters do not directly vote for the head of government. The American presidential system is based on the assumption that the quasidirect election of the head of government (ignoring for the present whatever complications the electoral college poses for this argument) is the best means of insuring the popular control of the occupant of that role. In the parliamentary system, the government's accountability is constitutionally to the legislature rather than to the electorate directly, and Americans, who do not readily trust politicians, are uneasy about giving control of the presidency to another group of politicians.

Yet, it may be argued that a legislative body is much better equipped to exercise meaningful control over a remote and powerful head of government than are atomized individual voters. One may legitimately have serious doubts as to what extent the options of the president are actually constrained by the fear of a ground swell of spontaneous popular disapproval. Research on behavior and opinion clearly shows that the typical voter in all industrial democracies, including the United States and Great Britain, is overwhelmingly uninformed and inactive.[29] Research further indicates that politically skilled and somewhat charismatic heads of government have a powerful capacity to lead public opinion in the directions they choose. Public opinion, far from being a spontaneous force that serves as a constraint on a head of government, is mobilized by opinion leaders, including the government that the opinion is supposed to constrain. Public opinion is more likely to be a tool mobilized by the government as a base of support than a critical and independent constraint on governmental discretion.

Compared to the isolated and uninformed voter who is beset with the demands of daily living unrelated to his or her political role, the member of a legislature may be better equipped to hold the head of government accountable in a parliamentary system. Members of parliament (MPs) regard their political role as either their full-time occupation and at least one of their primary roles; hence, they are not faced with as many competing demands on their attention. Since politics is their primary or full-time job, they have more at stake in political outcomes than do ordinary citizens. Ordinary citizens, who are not directly affected by such outcomes, at least in the short run, may find that the expenditure of time and effort to acquire the information needed to participate rationally in politics exceeds any benefits derived by such rational action (i.e., supporting policy outcomes in one's interest); therefore, it may paradoxically be rational to be "irrational."

Moreover, MPs have access to information unavailable to the ordinary citizen, and they tend to possess individual attributes that better enable them to handle the kinds of information that affects issues in a mature industrial society. Being better educated and with greater political experience than the ordinary citizen, MPs not only possess but are better equipped to comprehend the information relevant to holding elites accountable to the public interest. In most parliamentary systems, members of the government are also required to be members of the legislature; hence, they are part of the legislative debate and available for interrogation by their fellow MPs about policies and activities for which they are arguably responsible. In fact, several of these nations regularly set aside a time for formally addressing such questions to members of the government. The members of the government, aware that they may be called upon to justify any controversial or significant activity in which they are engaged, may accordingly feel constrained to govern or behave in a way that they feel comfortable defending in a public forum. This may be contrasted to the American system, with its separation of powers, in which the claim of executive privilege has been advanced to limit the availability of members of the executive branch to congressional inquiry.

In a formal sense, therefore, that variety of parliamentary democracy sometimes known as cabinet government, which is apparently characterized by a concentration of decision-making power in the inner circle of the cabinet, offers a clear structure of accountability. Its advantages with respect to the apparently clear lines of responsibility have seductively appealed to many scholars, even to the extent that some variation of this model has frequently been advocated for the United States.[30]

On closer or more recent analyses, however, two major problems with this model have presented themselves. One is that the increasingly prevalent attributes of a postindustrial society alter the seemingly clear and formal lines of responsibility in ways not anticipated by classical democratic theory, a problem that will be addressed at some length below. Secondly, the ability of the legislature to end the tenure of its government by a simple majority vote, usually without reference to a criterion of justification, raises the danger of such frequent changes in the composition of the government that it is unable to develop and implement coherent programs and policies to deal with significant issues, a situation known as *cabinet instability.* This phenomenon has in fact characterized a number of major European parliamentary democracies in the twentieth century, severely inhibiting their ability to govern and possibly rendering them vulnerable to authoritarian challenges promising efficiency and order. At this writing, Italy has had 53 governments since World War II, and Belgium has had over 30. On the other hand, only 2 governments have fallen on no-confidence votes in Great Britain in the past hundred years, and the parliamentary democracies of the older Commonwealth nations have nearly matched this record of stability. Cabinet stability has similarly characterized the Scandinavian democracies. One party, the Social Democrats, controlled the Swedish government from 1935 to 1976 and then again from 1983 to 1990, a period characterized by one successful vote of no confidence. They recaptured the government in 1994, capping a remarkable record of nearly hegemonic control.

The degree of cabinet instability is frequently thought to be largely a function of the nature and operation of the political party system. The party system of a nation has been argued from a functionalist perspective (discussed in Chapter 1) to carry out certain functions needed for the successful operation of democracy, especially with regard to the structuring of accountability. The capacity of the several party systems of Western democracies to fulfill these various functions is another question addressed by a large literature on the subject, to which it is now appropriate to turn.

Party Systems and Cabinet Stability

The concept of the party system essentially refers to the pattern of interaction among the political parties in a nation. This pattern in turn is a function of the number of parties in a system and their relative electoral and legislative strength. The earlier, simplistic literature distinguished between two-party systems and systems involving more than two parties. The thinking was that a two-party system produces an automatic majority of seats for one party in the legislature. Since democratic governments operate on the basis of majorities both in resolving issues and in maintaining the support necessary to keep a parliamentary government in office, a two-party system was held to contribute to stable and effective parliamentary democracy.

Parties can exercise some control over the legislative voting behavior of their own members. This discipline probably depends largely on the extent to which some central party structure maintains veto power or another form of ultimate control over the nomination of candidates, and the ability to deny those who do not support party principles and legislative goals (within some boundaries of tolerance) the right to run on that party's label. Thus, when the British Tories denied the whip or effectively expelled eight of their MPs for voting against the government on an announced confidence question in 1994, the Conservative Central Office was putting pressure on their Constituency Associations to *de-select* (not renominate) the rebels. This pressure met with varying degrees of resistance from those associations, and Major's action against the rebels was probably unavoidable once the issue was officially declared to be a confidence question. The rebels were reinstated by Major a few months later, probably due to his small majority in commons. Party discipline leads directly to party cohesion, for when one party exercises such control over a majority of members of the legislature, the maintenance of a stable majority is facilitated.

Systems involving more than two parties cannot be counted upon to produce a majority under the control of one party. Governments and their legislative support must therefore be based on *coalitions,* alliances of two or more parties. Inasmuch as the leaders of one party have little or no control over MPs from other parties, coalition governments should tend to be more unstable or vulnerable to a no-confidence vote than those based upon a single party majority. Moreover, this disposition toward instability should increase with the number of parties required to compose the governing coalition.

A strategy of gamesmanship is involved in building governing coalitions in that two conflicting goals are at work. One goal is the need to have enough allies in the governing coalition to insure, insofar as one is able, that the coalition has sufficient support to gain and keep office. The other has to do with what William Riker calls the "size principle," which dictates that one should keep coalitions to the minimum size needed to win.[31] The more actors there are in the governing coalitions, the more one has to divide the spoils of victory and the fewer losers there are from whom to reap those spoils. In the case of cabinet coalitions, the more parties that make up the coalitions, the more that each party has to compromise its principles and legislative agenda. Riker qualifies the "size principle" with the uncertainty principle, or what he calls "the information corollary," which holds that there is never adequate information to calculate with confidence just how big the minimum winning coalition must be. Hence, those forming a coalition tend to try to recruit more partners than they objectively need, further diversifying the character of the government and intensifying its fissiparous forces (that is, rendering the coalition more likely to break apart).

Numerous parliamentary regimes with more than two parties and a tendency toward coalition governments have, despite the logic of the foregoing analysis, maintained a high degree of cabinet stability. Research has shown that cabinet instability is largely explained not by the number of parties in a coalition in and of itself but rather by an index that includes the relative size of the parties.[32] In systems in which one party has a dominant plurality of seats but less than a majority, a high degree of stability is maintained,[33] especially if the dominant party is part of the governing coalition. Coalitions of a number of weaker parties that leave the plurality party in opposition may also tend to fall quickly, as occurred in Sweden and in India. When one party maintains such a clear plurality of seats that it can fairly be characterized as dominant, it is usually not possible to exclude that party from the government. Weaker parties are then faced with the choice of becoming a junior coalition party or being in opposition. Because a decision to desert the governing coalition is fraught with serious consequences for the influence of the party, it is not to be taken lightly.

Yet, such a decision is sometimes made, especially in Italy, whose cabinet instability was noted. The raw number of times a vote of no confidence is passed in a system may be a misleading indicator of the actual instability of the regime with respect to the ability of an elite to expect to remain in power over a range of controversial issues and to develop a coherent program for processing these issues. In the Italian case, one party, the Christian Democrats, provided every prime minister of the first 52 governments, except for the Socialist government of Mr. Craxi. (The hegemonic hold of the Christian Democrats was broken in 1993 with the victory of the right-wing Freedom Alliance of Silvio Berlusconi, while the Christian Democrats, finally discredited by pervasive corruption, changed their name.) Many times, a vote of no confidence led to a government reconstituted with the same individual in the prime minister's role and only one or two changes in minor ministries. Hence, unless the measures of both the fractionalization of the party system and of cabinet stability are relatively complex and take account of a number of factors, the relationship between party system and cabinet stability may be quantitatively weak.[34]

Even when the measured relationship between complex indexes of party system fractionalization and weighted indexes of cabinet instability is the highest obtained thus far, that relationship explains less than half of the variation in cabinet instability. Clearly, the degree of cabinet instability is a function of numerous factors other than the party system, including the extent to which parties are rigidly principled or dogmatic and resistant to the compromise that could facilitate the maintenance of stable coalitions, the idiosyncratic traditions of each nation that cannot be subsumed in general propositions, and even institutional factors such as the power of dissolution.

Yet, democratic theory persists in positing a role for party systems in the political process. Although a literature has recently emerged questioning the role of party systems in the processing of issues themselves, which will be examined below, the effort to explain variations in the nature of party systems remains an important part of the work of comparative politics.

Explaining Party Systems: The Role of Electoral Systems

Electoral systems have held a prominent place in the literature that attempts to explain variations in the type or degree of fractionalization of party systems. *Electoral systems* are the rules by which votes by the electorate are translated into the allocation of offices or legislative seats among parties or candidates for major political offices.

There are two broad types of electoral systems: proportional representation and the single member district system with plurality vote. *Proportional representation* is actually a generic name given to a class of specific electoral systems that vary a great deal. The term also implies an ideal in which the percentage of votes that a party receives nationally shall equal the percentage of its total seats in the legislature. This concept of pure proportionality is based on votes being distributed on an at-large basis—that is, without the electorate being divided into distinct electoral districts.

Actually, there are no systems of pure proportional representation. Rather, there are a number of electoral systems that in varying degrees disproportionally favor weaker parties in the allocation of seats. These systems are generally based on multimember election districts from which more than one winner emerges or more than one seat in the legislature is awarded. The French Third Republic was an exception in that it used a single-member district system with a majority vote requirement, which usually forced a runoff and gave smaller parties a chance to form alliances to defeat stronger candidates. This system also somewhat exaggerated the strength of weaker parties.

Among the more popular models of proportionality is the Hare system, also known as the Single Transferable Vote. In this system, the voters express their preferences in terms of first, second, and so forth choices among the parties. A quota is then calculated based upon a ratio of votes cast and seats to be allocated. When a party reaches this vote total, it gets the first seat to be allocated, but when this party appears as the first choice on subsequent ballots, the voters' second choice is counted. This process continues until all the seats in the district have been allocated. Since counting usually gets down to second and third choices, weaker parties are clearly given exaggerated representation. Another variant of proportional representation is the D'Hondt system of the "greatest remainder." In this system, when a party reaches the quota and achieves a seat, its subsequent votes are divided by two. If a party should nevertheless win two seats in a constituency, its subsequent votes would be divided by three. This system is based upon the principle of penalizing electoral strength and thereby rewarding electoral failure; hence, weak parties are disproportionally allocated seats.

Several scholars have argued that by exaggerating the strength of weak parties, proportional representation contributes directly to the fragmentation of the party system and ultimately to cabinet instability.[35] An implicit causal model runs through this literature as follows: proportional representation → fragmented party system → ideological extremism → cabinet instability → breakdown of democracy. Thus, one of these scholars suggests that the failure of a number of European parliamentary democracies in the years immediately preceding World War II could have been averted by the simple tactic of changing the electoral system from variations of proportional representation to the Anglo-American system of the single-member district with plurality vote (hereafter referred to as the plurality system). By exaggerating the strength of weaker parties, the proportional system gives representation to small political movements that achieve political power not by earning any significant amount of electoral support but by mobilizing their true believers. Once in the legislature, they may even become a balance-of-power force in the government, as is the case with Israel's tiny but disproportionately powerful extremist religious party that has imposed a regimen of religious orthodoxy on a largely secularized nation. These small parties may retain their principles or agendas in their extreme form without the necessity of compromise. We have seen how such doctrinal rigidity is dysfunctional for the goal of maintaining stable coalitions.

Does proportional representation (PR) actually *cause* party system fragmentation, doctrinal extremism and rigidity, and the breakdown of parliamentary systems? The data are not fully supportive of this proposition. Belgium, for example, adopted PR in the early twentieth century while maintaining a stable three-party system for decades thereafter. The fact that the Belgian party system began to fragment to some extent in the 1960s was due to the rising salience of the issues surrounding the linguistic and cultural divisions discussed above, and was certainly not directly caused by the electoral system that had been adopted decades earlier.

For decades after PR was adopted, the Swedes maintained a five-party system with a strongly dominant Social Democratic Party that won close to half the votes and seats. In the 1994 election, seven parties gained seats in the Swedish Riksdag, but this slight increase in the number of parties was more a result of changing political cleavages along the lines proposed by Ronald Inglehart (See note 13) and his followers. A Green Party gained seats (18 of 349) for the first time, thus following the pattern of the emergence of such ecology parties throughout the Continent. The Social Democrats meanwhile maintained the dominant position that they have held for over half a century, winning more than twice the vote percentage and twice the number of seats of their nearest competitor (the Moderates) in 1994. Clearly, a five- to seven-party system in which one party approaches a majority of votes and seats will function differently than a system with the same number of parties of relatively equal strength. This dominant party system may produce the long-term hegemony of power seen in Sweden and Italy due to the fragmented nature of the opposition.[36]

The goal of PR, it will be recalled, is to have the distribution of seats among the political parties mirror the distribution of opinions and loyalties in the electorate. Thus, it seems reasonable to suggest that PR allows a fragmentated system of social or cultural cleavages to be reflected in the party system; hence, PR will result in a fragmented party system when it is used in a fragmented sociocultural context. In fact, the pressure to adopt PR in the first place frequently comes from a perception that there are important opinions or interests that are not fairly represented in the current party system.

While one cannot say that PR causes party system fractionalization, one may have a stronger case arguing that the Anglo-American plurality system generates solid pressure for a highly aggregated party system regardless of the sociocultural context. Maurice Duverger, the author of a classic treatise on political parties in the Western world, characterized the relationship between the plurality electoral system and the two-party system as being so invariable as to approach the status of a "sociological law."[37] This, of course, presumes we can agree on what we mean by the term "two-party system." Since no major system has only two parties contending for major political office, its meaning is more complicated than would appear at first glance. Some would argue that a two-party system is one in which only two parties have a genuine chance to gain power in the sense of controlling the national government or providing the head of government. Others, like Leslie Lipson, would add that in a two-party system, one party normally can gain power and stay in office without help from a third party.[38] Yet, even this definition would not include party systems whose pattern of interaction and political impact are closer to the classic British two-party model than to the fragmented party model. For example, Australia was governed either by an invariable coalition of the Liberal Party and the Country Party or by the Labour Party. The Liberal Party is liberal in the classic nineteenth-century sense of that concept and clearly to the right of center, while the Country Party was much more to the right. The Labour Party is on the political left, trade union based and mildly collectivist; hence, it is not a party with which the Country Party could have conceivably allied itself. The result was that the alliance between the Liberal Party and the Country Party was a rather permanent one that stably controlled the Australian government for much of the post–World War II period until the 1980s, when Labour came to power. Since one party did not control the government by itself and since the parties did not alternate in and out of office regularly, the Australian system would not have qualified as a two-party system by Lipson's widely cited definition. Yet, the system operated as a contest between two stable political forces with a viable opposition; therefore, it performed the functions of providing a stable majority, a viable opposition, and a manageable amount of competition that are normally filled by a two-party system.

The Canadian party system had similarly exhibited a pattern of interaction that fit the two-party model much more closely than the fragmented party model; yet, with five parties that normally received a significant number of seats on the House of Commons, governments were frequently composed of a coalition of two or more parties, thus disqualifying the Canadian system from Lipson's two-party category. Of course, with one of the erstwhile major parties now virtually eliminated from parliamentary representation in the last election and the second strongest party an antisystem party with an ethnically and regionally defined constituency, whatever pattern may have existed in that party system has been broken, and the system is difficult to classify. The Liberal Party has normally controlled the Canadian government by being a provincial rights party that appeals to the antinational government proclivities of the *Québeçois* subculture. The Progressive Conservatives are the only other party that has ever controlled the national government, thus fulfilling one of the two-party system requirements, but they have only provided two prime ministers since World War II and were virtually eliminated from the House in their electoral debacle of 1993. The New Democratic Party, formerly known as the Cooperative Commonwealth Federation, a curious small-farmer-based collectivist party, has controlled two of the prairie provinces for much of the post–Great Depression era and regularly places around 25 members in the 265-member House of Commons. (In the 1993 election it dropped from 43 seats to 9 seats.) An even more curious farmers' party of the right, the Social Credit Party, controlled Alberta for much of this period and regularly elected 10 to 15 members to the House of Commons. It was replaced in the last election by the Reform Party, a right-wing populist party with a constituency confined to Alberta and eastern British Columbia, an illustration of the "new right" discussed below. A third "minor" party has appeared and reappeared under various names, such as the *Ralliament de Creditistes, Québec Libre,* and now *Bloc Québeçois,* to speak for the separatist sentiments of the French Canadian subculture. While formally placing only 10 to 15 members in the House of Commons, this party became the official opposition in 1994.

Germany offers another example of an almost two-party system that seems to blur the clear theoretical distinction between two-party systems and fragmented party systems. In Germany, the Christian Democratic Union (and its Bavarian branch, the Christian Social Union) is the major center-right party. The Social Democratic Party has been a slightly left-of-center party but clearly centrist since 1959. Together, these two parties control about 90 percent of the vote. A centrist but more classically liberal minor party, the Free Democratic Party, controls less than 10 percent of the vote but frequently has disproportionate influence as a balance-of-power party that can determine which of the major parties gets to form a government. This disproportionate power of the Free Democrats was especially apparent in 1994, as their percentage of the vote dropped but, because of Chancellor Kohl's very narrow victory (his party won only 294 of 672 seats), the Free Democrats' 47 seats were needed more than ever to produce a center-right majority. Here again is a party system on the verge of transition. The 1994 elections saw the Free Democrats dropping from 11 percent of the vote to a mere 6.9 percent and slipping into third place behind the rising Greens, a trend consistent with Inglehart's thesis on the rise of postmaterialist values and with our previous discussion of the decline of classical liberalism.

Thus the distinction between a two- and a more-than-two-party system has virtually no applicability in the real world. Even Great Britain, Lipson's quintessential model of the classic two-party system, not only regularly places candidates from more than two parties in Parliament but in recent years has been characterized by minority governments. A more useful way of defining the differences among party systems would be to classify them along a continuum of more or less fragmented or aggregated, as suggested in the above discussion of party systems and government stability.

The essence of the plurality electoral system is that only the party that comes in first in a district gets any representation from that district; finishing a close second among a number of parties means nothing. Although an uneven distribution of support in the nation will mean that the second strongest party will finish first in some districts, the strongest party will still win most districts by a varying margin, and its margin of victory in total seats will be exaggerated. Third strongest parties will come in second in some districts but only rarely will they actually win the district; hence, they will be severely underrepresented relative to their total national support. Even weaker parties will face even more severe electoral system bias. Moreover, the support for the third strongest and weaker parties is further eroded by what is called the *wasted vote psychology*, as people who might otherwise prefer one of the weaker parties will assume that their party cannot win the district and thus decide to choose the less objectionable among the two major parties in order for their vote to have any impact. This factor helped to hasten the decline of the Liberal Party in Great Britain. Clearly, it is very difficult to maintain a viable multiparty system (i.e., more than two) with a plurality electoral system.

If obtaining a two-party system, which is most clearly associated with stable, effective democracy, is as simple as adopting the plurality electoral system, why then do not all democracies adopt that system? The suggested answer is that the electoral system is a tool that allows the party system to reflect the imperatives generated by the culture and cleavage structure in which it operates. When a noncompromising culture and a fragmented set of socioeconomic cleavages require the representation of several distinct perspectives in the system of party competition, the pressure to adopt a version of PR to accommodate those divisions will be great.

For example, in Great Britain through the 1980s, there was widespread dissatisfaction with the choices presented by the two major parties, the Labour and Conservative Parties, because during that period each moved away from its traditional centrist position, a phenomenon that will be discussed in greater detail in Chapter 3. This led to support for a third alternative, an alliance between the Liberal Party and the newly formed Social Democratic Party; this support virtually equalled that given to the Labour Party in terms of votes in the 1983 general election. However, the considerable frustration felt by the supporters of the alliance due to its severe underrepresentation in seats under the Anglo-American plurality electoral system, led to its demise just a few years later. The alliance and its present-day heirs, the Liberal Democrats, lead a chorus demanding reform of the electoral system away from the plurality system so lauded by F. A. Hermans and other students of electoral systems and toward PR, the system that is frequently identified as the villain in the destabilization of European parliamentary democracies.

To take another example, in the U.S. presidential election of 1968, the nominees of both major parties were widely perceived as supporting the war in Vietnam; hence, there was no outlet for the antiwar passion in the electoral process. The point is that two parties may not allow for the range of choices that are demanded by the level of political sentiment and the stratification system that are salient in a given society at a given point.

It seems reasonable to conclude from the foregoing that nations ultimately need a party system that reflects their system of soci-

etal cleavages, and will adopt an electoral system that encourages or permits that kind of party system. That parties and party systems will reflect the unique set of cleavages in a particular setting was illustrated by the breakdown of the Irish coalition government in 1994. Prime Minister Albert Reynolds led his *Fianna Fail* Party in coalition with the Labour Party under Dick Spring in the context of economic prosperity and a promising peace process for the first time in decades. Yet, Labour withdrew from the coalition over Reynolds's appointment of his attorney general to the presidency of the High Court, an apparently trivial issue. The controversy arose because the appointee had blocked the extradition of a priest back to Ulster to face charges of pedophilia, an issue that raised fundamental questions of the role of the Church in this most Catholic of political systems. Spring ultimately led his Labour Party into a new coalition with *Fine Gael*'s uninspiring leader, John Burton, without calling for new elections. The episode seems to contradict the generalizations made earlier about the number of parties and cabinet stability; here there were just three important parties involved. Cleavages based upon class—epitomized by the Labour Party—were mixed with parties representing other important sociocultural cleavages.

The debate among the advocates of the different types of electoral systems reflects a basic disagreement about the ideal type of party system in a democracy, and this in turn reflects different assumptions about the nature of democracy. Since these assumptions are frequently left implicit, advocates of the different types of electoral systems and party systems are arguing past one another. On the one hand, the advocates of proportionality are fully aware that that kind of electoral system will permit a fragmentation of the party system; however, they assume that the primary function of an electoral system is to produce a party system that mirrors the spectrum of opinions in society as closely as possible. In this, the representative and expressive functions of a party system, granting each interest its spokesperson in the political decision-making process, are given priority over competing values. On the other hand, the advocates of a plurality electoral system, which is designed to compel an aggregation of the party system, view democracy as a system that maximizes the responsiveness of public policy to shifts in public opinion and the lines of accountability between political decision makers and the society they allegedly serve. In a two-party system, important strains of opinion and significant interests may go unrepresented; however, in that system small shifts of a few percentage points in the political allegiances of the electorate may result in one government being completely replaced by another. In a fragmented party system, all variations of opinion and interests may have their representatives in the legislature and many of them in the government; yet, a larger shift in political allegiances in the society may not affect the relative strength of the parties or the composition of the government and its output. Since these conflicting values and interpretations of the essence of democracy cannot be objectively resolved, much of the debate between advocates of different types of electoral and party systems takes on the nature of a polemic rather than of scholarly analysis.

TRENDS IN PROGRAM AND PRINCIPLE AMONG WESTERN POLITICAL PARTIES

Thus far, the discussion of political parties has been concerned with the pattern of interaction among the parties in a political system. Within those systems, however, individual parties possess attributes of theoretical significance that have been the subject of a large literature. Among these attributes is the set of principles or programs on which a party bases its electoral appeal. In this regard, a tripartite classification scheme has been suggested to distinguish among parties of principle, programmatic parties, and expediential parties. Parties of principle are those whose reason for being is the advocacy and ultimate realization of a set of principles, or an ideology. Policy choices are advocated or political courses of action undertaken to implement the values implied by the principles or ideology.

The terms *principles* and *ideology* have thus far been used interchangeably, a confusion adding to the debate about the continuing role of ideology in modern society. A distinction between the terms has been frequently made, however, which that will be honored in this book. Principles are any general rules or standards that serve as guides to the determination of truth or action. Such rules may be general statements about the real or sensory world and may be made accountable to the evidence from that world; they may be about transcendent phenomena (in the world of ideas rather than of sensory reality); or they may be overtly normative. Clearly, all parties operate on the basis of principles so defined to a greater or lesser extent.

An ideology is a particular subset of the concept of principles. An ideology is a *closed* and relatively *comprehensive system* of principles. A system of principles is a set of principles that are logically interrelated. A system of principles is comprehensive to the extent that it attempts to answer all questions and to cover all aspects of life. A thought system is closed to the extent to which the conclusions it generates are not sensitive to or subject to change on the basis of new information from outside that system. Closed thought systems change their truth claims or conclusions only on the basis of the dictates of some internal authority figure or institution. For example, the claims of Marxism did not change because of world events that are inconsistent with that theory but on the basis of a new line from the Kremlin. Many religions are closed systems in that they alter their truth claims based not on unfolding evidence but on a promulgation from the leading ecclesiastic of the faith.

Clearly, the use of an ideology, in the narrow sense of a closed, comprehensive thought system, as a guide to action is dysfunctional for the realization of sensory world values in that it by definition is not adaptable to the changing realities of that world. Parties that exist to promote an ideology in that closed sense of the term tend to lose sight of the imperatives of seeking power and ignore plausible solutions to the salient issues of the society. Ideological principles, being insensitive to changing realities, may perpetuate past conflicts and issues while disregarding current ones. For example, Marxists are frequently fighting a class struggle based upon a nineteenth-century reality of a large, undifferentiated, exploited, and progressively radicalized urban working force, while twentieth-century reality finds a specialized, unionized, prosperous, and relatively conservative working class. As we shall see, many parties with a pre–World War II history are rooted in economic or class-based issues, which in the postwar era have declined in salience relative to noneconomic symbolic or life-style concerns. The rigid anticlericalism of the French left during their Third and Fourth Republics prevented them from forming a stable coalition with the French manifestation of that European phenomenon known generically as Christian Democracy; hence, the natural French center could not effectively govern.

Certain parties seem more interested in eschatology than in policies directed at problem solving. When such parties are able to acquire the power and responsibility for governing a nation, they tend to lack a theoretical basis for dealing with the actual problems of their society. A classic manifestation of this point may be found in the experience of Germany's Social Democratic Party (SPD). Although it was the original Marxist party, its reformist faction triumphed over the ideological purists at the outset, resulting in the distinctly reformist Gotha Programme of 1875. However, the repressive policies of Bismarck rendered the party more receptive to revolutionary Marxism and in 1891 led to a schizophrenic bifurcation of the party program into a revolutionary socialist component and an immediate program of pragmatic policy proposals that historian Carl Schorske has called the "Erfurt Synthesis."[39] The irrelevance of the utopian visions of an international workers' cooperative for dealing with the real world of international politics became manifest during World War I, when the Marxist maxim, "To this system, no man and no penny," was easily replaced by the slogan, "In the hour of danger we shall not leave the fatherland in the lurch."[40] After World War II, the party again faced the dilemma of the conflicting imperatives of the loyalty to the symbolic Socialist ideological baggage that to many of the old Marxists provided the party's very identity and the fact that in an emerging two-party alignment that very ideological baggage was permanently alienating the middle-class support that was essential if the party was ever to get a share of power. Again the imperatives of real world politics made the Marxist ideological baggage a luxury the party could not afford if it desired an impact on the policy-making process. Hence, in the 1959 Basic Program adopted at Bad Godesburg, the party stated that "private ownership of the means of production can claim protection by society as long as it does not hinder the establishment of social justice."[41] This statement among others heralded a virtual abandonment of the socialist goal that had defined the essence of the SPD.

This eschewal of the socialist roots of a party representing the urban working class was reenacted to an extent at the 1994 British Labour Party's annual conference, where the new party leader, Tony Blair, led a fight to revise the party constitution to exclude the clause committing it to public ownership of the means of production as part of his effort to steer Labour to the political center. Blair lost the vote on this emotionally and symbolically charged issue at the conference; however, he later had his way on this critical question.

One generalization that may be drawn from the experience of Western Socialist or working-class-based parties such as the SDP, the Australian and British Labour Parties, and the Austrian Socialist Party is that socialist doctrine tends to be modified or abandoned to the extent that a party either obtains or perceives a realistic opportunity to obtain the power and responsibility of government. Even the Italian Communist Party, according to Joseph LaPalombara, qualified its Communist ideology in the 1960s, probably because it saw that as the second strongest party in the country, it had a realistic chance of obtaining or sharing power in the existing democratic process.[42]

One may discern certain patterns in the ideological or principled bases of parties in Western democracies. The similar categorization of parties according to their ideological or programmatic appeal is found, with slightly different names, in most of the nations under consideration. For example, *Christian democracy* appears in the Federal Republic of Germany as the Christian Democratic Union, in Italy as Christian Democracy, in Belgium as the Social Christian Party, and in France as the Popular Republican Movement. Generically, Christian democracy refers to the political parties of the center right

that have what might be termed a confessional base. That is, Christian Democratic parties are frequently more or less loosely affiliated with the Catholic Church and have predominantly appealed to religious Christians in general and to Catholics in particular. These parties have attempted to broaden their appeal to all Christians in nations with a strong Protestant population, such as Germany, in order to include all those in the center right who are repelled by the collectivist image of parties of the left, whether or not these people are particularly religious.

This broadening of the appeal of these parties has been at the expense of their principles, thus rendering them classic examples of what Otto Kirchheimer called "catch-all parties."[43] Kirchheimer's famous thesis is that Western European parties are moving in the direction of deideolization and aggregation and that the parties of the future will be broad coalitions of ideologically and even programmatically diffuse groups. In addition to the German SPD and the French Gaullists (the Rally of the French People in the Fourth Republic and the Union for the New Republic in the Fifth), the Christian Democrats are a major example of the Kirchheimer thesis. He could have mentioned the Dutch Catholic Party, which was the strongest one in the Netherlands for decades. More recently, however, with an increasingly secularized society, Dutch Catholics are no longer voting their religion, and the party has lost considerable support. In response, the party tried to broaden its appeal to be regarded as a generic Christian party and merged with the the two orthodox Protestant parties in a "confessional bloc." The party found itself in a kind of vicious circle, however, for as long as most of its supporters and officeholders are Catholic, non-Catholics still regard it as a Catholic party, and as long as it is still regarded as a Catholic party, its supporters and officeholders will be overwhelmingly

Catholic. Ultimately, the Catholic Party disappeared as an independent entity, and Dutch religious voters now support the Christian Democratic Appeal, a party that still lost considerable support in the 1994 election, with the continuing secularization of Dutch society forcing Prime Minister Ruud Lubbers to resign after 12 years in office.

Throughout the democratic world, the phenomenon of parties based on the support of the industrial labor force is manifested under various names. These parties frequently embrace a loosely articulated philosophy known as *social democracy*. This position entails the idea that an economic position of aggressive egalitarianism based on a vigorous application of the welfare state, often combined with widespread state ownership of the major means of production, distribution, and exchange, is compatible with political democracy.

These labor-based parties vary a great deal in the vigor and seriousness with which they espouse state socialism as an ideological or policy goal. Some, like the British Labour Party, have been primarily trade union parties whose programmatic goal has been to advocate and advance the interests of the trade union laborers. Trade unionists, whose tactics emphasize collective bargaining with management, have no interest in turning management over to the powerful arm of the state, which is clearly a tougher bargaining agent. Such trade union–dominated parties always seem to have their more principled left wing; in the case of Labour, it is the Fabian Society's democratic socialist wing that sees political conflict almost exclusively in terms of class conflict. Other parties, like the Australian Labour Party, attempt to divide their goals into a "fighting platform" of short-term, realistic trade union goals and a long-range platform that clings to the mobilizing symbolism of a socialist objective. Still others, such as the defunct French Section of the Workers' International, cling to the symbolism of a pan-national workers' movement that is inherently opposed to the capitalist system, without actually proposing any sudden dismantling of the existing economic system, let alone opposing political democracy. Such ideological parties have tended to disappear in favor of parties with more pragmatic goals.

The Postmaterialist Revolution and Class-Based Parties

What these parties have in common is that they presume the predominant salience of the politics of social class, a salience that has been brought into serious question by the research of Ronald Inglehart.[44] Inglehart's widely cited and discussed thesis holds that there has been a fundamental shift in Western European values away from an emphasis on economic and material well-being and toward an emphasis on life style and civil liberties, which he calls postmaterialist or post-bourgeois values. Thus, those on the political left who are concerned with material values might advocate such goals as higher wages and jobs for the industrial labor force or other redistributive policies, while leftists concerned with postmaterialist values might support such objectives as greater tolerance of nonconformity with middle-class life styles, environmentalism, or nuclear disarmament. Clearly, the rise of Green Parties across Europe epitomizes the postmaterialism envisaged by Inglehart. *Die Grunen*—Germany's Greens, the most famous of such parties—captured 49 of the 672 seats in the Bundestag in the 1994 election, with 7.3 percent of the vote in the newly reunited Germany. Moreover, although less successful thus far, there are the Italian, French, Dutch, British, and Belgian Greens. These parties have tended to evolve into something more than mere conservationist parties. Rather, they have in some cases, most notably in Germany, become generalized new left parties espousing a broad anticapitalist, anti-Western agenda, as discussed by Russell Dalton.[45] Their support comes from the well educated but unemployed or underemployed (in the sense of having to take jobs for which they are educationally overqualified) middle class.[46]

To the extent that it is valid, this postmaterialist revolution in values would reverse the relationship between class cleavages and one's position on the left-right continuum of the political spectrum. The working class is on the left wing on the materialist or economic values and as such is the natural constituency for labor-based parties. However, leftist positions on postmaterialist or postbourgeois values are generally correlated with higher education and are hence more prevalent among the middle and upper-classes. The working class is more likely than the middle to upper classes to be protective of values such as middle-class morality and an ethnocentric variety of patriotism, positions that are definitely conservative. Hence, the natural working-class clientele of labor-based parties is generally opposed to the issue positions that are defined as liberal in the postmaterialist world.

Labor-based parties tend to define themselves as leftist, but they also tend to define themselves in terms of the issues that were salient in their formative period. Inglehart's research suggests that these issues are becoming less salient with time. It is largely a generational division. People who themselves or perhaps whose parents developed their values in a time of scarcity in the 1920s and 1930s tend to be characterized as materialist in their value priorities. Those who developed their political values during the long-term postwar prosperity tend to be characterized as postmaterialist or postbourgeois in their value priorities. Obviously, over time the former generation is becoming an ever-smaller portion of the population.

Labor-based parties thus find themselves in an ideological dilemma. To appeal to their natural working-class constituency, they must take a conservative position on postbourgeois issues, something that is emotionally difficult for politicians with a lifelong attachment to the idea of liberal if not radical politics, and something that would threaten the symbolic and ideological essence of these parties. Those educated people from a professional or business family background may have greater affinity for leftist positions on postbourgeois issues, but it is emotionally difficult for them to support parties that are symbolically associated with trade unionism if not with a modified Marxism. Labor-based parties therefore find themselves advocating issue positions that are decreasingly salient to their natural working-class clientele or that are salient to an increasingly contracting segment of the working class.[47]

It would seem that support for labor-based parties would diminish in times of prosperity but would resurge in times of economic recession. The evidence that the widespread and long-term economic prosperity of the West since World War II may be leveling off if not declining should, by this logic, presage a new era of political success for labor-based parties. The scarcity of resources and the geometrically higher cost of energy may be placing a finite upper limit on the economic growth that the West has come to take for granted, a phenomenon that should give new salience to economic or materialist concerns.

Inglehart's findings indicate, however, that the value orientations of the citizens of Western nations reflect the economic conditions that existed when those values where formed during their childhood and do not change as economic conditions fluctuate during their adult life. People who were raised during the Great Depression tend to be materialist, even though they have lived most of their adult life in a period of steady prosperity. People raised in the postwar era of prosperity will probably remain postmaterialists even if an age of scarcity develops. The materialists of the Depression era are dying out; hence, the politics of the foreseeable future should be dominated by postmaterialist values, regardless of the strength of Western economies. Meanwhile, leftist parties are emotionally tied to materialist or class-based values. To the extent that the "new left" of the postmaterialist age supports parties of the left, such parties are in danger of being divided, as we will see is the case of the British Labour Party and the American Democratic Party since the development of its so-called McGovern wing. Actually, Inglehart finds that many supporters of new left values do not support the old left-wing or class-based parties but seek political expression in a new set of parties such as ecological parties.[48] He notes the rise of the Green Party in Germany as an example of this trend. However, these parties still command the support of but a small portion of the electorate, and he may overstate their significance. These new left parties tend to be more ideological in the closed, consistent sense of the term than the old class-based, trade union parties. The German Greens, as we have noted, are much more than the ecological party that Inglehart discusses.

Scott Flanagan argues that Inglehart's dichotomy between materialist and postmaterialist value orientations is too simplistic in failing to distinguish between the new left and the new right.[49] Positions such as those that hold that the military should be strengthened, that crime and terrorism can be deterred with severe punishment, that the poor try to avoid work, and that there are moral absolutes whose violation should be criminalized are not materialist, nor are they reflected in Inglehart's conceptualization of postmaterialism, which seems to be exemplified by such issues as environmentalism and

disarmament. The former positions would be classified as post–materialist, or "new" right, while the latter are also post–materialist or "new" left.

Supporting Flanagan's argument that postmaterialism is not necessarily an exclusively left-wing phenomenon is the rise of a set of parties in Europe that may be characterized as a "new right." They have an electoral constituency and programmatic or principled base that are different from the more traditional and mainstream parties of the right such as the British Conservatives; the various Christian Democratic parties in Germany, Belgium, Italy, the Netherlands, Norway, Denmark, and Austria; and the Progressive Conservatives of Canada. The British and Canadian Conservatives stress such principles as the natural inequality among people, a need for continuity with an evolving past with a respect for traditions, and an organic structure of society. Christian Democratic parties further tie such principles to originally Catholic and now more broadly Christian social doctrine. All of these parties mainly represent the interests of the middle classes or higher, as opposed to the industrial working or underclass, by being concerned with property rights, contractual obligations, and the free market.

The newer group of parties of the right are not representative of the upper and middle class or bourgeois interests. In fact, they tend to have a more populist ideology and a working-class clientele, and may be classified as populist. They are frequently concerned with the preservation of subcultural autonomy, and in a number of cases advocate separatism or secession from the nation of which they are a part. Others have, in contrast, promoted a xenophobic nationalism and nativism that have taken the form of anti-immigrant programs and hostility toward various racial, ethnic, and religious minorities. In this, they resemble the fascists parties of the

1930s. These new parties are therefore parties of a social rather than an economic right.

While traditional conservative parties such as the British and Canadian Conservatives are on the electoral ropes, and while Christian Democrats have been losing electoral ground, the nativist and anti-immigrant parties and the parties of cultural defense have been making significant electoral gains. Having started from ground zero, however, they are for the most part short of major party status in their respective nations. Among the separatist parties that have experienced electoral success in the past decade are Canada's *Bloc Québeçois* and Italy's Northern League. Of course, each of the nine Belgian parties has a component of subcultural defense. Among the anti-immigrant and nativist or right-wing populist parties are France's National Front, Italy's National Alliance, the Netherland's Centre Democrats, and Belgium's *Vlaams Blok*. The Reform Party of western Canada is a curious blend of right-wing populist elements, and the Country Party of Australia exhibited some crypto-fascist characteristics.

The point of Inglehart's research on party ideology is that while the raison d'être and electoral appeal of the major Western parties are focused around economic or class-based issues, such issues have a "diminishing marginal utility" to mobilize voters in the postindustrial world. The interparty struggles are, therefore, increasingly irrelevant to the issues of greatest salience to these societies. These issues in fact may not be resolved by the outcome of electoral competition among the parties but in other arenas, such as direct action in the streets or in the neocorporatist processes discussed below. Thus, the results of these electoral contests may not make very much difference for policy outcomes.

Labor-based parties are not the only type that have found their ideological or programmatic appeals increasingly irrelevant to the political cleavages of mature industrial democracies. A striking example of a viable ideology that became atavistic is *classical liberalism*. Classical liberalism should be distinguished from the politics of the present-day left. Classical liberalism, which is sometimes known as Manchester liberalism, is associated with the reaction to the formative or earlier stages of industrial democracy in nineteenth-century England. Articulated most clearly in the writings of John Stuart Mill and his utilitarian progenitors, it has its roots in the works of John Locke and the economic theories of Adam Smith.

The basic principle of classical liberalism is individualism, the belief that law and social policy should treat people as individuals rather than as members of a social group, and should allocate rewards and punishments on the basis of achievement rather than ascription. Classical liberalism, therefore, has as one of its principal policy goals equality under law, which means that the law should avoid categorizing people except insofar as there is a widespread consensus that such categories reflect actual behavioral distinctions and serve a valid and compelling public purpose.

The public policy agenda of classical liberalism was based upon the presumption that governmentally ascribed privileges and status constituted the only important barriers to the realization of one's human potential; hence, the maximization of individual freedom requires the minimal amount of governmental power and activity. As Ralph Waldo Emerson put it, "The less government we have, the better," and in the words of Henry David Thoreau, "That government governs best which governs least." Many of the great theorists in the liberal tradition began with the assumption that there was a state of nature in which people had numerous "self-evident" rights that could be discerned by proper reason, and that people were inherently reasonable and disposed to accept the fact that others also have natural rights. Hence, the only justification for government intrusion on this essentially benign state of nature is to protect these rights from abuse, an idea epitomized by the social contract idea of Locke, Jean-Jacques Rousseau, and their followers among the theorists of the American Revolution. The specific political policy goals of classical liberals included the eradication of the last vestiges of aristocratic privilege, the achievement of universal male suffrage based on the principle of one man–one vote, and the maximization of civil liberties by restraining the exercise of governmental authority over the individual. In the economic sphere, classical liberals favored a policy of laissez faire, or the avoidance of governmental interference in the supposedly self-regulating market. This theory of the self-regulating market holds that the price and the allocation of goods and services are determined not by the conscious decisions of economic actors but rather by the impersonal forces of supply and demand. Drawing upon the powerful arguments for universal free trade and against the economic protectionism of mercantilism made by Adam Smith in *An Inquiry into the Causes of the Wealth of Nations* in 1776, liberals argued that the public good is best served by freely allowing men to pursue their rational economic self-interest. A corollary is that a process of natural selection (sometimes referred to as Social Darwinism) leads to the survival from economic competition of those individuals or economic actors that best serve the needs of society. Both the political and the economic agendas of classical liberalism assume that people follow their rational self-interests, an assumption that further presumes that they possess the information necessary to do so. In the complex world of a mature industrial society, this corollary is increasingly questionable. Moreover, the theory of the self-regulating market presumes that economic motivation overrides all others. Human motivations, however, are clearly more complex.

As classical liberalism was one of the major ideological traditions in the history of Western ideas, the parties of classical liberalism were among the strongest and most venerable in their respective countries from sometime in the nineteenth century until well into the twentieth. These parties were called liberal parties in some nations (e.g., Great Britain, Australia, Canada, Norway, Italy, and Sweden), but have also appeared under various other labels, such as the Radical Socialists in France, the Party of Liberty and Progress in Belgium, and the Free Democrats in West Germany. Whatever the specific label, classical liberalism was represented by some party in each of the Western industrial democracies for some part of this period.

Either shortly before or shortly after World War II, these once great liberal parties began to decline in electoral strength and faded from major to minor party status. (The Liberal Parties in Canada and Australia are exceptions to this trend, as they have managed to transform themselves into Kirchheimer's type "catch-all" parties of the political center to center right.) The decline of liberal parties may be attributed to the fact that their political agendas have more or less been fulfilled and their economic agenda appears increasingly untenable in today's postindustrial world.

On the political side, universal male suffrage had been realized throughout the West by the early twentieth century, aristocratic privileges are a thing of the past, the secular powers of religious institutions have largely been curbed, and the civil rights of individuals are generally respected. On the economic side, the self-regulating market has increasingly been perceived as inadequate to deal with the imperatives of an advanced state of technology. As John Kenneth Galbraith has argued, the imperatives of technology require producers to concentrate capital at a level that is incompatible with market theory, in order to create demand and to set prices according to the costs of production.[50] The economies of size are too great, the costs of production too staggering, the time needed for production too long, and therefore the risks too unbearable to rely on the impersonal and unpredictable forces of the market in advanced industrial societies. Moreover, in the second half of the twentieth century scholars have increasingly questioned whether equality under law actually produced equality of opportunity to realize one's human potential, unhindered by external barriers that are not equally distributed among the population. Equal laws have unequal impacts on unequal persons, or, as Anatole France once said, "The law, in its majestic impartiality, forbids the rich as well as the poor to beg in the streets, sleep under bridges, and steal bread."

The economic stagnation that beset many Western nations in the 1980s led to a disillusionment with the policies of welfare state capitalism in some quarters and a renewed interest in a reliance on market forces. This reawakened interest in some of the economic policies of classical liberalism did not produce a great resurgence in the now dormant liberal parties, however. Rather, the political benefit fell to the major parties on the center right, such as the Christian Democrats or, in the British case, Thatcher's Conservative Party. The political and social agendas of liberals have largely been coopted by parties of the left, while their economic agendas have largely been coopted by parties of the right.

Clearly, the ideological spectrum has changed in Western societies; the ideologies that once motivated people no longer seem applicable to the problems these societies face or the issues that are salient to their citizens. A debate appeared in the literature in the mid-1950s on whether the salience of ideology itself had declined. Critics of this "decline of ideology" school argued that while the content of ideology had changed as the old ideologies such as Marxism or classical liberalism had largely been rendered irrelevant to the values and issues of mature industrial societies, new ideologies had risen to take their place. These new ideologies have been identified as including such phenomena as feminism, peace and disarmament, and cultural defense for newly assertive subcultures. These ideologies do constitute sets of principles but not the kind of closed, comprehensive belief systems identified by such proponents of the "decline of ideology" thesis as Seymour Lipset and Daniel Bell, who were using the term *ideology* in a narrower, more restrictive sense than their critics. The debate may, to a large extent, have been based upon different conceptualizations of the term.

A Functional Perspective on Political Parties

The foregoing analysis presumes that the models of democracy discussed above entail certain functions for political parties—contributions to the effective operation of the system—and that these functions are not being adequately performed by Western party systems. It also presumes that parties perform the function of identifying and transmitting interests and demands from the society to the political decision-making process, which Gabriel Almond has called *interest articulation*. In the course of doing this, however, parties are also supposed to perform what Almond has called *interest aggregation*, the filtering and consolidation of interests and demands into a number that is manageable for the system.

Parties are not only supposed to react to the spontaneously arising demands of society but to shape those demands positively. Public opinion is not spontaneously formed on specific issues but largely developed by opinion leaders. As one type of these opinion leaders, parties are expected to present, explain, and sell to the voters clear and manageable alternatives of public policy on the salient issues of the day. Parties thus are supposed to structure the debate on public policy.

Parties are expected to present not only policy alternatives but also personnel alternatives by selecting and training candidates for public office. In nonpartisan elections, the average voter frequently is unable to possess the information needed to judge the potential ability and values of each contender for public office; however, party labels offer an approximate means of making such judgments while by-passing the substantial information costs. It will be shown that in parliamentary systems, the MPs rise through the party from backbench to lower ministerial to inner cabinet positions, all the while demonstrating and acquiring the very skills they will need to govern the country. Politics, after all, is a skill involving the exercise of power and the manipulation of rewards and punishments to make others perceive that it is in their best interest to do what the power wielder wants them to do and what they otherwise would not have done.

The literature suggests that various parties and party systems are widely perceived as not adequately filling the above functions and that others perform these functions with varying degrees of effectiveness, depending on their attributes. For example, fragmented party systems more effectively articulate or transmit demands, while aggregated party systems clearly aggregate or consolidate demands more effectively. Programmatic parties more effectively present clear policy alternatives to the voters, while "catch-all" parties do so less effectively; however, the latter type of party reduces the voters' choices to a manageable number and is more likely to be able to organize the governance of the nation by providing a cohesive majority behind a single set of elites.

At the heart of the skepticism about the actual role of parties in Western democracies is the perception of scholars such as Richard Rose and Anthony King that parties, being structured along increasingly atavistic lines of cleavage, no longer offer meaningful alternatives on the salient issues of the day.[51] Accordingly, a growing percentage of the voting public in some Western democracies no longer psychologically identifies with one of the parties, a phenomenon called *dealignment*. In other nations, the disillusionment with the choices provided by the established parties has led to a shift in the party identification of large segments of the voting public to newer parties often espousing postmaterialist values, a phenomenon known as *realignment*. Inglehart refers to the rise of environmentalist parties in this regard.[52] The rise of parties of cultural defense and the appearance of Democrats '66 in the Netherlands may also illustrate this realignment phenomenon. There is a growing empirical literature that documents the strength of both realignment and dealignment in Western democracies.[53] It does seem clear that party systems throughout the Western world are in a state of fundamental flux, a transition brought about by a widespread perception that the established parties and party systems are no longer performing (if indeed they ever did) the functions allocated to them in the democratic model and in particular are not structuring the debate or offering solutions to the salient issues of the day.

If the foregoing is correct and the party systems do not function in the classic role of processing issues and offering policy solutions to these issues, the question arises as to where in the modern democratic state are these functions performed. The following sections suggest that they are increasingly performed outside the formal political process itself, in the administrative sector and in what are called neocorporatist processes.

THE ADMINISTRATIVE STATE
AND DEMOCRATIC THEORY:
THE ROLE OF THE TECHNOCRACY

The term *administrative sector* refers to that part of the state whose formal function is to implement the policy decisions emanating from the political sector. Theoretically, governments (i.e., prime ministers, cabinets, and legislative assemblies) formulate and adopt policy resolutions on political issues, and the civil service or administrative sector puts these decisions into effect. The structure designated for this purpose is the public *bureaucracy*.

Bureaucracy refers to the form that large organizations tend to take in order to maximize the rational efficiency of implementing tasks or attaining goals already adopted. Administration is what bureaucracies do. The key point in classical administrative theory is this presumed separation of politics and administration.

The statement that bureaucracies are designed to maximize rational efficiency seems strange to many people to whom the term *bureaucracy* conjures up pejorative images of monumental inefficiency. The term is associated for many with visions of bespectacled clerks in green eyeshades mindlessly impeding the self-evidently just and reasonable solutions to problems in a sea of pointless regulations and procedures that are popularly called "red tape." In particular, the idea of "the bureaucrats" as a stereotyped group of villains blocking the will of "the people" has had a reliable appeal to politicians with a consciously populist image, and to the kinds of people who fear and resent the complex interdependence of the postindustrial era

and who yearn for simple solutions to simple problems of a partially apocryphal past.

The confusion here stems from the invalidity of the key assumption of classic organization theory—the separation of politics (goal setting, policy formulation, and allocative decision making) and administration (the application or implementation and enforcement of policy). Scholars dealing with less modernized nations began to suggest that in those nations, beset with weak political and representative structures, putatively administrative structures in fact played an important political role. In particular, Fred Riggs's concept of "the heavy weight of bureaucratic power" implies that colonial powers developed administrative structures while repressing political ones, which in turn led to a "formalism" in which the actual decision-making powers rested in the hands of such administrators despite a constitutionally designated format placing such power in politically accountable hands.[54]

The essence of complex advanced industrial societies, however, generates imperatives for the inexorable devolution of political authority from the political to the administrative sector. Despite the legal or conventional constitutional principles that clearly place the responsibility for the formulation of policy and the allocation of values in the hands of politically accountable legislatures or governments, bureaucrats in the administrative sector of such societies are increasingly exercising a great deal of discretion in the application and implementation of policies, discretion that amounts to policy making. This growing political role of bureaucrats may be one of the most important developments in the nature of industrial democracies, one that can only be understood with reference to the nature and attributes of the classical model of bureaucracies.

Max Weber, a German sociologist of the early twentieth century whose writings have had an enormous impact on modern social science, was the first to specify the attributes of large organizations in order to maximize the goal of rational efficiency. His ideal type or model of bureaucracy consisted of the following characteristics:

1 A comprehensive set of impersonal rules. (This means that the proper response for the occupant of each role is spelled out for each possible eventuality, regardless of who occupies that role. This routinization provides the all-important value of predictability.)
2 Allocation of tasks on the basis of the specialization and division of labor. (This is the manner in which the organization handles the great increases in the flow of knowledge and information necessarily associated with modern technology. As technology expands, it becomes increasingly impossible to master the corpus of human knowledge and skills, even on one task or subject. For example, while the Wright brothers could build an airplane from start to finish, it takes an array of highly trained specialists to construct a modern aircraft. Specialization permits an aggregate of ordinary people to function as a collective genius.)
3 A hierarchical structure. (Each office is under the supervision and control of a higher one in order to give coherence and coordination to the organization as a whole.)
4 Members are subject to authority and responsibility only with respect to their official roles.
5 Candidates are selected for offices on the basis of demonstrated competence and given tenure of office. (Since the bureaucrats are chosen on the basis of their expertise, they can only be fired for dereliction of duty, and are thereby insulated from political or social pressures.)
6 Compensation of officials by a fixed salary. (They can implement policies and perform other tasks on the basis of expertise rather than for financial gain.)[55]

The Weberian model details the model of rational efficiency for the role of implementing goals in a technologically advanced society. As such, this routinization and bureaucratization of the processes of society were to Weber almost coterminous with the process of modernization itself. Besides the questionable validity of the assumed separation of politics and administration, however, the model is internally flawed.

In Weber's model, the integration and coherence of the organization are provided by the principle of hierarchy, whereby each role is subject to the oversight of a higher role. The principle of specialization, however, implies that the knowledge and information possessed by the occupants of each role are esoteric to themselves. Thus, the occupants of each subordinate role possess esoteric knowledge about that role that is not shared by their superiors, to whom they are ostensibly responsible. Hence, each role is isolated both vertically and horizontally from each other distinct role in the organization, effectively breaking down the principle of hierarchy.

Thus by definition the public bureaucracy is the part of the political system in which one finds the technically trained experts who possess the knowledge and skills to understand the complex issues and to formulate policy decisions in an advanced state of technology. Legislatures and governments are usually composed of generalists such as lawyers or businesspeople who lack such knowledge. For example, what does such a generalist know about the standards needed to protect the air and water from chemical pollution?

Consequently, the politically responsible institutions—governments and legislatures—increasingly delegate the power to make the actual decisions in the form of bureaucratic regulations having the force of law. Because more and more of the government is conducted by these technically trained people, they are collectively referred to as the *technocracy* and individually as *technocrats*. This devolution of power from the political to the administrative sectors constitutes one of the most important developments in the actual operation of mature industrial democracies, because it drastically alters if not negates the entire structure of accountability in such systems and furthermore has serious implications for the capacities of these systems to perform adequately. The reasons for these consequences lie partly in the essence of bureaucracy itself and partly in the kinds of attitudes and behavior patterns it fosters among its officeholders.

Because bureaucracy is designed to implement policies already adopted on the basis of objective knowledge and expertise, it is intended to foster the following values: insulation from political and social pressures, as opposed to responsiveness; routinization and predictability, as opposed to creativity and adaptability; and value neutrality, as opposed to representativeness. For political structures, however, the foregoing value dichotomies should be diametrically reversed. Especially in a democracy, political institutions should be responsive, creative, adaptable, and representative of the spectrum of social values. Thus, when an institution such as a bureaucracy finds itself performing a function or set of functions for which it was not designed, it discovers that it is poorly suited to the task at hand.

The imperatives of bureaucracy generate attitudes and behavior patterns that are dysfunctional for the political role played by administrators, as shown in research by Robert Putnam,[56] Michael Crozier,[57] and others. Their data of course show that administrators or bureaucrats vary individually and that on the national level they vary with respect to the extent to which they manifest "classic" bureaucratic attitudes and behaviors. For example, according to Putnam's data Italian civil servants vary among themselves with respect to these attitudes, but Italians in the aggregate tend to have a significantly greater tendency to exhibit classic bureaucratic attitudes than do British civil servants.

Classic bureaucrats tend to do things "by the book," following established procedure as literally and rigorously as possible rather than showing some flexibility in the application of rules and procedures in the light of changing circumstances. This means they tend to create a greater margin of safety for their position and are less disposed to engage in risk-taking behavior. Of course, rigid adherence to a system of impersonal rules and procedures stifles creativity. By such behavior, the classic bureaucrat avoids the reality of what Crozier calls "the problem of power."[58] *Power* is a concept that refers to a relationship that allows the power wielder to cause others to do what the power wielder wants and that they otherwise would not have done. This ability to control the behavior of others is based upon the creation of a perception that one can and will manipulate resources into the threat of rewards and punishments that makes others believe that they will be better off doing what the power wielder wants. Power relationships are at the heart of what we mean by the political and are the basis of the bargaining process by which political issues are resolved in any society. Obviously, in an autocratic system the power relationships are much more asymmetrical than in an open or democratic system. Clearly, the search for perfect rationality and the suppression of the bargaining process impede the adoption of viable but imperfect solutions to issues that, after all, involve values more than a rational calculus.

Classic bureaucrats are impatient with political or social pressures or inputs. By perceiving that their role involves applying rational criteria based upon technical expertise rather than resolving the conflict between values or real interests, they diminish their system's responsive capacity.

Classical bureaucracy, by its emphasis on the functional specialization of each role based upon esoteric knowledge, tends to isolate the offices or roles in the organization from one another. Not only are the coherence and coordination of the organization diminished, but the possibility of applying the core democratic goal of accountability is seriously impeded. One is hard-pressed to hold an official accountable for doing his or her job effectively when one does not understand that job. Supervisors accordingly can exercise little control over their nominal subordinates, and thus the principle of hierarchy breaks down.

The breakdown of the separation of politics and administration is but one manifestation of the delegation of the actual decision-making function from politically accountable roles to the technocracy. Another manifestation of the growing role of the technocracy is the increase of an imprecisely defined phenomenon known as *neocorporatism.*

NEOCORPORATISM AND THE DOMINANCE OF THE TECHNOCRATS

It is somewhat strange that the literature applying the concept of corporatism to the industrial democracies can be accurately called one of the real "growth industries" in the field of comparative politics. The concept of corporatism was developed to describe a set of politico-economic arrangements unique to Benito Mussolini's Fascist Italy, and as originally formulated is clearly inapplicable to the liberal democracies of the Western world. Hence, we see the prefix *neo-* frequently affixed to its democratic applications. (This prefix is widely used to justify or hedge an obviously inappropriate use of a term in social and political polemics. For example, the United States, which was never more than marginally in the business of acquiring political sovereignty over less-developed lands, may still be called "neo-imperialist," and various liberal democracies whose formats bear not the slightest resemblance to the World

War II dictatorships in Italy and Germany may still be called "neofascist.")

The "corporations," in the Italian version of corporatism, were structures created by the state to regulate an economically defined sector of the society (e.g., agriculture, industrial workers, or medicine) in the interest of the state. The term *corporation* in its corporatist usage is not related to its current Western usage referring to the legally defined structure of a large business involving the formal separation of ownership and management. Since Italian corporatism by definition involved the control of the economy and society in the interest of the state, that term is clearly inapplicable to Western systems in which the economy is run either for profits or, in social democracies or welfare state capitalism, for some conception of the public interest.

Led by Phillipe Schmitter and Gerhard Lembruch, a number of prominent scholars have produced a substantial body of literature attempting to revive and reshape the concept of corporatism some four decades after the fall of Fascist Italy.[59] By developing such qualifying concepts as "liberal corporatism" or "societal corporatism," they are using the concept to describe a pattern of decision making that is becoming increasingly widespread and institutionalized throughout the industrial democracies.

As conceptualized by Schmitter, Lembruch, and others, the democratic manifestation of corporatism refers to a pattern of domestic policy formulation in which the administrative sector of the state recognizes a peak interest association that has emerged in each sector of society (such as the AMA for medicine or American Bar Association for law) and in effect grants that association a representational monopoly over that sector of society. In return, that association agrees to work cooperatively rather than competitively with the appropriate agencies of the higher civil service in the formulation and implementation of policy. This means that the association in effect guarantees that its membership will facilitate the implementation of whatever policy outcomes emerge from the cooperative bargaining process between the association and the bureaucratic agency. In this process, it is not clear that the interests of the ordinary members of society are given careful consideration. It is clear that the policy proposals formulated in this process will necessarily be formalized into law with very little revision or oversight by the politically accountable institutions; when all of the relevant interests with respect to a policy question (e.g., labor, management, middle management, etc.) and the relevant civil servants all agree on a policy solution, any other solution will not be viable or capable of being implemented.

Hence, neocorporatism involves another process of policy making outside the formal political process, thereby fundamentally altering the entire structure of accountability in democratic societies. It refers to the institutionalization of a bargaining process among members of the technocracy whose institutional position and esoteric knowledge render them insulated from accountability to the electorate. The processes referred to as societal corporatism by Schmitter or liberal corporatism by Lembruch are institutionalized in a pattern of structures that has arisen in many of the advanced industrial democracies of the West. These structures consist of representatives from the designated peak interest groups and members of the higher civil service with the formal responsibility to present policy proposals or economic plans to the political process for ratification into law. The first of these structures originated in Sweden with an informal process of bargaining widely referred to as "Harpsund democracy," after the city where it first occurred. It was eventually formalized as the Planning Board. In Great Britain, the National Economic Development Council, known as "Neddy" and made up of representatives from trade unions, management groups, and higher civil servants, was founded in 1961 to hammer out industrial policy; however, in the 1980s the Thatcher administration, with its ideological commitment to market forces, reduced its direct impact on policy making. In France, the General Commissariat of the Equipment Plan and of Productivity grew out of a structure started by Charles de Gaulle, who highly praised its work. Hence, planning was clearly not an exclusive franchise of the political left. (No direct manifestation of such liberal corporatist structures has appeared in the United States, partially due to the absence of obviously peak organizations in most sectors of the economy.)

These and other manifestations of neo-, liberal, or societal corporatism thus appear to be a product of the imperatives of the advanced state of technology that inevitably affects public policy issues in a mature industrial society, imperatives that require an increasing delegation of the policy-making function to the technocracy and that may require an increasing reliance on planning rather than on market forces in the formulation of economic and industrial policy. The implications of these imperatives give new life to a suggestion that has been advanced and then rejected on numerous occasions— that the structures and processes of policy making (as opposed to the substance of policy) may be more a function of the imperatives of the state of technology than of the variations in the constitutionally designated structures of government.

The idea that the state of technology determines political structure and process and therefore that advanced industrial democracies and industrial dictatorships are becoming increasingly similar in that respect is called *convergence theory*. It amounts to a technological determinism. In its more extreme versions, convergence theory is suggested to explain not only process but policy as well. Although some political radicals have contended that the choice between American and Soviet influence is morally neutral, the contention of convergence with respect to policy would be hard to sustain. Policy choices are affected not only by technology but by normative considerations, the values that constitute the very essence of a political system. However, the contention of a qualified convergence with respect to structure and process is given some support by the literature indicating a pattern in the growth of neocorporatism and the administrative state in advanced industrial societies.

The pattern of growth in what are imprecisely identified as neocorporatist processes may be attributable to a widespread perception that the advanced state of technology relies heavily on market forces that are increasingly unreliable. We have already discussed economist John Kenneth Galbraith's argument that the advanced state of technology in mature industrial states makes planning imperative.[60] Hence, planning in economic and industrial policy has generally become the norm in the democratic world, and these nations have adopted institutions for that purpose that have generally been grouped under the neocorporatist label. In the 1980s, the resurgence of the political right epitomized by the Reagan, Thatcher, and Kohl administrations was accompanied by a rediscovered interest and faith in market forces. As noted, this led to some curbing of the forces of planning and of neocorporatism, as seen in the somewhat diminished role for "Neddy" in Great Britain. Yet, to some extent this nostalgia for market economics was more rhetorical than real. While cuts in welfare state spending were significant in some areas, none of these conservative administrations seriously threatened the core of their respective welfare state systems. In the United States the Reagan budget was at record levels, and most of Britain's welfare state remained intact under Thatcher, despite the promarket, conservative image of both of these leaders. One may conclude from the discrepancy between ideology, rhetoric, and programmatic intent on the one hand and political reality on the other that the active economic role of the state and its abandonment of market forces are more a function of contextual factors rather than political or ideological choice. The persistence of planning and the welfare state under the regimes of these ideological conservatives supports the thesis that the state of technology requires planning and the structures that support it, including what we have called neocorporatism and the expansive political role of the higher civil service.

CONCLUSIONS: THE CRISIS OF DEMOCRACIES

Democratic government has always lived with a certain tension between the imperatives of the responsiveness that is part of its essence on the one hand and stability on the other. The responsive capacity entails the accountability of the elites to public opinion, while stability—the control of change within the confines of existing structures—entails a degree of insulation from the inevitably shifting currents of public opinion that gives government the discretion inherent in its core function of governing. Hence, one may regard responsiveness and stability as somewhat conflicting imperatives in modern democratic states.

We have attempted to show that the complexities of the modern world limit the role of the public in the policy-making process of a modern state and even the extent to which such a state can in fact be responsive to public opinion. Eric Nordlinger has written persuasively that even democratic states remain largely autonomous of public opinion.[61] Public opinion itself is not autonomous of the elites it is supposed to control; rather, it is largely created by opinion leaders.[62] Yet, it was suggested above that a widespread perception of political efficacy is one of the cultural requisites of democracy, and is based upon the assumption of some level of governmental responsiveness to the needs and demands of its people.

We have further suggested that democratic governments must be legitimate to survive. Legitimacy, it will be recalled, is the widespread acceptance of the government's authority, regardless of one's feelings about specific governmental performance. Legitimacy has therefore always been assumed to be independent of performance.

Recent evidence, however, indicates that long-term performance can in fact affect the level of legitimacy in either direction. In a positive example, we will show in Chapter 5 how the legitimacy of the democratic political format of Germany significantly increased in the 1960s after several decades of highly successful political and economic performance. This and other data indicating a strong shift in Germany toward the attributes of what Almond and Verba called the "civic culture" indicate that culture is highly malleable when faced with external influences and far from the unchanging phenomena that it may have been perceived to be in some quarters. Of course, as will be discussed in Chapter 5, the postwar prosperity of Germany has now been severely compromised by the enormous costs of reunification. Germany's GDP actually shrank 1.9 percent in 1993, and the country had a "structural deficit" (the share independent of the business cycle) of 5.2 percent of the GDP right after reunification in 1991. This figure had improved only slightly to 3.1 percent by 1993.

The narrow reelection of Chancellor Kohl in 1994 indicates a rising public dissatisfaction with government's performance. It is unclear what this will mean for German commitment to the "civic culture."

On the other more negative side, the data indicate that these "civic culture" attributes significantly declined in Great Britain following decades of consistently poor economic performance and the loss of world empire and international stature. In particular, the deference to authority and to the nature of the system that had been thought to be uniquely strong in Great Britain was judged to have been substantially eroded, which suggests that performance- and policy-specific dissatisfaction can diminish legitimacy in the long run.

It will be shown in Chapter 3 that there have been more recent indications of improved performance in some areas by the British political system. To have an impact on the legitimacy of the system, this improvement would have to be sustained over a significant period. In other words, it appears that policy performance affects legitimacy when the performance pattern is of fairly long duration, possibly measured in decades.

A number of scholars have been raising the question of whether, in the postindustrial world, it is still possible for democratic governments to sustain the perception of effective and responsive policy making over a long period. They are suggesting that there may be no socially and politically acceptable solutions for the salient issues of our time available to the politically accountable elites, thus creating an inevitable dissatisfaction with those elites, regardless of their political or ideological orientation. The reasons for this lie in the nature of postindustrial societies and of the world system in the present state of technology.

First, it is commonplace knowledge that the world is interdependent to an unprecedented extent, but the impact of this interdependence is just beginning to be explored. Markets are now world markets; hence, economic decisions taken outside of any given nation may have major impacts on that nation's prices, employment, and other economic factors. A significant part of the high levels of inflation that gripped much of the Western world in the 1970s was caused by the geometric rise in the price of crude oil that was due to the actions of OPEC (Organization of Petroleum Exporting Countries) and to Middle East politics in general. The trade imbalance that closes factories and costs industrial laborers their jobs in the United States is in part due to industrial policies of other nations such as Japan.

Long-term economic growth capable of absorbing population increases and alleviating issues involving the distribution of material well-being can no longer be routinely assured. Such growth, which had formerly been taken for granted, promised to raise everyone's standard of living absolutely if not relatively, thus plausibly pacifying the less competitively successful with the old aphorism that a rising tide floats all boats. However, the finite supply and inevitable scarcity of resources as well as limits on the ecological capacity of the planet to absorb the by-products of infinitely increasing productivity must at some point put an upper cap on economic growth. We will increasingly live in a zero sum world, one in which the values are finite; hence, any policy that allocates more to some must take away from others. There will now be winners and resentful losers generating increasingly intense conflict among interests over the allocation of social values. Significant policy decisions will almost inevitably alienate some portion of the electorate.

These are the conditions of the world at the present advanced state of technology that raise the question of whether advanced industrial societies are governable in terms of

having policy choices that promise solutions or at least partial solutions to the salient issues of the time. The suggestion that there may not be such policy solutions should apply to both advanced industrial democracies and industrial autocracies as well, as we will point out in Part Three.

The realities of mature industrial society pose an additional problem that is is unique to the democratic world. It was pointed out above that one of the cultural requisites of democracy is a widespread perception of civic competence, which entails the belief that the government is accountable to the citizens, that the citizens maintain some control over their government, and that the government has a responsive capacity. Yet, the growing and inexorable delegation of power to the technocracy threatens this perception of democratic accountability. Moreover, as issues become increasingly complex and beyond the capacity of the ordinary citizen to understand, the citizens are going to lose the sense that they can control the decisions that affect their lives.

Part of the legitimacy of democratic governments comes from the popular perception that such governments are structurally accountable and responsive to their citizens. To the extent that citizens no longer perceive that they can exercise popular control over the outputs of government, democratic governments stand to lose some of the legitimacy that they have acquired in the Western world. This threatens not only their stability and effectiveness but also their very nature. The question that this chapter has implicitly posed is whether democratic government as conceptualized here is compatible with the imperatives of a mature and technologically advanced industrial society. Can technocracies be held meaningfully accountable for their allocative decisions? This is a most relevant question in light of the recent wave of democratization among states that are, for the most part, at a less advanced stage of industrialization. While mature industrial society is a recent enough phenomenon that one should not be premature in drawing a final conclusion, the analyses of this problem are not encouraging. It is clear that the reconciliation of the imperatives of advanced technology and the value of accountability is one of the most important and difficult challenges faced by Western democracies.

NOTES

1. Samuel Huntington, *The Third Wave: Democratization in the Late Twentieth Century* (Norman, OK.: University of Oklahoma Press, 1991).

2. See e.g., Daniel Bell, *The Coming of Post-Industrial Society* (New York: Basic Books, 1973); and Leon Lindberg, ed., *Politics and the Future of Industrial Society* (New York: David McKay, 1976).

3. Lawrence Mayer and John Burnett, *The Politics of Industrial Societies: A Comparative Perspective* (New York: John Wiley and Sons, 1977), p. vi.

4. See n. 2.

5. Sidney Verba, Norman Nie, and Jae-on-Kim, *The Modes of Democratic Participation: A Cross-National Comparison* (Beverly Hills: Sage Publications, 1971); Sidney Verba, Norman Nie, and Jae-on-Kim, *Participation and Political Equality: A Seven Nation Comparison* (New York: Cambridge University Press, 1978); and Samuel Barnes et al., *Political Action: Mass Participation in Five Western Democracies* (Beverly Hills: Sage Publications, 1979).

6. Arend Lijphart, *Democracies: Patterns of Majoritarian and Consensus Government in Twenty-One Countries* (New Haven: Yale University Press, 1984), p. 1.

7. Eric Nordlinger, *On the Autonomy of Democratic States* (Cambridge: Harvard University Press, 1981).

8. Walter Lippman, *Public Opinion* (New York: The Macmillan Co., 1922, and Penguin Books, 1956); and Walter Lippman, *The Phantom Public* (New York: Harcourt Brace, 1930).

9. Joseph Schumpeter, *Capitalism, Socialism, and Democracy* (New York: Harper and Row Torchbooks, 1950), p. 269.

10. Anthony Downs, *An Economic Theory of Democracy* (New York: Harper and Row, 1957), pp. 116 ff.

11. Ibid., p. 101.

12. Otto Kirchheimer, "The Transformation of Western European Party Systems," in Joseph LaPalombara

and Myron Weiner, eds., *Political Parties and Political Development* (Princeton: Princeton University Press, 1966), pp. 184–200.

13. Ronald Inglehart, "The Silent Revolution in Europe: Intergenerational Change in Post-Industrial Societies," *The American Political Science Review,* vol. 65, no. 4 (December 1971), pp. 991–1017.

14. Ibid., p. 994. See also Ronald Inglehart, "Value Change in Industrial Societies," *American Political Science Review,* vol. 81, no. 4 (December 1987), p. 1290.

15. See, e.g., Russell Dalton, "Cognitive Mobilization and Partisan Realignment in Advanced Industrial Democracies," *Journal of Politics,* vol. 46, no. 1 (February 1984), pp. 264–85; and Harold Campbell and Marianne Stewart, "Dealignment of Degree: Partisan Change in Britain, 1974–1983," *Journal of Politics,* vol. 46, no. 3 (August 1984), pp. 689–719.

16. Gabriel Almond and Sidney Verba, *The Civic Culture* (Boston: Little Brown, 1965).

17. Sidney Verba and Norman Nie, *Participation in America: Political Democracy and Social Equality* (New York: Harper and Row, 1972), pp. 31, 79–80.

18. Harry Eckstein, "A Theory of Stable Democracy," Appendix B in *Division and Cohesion in Democracy: A Study of Norway* (Princeton: Princeton University Press, 1966), p. 266 passim.

19. See, e.g., Dennis Kavanaugh, "Political Culture in Great Britain: The Decline of the Civic Culture," in Gabriel Almond and Sidney Verba, eds., *The Civic Culture Revisited* (Boston: Little Brown, 1980), pp. 124–76; and Samuel Beer, *Britain Against Itself : The Political Contradictions of Collectivism* (New York: W. W. Norton, 1982), esp. chap. 4.

20. Lee Sigelman and Syng Nam Yough, "Left-Right Polarization in National Party Systems: A Cross-National Analysis," *Comparative Political Studies,* vol. 11, no. 3 (October 1978), pp. 355–81.

21. Robert Alford, *Party and Society: The Anglo-American Democracies* (Chicago: Rand McNally and Company, 1963).

22. Herbert J. Spiro, *Government by Constitution* (New York: Random House, 1959), pp. 39ff.; Raymond Grew, ed., *Crises of Political Development in Europe and the United States* (Princeton: Princeton University Press, 1978).

23. Mayer and Burnett, *Politics of Industrial Societies,* pp. 44, 63–64.

24. Samuel Huntington, *Political Order in Changing Societies* (New Haven: Yale University Press, 1968), pp. 266ff.

25. Martin O. Heisler, "Institutionalizing Social Cleavages in a Cooptive Polity: The Growing Importance of the Output Side in Belgium," in Martin O. Heisler, ed. *Politics in Europe: Structures and Processes in Some Post-Industrial Democracies* (New York: David McKay, 1974), pp. 178–220, esp. pp. 290ff.

26. Martin O. Heisler, "Political Community and Its Formation in the Low Countries," Ph.D. dissertation,

University of California, Los Angeles, 1969, pp. 298–99.

27. Arend Lijphart, *The Politics of Accommodation: Pluralism and Democracy in the Netherlands* (Berkeley: University of California Press, 1968).

28. *London Times,* December 4, 1994, p. 2.

29. Almond and Verba, *The Civic Culture;* see also n. 5.

30. E. E. Schattschneider, *Party Government* (New York: Rinehart and Company, 1942); "Toward a More Responsible Two-Party System: A Report of the Committee on Political Parties of the American Political Science Association," *American Political Science Review* (supplement), vol. 44, no. 3, pt. 2 (September 1950).

31. William Riker, *The Theory of Political Coalitions* (New Haven: Yale University Press, 1962), chaps. 2 and 3.

32. Michael Taylor and V. M. Herman, "Party Systems and Government Stability," *American Political Science Review,* vol. 65, no. 1 (March 1971), pp. 28–37; Lawrence C. Mayer, "Party Systems and Cabinet Stability," in Peter Merkl, ed., *West European Party Systems* (New York: The Free Press, 1980), pp. 335–47.

33. Alan Arian and Samuel Barnes, "The Dominant Party System: A Neglected Model of Political Stability," *Journal of Politics,* vol. 36, no. 2 (August 1974), pp. 592–614.

34. Mayer, "Party Systems," pp. 345–46.

35. F. A. Hermans, *Democracy or Anarchy: A Study of Proportional Representation* (Notre Dame, IN: Notre Dame University Press, 1941); Andrew Milnor, *Elections and Political Stability* (Boston: Little Brown, 1969).

36. Cf. nn. 33 and 34.

37. Maurice Duverger, *Political Parties,* trans. Barbara North and Robert North (New York: John Wiley Science Editions, 1963), p. 217.

38. Leslie Lipson, "The Two-Party System in Great Britain," *American Political Science Review,* vol. 47, no. 2 (June 1953), pp. 337–58.

39. Carl Schorske, *German Social Democracy, 1905–1917: The Development of the Great Schism* (New York: John Wiley and Sons Science Editions, 1953).

40. Ibid., p. 285.

41. *Basic Program of the Social Democratic Party,* p. 11.

42. Joseph LaPalombara, "The Decline of Ideology: A Dissent and Interpretation," *American Political Science Review,* vol. 40, no. 1 (March 1966), p. 1.

43. Kirchheimer, "Transformation."

44. Inglehart, "The Silent Revolution"; and Ronald Inglehart, "The Changing Structure of Political Cleavages in Western Societies," in Russell Dalton, Scott Flanagan, and Allen Beck, eds., *Electoral Change in Advanced Industrial Democracies* (Princeton: Princeton University Press, 1984).

45. Russell Dalton, *The Green Rainbow* (New Haven: Yale University Press, 1994).

46. Hans George Betz, "Value Change and Post-Materialist Politics: The Case of West Germany," *Comparative Political Studies,* vol. 23, no. 2 (July 1990), pp. 239–53, esp. pp. 244–48.

47. Risto Sankiaho, "Political Remobilization in Welfare States," in Dalton, Flanagan, and Beck, *Electoral Change,* p. 86.

48. Inglehart, "Value Change in Industrial Society," *American Political Science Review,* vol. 81, no. 4 (December 1987), pp. 1299, 1301.

49. Scott Flanagan, "Changing Values in Industrial Societies Revisited: Toward a Resolution of the Values Debate," *American Political Science Review,* vol. 81, no. 4 (December 1987), pp. 1303–19.

50. John Kenneth Galbraith, *The New Industrial State,* 2nd ed. (New York: Mentor Books, 1971), pp. 48ff.

51. Richard Rose, *Do Parties Make a Difference,* 2nd ed. (Chatham, NJ: Chatham House, 1984); Anthony King, "Political Parties in Western Societies: Some Skeptical Reflections," *Polity,* vol. 2, no. 2 (Winter 1969), pp. 111–41.

52. Inglehart, "Value Change in Industrial Society," pp. 1297–98.

53. See n. 15.

54. Fred Riggs, *Administration in Developing Countries: The Theory of the Prismatic Society* (Boston: Houghton-Mifflin Company, 1964), pp. 222ff. Cf. Lee Sigelman, "Do Modern Bureaucracies Dominate Underdeveloped Politics? A Test of the Imbalance Thesis," *American Political Science Review,* vol. 66, no. 2 (June 1972), pp. 525–28; and Lee Sigelman, "Bureaucratic Development and Dominance: A New Test of the Imbalance Thesis," *American Political Science Review,* vol. 67, no. 2 (June 1974) for a critical analysis of Riggs's thesis.

55. Weber's writings on bureaucracy appeared in *Wirtschaft and Gesellschaft,* published posthumously in 1921. This list is distilled and paraphrased from H. H. Gerth and C. Wright Mills, eds. and trans., *From Max Weber: Essays in Sociology* (New York: Oxford University Press Galaxy Books, 1958), pp. 196–98; and N. M. Henderson and Talcott Parsons, eds. and trans., *The Theory of Social and Economic Organization* (New York: The Free Press, 1964), p. 333.

56. Robert Putnam, "The Political Attitudes of Senior Civil Servants in Western Europe," *British Journal of Political Science,* vol. 3, no. 3 (July 1973), pp. 257–90.

57. Michel Crozier, *The Bureaucratic Phenomenon* (Chicago: University of Chicago Press, l964), pp. 178ff.

58. Ibid., pp. 145ff.

59. Phillipe Schmitter, "Still the Century of Corporatism" and "Modes of Interest Mediation and Models of Social Change in Western Europe," in Phillipe Schmitter and Gerhard Lembruch, eds., *Trends Toward Corporatist Intermediation* (Beverly Hills: Sage Publications, 1979), pp. 1–62, 63–93. For a critical

perspective on the use of this concept, see Andrew Cox, "Corporatism as Reductionism: The Analytic Limits of the Corporatist Thesis," *Government and Opposition,* vol. 13, no. 3 (Winter 1981), pp. 78–95; and Les Metcalf and Will McQuillan, "Corporatism or Industrial Democracy," *Political Studies,* vol. 27, no. 2, pp. 266–82.

60. Galbraith, *The New Industrial State,* pp. 114ff.
61. Nordlinger, *On the Autonomy of Democratic States.*
62. Lippman, *Public Opinion.*

3
Government and Politics in Great Britain

> "This precious stone set in the silver sea,
> Which serves it in the office of a wall,
> Or as a moat defensive to a house,
> Against the envy of less happier lands;
> This blessed plot, this earth, this realm, this England."
>
> *William Shakespeare,*
> Richard II, *act II, scene I*

These immortal lines of John of Gaunt reflect the almost conventional wisdom among modern students of politics that the political format of England provides the standard of excellence that other nations aspiring to stable, successful democracy ought to emulate.[1] Indeed, as late as the early 1950s, a select committee of the American Political Science Association presented a widely touted and cited report that in effect argued that the American political party system ought to become more like the British party system.[2] This perception of the so-called mother of parliaments as the ideal model of how democracies ought to function has resulted in the fact that the overwhelming preponderance of democratic governments (as well as some with democratic pretentions) have to greater or lesser extent tried to base their political format on the British example. Because of the longstanding status of the British political system as a model democracy, it is a mandatory part of all comparative politics books.

Yet, this chapter will show that the performance of the British system has been in decline in the post–World War II era, and that this decline has been accompanied by a decline in the status and long-lived respect for that system. Britain has in effect been transformed from a model of a successful democracy to a model of a democracy in decline. Many of the attributes that have been hailed as the reasons for its early strength and success now either are no longer characteristic of the British system or are contributing to its decline. Structures that had been regarded as immutable, such as the nation's essentially two-party system, predominantly class basis of cleavage, and the monarchy itself, are now regarded as being in a state of flux and perhaps permanently altered.[3]

The ability of the British system to function effectively in the postindustrial age is still an open question, however. After years of decline, of being labeled by some as the new "sick man of Europe," the economy appeared to be on the road to recovery by the mid-1990s, according to several indicators. After reaching a high of 18 percent in 1980, inflation had been brought down to 1.9 percent by December 1993, although it climbed back slightly to 2.5 percent by late 1994. Unemployment had remained persistently in the double digits, partly due to the government's decision to grant priority to the fight against inflation, which, in the Keynesian economic universe, tends to be inversely related to unemployment. However, after years of double-digit unemployment, the unemployment rate in the United Kingdom fell to single digits in the early 1990s (8.9 percent by November 1994, and, unlike the situation in other major European powers, falling). The trade deficit of £13,400 million in 1992 fell to £9,300 million in 1993. In 1994, the overall economic picture for Britain did not compare that badly with that of its European neighbors, as shown in Table 3-1. Meanwhile, real average earnings had grown by around 16 percent in the 1980s, growth that was even higher in the white-collar classes. Although certainly no longer an imperial power, in any meaningful sense of that term, nor even one of the international major powers, Britain probably still exercises an influence in international affairs that is disproportionate to her size and resources.

This chapter will attempt to describe the early economic and political success of the British system as well as its apparent postwar decline and failures, and to examine and evaluate some of the explanations of these phenomena in the light of the theories of stable democracy discussed in Chapter 2. In other words, this chapter will describe the major attributes of the structures and processes of the British political system as well as of the social and cultural context in which it operates, and note how these attributes seem to have changed.

Some of the confusion about the characteristics of the British system resides in the confusion over the subject under analysis. Too much of the literature casually uses the terms England, Great Britain, and the United Kingdom interchangeably, and thereby implicitly attributes characteristics of England as a social system to the broader systems of Great Britain or the United Kingdom. The island comprising England, Scotland, and Wales is known as Great Britain. This island of Great Britain, together with Northern Ireland, forms the United Kingdom. The government of the United Kingdom still retains a loose but special relationship with independent nations that once were part of the British empire, collectively known as the British Commonwealth. While the nations of the Commonwealth are sovereign and formally independent, they enjoy a special relationship with one another in terms of economic and political cooperation that is symbolized by their common recognition of the British monarch as "Head of the Commonwealth," a purely symbolic and ceremonial role.

TABLE 3-1   Leading Economic Indicators in Western Europe, November 1994

Country	GDP	Unemployment 1993	Unemployment 1994	Inflation
Great Britain	+3.6%	10.3%	8.9%	1.9% (12/93)
France	+2.0%	12.1%	12.7%	2.3%
Germany	+2.3%	7.7%	8.3%	3.7%

Source: The Economist, vol. 333, no. 7888 (November 5, 1994), p. 141.

England, Scotland, and Wales are distinct cultural systems that are now governed from Whitehall but have a history of over five centuries as separate political entities. Mary Queen of Scots (Mary Stuart) was forced to abdicate the Scottish throne in 1568 and was finally beheaded in 1587 as a result of a conflict with Elizabeth that was in part a conflict between Elizabeth's Protestantism and Mary's Catholicism and in part a conflict over Scottish resistance to political absorption and domination by England. The political absorption in 1603 only integrated the two kingdoms under a single ruler, and the current provisions of union did not occur until 1707, although the Scots were left with their own church and legal system. Actually, the Scots, who were at this point largely Presbyterian and hence resistant to attempts by the ill-fated Charles I to impose the Anglicanism upon them, joined forces with the armies of Parliament in the English Civil Wars in1640 and 1643. Even after the Act of Union of 1707, many Scots rebelled against George I in 1715 and 1745. The citizens of Scotland to this day most clearly do not regard themselves as English, as in the recent argument for the devolution, or political autonomy, of Scotland from England after the North Sea oil revenues were being provided by Scotland and used by England reflects. (In fact, the 1973 Kilbrandon Report proposed legislative devolution for Scotland and Wales, but these proposals were not implemented.)

Wales has similarly had an independent identity, as suggested by the fact that the majority of its citizens were primarily Welsh speaking into the twentieth century. As of 1971, 21 percent of its citizens still were primarily Welsh speaking, although Wales had been economically as well as politically integrated in the British system. Wales was formally united with England in 1536, but the Welsh remain zealously resistant of being culturally absorbed by the English. Many street signs in Wales are still in Welsh (a Gaelic language) as well as in English. The issue of the devolution of power to the constituent nations within the United Kingdom remains salient, with the opposition party's proposal in 1994 to establish a Scottish Parliament and a Welsh Assembly.

Ireland has never been effectively integrated with England, despite the fact that it was governed by Whitehall from 1801 to 1922. Since then, the six northern provinces known as Ulster remain under a troubled British rule.

Some of the attributes commonly associated with the British political system, such as the lack of politically salient regional diversity and the pan-national importance of social class, are really more characteristic of England than of Great Britain or the United Kingdom. Therefore, despite its reputation as a political system that operates in a context of great sociocultural homogeneity, the United Kingdom has had to balance and reconcile a great deal of barely repressed geographically defined diversity. The development of this balance of diversities is part of the historical tradition that plays such a major role in modern British politics (see Table 3-2). Tradition probably has as strong a political role in the United Kingdom as in any political system in the world. It is to the development of this tradition that we now turn.

POLITICAL HISTORY: THE IMAGE OF CONTINUITY

The United Kingdom is widely regarded as the model of a system based on evolutionary and peaceful rather than violent and discontinuous change.[4] Yet, this impression is founded more upon illusion than reality.[5] One merely needs a cursory familiarity with Shakespeare's history plays (e.g., *Richard III,*

TABLE 3-2 Facts and Dates from British Political History

Date	Event
1066	Battle of Hastings and the Norman conquest
12th–13th centuries	Development of common law
1215	Magna Carta
1284	Wales conquered by England
1327	Regicide of Edward II
1337	Beginning of the Hundred Years' War
1349	Regicide of Richard II
1485	Conclusion of the War of the Roses
1509	Henry VIII begins his reign
1534	Act of Supremacy—Henry VIII becomes head of the Anglican Church and independent of Rome
1559	Elizabeth I begins her reign
1568	Mary Queen of Scots forced to abdicate
1603	England and Scotland united under a single ruler
1640	Long Parliament meets
1642	Civil War breaks out
1649	Charles I decapitated
1653	Oliver Cromwell takes the oath as Lord Protector of his republic
1660	Restoration of Charles II and the beheading of Cromwell
1688	Glorious Revolution deposes James II
1689	Parliament begins annual meetings
1701	Act of Settlement brings William and Mary of Orange as monarchs
1701	England and Scotland united as a single political unit
1707	Anne withholds royal assent for the last time in British history
1714–26	George I allows the cabinet to function in his absence
1721–42	Robert Walpole serves as the first prime minister
1750–1800	Enclosure movement and beginnings of capitalism
1798	Speenhamland Law, the first minimum income bill
1801	English assume rule over Ireland
1832	First Reform Act largely enfranchises the middle class
1846	Corn Laws repealed
1867	Second Reform Act enfranchises the urban working class
1911	Parliament Act circumscribes the veto power of the House of Lords to a two-year delay
1918	Representation of the People Act enfranchises men at 21 and women at 30
1922	England relinquishes control of Ireland except for Ulster
1936	Edward VIII abdicates
1937	Ministers of the Crown Act pays a salary to the leader of the opposition
1948	University vote abolished
1945–51	Attlee government (Labour)
1951–55	Churchill government (Conservative)
1955–57	Eden government (Conservative)
1957–63	Macmillan government (Conservative)
1963–64	Home government (Conservative)
1964–70	Wilson government (Labour)
1970–74	Heath government (Labour)
1974–76	Wilson government (Labour)
1976–79	Callaghan government (Labour)
1979	Callaghan government's loss of a vote of confidence is the first in this century
1979–90	Thatcher government (Conservative)
1990	Thatcher becomes the first prime minister replaced as the leader of own party
1990–	Major government (Conservative)
1994–	Tony Blair becomes leader of the Labour Party and challenges its commitment to socialism
1994–	Eight members of the Tory Party expelled for violating whip-making Tories a minority government

Henry IV, Parts 1 and 2, Henry V) to realize the extent to which England's political history was shaped by violent revolution and regicide. Keith Thomas, in fact, suggests that "until the eighteenth century England was notorious for her political instability."[6] Charles I lost his head over the issue of royal absolutism, and Edward II suffered a most painful and undignified demise. The War of the Roses between the rival claimants to the throne—Richard, the Duke of York, and Henry VI of the House of Lancaster—was another case of internal violence that disrupted parts of the country for some 30 years in the mid-fifteenth century.

Yet, not only has the system enjoyed three centuries of peaceful, evolutionary development from 1688 to the present, but it is arguable that the threads of continuity stretch back many centuries further. The principle of constitutional monarchy, a system in which the discretion available to the king or queen is constrained by a set of consensually accepted fundamental principles, was in effect established by the Magna Carta in 1215. This landmark document formally stipulated a list of baronial rights that are now completely irrelevant but symbolically established the principle that there are rules that constrain the actions of the crown. The *crown*, a concept referring to the repository of political power, has a unique meaning in British politics.

It was suggested in Chapter 2 that there is a sequential question about a nation's history that is critical in determining whether that nation will have a stable and successful political system. Nations that face and resolve their major developmental problems one at a time and that in particular settle the question of what kind of regime they will establish are more successful in arriving at legitimate and viable solutions to the controversial issues faced by all modern nations. Britain was blessed by an island setting that provided insular borders and freedom not only from for-

eign invasion but also from the centrifugal forces that beset regimes attempting to assert their authority over territory whose borders were not self-evident. This enabled the monarchy, exercising the power of the crown, to establish its effective control over the territories and inhabitants over which it reigned (thus solving the so-called crisis of penetration) much earlier that was the case in France and Germany. Since these latter two nations, situated on the broad European plain running from the Atlantic coast to the Ural Mountains, were unable to resolve the crisis of penetration until much later, this left the question of the nature of their regimes equally unresolved. Consequently, when the mobilization of the masses and the onset of the industrial revolution generated controversial issues and intense conflicts of interest in France and Germany, those conflicts were debated in terms of the question of regime. However, no regime enjoyed sufficient legitimacy to impose a resolution of such issues.

The legitimacy of a system refers to the extent to which its structures and processes are widely accepted regardless of at least its short-run performance. A system acquires legitimacy largely by having functioned adequately over time. Because the question of regime was essentially resolved in Britain before the serious divisive issues of the eighteenth and nineteenth centuries, British institutions were able to become legitimate without the strain of substantive conflicts. Although it is true that British history is rife with rebellions and political violence, the roots of an essentially evolutionary and peaceful development go back over three centuries.

Tradition thus has a value in the British context that is almost unique among nations and that is related to its role in the establishment of regime legitimacy (Figure 3-1). Consequently, the British preserve numerous apparently atavistic institutions whose functions disappeared sometime in the past, thus creating a unique blend of tradition and modernity in an effort to preserve the link with tradition. For example, the Privy Council and the Warden of the Cinq Ports, an official charged with keeping watch for an invasion by Napoleon's fleet, are among the many atavistic roles that are maintained with a paper existence. Legal fictions that are at variance with contemporary political reality, such as the fact that a bill becomes law not when it is passed by Parliament or signed by the prime minister but when the clerk of the House of Lords informs the Lord Chancellor that the monarch has given her royal assent. Sometimes it is done verbally, with the clerk, using French from the tradition of the Norman conquest, says, "La reine le veult" (The queen wills it). In the case of "supply," or appropriation, bills, the clerk says, "La reine remercie ses bon sujets, accepte leur benevolence, et ainsi le veult" (The queen thanks her good subjects, accepts their kindness, and thus wills it.") Of course, the monarch no longer has the practical or politically viable option of in fact refusing to "will it" by declaring that she takes it under advisement ("La reine s'avisera"), an option that was last exercised by Queen Anne in 1707. Out of the struggles between king and Parliament grew the rule that one could not at the same time be a member of Parliament and a member of the royal household. Therefore, in modern times, when Parliament wants to expel a member, or if the member wants out without formally or openly resigning, he or she is appointed to a now defunct role in the royal household—the groundskeeper for a large royal estate, the Chiltern Hundreds, a job that carries no formal duties. The fact that the British choose to keep accomplishing a

FIGURE 3-1 The British commitment to the preservation of tradition is illustrated by the elaborate guard-changing ceremonies at the royal residences, shown here as part of the daily ritual at Windsor Castle.

very simple function in this convoluted way rather than simply changing the relevant rules to fit reality illustrates the extent to which they will go to preserve tradition.

One may therefore discern in the British system a pattern of continuity with the past, an evolution toward an increasingly circumscribed constitutional monarchy that may be traced back at least to Magna Carta, if not to Henry II or even William the Conqueror. This evolution of British decision-making machinery may be seen as a series of practical (in the sense of nonprincipled), ad hoc responses to given needs or problems as they arose. Royal consultation with the nobility, leading to the antecedents of Parliament, was regularized about the time of the Hundred Years' War and based largely on the need for funds to finance that adventure and on the financial independence of the English nobility. The latter was due to the persistence of the feudal system, which the English kings had not acted to suppress, unlike the French monarchs with their centralizing impulses.[7]

Commoners were also summoned to the *parlement* (French for "speaking"), as a consequence of their success during the commercial and industrial revolutions, which enabled them to bargain for concessions against the monarch. The power of the crown thus began a long process of flowing *"out of court,"* a term that refers to the increasing exercise of the powers of the crown by actors or structures other than the monarch but in the name of the monarch or ultimately in the name of the crown.

This going out of court as a result of the process of monarchial bargaining with independent sources of wealth should be contrasted with the situation in France, where the monarch was able to maintain a virtual monopoly on significant sources of wealth. While the early success of the commercial and industrial revolutions in England and the Enclosure Movement, fencing off common lands for the raising of sheep or farming in about the sixteenth century by well-off landowners, led to a financially independent middle class and aristocracy, respectively, the failure of such classes to emerge on the Continent contributed there to the growth of royal absolutism. Enclosures also drove the tenant farmers off the land minimizing the impact in Britain of the frequently troublesome peasantry.

This ad hoc development of British institutions may also be seen in the evolution of the office of prime minister. The Hanoverian kings, especially George I, were culturally and psychologically German, and had little interest in governing England. George I, in fact, spoke little or no English. He therefore chose to reign but not rule and accordingly designated the first lord of the treasury to get on with the mundane business of governing in his name. To this day, the prime minister officially holds this post (but now he or she must be a commoner). Although it became institutionalized for the monarch to designate the first lord of the treasury to act as his first, or prime, minister and to in effect govern, the monarch is nowhere required by law to make such a designation. That the British are able to leave something that is so fundamental to their political system to the force of custom or tradition indicates the strength of that force and the depths of the roots of tradition.

The concept of political culture was discussed in Chapter 2 as a systematic way of conceptualizing the character or soul of a nation. The essence of this character or soul is frequently reflected in the ideas of one or more of the nation's preeminent political philosophers. It thus may be said that Edmund Burke, the so-called father of classical conservatism, reflects a good part of the character of Great Britain.

Burke used the phrase "the collective wisdom of the ages" to argue that civilization is built in a cumulative fashion over many centuries. He reasoned that it would be presumptuous for any generation to believe that it could start from scratch and improve on its civilization in its own time. Burke therefore emphasized maintaining continuity with the past and confining change to small trial-and-error adjustments to an evolving status quo. This approach to policy making, known as *incrementalism*, has characterized the British political style, which has sometimes been called *muddling through*.[8] Such a respect for the institutions of the past and for incremental change implies a skepticism about the capacities of human rationality and a sense of the limits of mankind that contrast with the optimism that has characterized the social and political left.

This strong role of tradition has so legitimized the fundamental British institutions that Britain remains unique among modern democracies in having no formal written constitution. There is no written law in the United Kingdom that is legally superior to an act of Parliament. Yet, people still speak of the British constitution. The concept of a constitution in this sense refers to those principles of the system that are part of its very nature. Without them, Britain would be a different kind of system.

All political systems must adapt to an ever-changing and unfolding environment. The decisions that constitute responses to the evolving circumstances in which the system finds itself are characterized as *circumstantial*. Circumstantial decisions or policies reflect those things that are expected to change while the fundamental principles remain constant. The British concept of the constitution, therefore, embodies the distinction between those things that are expected to be stable and resistant to change and those things that must be flexible and easy to adapt to new circumstances.

These fundamental principles in Britain are embodied in four types of sources. First and most important is the strong tradition that shapes the system. Second are certain landmark documents, such as Magna Carta, with symbolic meaning that extends beyond their literal content. Third are some acts of Parliament. Fourth are some principles of common law. The question arises as to which traditions, which documents, which acts of Parliament, and which common law rules take on constitutional significance. The answer is those principles that are fundamental to the nature of the system.

Only two types of constitutional principles are legal in Great Britain, certain common law rules and certain Acts of Parliament. The principle that the monarch is obligated to "will" acts duly passed by Parliament is purely customary. Legally, Elizabeth II has as much power as did Henry VIII or James I. However, if Elizabeth II were to cause the clerk of the House of Lords to say, "La reine s'avisera," thereby withholding her royal assent to a duly passed act, she would be within her legal right but she would be provoking a constitutional crisis. In Great Britain something may be perfectly legal but unconstitutional, because the constitution is basically not a legal document.

Every nation that expects to last must somehow establish the legitimacy of its fundamental principles. The United Kingdom is unique in being able to rely heavily on the force of tradition for its legitimacy. Nations that do not enjoy such strong and deep roots to their past must therefore normally rely on a written constitution to afford their fundamental principles such legitimacy. Because the mobilization of the masses is nearly a universal reality, the ability to acquire legitimacy over time has probably gone forever, and the United Kingdom will doubtless remain unique in its reliance on custom to guarantee the persistence of that which it regards as fundamental.

American students, used to regarding their written constitution as a bulwark against the potential abuse of power, frequently see mere custom as a weak guarantee against such abuse. It seems dangerous to say that the queen would not usurp power that she legally has but is constitutionally denied simply because that is not what one does. Such skeptics about the force of tradition may note that there are parts of the American fundamental rules that are not embodied in the legal constitution. For example, there is no law requiring the electoral college to vote in accordance with the popular vote. Moreover, the world has seen too many examples of rights and checks on the abuse of power being ignored even when they are enshrined in written law. The Russian constitutions of 1936 and 1977, for example, had rigorous bills of rights. The English may be relying on the principle that rights are as viable as their cultural support, regardless of whether they are recorded in law.

The importance of tradition and the consequent evolutionary and incremental approach to policy making in Britain that have been so admired for so long by students of democratic governments have in recent years come under critical analyses. Recall from the opening sentences in this chapter that the Britain that has so long been regarded as the epitome of democratic success has now come to be widely regarded as a model of democratic decline and ineffectiveness.[9] Not only has the sun finally set on the British Empire, for all intents and purposes, but perhaps even more significantly Britain had one of the worst postwar rates of economic growth among industrial nations until Thatcher came into power in 1979, and then inflation seemed to be out of control. We have noted the accomplishments of that government in increasing real income and lowering inflation. However, these successes came at a cost of double-digit unemployment and · zero

growth until the early 1990s. In addition, Britain, widely seen for years as the model of a racially and ethnically homogenous society, free of the social problems of racial strife and grinding poverty that have plagued American inner cities, has been experiencing growing racial and ethnic heterogeneity from the nonwhite population immigrating largely from areas that were formerly part of its far-flung empire. Along with this increased heterogeneity of the population is the development of a British underclass that exhibits much of the same alienation and propensity toward crime and violence that has been widely noted in the American underclass, as the American Charles Murray has observed.[10]

The crisis of democracies that was discussed in Chapter 2 seemed to apply particularly well to Great Britain, as neither of its major parties appeared able to provide any solutions to its growing problems. In the face of such problems and such performance failure over a period of decades, many feel that the British need to make the sort of bold, creative, and innovative decisions, including structural changes, that are inhibited by their reverence for tradition and incrementalism. Pragmatic tinkering and slow, evolutionary adjustment may not yield reaction that is fast enough and extensive enough for the imperatives of a postindustrial world. Thus, the very force of tradition and the incremental approach to policy making that have long been held as the traits that enabled Britain to stand out as the epitome of stable, successful democracy are now being blamed for perpetuating if not partly causing Britain's recent decline.

The insular position of Britain has also contributed to its relatively stable development in modern times by eliminating the need for a large standing army. Since the British were not faced with the imminent threat of foreign invasion, the military never became the indispensible and therefore dominant force in the political life of the nation. This is significant, because large standing armies can be a potentially disruptive force in the politics of developing democracies. The military can become a source of coercive power that is independent of the government and therefore can be used to provide the resources and organization for mobilizing extra-constitutional opposition to the regime. It is even more likely that the government will use the military to suppress opposition to the incumbent rulers or regime. Not only would such action generate intense feelings of frustration and alienation among the citizens, but the very potential of such suppression might tempt the government to be less responsive to the needs and demands of the society. A large military establishment without wars to fight looks for other ways of using its might. Such a force frequently involves itself in domestic politics, assuming the task of maintaining internal order or security or of defending the interests of the class from which its leaders are largely drawn. Nations whose history has been characterized by a long, violent struggle to establish and preserve permeable national boundaries have often been known for a strong military and the general glorification of martial values. Germany might be a classic case, with the exuberant celebration of military ideals by such philosophers as Heinrich von Treitschke and Georg W. Hegel. Although to a lesser extent, we will see that a powerful standing army is also part of the French heritage, as manifested in the Affair.

A powerful standing army is but one of several groups that have repeatedly proved to be a disruptive force in the affairs of nations. Mark Hagopian offers the concept of "the crisis strata" to refer to those groups, or strata, of society "whose livelihood, social status or scheme of values is imperiled by existing conditions or trends."[11] The peasantry and the lower middle class are two groups that are frequently mobilized for antisystem movements of either the right or the left. The conditions or trends that threaten their values and economic status are virtually defined by the process of modernization itself; hence, since modernization cannot be undone, their grievances cannot realistically be redressed. The peasantry in France provided a significant portion of the support for the early stages of the French Revolution and shortly thereafter provided the basis for a counterrevolutionary uprising in the Vendé. Peasant revolts occurred in Germany in 1524 and in England in 1381. The peasantry and the lower middle class also provided the earliest and strongest electoral support for the Nazi Party in Weimar Germany. Nations in which these groups have remained strong have had a rather poor record with respect to the achievement and maintenance of stable, effective democracy.

The peasants were eliminated as a significant political force in Britain when they were driven off the land by the early enclosure of common land in the fifteenth century, as rich landowners switched from growing crops to raising sheep, and by the Enclosure Acts of the eighteenth century, which consolidated agricultural holdings to the disadvantage of the small landholder. The early advent of the industrial revolution in England, partly due to the accumulation of the necessary capital from the country's success in agriculture, maritime commerce, and empire, spread the benefits of that economic growth throughout the middle class and did not leave a large shopkeeper class threatened by modernization.

Early industrialization, the commercial revolution, and their attendant prosperity in England were all facilitated by another factor in which England stands in sharp contrast to France and Germany: the early resolution of the conflict between church and state. To be sure, England has not been immune from religious conflict both between Catholics and Protestants and between branches of Protestantism. The struggle between adherents of the Roman Church and of the newly established Protestantism was revived by Mary Stuart, Queen of Scots, with her challenge to the English throne. Mary's forces failed, however, and she was imprisoned and eventually beheaded by the command of Elizabeth I. The Tudor monarchy had become well enough established by this time for Henry VIII to impose a solution to the religious question in response to Rome's reluctance to sanction an annulment of his marriage to Catherine of Aragon. Henry's break with Rome was based upon personal interest rather than any theological or philosophical dispute. Nevertheless, the fact that the Protestant character of England was effectively established by a monarch freed England from the kind of religious strife that in effect destroyed Germany in the seventeenth century. Parliament's struggle with Charles I in the 1640s was decided by the Scottish forces who also opposed Charles because of his attempt to impose the use of the Anglican prayer book on the Scottish followers of John Knox, the founder of modern Presbyterianism. The key here is not how the religious question was resolved in England but that in fact it was resolved early and effectively. The religious question was similarly resolved in Scandinavia by Gustaf Vasa's expulsion of the Catholics, partly out of greed for church properties, thereby also affording those nations centuries of freedom from the divisive impact of religious conflict.

The early elimination of religion as an important political factor contributed to the stability of English politics because religious issues are especially difficult to resolve. Framed in terms of moral absolutes that do not lend themselves well to compromise or tolerance of opposition, they are among the most difficult kinds of issues to resolve by democratic

means and add significantly to the intensity of partisanship. It will be elaborated below how a secular culture contributes to stable, effective democracy. For now, it should be recalled that England achieved such a relatively secular culture due to the early resolution of the church and state issues by a monarchy strong enough to impose such a solution. A 1989 survey shows that only 20 percent of British citizens attend religious services "regularly" (at least once a month) compared to 54 percent of Americans, 45 percent of Italians, and 29 percent of West Germans. Moreover, almost 80 percent of the British believe the scientifically accepted Darwinian explanation of man's origin, while over half of Americans prefer the biblical explanation.[12] By these criteria, Britain appears as the least religious of all Western democracies.

Moreover, the relatively early elimination of the dominance of the Roman Church in England may have contributed to the early manifestation of the commercial and industrial revolutions in that country. The Universal Roman Church, as it existed throughout Europe from the Middle Ages until modern times, was dysfunctional for economic, industrial, and political modernization in several ways. First, the dominant secular authority of the papacy rendered the establishment of legitimate secular authority more difficult. Second, the church fostered an otherworldly orientation in which salvation was the most important value, superseding such values as the search for knowledge about the physical world and the advancement of technology and human well-being. It was no accident that the zenith of the power of the medieval church coincided with the nadir of the advancement of science, knowledge, and human well-being in the West, including the advancement of the technology that was the backbone of industrial modernization. Third, the church maintained religious taboos against the very behaviors that were the foundation of the commercial revolution and modern capitalism. Usury (making money from money, or capital gains) was banned, and poverty and asceticism were positive values. Although it is not universally accepted, Max Weber and R. H. Tawney have advanced a thesis that the Protestant Reformation made the rise of capitalism and the commercial revolution possible by allowing usury and giving moral sanction to competitive success in the acquisition of worldly goods. Whatever the merits of that thesis, modernization, industrialization, and capitalism came to England and the other Protestant nations long before they arrived in the Catholic nations.

Hence, although England has an established church, the Anglican Church (the American equivalent is Episcopalian), religion does not frame political issues. In this sense, England is more secularized than the United States, where, despite the absence of an established church and a constitutionally mandated separation of church and state, religion is still politically important. The 1980s saw the rise of a religious right with a controversial, religiously based social agenda that it sought to impose by law on the nation at large, a movement that reasserted itself in the massive Republican victory in the 1994 midterm elections. It would be difficult to imagine a parallel set of issues in England, where the concept of an established church only means that the state gives monetary support to the church and has an official role in naming its major prelates (the monarch names the Archbishop of Canterbury on the advice of the prime minister), and that the monarch must be a member of that church. This means that Elizabeth is Anglican when in England but Presbyterian when in Scotland, where that latter sect is the established church.

The secular nature of British society is due to the early consolidation of the power of the national government by an authority figure strong enough to impose a resolution of the issues arising out of the relationship between religion and the political system. This early consolidation was in turn facilitated by the insular geographic location of Great Britain, which then also contributed to the absence of a tradition of a large standing army that might conflict with civilian authority. Britain's geographical setting encouraged both grazing and maritime power. These two factors then encouraged the enclosure movement that effectively eliminated the peasantry as a potentially disruptive social force.

Its relatively easy consolidation of the legitimacy of its regime also permitted Britain to resolve difficult issues sequentially, beginning with the question of regime. Nations that had to settle this question after the mobilization of the masses in the late eighteenth to early nineteenth century experienced considerably more difficulty establishing the legitimacy of their constitutional format.

It thus appears that Great Britain's island location at a particular point in history and at a particular state of technology did much to shape the context of modern British politics. It is the nature of that context to which we now turn.

THE SOCIOCULTURAL CONTEXT OF BRITISH POLITICS

The British political culture contains a number of unique attributes that were in turn shaped by the unique aspects of the British historical experience described above. The properties of the British political culture then help shape another important contextual dimension—*the social stratification system*—the criteria by which the members of a society are grouped and divided (e.g., by socioeconomic class, religion, language, ethnicity, etc.).

A nation may be categorized by the style of its problem-solving or decision-making process,[13] which goes a long way in characterizing its political culture. A nation's political style refers to the kinds of rationales it uses in choosing among possible resolutions to the issues they face. As such, political style is not identical to the concept of political culture, although cultural factors help shape that style.[14] Perhaps more than any other nation, Britain possesses a pragmatic political style.[15] Pragmatism as a political style is used here in contradistinction to ideologism. A pragmatist chooses among policy alternatives by what seems to work on a trial-and-error basis of continual tinkering and readjusting, irrespective of the consistency of policies to logic or to any a priori principles. An ideologue, on the other hand, chooses among alternative courses of public policy according to their consistency with given principles, irrespective of their actual impact. The British disdain for abstract principle or logic has been noted elsewhere as an aspect of their penchant for "muddling through."

The British pragmatic style is clearly manifested in the evolutionary development of British institutions as ad hoc responses to a contingent need or development. The office of prime minister was shown to be a pragmatic adjustment to the disposition of the early Hanoverian monarchs to enjoy reigning over Britain without having the responsibilities of actually governing. The development of the House of Commons was largely a response to the need for funds to fight the Hundred Years' War and the realization that commoners in the early stages of the commercial revolution frequently possessed considerable amounts of such resources. The king's need to bargain with the invited commoners for these funds led to the flow of power "out of court."

The pragmatic orientation of the British is also apparent in the English system of common law, which is combined with aspects of the civil law system in Scotland, and in the United States. The civil law, which prevails on the European Continent, is characterized by legal principles embodied in a comprehensive legal code drawn up according to considerations of logic and abstract justice in advance of the disputes to which they are applied. Common law principles, by contrast, emerge inductively and impersonally from patterns in the way actual disputes have been viably resolved.[16] Thus, the outcomes of cases take on legal significance. The great Justice Oliver Wendell Holmes, Jr., characterized the process thusly: "the life of the law has not been logic; it has been experience."[17]

The development of common law was related to the effort of the first Plantagenet ruler, Henry II, to solve the crisis of penetration by establishing the legitimacy of the crown throughout the realm by curbing baronial autonomy. Henry attempted to establish what has been called "the king's peace" by "replacing the multitude of manorial courts where local magistrates dispensed justice whose custom and character varied with custom and temper of the neighborhood" with "a system of royal courts which would administer a law *common* to all England" (italics added).[18] Since the development of common law was part of the strategy of establishing the legitimacy of royal authority, the courts attempted to resolve disputes in the most viable way possible, abstract conceptions of justice or truth notwithstanding. To this day, common law emphasizes the pragmatic goal of the resolution of disputes rather than abstract justice; hence the need for a complementary system of equity.

Disputes in common law are resolved by adversary jurisprudence meaning that the parties to litigation are responsible for presenting their respective cases in the best possible light. The court assumes the role of a neutral arbitrator (rather than the judge found in the civil law system) who conducts the inquiry seeking truth and justice. The pragmatic nature of common law is thus manifested in the fact that its principles and even its forms of action grow out of experience and actual need, while the principles of civil law are embodied in a comprehensive legal code drawn up in advance of disputes by criteria of justice and logic. For example, the basic remedy to injury once lay in the writ of trespass, which only applied to direct and obvious injury. However, after the reality of indirect injuries had to be dealt with by convoluted legal fictions, the writ of case was developed specifically to cover indirect injuries. The writ of assumpsit, a principle that underlies much of modern contract law, was developed to treat the failure to fulfill an obligation (nonfeasance) as no less a wrong than actively committing a wrong (misfeasance). The concept of equity itself was developed out of a perceived need to remedy harshness, the failure to provide adequate remedies, and areas not covered in common law.

Thus common law reflects the British disposition to formulate ad hoc remedies to needs or problems without serious regard to logic or long-term principle, or in other words, the British disposition to "muddle through." Many, however, are now questioning whether this style of politics, which had apparently worked so well for the British until the postwar period, is now adequate to solve to the rapidly unfolding problems of a postindustrial age. While the British pragmatic style implies a trial-and-error tinkering involving small incremental changes, many feel that, given the extent and speed of changes in the postwar world, and the poor British performance in that world, the British political system needs rapid and fundamental change.

Prime Minister Thatcher was perceived by some as the most principled or ideologically motivated British leader in modern times, a trait that generated a measure of resentment toward her. It further generated a perception of her cabinet as "arrogant" and of her as an "outsider" relative to the type of person most generally found as British prime minister.[19] This style was manifested by her practice of "sacking" (dismissing) or causing the resignation of leading cabinet members who deviated from the ideological purity of her positions. In 1990, for example, Sir Geoffrey Howe, leader of the House (in effect, deputy prime minister), was dismissed following the resignation of Nigel Lawson as the Chancellor of the Exchequer in the fall of 1989, when he could no longer accept the pure moneterism of Thatcher's financial policy. The vigor of the criticisms of her perceived ideological rigidity on several dimensions illustrates the British commitment to pragmatism.

Among the cultural phenomena that are frequently mentioned as politically relevant are attitudes about or conceptions of authority, which are often categorized into three types: *submissive,* or *authoritarian,* patterns, in which some people are recognized as being more fit to govern than others and in which the masses owe their leaders unquestioning obedience; *egalitarian* patterns, in which it is presumed that all people are equally capable of making political judgments or of occupying leadership roles and in which the masses exercise close control over their leaders; and *deferential* patterns, in which it is accepted that some people are more fit to rule than others, and in which the leaders are somewhat insulated from the day-to-day passions of mass opinion but still are obligated to govern in the public interest and are ultimately held accountable for so governing.

Clearly, authoritarian conceptions of authority are dysfunctional for fostering the democratic value of accountability. A widespread disposition toward unquestioning obedience will not make elites conscious of a need to justify their policies in terms of the public interest. The aforementioned expectation that the prime minister should accept a collegial relationship with her cabinet demonstrates the lack of an authoritarian orientation in the British culture. It was the perception that Thatcher had violated this expectation that led to the rising dissatisfaction with her leadership style and that, as much as disagreement over policy, generated the 1991 challenge by the Right Honourable Michael Heseltine that ended her tenure as party leader.

While it may be supposed that egalitarian attitudes are best suited for democracy, critics point out that egalitarian cultures do not grant elites the insulation from the shifting passions of public opinion that they require for stable, effective government over time. Harry Eckstein has hypothesized that stable government requires some congruence in authority patterns between those in society and those in the constitutional format.[20] If people are taught to obey all those in authority, such as parents, school officials, and work superiors, they will have to make a significant change in their role orientation, which will cause them psychological strain, to be able to regard their political authorities as their equals who are answerable to them. It almost follows from Eckstein's analysis that a highly egalitarian constitutional format will be non-congruent, because nowhere is egalitarianism the social norm. Even in such a supposedly egalitarian society as the United States, issues between parents and children or between teachers and students are not resolved by majority vote. Since authority is exercised in all societies, the criterion of congruence suggests that a degree of authoritarianism is healthy in any system.

Because of the foregoing considerations, most scholars have concluded that a deferential attitude toward authority is the most conducive to stable, effective democracy. Great Britain has been widely identified as the epitome of a deferential political culture since that term was advanced by Walter Bagehot in his classic disquisition on the English constitution over a century ago.[21] The characterization of Britain as a deferential system in modern times is based on both the impressionistic judgments of long-time students of the system such as Samuel Beer as well as survey data, most prominently those presented in Gabriel Almond and Sidney Verba's *Civic Culture* study and in Eric Nordlinger's attempt to apply that theory.[22] This British deference was manifested in acceptance of the class system by those in the lower or manual labor classes and by an acceptance of political authority. For example, David Butler and Donald Stokes's 1963 data show a remarkable 53 percent of the respondents identifying themselves as working class in a classification scheme of upper class, upper middle, middle, lower middle, upper working, working, and lower working.[23] This is in sharp contrast to the United States, where a majority of citizens retain a self-image of middle class, even among those in objectively manual occupations. The British class deference was related to political deference in that the British widely believed that some people were more "fit" to rule than others. Thus, the British would not have subscribed to the American assumptions that anyone can grow up to be president or that their political leaders are very ordinary people (as manifested in the so-called log cabin tradition in American politics in which candidates stress their putatively humble origins). The British, by contrast, have preferred their leaders to be extraordinary people either born to high station or having achieved entry into the elite by educational or other achievement against great odds.

This deferential attitude toward political authority has supported the legitimacy of a British political format that is more highly centralized and more insulated from the public than would ever be tolerated in the American context (as we shall see below in the section on political processes). Thus, the essence of the British system has largely presumed deference and could not operate, as it has been commonly understood to operate, without it.

Yet, recent data indicate that this vaunted British deference has significantly diminished. The acceptance of the system and of the competence of those who run it is no longer as strong as conventional wisdom has always said it was.[24] This is reflected in the greater mistrust of politicians and their conduct of government,[25] in challenges to the supremacy of Parliament, in increased criticism of such venerable institutions as the House of Lords and the monarchy, and in a decline in working-class acceptance of material inequality and of institutions that foster and perpetuate such inequality. An example of this diminished tolerance of inherently inegalitarian institutions was the abolition of the "eleven-plus exam" in the state-supported school system. This exam consisted of a comprehensive general abilities test, given at about age eleven, that selected out more than three-quarters of the students as fit only for terminal, vocational education. The grammar schools that provided the academic track education for those who passed the exam and the secondary schools that provided the vocational education for those who did not pass virtually disappeared from the British scene in favor of "comprehensive schools." Some grammar schools have survived independently, and in 1989 the Thatcher government announced plans to subsidize the reestablishment of some six hundred grammar schools, a plan strongly opposed by egalitarian-oriented forces in British society. These plans were never realized, however, and at present there are less than two hundred academically selective secondary schools in the state-financed system. Mean-

while, the egalitarians have so shaped the comprehensive schools that many of them try to include all ability levels within each "tutor group" that takes classes together, so that a given math group may contain students ranging from those doing advanced algebra to those who can barely count. This complete rejection of ability grouping in the name of egalitarianism is further testament to how far the British have come from their deferential culture. (Recent attempts to allow a few comprehensives a measure of selectivity in reaction to the poor academic performance of British students is discussed below.)

The deferential attitudes that were part of the British culture presumed a strong element of trust in political authority. The extent of this trust in Great Britain relative to the other nations under consideration was clearly shown in the original *Civic Culture* data.[26] This kind of diffuse trust in the political system, which is not predicated upon satisfaction with specific short-run performance, is closely related to legitimacy. Legitimacy, it was suggested in Chapter 2, is acquired by satisfactory performance over a longer period. Therefore, the deference that the British had accorded the political and other authorities was a product of the centuries of relative success of the system. It is therefore not suprising that the postwar economic and political decline of Great Britain over decades might be accompanied by a decline in both the legitimacy of the system and the deference shown to authority, political and otherwise.

The British deferential attitude toward authority had also supported the attribute that was thought to characterize the British social stratification system—the predominance of class. A nation's *social stratification system* refers to the criteria by which the individuals in a society are grouped or divided. These criteria may include social class, religion, ethnicity, language, or some combination of the foregoing. A class-based politics means that socioeconomic status is the most salient basis of self-identification, that, for example, an industrial laborer thinks of himself as a laborer sharing common interests with other laborers more than with fellow members of his religion, ethnic groups, etc. Robert Alford has hypothesized that class-based politics makes for more stable democratic politics than other possible bases of political division, because class-based issues are related to the allocation of material values.[27] Being based upon such questions of who gets how much, such issues more readily lend themselves to compromise than do nonmaterialist issues based upon claims of right versus wrong, truth versus falsehood, or cultural superiority versus barbarism. Nonmaterialist issues are framed on mutually exclusive, either/or alternatives that do not lend themselves to compromise and that instead tend to exacerbate the intensity of conflict, which often reduces the tolerance of those with whom one disagrees. Since in a democracy issues are resolved by compromise and the system presumes accepting the legitimacy of opposition, class-based politics appears obviously conducive to stable, effective democracy, which the success of Great Britain when it was the epitome of a class-based democratic system, seemed to confirm.

The characterization of Great Britain as the epitome of a class-based system was based upon both some hard survey data and the impressionistic judgments of long-time observers. Alford and others had presented hard data in the form of an index of class-based voting in which Britain scored higher than any of the other Anglo-American democracies.[28] (The Alford data predated the enormous changes of the 1970s.)

Less precise judgments about the salience of social class may be based upon the following indicators suggested by psychologist Roger Brown: class consciousness; the striking uniformity of life style within each stratum and the striking contrasts in life style between strata; and individual interactions patterned by strata.[29] By Brown's indicators, life styles and patterns of interaction were largely determined by social strata. These class-related differences seemed to pervade patterns of speech, dress, taste, and choice of leisure-time activities. Although regional speech variations—such as between southeast England, the Midlands, and the Highlands—are hard to detect with the untrained ear, the difference between the Oxford speech patterns of the upper middle and upper classes and the Cockney accent of the working classes is apparent to anyone. While upper classes prefer to drink sherry and whiskey, the lower classes prefer room-temperature ales. Rugby and football (soccer) fans are mostly working class, while theater and opera goers are mostly upper class. Styles of dress have been patterned along class lines as well. (Recalling our earlier caveat about the cultural differences between England, Scotland, and Wales, it should be noted that class-related distinctions in life style and speech are not as apparent in the latter two areas as in England. In Scotland, for instance, a more basic distinction has been made between "Clydeside" urban dwellers and rural dwellers.)

These life-style differences are deeply rooted and hard to eliminate. By satirically describing a fictional transformation from lower to upper class speech, taste, and life style, the famous musical play *My Fair Lady*, based upon George Bernard Shaw's *Pygmalion*, was emphasizing the virtual implausibility of such a transformation. These objective traits may have helped support the subjective consciousness of class identification, yet, it is that conscious salience of class identification as well as an acceptance of the social implications of such a self-designation that has proven to be less permanent than the life-style indicators of class.

With the decline of deference to authority has apparently come a decline in the salience of class as a primary basis of self-identification, primarily among the working class. Scholars such as Richard Rose and Ian Mc-Callister have offered data documenting the declining salience of class in British politics as well as what they view as the end of the dominance of the traditional two-party system that has been considered axiomatic in British politics.[30] (The validity of their analysis with regard to the party system will be examined below.) What Samuel Beer has called the "new populism" is a rising egalitarianism that no longer accepts the necessity or justice of the disproportionate political influence and material well-being of the upper middle and upper classes. The aggressive demands of trade-union labor and other groups upon the British system for the highest possible wages and other public benefits manifest a rising unwillingness among these groups to subordinate their own interests to the general interest. As Beer points out, unless one has confidence that competing interests are prepared to make similar sacrifices, such altruistic behavior would put one's own interest at a competitive disadvantage.[31] Moreover, given the pessimistic outlook for the fortunes of the British political system as a whole that has pervaded the post–World War II era, the acceptance of relative inequality on the presumption that it will lead to absolute gains no longer seems appropriate. When a healthy rate of economic growth cannot be taken for granted, the politics of the distribution of the increasingly finite resources becomes much more intense.

The declining salience of class in England in particular and in Great Britain in general is probably a function of three major postwar trends. One is the overall decline in deference to authority, a phenomenon that has been suggested to be related to the declining performance and prospects for the system as a whole. Second is the emergence of competing bases of self-identification that are becoming increasingly important in the Western world. The growing salience of regionalism, as indicated by the Scottish devolution issue, is one example of this, as are the issues arising out of the increasing racial and ethnic heterogeneity of England. Racial and ethnic homogeneity had long been an identifying trait of England, and thus racial and ethnic factors were not present to supersede class identification. However, in the postwar era, England has experienced an unprecedented wave of immigration of nonwhite people, especially from Commonwealth nations such as India, resulting in a distinctly un-British wave of racial conflict. The notoriety some years ago of ultraright-wing MP Enoch Powell as a spokesperson of white resentment was a manifestation of the salience of this conflict. Third is the basic shift in values away from materialism that was documented by Ronald Inglehart and discussed in Chapter 2. To the extent that issues of material well-being are less salient, class identification based upon such issues will similarly decline in salience. Due to continued weaknesses in the manufacturing sector of its economy, Britain faces some austere economic prospects in the 1990s, the greatest burden of which will fall on the lower middle to working classes. It is unclear whether this will result in a resurgence of working-class support for the Labour Party, but 1991 poll data showing Labour surging to a 51 percent to 37 percent lead over the Conservatives suggests some movement in this direction.[32] By 1995 things had become so bad for the Conservatives that a Gallup Poll found only 7 percent of the respondents thought the Conservatives would win the next election, and only 10 percent had a favorable opinion of the Conservatives as opposed to three-fifths for Labour (cited in *British Politics Group Newsletter,* no. 81, summer, 1995, p. 18).

To whatever extent the political salience of class has been replaced by postmaterialist criteria of stratification, the prospects for compromise and the peaceful resolution of issues as well as the relevance of the party system for addressing the salient issues of society will be seriously diminished, a problem that will be discussed below.

THE BRITISH PARTY SYSTEM: MYTH AND REALITY

Those who have admired the British political system frequently point to the British party system as the core of that system. The famous report of the American Political Science Association on reforming the American party system clearly proposed a modified version of the British system as the model of the way a democratic party system ought to operate.[33] It is useful to examine the image of the British party system that has been widely assumed to exist and then to contrast that image with the reality of the system today.

The essence of that model is what is frequently called *responsible party government*. That term describes a system in which one party effectively controls the political decision-making processes of a nation and proceeds to govern according to a *mandate* received from the voting public at the previous election. A mandate means here an understood authorization from the voters to support and implement certain policies and values. In order for the concept of a mandate to be meaningful, the party had to stand on some relatively unambiguous principles or policies in the electoral contest. When the party that wins the election has the power to govern according to its mandate, it can be held responsible for the consequences of how it has governed. The party that wins the election cannot effectively implement its mandate and accordingly assume responsibility, however, unless it does control the nation's political decision-making process. This in turn requires either a two-party system or one that is sufficiently aggregated so that one party can control the government without the necessity of compromise with coalition partners, in effect, a system in which one party normally wins a majority or a near majority of seats in the legislature. This model also requires a political format in which power is concentrated so that the same party will control all of the nation's decision-making processes.

If the system of responsible party government were to function according to this idealized model, the outcome of the election would in effect determine the policy direction as well as the personnel of the government. The democratic values of accountability and of responsiveness to patterns of public opinion as well as the general political values of effectiveness and stability would be maximized. The party, which may be the only institution capable of doing so, would organize a majority of the electorate for the purpose of governing, and, as E. E. Schattschneider argued in his famous brief for importing the party government model to the United States, "If democracy means anything at all, it means that majorities have the right to organize for the purpose of taking over the government."[34] In the real world, however, the party government model could not work in the United States and does not even accurately describe the British system today. In fact, there is doubt that it ever did.[35]

The British political system has or was assumed to have had certain attributes necessary for the operation of party government that are not found in the American system. In the first place, party government requires a concentration of power. While the British cabinet system permits such a concentration of formal power, the American political format fragments power. Thus frequently one party controls the presidency and the other one controls Congress.

Moreover, the American parties have little control over their individual members, so even if one party controls both the presidency and Congress, there is still no certainty that the president's program will be enacted. However, because British parties are able to exercise discipline over the individuals who run for public office under their label, they effectively vote as a bloc. This discipline is a result of tradition and the fact that British parties have some ultimate control over who can be nominated under the party label.

British candidates are in fact normally selected by constituency party organizations, but the national party organization has the understood power to veto any candidate egregiously unacceptable to party elites. Because central party organizations have used that power with restraint on policy grounds, some observers have concluded that it is without effect.[36] However, that disuse probably has been due to the fact that British MPs, aware of the power of the party, show restraint in violating leadership expectations. In fact, such discipline was exercised in the fall of 1994, when the Tory government of John Major sought to push through a bill increasing Britain's financial contribution to the European Community in the face of determined opposition from "Euro-skeptics" on the Tory back bench. Major declared the vote to be a question of confidence (meaning that the government would resign if it lost) and then proceeded to apply all the pressure he had at his disposal to bring the back bench in line on the crucial division. The Conservative Party headquarters was on the phone to the constituency associations of leading rebels, telling them to *deselect* for renomination the offending MPs who defied the whip. The central party organization may also have reminded the constituency associations that it could disband them if they defied the in-

structions. Most rebels fell into line, swallowed principle, and supported the government on that vote. However, eight MPs chose to abstain. All of these intrepid souls received a letter telling them that the whip had been withdrawn from them. This in effect meant that they had been blackballed from the parliamentary party; they would no longer receive written whips; they could not vote in parliamentary party affairs, especially in those choosing a leader; and they could not attend meetings such as those of the 1922 Committee. Had they not been reinstated, they might have been deselected because such politically emasculated candidates would clearly be less attractive to the constituency associations. Such strong punishment for the mere act of abstention, especially when the government carried the division by a comfortable 27 votes, was not an act of reprisal but rather a message to prospective rebels that one violates a three-line whip at one's own peril. This is important in maintaining the level of party cohesion necessary to survive confidence votes with a narrow majority and thereby provide stable cabinet government.

On the one hand, the egalitarian political culture in the United States has produced a system of selecting candidates in popular primaries in which people can acquire the party nomination while disavowing all principles and policies for which the party seems to stand. The nomination of followers of radical right-wing leader Lyndon LaRouche for important statewide offices on the Democratic ticket in Illinois in 1986 is a case in point. Such parties cannot be said to stand for anything in particular. By contrast, the British parties, with some control over whom they may nominate, can stand for a more coherent set of policies and principles and ensure a stable support for its leadership over a range of issues. This could produce what Rose has called the adversary model of party competition, in which the opposition party offers voters a distinct and meaningful choice from the government party in terms of policy and principle. In this model, when a party assumes office, it undertakes to implement what Rose calls its "manifesto," the principles and programs for which it received a mandate at the election.[37] Elections in Great Britain are therefore assumed to be (and, compared to the United States, have been) more about choices between manifestos, or alternative ways of governing the country, than about the personalities of the candidates for Parliament or even for prime minister.

However, the reality is that British parties have not offered the clear policy choices that conventional wisdom would suggest. Parties in Britain have not been as principled as the ideal model would suggest but instead resemble organizations presenting a "team of candidates seeking office."[38] The reality is that the British parties have not significantly differed from one another in terms of policy and principle for most of the postwar era but in fact have shared a broad consensus.[39] The Conservative acceptance of the essence of the welfare state (as indicated by the fact that numerous Conservative governments left a significant amount of the nationalization of industry intact, including the once controversial National Health Service) and the Labour understanding that the welfare state will not be significantly extended are manifestations of this consensus. Both the Labour and Conservative Parties supported the basic principles of British foreign policy, including participation in NATO and a policy of deterrence vis-à-vis the Soviet Union. However, in 1989 important differences emerged between Thatcher's Conservative government and Kinnock's Labour Party with regard to the breakdown of Communist control in most of the Warsaw Pact nations and Britain's role in the European Community, with the

possible modification of aspects of British sovereignty. The right wing has been much more cautious about British participation in European union, beginning with the European monetary system, while Labour strongly endorses such participation. Thatcher experienced significant challenges to her position on this issue even from within her own party, challenges outlined in a letter of protest to her position sent to the *Times* by virtually the entire Conservative delegation to the European Parliament and manifested in Anthony Meyer's abortive challenge to her leadership of the party in 1989. Subsequently, the Major government assumed a more ambiguous position on Britain's role in Europe and continues to be challenged on this issue by a group of "Euro-sceptics" on the party's right wing.

For much of the postwar period, as successive Labour and Conservative governments alternated in and out of office, the basic structure of British economic and foreign policy did not significantly change. The consensus model, in which the major parties did not offer a distinct and meaningful choice about principles and policies for governing the country, would render the classic responsible party government model inapplicable.

This consensus model became significantly less descriptive of the British party sytem when the backbench revolt of left-wing militants in the Labour Party elevated Michael Foot to party leadership in 1980, and when the Conservative Party moved toward the right with the ascendancy of Thatcher. Before these developments, the Labour Party was a trade union party more than a party of socialism or of the principled left. While intellectual adherents of nonrevolutionary Fabian socialism had always found a home within the Labour Party, and while the party's back bench included a number of left-wing ideologues representing the Trade Union Congress, who are guaranteed the largest bloc of seats at the party conferences, its raison d'être had been to promote the interest of the working class.

The ascension of Michael Foot to the post of party leader reinforced Labour's movement into an advocacy of aggressive nationalization and egalitarianism domestically and unilateral disarmament and anti-western positions internationally, which alienated the substantial middle-class support that the party has always enjoyed. Many of its leading moderates broke away and formed a new party of the moderate left, the Social Democratic Party. This new party created an alliance with the Liberal Party that quickly became a third force in the party system, garnering nearly as many votes as Labour in the 1983 election (over a quarter of the votes). This, together with the advantage that the Anglo-American plurality electoral system gives to the plurality party (discussed at length in Chapter 2), enabled Thatcher's Conservative Party to win a majority of the seats (61%) with a minority of the votes (42.4%). With the tyranny of the electoral system denying the Alliance anything close to its proportionate share of seats, it quickly disappeared as a distinct political entity by 1987.

A few former Alliance members now run under the new banner of the minuscule Social and Liberal Democrats, known simply as the Liberal Democats. This remnant of the Alliance, under the leadership of the popular Paddy Ashdown, climbed back to earn some 15 percent of public support by the spring of 1992, with the failure of either John Major, the new Conservative leader, or Neil Kinnock, the Labour leader, to generate much enthusiasm among the British public. Ashdown's Gallup Poll approval rating in the fall of 1991 was 56 percent, higher than that of either Major or Kinnock.[40] However, the "wasted vote" psychology that works against minor parties under the Anglo-American electoral system (discussed above) had reduced the level of Social and Liberal Democ-

ratic support by the spring of 1992 to a mere 23 of 651 seats. Meanwhile, Kinnock had a difficult time shaking his image as a hard-line pacifist from the party's left; hence, after his unsuccessful challenge to the long-term Conservative hold on the government in 1992, he resigned as Labour Party leader. With the end of the Cold War and the collapse of the Soviet Union in 1991, these issues disappeared from the electoral arena.

After a decade and a half of their respective polarization, the major British parties appear to be struggling to recapture the ideological center. The short reign of John Smith, Kinnock's successor as head of the Labour Party, ended with his premature death in 1994. Smith's successor, Tony Blair, has moved strongly toward directing the party away from the ideological left, as most dramatically demonstrated at the party's 1994 annual conference at Bournemouth, when Blair proposed to drop the clause in the Labour Party constitution that committed it to the long-range goal of public ownership of the major means of production (i.e., state socialism). That this proposal was voted down by the party membership at the conference, a membership still sensitive to the sympathies of the party's left, may be less significant than the fact that the proposal was even made by the party leadership. In his speech, Blair also called for the party to drop its "tax and spend image" and to challenge the Conservative Party's claim to be the party of the free market, low spending, and low taxes. Furthermore, the Labour Party, under John Smith, set up a Commission on Social Justice that produced a 418-page proposal for reform of the welfare system, which had been at the heart and soul of the party. The essence of the report is a plan to get the long-term unemployed back into the work force by giving them "a hand up rather than a handout."[41] Since the proposal was the product of an outside commission, Labour Party leadership has been able to claim independence from it and pick from among its provisions according to political expediency, eschewing those parts that are vulnerable to charges of entailing more public spending. If Labour can sucessfully transform its image in the direction that Blair has laid out, it will have come a long way from its leftist image of the late 1970s. It seems likely that Blair will eventually succeed in modifying the socialist image that has been so important to the party's left wing but that has also provided a convenient bogeyman against whom the conservatives could run. However, since unreformed leftists among the Labour MPs, such as Peter Hain, Tony Benn, and labour leader Arthur Skargill, remain determined to resist Blair's efforts, the outcome of the struggle is still undecided.

The ruling Conservative Party also remains a party deeply divided and in search of its essential nature. Its right wing consists primarily of former Thatcherites such as Michael Portillo, while Prime Minister John Major's faction includes many of the "old guard" Tory leaders such as former Prime Minister Ted Heath, Minister of Trade and Industry Michael Heseltine, and Foreign Secretary Douglas Hurd. The European Community remains the most divisive issue, with the right taking the "Euro-sceptic" position, of opposing Britain's support of the European integrationist movement centered in Brussels. The Euro-sceptics fear that an economically united Europe inevitably means a politically federalized Europe dominated by Germany's Chancellor Helmut Kohl, a leading advocate of such a result whom the *London Times* dubbed "Bismarck in a cardigan." They point out that the value of the pound sterling plummeted severely on "Black Wednesday" in 1992, when Britain lost control of its own currency as a member of the European Rate Mechanism (ERM). They further note how the British economy has grown faster than that of most other Western nations in the past decade, how inflation has hit its lowest point in decades, and how the pound has stabilized since Britain's withdrawal from the ERM in 1992. The right wing on the Tory back bench showed its independent clout in November 1994, when they forced the Major government to abandon its plan to privatize the Royal Mail Service and prompted it to declare its bill to increase contributions to Brussels to be a question of confidence. This meant that a government defeat on the division on that bill would have been tantamount to a vote of no confidence that would have resulted in a dissolution of Parliament, forcing every MP to stand for re-election, which was a way of pressuring the back-bench rebels not to take their threatened defiance of the party whip lightly. In this instance, the threat was sufficient to produce a comfortable government victory. It is interesting that the rebels opposed the privatization of the Royal Mail, since privatization was touted as virtually an economic cure-all for the Thatcherite right. Perhaps with most of the former public sector already returned to private hands, privatization is no longer the defining issue for the party that it once was.

The idea of an aggregated party system being the British norm from time immemorial, as held by conventional wisdom,[42] is belied by the facts. For most of the time since the achievement of universal male suffrage, the British party system has had more than two parties. Much of the period between the two world wars was characterized by a three-party arrangement in which the formerly major Liberal Party was being overtaken by the rising Labour Party. (The pattern of the decline of liberal parties in the West was discussed in Chapter 2.) During this time, coalition government was the norm, and single-party governments the exception. Ten distinct parties (including the Alliance in

1983) have won seats in the House of Commons in post war elections. (There are eight in 1994.) The fortunes of several minor parties, such as those of cultural defense (e.g., the Scottish Nationalists and the Welsh Plaid Cymru), remain unstable and uncertain with the fluctuating popularity of devolution (the transfer of power to Scotland and Wales, giving them virtual political autonomy within the British crown). After a peak in the early 1970s, sentiment for devolution has waned for the moment; however, Scottish and Welsh nationalism remains alive and well, and could reappear given the proper stimulus, especially since Blair's Labour Party has supported the establishment of national parliaments in Scotland and Wales.

Thus the assumption that the British party system will always produce a majority of seats for one party, thereby allowing it to form a coherent government, is not corroborated by the long-term perspective in British history. The prospect of a *hung Parliament* in which no party has a majority in the House of Commons, arose again in late 1994, when eight members of the narrow Conservative majority had "the whip withdrawn," in effect being drummed out of the parliamentary party for defiance of the written whip on an important division (discussed below). If the Ulster Unionist Party would have failed to support the Tories and the eight dissidents had sided with the opposition, the government stood to lose important divisions. This is probably why John Major reinstated the unrepentant rebels. Multiparty coalitions that are based upon compromises of personnel and policy negotiated after the election cannot be said to be governing on the basis of a mandate that is assumed by the theory of responsible party government.

Another question concerns the probability that the increased strength of minor parties, whether the Liberal Democrats or the parties of cultural defense, could result in a hung Parliament, with no party receiving a workable majority of seats. This probability is affected by the outcome of the debate about electoral systems, which argues that the Anglo-American plurality system unacceptably distorts the representation of politically relevant principles and interests, and should be replaced by a variant of proportional representation (PR). While the Labour Party, with 27.6 percent of the popular vote in the 1983 general election, was rewarded with 32.2 percent of the seats in the House of Commons, the Alliance, with 25.4 percent of the vote, received only 3.5 percent of the seats. The tyranny of the British plurality electoral system can be further seen in the discrepancy between voting percentages and seats in recent elections, as shown in Table 3-3. Since the parties that would have the most to gain from such a change are by definition not in a position to impose and imple-

TABLE 3-3 Election Results for the Strongest Three British Parties, 1983–92

Party	1983		1987		1992	
	Votes (%)	*Seats*	*Votes (%)*	*Seats*	*Votes (%)*	*Seats*
Conservative	42.4	397	42.3	375	42.8	336
Labour	27.6	209	30.8	229	34.4	270
Alliance	25.4	23	22.6	22	–	–
Liberal Democrats	–	–	–	–	17.8	20

Source: Vacher's Parliamentary Companion, no. 1075 (August 1994); and *Keesing's Record of World Events,* 1983, 1987, and 1992.

ment that change, and those who are most likely to remain in power benefit from the distortions of the present system, the prospects for the early adoption of PR are not good. However, if the Liberal Democrats were able to force a *hung* Parliament, they might be able to coerce electoral system reform as the price of their coalition support. This strategy, if successful, could force a permanent realignment of the party system, with such coalition governments becoming the norm. The experience of modern British history, however, cautions against such an expectation, as major parties in Britain have generally found a way to coopt enough minor party support to produce a government without making fundamental concessions to such parties.

Although economic issues seem to be dominating the British agenda in recent years, part of the fundamental, longer-range troubles of the Labour Party might be related to the problems presented to Western party systems in general by the value change in European populations reported by Ronald Inglehart. The relevance of this research for political parties is that parties defined their identity in the era of materialist values. Parties of the left, in particular, see their reason for being as the promotion and protection of the working classes. Even traditional parties that have not been essentially class based, such as Europe's numerous parties of Christian Democracy, have in these times of increasing secularization become identified with the antisocialist middle class. But to the extent that the currently salient issues are postmaterialist, the parties have not given them adequate emphasis. Therefore, the outcomes of the elections do not provide the governments with a mandate for dealing with such issues.

Parties of the left have been particularly hurt by this lack of congruence between the materialist basis of their self-identification, their manifestoes, and their traditional clientele on the one hand and the salience of postmaterialist issues on the other. These parties almost by definition are anti-establishment. Research shows that anti-establishment people have a greater sense of political efficacy and a higher degree of participation, and are most affected by the transformation to postmaterialist values.[43] Therefore, parties of the left suffer the most from a split between a materialist and a postmaterialist wing. The division in the American Democratic Party between its so-called McGovern wing and its traditional working-class clientele in 1972 illustrates this dilemma. The ability of the British Labour Party both to mobilize its pacifist and other militant leftist supporters and to retain its middle-class support is questionable. As Labour identifies itself as a party of the left, it cannot ignore or disavow the anti-establishment values of the day.

Whether the aforementioned difficulties of the Labour Party will prevent it from displacing the Conservatives as the government party for the time being, Labour is even less likely to be displaced in the foreseeable future as the major party of opposition. (At this writing, Labour has a solid lead in the polls.) We have seen how distortions of the electoral system have operated to keep the Liberals, the Alliance, and their Liberal Democratic heirs in minor party status.

It has been implied that the British parties are much more coherent than their American counterparts in the sense of both standing for a set of identifiable principles to which all MPs must more or less subscribe and imposing a high degree of discipline in legislative votes or divisions. An MP who may disagree with the mandates of the party whip because of conscience or constituency pressure will normally try to work out these differences in consulatation with the party leadership, or, failing that, simply abstain from voting on that particular division. A move to the division lobby of the opposition is a move of the last resort and occurs infrequently, although it has become somewhat more common in recent years. However, this image of party coherence should not be taken to imply that British parties are immune from serious internal disagreements over policy.

The intense split between the pro-Europe and Euro-sceptic wings of the party, already noted, flared up at the opening of Parliament in November 1994, when the Euro-skeptics threatened to defeat a government bill to increase British contributions to the European Union, thus fulfilling an obligation negotiated by the government at the Edinburgh Summit of 1992. Prime Minister Major was forced to declare the bill a question of confidence to quell the rebellion.

The coherence that supposedly differentiates British parties from their American counterparts, according to the responsible party government model, is reflected in the organization and structure of the British parties. The existence of a central party organization separate from the annual conference and from the parliamentary party has already been mentioned with reference to party discipline and control of the party nominations. The Conservative Party has a Conservative Central Office and a National Union of Conservative Unionist Associations, the latter being an instrument of the various constituency organizations. The Labour Party has the National Executive Committee, which participates in the drafting of the election platform of the party. The Conservatives have been concerned that the extraparliamentary party organization be viewed as an instrument of the parliamentary party, while Labour, with its theoretical emphasis, has in a sense taken the reverse position. Labour's egalitarian ideology has implied a commitment to rank-and-file control of the leadership. It sees its parliamentary party, after all, as the political instrument of a socioeconomic movement, while the Conservative

Party, originating as a faction of the House of Commons, has a much more elitist perspective. Therefore, the Labour Party leader, the individual who becomes prime minister when the party controls the House of Commons, had to face annual election by the parliamentary party and, since 1981, by an electoral college that is not dominated by the Trade Union Congress.

These alleged differences in the degree of rank-and-file control of party leadership have been argued to have disappeared in practice by the landmark study of British parties by R. T. McKenzie, who claims that the Labour leader is not nearly as accountable to party rank-and-file, and that the Conservative leader is not as autonomous of rank-and-file influence as their respective ideologies would suggest.[44] The annual reelection of the leader of the Labour Party is usually a mere formality and is certainly so when the party controls the government. At the same time, the 1922 Committee has institutionalized bank-bench input into the Conservatives' legislative agenda and its principles. Moreover, the selection of the Conservative Party leader has been institutionalized into an electoral process after the confusion over the elevation of Sir Alex Douglas Home in 1963, replacing the previous process by which the leader "emerged" by informal consultation among the party's "magic circle," which kept the leadership post from popular party stalwart R. A. Butler. The challenge to Thatcher in 1989 and her defeat in 1990 demonstrate the reality of a measure of rank-and-file control of the party leadership within the Conservative Party. McKenzie suggests that the autonomy of the party leader is a function more of the imperatives of the nation's constitutional format than of the Conservatives' ideological or political perspective.

The imperatives of the British cabinet system demand a cabinet that is accountable and responsive to the interests and demands of the whole political system, and hence reasonably independent of the fluctuating passions of one set of interests. Winston Churchill, a staunch Tory except for the nearly two decades he was a Liberal and then an independent, opined that the Labour Party may be unconstitutional, based upon the mistaken presumption that a Labour government would be the obedient servant of the Trade Union Congress. The imperatives of the cabinet system also demand that a cabinet remain to some degree responsive to the concerns of ordinary backbenchers. Both a Labour leadership functioning as clerical order-takers for the trade union movement or the socialist left, and a Conservative leadership functioning as a thoroughly independent elite, would be incompatible with these theoretic dictates of cabinet government.

Both Labour and the Conservatives are to some extent mass parties in the sense that large numbers of citizens are dues-paying, card-carrying party members, in addition to those who psychologically identify with the party or vote for its candidates. This phenomenon is more pronounced with the Labour Party, with about 6 1/2 million members, than with the Conservative Party, with only about 1 million members. The former party, originating as a social movement outside Parliament, has always placed more emphasis on its rank-and-file than do the Conservatives, who, originating as a faction within Parliament, view their membership as a support for the parliamentary party. Labour, with a lower per capita income among its members, gets a fair proportion of its revenue from their dues; hence, any provision to maximize the size of its formal membership is much to Labour's advantage. Much of Labour's membership comes automatically with membership in one of its constituent unions, with the dues automatically deducted from the paycheck unless the member specifically signs a paper eschewing such membership (*contract out*). A Con-

servative government reversed this arrangement so that a union member would not be a Labour Party member without specifically requesting such membership (*contract in*), and Labour Party membership dropped precipitously. A subsequent Labour government changed the arrangement back to contract out, and its membership size climbed to the old levels, indicating that party membership was largely a matter of inertia on the part of the working class. In fact, some trade union members of the Labour Party are unaware of their party membership.

The organization of the Liberal Democratic Party, rather than being largely based on indirect membership, as with both the Conservatives (through their constituency organizations) and Labour (through trade unions), is more centralized, as membership is recruited directly through the central party organization. Since the Liberal Party likewise recruited its members on an individual basis, this is the structure followed by the Liberal and Social Democratic heir of these two late organizations. Because these and other minor parties have not faced the prospect of governing the nation in modern times, the impact of the imperatives of the constitutional format on their organizations is not as great as it is for the major parties.

The putative class basis of the electoral support of the major British parties has always been somewhat overstated. In any highly aggregated party system, the electoral appeal and the clientele of the major parties will always move more generally in the direction of Otto Kirchheimer's "catch-all" model, discussed in Chapter 2, rather than coherently representing a social class, as implied in the party government model. There are many working-class supporters of the Conservatives and many middle- to upper-class supporters of Labour. These parties have been able to aggregate to a higher level of generality instead of representing specific sectors of society or groups of interests, partly because Britain has a well developed and legitimate set of secondary associations that articulate specific interests.

The representation of specific interests has been more legitimate in Great Britain than in the United States, where the concept of the "special interests," as contrasted with the public or general interests, carries a certain degree of insidiousness. The political burden of the 1984 Democratic presidential nominee Walter Mondale of being labeled a candidate of the "special interests" is a case in point. By contrast, in Britain, it is perfectly acceptable for a member of Parliament to assert that he or she speaks for a particular interest, a position that would probably be politically disastrous in the United States and also in France, with its general hostility toward secondary associations. In Chapter 2 it was shown how the Rousseauian concept of the leader as the direct embodiment of the general will, which pervades the French culture, lends itself to the idea of the mass society.

British MPs must, however, register their outside interests, and the 1994 "sleaze" scandals in the Tory Party show the limits to how far they may go in representing particular interests. In the 1994 scandals, one junior minister, Tim Smith, resigned, and Ministry for Trade and Industry Minister Neil Hamilton and Chief Secretary to the Treasurey Jonathan Aitken stood accused of accepting bribes from Mohamed al-Fayed, the owner of Harrod's, to table parliamentary questions relating to Fayed's effort to get British citizenship. Meanwhile, another minister, David Mellors, has admitted to ten consultancies that netted him a six-figure income, which did not help his involvement in another controversy over two extramarital affairs. (In Britain and the United States sexual indiscretions seem to be taken more seriously than in France, where the married President François Mitterrand recently acknowledged the existence of a grown "love child" with his long-time mistress with the reaction, "So what?")

The major "corporate" sectors of the British economy are represented by large federations of specific interest groups, much as in the United States. The Trade Union Congress, which is structurally tied to the Labour Party, is a federation of trade unions. British industry is represented through the Confederation of British Industries, formerly known as the Federation of British Industries. (The name change alleviates the confusion the earlier set of initials generated for Americans.)

Because of the legitimacy of group activity in Great Britain, thousands of groups attempt to influence public policy. Although an MP may speak for certain interests, party discipline dictates that he or she has little independence in voting. Accordingly, groups do not find that it is much in their interests to devote resources to influencing individual MPs. One of the chief services rendered by MPs is in the tabling or filing of questions at question time on behalf of their clients, a practice that has vastly increased the number of such questions to over 50,000 per year, at a cost to the British taxpayer of some £97 per question.[45] Alternatively, those groups that are identified as "peak" in their sector of the economy participate in "corporate" operations such as Neddy (discussed below), while others concentrate on the policy-making levels of the higher civil service, that bastion of the technocracy. (The role of the technocracy in the policy processes of mature industrial societies was considered at length in Chapter 2.)

The British party system thus has not fulfilled the role assigned to it by the classic responsible party government model for a variety of reasons. Among these reasons are the imperatives of postindustrial society that assign much of the policy-making role to the technocracy; the value revolution posited by Inglehart that renders the party manifestoes and principles incongruent with the actual social and political cleavages of today's Britain; and the internal splits in the major parties between their front-bench wings, competing for the moderate center, and their more ideological back-bench wings, trying to force their respective parties back to the polarized days of the 1980s.

This perception of the inability of any of the parties to offer meaningful and viable solutions to the salient problems of the system and of the growing irrelevance of party competition to the determination of significant policy choices has resulted in what several scholars have called *party dealignment.*[46] This term refers to the process by which a growing and significant proportion of citizens no longer identify with one of the parties beyond voting for it, or holding passive membership. It could once be said that independents, those that were not predisposed to identify with one party or the other, were mostly apathetic and uninformed, but now informed and concerned people increasingly lack such identification. This trend is manifested in Great Britain in the *dealignment of degree*, a decline in the strength of identification or commitment to parties rather than in the number of people that may identify, weakly or otherwise. This dealignment is one more example of the growing perception that the policies and principles offered by the major parties do not speak to the issues and concerns salient to British society. Clearly the parties, an integral mechanism in the British classic model of parliamentary democracy, do not fulfill the role assigned to them in that model.

POLITICAL STRUCTURES AND PROCESSES

The model of responsible party government discussed above requires a cabinet system of government, a political format that has been emulated with varying degrees of accuracy and understanding by a substantial portion of the world's democracies. Of course, any political format transplants imperfectly to a different sociocultural context. It will be argued in this section that there is a discrepancy between the way in which the British political system is designed to operate (and, to a large extent, has been assumed to operate) and the way in which it actually operates, especially with respect to the structure of accountability.

The British political format falls into that broad category of systems called *parliamentary democracies.* These systems are distiguished from the presidential system used in the United States in two important respects: first, in parliamentary systems, the roles of head of state and head of government are distinct offices; and second, in parliamentary systems, the head of government is chosen by and accountable to the representative assembly, rather than being directly elected and accountable to the general electorate, as in a presidential system.

The head of state, what Walter Bagehot referred to as the "dignified" as opposed to the "efficient" aspect of government, embodies the role of symbolizing the unity of the system and performing many of the ceremonial tasks emanating from that symbolic role. It is a role that is assumed to embody the sense of community for the nation as a whole and hence to be above the partisan divisions that necessarily characterize the politics of any open society. In Great Britain and in other constitutional monarchies, this role is filled by the royal family. In those parliamentary democracies that are republics, it is filled by a president. In either case, the head of state maintains as nonpartisan an image as possible. The political preferences of the British monarch have not openly been a matter of public discourse since Queen Victoria complained about "that dreadful Mr. Gladstone."

In a presidential system, by contrast, presidents combine both their partisan political role and their unifying symbolic role, a combination that some feel detracts from the optimum performance of both roles. A very conservative president, for example, might not be easily perceived by liberal Democrats as the symbol of all that the United States means to them. More importantly, presidents can utilize the diffuse support and prestige that accrues to them as the symbolic head of the nation to mobilize support for partisan political purposes. Moreover, the combination of both roles in the same office and individual means that the heavily burdened president must perform many routine ceremonial duties, duties from which the British monarch frees the prime minister. A notable example of this role was the heroic effort of George V to rally his people during the darkest days of World War II, an effort that effectively supplemented the more famous mobilizing performed through the eloquence of the charismatic Winston Churchill. Few leaders are likely to match Churchill in terms of eloquence and charisma; Prime Minister Major, whom the satirists color gray on British television, may be more the norm. Furthermore, the pomp and circumstance surrounding the royal family as well as their carefully guarded nonpartisanship may render them more effective in ceremonial and symbolic roles compared to an ordinary partisan politician.

The head of parliamentary government is the prime minister, a role designated by the monarch since George I tapped Robert Walpole to govern the country in the name of the crown. In practice, the monarch must choose the head of the majority party in the House of Commons, since only he or she can govern in the face of the confidence mechanism. We have already discussed the possibility that some future election may fail to produce a party with a majority of seats in Commons and perhaps even a dominating plurality. In such an eventuality, a strong-willed monarch could conceivably have some influence in the choice of the prime minister. Most observers had not thought of Elizabeth II as being the type of strong-willed person likely to exercise this remaining small area of monarchial discretion, although she is rumored to have been critical of some policies of the Thatcher government in a quiet, behind-the-scenes manner.

Moreover, in the British constitutional system, without judicial review of acts of Parliament and with tightly disciplined parties permitting a strong centralization of power, checks on the possible egregious abuse of power could become a concern. The monarch still retains the legal right to withhold royal assent in the unlikely event that the government transgresses the line of what in the British sense is "unconstitutional" although perfectly legal. It is not realistic to expect that this power will actually be exercised in the foreseeable future. However, governments are aware that this limit on their discretion exists, and they may be persuaded to guide their choices accordingly. The prime minister meets weekly with the queen for an extensive review of policy and politics. The queen is fully informed of all governmental business, secret or otherwise. One may suspect that she may express some reservations over certain aspects of governmental thinking. It is known, for example, that the queen and Prime Minister Thatcher did not particularly admire one another, and it is thought that the queen may have persuaded Thatcher to alter her plans on some matters.

This illustrates the remaining area in which a monarch might exercise some political influence, although it is doubtful whether modern monarchs affect policy very much. The monarch has the right to be kept informed and the right to be consulted. Since monarchs reign over a long period while governments come and go, and since monarchs do not have to worry about short-term public opinion and political fortune, they can offer a detached perspective on policy questions that is unavailable to political leaders concerned with keeping their jobs.

The institution of the monarchy has come under growing attack in recent years in the face of what some see as the declining role of that institution due to the extensive costs, and fueled by numerous and increasingly public scandals involving the offspring of Elizabeth II. The British taxpayers support the monarchy by an annual appropriation (*the civil list*) to cover the cost of fulfilling constitutional duties and maintaining royal residences. The civil list at present is some £7.9 million, a sum that some critics resent in light of the fact that the queen is reputed to be the world's richest woman, with a net worth of some £8 billion. Resentment boiled up when it was proposed that the taxpayers foot the bill for the extensive renovations of Windsor Castle after it was gutted by fire in 1990. The queen deftly defused some of this controversy by offering to pay taxes on her income for the first time.

The royal scandals have been even more troubling for the future of the monarchy. Marital discord has reached an unprecedented level in this generation of royals. The divorce of Princess Anne, the separation of Prince Andrew from his wife, Sarah Ferguson, and the estrangement of the Prince and Princess of Wales only highlighted the family's domestic problems. These may have reached a peak in 1994, when the Prince and Princess of Wales authorized the publication of biographies explicating details of their mutual dislike, his extramarital affairs, and their other all-too-human weaknesses, thereby removing some of the mystique that was so important to the effectiveness of the monarchy as an institution.[47]

In reality, the task of formulating public policy and initiating legislation has long since "gone out of court," passing from the monarch to the aristocracy and ultimately to the representatives of the commoners as a result of monarchial bargaining with independent sources of wealth, especially about the time of the Hundred Years War in the mid-fourteenth century. The term "going out of court" refers to the process of the power of the crown being exercised by individuals and structures other than the royal family but still in the name of the crown. Initially, nobles were summoned to Whitehall to finance that enterprise, and these nobles increasingly bargained for concessions in return for their money. The institutionalization of these meetings, the Great Council, was a carryover from the old Anglo-Saxon *Witan*. When the Great Council grew in size until it became unwieldy, a group within the council—the Small Council—increasingly controlled decision making.

Each time yet another decision-making body was established, pressures for ever-wider inclusion would expand it to an unwieldy size. Thus, the evolution of the role of head of government may be viewed as a set of concentric circles. Within the Small Council, a group of nobles took an oath to keep the business discussed with the king private. These individuals, thus entrusted with the role of advising the king on these private affairs of state, became the Privy Council, which became the real governing force of Tudor England. Once it became recognized as a center of actual power, it too expanded, and now contains some three hundred people. Today, the Privy Council membership is a way of bestowing honor and a title (The Right Honourable) without responsibility, and the paper existence of the Council is used to justify the perpetuation of several standing committees of the Privy Council that carry out certain specific functions. For example, a group from within the Council witnesses the signing of royal proclamations, and the Privy Council Office makes certain arrangements for the monarch. The Council in its entirety gathers as a body only at coronations. All members of the government, past and present, belong to the Council, since, because of its origins, membership in the Council confers access to classified material and a security clearance. Britain's court of last resort for both Great Britain and the otherwise sovereign members of the Commonwealth is the Judicial Committee of the Privy Council, known as the "law lords."

Eventually, a group from within the Privy Council began meeting in the king's chambers, or cabinet, and was so labeled. Today, the cabinet is recognized as the place to be for aspiring young politicians, which generates great pressures to include as many MPs from the government party as possible. Under such pressure, the cabinet has grown to an unwieldy number (it varies from around 17 to the 20s). The precise number is not fixed and changes from one government to another. (The Thatcher government started with 22. Major's government had 23 as of November 1994.)

A group within the cabinet carries out the functions of the head of government: the secretaries of state (the foreign secretary and home secretary); the Chancellor of the Exchequer; and two officers of the Privy Council, the Lord President of the Council and the Lord Privy Seal (the former is the government Leader of the House of Commons and the latter is the leader of the House of Lords). These Privy Council officials have no official duties as Council members; hence, they are free to act as policy generalists within the cabinet. Such offices that have lost whatever official responsibilities they may have once had are called *sinecure offices.* Beyond the Privy Council officials, the Chancellor of the Duchy of Lancaster is another *sinecure office* that always appears in British cabinets.

The role of party chairman is also a "minister without portfolio," meaning a minister without a ministry to run (a portfolio is a briefcase). Such an official can also function as a generalist. Which other cabinet roles make up the inner circle will depend on the personalities of the individuals who occupy those roles. For example, the post of president of the Board of Trade and Department of Trade and Industry has probably achieved major status due to its high-profile occupant, the Right Honourable Michael Heseltine.

In a parliamentary system, the cabinet, including the prime minister, is known as the government. The cabinet is collectively responsible to the House of Commons. It is "constitutionally" expected that the prime minister and this inner circle of the cabinet jointly govern the nation. Thatcher, however, relied more heavily on advisers outside of the cabinet and made more policy decisions independently of cabinet consultation than any other modern prime minister. This raises questions about the validity of conventional wisdom about the role of the cabinet. Thatcher's reliance on Sir Alan Walters, an economist without a government post, over her own Chancellor of the Exchequer, Nigel Lawson, on the question of joining the European Monetary System in 1989, was only the latest episode in her career disposition to rely on individuals outside the largely public school, "Oxbridge" elite that has traditionally dominated the inner circles of the Conservative Party. Even within her own cabinet, Thatcher relied on those outside the traditional Tory elite. Lawson himself was a journalist and the son of a Jewish tea merchant, and John Major, his successor as Chancellor of the Exchequer and her successor as prime minister, is the son of a circus trapeze artist.

The responsibility of the cabinet to Commons means that Commons can compel the resignation of the entire cabinet by a simple majority vote, with no restrictions as to the reasons for taking such a vote (see Figure 3-2). Unlike some systems, such as Italy, the vote of no confidence does not apply merely to the prime minister or any one minister, leaving the remainder of the cabinet intact. Thus, the furor generated in the press in 1994, when it was revealed that the entire cabinet had agreed in a so-called suicide pact to resign if the government lost the vote on funding the European community, was misplaced excitement. Once the vote was declared to be a matter of confidence, the mass resignation of the cabinet would have been constitutionally required in the event of a governmental defeat, so the "suicide pact" was not news.

However, when the reputation or integrity of any single member of the cabinet, including the prime minister, is brought into ques-tion, thus threatening the tenure of the en-tire government, that minister may resign without a confidence vote—and sometimes to forestall such a vote—leaving the remain-der of the cabinet intact. The prime minister may even resign as party leader, leaving his party still in control of the government. This was the course of action of Neville Chamber-lain, the prime minister who had engineered the Munich concessions to Hitler, after the Nazis invaded Poland and exposed the fail-ure of that policy. The resignation of Por-fumo from the cabinet after he was revealed as having been intimately involved with a woman who was also involved with a Soviet agent and then lying about the affair to Com-mons, was probably necessary to forestall a confidence vote on the government as a whole.

FIGURE 3-2 The Palace at Westminster, where Parliament meets, as viewed from across the River Thames. Big Ben looms from the corner of the building near the Westminster Bridge.

The collective nature of cabinet responsibility is carried to the point that a member of a cabinet would never publicly criticize its decisions. When Anthony Eden was foreign secretary under Neville Chamberlain, he was passionately opposed to Chamberlain's policy of rapprochement with Adolf Hitler. Nevertheless, Eden suffered his doubts in silence through Munich and did not speak out until he had resigned from the cabinet. Similarly, Nigel Lawson did not publicly express his reservations about Thatcher's monetarism until he had resigned. More recently, in 1994 Tory MP David Martin resigned from a sub-cabinet-level post to be free to speak out against his government's policies.

As explained in Chapter 2, the government's responsibility to the legislature is maintained through the vote of no confidence. Since that vote has been used to oust a government only once in the twentieth century, many feel that its availability is meaningless, since everyone knows that with party discipline the government can effectively control the outcome of all significant divisions. (This is Britain's method of legislative voting. It involves supporters of the *yea* position filing into halls called "division lobbies" behind benches on the right side of the house (viewed from the front) and being tallied by the whips, while opponents of that position are tallied from the lobby across the floor. An MP voting against his or her party's position would literally have to cross the floor in a very public gesture and mingle with his or her usual opponents in the lobby. Some suggest that this may also help discourage breaking party discipline.) Voting with the opposition is not unheard of, despite these restraints; however, with the force of party discipline, it is most likely to occur when such an act reduces a large government majority but does not threaten the government with a loss on a division that entails a confidence question that would compel a government

resignation. For instance, there was a large defection from the huge Conservative majority in protest to Neville Chamberlain's policies, most notably his concessions to Hitler at Munich, a defection that did not bring the government down but did contribute to pressure for Chamberlain's resignation in favor of another Tory, Winston Churchill. More recently, 28 of the 376 Tories voted against the government in April 1988 to protest the Thatcher government's policy of terminating free dental and eye examinations. Because of the relatively small amount of money at stake, this action was to a large extent a symbolic protest against the austerity measures of the Thatcher government chipping away at the still widely popular welfare state (discussed below). Backbenchers may vote against their front bench or whip on issues that are not questions of confidence without fear of a penalty from the front bench or national party organization. However, a pattern or reputation of being a rebel against one's party whip will at a minimum lessen one's chances of rising to front-bench status and may ultimately cost one the right to be renominated under the party label. A government may declare any given vote it considers crucial to be a question of confidence. This is tantamount to a promise to resign if the government position is rejected. The potential rebel is then confronted with the prospect of facing a general election and of possibly of losing one's seat or of being forced to the opposition benches. In November 1994, John Major quelled a rebellion among his back bench over the bill to increase Britain's financial contribution to the European Community by declaring the vote to be a question of confidence.

The importance of the vote of confidence is not a function of the frequency with which it is used, however. Governments are aware that such a vote is an available option and generally adjust their behavior and policy goals accordingly. The possibility or even implicit threat of the use of a no-confidence vote is more important than its actual use. In this way, the confidence mechanism may be compared to the presidential veto power in the United States, where Congress will frequently adjust what it passes to avoid the veto. Thus while governments need only the passive consent of Parliament in order to govern, they are aware that there are limits even to that level of acceptance and that without such acceptance they cannot govern. Governments regularly consult with their back-benchers, ascertain the limits of their tolerance, and compromise their policy agenda before that agenda is formally introduced in the House. Both major parties have party *whips*, officials who serve as liaisons between back-bench and front-bench MPs. In 1994, the Tory government had 12 whips, a chief whip, and a deputy chief whip. (These officials should be distinguished from written whips, or notices from the front bench to back-bench MPs that a division is expected at a certain time and that their suppport is requested. This may come with one, two, or three underscores to indicate the importance with which the front bench regards compliance. See the sample whip in Figure 3-3). The Conservatives have a formal organization of backbenchers, the 1922 Committee, that serves to keep their party leadership informed of back-bench opinions and passions. (This committee is so named having originated in that year as a response to Stanley Baldwin's disastrous decision—from the party perspective—to dissolve Parliament and go to the country over the tariff issue.)

By contrast, President Nixon's defiance of the will of Congress in the early 1970s—as manifested in such actions as his impoundment of funds appropriated by Congress and upheld in a clear veto override and in his declaration of an extreme interpretation of executive privilege in response to Congress's request for information about the administration's activities—was probably supported by his judgment that impeachment was not a realistic option and that his tenure in office was secure regardless of the will of the legislative body. While the Official Secrets Act in Britain, applied more extensively by the Thatcher government than by any other modern British government, gives the British prime minister greater leeway to withhold information from Commons than is expected from an American president, the point is that Nixon could feel bolder in defying congressional expectations given the then-remote possibility of impeachment than a British prime minister could feel in ignoring his or her bounds of discretion.

The relationship of the government to Parliament is one based upon the familiar principle of checks and balances. The implicit threat to the tenure of a government posed by the power to vote no confidence, a result that may be obtained either by a direct no-confidence vote or by the legislative rejection of a significant piece of legislation introduced by the government, keeps the government operating within the broad bounds of discretion set by Parliament. Parliament no longer is the source of any legislation or public policy; its function is essentially what it was at the time of the Great Council: to use the power of the purse, the threat of the power to vote no, and to use public debate to circumscribe the discretion of the executive.

Against these parliamentary powers, the executive has the power to ask the monarch to dissolve Parliament at any time and force the House to stand for reelection, a request that the monarch constitutionally must grant. (There was some discussion in 1994 that, if the government had resigned over the funding of the European Community, the monarch retained the prerogative not to grant the expected request for dissolution if she thought another leader or coalition

PARLIAMENTARY LABOUR PARTY

TUESDAY 11th January, 1994,   the House will meet at 2.30 p.m.

1. Defence questions,   tabling for Health.

2. CRIMINAL JUSTICE BILL: SECOND READING.
   (Tony Blair & Alun Michael)

   YOUR ATTENDANCE BY 9 P.M. IS ESSENTIAL.

   ▬▬▬▬▬▬▬▬▬▬▬▬▬▬
   ▬▬▬▬▬▬▬▬▬▬▬▬▬▬
   ▬▬▬▬▬▬▬▬▬▬▬▬▬▬

3. Money resolution relating to the Non-Domestic Rating Bill.
   (Doug Henderson)

   YOUR CONTINUED ATTENDANCE IS REQUESTED.

   ▬▬▬▬▬▬▬▬▬▬▬▬▬▬

WEDNESDAY 12th January,   the House will meet at 2.30 p.m.

1. Trade & Industry questions,   tabling for Scotland.

2. NON-DOMESTIC RATING BILL: PROCEEDINGS.
   (Jack Straw & Doug Henderson)

   YOUR CONTINUED ATTENDANCE FROM 3.30 P.M. IS ESSENTIAL.

   ▬▬▬▬▬▬▬▬▬▬▬▬▬▬
   ▬▬▬▬▬▬▬▬▬▬▬▬▬▬
   ▬▬▬▬▬▬▬▬▬▬▬▬▬▬

3. Motion on the Insider Dealing (Securities and Regulated Markets) Order.
   (Alistair Darling)

   YOUR CONTINUED ATTENDANCE IS ESSENTIAL.

   ▬▬▬▬▬▬▬▬▬▬▬▬▬▬
   ▬▬▬▬▬▬▬▬▬▬▬▬▬▬
   ▬▬▬▬▬▬▬▬▬▬▬▬▬▬

THURSDAY 13th January,   the House will meet at 2.30 p.m.

1. Home Office questions,   tabling for MAFF.

2. Opposition Day   1st allotted day.

3. There will be debate on a BUREAUCRACY AND WASTE IN THE NATIONAL HEALTH
   SERVICE, on an Opposition Motion.
   (David Blunkett & Dawn Primarolo)

   YOUR ATTENDANCE BY 9 P.M. IS ESSENTIAL.

   ▬▬▬▬▬▬▬▬▬▬▬▬▬▬
   ▬▬▬▬▬▬▬▬▬▬▬▬▬▬
   ▬▬▬▬▬▬▬▬▬▬▬▬▬▬

FIGURE 3-3 This is a party "whip," a notice sent to each MP in the major parties by party leadership, informing the MPs of upcoming divisions and the party's position on the divisions, which the MPs are expected to support. The number of lines under an item indicates the importance the leadership attaches to winning the division and, hence, the seriousness of probable consequences to the MP who does not vote as the leadership expects. The term *whip* also refers to the party officials who provide a link between the front and back benches and mobilize support for party positions among backbenchers.

could be found without a general election. While this constitutional speculation was not put to the test since the government prevailed on the division, most scholars still believe that the royal prerogative could only be exercised in the most extreme circumstances, if at all.) Some scholars have suggested that this power of dissolution counterbalances the legislative power to vote no confidence and prevents no-confidence votes being called for frivolous reasons. They point to the frequency with which governments were voted out of office on confidence motions in the Third and Fourth French Republics and in Weimar Germany when the power of dissolution was not an effective option of those governments. However, it was tradition and culture that prevented the use of the legally available power of dissolution in the Third Republic, and it is probably more tradition and party discipline that prevent the frivolous use of the confidence vote in Britain, rather than the institutional factor of the power of dissolution.

Despite the parliamentary power to check and constrain the policy-making discretion of the government, that discretion is quite broad. The cabinet in fact dominates the policy-making process to the extent that some prefer to call the British system cabinet government rather than parliamentary government. This concept is based upon the idea of collective cabinet responsibility for policy making, an idea that has only an imperfect correspondence to political reality for two reasons. The first reason is that prime ministers to a greater or lesser extent dominate the policy-making role of the cabinet; they are clearly not just one more member of a collegial body but, at the very least, *primus inter pares* (first among equals). As pointed out by two British scholars, while many foreign secretaries or chancellors of the Exchequer have schemed to become prime minister, there is very little record of the reverse—prime min-

isters wanting to become foreign secretaries or chancellors.[48] The second reason is that cabinet ministers compete with one another for power and scarce resources and often identify with their individual role as the head of a department more than their collective role as a member of the cabinet. The dominance of the prime minister is to a large extent related to the personalization of politics and the charismatic basis of that person's power.

Coordination of the diverse and often conflicting perspectives within the government is of course mainly the job of the prime minister, but the treasury plays a major role as well. Treasury control is an important concept in understanding the policy making process in Great Britain. This control is effected by the role of the treasury in recommending the allocation of expenditures among departments, a role that requires that the treasury review, evaluate, and establish priorities among the programs of the various departments. The detailed examination of the expenditure of public money with regard to how policy goals may be most economically met is done in the Committee on Estimates, while the Commitee on Public Accounts insures that money is spent as the House has authorized.

It has been noted above that among the principal tools available to Parliament in constraining the discretion of the government and therefore of structuring its accountability is the role of debate in general and of the question period in particular. The latter phenomenon refers to the time set aside during the first hour of each session of the House of Commons on Monday through Thursday in which any member of Commons may address a previously written question to any member of the government with respect to the responsibilities or activities of that minister. The principal members of the government to whom questions are scheduled to be addressed are of course present. Due to the fusion of power that is inherent in the essence of parliamentary as opposed to presidential democracy, these officials must be members of Commons. The prime minister normally appears twice a week (Tuesdays and Thursdays, from about 3:15 to 3:30 P.M.) to field questions, which tend to be challenges to the broad thrust of foreign or economic policy rather than attempts to garner specific facts. Sometimes the criticism levied at government policy takes the form of a follow-up to a question about how the prime minister has spent the day—how much time had been devoted to which appointments and tasks. The several ministers deal with the requests for information about their departments. Other cabinet ministers appear to field questions on a rotating basis. These sessions (the question periods are from about 2:45 to 3:30 P.M.) are usually well attended compared to the frequently sparse attendance at ordinary debates, and the debates in which the prime minister squares off against the leader of the opposition tend to be rousing affairs with much cheering and jeering from the other MPs. Since question time is not long enough to allow all questions to be fielded orally, there are a large number of written questions to which the MPs receive written answers from the minister. Both written and oral questions are printed in advance on the Orders Paper, one of which is reproduced as Figure 3-4.

This requirement that the government be members of Commons is a logical evolution of the structure of the government's accountability to the House. It was understood to be logical that these officials be present to answer to Commons. Hence, the American concept of executive privilege by which some presidents have claimed the power to refuse to answer the demands of Congress for an appearance or information or even to allow other members of the administration to answer congressional subpoenas, insofar as it constitutes a denial of executive accountability to Congress, contrasts with the British tradition. The claimed powers of the British government to withhold information from Commons are based upon a controversial act of Parliament, the Official Secrets Act of 1911, not upon constitutional doctrine. While the broad language of the act and its zealous implementation most recently under the Thatcher government result in more information being withheld in Britain than in the United States (with the latter's Freedom of Information Act), the principle that members of the government must appear to face the questions of Commons is well established in Britain, most notably but not exclusively by the question time, while the principle that members of the executive may not be so compelled to appear is protected in the United States by the concept of executive privilege.

The constitutional requirement that the prime minister also be a duly elected member of Commons became established shortly into the interwar period, when it was widely recognized that the most prestigious man in the Conservative Party, Lord Curzon, could not ascend to the post of party leadership because, due to his peerage, he was ineligible to seek election to Commons. This problem came up again in 1963, when the Conservative Lord Hailsham sought a seat in Commons as Quentin Hogg, and Anthony Wedgewood Benn, a radical aristocrat then known as Viscount Stansgate, wanted election as a Labour MP because it was apparent by this time that potential prime ministers and probably the most influential members of the government would have to be members of Commons. The two major parties agreed on a solution in the form of the Peerages Act of 1963, which enabled newly named peers to resign their peerage within a year after receipt and current peers to disclaim their peerage within a year of the passage of the

| No. 7 | **Order Paper: 24th November 1994** | **173** |

QUESTIONS FOR ORAL ANSWER—*continued*

★28 **Mr John Whittingdale** (South Colchester and Maldon): To ask the Secretary of State for the Home Department, how he intends to improve the disciplinary regime in prisons; and if he will make a statement.

★29 **Mr Jeff Rooker** (Birmingham, Perry Barr): To ask the Secretary of State for the Home Department, if he will bring forward proposals for the registration of political parties.

★30 **Mr Geoffrey Hoon** (Ashfield): To ask the Secretary of State for the Home Department, by how many the number of police officers has increased since 1992.

Questions to the Prime Minister will start at 3.15 p.m.

★Q1 **Mr William McKelvey** (Kilmarnock and Loudoun): To ask the Prime Minister, if he will list his official engagements for Thursday 24th November.

★Q2 **Mr Christopher Gill** (Ludlow): To ask the Prime Minister, if he will list his official engagements for Thursday 24th November.

★Q3 **Mr Robert Ainsworth** (Coventry North East): To ask the Prime Minister, if he will list his official engagements for Thursday 24th November.

★Q4 **Mr Mike Hall** (Warrington South): To ask the Prime Minister, if he will list his official engagements for Thursday 24th November.

★Q5 **Mr Mike Gapes** (Ilford South): To ask the Prime Minister, if he will list his official engagements for Thursday 24th November.

★Q6 **Lynn Jones** (Birmingham, Selly Oak): To ask the Prime Minister, if he will list his official engagements for Thursday 24th November.

★Q7 **Mr Jacques Arnold** (Gravesham): To ask the Prime Minister, if he will list his official engagements for Thursday 24th November.

★Q8 **Mr Derek Enright** (Hemsworth): To ask the Prime Minister, if he will list his official engagements for Thursday 24th November.

★Q9 **Mr Andrew Welsh** (Angus East): To ask the Prime Minister, if he will list his official engagements for Thursday 24th November.

FIGURE 3-4   An Order Paper for the British House of Commons, listing questions to be posed at question time. Note that questions asking the prime minister for an account of the official engagements for a specific day are a well-understood opening for follow-up questions on the substance of the prime minister's meetings.

law. That same year, the Earl of Home emerged as the compromise choice for leader of the Conservative Party and accordingly disclaimed his title and entered Commons as Sir Alec Douglas-Home.

Due to the partisan nature of debate in Commons (discussed below), it is usually a member of one of the opposition parties who addresses critical questions to the minister. The only limit on the content of the question is the constraint of national security considerations; ministers may not decline to answer questions for political or personal reasons. This means that members of the government formulate policy informed by the realization that they may be called upon to justify that policy in the public forum of Commons. The typical British citizen, of course, does not read the official reports of the debates in the House (*Hansard*) any more than the average American reads the *Congressional Record;* however, the opinion leaders follow these debates to a greater extent than is done with respect to Congress, and they transmit relevant parts to the politically active public through the serious public media, such as the *London Times* or the *Manchester Guardian.*

The debate in the British House of Commons sometimes more seriously involves the postulation of policy positions, critiques, and responses as well as the exchange of ideas than does the debate in Continental assemblies, such as the German Bundestag or the French Assembly, and in the Congress, where "debate" tends to consist of a series of unrelated formal speeches. Debate in Commons tends to take the form of either criticism or defense of government-formulated policy. Recall that the policy formulation function is monopolized by the government because decentralized representative assemblies are inherently incapable of taking coherent action in the absence of centralized leadership structures, which never exist independently of the government. The policy proposals of the government in a sense structure the debate.

Because the House of Commons usually cannot alter the essential content of government bills, debate usually focuses on the general principles of the bills. Governmental rewards cannot be effectively reallocated to the special interests of the constituents of various MPs; hence, there is less attention to the defense of such interests. Debate in Commons is rather more likely to focus on general policy questions on a higher intellectual level than is found in the Congress or other legislatures with more effective power to add benefits for special constituencies. Various events or motions function as understood cues to initiate such general policy debates as the debate on the Speech from the Throne, which is read by the monarch to open each session of Parliament but written by the prime minister to outline the government's policy agenda. The speech is somewhat analogous to the American State of the Union Address. The explanation for the almost unique nature of the debate in the British House of Commons probably lies mostly in tradition and in the manner in which the system has evolved.

However, there are those who suggest that the physical structure of the House itself may play a role in the character of the debate carried on inside. Rather than the semicircular arrangement of seats found in other legislative chambers, in which all seats face some sort of dias or podium, seats in the House of Commons consist of benches arranged in two sets of four tiers, with the two sets facing one another (see Figures 3-5 and 3-6). The only raised seat is occupied by the speaker of the House, a nonpartisan presiding officer. A table between the two sets of benches provides a place for the clerks of Commons to keep records. The government party occupies the benches to the right of the speaker, and the opposition parties occupy the benches to the speaker's left. The members of the government itself occupy the front tier of bench on its side of the room, while the

FIGURE 3-5 The British House of Lords. The monarch reads the Speech from the Throne seated on the gold throne at the head of the room. The Lord Chancellor, presiding over the House, sits on the woolsack. The bar of the House, behind which stand Commons and the government for the opening of Parliament, is directly below (not visible).

members of the "shadow cabinet," those members of the major opposition party who are designated to become the government if their party should win the next election, occupy the front tier of benches facing the government to the speaker's left. Members of the smaller minor parties occupy the benches to the speaker's left behind an aisle midway back in the room. It is obvious that the physical arrangement of the seating presumes a dichotomized government, for there is no logical place for third and fourth parties. The front benchers may speak from small podiums called the dispatch boxes on either side

of the speaker's table, but backbenchers must speak from their places. MPs are not supposed to read their speeches. They speak with the aid of notes but mostly extemporaneously from their benches, a situation in which speech making would seem entirely out of place. While the MPs in fact address one another, in a formal sense all remarks are directed to the speaker, as in, "Madame Speaker, I hope that my honourable friend understands his error. . . ."

The idea of trying to limit the intensity of acrimony in the debates is reflected in the lines on the carpet running in front of the

FIGURE 3-6   The British House of Commons, as seen from the Strangers' Gallery, looking toward the front of the House. The doors to the division lobbies are at the rear, just beyond the bottom of this view.

two front benches; the space between them equals, it is said, two sword lengths. Members are supposed to stay behind the line. This is to prevent argument from degenerating into sword play, a presumably purely symbolic concern in modern times.

This physical arrangement in the House of Commons is also said to encourage party discipline. Voting is done by having the MPs file from the respective division lobbies behind either side of the House to be counted by tellers—the party whips and their deputies. For a member of the government to vote with the opposition, he or she would have to walk past his front bench and cross the floor of

Commons to file into the division lobby of the other side and mingle there with members of the opposition, a task that cannot be accomplished as subtly as pushing a button or raising one's hand. After the division, two tellers from each side—the winners on the speaker's left and the losers on the speaker's right—stand stiffly in front of the mace on the table of the House, while the tellers on the right announces the results. Figure 3-7 shows the tellers announcing the government's surprising loss of a crucial vote to raise taxes on heating fuel in a raucous session of Commons on December 6, 1994.

The faith in the positive impact of the

FIGURE 3-7 Standing in front of the mace, tellers announce the government's defeat in a historic and raucous division on the bill to raise the value-added tax on heating fuel near midnight on December 6, 1994. Such government defeats on their budget are rare. Jubilant members of the Labour Party may be seen behind the table. *Source: London Times,* December 7, 1994, p. 1.

physical disposition of Commons is such the point that when German bombs destroyed the House in May 1941, the British rebuilt a virtual replica of the House in the belief that its physical arrangements shapes the character of the debate and helps the maintenance of party discipline. Furthermore, the physical arrangement of the House is itself part of the tradition, and reflects and facilitates the imperatives of that tradition.[49]

Clearly, the House of Commons does not perform the function of legislating for the United Kingdom in the sense of formulating and authoritatively adopting public policy al-

ternatives. Under the system of disciplined parties that provides Commons with approval for virtually every serious policy initiative of the government, it appears to many that Parliament has essentially become a "rubber stamp" for cabinet government. This perceived "crisis of parliamentarianism"—the realization that modern legislatures can no longer function as autonomous legislative bodies—is based upon the myth of what Karl Bracher has called "the fiction of partyless parliamentarianism."[50] This myth is the idea that since the classic and proper role for parliaments is to legislate and the role of political executives is to implement, Parliament therefore has lost a role that it had always properly had. However, it was suggested above that the role of the evolving antecedents of Parliament was to provide a constraint on the discretion of the crown, and it was always the crown, broadly construed, that was the policy formulator for the system. In modern times, we have pointed out, the cabinet exercises this function of crown power.

The procedures and style of Commons are deeply set in traditions that have long since lost whatever original purpose they may once have had. For example, the tradition of slamming the door on the royal messenger, "Black Rod," when he is sent to summon Commons to the throne room to witness the monarch read the Speech from the Throne at the opening of Parliament is a throwback to the conflict between the crown and parliamentarians who were only being summoned to contribute more funds. Some would argue that the House is trapped in the strait jacket of tradition and must be substantially reformed if it is to cope with the imperatives and exigencies of the modern world.

For example, the "sleaze" scandals of late 1994, which revealed that some MPs had accepted gifts in return for such favors as the tabling of questions in behalf of a client and that others had had excessive consultancies, led to the cry that MPs should be limited to one job and in their sources of outside income. The midafternoon starting time for Parliament—2:30 P.M. Monday through Thursday—is set in part to allow MPs to maintain their nonpolitical professions. They used to be so poorly paid that an outside income was almost assumed. Now, however, an MP receives £31,687 per year in salary, plus about another £40,000 or so for office help and a living allowance to maintain a flat within eight minutes of the House. Members of the government and of the shadow cabinet receive an additional salary for their more re-

sponsible and demanding roles. Prime Minister Major's salary, for instance, as of late 1994, was £78,292. However, the government at this time voted themselves a 4.5 percent pay boost, twice the rate of inflation, a proposal that has generated vociferous opposition.

Such cries for the "reform of parliament"[51] contain lists of suggestion for better enabling Commons to cope with the demands of the postindustrial age: more staff and assistance for MPs, better access to technical information, better trained and paid full-time MPs, more sitting time in the House, etc., all of which are to some extent based on the classic structure of accountability. Such reforms implicitly presume a significant discretionary role for Commons. However, if its main function is not to formulate policy in detail but to critique policy on general terms, it is not necessary for MPs to master more technical detail. Much of the critique of the operation of Commons presumes an autonomous legislative role that it does not have, and with perhaps a short-lived partial exception during the so-called golden age of Parliament—the period from the establishment of parliamentary supremacy over the monarchy in the seventeeth century to the emergence of disciplined parties in the nineteenth—a role that Commons never did have.

With the structure of accountability with respect to the vote of confidence mechanism and the question hour exercised exclusively through the House of Commons, one can overlook the bicameral nature of Parliament. In fact, many have echoed the sentiment that the House of Lords, lying outside the logical structure of the system, has outlived its usefulness and ought to be abolished. The House of Lords, whose official membership is dominated by the hereditary aristocracy, is an institution that inherently offends pure democratic values, thus adding to the chorus of egalitarian opinion that holds that its usefulness has been outlived.

Much of the argument that the upper house of Parliament has become atavistic is based upon a misconception of the actual role of democratic legislatures in general and of the House of Commons in particular. By the Parliament Act of 1911, the House of Lords lost whatever stature it had had as a co-equal house by having its legislative power limited to the power to delay the passage of an act of Parliament for two years. That power was further circumscribed to the power to delay an act of Parliament for one year by the Parliament Act of 1949. This power to delay legislation, an action that does not entail the termination of the government, as would a rejection of government policy in Commons, has been used on several occasions in the 1980s. Specifically, the Lords defeated the government 233 times from 1979 to 1994 and even forced a one-year delay once during that period. Other times, Lords has forced the government to amend their bills to avoid such a delay. For example, the Lords prevented the government from imposing cuts in rural school transport and in the external services of the BBC, and in 1994 Commons had to reconsider its controversial criminal justice bill after initial rejection by Lords. In the three sessions—1991–92, 1992–93, and 1993–94 (to November 1994)—the House of Lords added 1,583, 2,079, and 1,441 amendments, respectively, to government bills that then passed in their amended form. Hence, the House of Lords continues to function as an additional check on Britain's highly centralized legislative process.

The House of Lords is composed formally of all of the people who hold peerages (aristocratic titles). The total number is not fixed, but today is around twelve hundred. This most emphatically does not mean that one can expect a thousand individuals to show up for any given session of the House of Lords.

Slightly over five hundred have ever attended any session, and only about a third of those eligible attend with any regularity.

Naturally, as one would expect among aristocrats, there has always been a strong majority of Conservative party sympathizers among the peers; hence, the Conservative Party has been a stronger and more consistent supporter of the existence and prerogatives of the House of Lords. As a partial attempt to remedy this imbalance, the Life Peerages Act of 1958 enables the monarch, on the advice of the prime minister, to confer titles for life on selected commoners, titles that are not passed on through inheritance to their progeny. Life peerages were intended to supplement the hereditary principle by naming people who might be more able to carry on the work of that house and who would reduce the overrepresentation of Conservatives by supporting Labour. Life peers are frequently people near retirement age who have established reputations in the House of Commons or other sectors of public life. This serves to increase the rather advanced average age of members of the House of Lords (69); consequently, one frequently finds several peers napping on their plush red benches during a session of Lords. Over three hundred of the some twelve hundred peers are of this life peerage variety. Considering that the essence of a classic Labour politician is the representation of working-class constituents and interests, the concept of a Labour lord is almost an oxymoron. Labour Party leader Tony Blair, offended, like most of his egalitarian colleagues, by the concept of a hereditary upper house, has promised that soon after becoming prime minister, he would "reform" the House of Lords by denying the hereditary peers the right to sit and to vote in Lords. Of course, life peers are not as overwhelmingly Tory, so such a measure would be to Labour's political advantage.

Given the constraints of time, the House of Commons is unable to give each issue and each bill the attention they deserve. Lords can give deliberate consideration to such bills, since that house, unlike Commons, is under no obligation to discuss all bills. The quality of debate in Lords is quite high, despite the fact that its debates are not as widely followed as are those in Commons. This power to engage in informative debate and to place public policy in the glare of publicity is very close to the main function of Commons. Thus while the importance of the actual role of Commons in the political process may be exaggerated by the model of cabinet government, the role of the House of Lords may be understated. While Commons is still clearly the more significant actor in the process, the roles of the two houses of Parliament appear to have to some extent converged, once the real role of legislative assemblies in modern parliamentary democracy—the role of constraining the discretion of the government and structuring its accountability largely by publicity and an informed critique of government policy and behavior—is properly understood.

Nevertheless, there is a widespread feeling, especially on the political left, that the House of Lords is an anachronistic institution that offends egalitarian and democratic sensibilities. The "shadow" Home Secretary, Jack Straw, has indicated that a Labour government would quickly move to ban hereditary peers from sitting or voting in the House of Lords to render that body more compatible with a democratic and "classless" society.

PUBLIC POLICY AND PERFORMANCE: THE FUTURE OF THE BRITISH SYSTEM

Great Britain led the Western world into the modern era. It was in England that the industrial and commercial revolutions first appeared. With the advantages of being first and of having an empire, Britain was a Western economic and industrial leader through World War II.

The end of that war saw the virtual demise of the British Empire (along with the achievement of independence of almost all other former colonies of Western powers), and Britain sank to the status of a second-class power after having played such a leading role on the world's stage. The postwar era, through the 1970s, saw such a decline in its economic performance that this nation, once the economic leader of much of the industrialized world, was known as "the sick man of Europe," in a coopting of the term that originally referred to Turkey on the eve of World War I. Unemployment and inflation each hit high levels in Britain, in disastrous conflict with the Keynesian principle that a rise in the one ought be accompanied with a decline in the other. The Phillips Curve principle of a trade-off between these two "evils" was finally applied with devastating severity by the Thatcher government, whose austerity policies swapped a reduction from double-digit inflation at the end of the 1970s to an acceptable rate of a little over 5 percent by the mid-1980s for an increase in the rate of unemployment from around 5 percent to over 13 percent in that same period. The rate of economic growth in Great Britain was one of the slowest in the Western world from the end of World War II through the 1970s.

Great Britain's generally poor performance both in the assertion of national power and the protection of national interests in the international arena and in economic performance led many people to question the heretofore assumed superiority of the British institutions and political style, and led others to criticize the collectivist economic policies of the advanced welfare state adopted by both Conservative and Labour governments in the postwar era. Having blamed Britain's economic failures on its apparent abandonment of capitalism and the market economy since World War II, many critics then blamed the country's continuing poor performance into the first half of the 1980s on the putative failure of Thatcher's Conservative economic retrenchment.

Having been one of the leaders in the development of the theory of market capitalism and the self-regulating market (Adam Smith, the philosophical father of economic laissez faire, was, after all, British), the British led the way in the modification of market capitalism with what they perceived to be pragmatic adjustments to economic and social realities. Recall that Britain is one of the least likely nations to be constrained by the imperatives of theory in the face of contradictory realities. As Karl Polyani asserted in his classic, *The Great Transformation,* the British compromised their commitment to the idea of the self-regulating market with the Speenhamland Law, the West's first guaranteed minimum income law, at the end of the eighteenth century. Hugh Heclo reminds us, however, that the concept of Social Darwinism, with its corollary principle that the poor are responsible for their own predicament, died hard. The Poor Law of 1834 limited public assistance to what was called "indoor relief"—working for one's sustenance in workhouses—in a persistent attempt to distinguish the "deserving" from the "undeserving" poor.[52] Nevertheless, the British, less committed to principle than their American cousins, have had an easier time accepting modifications and violations of market theory. Whatever long-term social benefits that may or may not ensue from strict adherence to market principles, the social and human costs were apparent, real, and increasingly unacceptable. Market theory ultimately regards labor as a commodity whose price should be determined by impersonal market forces. In the social dislocations that resulted

from regarding labor as a commodity, human misery was severe. Subsistence-level wages, long hours to the limits of human endurance, unsafe working conditions, widespread child labor, and the use of women at heavy labor were commonplace. In fact, the passionate description of the human misery of early unregulated capitalism in England occupies a central place in the first volume of Karl Marx's magnum opus, *Das Kapital.* The periodic fluctuations of the uncontrolled business cycle resulting in the human costs of uncontrolled inflation and unemployment further generated pressure for modification of classic market capitalism.

It was a British aristocrat, John Maynard Keynes, who suggested that governments utilize fiscal policy, taxing and spending decisions, and direct control over the money supply to control the level of investment and thereby control the business cycle. Yet, postwar Great Britain, especially under a series of Labour governments, went well beyond Keynesian modifications of market economics. The nation adopted a mixture of state socialism and welfare state capitalism, the latter being an economic system that combines the principle of the private ownership of production run for profit with the principle that many of the values of material well-being, such as access to medical care, child care, and decent housing, attributes that are still allocated in the United States on the basis of the ability to pay, are matters of entitlement or right.

The welfare state in Britain had been to a signficant extent combined with a greater amount of public ownership of the major means of production in a system known as state socialism. A clause in the constitution of the Labour Party commits it to such public ownership; it is this clause that was challenged by the centrist Labour leader Tony Blair. At one point, Great Britain had a greater proportion of its gross national product from state-owned enterprises than any other Western nation; the only one that was close was France. The British also had a state-owned broadcast network, coal industry, steel industry, airline, car industry, and perhaps most famously, the National Health Service, through which most health services are provided without charge to British citizens by health care professionals paid by the state.

This extensive public sector did not mean that Britain did not have a private sector. Commercial broadcast networks compete with the BBC with fare that more realistically caters to popular taste, Virgin Atlantic competes with British Airways, and physicians may and occasionally do enter private practice.

One of the principles driving the regime of Margaret Thatcher, that most principled of prime ministers, was a belief in the self-regulating market. Among other elements of this belief is a deep aversion to public ownership. Hence, the Thatcher years saw a virtually complete dismantling of Britain's system of publically owned industries. *Privatization,* almost a defining Thatcherite principle, extended to cars, steel, and British Airways. By 1994, public enterprise was pretty well confined to coal, British Rail, the Royal Mail, and of course the popular and politically unassailable National Health Service. Attempts in 1993 and in 1994 to sell off 51 percent of the Royal Mail were blocked by a motley collection of back-bench rebels in the Tory Party for a complex of reasons, including the fear that a for-profit mail service would abandon sparcely patronized rural mail areas. Plans were also underway to sell off the coal industry and to sell British Rail to some 25 smaller companies by 1996. Some public corporations have had their shares sold to the public, as in the case of British Aerospace and British Telecom, while the National Freight Corporation was sold to a consortium of employees and managers. Parts of other publicly owned

companies, such as the Jaguar division of British Leyland, were also sold. (This action provoked a great deal of controversy in 1989 with the revelation that the government, relying on only one bidder, sold the operation to British Rover for a good deal less than its market value.) It was clear that the ideal of the nationalization of industry as a panacea for the socioeconomic ills of mature industrial societies had fallen into such widespread disrepute by the late 1990s that the Labour Party leader Tony Blair made one of his main goals in 1994 the explicit rejection of that part of the party constitution that cites nationalization as one of its basic objectives (clause 4). This move drew stiff opposition from many parliamentary party and rank-and-file members, who, by majority vote at their 1994 Bournemouth convention, rejected the Blair proposal. It is clear, nevertheless, that even a Labour government in the hands of a pragmatic centrist like Blair will not try to reverse Thatcher's legacy of privatization. The difference between the parties in this regard appears to be how much further, if at all, the Tories will go to privatize what is left of the public sector.

The ideal of the democratic socialists is that, because the state is democratically accountable, state-owned enterprises would run in the public interest instead of for profit. In contrast, these socialists argue, market forces do not realistically hold large oligopolist and remote corporations accountable to the public, and there is no necessary correspondence between private profit and the public interest. However, in reality, state-owned industries are not run by the democratically accountable parts of the government but rather by experts in the equally unaccountable higher civil service, specifically by boards of ten or more people appointed by the relevant minister. Often the same people who served on the corporate boards of directors when these industries were in the private sector manage these industries for the public sector, and ministerial control of these boards has proved difficult.[53]

Hence, as Joseph Schumpeter argued in *Capitalism, Socialism, and Democracy,* modern corporations and public enterprises are both a type of bureaucracy, an organizational form that is by definition not conducive to creativity, risk-taking innovation, or accountability.[54] The choice between corporate capitalism and state socialism at this stage of technology is a choice between private bureaucracies and public bureaucracies. Since the imperatives of bureaucratic behavior apply equally to public and private bureaucracies, the choice between state socialism and welfare state capitalism, as those systems are actually practiced in advanced industrial democracies, may not be all that significant in a practical sense although the issue has great ideological force. The Thatcher government was ideologically committed to the goal of privatization as part of its commitment to the principle of market economics.

The National Health Service (NHS) may be the best known nationalized industry in Britain. Under this system, hospital and other health-care facilities are owned and managed by the state, and health-care personnel, including physicians and nurses, are paid standard fees directly by the state for each patient treated.[55] Some of the hospitals have been granted their own budget and the power to allocate care within the confines of that budget (known as "self-governing trust status"), a move by the Thatcherites to inject a measure of competition (what they called "an internal market") and efficiency in the system. Similarly, almost half of the British population is treated by general practice physicians (with practices of over 7,000 patients each) who receive an individualized budget that supposedly covers the costs of running the practice, buying drugs, and using certain nonemergency hospital services. These doctors have a financial incentive to process each patient as economically as possible.

The NHS is supported by taxes and provides most forms of medical care (with the recent exceptions of eye and dental examinations and the long-established charges for spectacles themselves) to citizens of the realm without cost; hence, medical care is available on the basis of need, without regard to the ability to pay. Hence, when anyone on British soil has a medical emergency, they can immediately receive all necessary care at a NHS hospital without charge. There are no questions about insurance coverage or the ability to pay. The patient chooses his or her physician and can continue to develop a doctor-patient relationship with the same primary-care physician or specialist if recurring treatment is needed, just the same as when these physicians are in private practice.

The evidence does not support allegations of widespread unnecessary use of the NHS because it is free; one does not normally take trips to the doctor, dentist, or hospital for fun. Health-care professionals make better than average compensation but less than they would in a system of fee for service with unregulated costs, as is used in the United States.

For nonessential NHS services, however, there is a wait that lengthens with the seriousness of the care in question. One may wait several years for some forms of surgery. Moreover, there are charges for nonessential medical care for noncitizens of the United Kingdom; however, these charges are considerably less than one would pay for comparable care in the United States. In practice, however, it soon became apparent that the system could not afford to give all the care a consumer might want or from which he or she might benefit. Hence, a system of rationing evolved, initially on a more or less ad hoc and unofficial basis, using a loosely defined criterion developed by the NHS called "Quality Adjusted

Life Years" (QALYs). This standard refers to a judgment as to how many additional years of life a proposed treatment will afford, discounted by any reduction in the health and vigor in which the years would be lived (calculated from a table of levels of disability and distress). This judgment is balanced against the cost of the treatment to provide a cost-benefit analysis. Hence, it would not be considered good value to spend thousands of pounds on complex surgery for a crippled octogenarian, although such surgery is frequently performed in the United States if the patient can pay for it. Rationing in Britain frequently takes age into account and has progressed to the point that it is nearly impossible for someone past their middle forties with acute kidney disease to receive dialysis. Similarly, hip replacement surgery usually involves waiting for several years or moving to a remote area with empty beds.[56]

The overwhelming number of citizens approve of the National Health Service, but health-care professionals are less enthusiastic. While some efficiencies are achieved over the American private enterprise system of health-care delivery (for example, hospitals are not overbuilt, nor do they duplicate and overlap expensive equipment and services, and doctors' freedom to relocate is subject to an administrative decision that there is not an oversupply of physicians in the area to which someone wants to go), the overall cost of the NHS has risen to over £20 billion a year. However, by 1976, the United Kingdom was spending 5.8 percent of its gross national product on health care, compared to 8.6 percent in the United States and 9.7 percent in West Germany; hence, one cannot claim that the growing costs of health care are uniquely attributable to the British system of socialized medicine.[57] While the adoption of the NHS saw the initial exodus of a number of physicians who were primarily interested in the greater potential earning power of private practice in North America, Britain has been able to attract and keep an adequate supply of physicians in the Service, and currently ranks twenty-ninth among nations with respect to number of physicians per million population.[58]

The overall popularity of the National Health Service probably does not allow its complete abolition by the government. Thatcher's principled opposition to the idea of nationalization, a passion that led to the selling off of several nationalized industries for whatever price could be obtained, did not lead to a significant dismantling of the Health Service. Rather, Thatcher did and Prime Minister Major will probably continue to do some chipping away of the health-care delivery system at its margins, as seen in the spring 1988 bill to end free dental and eye examinations through the NHS. Considering the small sums at stake, the furor aroused by even that minor alteration in the role of the NHS is only a hint of the storm the government would face if it attempted to return health-care delivery entirely to the private sector.

Thatcher was committed to the goal of privatization to the extent that political realities would allow.[59] Her government came to power pledged to remedy the economic miseries of Great Britain with some tough policies on wage restraints, tight money, and inflation control. But the aforementioned Phillips Curve interchange of high levels of inflation for high levels of unemployment still did not generate enough economic growth to undo Britain's postwar image as "the sick man of Europe." Anticollectivists blamed Britain's economic woes on the abandonment of market principles; recently, the failure of the Thatcher government to reverse Britain's sluggish economic performance proved grist for the mills of critics of right-wing economic policies. In reality, and paradoxically, one of the reasons for the poor performance of Britain's productive system was the country's success in World War II. Britain's industrial plant was one of the few in the West to survive the war relatively intact; hence, unlike the other nations, Britain did not replace it with a more modern one. It therefore entered the postwar world with obsolete technology in a period of rapid and significant technological change. Much the same thing, incidentally, could be said about the American industrial plant, which was also rendered obsolete compared to that of much of Europe and Japan, rendering the United States also at a competitive disadvantage with those nations. It is difficult to blame the Thatcher government for its failure to turn Britain's economy around in its first term in office, because any given government does not transform the legal and policy structure of a nation overnight. During its term any government can only be held responsible for perhaps 10 percent of all the laws on the books.[60]

Despite all of this, Britain's economic performance did improve in the late 1980s. In the four-year period from 1984 to 1988, real GDP growth averaged 3.7 percent—the fastest rate in either Europe or North America,[61] and by 1994 it had reached 4.2 percent. Manufacturing output was growing at an annual rate of 6.5 percent in 1988, and a healthy budget surplus of about £16 billion was projected for fiscal year 1988–89. Meanwhile, by October 1994 unemployment had fallen to the unexpectedly low rate of 8.9 percent, and the underlying rate of inflation fell to a 27-year low of 2 percent.[62] This apparent resurgence of Britain's economy during the decade of Tory rule may counter the increasing predictions in the literature of the decline and fall of Great Britain as a viable political system.[63] However, these positive numbers can be used to mask some underlying difficulties. A large number of the individuals listed as employed are in low-paying

(under £75 per week), often temporary work. About a third of the women in the work force have such jobs, and that figure balloons to over 50 percent in some of the manufacturing areas, such as Manchester. This indicates that Britain has still failed to resolve the fundamental problem of structural unemployment, unemployment due to the unemployability of those seeking work, which in turn is a consequence of the evolving state of technology.

CONTINUITY AND TRADITION IN A CHANGING WORLD: THE ROLE OF EDUCATION

We have made a point about the unique role of the force of tradition in Great Britain as a constraint upon social and political change. Great Britain has long been known for its incremental approach to policy making, its preference for a small step-by-step, trial-and-error approach to the development of public policy.[64] In fact, the system has been criticized for its inability to undertake the kind of fundamental and far-reaching reassessment of its policies and institutions that many people feel is required in today's postindustrial world.

The importance of tradition and of the institutions supported by tradition in Britain contributes an element of continuity in the face of pressures for rapid social change. For example, the declining salience of class was noted above with respect to some of its causes and implications. However, one can overstate the extent to which class consciousness has faded in the British context. The partial assault on the institutions that perpetuate class stratification in Britain can be seen with references to an institution that has been an important pillar propping up that stratification—the education system. Many scholars have focused on the 11-plus examination system in the state-supported schools as an important barrier to obtaining the higher education and credentials needed for elite status for the bulk of the population who were economically restricted to those schools. The reasons why the system would disproportionately winnow out students from working-class backgrounds involve the reality that bright individuals seeking to overcome a culturally and educationally deprived background are likely to need more time to acquire these skills than students to whom educated parents impart these skills and values at an early age. Yet, the exam given in the fifth grade was certainly winnowing out "late bloomers." As noted above, under egalitarian pressures from Labour governments, the 11-plus system was formally abolished in the early 1970s, and "comprehensive schools" replaced the distinction between "grammar schools," meant to provide university preparatory education for those who passed the exam, and "secondary modern schools," meant to provide vocational or other terminal education for those who did not.

Such comprehensive schools frequently promote egalitarian values so that each "tutor group" contains students with the full range of ability levels; ability grouping or tracking is eschewed. This, of course, entails a sacrifice in the academic rigor of the instructional level offered to the brighter students. Some comprehensives have been granted the right to "opt out" of government control and a budget to allocate as they see fit. Schools interview and admit prospective students according their own criteria. Consequently, some more academically selective institutions or instruction may be found within state-supported secondary education. There are even religious-oriented and single-sex schools among the state-supported secondary schools.

Hence, it would be deceptive to conclude that the educational system no longer oper-

ates in a selective manner that perpetuates the disproportionate number of individuals from upper-middle to upper-class backgrounds in elite roles in Great Britain. It remains true that the overwhelming preponderance of political leaders (i.e., MPs—especially front benchers—and members of the higher civil service) are university educated, and a disproportionate number of them are graduates of the prestige universities (i.e., Oxford and Cambridge). Of 18 twentieth-century prime ministers, 11 were graduates of a university, and 9 of these were from either Oxford or Cambridge. While some graduates of state-supported schools pass the difficult entrance exams and attend "Oxbridge," it is much more common for the university-track graduates of such state-supported schools to attend one of the respectable but less prestigious universities.

The more likely road to Oxbridge is via one of Britain's famed "public" schools—a set of expensive and academically demanding private boarding schools, including those with such legendary names as Eton, Rugby, Winchester, Shewsbury, and Harrow, schools in the "Mr. Chips" tradition that methodically train their pupils in the lore of classic education that they need to gain admission to the Oxbridge universities (see Figure 3-8). For example, of the 13 leaders of the Conservative Party in the twentieth century, 9 were graduates of the prestigious public schools, and 11 graduated from a university. (Three of the four non–public school graduates are the three most recent leaders, perhaps indicating a weakening of that tradition. Thatcher made it to Oxford from a grammar school background by passing her "11-plus.") The common feeding institutions for the very selective public schools are private primary boarding schools, such as Sunnyvale, that rigorously prep their youngsters in the skills they need to pass the tests to get into a public school. Moreover, even if a very bright

FIGURE 3-8   Students going to class at Eton College, one of Britain's most prestigious "public" schools (private boarding schools). Note the full dress uniform the boys are required to wear, a uniform that the student body recently voted to keep as a mark of their distinctiveness.

working-class youngster were to pass the exams to get into a British public school, there would still remain the problem of the steep tuition. Eton, for example, charges over £10,000 per year per child in a nation in which the median income is a little over £12,000. Only a very limited number of scholarships are available.

Thus while the abolition of the 11-plus exams and of the clear distinction between the university-track grammar schols and the terminal-education secondary modern schools in favor of comprehensive schools appears to end the highly selective process of recruiting political elites, in reality the public school tradition continues to reduce the ap-

plicant pool for elite roles significantly. Furthermore, a growing dissatisfaction in some circles over the quality of education provided by comprehensive schools has resulted in a government attempt in 1989 to subsidize the building of some six hundred selective grammar schools, a move that has been vigorously opposed by the Labour Party and by egalitarians throughout the system. At present over one hundred grammar schools have in fact been reestablished.

Student performance has been measured by a comprehensive exam taken at the end of secondary education at the age of 16: the GCSEs. Performance on these exams has been unsatisfactory compared to performance on similar exams in other European nations, but improved somewhat in the figures released in 1994. Meanwhile, in 1995 students will again be taking an 11-plus exam, not to segregate them into academic or terminal education, as before, but to provide a basis of guiding them and evaluating their progress. Students who do well on their GCSEs may be advised to study another two years for their "A levels," which measure how many subjects they have mastered at the advanced competency levels. Successful performance on the "A levels" is the key to admission to the prestigious universities.

The appearance of egalitarian change did not alter the essence of the educational system, especially its tendency to perpetuate the existing class stratification. Also unchanged is the tendency to emphasize classically educated generalists as opposed to technically trained specialists, despite the imperatives of a postindustrial society for trained technocrats. The cream of British university students still eschew business or technical professions in favor of the civil service, politics, teaching, the clergy, or military service. Thus both the educational system and its students have been slow to adapt to the demands of the postindustrial world, possibly to Britain's competitive disadvantage.

Thus, the tradition and continuity that many people had identified as a source of strength in the British system are now seen as an impediment to its successful adaptation to a world that is rapidly changing. The inability of the party system to adopt to and represent the newer postmaterialist values alluded to above has resulted in a widespread dealignment and diminished relevance for that system. Change is coming, as one can see from the flux that is engulfing the party system that not too long ago had been accepted as a fixture on the British landscape. However, the change is being resisted to a large extent by that system, as seen in the apparent

demise of the Alliance and its successors, the Social and Liberal Democrats, as a major force threatening the monopoly of Labour on the role of the loyal opposition. This attests to the resiliency of the essentially two-party system.

THE GOVERNMENT IN DISARRAY: DIVISION OVER THE NATURE OF CHANGE

Change in British politics is unplanned, erratic, and still resisted to a large extent. The British, with their commitment to incrementalism, appear incapable of thinking systematically about the future. Their uncertain commitment to change may be seen in the end of the reign of Prime Minister Thatcher, the "Iron Lady," in December 1990, and in the deep splits within the ruling Conservative Party over fundamental issues, including what some see as the most basic issue faced by a modern British government—Britain's participation in and possible subsumption within a European federalism based in Brussels and dominated by either Germany or a Franco-German alliance.

Recall from our earlier discussion that there has been a split in the Conservative Party between the supporters of Thatcher and those who opposed her on grounds of both style and policy substance. This opposition was first mobilized in the unprecedented challenge to a sitting prime minister as party leader by Sir Anthony Meyers in the fall of 1989, a challenge that apparently legitimized such a stand. Not only was Thatcher ultimately deposed in 1990, but in the fall of 1994 there was serious talk of a challenge to Prime Minister John Major over the continuing split in the Tory Party, to a large extent driven by the issue of integration with Europe.

Thatcher and many of her followers

strongly resisted pressures to surrender aspects of Britain's sovereign prerogatives to the concept of European unity. Those in the party who supported a commitment to Europe were called the "wets," while those who resisted that commitment were called the "drys." This conflict reflects a longstanding British ambivalence about becoming part of Europe rather than concentrating on older Commonwealth and Anglo-American ties. In the fall of 1990, the Lord President of the Council and leader of the House of Commons (in effect, deputy prime minister), the Right Honourable Sir Geoffrey Howe, resigned from the cabinet and then gave a notable speech in the House excoriating Thatcher's reluctance to commit to Europe. On top of the numerous other cabinet resignations that we have noticed, this loss of one of the most respected men in the party seriously weakened Thatcher's political position.

Meanwhile, the Right Honourable Michael Heseltine, a charismatic figure from the traditional wing of the party and an earlier defector from the Thatcher government, had been circulating about England in numerous public appearances, and, while not declaring himself a candidate to succeed Thatcher, allowed himself to become identified as the focus of the opposition to her. Finally, in December 1990, Heseltine formally challenged her reelection as party leader.

Heseltine surprised most observers of British politics by receiving enough support to prevent Thatcher from achieving a first-ballot victory. The rule, which Thatcher had engineered and used to unseat party leader Ted Heath when she assumed the leadership role, is that the winner must win by a margin of 15 percent of the votes cast. Of the 374 Conservatives in the House, Thatcher received 204 votes and Heseltine 152, with 18 abstentions. This was two votes short of the 15 percent majority that she needed to claim a first-ballot victory.

For a second-ballot victory, a candidate only needs a majority of the votes cast, but other candidates may now enter the contest. Accordingly, the Right Honourable John Major, Chancellor of the Exchequer, and the Right Honourable Douglas Hurd, the foreign secretary (technically, secretary of state for foreign and Commonwealth affairs), submitted their names. Thatcher was quickly informed of a defection in her intitial support, as some of those supporting the prime minister out of loyalty were eager to have her replaced with someone more electable and less divisive within the party. Thatcher, rather than go down to defeat, resigned and threw her support to Major, who had been a Thatcher protégé. In the ensuing three-way vote on the second ballot, Major fell two votes short of the majority he needed; however, Heseltine and Hurd withdrew in his favor, and Major's election was declared to be unanimous.

By resigning in his favor, Thatcher was instrumental in the selection of her successor, John Major. Although considered her protégé, he has turned out to be a very different kind of prime minister. He has been much more of a conciliator than a person driven, as Thatcher was, by principle. Consequently, he has been perceived as weak by many from the Thatcherite wing of the party, as when, in 1994, he backed off from plans to privatize the Royal Mail in the face of strong backbench opposition. More significantly, Major has moved away from the Thatcherite position on the question of Britain's commitment to Europe.

Thus, when, in November 1994, he tabled a bill to increase Britain's financial contribution to the European Community, a revolt was generated by the Euro-skeptics on the Tory back bench. Major not only quelled the revolt by declaring the issue to be one of confidence, but withdrew the whip from those eight MPs who did not support the government's position. Withdrawal of the whip effectively means that the MPs so stigmatized cannot participate in the affairs of the parliamentary party, such as voting on party leader or attending meetings such as the 1922 Committee. The eight unwhipped MPs, plus one more who voluntarily resigned from the parliamentary party, crossed the floor to defeat the government in the crucial division on raising the value-added tax on heating fuel on December 6, 1994. This is further evidence of the weakening of the once vaunted British party discipline, a trend that, if it continues, would threaten the stability of Britain's cabinet system of government. As of December 1994, Major's beleaguered Conservative government was a minority government, and a vote of no confidence before the next scheduled general elections appeared possible. Although the reinstatement of the rebels makes such a removal of the Major government unlikely, that government continues to be attacked from its own backbenches as well as from across the floor. In summer, 1995, Major, in a move to confront his critics, resigned as party leader and then stood for reelection. He won that election against a weak challenger, Secretary of State for Wales, John Redwood. Major thus strengthened his position within the party but the party remained some 50 points behind Labour in the polls as of 1995.

Thus, it is now clear that Major is no Thatcher. He lacks her charisma and has already shown that he cannot rouse the passions during prime minister's question time in Commons, as did the "Iron Lady" from time to time. He is the second British prime minister in this century and the first from the Tory Party who did not attend college or university. Major finished his formal education at the age of 16, like nearly all Britishers who do not go on to college. In this, he is as much outside the "old boy network" as was Thatcher. Major is a self-made man who can

more readily identify with and garner the support of working-class Tories, many of whom were alienated by Thatcher's austere and elitist style. More importantly, Major appears to be less of an ideologue and more amenable to the collegial style demanded by the British cabinet tradition; therefore, he may be more amenable to the British pragmatic and incremental style of politics.

The Labour Party also appears to be badly divided over the abandonment of principle by a more pragmatically driven leadership. Tony Blair's move to modify Labour's commitment to public ownership has angered the party's militants and its left wing, as noted. In 1994, he aroused another negative reaction among the Labour left by choosing to send his son to a grant-maintained secondary school. (Recall that such schools may "opt out" of control by local education authorities and set their own policies.) These schools, including the one selected by the Blairs, tend to be academically selective, which offended the egalitarian sensibilities of the Labour left. Labour is therefore on the record as opposing the option of grant-maintained independence for selected government schools putting Blair in direct conflict with the policies of his own party.

Despite some convergence of the two major parties toward their respective pragmatic centers, fundamental differences in their constitutional import remain. The Labour Party is committed to a basic restructuring of the House of Lords, the establishment of national parliaments in Scotland and Wales, and a more unequivocal support of British integration into the European Community. Moreover, Labourites have suggested that they would reconsider the question of reform of the electoral system to accommodate a measure of proportionality, and Labour's commitment to the preservation of the beleaguered monarchy is clearly in question. It is arguable that these moves would fundamentally alter Britain's constitutional structure. Perhaps the most controversial prospective change is the announcement by "shadow" Home Secretary, Jack Straw, in December 1994 that a Labour government would reduce the scope of monarchial activities, lower the number of the members of the royal family expected to perform official duties from the present 15 or so to a core of about 6, and abolish the royal prerogative to dissolve Parliament and give or withhold assent to acts of Parliament. Straw argued that the current monarchy represents privilege, as opposed to a simpler monarchy appropriate for a "classless society." Support for reforms of the monarchy along some of these lines, especially the trimming of the size of the state-supported royal family, may be widespread among the British, including the queen and the Prince of Wales. However, support for the monarchy as a constitutional symbol remains strong among the British public, and there was fear among some Labour supporters that just when the party had shed its radical image among middle-class voters, Straw and his followers may have renewed grounds for middle-class distrust of a Labour government.

It is unclear at this writing whether the British public is committed to such basic change in their constitutional system. Major's perceived weakness as a leader, disarray in the Conservative Party, public disenchantment with a party that has been in power for a long time, and the wide, charismatic appeal of the youthful Tony Blair have combined to give Labour a substantial lead in public opinion polls two years before the scheduled general elections. How the issues of constitutional change will be received by the British voters in those two years remains to be seen.

There is much to recommend Britain's style of pragmatic incrementalism in policy making, as attested by its record as one of the world's first successful modern democracies and one of the world's great powers for centuries. The open question is whether that style can adapt to the very different imperatives of a postindustrial world that is changing more quickly and more fundamentally than at any time in human history.

NOTES

1. Richard Rose, *Politics in England,* 4th ed. (Boston: Little Brown, 1986), p. 3, describes England as "the prototype of a country enjoying both stable and representative government. Its political institutions have served as a model on every continent."

2. "Toward a More Responsible Two-Party System: A Report of the Committee on Political Parties of the American Political Science Association," *American Political Science Review* (supplement), vol. XXLIV, no. 3, pt. 2 (September 1950).

3. Cf. Leslie Lipson, "The Two-Party System in British Politics," *American Political Science Review,* vol. XLVII, no. 2 (June 1953), pp. 337–58; with James Alt, "Dealiagnment and the Dynamics of Partisanship in Britain," in Russell Dalton, Scott Flanagan, and Paul Beck, eds., *Electoral Change in Advanced Industrial Societies* (Princeton: Princeton University Press, 1984), pp. 298–329.

4. For example, Rose, in *Politics in England,* p. 13, writes, "In England politics has evolved very gradually."

5. Keith Thomas, "The United Kingdom," in Raymond Grew, ed. *Crises of Political Development in Europe and the United States* (Princeton: Princeton University Press, 1978), p. 45.

6. Ibid.

7. Barrington Moore, Jr., *The Social Origins of Democracy and Dictatorship* (Boston: The Beacon Press, 1966), p. 28.

8. Charles Lindblom, "The Science of Muddling Through," *Public Administration Review,* vol. 29, no. 2 (Spring 1959), pp. 79–88. See also Robert Jessop, *Traditionalism, Conservatism, and the British Political Culture* (London: George Allen and Unwin, 1974).

9. For a summary of some of this literature, see William Gwyn, "Jeremiahs and Pragmatists: Perceptions of British Decline," in Richard Rose and William Gwyn, eds., *Britain—Progress and Decline* (London: The Macmillam Co., 1980).

10. Chas. Murray, "The Underclass: The Alienated Poor Are Devastating America's Cities. Is the Same Thing Happening Here?" *The Sunday Times Magazine,* November 26, 1989, pp. 26–51.

11. Mark Hagopian, *Regimes, Movements, and Ideologies*, 2nd ed. (New York: Longmans, 1984), p. 25.

12. *London Times*, November 16, 1989, p. 7.

13. The concept of political style is eloquently developed by Herbert Spiro, *Government by Constitution* (New York: Random House, 1959), chaps. 13–15.

14. On the relationship between political style and culture or national character, see Ibid., pp. 192–93.

15. See James Cristoph, "Consensus and Cleavage in British Political Ideology," *American Political Science Review*, vol. 59, no. 3 (September 1965), p. 631.

16. Bejamin Cardozo, *The Nature of the Judicial Process* (New Haven: Yale University Press, 1921), p. 23. Cardozo's book is a classic exposition of the nature and spirit of the common law.

17. Ibid., p. 33.

18. Winston Churchill, The Birth of Britain (New York: Dodd Mead, 1956), p. 216.

19. Anthony King, "Margaret Thatcher: The Outsider as Political Leader," paper presented to the 1989 meeting of the American Political Science Association, September 1989, Atlanta.

20. Harry Eckstein, "A Theory of Stable Democracy," Appendix B in *Division and Cohesion in Democracy: A Study of Norway* (Princeton: Princeton University Press, 1966), pp. 225–88; Harry Eckstein, "Authority Patterns: A Structural Basis for Political Inquiry," *American Political Science Review*, vol. 67, no. 4 (December 1973), pp. 1142–61; Harry Eckstein, "Authority Patterns and Governmental Performance: A Theoretical Framework," *Comparative Political Studies*, vol. 2, no. 3 (October 1969), pp. 269–326.

21. Walter Bagehot, *The English Constitution* (New York: Doubleday Dolphin Books, 1872), p. 13.

22. Gabriel Almond and Sidney Verba, *The Civic Culture* (Boston: Little Brown, 1965), p. 315; Eric Nordlinger, *Working Class Tories* (London: McGibbon and Kese, 1967). Cf. Samuel Beer, "The British Political System," in Samuel Beer and Adam Ulam, eds., *Patterns of Government*, 3rd ed. (New York: Random House, 1973), p. 130.

23. David Butler and Donald Stokes, *Political Change in Britain: Forces Shaping Electoral Choice* (New York: St. Martin's Press, 1969), p. 67.

24. See, e.g., Dennis Kavenaugh, "Political Culture in Great Britain: The Decline of the Civic Culture," in Gabriel Almond and Sidney Verba, eds., *The Civic Culture Revisited* (Boston: Little Brown, 1980), pp. 156–60. Cf. Samuel Beer, *Britain Against Itself: The Political Contradictions of Collectivism* (New York: Norton, 1982), part 3, "The Collapse of Deference," along with his earlier assessment of the British culture cited in n. 22. Cf. also Dennis Kavenaugh, "The Deferential English: A Comparative Critique," *Government and Opposition* (1971).

25. Alan Marsh, *Protest and Political Consciousness* (London: Sage, 1978).

26. Almond and Verba, *The Civic Culture.*

27. Robert Alford, *Party and Society* (Chicago: Rand McNally, 1963).

28. Ibid., p. 102.

29. Roger Brown, *Social Psychology* (New York: The Free Press, 1965), p. 114.

30. Richard Rose and Ian McCallister, *Voters Begin to Choose: From Closed Class to Open Elections in Britain* (Beverly Hills: Sage Publications, 1986).

31. Samuel Beer, *Britain Against Itself,* pp. 30–31. Beer refers to these aggressive individual and group demands as the "pay scramble," the "subsidy scramble," and the "benefits scramble."

32. *London Times,* November 26, 1989.

33. See n. 2.

34. E. E. Schattschneider, *Party Government* (New York: Rinehart and Co., 1942), p. 208.

35. Richard Rose, *The Problem of Party Government* (London: The Macmillan Co., 1974).

36. Cf. Leon Epstein, *Political Parties in Western Democracies* (New York: Praeger, 1972), p. 323.

37. Richard Rose, *Do Parties Make a Difference?* 2nd ed. (Chatham, NJ: Chatham House, 1984), pp. 20–27.

38. Ibid., p. 44.

39. See ibid., p. 47.

40. *Washington Post*, September 15, 1991, p. A31.

41. *London Times*, September 28, 19__, p. 9.

42. Lipson, "The Two-Party System."

43. Risto Sankiaho, "Political Remobilization in Welfare States," in Dalton, Flanagan, and Beck, *Electoral Change*, p. 82.

44. R. T. McKenzie, *British Political Parties* (New York: St. Martin's Press, 1963).

45. Two Tory MPs, Graham Riddick and David Tredinnick, accepted £1,000 each for asking questions in commons in Summer, 1994. *The Guardian*, December 8, 1994, p. 3.

46. Harold Campell and Marianne Stewart, "Dealignment of Degree: Partisan Change in Britain, 1974–1983," *Journal of Politics*, vol. 43, no. 3 (August 1984), pp. 689–719.

47. See, for example, Jonathan Dimbleby, *The Prince of Wales: An Authorized Biography* (London: Little Brown, 1994); Andrew Morton, *Diana: Her New Life* (London: Michael O'Mara Books, 1994); and Anna Pasternak, *Princess in Love* (London: Bloomsbury Publishing Co., 1994).

48. A. G. Jordan and J. J. Richardson, *British Politics the Policy Process* (London: Unwin Hyman, 198__ 149.

49. See the discussion of the impact of the phy of the House and the decision to rebuild been before it was bombed in Eric Tayl *of Commons at Work* (Baltimore: P 1963), chap. 1.

50. Karl Bracher, "Problems of Parliamentary Democracy in Europe," *Daedalus* (Winter 1964), pp. 179–98.

51. E.g., Bernard Crick, *The Reform of Parliament* (New York: Doubleday Anchor, 1965).

52. Hugh Heclo, *Modern Social Politics in Britain and Sweden* (New York: Yale University Press, 1974), p. 87.

53. See W. A. Robson, "Ministerial Control of Nationalized Industries," *Political Quarterly* (1969) A. H. Hanson, *Parliament and Public Ownership*

54. Joseph Schumpeter, *Capitalism, Socialism and Democracy* (New York: Harper Torchbooks, 1950).

55. The most complete discussion of the National Health Service to date is Rob Baggot, *Health and Health Care in Britain* (New York: St. Martin's Press, 1994). See also Harry Eckstein, *The English Health Service* (Stanford: Stanford University Press, 1958); and Harry Eckstein, *Pressure Group Politics: The Case of the British Medical Association* (Stanford: Stanford University Press, 1960).

56. On rationing in the British system, see Robert Baker, "The Inevitability of Health Care Rationing: A Case Study of Rationing in the British National Health Service," in Martin Strosberg et al., *Rationing America's Health Care: The Oregon Plan and Beyond* (Washington, DC: The Brookings Institute, 1992), pp. 208–30.

57. Cited in Clarke Cochran, Lawrence Mayer, Joseph Cayer, and T. R. Carr, *American Public Policy,* 2nd ed. (New York: St. Martin's Press, 1986), p. 228.

58. Charles Taylor and David Jodice, *World Handbook of Social and Political Indicators,* 3rd ed., vol. 1 (New Haven: Yale University Press, 1983), p. 15.

59. R. M. Punnett, *British Government and Politics* (Chicago: The Dorsey Press, 1986), p. 388.

60. Rose, *Politics in England,* p. 385.

61. Michael Elliot, "Sammy and Rosie Get Paid," *The New Republic* (February 15, 1988), p. 15.

62. *The Economist,* vol. 333, no. 7891 (November 26–December 2, 1994), p. 35.

63. E.g., R. Emmett Tyrell, Jr., ed., *The Future That Doesn't Work: Social Democracy's Failures in Britain* (Garden City, NJ: Doubleday, 1977).

64. Lindblom, "Muddling Through."

4

Government and Politics in France: The End of French Exceptionalism

"*Plus ça change, plus c'est la même chose* (The more things change, the more they remain the same)."
"The French Revolution is now ended."

François Furet, 1988

The epigrams for this chapter suggest a steadfast consistency within France, which the French scholar Raymond Aron also suggested in the title to his 1959 book: *France Steadfast and Changing*.[1] They connote a nation that has been locked into a two-hundred-year-old pattern of ideologically refighting the issues generated from the Revolution of 1789, resisting the attributes of modernization found elsewhere in the Western world, and reeling from one political crisis to the next. The lasting impact of the Revolution made France in important respects unique among nations in the West, a position that Ronald Teirsky insightfully calls "French exceptionalism."[2] Hence, the image of the French political system that a casual student of French political history may acquire is one of extreme constitutional and, in some regimes, cabinet instability. Indeed, at this writing, France has experienced some 12 constitutional changes since 1789 (see Table 4-1). Yet, despite all of this political upheaval, France has shown a rather consistent pattern in its constitutional formats and in its approach to resolving political issues; this is the source of the changing yet steadfast image that formed the basis of French "exceptionalism." Hence, the first quotation is intended to indicate that after the turmoil of all of its constitutional instability over the past two hundred years, the essential style of French politics has consistently reflected an unresolved contradiction in the French conception of authority, a contradiction that was itself manifested in the major forces in the Revolution of 1789.

This image of persistent "exceptionalism" must be contrasted to François Furet's now widely quoted declaration, "The French Revolution is now ended."[3] Furet means that the ideological struggles of that cataclysmic event have finally been played out, and that the unique aspects of French politics have given

TABLE 4-1   French Regimes

Until 1789	*Ancien régime*
1789–91	Constituent Assembly (constitutional monarchy); ended with the Revolution
1792–99	Convention and Directory (First Republic); ended with a coup
1799–1804	Consulate ⎫
1804–15	Empire ⎭ Napoleonic dictatorship
1815–30	Bourbon restoration of Louis XVIII (to 1824) and Charles X (to 1830); ended with revolution
1830–48	July Monarchy of the Orleanist Louis Philippe; ended with revolution
1848–52	Second Republic with Louis Napoleon as president
1852–70	Second Empire with Napoleon III; ended with military defeat
1870–1940	Third Republic; ended with military defeat
1940–44	Vichy under Marshal Pétain, an Axis collaborationist
1946–58	Fourth Republic; ended with the threat of military uprising
1959–present	Fifth Republic (originally called the de Gaulle Republic)

way to the politics of negotiation and compromise over pragmatic questions of interest and of the allocation of the scarce resources of the society. This chapter will attempt to show that while for nearly the two centuries following the Revolution France was unique among Western powers in remaining an imperfectly modernized, segmentally divided, and ideologically rent society, recent decades have witnessed a transformation of that society to one that more closely resembles other Western powers. The France of today is more modernized, less ideologically oriented, more legitimate, and thus less unique than the France of the immediate post–World War II period.

Although France cannot boast of the evolutionary heritage that, as we saw in Chapter 3, characterizes England, the impact of the past is no less influential on present French politics. Indeed, many have concluded that France has continued to fight atavistic battles stemming from that cataclysmic revolution until recent decades. (Even if the struggles of the Revolution are over, their impact has so shaped modern French politics that one must understand the past in order to understand the present.)

THE IMPACT OF THE PAST: FRANCE'S REVOLUTIONARY LEGACY

Paradoxically, France, a nation that has been widely perceived in modern times as a less successful democracy than Great Britain, has been aptly characterized as more quintessentially modern than Britain. *Modernization* in this school of thought implies the centralization of authority and the subordination of competing sources of authority, such as the nobility or feudal institutions; the concomitant development of the concept of *sovereignty* (the final or ultimate power to make and enforce law over individuals) as opposed to the medieval and ultimately common law concept that the law is somehow "found" in the customs and practices of the community, and the rationalization and impersonalization of authority as manifested in the growth of centralized bureaucracies.

Beset with the centrifugal forces of permeable borders, France, like Germany and the other nations on the broad plain of Europe running from the Atlantic to the Urals, had a more difficult time with the nation-building process than did the geographically isolated Great Britain. Specifically, the English monarchy resolved what Lucien Pye called "the crisis of penetration,"[4] or the establishment of the authority of national government in the various corners of the realm over which it supposedly reigned, at about the time of Henry II, who ruled in the second half of the twelfth century. The more or less effective consolidation of France under control of the monarchy occurred under Louis XI in the late fifteenth century, about the same time as the consolidation of Sweden under Gustav Vasa (in about 1500). The key point here is that the effective consolidation of France lagged several centuries behind the idea of a French nation, which can probably be traced back as far as Phillip Augustus (1180–1223), while in England the process of nation building more or less coincided with the growth of the idea of an English nation. Hence, due to the difficulty experienced by the French monarchy in subjecting autonomous and centrifugal forces to its control, the French monarchy was less tolerant of the retention or growth of the power of such independent forces—the process of *going out of court* discussed in the previous chapter on Britain.

The centralizing imperatives of the French monarchy were exacerbated during the Hundred Years' War (1337–1453), when the French nobility, unlike their English counterparts, lacked an independent financial base and grew more dependent on the court for protection against the bands of English brigands who roamed about French soil attempting to regain the Normandy that English kings had claimed for themselves some 138 years after the Norman Conquest of 1066. While English monarchs were compromising first with their nobility and then with the rising institution of Parliament, the French monarchy was evolving into the model of royal absolutism epitomized by the Sun King, Louis XIV, whose reign might have best been characterized by his probably apocryphal

claim, "L'Etat c'est moi" ("I am the state"). The resulting decentralization of the English system that recognized or even restored feudal and baronial prerogatives and degrees of local autonomy facilitated that nation's evolution toward more democratic forms, but this decentralized regime was less modern, according to Samuel Huntington, than the simple, centralized, and rationalized regimes of the Continent.[5] Huntington further suggests an inverse relationship between the modernization of governmental institutions on the one hand—the growth and rationalization of bureaucracies, including the functional differentiation of structures, and the legitimation of the sovereignty of the central government—and the growth of citizen participation and the evolution of democratic forms on the other.[6]

While by the sixteenth century France had evolved into one of the most centralized and, in the sense of actually exercising control over the citizens of its realm (collecting taxes and the like), efficient monarchies in the West, in the beginning of the fourteenth century France remained a collection of autonomous feudal principalities, some of which were ruled by the French kings (e.g., Normandy, Picardy, and Champagne). Other fiefdoms, such as Valois, Anjou, and Bourbon, were under the control of relatives of the French kings, giving those kings an indirect control. However, other areas, such as Armagnac, Artois, Blois, and Limoges, were governed by feudal lords frequently in conflict with the emerging French monarchy.[7] Some parts were controlled by Edward III of England, and even more, such as the important cities of Crécy, Calais, and ultimately, Poitiers, were lost to Edward, the "Black Prince," in the Hundred Years' War. These defeats, combined with the spread of the bubonic plague of 1348–49, a rat-borne bacterial infection that killed perhaps a quarter of all the people in Europe, brought chaos to

France and greatly impeded its nation-building process.[8] However, the plague also contributed to the undermining of feudalism by eliminating about 40 percent of the tillers of the land. Fourteenth-century France thus stood in sharp contrast to England, with its relatively efficient monarchy that had evolved almost a century earlier.

These difficulties in the French nation-building process created a monarchy that was highly centralized and increasingly out of touch with and unconcerned about the social forces and demands that were coming into being with the onset of the modern age. The monarchy had largely consolidated its power by the late sixteenth century under the reign of Henry IV. Henry was assassinated, however, in 1610, and Louis XIII, a boy of nine, ascended to the throne. The real power fell to the austere and autocratic Cardinal Richelieu, who set about suppressing the nobility, local officials, and finally the Estates General as competing and balancing powers to the throne.

France emerged in 1648 from the Thirty Years' War, the last of a series of religious wars that decimated much of Europe, especially Germany, as the preponderant power in Europe. The Huguenots (French Protestants), after having suffered the Saint Bartholomew's Day massacre in which some ten thousand were slaughtered in 1572, were merely tolerated under the Edict of Nantes and never became a sociopolitical force in France. They were ultimately driven from France in 1685, and the Catholic Church and the monarchy became mutually supportive. The effective suppression of the Protestants removed the religious struggles emanating from the Reformation from the French sociopolitical agenda; hence, France was to a large extent spared the devastation that these conflicts brought to Germany and other areas.

French absolutism peaked with the reign of the powerful and effective Louis XIV. His successor, Louis XV, was preoccupied with his mistresses and indifferent to affairs of state. Louis XVI was similarly indifferent to the affairs of state; clocks were his passion. The profligate spending to maintain the opulent court that Louis XIV made famous, and the exemption of the first two estates—the nobility and the clergy—from the principal tax, helped create a government that was chronically short of money in a relatively prosperous society.[9] This situation in turn led to a government that was inefficient and vulnerable to criticism and a society with the comfort and leisure to undertake that criticism.

The eighteenth century brought the Enlightenment, or the Age of Reason, a period in Western history characterized by the breakdown of the pieties and certainties of the Age of Faith, or the Middle Ages, which had been characterized by the dominance of the Universal Church, or *Pax Christiana*. The Enlightenment was an age of intense intellectual activity, much of it critical of established institutions, as intellectuals are wont to be. The institution of monarchial absolutism was especially vulnerable to the intellectual assault on the irrational and traditional, an assault that was especially strong among French intellectuals such as Voltaire, Condorcet, Montesquieu, and Rousseau. Crane Brinton, in his now classic theoretical perspective on revolutions, asserts that the "desertion of the intellectuals"—the tendency for people of ideas to attack the most fundamental and essential institutions of their system rather than merely to advocate their change or reform—is a consistent pattern of societies in the decades immediately prior to the great revolutions.[10]

Jean-Jacques Rousseau's philosophy had an especially strong and unique impact on French thinking about government in general and about the issue of liberty versus authority in particular. His book, *The Social Con-*

tract, has been called the Bible of the French Revolution. Beginning with an assumption of a state of nature in the tradition of John Locke and Thomas Hobbes a century earlier, Rousseau argued that the only legitimate purpose of government intrusion on this natural freedom is that the rulers serve what he called "le volonté generale" (the general will). The revolutionary implications of this statement are that disobedience and ultimately revolution become justified against any rule that fails to serve the general will. However, unlike the individualistic orientation of Locke, who was so influential in Anglo-American political thought, Rousseau's general will was conceptualized in a mystical, communitarian sense. Rousseau was a romantic, stressing emotions and remaining fundamentally at odds with the rationalism of the Enlightenment. He conceived state to be an organic reality over the sum of individuals who dwelt therein, a community that entailed essential and knowable values and was capable of possessing a will that was distinct from the demands of any proportion of its individual citizens, majority or otherwise.

In this way, Rousseau's general will had implications that has served the purposes of modern dictatorships as well. A ruler's legitimacy derives from the fact that he, she, or they embody the general will; yet, this general will, being undefined by any regularized procedures such as elections, legislatures, or majority rule, is left to the ruler to identify. In this way, a Hitler could legitimize his rule as embodying "the spirit of the folk," the essence of which was defined by the Nazis themselves.[11] Hence, far from being a constraint upon a ruler and a force for accountability, the concept of the general will could be used by an unrestrained ruler as an instrument for the mobilization of the masses.

Rousseau argued that the presence of "intermediaries" between the individual citizen and the ruler would distort the expression of the general will. Hence, the Rousseauian model does not fully accept the legitimacy of political parties, interest groups, or even representative assemblies. Rather, its vision of democracy is what William Kornhouser called a *mass society,*[12] one composed of atomized individuals with a low level of associational life between such individuals and the state. Not only are these individuals vulnerable to mobilization from above, but the state is uninsulated from the momentary and often irrational passions of the masses and hence unable to govern. Such a society by definition lacks the level of *institutionalization,* the legitimation of established patterns of procedure and interaction, that Huntington and others have shown to be requisite for stability.[13] This distrust of secondary associations was echoed certainly by Charles de Gaulle and contributed to a lowered level of associational life when he was in power; however, more recent decades have brought such a substantial growth in secondary associations in French society that by 1977, a poll indicates that some 61 percent of French men and 43 percent of French women belong to at least one secondary association. However, France, while now more pluralist than it traditionally had been, still is less so than other Western powers. For example, Henry Ehrman and Martin Schain show that a significantly smaller percentage of the salaried work force in France is unionized than in other Western nations (See Table 4-2).

France has retained a deep distrust of parties and legislative assemblies, a distrust that has at least been nurtured and exacerbated by the impact of Rousseau. The need for a symbolic, direct connection between the ruler and the general will is manifested in the plebiscitary form of democracy manifested in the present Fifth Republic. These plebiscites ask the public to approve a policy that has already been adopted by the elites, without a

TABLE 4-2 The Unionization of the Salaried Work Force in Industrialized Nations, 1989

Country	Percent of Work Force Unionized
France	10
United States	18
Japan	28
West Germany	43
Great Britain	40
Italy	39
Belgium	75
Sweden	83

Source: Henry Ehrman and Martin Schain, *Politics in France,* 5th ed. (New York: Harper-Collins, 1992), p. 177.

satisfactory alternative to such approval, as opposed to asking the public to choose directly between viable alternatives of policy. Such plebiscites thus offer the symbolism of mass participation without the reality of mass impact on policy choices. While by-passing and denigrating the role of representative institutions and intermediary groups that could impose a structure of accountability on a powerful national executive, decisions by plebiscite in effect transform the decisions of that unaccountable elite into a kind of general will.

Rousseau's communitarian conception of the general will is also incompatible with the concept of *pluralism,* the legitimacy of different interests and perspectives on the public good and policy as the outcome of bargaining and compromise among the organized manifestations of these differing perspectives. Community theory stresses the existence of knowable values that define the essence of the community and has little place for the institutionalized tolerance that characterizes the open society of Anglo-American democracy.

This monistic interpretation of the Rousseauian perspective was clearly mani-

fested in the meteoric career of Maximilien Robespierre—a lawyer, passionate disciple of Rousseau, and director of the radical Committee of Public Safety. The Committee, under Robespierre's direction, carried out what has been called the "Reign of Terror," the guillotining of perhaps some forty thousand persons, including entire families of nobles or suspected royalists, and anyone else suspected of disloyalty to the Revolution. This disloyalty became broadly defined as any disagreement with Robespierre and the Committee, and the condemned included many bourgeois and peasants as well as those early leaders of the Revolution such as Jacques Danton, who broke with Robespierres's radical faction over the extent of the terror. Ultimately, Robespierre himself met the fate to which he condemned so many others, and the radical Reign of Terror came to an end.

With the end of the Reign of Terror, the radical phase of the Revolution was supplanted by the Thermidorian Reaction, which fits with Brinton's theory on the pattern of great revolutions: a moderate phase followed by an anarchic radical phase, followed in turn by an authoritarian retrenchment or a stabilizing period of institutionalizing change and returning to order. The French Thermidorian Reaction was coopted by Napoleon Bonaparte's Consulate in 1799, a regime that might be characterized as an enlightened dictatorship.

The impact of the Revolution on subsequent French history and on modern French politics has been substantial in a number of respects. First, while the aforementioned difficulties in nation building produced a need in the French culture for a strong, centralized national government, the Revolution produced a need for a limited role of the state and an antipathy and perhaps a fear of face-to-face, direct authority relationships. As Stanley Hoffman has explicitly pointed out and other scholars have clearly implied, the need to reconcile these conflicting conceptions of authority was the constants in the various political systems that followed the Revolution.[14] Nicholas Wahl claimed that these "conflicting ideals of authority" have led to an alternation between two constitutional traditions, respectively representing "two approaches to the solution to political problems that have never been successfully merged or brought into compromise."[15] He calls these the "administrative" tradition and the "representative" tradition, respectively, the former embodying the need for a centralized authority and the absence of intermediary associations, and the latter embodying the extreme individualism and fear of authority that also emanated from the Revolution.

The Revolution was followed by the "benevolent dictatorship" of Napoleon Bonaparte from 1799 to 1814 (plus the "100 days"); the Bourbon restoration of Louis XVIII; the "July Monarchy" of Louis Philippe, brought about by the revolution of 1830 in reaction to Charles X's heavy-handed attempt to reconstruct much of the *ancien régime;* and the Second Empire of Louis Napoleon, nephew of the great Bonaparte, who made himself emperor of the French in 1852, after having been overwhelmingly elected president of the Second Republic following the French version of the revolutions that swept Europe in 1848. All of these regimes were in the administrative tradition of a strong centralized authority at the expense of representative or parliamentary institutions. Hence, after the chaotic cataclysm of three revolutions (1789, 1830, and 1848) overthrowing autocratic monarchs, France was governed by an autocratic monarch. "The more things change, the more they remain the same."

The "success" of three revolutions in a little over half a century left the legacy of the legitimation of violent revolution as a means of redressing political grievances, the so-called barricade tradition in French politics. (The term comes from the effective use of crude barricades to stop a modern army and neutralize its advantages in firepower and numbers in the very narrow streets of Paris.) Even more importantly, this revolutionary legacy legitimized the framing of political grievances in constitutional terms. Political forces dissatisfied with what is going on are prone to seek fundamental constitutional change as the means of redressing those grievances. By contrast, British and American forces have been generally more prone to take the fundamental rules of the game as givens and seek political goals through those rules.

Compared to the British experience described in Chapter 3, the French, due to their great Revolution and subsequent revolutions, were, until the Fifth Republic, unable to resolve the question of regime (i.e, what constitutional format should be used to govern the country) before the great divisive issues that all modern societies have had to face were generated by the politicization of the masses. This mobilization has been identified as one of the defining attributes of modernity because it generates a broad range of demands and expectations to which the state must adapt and react. While some scholars, such as Karl Deutsch, assume that the increased capacity of the political system to process issues is an inevitable result of the stress placed upon it by the increased quantity and complexity of demands, others, such as Huntington, distinguish the modernization of the demand-generating society from that of the political system that would have to satisfy those demands.[16] Thus, social modernization, as manifested in the *levée en masse* (the rising and politicization of the masses) that was one of the legacies of the French Revolution, came before the political effectiveness that is a concomitant of modern political institutions. This sequence is a formula for political and constitutional instability. The Revolution put the essence of the French regime itself on the table in the late eighteenth century (and for a century and a half thereafter), alongside the divisive issues that accompanied mass mobilization and the onset of the modern era, issues such as the relationship between church and state (temporarily resolved in what Stanley Hoffman calls "the republican synthesis" embodied by the Third Republic but remaining important enough to prevent practicing Catholics from ministerial roles through the Fourth Republic), and the social dislocations emanating from the process of urbanization and the industrial revolution. Issues such as these would be argued in terms of alternative types of regimes.[17] For example, the forces of privilege and tradition tended to favor a regime in the pattern of bureaucratic authoritarianism in the Bonapartist tradition discussed above, while the working classes and less traditional or less religious forces tended to favor the assembly-dominated republics in the tradition of the Third and Fourth Republics.

The Bonapartist military campaigns were fought in the name of the ideals of the Revolution: liberty, equality, fraternity, and the rights of man, although the institutions of Bonapartist France were certainly no manifestation of those ideals. Bonaparte's campaigns did spread the heretofore revolutionary concept that the masses had a legitimate role to play in politics and that they had rights that governments had an obligation to serve and respect. Once these concepts gained widespread dissemination and acceptance, the resolution of the question of regime would henceforth be rendered infinitely more difficult. Nations such as Great Britain and the Scandinavian regimes that essentially resolved this question before 1789 experienced much greater constitutional stability than those nations, such as Germany and Italy, that did not. Thus, the French Rev-

olution of 1789 and the Napoleonic wars fought in its name constitute a watershed in European history in the sense of their mobilization and politicization of the masses and their dissemination of the ideas of liberty, equality, fraternity, and the rights of man, even though the Revolution itself substantively resolved little.

This tendency to frame substantive issues in constitutional terms emanating from France's inability to resolve the question of regime is epitomized by the persisting issue of the relationship between church and state. As noted, the church and the monarchy in the *ancien régime* became mutually supportive, and in fact, leading ecclesiastics such as cardinals Richelieu and Marazin became among the most powerful figures in the secular political system. After Louis XIII assumed the throne at the age of nine, Richelieu became the real power behind the French throne. The church was understandably wary of any challenge to authority and traditional values. Moreover, the Constituent Assembly of the Revolution foolishly confiscated church properties, further incurring the enmity of the clergy and of serious Catholics. Consequently, the church opposed the Revolution at every stage and remained, for that matter, in a state of tension with liberal movements throughout Europe. In turn, advocates of republican formats in France saw the church as their enemy, to the point where practicing Catholic politicians were at a distinct disadvantage in the Third and Fourth Republics.

The conflict between French republicans and the forces of tradition including the church and the military came to a head in the notorious Dreyfus Affair in the early years of the Third Republic (1894–1906). The conflict became such a *cause célèbre* that *l'affaire Dreyfus* became simply known as *l'affaire*. Briefly, in the wake of the French defeat in the Franco-Prussian War, out of which the Third Republic was born, the French military elite and its supporters began to search for a scapegoat. Captain Dreyfus, the first Jew to reach the French general staff, was convicted of treason and sent to Devil's Island in a context of a deep strain of French anti-Semitism in which a Jew was regarded as somehow alien and therefore a perfect scapegoat. Amid growing evidence that the real traitor was an aristocratic Catholic royalist, the forces of the right fought to uphold the conviction so as to uphold the honor of the army and the church and to discredit the entire republic. The army was asserting its independence of public accountability in its decision to continue this punishment of a man they knew to be innocent for *raison d'état.* The affair was blown all out of proportion and was seen as a decisive battleground for the future of the Republic. Ultimately, the republican forces, led by such articulate intellectuals as Emile Zola in his article *J'Accuse,* carried the day, and Dreyfus was pardoned in 1899 and exonerated in 1906. *L'Affaire* further contributed to the discrediting of the church and its leaders among republicans. Its resolution ended the last serious onslaught on the republic by the forces of the traditional right, and the Third Republic, born out of defeat and characterized by its first president, Adolph Thiers, as "the regime that divides us the least," was France's longest lasting regime since the Revolution to date.

The Third and Fourth Republics were characterized by a weak executive, consequent cabinet instability, and a growing inability to govern through a crisis. France's traditionally fragmented party system (discussed below) meant that elections did not produce majorities or even strong pluralities; hence, all government consisted of coalitions that, in the divided and ideological cultural context to be described, did not easily reach the compromises needed to maintain them in office over a range of issues. The rise of the socialist left, culminating in Leon Blum's Popular Front of the 1930s, alarmed the conservative and even the centrist forces in the nation, rendering it more difficult to find a moderate republican majority to govern. Besides the antirepublican right and the radical left often being able to combine for a negative majority on confidence votes, individual deputies or even ministers in the government frequently voted no on confidence questions in the hope of obtaining a higher ministry in a reconstituted government. When Marshal MacMahon, the second president of the Third Republic and a monarchist, dissolved the Chamber of Deputies because it refused confidence to an antirepublican, conservative government, the power of dissolution became associated with antirepublican machinations and was consequently rendered politically unusable. In the Fourth Republic, the power of dissolution was constitutionally circumscribed by the requirement that it could only be used when governments fell by an absolute majority of the National Assembly, while governments regularly fell by relative majorities. Hence, deputies in the Third Republic or members of the Assembly had nothing to lose by voting a government out of power. The weakness of the political executive in the Third and Fourth Republics led to a stalemated political process for which the French had a name—*immobilisme.* The anti-authoritarian imperatives of the French culture manifested in the constitutional formats of the Third and Fourth Republics were balanced with the acceptance of a strong centralized bureaucracy that epitomized France's other authority tradition, as discussed below.[18] This balance between the conflicting "paradoxes of the French political community" made up part of what Hoffman refers to as "the Republican synthesis."[19] These systems were characterized by the strong, potentially centralized authority of the administrative structure, combined with a political structure that Hoffman calls non-interventionist in that it had neither the capacity nor the inclination to make and implement solutions to actual issues. Indeed, the Chamber of Deputies has been characterized as "the house without windows," signifying the extent to which the deputies in their political maneuvering were out of touch with public passions and needs.

In both the Third and Fourth Republics, governments fell and were reconstituted without recourse to the electoral process; hence, the lines of accountability as expressed through that process were severely compromised. Despite the egalitarian and individualistic sentiments of the architects of these two republics, governments under them were under little pressure to be highly sensitive to shifts in public opinion, a factor that may have contributed to their weak public support in times of crisis. Between the Third and Fourth Republics, France was divided between a zone occupied by the Nazis and a larger zone ostensibly ruled by the French but in reality governed by a collaborationist and authoritarian government in the aforementioned administrative tradition under the leadership of aging military hero Marshal Pétain. Named for its capital, Vichy France symbolized the deep divisions of the French system: an authoritarian, Catholic, and monistic cultural strain that was at ease in its collaboration with the Nazis, and the individualistic, anti-authoritarian cultural tradition that, together with strong Communist participation, produced the *Maquis,* the French resistance of World War II.

The history of France may therefore be seen as an alternation between two types of constitutional formats, each of which retained some symbolic elements of both of the conflicting conceptions of authority. The return to the bureaucratic authoritarianism of the Fifth Republic indicates that, despite the apparent history of rampant constitutional instability, a pattern exists, a pattern perhaps rendered inevitable by a necessary "congruence" between the authority relationships found in a nation's culture and in its constitutional format.[20]

THE SOCIAL, ECONOMIC, AND CULTURAL CONTEXT OF FRENCH POLITICS

The cultural attributes described in the preceding section as emanating from France's historical legacy have been used in conventional wisdom to characterize the context of French politics; however, these attributes are seen by more recent students of France to be changing in the face of the impact of the postindustrial world. Nonetheless, the cultural attributes of France remain distinct from those of Great Britain, and some of these French attributes have arguably had an impact on the relative lag of the French in modernizing their economy. The changes in these attributes, however, have also been a factor in an economic resurgence of France in recent decades.

Compared to the British, the French have tended to think about politics in terms of broad, abstract principles, a political style that Herbert Spiro refers to as *ideologism.*[21] Recall that the British in the last chapter were characterized as intensely pragmatic, meaning that they had a disposition to derive their institutions from experience on the basis of need and to modify them incrementally on a trial-and-error basis. The French, on the other hand, formed many of their political ideas divorced from any opportunity to implement them.

This lack of opportunity to apply one's political ideas stems from two sources. It will be recalled from the preceding section that French intellectuals engaged in a flurry of activity in the period before the Revolution, when political influence was monopolized by the inner circles of the court. The degree to which a political culture exhibits a tendency toward ideologism is to some extent a function of a gap between the time at which the groups or social forces in that society become aware of their distinct interests, thereby generating claims on the political process, and the time at which they are actually admitted to participation in that process.

The exclusion of groups from German politics, especially after the failure of the Frankfurt Assembly, was even more acute, and perhaps led to an even stronger disposition to romantic ideologism in the German culture. Yet, the German case provides support for the suggestion that participation in the political process tends to moderate a disposition to think in ideological terms. The original Marxist Party, the Social Democratic Party of Germany (SPD), found itself in power during World War I. In control during the wartime emergency, its slogan changed from "To his system, not one penny, not one drop of blood," to "In the hour of need we will not leave the fatherland in the lurch."[22] Accordingly, the abortive Sparticist rebellion led by Marxist "purists" Karl Liebknecht and Rosa Luxemburg was forcibly repressed by the SPD government, and its leaders were killed. After World War II, the party, seeing another opportunity to win power through the electoral process, abandoned its socialist manifesto in its Basic Program of 1959, and praised the socially responsible use of private property and pursuit of the profit motive.

The role of ideologism in French politics has been manifested in the atavistic perpetuation of issues that are no longer relevant to France's real problems. The persisting anticlericalism of republican politics stemming from the aforementioned stance of the church in the revolutions and the growing secularization of French society is a case in point. This pro-Catholic versus anticlerical split among the French nonsocialist republicans made it difficult to aggregate a centrist majority to govern during much of the Third and Fourth Republics. During the Third Republic, the strain and hostility in the relations between the republic and the Vatican greatly intensified. In this period, the republic repealed its concordat with the Vatican and declared a strict separation of church and state, while the Vatican responded by excommunicating every deputy who voted for the repeal. While the anticlerical stance of the republic was softened somewhat during the Fourth Republic, it was the Fifth Republic, under Charles de Gaulle, that restored the faithful to a position of respect in French politics.

While the intensity and rigidity of the pro- and anticlerical split has subsided, certain issues (such as the criminalization of abortion and the pill, RU-486, developed by French scientists to permit early stage abortions in the home) have proven in recent years that this symbolic cleavage still has the power to reawaken old political passions. Religion has come to terms with the more authoritarian Fifth Republic in the light of the identification of the church with the more conservative factions in French politics that dominated the first couple of decades of that republic and the limited hold that religion has on the population in general. In a nation that is nominally over 80 percent Catholic, less than 15 percent attend mass regularly and over half never attend at all.

This division between the faithful and the secular-agnostic French more or less coincides with the cleavage between the political left and the political right, and with the one between the bureaucratic-authoritarian model of authority relations and the republican—egalitarian model that dominated the Third and Fourth Republics. Hence, support for the Vichy regime of World War II came largely from among the Catholic antirepublican right. This bloc is also where one finds most of the anti-Semitism in French culture, which surfaced explicitly in the Dreyfus Affair; in the widespread French support for the philo-Nazi Vichy regime; and in the sudden switch of France under the Gaullist regime from being one of Israel's strongest supporters, as it was during the Fourth Republic, to one of its strongest critics. De Gaulle was undoubtedly echoing a widespread French sentiment when he referred to the Jews as being an inherently "alien people" wherever they reside, a statement that reflects an underlying xenophobia in the French culture and the sense that French culture embodies the values of Western civilization itself.

This cleavage between the bureaucratic-authoritarian, religious, and more likely anti-Semitic right wing and the egalitarian, secular, prorepublican left wing is also congruent with the division between the contrasting conceptions of authority developed in the preceding section: the split between the need for strong, centralized authority on the one hand and the distrust of face-to-face authority on the other. While the republican, legislative-dominant republics were controlled by anticlerical elites, the regimes in the Bonapartist tradition were generally led by people supportive of the church, culminating in the strongly pro-Catholic Gaullists who led the founding of the Fifth Republic.

The conflict between these ideals of authority was largely resolved in the Bonapartist type of regime, which Michel Crozier refers to as "the bureaucratic model."[23] In this model, bureaucratic forms of organization dominate the system with a very strong degree of centralization that preserves the need for an arbitrary and absolute authority in principle but removes that authority to a safe distance from those ultimately affected by the exercise of it. The bureaucratic form of organization, moreover, is compatible with the French cultural need to avoid direct power relationships by the *rationalization* of author-

ity. This concept, stemming directly from the writings of the famous German sociologist of the early twentieth century, Max Weber, who created the concept of bureaucratization as the essence of institutional modernization, involves the subjugation of the occupants of large organizations to a comprehensive set of impersonal rules that maximize predictability in interpersonal relationships and efficiency in implementing policy decisions.[24] In this kind of institutional arrangement, all individuals are equal under the rules; hence, face-to-face power relations are avoided. Yet the idea of the centralization of authority in principle is preserved.

French administration is not only a pervasive element in French society because of the weakness of French political institutions, as suggested earlier, but because the French administrative style reflects and accommodates the conflicting conceptions of authority in the French culture.[25] French bureaucracy is more centralized than most. One hyperbolic story says that the French minister of education in Paris, by looking at his watch, can tell you what verse or passage is being recited in a given grade at every school in the nation at that moment. The rigidity of its system of impersonal rules is also carried farther in the French bureaucratic model than in other administrative systems, thereby avoiding the reality of the exercise of power that is present in all large organizations. Thus, decision makers are protected against personal pressures and reactions by those to whom the decisions apply.

This form of bureaucratic organization has rendered it difficult for the French political system to function effectively. One reason is that the routinization entailed by the dominance of impersonal rules prevents the system from effectively adapting and responding to the changing needs and demands of the postindustrial era. It creates what Crozier calls, "the stalled society," one incapable of effectively adapting to the rapidly changing needs of the postindustrial world, not to mention of bold, innovative policy making, and a profoundly conservative society in which routinization is built into its social and political structures and institutions.[26] Second, in this highly centralized organizational setup, those who are competent to make decisions are so far removed from the impact of those decisions that they lack the necessary information on which to base those decisions. In short, those who have the power, lack the requisite knowledge, and those who have the knowledge, lack the power. The role and prestige of the highest level of the civil service in France are much greater than those of any civil service career in the United States. The personnel of the higher civil service is to a large extent fed from the most prestigious of the *Grandes Ecoles* (Great Schools)—the National School of Administration. Among its graduates are both of the leading Gaullist presidential candidates of 1995, Premier Eduard Balladur and former Premier and now President Jacques Chirac.

The Rousseauian impact that was referred to earlier has left a cult of individualism and a distrust of secondary and representative associations. This translates into a distrust of larger forms of association in the private sector, which led to a later modernization of economic institutions than was the case in other Western industrial societies. What Jessie Pitts called "the cult of prowess,"[27] an assertion of militant individualism, was manifested in the preservation of the small shopkeeper as opposed to larger corporate units of production and distribution and the preference for small, family-size, multicrop farms as opposed to larger, specialized units of agricultural production. These inefficient family farms were subsidized for a long time, thus delaying a much needed reorganization of French agriculture, and the small shopkeeper mentality was manifested in the Pou-

jadist Movement, a neofascist party with a small-shopkeeper electoral base during the Fourth Republic. This attitude contributed to the lag in French economic modernization. From the onset of the industrial revolution in the late eighteenth century to the 1950s, France had the slowest rate of economic growth of any of the "developed nations."[28] However, in the late 1950s, France began to modernize its economic system to the point where the country experienced three decades of rapid economic growth (referred to as "thirty glorious years"), suggesting a possible moderation of the strength of this aspect of French individualism.

Compared to their British counterparts, the French have had less trust of politicians and of the political system. In the first place, the egalitarian conception of authority present in the French culture precludes the kind of deference that was attributed to the British culture for so long. In the second place, the weakness of diffuse support given any constitutional format after two centuries of constitutional instability detracts from the trust, independent of the performance of any particular format. In any event, the French not only express significantly less pride in their system than did the British at the time of the original *Civic Culture* study, but they also manifest this *alienation* from the political system by massive tax fraud and tax avoidance and perhaps military service avoidance. Alienation in this sense refers to a feeling of not really belonging to the political system (as opposed to the broader social abstraction called France), a feeling of not really having a stake in the survival and well-being of the constitutional format. This feeling in France is also manifested in the significantly higher levels of distrust of politicians, a lower level of a sense of obligation to participate in the political process, and less of a sense of civic competence compared to the people of the Anglo-American democracies. This distrust of politicians is one aspect of a broader distrust of what Laurence Wylie identified as *les autres* ("the others," the term generally given by French villagers to those outside of one's extended family).[29] Edward Banfield found that this same distrust of outsiders characterized the occupants of a small village in southern Italy, another setting in a European democracy in which the "civic culture" has been conspicuously absent.[30] The absence of civic-mindedness or alienation has even been given a name by the French—*incivisme* (incivility)—although one finds such feelings of alienation and distrust present to an even greater extent in Italy, another less stable and less effective democracy.

The analysis of Crozier and others referred to above suggests a predominant role of administrative structures in French political life. It is therefore worth noting that recruitment to these structures and to the French political elite in general is largely drawn from a very tiny fragment of the population, a fragment that has been produced by a rigorously selective and highly competitive education system (discussed below). The role of an elite-oriented education system in selecting and socializing a narrowly based political elite is similar in France to the role of the educational system in Great Britain. In general, admission to higher education is much more selective in Britain and France than in the United States. While a little over 5 percent of the total population of the United States is enrolled in higher education (which would be a much higher figure if only college-aged people were used as the base), the corresponding figure for the United Kingdom is a little over 1 percent and the figure for France is just under 2 percent. Thus an individual in the United States is five times as likely as one in the United Kingdom to enroll in some form of higher education, and over two and a half times as likely as an individual in France to be so enrolled.

Clearly, the survivors of this educational winnowing process in France are not ordinary people. They are the best and brightest children of a very small portion of the top of the French social stratification system, children whose parents were well educated and well off. There is a strong correlation between one's social class and access to higher education in France. Pierre Bourdieu reported as of 1966 that the son of a higher civil servant was 80 times more likely to enter a university than the son of an agricultural worker, and twice as likely as the son of a middle-level civil servant.[31] Access to a university has actually become less selective in recent decades. Between 1958 and 1977 the number of students in higher education increased from 170,000 to 850,000, and included a greater proportion of the children of the working class and of farmers.[32]

Herein lies a notable difference in the pattern of political recruitment in Britain and France on the one hand and in the United States on the other. In the former nations, citizens tend to favor bestowing political or administrative authority on individuals who have demonstrated extraordinary achievement or intellectual capacity, while Americans seem to favor bestowing power on ordinary individuals who reflect the intellectual and achievement mediocrity of the masses. The Anglo-French preference for elites emerging from a highly selective educational experience is a force for perpetuating the powerful grip that the educated classes in those nations have on access to elite status. It would be uncommon for the children of uneducated working-class people to rise to elite status in those nations. Hence, there is some legitimate concern that the French elites in general and their administrative elites in particular are out of touch with the needs and concerns of ordinary citizens.

The description of the French political culture given thus far constitutes an oft-repeated and almost classic characterization of that culture. It is a description, however, that may be increasingly at odds with political and economic realities. One may therefore infer that the French culture may be in a process of modification in some respects.

Clearly, for example, the description of the cultural attribute of a passion for individualism that translates into a struggle to preserve units of industry and farming that have been dysfunctional for the postindustrial world (e.g., Poujadism and the subsidization of inefficient multicrop family farms) does not square with the "thirty glorious years" of economic prosperity and modernization.

Perhaps more fundamentally, there are indications that the aforementioned ideologism may be less characteristic of French society now than it had been through most of modern French history. France has traditionally stood out among European nations with respect to the political activity and impact of intellectuals (those whose primary occupation is the formulation and dissemination of ideas), a concept that was invented by the French. The role that the people of ideas played in mobilizing the masses behind a sense of injustice prior to the French Revolution has already been discussed. Subsequently, *l'affaire Dreyfus,* in which the impassioned manifesto and ongoing campaign by Emile Zola, Anatole France, Marcel Proust, and others succeeded in exonerating Dreyfus and largely discrediting the French right, provided a direct demonstration of the impact that intellectuals could actually have on the political process.

The almost exaggerated role of the intellectuals in French politics has traditionally and historically been on the left, a relationship that was made very apparent in the wave of manifestoes and intellectual support for the "events of 1968," the term given to the massive strike and student protest movement of May 1968. In fact, an attempt to organize a forum of right-wing intellectuals in December 1981, under the title "Alternatives to Socialism," was a resounding failure. Leading French intellectuals became enamored with classical Marxism as a realistic explanation of the gap between the egalitarian ideal of the French culture and the stratified reality of French society in a wave of Russophilia that swept the French intellectual community in the 1920s. The mesmerization with Marxism and the Soviets persisted under the leadership of famous intellectuals such as the philosopher and writer Jean-Paul Sartre. Frank Wilson, for example, has written on "The Persistence of Ideologism on the French Democratic Left."[33] The French Communist Party, one of those that most consistently adhered to the orthodox Moscow line, used to receive substantial electoral support, with around a quarter of the national vote in the earlier years of the Fourth Republic.

In recent years, however, this support has dwindled to insignificance in contrast with the more iconoclastic Italian Communist Party, which ostensibly accepted the electoral process and continued to receive substantial electoral support right up to the collapse of communism in Eastern Europe and the discrediting of undisguised Marxism. In the 1994 Italian elections, the former Communists ran under the label of "Communist Refoundation" and received only 6 percent of the vote. In the 1993 elections to the French National Assembly, the Communist Party received only 23 of the 577 seats, a loss of 3 seats. Several French intellectuals who were formerly Marxist ideologues have now been crusading against Soviet Communism with a zeal one finds in converts. Jean-François Revel's book, *The Totalitarian Temptation,* is one of the more visible of the manifestations of the disillusionment of the French left with classical Marxism, which grew out of the increasingly obvious oppressiveness of the Stalinist dictatorship. Bernard-Henry Levy (whose most noted book is *Barbarism with a Human Face*) and Andre Glucksmann (author of *The Master Thinkers*) are other members of the new breed of French intellectuals known as *Les nouveaux philosophes* (the new philosophers), a group once captivated by the romance of Marx, Lenin, and Che Guevara, but now under the intellectual leadership of Friedrich von Hayek (one of the most conservative of the free market economists), Raymond Aron (the leading spokesperson of the French pragmatic right), or even the American "Reaganites."[34]

The discreditation of the former hard-line role of the French Communists was probably completed and affirmed after the 1993 elections with the resignation of the venerable hard-line leader of the party, Georges Marchais, who had headed the party since 1972. Marchais was replaced with M. Alain Bocquet, who even adopted a new title, "National Secretary," in keeping with the party's decision to abandon "democratic centralism." The abandonment by parties of the left of the collectivist goals that had been their defining soul now seems to be a pattern of the postindustrial world, which is traceable perhaps most notably to the transformation of the German Social Democrats in 1959, discussed in Chapters 2 and 5, and continuing through the agonizing struggle by the new leader of the Labour Party in Britain, Tony Blair, to drop the commitment to nationalization in their party constitution at the landmark 1994 party conference. This pattern is also seen in the French Communists' formal abandonment of their defining goal (and even of their traditional name) and the *embourgeoisement* of the French Socialists under the embattled Mitterrand.

The May 1981 general elections brought to power the first left-wing government to head France in over three decades with the election of the Socialist François Mitterrand as president. The ideologues on the French left had hoped that this would usher in an era of seriously redistributing wealth, nationalizing many industries, reducing the role of private enterprise, and taking a more pro–Third World and anti-Western foreign policy, orientations suggested by the rhetoric of the students and intellectuals leading "the events" of 1968. These ideologues were disappointed, however, by the middle-of-the-road course the administration actually took. Although Mitterrand nationalized some 11 sectors of the French economy, including the banks (which he later reversed—see below); reduced the work week to 39 hours, and lowered the retirement age to 60, he also advocated the installation of U.S. missiles in Europe, cut government spending, restrained wages, and allowed the closing of outmoded industries, thereby generating short-term unemployment. Although ecology is a principle dear to the hearts of the European romantic left, in the Greenpeace scandal the administration first denied and then admitted scuttling a ship owned by that environmental group to prevent their protest of French nuclear testing in the Pacific. The moderate rather than leftist tendencies of the administration were reinforced when the legislative election of 1986 returned a rightist majority to the National Assembly, forcing Mitterrand to ask the leader of the neo-Gaullist party, Jacques Chirac, to form a government and become prime minister. The situation of a president from one political force and a premier or prime minister from the president's opposition is known as *cohabitation*. The 1986–1988 arrangement is known as *cohabitation I* to distinguish it from the current divided government emanating from the decisive rejection of the left in the 1993 National Assembly elections, an arrangement called *cohabitation II.* Even the initial wave of nationalization was reversed by this very centrist Socialist, who was being pulled further to the right by his conservative premier of *cohabita-*

tion II, when in 1993 legislation was adopted privatizing 21 formerly public sector industries, including automobiles, aerospace, chemicals, and banking.

Despite the apparent metamorphosis of French politics from its barricade tradition and romantic ideologism to the politics of pragmatism with the aggregation of the party system (discussed below) into catch-all parties epitomized by the moderate course of the socialist Mitterrand administrations, it may be premature to declare that metamorphosis a permanent attribute of the French cultural landscape. This tradition, which was both a legitimate expression of the populist strain in the French culture and a symbolic reenactment of that great French historical watershed of 1789, has been thoroughly romanticized (as in the classic Victor Hugo novel and current hit musical *Les Misérables*) and embedded in the French national psyche for better than two centuries.[35] Moreover, the aforementioned "events"—*les événements*—of May and June 1968 shut the nation down with a general strike lasting several weeks without a specific set of political objectives. The strike began typically with a student protest in the Faculty of Letters in Nanterre, a subsidiary of the Sorbonne, on March 22. The Twenty-Second of March Movement seemed to focus on the relative merits of Trotskyite and Maoist ideologies, hardly a pressing question to the problems of 1968 France. The most concrete complaint was that of the student activist, anarchist, and self-styled "Bakunin Marxist" Daniel-Cohn Bendit, that the entire university system was an oppressive tool of the bourgeois establishment. The "events" spread to an industrial strike that shut down much of the nation's economy. The target of the "events" seemed to be authority in general, a target in line with the French cultural antipathy to direct authority relations. This reemergence of the barricade tradition of taking to the streets

against established authority in general and of a romanticized ideological style of political discourse reinforces the chapter's theme of continuity amidst apparent chaos in France's cultural context.

Nevertheless, France may not be an exception to the imperatives of structural convergence discussed elsewhere in this book. Especially under the growing influence of European integration as well as the inescapable imperatives of the postindustrial age in a world economic system, French exceptionalism may have become impossible to maintain. What has been called by many "the French theater of revolution" may have alas played its final curtain.

THE CONSTITUTIONAL FORMAT: PARLIAMENTARY DEMOCRACY TO PRESIDENTIAL DOMINANCE

With France having become identified in the public mind with unstable, assembly-dominated parliamentary democracy since the late nineteenth century, it seems strange to reclassify it as a politically stable presidential system. Most observers of the French scene have a difficult time describing the Fifth Republic that came into being in 1959 as a presidential system; hence, they use terms such as "quasipresidential" to refer to the format now in place. The distinction between presidential and parliamentary has to do with the identification and means of selection for the role of head of government, the occupant of which is understood to have the primary responsibility to formulate national policy and to set the legislative agenda.

In a parliamentary system, as we have seen in the preceding chapter on Great Britain, the head of government is a member of the legislature and accountable to that legislature through the mechanism of the vote of no-confidence or censure. The head of government is chosen by the identical process that determines the composition of the legislature; hence, a cooperative relationship between the government and the legislative majority is built into the constitutional format.

The head of government in a presidential system is chosen by a process that is independent of the process that determines the composition of the legislature. Hence, a certain tension in executive-legislative relations is built into that format.

By any reasonable definition of the concept, the president of the republic, until the appearance of the *cohabitation* phenomenon, functioned as the head of government as well as the head of state in the Fifth French Republic. The president not only dominated the policy formulation and agenda-setting process but wielded powers to enact his legislative agenda in excess of those possessed by the American president. The prime minister, named by the president but accountable to the Assembly with a circumscribed confidence mechanism, is not necessarily a member of that assembly, and, until the accession of the Gaullist (RPR) Jacques Chirac to the post in1986, functioned largely as the president's deputy and liaison to the Assembly. This situation of a socialist president and Gaullist prime minister from 1986 to 1989 and again in 1993, with the ascension of the RPR's Edouard Balladur to the premiership, is discussed below.

The constitutional powers of the president of the Fifth French Republic to impose his will on the policy-making process and effectively to nullify any check and balance function of the other political institutions of that regime are impressive indeed. This has been true despite the apparently explicit provision in Article 20 of the 1958 constitution that says, "The Government (meaning the premier and his cabinet) shall determine and direct the policy of the nation."

However, the Constitution has given pow-

ers, and early presidents have by force of their personality and style further established powers, that have undermined the apparent intent of Article 20. To begin, the president has the power under Article 16 of the Fifth Republic Constitution to declare a state of emergency without precise restrictions on the circumstances in which such a state may be declared (a presidential finding that "the institutions of the Republic, the independence of the Nation, . . . or the fulfillment of its international commitments are threatened in a grave and immediate manner") or the length of time the emergency may last. During the emergency, the president rules by fiat, with presidential orders unchecked by any structure of accountability. This emergency power, compared by some to the emergency powers of the president of Germany's Weimar Republic that were used to end the republican regime and begin Hitler's dictatorship, was invoked once in the Fifth Republic by the charismatic Charles de Gaulle. This occurred during the abortive rebellion of the generals in Algiers in 1961, a time of actual crisis, and has not been used since. Nevertheless, the presence of such unchecked power is another manifestation of the French conception of democracy, a conception that devalues meaningful accountability and checks and balances in favor of a populistic version of popular sovereignty.

This devaluation of structured accountability in favor of a vague, Rousseauian conception of legitimate authority as the embodiment of the general will is also manifested in the president's plebiscitary power. When the legislature refuses to enact a bill that the president supports, he may present the bill to the general electorate for a yes or no vote. Although called referendums by the constitution, these exercises in popular sovereignty qualify as plebiscites in that they present one policy choice initiated by the government for the electorate to approve or disapprove, in a context in which the status quo is not acceptable. In light of the aforementioned ability of a head of government to mobilize public opinion, the outcome of such a vote will normally go the president's way. In fact, when De Gaulle presented his five plebiscites to the public, he announced that he considered these votes a vote of confidence in his presidency. Accordingly, when he lost the fifth one, he resigned the presidency and retired from public life. When the president's position wins, but not overwhelmingly, the outcome is considered a mild rebuke to the president, as in the case of President Georges Pompidou's plebiscite over the question of British entry into the Common Market. While the plebiscitary powers are not without restriction in the constitution with regard to subject (Article 11), the restrictions are vague and susceptible to rather broad interpretation. For example, while the writers of the constitution provided a procedure to amend the constitution in Article 89 and clearly did not intend for the plebiscitary procedure in Article 11 to be used for that purpose, De Gaulle used the plebiscite to amend the constitution in order to provide for the direct election of the president. Thus, while this provision was not intended to give the president blank-check power to by-pass the legislative process on any matter he chooses, it was used almost to that effect by De Gaulle and remains a potential source of presidential domination of the policy-making process.

Another power of the French president new to the Fifth Republic is the effective power to dissolve the Assembly no more than once a year without the formal consent of any other actor. The impact of the absence of this power on the infamous cabinet instability of the Third and Fourth Republics has been exaggerated. Moreover, it is tempting to overstate its significance in the Fifth Republic, during which this power has been exercised twice (once by De Gaulle and most recently

by Mitterrand in 1988). President Mitterrand accepted the rightist majorities in the legislative elections in 1986 and 1993, and named Gaullists Jacques Chirac and Eduard Balladur, respectively, as premier, and the president from the Federation of the Right, Valéry Giscard d'Estaing, hinted that he would have named the head of the Federation of the Left (Mitterrand) premier in 1976 if the left had won the parliamentary elections of that year as predicted. Apparently, there may be political risks in resorting to the power of dissolution to nullify the will of a legislature with a strong public mandate. However, the understood threat that the availability of this power poses to the Assembly may make members of that body somewhat less eager to challenge the clear will of a popular president.

There are grounds for the statement that an apparent division of labor between the president and premier, begun by De Gaulle himself, has evolved—especially out of the experience of the two *cohabitations*. The president should, in this view, concentrate on foreign policy, while the premier should have primary responsibility for domestic policy. De Gaulle permitted this largely because he was more interested in the grand schemes of international affairs, but he did assume the right of general oversight over policy as a whole. Georges Pompidou, De Gaulle's successor, implemented this implicit power of the presidency by a heavy-handed interventionist style. The Union for French Democracy president, the haughty Valéry Giscard d'Estaing, ran the country from the Elysée Palace to such an extent that his fellow Coalition of the Right leader Chirac was frustrated in the premiership with little to do, an experience that contributed to his decision to become mayor of Paris when he could have had the premiership in 1993 instead of Balladur. In each of these episodes of *cohabitation*, this division of labor was more or less understood. With the weakness of the increasingly ill and unpopular Mitterrand in the final years of his second term as president, the independence of the premier in the domestic sphere was greater for Balladur than it had been some seven years earlier for Chirac. The latter, however, a more aggressive personality than the more classic administrator Balladur, strove to assert the power of the premiership in various ways. For example, the competition between Chirac and Mitterrand to occupy the French chair at various international gatherings sometimes left others in a state of confusion if not bemusement.

The relationship between the president and the prime minister in the Fifth Republic is still evolving, and it is uncertain how much autonomy any future prime minister may be able to enjoy from a president from the opposing political faction. This uncertainty accounts for the disagreement as to the presidential—or quasipresidential—character of the regime. It has been noted that the key to identifying a parliamentary regime is whether the prime minister is in fact the head of government and is accountable to the majority of the legislature. The president's potential and often actual dominance of the policy formulation process has been noted. Although at times French presidents have been willing to allow their government to formulate important aspects of policy, these governments have done so with the acceptance of the president, except during *cohabitation*. While the presidential domination of the policy-making process is not actually written into the constitution, the precedent set by the strong-willed and charismatic De Gaulle was in the direction of such domination, a direction exacerbated by the styles of Pompidou and D'Estaing.

Thus, the parliamentary character of a regime is essentially defined by the relationship between the government (prime minister or premier and cabinet) that dominates the policy-making process and the legislature, a relationship of direct accountability to that legislature. This structured accountability has been weakened by the evolving interpretation of the constitution of the Fifth Republic. While Article 50 says that a premier who has lost a vote of no confidence or censure must submit his resignation to the president (constitutionally, the government must lose by an absolute majority of all members of the Assembly, as opposed to a mere majority of those voting), there is no clear requirement that the president must accept that resignation. Indeed, De Gaulle chose to retain Pompidou as his premier in 1962 after the latter lost a vote of no confidence, and in 1972 President Pompidou dismissed Jacques Chaban-Delmas as prime minister after the latter decisively won such a vote. More recently, Chirac resigned as premier after he lost the 1988 presidential election to Mitterrand, despite the fact that the conservative parties supporting Chirac retained a narrow majority in the Assembly. It seems that the confidence of the legislature is of uncertain relevance to the tenure of the government, which violates one of the defining attributes of a parliamentary regime. Yet, the phenomenon of a divided government with a president and premier representing opposing political forces seems likely to be a recurring one in French politics. The sorting out of the relationship between the president and premier will undoubtedly depend on the personalities of the individuals who occupy these roles.

The weakness of the Mitterrand regime has finally cleared the way for a return to a Gaullist-dominated presidency led by Jacques Chirac.

Chirac emerged after a struggle between himself, Balladur and long shot hopeful, former assembly president Phillipe Seguir. Chirac defeated former premier Edouard Balladur in the first round, and then defeated the Socialist candidate, Lionel Jospin, who emerged as the party's candidate when former European Community president Jaques Delores eschewed the race. Jospin actually led the voting in the first round, as the rightist votes were divided among Chirac and Balladur. The strength of the extreme populist right, whose rise over Europe is noted in Chapter 1, is confirmed by the fact that LePen's National Front and de Villiers' anti-Maastricht Movement together polled nearly 20 percent of the vote (see Table 4–3).

Of course, the run off system and the singular prize of the presidency narrowed the field to Chirac and Jospin for the second round on May 7, 1995. Of the 29.5 million votes cast, Chirac received 52.6 percent compared to Jospin's 47.4 percent, once more turning the country over to Gaullist hands. Chirac named Balladur's former Foreign Secretary, Alaine Juppe, as his premier, once more ending cohabitation.

The Gaullists had suffered from an outbreak of corruption scandals from within the Balladur government, with one minister, Gérard Longuet (industry), forced to resign and another, Alain Carignon (communications), already in jail.[36] Séguin, who represents the right wing of the RPR, led the fight against French acceptance of Maastricht and entry into the European union, while Delors, who spent the past decade in Brussels thinking he was president of something, personifies the drive to assimilate France and other European nations into the bureaucracy at Brussels. The 1995 presidential election, temporarily promised to be another referendum on European union, until Delors dropped out.

The presidential domination of the political process in the first three and a half decades of the Fifth Republic in part may be seen as a reaction to the Assembly domination and executive impotence of the classic parliamentary regimes of the Third and Fourth Republics. In each, the various governments were composed of shaky coalitions not only of disparate parties but also of parliamentary groups and cliques that were only loosely congruent to party lines. Deputies in their "house without windows" tended to engage in a process of political bargaining and gamesmanship without primary concern for the issues and needs of the country, activity designed to enhance their own roles and careers more than to formulate policies and resolve issues. Deputies, for example, even including members of the government, would vote to bring down a government not on matters of principle but in the hope of getting into or getting a better ministry in the next government. We have seen how the power of dissolution was circumscribed by political

TABLE 4-3   First Round Results

Candidate	Party	Percentage of Vote
Lionel Jospin	Socialist	23.3%
Jaques Chirac	RPR	20.8
Edouard Balladur	RPR	18.6
Jean LePen	National Front	15
Robert Hume	Communist	8.6
Arlotte Leguiller	Leftist Workers	5.3
Phillippe de Villiers	Anti-Maastricht Nationalist Movement of France	4.7
Dominique Voyret	Greens	3.3

FIGURE 4-1   The French National Assembly, as seen from the Place de la Concorde in Paris (the large square where the execution of Louis XVI as well as other guillotining took place during the French Revolution). The River Seine runs behind the building.

considerations in the Third Republic and by constitutional restrictions in the Fourth Republic. Since the government could only dissolve the Assembly when that body voted censure by an absolute majority, while governments regularly fell by relative majorities, governments were constantly being reconstituted without input from the electorate. Hence, the egalitarian framework of the Assembly-dominated republics paradoxically weakened the accountability of governments to the electorate.

The legislature in Fifth Republic France is bicameral, being composed of a National Assembly and an indirectly elected Senate (see Figure 4-1). The Assembly, the lower house, is chosen by a single-member district system with majority vote and a runoff election provision, as was used in the Third Republic (although a version of proportional representation was tried once, in the 1986 parlia-

mentary elections). While lacking the aggregative force of the Anglo-American plurality system, the French double-ballot system appears not to be as conducive to party system fragmentation as are the various forms of proportional representation. In any event, the number of parties has been reduced since the Fourth Republic era, as we will see below.

The Senate, or upper house, is chosen by an electoral college of over 100,000, composed of the members of the Assembly and local officials, a group whose composition gives disproportionate representation to smaller towns and rural areas. While the Senate can and sometimes does amend or alter bills, the Assembly can override Senate objections to a bill, leaving the Senate in effect with a delaying power, similar to the remaining power of the British House of Lords but without that latter body's traditions, legitimacy, and quality of debate. This emascula-tion of the effective power of the Senate in both the Fourth and Fifth Republics was in part a reaction against the powerful Senate of the Third Republic. The overwhelming pre-ponderance of legislation in France origi-nates with the executive rather than with members of the legislature, and the over-whelming preponderance of the few bills of legislative origin originate in the Assembly rather than in the Senate. The Senate has tended to reflect a political orientation that is both more conservative and less urban than that of the Assembly, which has further de-tracted from the relevance of the Senate for a rapidly modernizing society. Because the Senate represents agricultural interests, its positions on such matters receive some con-sideration. Although the impact of that house on the overall policy process is re-stricted, the French people rejected a Gaullist plebiscite in 1969 intended to dilute the autonomous power of the Senate, per-haps as a backlash to President De Gaulle's then growing dominance of the French polit-ical process.

The Assembly had, until 1986, reflected the political orientation of the president; hence, the prime ministers were little more than deputies to the president and liaisons between the president and the Assembly. However, when the parliamentary election of 1986 produced a conservative majority in the Assembly, Mitterrand, as noted, felt com-pelled to name his former opponent in the presidential race and leader of the Gaullist party, Jacques Chirac, as prime minister. The then unprecedented situation of a president having his political opponent as premier seemed unique enough to merit a special term, *cohabitation*. This arrangement lasted until the presidential elections of 1988, which returned François Mitterrand to office with a clear majority of 54 percent of the vote on the second ballot. "Black" Jacques Chirac,

Mitterrand's opponent on that ballot, re-ceived only 45.98 percent of the vote, the largest margin of victory in a presidential election since the election of Pompidou in 1969. Chirac, accordingly, resigned as pre-mier and was replaced by a Socialist, Michel Rocard. Mitterrand then used his presiden-tial power to dissolve the Assembly and force new elections. In the parliamentary elections of 1988, despite polls that predicted a sub-stantial Socialist victory, the Socialists won only 276 of the 575 seats up for reelection in the 577-member assembly, or 47.8 percent of the seats. The Conservative alliance of the Union for French Democracy (UDF, the cen-ter-right group that produced former Presi-dent Giscard d'Estaing) and the Gaullist RPR won 271 seats. Neither group received the 289 seats needed for a majority. The Com-munists won only 27 seats, or about 4.7 per-cent, down from 44 seats, and Jean-Marie Le Pen's ultrarightist National Front won only 1 seat, down from 33. Although these were en-couraging results from the standpoint of an assumption that the decline of the strength of extremist parties would have a salubrious impact on the prospects for stable, effective democracy in France, we will see that ex-tremist parties of the right enjoyed a resur-gence in the 1993 elections.

Apparently, since the French public awarded a significant majority of seats to the center-right coalition again in 1993, it has be-come comfortable with the concept of a Na-tional Assembly with a different political ori-entation than the president, perhaps moving toward a check-and-balance format along the lines of the American system. Whether that produces once again the stalemated political system that the French called *immobilisme* and observers called "the stalled society"—a gov-ernment that was too fragmented to be able to act, such as those of the Third and Fourth Republics—remains to be seen.

The inability of the Senate to check either

the government or a strong president is nearly matched by that of the Assembly, whose autonomy under the Fifth Republic is potentially compromised by three constitutional provisions: Articles 40, 44, and 49.3. Article 40 removes from the Assembly the power of the purse—the power to initiate bills involving public expenditures. We have seen in Chapter 3 how this power was crucial in bringing about the flow of power "out of court" in Britain. Article 44, the so-called blocked-vote provision, enables government to refuse to recognize any amendments the Assembly may have made to a government-initiated bill, a power that effectively nullifies any legislative action other than outright rejection or total acceptance of government policy. This was used extensively during the earlier years of the Fifth Republic. More recently, government has tended to resort to Article 49.3, by terms of which the government may engineer the passage of a bill that has been rejected by a majority of the Assembly. When this occurs, the government may invoke the article under which the bill automatically becomes law if the Assembly fails to pass a motion of censure (no confidence), which must be approved by an absolute majority of the members. This provision has been invoked nearly 20 times to reverse a negative decision by a majority of the Assembly. These three provisions, which can and have been used, are in conflict with the principle of majority rule and with the logic of a parliamentary regime, a fundamental principle of which is a legislature able to check and balance the policy inclinations of the executive.

Another attribute common to parliamentary regimes in Europe is a cabinet that is in essence a political institution collectively participating in the process of policy formulation. As such, cabinets are primarily composed of individuals with a political (meaning legislative or party) background. In Fifth Republic France, however, the cabinets under the several conservative or centrist presidents have been to a large extent composed of people with an administrative background, indicating that the French cabinet has functioned less as an integral part of the head of government than as an administrative tool of the president. The background of the Mitterrand cabinet has been much more political than administrative. However, even more than in the British cabinet, its size renders it too unwieldy to operate as the collective head of government. The cabinet under Mitterrand's first term as president had over 40 members.

Thus the ambiguity of the essence of the French system has been revealed by its apparent changes over recent decades. A supposedly quasiparliamentary regime was undermined by the nearly monarchial powers of the first three presidents: De Gaulle, Pompidou, and D'Estaing. The phenomenon of divided rule that occurred twice under Mitterrand raised the specter of stalemated government revisited more than executive omnipotence—"The more things change. . . ." However, the rediscovery of true parliamentarianism by the potential autonomy of the government from the president is compromised by the lack of autonomy of the Assembly as a check on the executive. The French seem to be still seeking a balance.

THE TRANSFORMATION OF PARTY POLITICS IN FRANCE

The transformation of the constitutional format in France from one of an unstable, Assembly-dominated parliamentary regime to what appears to be a stable, executive-dominated, quasipresidential regime has been accompanied by and is not unrelated to a transformation of the French party system. Until recent decades, the French party system has been widely identified as the epitome of a highly fragmented, ideological party system incapable of aggregating or consolidating interests and perspectives to permit the formation of stable majorities that could govern the country. During the Third and Fourth Republics, some six or seven distinct parties typically had significant numbers of seats in the lower house, and with these parties were an indeterminate and shifting array of parliamentary groups (something like a caucus in the American context, except that these groups did not necessarily correspond to the cleavages among parties). Some significant fraction of the seats were typically held by parties having as their raison d'être a fundamental alteration of the regime itself (the Stalinist-oriented French Communist Party typically received over a quarter of the vote in national elections throughout the Fourth Republic, and the extreme right received over 13 percent of the vote in 1956). Consequently, it was frequently possible to mobilize a majority of deputies against a government, deputies from the extremes of the political left and right who could never agree among themselves on the character of any government that they could support.

In such a fragmented system, party leaders could reasonably hope to be included in a government even though their party or parliamentary group controlled only a small minority of the seats in the lower house. Hence, party leaders were under no particular compulsion to moderate or compromise the purity, rigidity, or extremism of their programs and principles in order to attract broad electoral support. Rather, these rigid and pure ideological stances were emphasized to distinguish each small party from other small parties close to it on the ideological spectrum and to mobilize the faithful.

Moreover, since no party could hope to govern by itself or even really to dominate a government, no party platforms were actually implemented, thus further reducing the incentive to take a pragmatic view toward problem solving and issue resolution. Instead of addressing the real problems and issues of the society, French political leaders were busily making deals to obtain the best possible government post or ministry or concerning themselves with ideologically generated questions, the latter having the effect of perpetuating past conflicts. The failure of French parties under this system to perform the functions widely ascribed to democratic party systems doubtlessly contributed to a generally weaker confidence in and attachment to particular parties compared to the Anglo-American context. This weaker attachment in turn facilitated the transformation of the system under the Fifth Republic.

During the Fifth Republic, the French party system changed with respect to all of the aforementioned characteristics of the party system under the Third and Fourth Republics. The number of parties was sharply reduced at the onset of the Fifth Republic, as the surviving parties became more aggregated and appealed to a more diverse clientele. In the process, the importance of ideology declined, rendering France a prime example of Seymour Lipset's decline of ideology thesis and Otto Kirchheimer's thesis on the transformation of Western European party systems, discussed in Chapter 2.[37] This process of conversion from the politics of grand ideology toward the politics of interest, a pattern found throughout Western democracies, is further evidence of what Tiersky has called "the end of French exceptionalism."[38]

Two phenomena in particular stand out in the rapid transformation of the French party system. First was the rapid decline in support and in some cases the virtual disappearance of some of the strongest parties of the Third and Fourth Republics. The Communists, for instance, declined from the steady 25 percent-plus to less than 20 percent of the vote in the early years of the Fifth Republic, falling to 3 percent in the runoff in 1988, and only 23 seats in the 577-seat Assembly by 1993, or just under 4 percent. More striking in the early years of this regime was the virtual fading out of the Radical Socialists and the Popular Republican Movement (MRP), two of the most venerable and dominant parties of the preceding republics. The Radical Socialists, neither radical nor socialist in the generally accepted meaning of those terms, was the French party equivalent of classical liberalism, and suffered the fate of such liberal parties throughout the Western world. The Popular Republican Movement was roughly the French equivalent of Christian democracy, a politically difficult position in France given the Gaullists' and others' cooptation of the religious right and the illegitimacy of Catholicism among supporters of the republican left. As with some other Catholic parties on the Continent (e.g., the Dutch Catholic Party) faced with a declining tendency of people to vote their religious affiliation, the MRP tried unsuccessfully to expand their image and appeal beyond their religious base, eventually changing the party's name to Progress and Modern Democracy. The second phenomenon was the rapid rise to a dominant position of the ideologically amorphous Gaullist party—the Rally of the French People (RPF) in the Fourth Republic and the Union for the New Republic (UNR)—in the early part of the Fifth Republic.

These two phenomena epitomize the transformation of the French party system, as dominance shifted from parties of principle—parties defined by relatively closed, romantic ideologies marginally relevant to the issues facing the country—to ideologically amorphous, "catch-all" parties and a related aggregation of the party system. This system has virtually become the conflict between two political forces—the Conservative alliance dominated by the Gaullists and the independents (now represented by the Union for French Democracy [UDF]), and the union of the left dominated by the Socialists.

This aggregation was certainly encouraged if not to a large extent caused by the adoption of the presidential format in the Fifth Republic. The presidency has now become the dominant prize of the electoral process. Under the previous two Assembly-dominated formats, a party with a strength in seats well below a majority still had an opportunity to become part of a coalition government; hence, there was no pressure to aggregate the kind of diverse and broad support necessary to win a national majority. A party's influence in the national policy-making process was not diminished by the party's retention of a closed, electorally restricting ideological position. However, in the Fifth Republic, any substantial fraction of votes that cannot be aggregated to a national majority by the second ballot (or, as originally provided, a majority of the electors) will leave that party totally excluded from the head of government.

Thus, for example, the Radicals, the leading party of the Third Republic, participated in many governments of the Fourth Republic, and even provided one of its most famous prime ministers, Pierre Mendes-France, while receiving only 10 to 13 percent of the vote and sometimes less than 10 percent of the legislative seats during that regime. Under the Fifth Republic, the Radicals, like many other Continental parties of classical liberalism, found that its message of anticlericalism and economic individualism had lost relevance, and the party, unable to hope to attract a national majority, merged partly with the coalition of the left and more so with the coalition of the right, thus losing its independent identity. The left Radicals, or MRG (*Mouvement des Radicaux de Gauche*), aligned with the Socialists in deference to the strong anticlerical tradition of the old Radicals (the right is Catholic oriented), while the other

TABLE 4-4   The French Party System, 1994

Party	Leader
Coalition of the Right	
Gaullist Rally for the Republic (RPR)	Jacques Chirac
Union for French Democracy (UDF)	Valéry Giscard d'Estaing
Center of Social Democracy	
Social Democratic Party	
Radical Socialists	
Perspectives and Realities	
Other Parties of the Right	
National Front (fascist—nativist, populist, nationalist)	Jean-Marie Le Pen
Parties of the Left	
Socialist	Lionel Jospin
Communists	Alain Bocquet
Greens	Dominique Voynet
Ecology Generation (more Greens)	Brice Lalonde
Movement of the Radicals of the Left (MRG)	Jean-François Hory
Movement of the Citizens	Jean-Pierre Chevénement

Source: Keesing's *Record of World Events: 1994.* (London: Longman's, 1994).

Radicals aligned with the coalition of the right in deference to the strong bourgeois tradition of the old Radicals. The MRG was down to slightly over 2 percent of the vote by the late 1970s.

The Catholic-based MRP, one of the strongest parties in the Fourth Republic claiming to reconcile Catholicism with republicanism, similarly disappeared after it became plain that the French were unlikely to vote their religion. Further contributing to its decline was the fact that the Gaullists provided an alternative vehicle for the reconciliation of Catholicism with commitment to the existing republic. Thus, the singular prize of the presidency, the pressures of the single-member district majority electoral system, and the transformation of the French culture along less ideological lines have resulted in a considerable consolidation of the French party system into two broad political forces comprised of only three parties with a realistic chance of producing a president. The current lineup of parties is summarized in Table 4-4.

The Socialist Party has also reflected the deideologization of the party system. Under the Third and Fourth Republics and until 1970, the party was known as the French Section of the Workers' International (SFIO). The Workers' International was of course the theoretical organization reflecting the idea of an international solidarity of the working class transcending national loyalties; hence, the party's very name reflected its Marxist self-image. The party had included the strain of syndicalist anarchism of the followers of the famous French political philosopher Georges Sorel, whose magnum opus, *Reflections on Violence,* reveals both a romantic and nihilistic orientation toward the class struggle.

Yet, it has been noted how the Mitterrand administration has greatly disappointed the hopes of the doctrinaire leftists while pleasing its middle-class supporters by instituting an austerity program, privatizing most of the publically controlled industries, and steering a very centrist course. The Socialists for years faced the dilemma of how to obtain the Communist support they needed to capture the presidency without alienating their substantial middle-class voting clientele and membership. The very background of the Socialist deputies elected to the French Assembly in 1981 reflects the clear *embourgeoisement* of the party. Among the 268 deputies, only 2 were from the working class, while the others were from professional and academic backgrounds that reflected a considerably higher education and social status.[39]

Nevertheless, the appeal of the political left seems to be waning in France, as it is in much of the industrialized world. The Socialist Party of President Mitterrand received a sound electoral trouncing in 1993, losing 198 of its 242 seats in the face of prolonged recession and the perception of gross government incompetence. The sagging French economy produced a level of unemployment of 10.3 percent by the end of 1992 and then soared to 11.7 percent in 1993, a large tax increase was introduced in 1993 to reduce the budget deficit, and the accusations of incompetence forced Mitterrand to dismiss his outspoken Premier Edith Cresson (the first woman to hold that post) and replace her with Pierre Bérégevoy (who served only until the ascension of Balladur in March 1993). Parties of the right, both major and minor, including Le Pen's National Front, received

significant gains. The results of the 1993 elections may be seen in Table 4-5.

Meanwhile, the dilemma of the Socialists with respect to the Communists has been considerably ameliorated by the rapid decline of the latters' electoral strength. The French Communist Party (PCF) has been one of the more faithful in following the Kremlin line and remaining more unapologetically Stalinist compared to other Western European Communist parties, who were reflecting the movements known as "polycentrism" and "Eurocommunism." (The former is the idea that world Communism can have as many centers of power as there are national Communist parties, as opposed to a monolithic movement directed from the Kremlin. The latter refers to the idea that Communism in Western Europe can take on a distinct character that is reconcilable with the democratic character of those societies.) Despite its unreformed stance, the French Communist Party received what was apparently a protest vote amounting to over a quarter of the vote in most Fourth Republic elections. That most of these voters did not intend for the Communists to control the government is indicated by the very rapid decline in the party's support under the presidential system of the Fifth Republic. Given its

TABLE 4-5   Results of the 1993 Elections to the National Assembly

Party	Seats	Gain or Loss Since 1988
Coalition of the Left		
Communists	23	−3
Socialists	54	−198
Left Radicals (MRG)	6	−4
Ecology Generation	0	−
Greens	0	−
Coalition of the Right		
Gaullist Rally for the Republic (RPR)	247	121
Union for French Democracy (UDF)	213	82
Other rightists, including the National Front	24	13

Source: Keesing's Record of World Events: 1994. (London: Longman's, 1994).

hard-line tradition, the coherence of the party's position was undoubtedly placed under a strain by the *glasnost* and *perestroika* of the Gorbachev regime in Moscow. The PCF made significant ideological concessions to the Socialists in return for four relatively minor cabinet positions. The PCF's share of the seats fell to a low of 4.7 percent and 26 seats in the 1988 parliamentary elections, and the party then lost 3 more seats in 1993, placing it in a decidedly subordinate position in the electoral alliance with the Socialists. After the 1993 election, the party's long-time hard-line leader, Georges Marchais, retired and his successor tried to distance himself from the party's past by assuming a new title. In the face of the collapse of Communism in the Soviet Union and Eastern Europe, the future of the PCF appears bleak.

The collapse of support for the PCF did not necessarily signal a move of its former supporters to embrace the more moderate parties. Robert Hume, the Communist candidate, still received 8.6 percent of the vote in the first round of the 1995 presidential elections. Many of the blue-collar workers who formerly supported the PCF have now shifted their support to Le Pen's National Front, a nativist, antiforeigner party of the far right. Le Pen's party received nearly 5 percent of the national vote between the general and presidential elections in 1988 and 15 percent of the first round vote in the 1995 presidential elections. This is part of the broader phenomenon of the rise of parties of the populist right. Note that a leftist Worker's Struggle party and an anti-Maastricht Nationalist party captured 10 percent of the vote between them in the first round of the 1995 elections.

This aggregation, deideolization, and moderation of the French party system raises the question of its perceived effectiveness in the articulation of salient interests in French society. Presumably, the French party system has been a reflection of the intensity of the salience of the actual cleavages found in that society; a sharply fragmented political and social culture produces a fragmented party system. For instance, does the decline in the support for the French Communist Party signify a decline in the alienation of the French industrial worker, as the earlier strong support of that party indicated a high degree of such alienation? It can reasonably be inferred from "the events" that a substantial degree of alienation persisted among the French left as late as 1968. This raises the question of the extent to which the French, having perceived that their party system is not performing the function of structuring the vote by offering plausible policy alternatives to the issues of society, have taken to resolving issues outside the party system, thereby rendering that system essentially irrelevant.

INTEREST MEDIATION IN A MASS SOCIETY

The fragmentation of the French party system has to some extent been a product of the failure of the system of associational life to perform the function of the articulation and transmission of interests and grievances. The traditional weakness of the level of associational life in France, itself in part a product of the Rousseauian model of democracy, has been discussed above. This ingrained hostility to secondary associations was manifested by *Loi Le Chapelier* in 1791, which declared all secondary associations to be illegal, a law that was not repealed until 1884. It was not legal for groups to be formed without government authorization until 1901.

When, on the one hand, a well-developed system of legitimate interest groups effectively articulates the interests of society at the necessary level of specificity, parties then are freed, as it were, to aggregate interests at a higher level of generality. When, on the other hand, the interest groups fail to perform that articulation function, the party system tends to fill that gap at the expense of the aggregation function. The party system of the Third Republic was essentially in place at the time that interest groups were legalized, and, as the complexity of society grew with the modernization process, these groups became closely allied to the parties that were already in place.

This weakness in associational life that characterized France until well into the postwar period no longer accurately describes the country, which is fairly regularly beset by organized demonstrations and strikes. This growing level of associational life in France is in large part a reflection of the transformation of French culture and society from a focus on ideological struggles to the politics of pluralistic bargaining. This in turn is a manifestation of the convergence of mature industrial societies toward the structural imperatives of an advanced state of technology. This convergence theory has been discussed earlier and is addressed in the conclusions.

The largest and oldest of the secondary interest associations in France are the trade unions. The effectiveness of the largest and oldest of these—*Confédération Générale du Travail* (General Confederation of Workers, of CGT)—has always been limited by its close connection to the Communist Party and its focus on the ideological and revolutionary goals of Marxism rather than on the material well-being of workers. This led to a split in the working-class movement, with many Catholic workers forming the *Confédération Française des Travailleurs Chrétiens* (French Confederation of Christian Workers, or CFTC), and other non-Communist workers establishing the *Force Ouvrier* (Workers' Force, or FO), a union that was associated with the old SFIO. The CFTC was associated with the centrist, Catholic, and now defunct

MRP. Focused as it was on the mobilization of Catholic workers for the goals of the church, rather than on the material well-being of the working class, the CFTC did not fulfill the needs of those workers who had material interests as workers, and the CFTC has largely been absorbed by the CFDT (described below). While the FO has attempted to function as an American union, utilizing collective bargaining to promote the pragmatic interests of the working class, its effectiveness was limited by the division of the working class in three sets of associations. The FO has become more centrist, although it is still more closely associated with the Socialists than any other party. In recent years, since the collapse of Communism in Europe, the CGT has declined sharply and has been eclipsed in strength by the FO. The *Confédération Française Démocratique du Travail* (French Democratic Confederation of Labor, or CFDT) is the main Socialist-oriented union and has remained the second strongest in France, having absorbed many former members of the CFTC. The perceived independence of unions is compromised when it is hard to tell where the organization ends and the political party begins.

Beyond the division of the trade-union movement, the movement in general is basically limited by the weaker commitment to organizational activity in France, and, with the possible exception of the FO, French unions seem more concerned with ideology and romanticized Marxian myths of a mobilized and unified working class than with the mundane business of collective bargaining. The CGT in particular eschewed collective bargaining with the capitalist enemy, although it would implement and allow its members to enjoy the fruits of collective bargaining agreements negotiated by others. French unionism in general has declined in strength, while the strength of other groups in French society was growing. Only about a tenth of the French work force is organized into any unions, compared to about 40 percent of British workers. Compared to the French, the American figure has fluctuated around 20 percent, reflecting, perhaps, a basic hostility in the United States to the concept of class-based politics. Thus, while trade-union strength has declined throughout much of the Western industrial world, indicating the declining salience of class-based political conflict, that strength has declined more in France than in the other nations, and today the French unionized work force is the smallest in any Western industrialized nation (see Table 4-6).

The legitimacy of business in France has been largely restored after its World War II collaboration with the Vichy regime and is primarily represented through the *Conseil National du Patronat Français* (National Council of French Employers, or CNPF). This organization has incorporated a variety of types of businesses and dominates the management side of the economy. The movement of top civil servants back and forth between the highest offices in French industry and the civil service, without jeopardizing their lifetime tenure in the civil service, has become so regularized that the French have a term for it—*pantouflage*, or "putting on the slip-

pers." Clearly, this phenomenon vitiates the ability or disposition of the civil service to control industry in the public interest.

Agriculture is dominated by the *Fédération Nationale des Syndicats d'Exploitants Agricoles* (National Federation of Syndicates of Agricultural Landowners, or FNSEA), an organization that has been given almost official status by the relevant parts of the higher civil service and that therefore maintains what amounts to a neocorporatist relationship with the government. The FNSEA, a federation of many independent farmers' groups, tends to be centrist, pro-Catholic, and, according to some of its critics, disposed to defend the interests of those with large landholdings rather than owners of small, family-style farms. Hence, rival agricultural groups have appeared, such as the *Confédération Nationale Syndicale des Travailleurs-Paysans* (National Confederation of Interest Groups of Agricultural Workers, or CNST), aligned with the Socialist Party. The appearance of such rival groups constitutes a further fragmentation of the representation of agricultural interests. Meanwhile, the small farmer, a remnant of the peasant class that had disproportionately characterized French society into the postwar era, is finally being rapidly displaced by the more efficient and mechanized large farms. The small farmer, or *paysan* (literally "peasant"), has been aggressive in demanding and receiving large agricultural subsidies from the government in an effort to stave off extinction. This subsidizing of inefficient small farms is of course in conflict with the Common Agricultural Policy (CAP) of the European Community, of which France is a member, a reality that further dims the prospects for the survival of the French *paysans*.

The significant reduction in the membership of groups representing some of the traditional corporate sectors of society (such as labor and small farmers), has been offset

TABLE 4-6 Strength of Trade Unions in Western Nations

Nation	Percent of Work Force Unionized
France	10
Great Britain	40
United States	18
West Germany	43
Belgium	75
Sweden	83

Source: Ronald Teirsky, *France in the New Europe: Changing Yet Steadfast* (Belmont, CA: Wadsworth Publishing Company, 1994), p. 155.

by the growth of a newer breed of association in France—noncorporatist, issue-oriented groups such as Operation Greenpeace, Doctors Without Borders, and a human rights organization calling itself S.O.S. Racism.

Although France has a full range of interest groups and secondary associations far too diverse and numerous to list here, the strength and effectiveness of interest mediation are not as great in France as in other Western nations. As suggested, the persisting impact of the Rousseauian conception of democracy has detracted from the legitimacy of the representation of particular interests. The idea persists in the French psyche that there is a general, knowable public interest that is distinct from any particular interests (as opposed to the pluralist view that even if the general interest essentially exists in the Platonic sense, it is not knowable by any actor, who is, after all, inexorably enmeshed in a particular role in society, which generates a particular perspective and particular interests). In the pluralist and Anglo-American view, we cannot view society as objectively as a scientist views matter through a microscope, because we are all on the slide. Hence, the public interest, in the pluralist perspective, can only be approached as an impersonal outcome of the bargaining process among particular interests. There is no objective general interest apart from the various particular or special interests that comprise society.

Given the French suspicions about the legitimacy of the role of interest group representation and mediation, French bureaucrats are less receptive to outright pressures and lobbying by interest groups than are their counterparts in the British or American civil service. Compared to their British or American counterparts, French bureaucrats are more likely to view themselves as objective and properly insulated experts who can speak for the general or public interest

rather than the special interests of the interest groups.[40] This attitude fosters a disposition toward neocorporatism in the sense of a regularized cooptation of peak interest associations to secure the cooperation of the membership of those associations in the interpretation and implementation of public policy. The French characteristically have a name for this corporatist relationship that has evolved between what remains of French unions and management—*partenaires sociaux* (social partners). The strength and dangers of these attitudes and their overall role in the French policy-making process can best be grasped after a closer examination and understanding of the nature of the French civil service and its role in that process.

BUREAUCRACY IN THE FRENCH POLICY-MAKING PROCESS: THE STALEMATE SOCIETY

Bureaucracy in France fits the classical pattern outlined in the writings of Max Weber more closely than do its counterparts in the Anglo-American democracies. Furthermore, as is more or less true throughout the Western world, the French pattern of bureaucratic structures and behavior reflects that nation's political culture.

The classical, or Weberian, model of bureaucracy is based upon the presumption that administration—the implementation of policy—is a function clearly distinct from politics—the balancing of conflicting values and the allocation of scarce resources. The efficient implementation of policy—maximizing the politically determined values or goals with the minimum expenditure of resources—is best served by an organizational form with the following attributes: routinization and impersonalization to enhance predictability and to avoid having to determine anew each time the most efficient means of reaching given ends; functional specialization of roles to enable the occupants of each role to master the growing body of knowledge that characterizes technologically modern societies; selection of personnel on the basis of competence or expertise; and insulation from public opinion and sociopolitical pressures to allow the technocrats and experts in the bureaucracy to proceed in the right or technically efficient way rather than in the popular way.

Politics in a modern democratic system, in contrast, would be best served by structures with a different set of attributes: creativity, innovation, adaptability, justice to individuals, accountability and responsiveness to public opinion, and the use of power relationships. These attributes are almost diametrically opposite of those attributes of the classic administrative structure. Clearly, an elaborate set of impersonal rules is dysfunctional for the values of individual justice, power, and accountability. Routinization is dysfunctional for creativity, adaptability, and innovation. The insulation of personnel from public pressures is dysfunctional for the enhancement of responsiveness.

As pointed out in Chapter 2, the presumed separation of politics and administration is glaringly at odds with reality throughout the modern world. Bureaucratic discretion that clearly involves political functions is inexorably a fact of life in the modern world in general and in France most particularly. The strong impact of bureaucratic power and its influence in the policy-making process are well established in France, with its history of well-developed bureaucratic structures coupled with its history of regime weakness and instability.

The reasons for the important political role of the bureaucracy in general and in France in particular are well known. First, policy making in an advanced industrial society demands technological competence, and bureaucracy, based as it is on the principles of the functional specialization of roles and recruitment on the basis of demonstrated competence, is where one generally finds the technocrats. Chapter 2 discussed at length the growing role of the technocracy in the policy-making processes of all advanced industrial societies and the diminishing role of the political sectors of such societies.

Second, in a nation like France, characterized by a history of regime weakness and instability, the bureaucracy fills what amounts to a political vacuum. This reason is parallel to the "heavy weight of bureaucratic power" thesis associated with Fred Riggs and others with respect to less developed nations.[41] Riggs argued that colonial powers, concerned more with efficiently administering their colonies than with preparing them for the generation of nationalist demands and eventual self-rule, built Western administrative institutions in those colonies while not developing representative institutions. Consequently, in the new nations of the Third World, well-developed bureaucracies tend to dominate the poorly developed representative institutions in the political function, a role that is dysfunctional for the goal of sociopolitical change. Germany, which also has a history of regime instability, is characterized by a strong, classical administrative sector.

Third, the political role of the bureaucracy has been persuasively argued by Michel Crozier and others to reflect certain cultural imperatives that particularly characterize France.[42] As noted above, France, because of the symbolism and mythology of its revolutionary heritage, has a strong dislike of direct, face-to-face authority relations combined with a seemingly contradictory need for a strong, centralized authority.[43] Furthermore, the particular nature of French Catholicism has been shown by Jessie Pitts to foster a "doctrinaire-hierarchical orientation" in which the imperative is for "deductive chains of reasoning and hierarchy, the insistence upon the unity of the power center, and formulations where everything and everybody is *à sa place* (in its place)."[44]

The rigidity of the comprehensive set of impersonal rules that are said to characterize the French administrative system enable the French to avoid confronting the reality of power relationships. Power implies discretion; however, to impersonalize human interaction entails a lack of such discretion. Everyone is equal under the rules, thereby avoiding face-to-face power relations. This complete impersonalization is, of course, a fiction, and bargaining does occur among the occupants of various bureaucratic roles. However, the fiction that all behavior is guided by impersonal rules enables the French to justify bureaucratic behavior in terms consistent with French cultural imperatives.

The centralizing imperative of the French culture is also reflected in the French administrative style. Stemming back to Napoleon, administration in France has been highly centralized in the ministries in Paris. Reflecting also the Rousseauian myth of France as an undifferentiated political community, this high degree of centralization does not allow for adjustments to regional variations.

The centralization and impersonalization of French administration undercut the Weberian principle of hierarchy, the concept of a chain of command in which superiors can assume real responsibility for the job performance of their subordinates. Hierarchy is essential to provide coherence and coordination to an organization and to avoid both duplication and gaps in tasks performed. Clearly, to the extent that everyone's behavior is rationalized by a comprehensive set of impersonal rules, superiors lose control of the performance of their subordinates. The impersonalization of bureaucratic behavior,

coupled with a high degree of functional specialization and division of responsibility, results in a high degree of isolation of each office or role in the organization from other offices or roles. This includes not only the strata isolation discussed by Crozier as being dysfunctional for the effective operation of the principle of hierarchy, but the isolation of offices on a horizontal level as well. All of these characteristics create what Crozier calls a "bureaucratic vicious circle," a self-reinforcing bureaucratic system that "cannot correct its behavior by learning from its errors."[45]

The bureaucratic behavior pattern that emerges from the French style of organization is generally noncreative, routinized, and often somewhat arrogant and insensitive to public needs and expectations. These behavioral patterns are exacerbated by the recruitment pattern of the higher civil service, which resembles that of other Continental civil services in several respects. The expectations of a routinized orientation toward one's job in the bureaucracy do not fit well with the rigorous requirements for recruitment to the higher civil service that result in these roles being filled with the nation's intellectual and educational elites. Clearly, the survivors of the nation's most rigorous academic selection processes are not likely to adjust well to the role of a routinized implementer of a stagnant set of impersonal rules, or, as Robert K. Merton wryly put it, they are "unfitted by being fit to an unfit fitness."[46]

It has been shown above that the career path to the higher civil service in France is through a level of educational achievement generally favoring the offspring of that nation's educated and professional elite. In this, the French system resembles that in other Continental systems, notably in Germany and Great Britain. This recruitment pattern for the highest civil servants (*grands corps*) is by rigorous competitive examination, a procedure that gives the impression of equality. In reality, however, the ability to pass these examinations is largely limited to the graduates of a prestige university and more especially one of the aforementioned *grandes écoles.* The *Ecole Polytechnique,* which has been in existence since Napoleon's era, produces candidates with engineering or technical competence. The *Ecole Nationale d'Administration* (ENA), founded after World War II, now produces the bulk of other high civil servants, although various specialized *fonctionnaires* emerge from one of the growing group of specialized *grandes écoles,* such as the *Ecole Nationale des Impôts,* which trains tax officials. Admission to the ENA is by a rigorous competitive exam (*concours*) that selects a very narrow base of admittees. From 1964 to 1975, 75 percent of those who successfully passed the *concours* for the ENA came from the upper-middle to upper classes. Moreover, 736 out of 782, or 94 percent, of those who passed the *concours* during this period prepared at the prestigious *Institut d'Etudes Politiques de Paris* (IEPP). Only 3.94 percent of the 1,167 people who prepared at one of the institutes for political studies outside Paris successfully passed the ENA *concours,* while 16 percent of the IEPP graduates were admitted to the ENA.[47] ENA graduates are known as *enarchs.*

Thus, because of selectivity of the French educational process in general and especially of the ENA, which admits only about 10 percent of its applicants, there is a very strong tendency for the students at these schools and hence for the recruits to the higher civil service to come from highly educated, upper-class parents. In fact, a significant percentage of the recruits come from parents who themselves were members of the higher civil service, prompting Crozier's comment that the French bureaucracy is "one of the most entrenched of such closed systems of action that has existed in the modern world."[48] The French higher civil service is unrepresenta-

tive of the general population in terms of both demographics and attitude, in the sense of a sensitivity to the needs and demands of society or of other branches of government.

The expanded power of the executive branch of the government—especially the presidency—relative to the legislature and the prime minister accountable to it, has enlarged the area in which higher civil servants can formulate and implement domestic policies without the participation of any elective institution. Thus, several factors promote a powerful political role for this largely unrepresentative, rigid, nonresponsive, routinized, and impersonal institution that was designed for the implementation function—the weakness of the other parts of government in France; the imperatives of advanced technology that enhance the virtual indispensability and bargaining power of the technocrats; a set of attitudes among the French bureaucrats that, to a larger extent than among the higher civil servants of other Western nations, encompasses a sense of expertise and superiority to the politicians; and the ways in which the structure and behavior patterns of classic bureaucracy reflect the imperatives of the French culture. The result of the especially strong political role of the higher civil service with the aforementioned attributes is a political process that is unable to reconcile the reality of conflicting interests or to adapt to the inexorability of change in the environment of the system—what Crozier has aptly labeled "the stalemate society."[49] He in fact argues that the events of May 1968 did not constitute a serious attempt to overthrow the established order or to replace capitalism with some form of Marxist millennium. Rather, "the crisis of May 1968 thus appears as an attack upon the French style of action and as an instinctive revolt against what has been called the stalemate society."[50] Thus, France, perhaps to a greater extent than other Western democracies, is largely governed by a quintessentially bureaucratic apparatus that is by definition unsuited for assuming the political role needed in an advanced industrial democracy.

Clearly, the political role of the French bureaucracy has not been an absolute impediment to France's adjustment to the coming of postindustrial society. We have already alluded to the "thirty glorious years" that characterized the postwar economy of France. While France may have rapidly made up for lost ground during this period, the nation was one of the slowest in Western Europe to adjust fully to the modern age. The earlier French reluctance to abandon an economic organization based on shopkeepers and the family farm in favor of modern forms may be a case in point.

SOCIAL POLICY IN FRANCE: PROSPECTS FOR ADJUSTMENTS TO THE POSTINDUSTRIAL ERA

Despite the historic French attachment to individualism and the French cultural discomfort with state power, France is far more committed to an interventionist approach to managing the economy than is the United States, with its commitment to the idea of the self-regulating market. The French, along with the British and the Italians, had a greater portion of their productive capacity under public ownership than any of the other Western democracies.[51] This public ownership was initially expanded by the Socialist president Mitterrand, who nationalized some 12 industries and 36 banks. In 1982, in the face of rising unemployment and inflation, he backed off from expanding the public sector in favor of an austerity program featuring wage and price restraints and freezes on some public benefits, a move that had some of his erstwhile supporters complaining that his government was indistin-

guishable from those of his conservative predecessors. The rightward shift of this Socialist president continued. In 1993, the government introduced a tax increase to reduce the budget deficit and adopted legislation to privatize some 21 public sector industries, as noted. Perhaps the final betrayal of the principles of the French left by this Socialist president, whose administration was ushered in with a euphoric anticipation of a socialist millennium in 1981, came in October 1994, when the *London Times* reported that during World War II Mitterrand had served in the Nazi-protectorate Vichy administration under Marshal Pétain.

Despite the austerity moves, despite the domination of conservative administrations during the Fifth Republic before Mitterrand, despite the apparent political chaos before the Fifth Republic, and despite the cultural forces discussed earlier that are putatively dysfunctional for modernization, France today and in most of the postwar era exemplifies the most advanced and socially "enlightened" welfare state. Unlike the United States but like all other Western democracies, France has a system of providing access to the health-care system on the basis of need rather than on the ability to pay. And as in other Western nations that have striven to guarantee equal access to health care without regard to financial circumstances, France has found such an ideal to be beyond the financial resources of the state. Hence, French citizens now pay 20 percent of their health-care costs.[52] Unlike Britain, French physicians are in private practice and compensated on a fee-for-service basis, as in the United States. Moreover, income of French physicians relative to other roles in society and even relative to other professions is quite high. The gap between the income of the average physician and the average worker in France in 1973–74 was sevenfold, compared to 5.6-fold in the United States and 2.7-fold in Britain.[53] The

French accomplish this apparent contradiction with a comprehensive, compulsory, and subsidized medical insurance scheme combined with some cost controls. Thus, France spent $546 per capita on health care as of 1978, compared to $268 spent by Britain and $341 by the United States. In this, France ranks sixth among 141 nations of the world.[54] Measured as a percentage of the gross national product, France by 1985 spent 8.6 percent of its GNP on total health expenditures. Only the United States (10.7 percent) and Sweden (9.4 percent) ranked higher among industrialized nations. France also recorded the highest percentage increase in this statistic from 1980 to 1985 of any industrialized nation.[55] This massive financial commitment to the health of its citizenry is in part symptomatic of the French commitment to a policy of guaranteeing a level of well-being comparable to that in any other Western nation.

The French also subsidize university students, the construction of affordable housing, and mass transport, among other public benefits. Yet, the inequality of income distribution in France is one of the highest among Western nations. In France, the top 10 percent of the population received 30.4 percent of the national income in 1979, while the bottom 40 percent received 14.1 percent, compared to Britain, where the top 10 percent received 23.5 percent of the income and the bottom 40 percent received 18.9 percent, and the United States, where the top 10 percent received 26.6 percent and the bottom 40 percent received 15.2.[56] Thus, despite the much publicized widespread abject poverty in the inner cities of the United States and the "survival of the fittest" element in the American culture, the United States has a much more egalitarian distribution of income than the French, with their strong ideological commitment to equality, and estimates are that this did not change significantly under the Socialist administration of Mitterrand.

Another symptom of material inequality among the French is in the tax structure, which is among the least progressive in practice because of widespread, massive tax evasion, the opportunities for which are more pronounced among the wealthier segments of society. This disposition toward tax evasion has been so common for so long that it virtually constitutes a cultural attribute, which reflects the weaker legitimacy that government itself has had in France compared to other Western nations—the *incivisme* referred to above. To make up for the revenue shortfall in which income tax produced only 20 percent of the revenue in 1991, the French rely on a value-added tax (a kind of hidden sales tax) for 40 percent of their revenues. Like all sales taxes, it is highly regressive, placing a higher burden on those with lower incomes.

CONCLUSIONS: STABILITY AND CHANGE

The foregoing section illustrates the theme of this chapter—essential pattern maintenance and stability amidst the perception of fundamental change. The modernization of France into a somewhat greater congruence with what Samuel Beer has called "the collectivist age" has proceeded, despite the inability of the Fourth Republic to govern and despite the domination of the Fifth Republic by conservative governments not ideologically committed to these values of modernization. Nor has the development of the welfare state in France depended on the political or economic orientation of the government. We have seen that the Socialist government of Mitterrand did not produce economic policies substantially different from those of its centrist-rightist predecessors. Thirteen years of a Socialist presidency did not reduce the wide income inequalities among the French.

Despite France's reputation as epitomizing

the essence of political instability, we have seen that when the dust has settled after two centuries of social revolution and numerous regime changes, two patterns of political format have continually reappeared: the Assembly-dominated, anticlerical, weak-executive republics of the First, Third, and Fourth Republics, and the bureaucratic-authoritarian tradition to which the nation seemingly inevitably returns after its forays into executive impotence. The persistence of the dominant political role of nearly classic Weberian bureaucracy is more pronounced in France than in some other nations in the Western world; yet, the bureaucratization of political life is increasingly symptomatic of mature industrial societies. The domination of the Fifth Republic by the president, which characterized the regime until Mitterrand, is no longer a self-evident attribute of the government. After two experiences with divided government, or *cohabitation,* a format characterized by a greater check-and-balance relationship between the legislature and the executive may be evolving. In this, France may be coming to resemble other Western democracies.

The ideologism, the romanticism, and the greater readiness to frame sociopolitical issues in terms of questions about the nature of the regime—attributes in the French culture about which we have written—have constituted the French political style, a style in which there was a romance and mythology with the idea, or "theater," of revolution. The political style of a nation is of course unique to that nation and is a product of innumerable historic, geographic, demographic, and other factors. This style itself becomes a recurring pattern, as in reassertion of the barricade tradition in "the events" of May 1968 and in the university demonstrations against some educational reforms of Jacques Chirac in 1986.

However, the political format of a nation, the pattern and structures by which its collective decisions are made, and the pattern of socioeconomic decisions and policies actually adopted and implemented by a nation, may be more a function of the technological imperatives of mature industrial societies and may hence be more independent of the idiosyncrasies of a nation's political style or the ideological orientations of either its leadership or population. We have developed elsewhere the argument of a structural convergence among mature industrial societies, irrespective of ideological differences.[57] We have thus seen France adapting to the imperatives of the postindustrial era, despite its widely discussed sociocultural attributes that would seem to have worked against such an adaptation. These imperatives for structural and procedural convergence, with the realities of a pluralist nation beset by a multiplicity of mobilized interests demanding access to and influence on the process, may be the cause of France finally bringing down the curtain on its two-hundred-year romance with the "theater of revolution" and getting on with the business of negotiating incremental policy adjustments in the newly discovered politics of interests.

NOTES

1. Raymond Aron, *France, Steadfast and Changing: The Fourth to the Fifth Republic* (Cambridge, MA: Harvard University Press, 1960).
2. This term forms the theme of Tiersky's perceptive interpretation of contemporary France in his *France in the New Europe: Changing Yet Steadfast* (Belmont, CA: Wadsworth Publishing Company, 1994). Tiersky's analysis has strongly influenced the interpretations in this chapter.
3. François Furet, *La Révolution, de Turgot à Jules Ferry, 1770–1880* (Paris: Hachette, 1988), quoted in ibid., p. 19.
4. Lucien Pye, *Aspects of Political Development* (Boston: Little Brown, 1966), pp. 64ff.
5. Samuel Huntington, *Political Order in Changing Societies* (New Haven: Yale University Press, 1968), chap. 2, esp. pp. 95–96.
6. Ibid., p. 94.

7. Will Durant and Ariel Durant, *The Reformation*, vol. 6, *The Story of Civilization* (New York: Simon and Schuster, 1957), pp. 58ff.

8. See Barbara Tuchman, *A Distant Mirror* (New York: Ballantine Books, 1975).

9. See Crane Brinton, *The Anatomy of a Revolution* (Englewood Cliffs, NJ: Prentice Hall, 1952), for the thesis that revolutions tend to occur when a combination of a prosperous society and an impoverished government exists.

10. Ibid.

11. See George Mosse, *The Crisis of German Ideology: Intellectual Origins of the Third Reich* (New York: Schocken Books, 1981), for a classic historical analysis of the *"volkish"* essence of the intellectual foundations of Nazism.

12. William Kornhouser, *The Politics of Mass Society* (New York: The Free Press of Glencoe, 1959).

13. Huntington, *Political Order*, chap. 1.

14. Stanley Hoffman, "Paradoxes of the French Political Community," in Stanley Hoffman, ed., *In Search of France* (New York: Harper Torchbooks, 1963), p. 12.

15. Nicholas Wahl, "France: Conflicting Ideals of Authority," in Samuel Beer and Adam Ulam, eds., *Patterns of Government*, rev. ed. (New York: Random House, 1962), pp. 275–305.

16. Karl Deutsch, "Social Mobilization and Political Development," *American Political Science Review*, vol. 55, no. 3 (September 1961), pp. 493–514; Huntington, *Political Order*, pp. 93ff.

17. Hoffman, "Paradoxes," p. 3.

18. See Michel Crozier, *The Bureaucratic Phenomenon* (Chicago: University of Chicago Press, 1964), for a brilliant analysis of the distinctive attributes of French bureaucracy as a manifestation of the French political culture.

19. Hoffman, "Paradoxes," p. 3.

20. Harry Eckstein, "A Theory of Stable Democracy," Appendix to his *Division and Cohesion in Democracy: A Study of Norway* (Princeton: Princeton University Press, 1966), pp. 225–87. See also Harry Eckstein, "Authority Patterns: A Structural Basis for Political Inquiry," *American Political Science Review*, vol. 68, no. 4 (December 1973), pp. 1142–61; and Harry Eckstein, "Authority Relations and Governmental Performance: A Theoretical Framework," *Comparative Political Studies*, vol. 2, no. 3 (October 1969), pp. 269–326.

21. Herbert Spiro, *Government by Constitution* (New York: Random House, 1959), pp. 194–211, esp. p. 198.

22. Karl Schorske, *German Social Democracy, 1905–1917: The Development of the Great Schism* (New York: Wiley Science Editions, 1955), p. 285.

23. Crozier, *Bureaucratic Phenomenon*, pp. 221ff.

24. The essence of Weber's writings on this topic may be found in H. H. Gerth and C. Wright Mills, eds., *From Max Weber: Essays in Sociology* (New York: Oxford University Press, Galaxy Books, 1958), esp. pp. 196–255; and N. M. Henderson and Talcott Parsons, eds. and trans., *The Theory of Social and Economic Organization* (New York: The Free Press, 1964), pp. 329ff.

25. Crozier, *Bureaucratic Phenomenon*, pt. 4; and Michel Crozier, *The Stalled Society* (New York: The Viking Press, 1970), chap. 5.

26. Crozier, *The Stalled Society*.

27. Jessie Pitts, "Continuity and Change in Bourgeois France," in Hoffman, *In Search of France*, pp. 235–304. See also his "The Bourgeois Family and French Economic Retardation" (Ph.D. diss., Harvard University, 1957).

28. Henry Ehrman, *Politics in France*, 4th ed. (Boston: Little Brown, 1983), p. 18.

29. Laurence Wylie, "Social Change at the Grass Roots," in Hoffman, *In Search of France*, p. 207.

30. Edward Banfield, *The Moral Basis of Backward Society* (New York: The Free Press, 1967).

31. Pierre Bourdieu, "L'Ecole conservatrice: Les inégalités devant l'école et devant la culture," *Revue Française de Sociologie*, vol. 7, no. 3 (1966), pp. 325–47.

32. Ehrman, *Politics in France*, p. 87.

33. Frank Wilson, "The Persistence of Ideologism on the French Democratic Left," in Gary Byrne and Kenneth Pederson, eds., *Politics in European Democracies: Patterns and Problems* (New York: John Wiley and Sons, 1971), pp. 217–32.

34. Michael Dobbs, "French Intellectuals Abandon the God That Failed: Communism," *Washington Post National Weekly Edition*, March 4, 1985, pp. 23–24. See also Keith Reader, *Intellectuals and the Left in France Since 1968* (New York: Wiley, 1986), for a survey of the major writers involved in this transition. See also Jean-François Revel, *The Totalitarian Temptation*.

35. Tiersky, *France in the New Europe*, p. 39.

36. *The Economist*, vol. 333, nos. 22–28 (October 1994), p. 51.

37. Wilson, "The Persistence of Ideologism."

38. Tiersky, *France in the New Europe*, pp. 1–3.

39. William Safran, *The French Polity*, 2nd ed. (New York: Longman, 1985), p. 60.

40. Robert Putnam, "The Political Attitudes of Senior Civil Servants in Western Europe: A Preliminary Report," paper delivered to the annual meeting of the American Political Science Association, Washington, DC, September 1972.

41. Fred Riggs, *Administration in Developing Countries: The Theory of the Prismatic Society* (Boston: Houghton Mifflin Company, 1964). Cf. Lee Sigelman, "Do Modern Bureaucracies Dominate Underdeveloped Politics: A Test of the Imbalance Thesis," *American Political Science Review*, vol. 66, no. 2 (June 1972), pp. 525–28; and Lee Sigelman, "Bureaucratic Development and Dominance: A New Test of the Imbalance Thesis,"

American Political Science Review, vol. 68, no. 2 (June 1974), pp. 308–14.

42. Crozier, *The Stalled Society,* chap. 5; Cozier, *The Bureaucratic Phenomenon,* pt. 4.

43. Hoffman, "Paradoxes," pp. 8–9; Nicholas Wahl, "France: Conflicting Ideals of Authority," p. 281.

44. Jessie Pitts, "Continuity and Change," p. 239.

45. Crozier, *The Bureaucratic Phenomenon,* pp. 187, 193–94.

46. Robert K. Merton, *Social Theory and Social Structure* (Glencoe, IL: The Free Press of Glencoe, 1957), p. 198.

47. George Venardarkis, "The National School of Administration: Training for the Higher Levels of the French Civil Service," *International Journal of Public Administration,* vol. 12, no. 3 (1989), p. 568.

48. Crozier, *The Bureaucratic Phenomenon,* p. 308.

49. Crozier, *The Stalled Society,* p. 129.

50. Ibid.

51. Charles F. Andrain, *Politics and Economic Policies in Western Democracies* (North Scituate, MA: Duxbury Press 1980), pp. 22–23.

52. Arnold J. Heidenheimer, Hugh Heclo, and Carolyn Teich Adams, *Comparative Public Policy: The Politics of Social Choice in Europe and America* (New York: St. Martin's Press, 1983), pp. 79–80.

53. Ibid., p. 19.

54. Charles Taylor and David Jodice, *World Handbook of Social and Political Indicators,* 3rd ed., vol. 1 (New Haven: Yale University Press, 1983), p. 31.

55. Ibid., pp. 134–35.

56. Ibid.

57. Lawrence Mayer and John Burnett, *Politics in Industrial Societies: A Comparative Perspective* (New York: John Wiley and Sons, 1977), pp. 375–77.

5

Germany: Emerging Superpower with a Troubled Past

"We do not live to extenuate the miseries of the past nor to accept as incurable those of the present."

Fairfield Osborn, The Limits of the Earth

"I have often felt a bitter sorrow at the thought of the German people, which is so estimable in the individual and so wretched in the generality."

Johann von Goethe

Among the industrial democracies, perhaps no nation is as conscious of the potential impact of its past and no nation has tried as hard to escape that impact as Germany. In contrast to the image of continuity and evolutionary development that we discussed in Chapter 3 with respect to Great Britain, Germany has undergone the most profound and cataclysmic changes of the European nations in the second half of the twentieth century. The reuniting of the Federal Republic of Germany (West Germany) and the Democratic Republic of Germany (Communist East Germany, the name illustrating the deceptive nature of terms) took place in the fall of 1990. The democratic Federal Republic has in effect absorbed the nondemocratic Democratic Republic. This reunification is effecting the sudden transformation of the former East German system from an authoritarian to a democratic format, much as the Federal Republic itself effected that transformation at the close of World War II.

These transformations from authoritarian to democratic formats raise the question of the constraints of contextual factors on a political system. We have seen in Chapters 1 and 2 that scholars have long presumed that there are cultural and social requisites of democracy and that contextual factors constitute a major part of the explanation of the kind of political format a system adopts and sustains. A literature exists that argues that the almost unique historical experiences of nation building in what we call Germany have produced cultural attributes that to a large extent explain the uniquely brutal dictatorship known as the Third Reich.

If it is true that cultural attributes and historical experiences constitute a major determinant of a regime's propensity to adopt and ability to sustain political democracy, then the transformation of Germany into a successful democracy involves a transformation of cultural attributes overriding the antidemocratic imperatives of that society's troubled

181

past. It had always been assumed that culture is difficult to change. The concept of political culture refers to generalized orientations toward political objects that determine people's attitudes on specific political issues. As such, political culture is acquired early in the preschool years and tends to be rather persistent. Ronald Inglehart's seminal research on cultural change stresses that this is generational change emanating from the socialization of different age groups in very different contexts; the values acquired by individuals tend to persist, he finds, despite contextual change, during the course of their lives.[1] The prospects for successful democracy in a reunited Germany thus depend upon the reengineering of cultural atttributes from those supporting the uniquely horrifying Nazi dictatorship and, more recently, the Stalinist dictatorship in East Germany to those supporting democracy.

THE IMPACT OF THE PAST: A TROUBLING LEGACY

Germany is certainly not unique among Western democracies in having a dictatorial experience in its past. Yet, the amount of attention focused on Germay's Nazi period, spanning a mere 12 years, suggests a widespread perception that the Third Reich somehow makes Germany unique among Western nations.

This perception arises out of two factors. The first is that the Third Reich manifested a level and nature of horror and brutality that many people feel has been unequaled before or since. Many others argue that the Nazis' genocide (attempted extermination of a whole class of human beings) has been approached or even exceeded by other regimes, such as Stalin's purges and extermination of the Kulaks or as Pol Pot's "killing fields" of Cambodia. Others maintain that the Nazi genocide, even though it may have

been exceeded in raw numbers by the Stalinists, was uniquely horrible in that it aimed at the systematic, ignominious extermination of an entire body of humanity—men, women, children, and even babies—identified not by any behavior, not by any position in the social order that may be imagined as some kind of threat to the regime, not by any belief system or adherence to a set of ideas that the regime finds threatening or abhorrent, or not even, as in the case of the Native Americans, by the possession of land or ways of life that conflict with the greed or nation-building aspirations of the dominant group. Rather, the Nazis set about the task of the destruction of world Jewry, defined racially. The Jew was identified as an individual whose blood acted as a cancer on the social system, regardless of his or her religious beliefs and practices. Assimilated Jews, Jewish converts to Christianity, and even Jews who were supporters of other Nazi policies and aspirations were equally marked for extermination with their observant coreligionists. Thus the Holocaust went beyond the practice of *terror*, one of the defining attributes of regimes that approach the totalitarian model (widely used by Stalin's regime), in that terror had some political purpose, however misguided. For the Nazi elites, the implementation of their "final solution" to the "Jewish problem" became the ultimate end in itself and even took precedence over the pressing imperatives of winning the war. The guilt that has fallen upon Germany and that has been assumed by Germany from the Holocaust is in a sense curious, because the institutionalized anti-Semitism of Central Europe, which provided the widespread acceptance of and active support for the Holocaust, was certainly not unique to Germany, and in fact was more established and virulent in Austria and Poland than in Germany itself. It is said that Austria perpetrated two of the greatest "con jobs" on the West: that Austria was a victim of rather than an enthusiastic partner with the Third Reich, and that Hitler was a German instead of the Austrian he was. It was there that he acquired his fanatical hatred of Jews. With regard to Poland, it was no accident that the most infamous death camps, whose grisly business could not really be hidden from nearby residents, were located there.

The second factor is related to the first. The very unique brutality of the Third Reich, a brutality that seemed to defy the absolute essence of what it meant to be a civilized Western nation, stands in inexplicable contrast to the fact that Germany, by other standards, has been one of the most civilized, cultured, and advanced nations of the Western world. We are mesmerized by the puzzle of how a nation that has given the world the likes of Beethoven, Brahms, Goethe, Kant, and Schopenhauer has also produced the Third Reich. Prior to World War II, Germany had produced almost twice as many Nobel Prize winners as either Great Britain, France, or the United States. German engineering and mastery of modern technology, hallmarks of modernity, are world renowned. Thus, the German past is in important respects a study in vivid contrasts between the heights and depths of Western civilization.

There is a third factor that causes the West to focus on Germany among all the nations with a nondemocratic past. Only Germany has actually overrun or attempted to overrun Western Europe twice in the twentieth century, causing that country's nationalism to be perceived as more of a real threat by its European neighbors. France in particular has its present attitudes toward a reunited Germany affected by its collective memory of German troops marching into Paris a half-century ago. Part of the French and British reluctance to embrace a federal Europe dominated by Germany and its Bundesbank can be traced to their memory of the two World Wars.

In coming to grips with the factors that distinguish the German experience with nation building from the experiences of her more successful neighbors to the West, one is first struck by the delayed formation of the German nation-state and the continuing struggle over the question of regime. The German nation was not formed as an actual political entity until the close of the Franco-Prussian War, long after the idea of the German nation was well established. Germany did achieve the status of a sovereign, unified nation-state long before the majority of Third World nations; however, in most of the Third World nations, the *idea* of nationhood did not long precede the *achievement* of nationhood. The gap between the widespread acceptance of the idea of the German nation, the self-identification by many opinion leaders as Germans, and the actual achievement of a unified German state produced a widespread frustration in Germany over the failure to achieve the nation-state status of its closest neighbors. This frustration, in turn, produced an exaggerated and extreme form of nationalism, an extreme glorification of the nation-state that shows itself in the writings of the philosophers and scholars most influential in shaping the German political culture, some of whom are discussed below.

This delayed nation building was itself the product of geographical and social forces shaping the German past. Germany is located in Central Europe on a broad plain running from the Ural Mountains in Russia to the shores of the Atlantic. Throughout the history of the Western world, armies marched back and forth along this plain, disrupting the establishment and institutionalization of normal political processes. The eastern and western boundaries of what was called Germany are highly permeable, a fact that rendered them the subject of continuing disputes with both France to the west and with Poland and Czechoslovakia to the east.

The centrifugal forces normally encountered in the process of nation building and contained by insular borders, such as those associated with Great Britain and the Scandinavian nations, are difficult to control when borders are highly permeable.

When permeable borders render the containment of centrifugal forces difficult in the nation-building process, the concern for national defense and security becomes part of the national psyche. Large standing armies result, and martial values take on greater importance in the political culture. Nowhere were martial values given greater adulation than in German political thought. For example, in addition to his glorification of the German nation-state, the famed German philosopher at the University of Berlin Georg Wilhelm Friedrich Hegel also extolled the glories of war for its own sake. He argued, "It is in this state of war that the omnipotence of the state manifests itself." He further writes, "War has the deep meaning that by it the ethical health of a nation is preserved. . . . war protects people from the corruption which an everlasting peace would bring upon it."[2] A few years later, Heinrich von Treitschke, a popular professor of history at the same university, outdid Hegel in his glorification of war. He wrote, "War is not only a practical necessity but a theoretical necessity. . . . The concept of the state implies the concept of war." He even found that "martial glory is the basis of all the political virtues."[3] This central place of martial values in German thought allows the military to exist as a source of power autonomous from the constitutional regime and of potential opposition to any constitutional regime. Military power can also be used as a means of suppressing the internal political competiton that is the basis of democracy and political freedom.

The centrifugal forces generated or perpetuated by the difficulty of Germany's nation-building process include the divisive factor of religious conflict arising out of the Protestant Reformation. Recall that the potentially intense conflict between Protestant and Catholic was resolved in Britain and France by a ruling elite strong and legitimate enough to impose a resolution, an elite that had established its internal legitimacy before the Reformation placed that conflict on the table. In Britain, Henry VIII broke with the Catholic Church over papal disapproval of his marital escapades. By contrast, in France, Henry IV recognized the dominance of the Catholics and sought papal absolution for himself, while Louis XIV ushered in a period of official intolerance of the Huguenot (French Protestant) minority. In Germany, however, with over 30 autonomous principalities, no legitimate political authority existed prior to the religious conflicts following the Reformation. Accordingly, religious wars were repeatedly fought on German soil, such as the Schmalkaldic Wars (1546–55), which ended with the Peace of Augsburg, and culminating in the bloody Thirty Years' War (1618–48), which ended with the Peace of Westphalia. Religious conflict can stir the deepest of passions, the strongest of animosities, and the greatest brutality of which human beings are capable. The Thirty Years' War physically devastated Germany, and cost the lives of around *40 percent* of the people, and the resulting Peace of Westphalia confirmed the political disintegration of Central Europe and the Holy Roman Empire.

When nations experience difficulty in containing the centrifugal forces associated with nation building, and have a more difficult time establising the authority and legitimacy of the central government, they tend to be less tolerant of criticism of and opposition to the government. After a series of military victories ending with the Franco-Prussian War, Germany was united under the stern authoritarian leadership of Otto von Bismarck and the Prussian aristocracy in 1871. This was the culmination of a struggle for the realization of German nationalism—the struggle to unite all of the peoples who spoke the German language and identified themselves as German in a single German state—that had been going on for years and in a sense has never really been resolved. Some 30 years earlier, in 1848, the failure of the Frankfurt Assembly to establish a unified constitutional monarchy signaled the exclusion of the middle classes, professionals, and intellectuals from effective participation in Germany's decision making and allowed the authoritarian governments of the over 30 constituent states of "the Germanies" to regain control. Yet, these middle-class and professional groups had become conscious of having their own distinct interests and rights, a consciousness that had emanated from the spread of liberal ideas during the Napoleonic wars and the revolutions of 1830.

There was thus in the German context a frustration of nationalists over the long delay in the establishment of the German state and the frustration of other groups over their exclusion from effective participation in the political process. In the absence of an actual state within which to work and with the inability of intellectuals to participate effectively in politics with a pragmatic problem-solving orientation, a tradition evolved of thinking about politics in romantic, ideological terms. Since the failure of nationalist aspirations was the source of much of this frustration, the idea of the nation was especially romanticized and glorified by prominent German philosophers and intellectuals. Perhaps the most famous was the aforementioned Hegel, who wrote that "freedom" consisted of service to the state and that since "the state is the divine idea as it exists on earth . . . we must therefore worship the state."[4] The struggle to incorporate the German-speaking and German-identifying peoples in one state was again manifested in

Hitler's annexation of the Sudetenland of Czechoslovakia, his Anschluss with Austria just prior to the outbreak of World War II, and the 1990 reunification of Germany.

The German state unified in 1871 under Prussia and Bismarck, with Kaiser (Emperor) Wilhelm I as the head of state, was known as the Second Reich. The First Reich refers to the medieval Holy Roman Empire, a loosely knit collection of hundreds of autonomous principalities that was not holy, was not Roman, and was not an empire. It was formally abolished by Napoleon. The Second Reich ended with the defeat of Germany in World War I in 1918.

The collapse of the Second Reich led to the proclamation of a republic, a move strongly encouraged and influenced by the victorious Western powers. The constitution of the Weimar Republic, drawn up by some of the most eminent scholars of the day, emphasized a highly egalitarian and representative format. A highly proportional electoral system, discussed in Chapter 2, produced a greatly fragmented party system in which no party had enough of a clear plurality to dominate any potential governing coalition. Much has been written about how the highly egalitarian format of this system was inconsistent with the predominantly authoritarian German culture. While this conflict is so plain that the Weimar Republic has often been cited as the epitome of such a system, the causal connection between that incongruity and the failure of the system has not been conclusively demonstrated. Besides its lack of fit with the German political culture, the Weimar Consititution was badly flawed in other respects. The format was designed to produce a government that was as perfectly representative of the spectrum of opinion in society as possible. Also, with mechanisms such as referendums and recall provisions, the possibility of the abuse of power was so carefully guarded against that, short of effectively terminating the democratric process with the infamous Article 48, no government was able to act in ways that may have been necessary for the longer term in a crisis situation but were not widely popular in the present. Article 48, which permitted the Reich cabinet to declare and utilize emergency powers, was misused by Hitler to terminate the Weimar democracy. In short, the government was representative and highly constrained, but weak and unable to govern over a range of difficult and controversial issues. The founders of Weimar apparently did not believe that the first job of a government is to govern.

Yet, the Weimar Republic faced the most difficult of situations from the outset. Representing the losing side in World War I, the Weimar government was confronted with huge reparations and war debts in addition to the national humiliation of defeat in a country in which nationalism was such a strong force. The Weimar government had in fact negotiated the settlement ending the war, thereby rendering it vulnerable to the charge that it had betrayed the German war effort. The Bolshevik Revolution in Russia just before the republic was established produced a flurry of activism by Communists, including the abortive Spartacist insurrection led by Rosa Luxemburg and Karl Liebknecht in 1919, activities that convinced many anti-Communist Germans that a Communist revolution was an imminent and serious threat. A disastrous level of inflation in 1923 wiped out the life savings of many ordinary Germans. In that year, the rate of inflation was *26 billion percent!* A kilogram of potatoes that cost 20 marks in January cost 90 billion marks by October. Meanwhile, the Communists on the left and the ultra nationalists, monarchists, etc., on the right were able to agree on nothing except to defeat any attempt by the center to form a government capable of addressing these problems. The republic appeared

completely inept in confronting these growing crises; hence, it was unable to establish any level of legitimacy among a people for whom democratic values were not well established. When the Great Depression hit in 1929, the economic troubles of the young republic were compounded with a sharp rise in unemployment.

The failure of the Social Democratic governments to deal adequately with this new crisis further undermined the legitimacy of the democratic center and of the regime itself. The vote for the political extremes grew at the expense of the center. By 1932, the combined vote for the Nazis and Communists was over 50 percent, providing a permanent antidemocratic majority. Support for the Nazis themselves had gone from a tiny 2.6 percent in 1928 to 37 percent, giving them a plurality of electoral support among the parties in the Reichstag. As head of the plurality party, Hitler was the logical person for President Hindenberg to ask to become chancellor and form a government. Much of the initial support for the Nazis came from two groups most threatened by the modernization process—the peasantry and the lower middle classes. Peasants were particularly attracted to the "blood and soil" components of the Nazi racial ideologies in that the peasantry were identified as the truest backbone of the folk, the real Germans. However, by the time the Nazi vote share reached 37 percent, their support was clearly much more widespread. Some elements undoubtedly felt that support for Hitler was a means of controlling other forces, such as the Communists, and that Hitler could be controlled for their own purposes. Big business and some military leaders may have been in this category. Clearly, they underestimated Hitler's determination and the seriousness with which the Nazis took their own rhetoric.

In a real sense, the Nazis were elected in the last free election in the Weimar Republic;

they came into office with widespread public support and with their plans and programs well known. The Third Reich was not something that was imposed upon the German people; they adopted it enthusiastically, and the values that the regime espoused were widely shared by the population. Clearly, few Germans were aware of the full details and extent of the population exterminations perpetrated by the Nazi regime; yet, most knew that large numbers of people were being seized and were disappearing into some unpleasant fate. Moreover, one cannot effect the seizure and systematic extermination of over 12 million civilians without the active participation and support of a considerable number of otherwise ordinary people. The significance of this for present German politics lies in the questions that are raised about cultural attributes of the population that is today expected to support a Western liberal democracy—the extent to which there has been a cultural transformation to accompany the political transformation of West Germany in the postwar era, and the direction that the new united Germany, not as clearly dominated and influenced by the Western allies as was the Federal Republic, might be expected to take.

Although frequently called fascist, the Nazi dictatorship was in many respects a unique sociopolitical phenomenon. Ernst Nolte's classic book on fascism[5] and a survey of other definitions by A. James Gregor indicate a lack of consensus among scholars as to the nature of generic fascism, not to mention as to the fascist nature of the Third Reich.[6] The opinion of Gregor and other scholars seems to indicate a widespread conclusion that the Third Reich was fundamentally different from Italian Fascism and that the latter represents the "model" or ideal type of what is meant by the concept of *fascism*.[7] Chapter 6 presents and analyzes the arguments that Nazi Germany and the Soviet Union under

Stalin constitute the two real-world manifestations of a generic class of political phenomena to which the term *totalitarianism* is sometimes applied. Among the attributes of such a system is an official millenaristic ideology,[8] a thought system that posits the existence of a utopian period of great happiness for all. The critical difference between the two states, according to some scholars, is that while the Marxist and therefore Soviet millennium is set in the indefinite future, that of the fascists—especially of the Nazis—is the Middle Ages. A highly romaticized vision of the Germanic peoples of the Wagnerian legends held great appeal for the Nazi leaders. This romantic component of the movement appealed to emotion as opposed to reason, to a sense of community as opposed to Enlightenment individualism, and to an anti-intellectualism.[9] The glorification of the peasantry was the other side of a deep distrust of an industrial society. The Nazi phenomenon in particular may be viewed as a revolt against modernity.[10] The Nazi anti-Semitism may be seen as a response to the image of the Jew in this part of Europe at this time as quintessentially modern, rational, cosmopolitan, and international in orientation, a denial of the basic Nazi values. The Nazi thirst for land to the east—*Lebensraum*—is viewed in this interpretation as a means of reducing Germany's need for industrial production to trade for food and a place on which the displaced industrial workers may be resettled. The audacious Nazi aim was to free the German people from industrial society and return them to a simplistic and romaticized rural, peasant existence.

Such an audacious vision and goal involved the heavy, systematic socialization of the population in general and the youth in particular to values compatible with the Nazi world view. The breakdown of the Third Reich and the imposition of a democratic format by the Allied powers in the Federal Republic therefore involved one of the most difficult and challenging attempts to engineer basic and comperehensive cultural change seen in modern history.

ENGINEERING POLITICAL CULTURE: CULTURAL CHANGE IN POSTWAR GERMANY

The Third Reich, it has been suggested, reflected a cultural context that permitted and even facilitated its emergence. A number of themes have been identified in the cultural context of Germany that would be logically conducive to an appeal such as that of the Nazis gaining widespread acceptance. Clearly, the long-term legitimacy of a democratic political format such as that adopted by the Bonn republic in the postwar era requires modification of such cultural attributes to those more supportive of democratic values. Several questions emerge here. One is the extent to which the data actually support the characterizations of the German culture made by those who argue that it was supportive of the Nazis. Second is the extent to which the data indicate cultural change in the postwar era. If such change in a direction conducive to democracy is indicated, can one conclude that the persistence of a democratic format over time due to economic and political success (i.e., peace, prosperity, and national stature) will lead to the legitimation of such a format and the spread of cultural attributes and values supportive of democracy? In other words, although it has long been assumed that cultural attributes are a major determinant of political format, is it possible to reverse the independent and dependent variables on this equation and have the format as a determinant of cultural attributes?

Among the themes in the German culture that have been identified as conducive to the emergence of the Nazi dictatorship are the following: a submissive, authoritarian attitude toward authority; an anti-intellectual and antirational romanticism; what has been called *volkishness*—a combination of the anti-intellectual romanticism with a distorted populism and xenophobia; an exaggerated form of nationalism with a corresponding rejection of internationalism; a glorification of war and martial values; a hostility toward the West and modernism and their values; and a deeply rooted hostility to Jews.[11]

Several scholars conducted immediate postwar studies whose data indicate a strong strain of authoritarianism in the German family and in other social relations, such as those between teacher and student, employer and employee, and even husband and wife.[12] Related to this is the finding of the classic *Civic Culture* study that, compared to the citizens of the Anglo-American democracies, citizens of the Federal Republic of Germany felt less competent to participate effectively in political activity.[13] They tended to perceive that their proper role was to leave the business of politics to their leaders, who were presumably more able to understand it. It is clearly one thing, however, to show that there is more of tendency to submit to authority in Germany compared to, say, the Anglo-American democracies, but it is clearly something else to posit such a tendency as a proximate cause of anything so complex as the emergence of the Nazi dictatorship. Moreover, despite the findings of greater authoritarianism in Germany compared to the Anglo-American democracies, Germany was certainly not unique among Central and Eastern European systems in having such an orientation in the first half of the twentieth century.

In the chaos and frustration of failed nationalism in the nineteenth century, many German writers and thinkers expressed a desire to belong to something greater than themselves. The isolation of individuals by virtue of the Enlightenment appeared to be threatening, and the Germans sought a concept through which they could express their longing for unity in the absence of any immediate prospect of political unity.[14] That concept is the *volk,* which meant much more than its literal translation of "folk" and, as such, was central to the romantic strain in German thought. It refers to an organic concept or essence (a reality in the world of ideas in the Platonic sense) that is more than the total of a group of individuals. It is the essence of what defines and distinguishes "a real German" and comes close to the idea of the "soul" of the nation. As such, it implies a set of values such as "rootedness." The peasant, tied to the land in a mystical bond of blood and soil, constitutes the epitome of the folk.

The concept of the folk as the unifying symbol for the German nation, a concept implying a soul rooted in nature, further connotes a people that have a long history in a given setting. Consequently, volkish thinkers focused attention on the ancient Germanic tribes. The Roman historian Tacitus, whose book *Germania* expounded on alleged Germanic virtues in contrast with what he felt was a growing Roman degeneracy, was frequently cited.[15]

This view of the soul of the German people, the folk, rooted in their racial heritage from the ancient Germanic tribes, leads to a hostility to the modern world itself, a world that had not been kind to the Germanies. Germany was finally united under the auspices of the Prussian autocracy in a struggle with the liberal democratic and modern forces of the West, a fact that may have exacerbated the preexisting disposition of Germans against those values.

Anti-Semitism, hatred of Jews, has been identified as another central theme of Nazi ideology, not just a peripheral disposition. The Nazis diverted critical resources and elite personnel from the war effort to what they called "the final solution," the rounding up and extermination of the Jews of Europe. Obsessed with the ideal of racial purity, volkish theorists such as Paul deLagarde and Julius Langbehn focused on the Jews as a primary pollutant of Germanic blood. Since Jews became defined racially, forced conversions were not a solution; the problem was not one of belief and observance. Anti-Semitic attitudes continued to be expressed by some 30 to 40 percent of the German population in variously worded surveys throughout the 1950s, well after the full extent of the Nazi war against the Jews had become known to everyone who did not practice pathological denial. Anti-Semitism has had a long and legitimate history in Europe, and the programs for the persecution of Jews found a receptive and even enthusiastic audience among the German people as well as in the surrounding countries in occupied Europe.

Given that tolerance and the legitimacy of pluralism have been identified as core democratic values, this German anti-Semitism was not conducive to German democracy. This does not mean that democracy cannot coexist with a strong strain of anti-Semitism, which has been well established in France, as we have seen manifested in the Dreyfus Affair (see Chapter 4), in the enthusiastic French participation in rounding up Jewish children for shipment to Auschwitz, in the current popularity of Jean-Marie Le Pen's almost avowedly fascist National Front, and in the 1990 desecrations of the Jewish cemetery at Carpentras. Great Britain as well is no stranger to such sentiments; one of the leading philo-German racists and anti-Semitic propogandists of the early twentieth century was an Englishman named Houston Stewart Chamberlain. Yet, the 200,000 French men and women, including the elites of their nation, that marched in protest against the outrages at Carpentras, and the vigor of the campaign of the Dreyfussards at the turn of the century, give support to the expectation that the general acceptance in Germany of the 1935 Nuremberg laws (officially removing the remaining civil and political rights from Jews and even forbidding sexual relations between Jews and non-Jews) would be impossible in France without intense political controversy. Hence, the depth and extent of institutionalized racial and religious bigotry in Germany by the close of World War II may be viewed as an indication of the enormity of the task of resocializing the citizens of the Bonn republic in a cultural orientation compatible with stable, effective democracy.

The question for German democracy today, of course, is the extent of residual xenophobia in general and anti-Semitism in particular, and the extent to which whatever manifestations of such bigotry occur are condemned by the rest of the population. Xenophobia perpetrated by the radical right in the reunited Germany has largely been expressed in attacks against foreigners, attacks in part justified and perhaps exacerbated by the preception that foreign workers have been competing for scarce German jobs in a period of economic uncertainty.

In 1992, riots and attacks against foreigners broke out in the port city of Rostock. Clearly, in the eyes of the world, any such right-wing violent xenophobia in Germany raises the specter of a resurrection of Nazism. Moreover, in 1992 the federal police estimated that there were some 40,000 right-wing extremists in Germany, who, in 1991, had committed 1,483 acts of violence, a five-fold increase over the previous year.[16] All of these acts resulted, however, in just nine fatalities. Thus, the intensity of such violence is clearly not in the same category as that of Weimar Germany. Eighty-six percent of the Germans condemned the violence in a poll; however, that means that 14 percent explicitly did not condemn it when asked to do so. Anti-Jewish incidents also continued. On Sep-

tember 26, 1991, the memorial to Jews who had died in the death camp at Sachsenhausen was destroyed by arson. Chancellor Kohl condemned the incident.

These attacks should be seen in the context of a Germany economy that has been stagnating since reunification. Unemployment in Germany in 1992 averaged 6.4 percent, up from 5.7 percent the previous year. In the former East Germany, the unemployment rate was 13.5 percent. The gross domestic product for reunited Germany grew by only 1.5 percent in 1992, well below the growth rate of other European powers.

Moreover, antiforeigner xenophobia has been further exacerbated by an especially large influx of foreign workers, willing to work for lower wages than the typical German, an influx encouraged by the most liberal immigration and asylum laws in the West. In 1992, 274,000 people applied for asylum in Germany in the first eight months, a figure 94 percent above that of a year earlier.[17] Foreign Minister Klaus Kinkel complained that Germany had been assuming "disproportionate share" of the refugee burden.

Rather than taking vigorous action against its perpetrators, Germany's response to xenophobic and anti-Semitic violence was the predictably legalistic and nationalistic one of tightening its laws on asylum and immigration in May 1993. In that year attacks on foreigners fell by 42 percent from the 1992 levels, and incidents perpetrated by right-wing extremists fell by some 30 percent. In that same year there were only 46 attacks on Jews motivated by religious bigotry, compared to 63 such attacks the preceding year. One cannot say, based upon the data from one year, whether this reduced level of xenophobic violence is a long-term trend and whether it is in part a reaction to the tightened restrictions in the influx of foreigners.

The weak commitment to democratic values in the Federal Republic of Germany at the time of its establishment in 1949 is related to the weak commitment to democracy itself as a political format. Sidney Verba reports that in 1953, only about 57 percent of the polled public said that democracy was the best form of government for Germany,[18] while Karl Deutsch reports that approximately one-quarter of the respondents in a 1956 survey of the national electorate were "consistent defenders of democracy and approximately another twenty-five percent professed some degree of sympathy or preference for the anti-democratic extreme right and one in eight professed explicit Nazi sympathies."[19] Approximately one-quarter of these respondents also expressed favorable opinions of Hitler and his closest henchmen.

Thus, at the outset of the founding of the Federal Republic, the commitment to the regime was based upon its success in achieving policy objectives, specifically, the famed "economic miracle" in which Germany emerged from the almost total devastation of World War II to become, within a little more than a decade, one of the most prosperous and economically powerful nations in Europe. Germany attained its prewar level of industrial production by 1950, and in the next 20 years that figure increased by 500 percent! Support for the system was feared to be support for specific performance, which is subject to change over time. Memories of the collapse of Weimar in the face of severe economic crisis had pessimists wondering aloud how well the Federal Republic would fare in the face of the first economic crisis that all systems inevitably experience.

Legitimacy, we have seen in Chapter 2, is normally acquired when the institutions in question have been around for long periods without widespread and intense opposition. The most legitimate political formats in Europe have been those that were institutionalized and legitimized before the mobilization

of the masses generated new levels of demands and stress with which the systems could not cope. Hence, a kind of vicious circle was created for the systems, like Germany, that completed their nation building after the mobilization of the masses had occurred in the eighteenth century: they could not last long because they were not legitimate, and they could not acquire legitimacy because they could not last.

The Bonn republic seems to have broken out of this vicious circle by acquiring legitimacy because of persisting support for specific performance. The regime lasted in the decades after World War II because of the "economic miracle" and a resurgence of national prestige and security. As the democratic format remained in place over decades, the prevalence of democratic attitudes and values began to grow among the population, imparting value and legitimacy to the democratic format for its own sake regardless of policy performance. Attitudes and values of the radical right are held by a steadily diminishing proportion of the population. For example, in 1951, six years after the fall of the Third Reich, when knowledge of all of its policies and their consequences was inescapable, 42 percent of the West German population felt that Germany had been better off in the prewar years of that regime, compared to only 2 percent who chose the democratic Federal Republic. This result suggests that the principal complaint against the Nazis was not their total denial of civil liberties and freedom or their persecution of large numbers of men, women, and children but that they lost the war.[20] Another 45 percent chose the nondemocratic Second Reich. Hence, some two years into the current democratic format, around 90 percent of the population thought Germany had been better off during one of the earlier authoritarian formats, a fact that shows how narrowly held were democratic values for their own sake.

Yet, by 1962, the proportion of respondents claiming that Germany was better off in the Federal Republic had risen to 62 percent, while only 10 percent still chose the prewar Third Reich. Similarly, a 1956 poll showed 48 percent of the respondents agreeing with the statement that Hitler was one of Germany's greatest statesmen, but that figure had declined to 32 percent by 1967, the first year in which over half of the respondents specifically denied that claim.[21] Despite this manifest trend in a democratic direction, one might feel some uneasiness by the finding that as late as 1967, a third of the German respondents still would identify Hitler as a great statesman. One may justifiably wonder about the commitment to democratic values by the considerable number of people who could still so identify Hitler. In 1951, 32 percent, or just under a third of the respondents, thought that the restoration of the Hohenzollern monarchy (the Second Reich) would be a good idea, but that figure declined to only 11 percent by 1965.

What these and a plethora of similar data suggest is that upon its founding and for two decades or so thereafter, support for the democratic format of the Bonn republic was based upon its successful performance (prosperity, peace, and security) and the lack of a credible alternative to the regime in the short run, but that as the regime remained in place, its legitimacy for its own sake grew as democratic values became more widely held among the population, and support or nostalgia for Germany's dictatorial past became increasingly confined to a small, fringe portion of the population.

We have seen that the collapse of democracy under Weimar occurred in a context of economic catastrophe. We also believe from subsequent research and theorizing, such as the much cited work of Inglehart discussed at length in Chapter 2, which is based upon earlier psychological theorizing of Abraham

Maslow, that when the value of material well-being is in question, other values, such as liberty, are superseded and placed on the back burner. In the context of the extent of the economic catastrophe under Weimar, it is not suprising that Germans chose the promise of economic security and material well-being over the abstract civil liberties values of democracy. In 1947, a survey confirmed the priority of economic over democratic values. When a sample was asked to choose between a government offering economic security and one offering freedom, 62 percent chose economic security, while only 26 percent chose freedom.[22] This is consistent with the aforementioned Inglehart theory of value change, which posits that for a generation of people raised in a period of economic scarcity, the value of material well-being takes precedence over more abstract values such as freedom, and that this value priority persists throughout life, even when the objective conditions of economic scarcity are alleviated. On the other hand, when people are raised in an era of economic well-being, material values are replaced in importance by nonmaterialist values; hence, one might expect the value priorities to be reversed for that generation of West Germans raised in the era of the "economic miracle."

The evidence indicates that diffuse support for democracy as a political format is in fact growing and becoming well established among the West German population. We do not have similar data for the citizens of the former Communist East Germany, who are now citizens of united Germany. One possible disquieting fact is that the earliest and strongest electoral support for the Nazis came from areas that were part of East Germany. Second, since most of them never experienced democracy, it seems less likely that they will come to value democracy for its own sake, as have the citizens of the Federal Republic. It may be hoped that the former East

Germans will go through a process parallel to that of their western counterparts—initially favoring democracy for the material well-being it can provide and then later developing support for democracy for its own sake. This of course presumes that a united Germany can similarly deliver on performance, an assumption that some people may doubt and that will be examined in the last section of this chapter. We simply do not know for sure whether or what cultural change has occurred in that territory; the data we have on cultural change in Germany applies to West Germany, which is now part of a larger political system.

The problem of cultural change is that it deals with attitudes and dispositions that are formed early in the life of an individual and tend to persist regardless of external circumstances. Cultural orientations are thought to be a product of an individual's formative preschool years. Yet, despite that pessimistic assessment, the evidence is that tremendous changes have occurred in the German political culture. Support for Nazi principles and leaders has diminished to insignificant levels. Even the short-term, very modest increases in support for the right-wing National Democratic Party in the 1960s, which was widely labled as neo-Nazi, may be more attributed to the fact that the "Grand Coalition" of the two major parties at that time left only this minor party as an alternative avenue for the expression of political opposition.

Meanwhile, support for the concept of democracy for its own sake has clearly grown. For example, we noted above the amazing growth in the percentage of respondents to a national survey who thought that Germany was better off in the democratic format of Bonn rather than one of its authoritarian predecessors, which went from only 2 percent in 1951 to 62 percent by 1962 to over 80 percent by 1970. This seems to suggest that the democratic format of the Bonn republic

has acquired a legitimacy, or diffuse support, among its citizens. It is expected that the citizens of the former Democratic Republic will develop a similar commitment to democracy for its own sake now that the two Germanies are unified; however, we have no data on this question.

Moroever, as Kendall Baker, Russell Dalton, and Kai Hildebrandt have observed, it is one thing to voice approval of the political regime but it many be something else to internalize the values and norms of a democratic society.[23] For example, the norm of a sense of political effectiveness and of an obligation to participate are most closely related to education.

In addition to the growing legitimacy of a democratic format, there seems to be a decline in other attributes of the German culture that some had linked to the German support for the Third Reich, such as the submissive orientation toward authority and a deep-seated lack of acceptance of the egalitarian standards of equality for liberal democracies as manifested in the quintessentially sexist implication of the classic German phrase on the proper role of women: *kinder, kirche, küche* (children, church, kitchen). Evidence for the decline of such blatant German sexism may be found in David Conradt's finding that the percentage of German males who would be pleased by women becoming politically active increased from 27 percent in 1965 to 56 percent in 1971 to 62 percent in 1976, while the percent who reported that they would be displeased decreased from 52 percent in 1965 to 26 percent in 1971 to only 16 percent in 1976.[24]

The attribution of an authoritarian nature to the German family has often been supported by the results of a 1951 national poll on the values that should be stressed in child rearing. The choice of "love of order and industriousness" received the support of 41 percent of the respondents and the value of "obedience and deference" was named by 25 percent. The choice of "independence and free will," classic values of liberal democracy, was named by only 28 percent of the sample. Yet by 1976, obedience and deference were named as the most important values by only 10 percent, while independence and free will were named by 51 percent.[25] Thus, the values that adults think ought to passed on to the children are definitely more compatible with the idea of liberal democracy than were the values of four decades ago, and these data indicate that the stereotypical image of the authoritarian German family is no longer typical of the present day Bonn Republic.

There are several possible explanations of the apparent success in engineering cultural change. First, the decline of an authoritarian orientation after the war may be related to the belief that this orientation was learned in the authoritarian German family dominated by a powerful father figure. Yet, in the postwar era, many German youths grew up in fatherless homes because of the heavy loss of men in the war. The relative shortage of men also helped weaken the rigidity of the classic German attitude toward the role of women.

Second and most important, it is widely believed that a large part of this cultural change is a generational phenomenon related to the Inglehart theory of value change, discussed at length in Chapter 2.[26] The residual antidemocratic or pro-Nazi orientations until recently predominantly appeared among older Germans for whom the values of order and the Fatherland were a reaction to the chaos of the interwar years and the gap between the idea and the establishment of the German nation. Germans who have grown up and acquired their values in the postwar era take the values of order, economic security, national self-respect, and effective government for granted. For them, what Inglehart calls "postmaterialist" values, including such things as environmentalism,

feminism, life style, and personal freedom, have acquired greater relevance. Hence, the Green Party, a new left-wing ecology party, has acquired growing although still limited strength among the younger voters. Still, the anti-immigrant and anti-Semitic violence of the early 1990s has been largely perpetrated by younger, alienated Germans, especially among the so-called skinheads. It is not clear that this recent violence is a resurgence of Nazism as such. Rather, it is a manifestation of the fear of being displaced by these foreign workers, who are often willing to accept lower wages as they compete for increasingly scarce jobs in a nearly stagnant economy.

Thus, the transformation to democratic values in the 1970s was not so much a matter of voters abandoning their personal values and acquiring new ones as it was a matter of older voters dying off and being replaced by the next generation coming of voting age. If Inglehart is correct that the political orientation and values that one acquires in one's preschool years are affected by the context of those formative years, but are not easily affected by adult situations and experience, then the values acquired in the context of the postwar "economic miracle" will tend to remain permanent, even if the economy takes a downward turn, as it eventually must. The decline of antidemocratic or pro-Nazi sentiment is as much a function of older Germans dying off as of German disenchantment with values they once held. The present generation of Germans, growing up in postwar prosperity, take for granted the concern for economic security and order that drove their parents to abandon Weimar.

A third reason that scholars have noted for the apparent rise of diffuse support for a democratic format among Germans is the absence of a credible alternative to the present system.[27] The Nazi system was discredited by the utter devastation of World War II, and the restoration of the monarchy was never a realistic prospect in the Cold War period. The model of Communist rule in neighboring East Germany further discredited the authoritarian alternative. This may be contrasted with the experiences of Weimar, when, as the regime encountered difficulty, Hitler and his associates were ready with an alternative.

The fourth reason is that regimes may acquire legitimacy by being in place without significant, widespread opposition over time. Due to certain circumstances, the Federal Republic was able to offer security, national respect, peace, and unprecedented prosperity for over four decades. In the course of that time, the regime became identified with its substantive success and acquired legitimacy for its own sake. Recall the suggestion in Chapter 2 that while diffuse support for the regime is distinct from satisfaction with its output, the latter can over time operate to increase diffuse support for the regime.

The four decades of substantive satisfaction require explanation. Recall the crisis of democracy literature that suggests that widespread support for a regime's outputs over time is very difficult in an era of mobilized populations with high expectations and an interdependent world that places the resolution of many political and economic issues outside the control of the nation-state. Germany and Japan, the vanquished nations of World War II, were able to overcome the logic of this suggestion and provide just such widespread satisfaction with outputs due to the following special circumstances. First, because of the outbreak of the Cold War immediately after World War II, these defeated and devastated nations received massive infusions of American aid to build them up as bastions against Communist expansion. Second, because the Allied powers insisted on their virtually complete demilitarization, Germany and Japan were freed from assuming the costly burden of their own defense and security, thus releasing considerable capital for in-

vestment into the growth of their gross domestic product. Third, because their industrial plants were so devastated, they were rebuilt from scratch with more efficient postwar technology. Ironically, Britain and the United States, as the two industrial powers that emerged from the war with their prewar industrial plants virtually intact, suffered from the loss of productive efficiency in the postwar era. Almost in the tradition of classical tragedy, their very strength and success were a major source of their economic undoing.

The transformation of the German political culture may also be seen in the area of what Herbert Spiro has called political style (discussd in Chapter 2). The Germans had been ideological and romantic in their thinking about political issues. Ideologism involves thinking about politics in terms of a closed set of abstract principles rather than in terms of what alternatives actually exist and what works on a trial-and-error basis. Romanticism refers to an emphasis on feeling and emotion that appeals to an anti-intellectual, irrational orientation. Such aspects of the German philosophical tradition as the glorification of war and the exaltation of the as yet nonexistent German nationhood could not be justified on a rational or empirical basis; hence, they were promoted on a mystical level with reference to a largely apocryphal and heroic past.

Germans have also been characterized as legalistic in the sense of having a reverence for rules for their own sake and a norm of unqualified obedience to such rules. Legalists have an exaggerated reliance on the efficacy of laws to resolve conflicts. The exaggerated German reverence for rules as such is illustrated in two probably apocryphal stories about German revolutionaries in 1918 who would not step on the grass when rushing buildings or seize a railway station without first buying a ticket because they would not disobey the posted signs.

Subsequent analyses of the German culture have characterized the citizens of the Bonn republic as highly pragmatic, almost cynical, and without a strong emotional commitment to the system or to any other set of principles. It is as if having been badly burned by their recent passions for the Nazi ideology, Germans now reject ideologies altogether. Their penchant for legalism apparently remains, however, as is revealed by the German attempts to resolve political problems by tinkering with the rules. The brief rise in support for the ultra-nationalist National Democratic Party in the early 1960s was addressed not with respect to ameliorating whatever grievances may have impelled people to vote for such a party at that time but by relying upon the rule of the minimum percentage of votes a party must receive to be awarded any seats in the legislature.

Another area in which there was a transformation in Germany from cultural attributes that are conducive to an authoritarian political format to those that are conducive to a democratic format is political participation. The famed five-nation study on the cultural requisites of democracy conducted by Gabriel Almond and Sydney Verba (discussed at length in Chapter 2) characterized the West Germans of the late 1950s as a subject culture, one in which political participation was limited to formal activities such as voting and in which there was a lower level—compared to the "successful" Anglo-American democracies—of a sense of an obligation to participate in politics and a lower sense of competence to do so.[28] This lower sense of competence was particularly true with respect to a perception that one could effectively do something about an unjust law on both the local and national levels. The Germans expected "serious consideration" from their government and police, believed their rights were well defined, and were relatively well informed about public affairs. But there was still that perception that politics ought to be left to political leaders.

By the late 1970s, however, there were signs that the attributes of a participant culture were emerging in West Germany. From 1952 to 1977, the percentage of Germans in a national poll who stated an interest in politics steadily increased from a low of 27 percent in 1952 to 50 percent in 1977, while the percentage of those who said they were not interested steadily declined from a high of 32 percent in 1952 to 9 percent in 1977.[29] One key indicator of a sense of competence in and obligation toward involvement in the political process is the frequency with which people attempt to persuade others to their social or political points of view. Data indicate that Germans increasingly discuss politics outside their immediate family. In 1953, some 63 percent of a national sample reported that they hardly ever or never discussed politics with others, while only 8.6 percent reported that they did so daily. By 1972, the first category had declined to only 15.5 percent, while 50 percent reported discussing politics frequently.[30]

The Germans, oriented toward fulfilling such formal and legal obligations of citizenship as obeying the law, have had a high voting turnout throughout the years of the Bonn republic (86% of eligible voters in 1974) relative to many other Western democracies; the German figures are clearly higher than the embarrassing low figures for the United States. The change has been in the disposition of Germans to move beyond the minimal and formal levels of participation in ways that suggest that the typical German no longer views politics as something that the ordinary citizen had best leave to others.

While Germans may be less eager to assume the guilt for the activities of the Third Reich than many in the West would prefer to see, a reluctance that was manifested in the Bitburg incident, direct sympathy for the extremist right seems to have declined to an insignificant level, while positive support for the ideas and values of democracy appears to have grown to a level of strength comparable to that in other Western democracies. The Bitburg incident occurred on a 1985 trip to Germany by President Ronald Reagan in which he agreed, in response to an intiative from Chancellor Kohl, to honor a cemetery for German military dead and to foster a spirit of "let bygones be bygones" unity. When it was discovered that the remains of a number of the infamous Nazi SS troops were interred there (troops that were not part of the regular German army but that had special responsibilities in maintaining internal security and in implementing the "final solution"), many Americans, Jews in particular, vehemently protested. The Kohl government, however, put strong pressure on Reagan to go ahead with the visit, which he did. Kohl's persistence was in response to indications that the German public strongly felt that Reagan should stick to his plans. The significance of the German reaction to American concerns in this incident is that this generation of Germans feel that after over 40 years of stable democracy, Germany's Nazi past should now be regarded as irrelevant. The attempt, largely among conservative historians and scholars such as Ernst Nolte, to minimize the significance of the Third Reich in general and to deny the unique nature of the Holocaust in particular has generated something of a debate in intellectual circles.[31] Nolte argues that many of the traits of the Third Reich also characterize, of all things, Zionism: extreme racialism, disregard for the historic rights of others, and expansionistic nationalism. Of course, the attribution of these traits to the Jewish state is a matter of interpretation on which reasonable people disagree. The characterization of Zionism as racism at the UN by a coalition of Arab and Third World nations provoked widespread outrage among many people, and the "historic rights" of the Palestinian Arabs is itself a matter of controversy. That Israel, the state founded by the surviving victims of Nazism, should be so characterized by so eminent a scholar illustrates the extent to which Germans believe that their past was not so uniquely horrible.

Despite this rejection of guilt or responsibility for the sins attributed to the generation of their parents, this generation of Germans appears to have a well-established positive feeling toward a democratic political format and democratic values. However, the dwindling of support for right-wing extremism does not mean that extremism of either the left or right has completely disappeared from the German political scene, as the resurgence of right-wing xenophobic violence in the 1990s has shown. Left-wing radicalism by many Marxist-oriented middle-class youth and university students, epitomized by the Baader-Meinhof Gang, flourished in the late sixties and early seventies. Frustrated by the rightward turn of the Social Democratic Party in 1959 (discussed below) and the pragmatic, nonideological turn of the German population in a basically prosperous society, the new left turned to terrorism. This had an impact on the domestic tranquility of German society that was out of proportion to the actually small number of leftist terrorists. But although the number of terrorists is not large, the amount of such extremist activity has been greater in Germany than in other Western democarcies. If one takes seriously the argument made by the present authors, among others, that left-wing antidemocratic extremism is not essentially different from such extremism of the right, then the flurry of extremist and terrorist activity in German may add a mild note of caution to our conclusion that the German penchant for romantic, millenaristic, antiliberal ideologism is now a thing of the past and that the Germans have now apparently acquired the cultural foundations for stable, effective democracy.

THE CONSTITUTIONAL FORMAT OF THE BONN REPUBLIC: THE ENGINEERING OF STABILITY

The constitution of the Federal Republic of Germany is not called a constitution; it is known as the Basic Law. The reason for this is that the term *constitution* implies a permanent set of arrangements, while the founders of the Federal Republic did not wish to acknowledge the division of Germany as permanent. The Basic Law was drawn up by representatives of the *Länder,* or "states" (singular, *Land*) but under the supervision of the Allied occupation authorities for the Western zones. The United States, of course, was the dominant force among the three Western powers; hence, the Basic Law reflected the American perspective on the solution to what all the Allied powers saw as a primary concern of the occupation—how to prevent the abuse of a strong central authority, as had happened under the Third Reich, while avoiding the weak institutions of the Weimar Republic that had facilitated its collapse in the face of the interwar crises.

The Basic Law set up a federal system, which means that a national and constituent governments simultaneously rule over the same territory, and that the existence and power to operate of each level of government are guaranteed by fundamental written law, with the national government retaining sovereign or final power in the case of conflict between the two levels. The possession by the national government (Bund, in the German context) of this sovereignty is what distinguishes federal systems from confederations. Like the American Constitution, with its supremacy clause, several clauses of the Basic

Law guarantee the national government ultimate legislative authority in Article 31, which explicitly states, "Federal law shall override Länd law." These provisions clarify the disposition of the inevitable conflict that will arise from the fact that the activities of government cannot be neatly compartmentalized into national and state spheres of activity. Thus, while the education function is assigned to the Länder, education may have an impact on the function of providing for national security, which is assigned to the national government. The Länder may legislate in an area of concurrent jurisdiction only to the extent that this does not contradict the exercise of national powers in that area (Article 72).

The German concept of federalism reflects the fact that Bismarck's Second Reich had been a federation of some 25 autonomous states that had existed long before being assembled more or less voluntarily into the federation. As in the American situation, the constituent subunits acquired their legitimacy well before the formation of the Second Reich. There is only a slight historical continuity between the boundaries and composition of the subunits of the Second Reich and those drawn up for the Bonn Republic; hence, German citizens have less identification with and loyalty to their respective Länder than do most of Americans to their respective states. The German arrangement also reflects the American style of handling the problem of power by dividing it among autonomous institutions that then act as constraints against possible abuse of power by one another. The fear of a resurgence of another form of Nazism led to the Allied pressure for a decentralized state.

While the Basic Law provides the structure for a substantial participation by the Länder in the national decision-making process, and sets up a house of the legislature (Bundesrat) whose members are chosen by their respective Länder and whose function it is to represent the interests of those Länder, the impact of and constraints imposed by the Länder on national policy-making are not great and are diminishing. Part of the reason is that while Germany does consist of some significant regionally defined diversities, these diversities are not as significant as those in some of the segmented societies such as Belgium, Canada, and the former Soviet Union. Moreover, the Länd boundaries are by and large artificially drawn, and have only minimal congruence with the diversities and interests in the society.[32] Hence, the elites of the Länder and their representatives in the Bundesrat do not have a clear, coherent set of interests for which to speak. The sixteen Länder are listed in Table 5-1. It can easily be seen that they are vastly unequal in population and hence in political impact, as is the case with the states in the United States. They are also unequal in wealth and resources.

At the level of the Bund, or national government, the founders of the Basic Law and their Allied consultants set up a parliamentary form of democracy, which was the form Germany had previously experienced in its Weimar experiment with democracy. However, they strove to avoid the pitfalls and weaknesses of the assembly-dominated, impotent Weimar Republic with institutional safeguards. True to the legalistic strain in the German political style, the Germans tried to prevent the recurrence of the collapse of democracy by appropriate legal and constitutional provisions rather than by assuming that such events are caused by political, social, or economic problems. Thus, the repeated votes of no-confidence in the Weimar Republic, the results of a weak center and a high degree of ideological fragmentation, were addressed by requiring that a majority of the lower house, or Bundestag, agree not only on their opposition to the current government but also on the identity of the successor government, the so-called constructive vote of no confidence. The intention of this procedure was to prevent the kind of negative majorities that frequently occurred in the Weimar Reichstag, comprised of extremists of the left and of the right who could agree on nothing except the desire to prevent a centrist government from governing and to see the republic fail.

The Basic Law provides for a parliamentary form of democracy with the head of government, in Germany called the chancellor rather than the prime minister as in Britain or the premier as in France, accountable to the lower house of the legislature largely through this constructive vote of no confidence. Since the choice between governments has effectively become a dichotomous one, as we shall see in the section on political parties, the constructive requirement has not in practice been a factor. However, as in the British case, this very aggregation of the party system has been a major reason for cabinet

TABLE 5-1   German Länder

Länder	Population in Millions
Baden-Württemberg	9.6
Bavaria	11.2
Berlin	3.4
Brandenburg	2.6
Bremen	0.7
Hamburg	1.6
Hesse	5.7
Lower Saxony	7.3
Mecklenburg–Western Pomerania	2.0
North Rhine–Westphalia	17.1
Rhineland-Palatinate	3.7
Saarland	1.1
Saxony	4.9
Saxony-Anholt	3.0
Schleswig-Holstein	2.6
Thuringia	2.7

Source: Frank L. Wilson, *European Politics Today*, 2nd ed. (Englewood Cliffs, NJ: Prentice Hall, 1994), p. 245.

stability. There has been one successful vote of no confidence during the entire history of the Bonn Republic—the one bringing down the Schmidt government and putting the present Kohl government in power in 1982, when the small, balance-of-power Free Democratic Party defected from the Schmidt government. Yet, also as in the British case, the availability of this vote probably forces the chancellor to take greater account of the wishes of members of the Bundestag than the American president is compelled to do by the remote prospect of impeachment.

As in the British case, there is no doubt that the chancellor is intended to be the formulator and initiator of public policy. Unlike the British case, however, where the preeminent role of the prime minister evolved out of need and circumstance, the position of chancellor is clearly provided by the Basic Law. Article 65 makes the chancellor the actor who "determines and is responsible for general policy." The chancellor appoints the other members of the cabinet, who are in turn responsible to him or her, while the chancellor alone is responsible to the Bundestag. True to the German legalistic character, the decision-making rules of the cabinet are highly formalized in contrast to the highly informal and almost unspecified procedures for cabinet decision-making in Great Britain. However, the first chancellor, Konrad Adenauer, frequently by-passed and ignored his cabinet in conducting a highly personalized administration, thereby fulfilling the role of a modified *führer* (leader in a nondemocratic, fatherlike sense), to which the Germans had become accustomed. Adenauer, who held office for 13 consecutive years, far longer than any of his successors, shaped the institution of chancellor so that it appeared to be such an autonomous force in the policymaking process that the Germany system was referred to as "chancellor democracy." However, the autonomy of the chancellor today

may not be as great as appearances would indicate. German chancellors have always had to accept at least one junior coalition partner in order to govern; hence, negotiations keeping that partner as a contented part of the government constrain the discretion of the chancellor. Moreover, Adenauer's successors have had neither the personality nor the inclination to conduct the personal, autonomous style of government of *der alte* (the old man).

As noted, parliamentary democracy entails the separation of the roles of head of government and head of state. In Great Britain and other constitutional monarchies, the monarch fulfills the role of head of state. In republics, such as the Federal Republic, a president is chosen to fill that role. The German president is indirectly elected by Bundestag deputies and representatives from the several Länder; hence, he or she even lacks a popular base of support on which to act. Presidents have varied in perspective, style, and influence, depending on the personality of the occupant of the office. Besides serving the basic symbolic and ceremonial role of head of state, some presidents, by standing above partisan politics in the short range, have led the nation in a moral sense on some broad-ranging issues. For example, Gustav Heinemann worked actively to draw attention to West Germany's poor, a group frequently overlooked in all the attention devoted to the nation's famed prosperity, and Richard von Weizsäcker, who assumed office in 1984, made a now famous speech in which he implored Germans to face up to their complicity and responsibility for the atrocities commited by the Third Reich, a speech that drew favorable reaction throughout the free world. The prestige and dignity that Weizsäcker thus brought to the office may be contrasted with the spectacle of Austria's election of Kurt Waldheim to the presidency, a man who clearly had lied to the world about the extent of his involvement with the Nazi military and its extermination policies. In 1993, Roman Herzog was elected to succeed Weizsäcker, who retired.

As in most federal systems, the German legislature is bicameral (consisting of two houses), with the upper house (the Bundesrat) intended to represent the interests of the political subunits, the Länder. The members of the Bundesrat are selected by their respective Länd governments roughly in proportion to population, although smaller Länder are disproportionately favored. Each Länd delegation is expected to vote as a unit. The Bundesrat must consent to any legislation that is within the designated area of competence or jurisdiction of the Länder. By interpretation, the veto power of the Bundesrat now extends to over half of all federal legislation. However, this power was seldom exercised until the 1970s, when a situation developed in which one political force controlled the lower house and therefore the government, while another controlled the upper house. The center-right parties controlling the upper house used that position to block government programs and actions.

The Bundesrat has been far less active in challenging the government since both houses have been in the same hands since the early 1980s. The significance of the Bundesrat in representing Länd interests is constrained by the fact that the boundaries of the Länder are not congruent with politically important and geographically defined diversities, unlike the situation in, for example, Canada, where the boundaries of the province of Quebec are more or less congruent with the geographical definition of French Canadian consciousness. The elites of Quebec can and do see themselves as spokespersons for a distinct set of subcultural interests that are in a state of conflict with the dominant Anglo-based culture in a way that the elites of Schleswig-Holstein, North Rhine–

Westphalia, or Rhineland-Palatinate, for example, do not. The importance of an upper house designed to represent state, provincial, or other subsystem interests will be a function of how strongly the elites of those subsystems perceive a distinct set of interests or values to represent. The power and influence of upper houses in a parliamentary system are always constrained by the fact that upper houses are outside the structure of accountability that defines such a system. The upper houses become like the proverbial fifth wheel, without a logical role to play.

The Bundestag is the lower house of the legislature of the Federal Republic, the house to which the government is structurally accountable. Accommodating the Continental influence and the German heritage on the one hand, and the fear of the immobilizing fragmentation of Weimar on the other, the founders provided that half of the 496 deputies will be elected by the Anglo-American plurality system, which, as outlined in Chapter 2, generates great pressure for an aggregated party system. The other half of the delegates are chosen by a form of proportional representation, with the voter choosing from Länd party lists. The result is a party system that is highly aggregated but that still allows some relatively significant participation from at least one smaller party. The members normally serve a four-year term, unless the Bundestag is dissolved early. This is not something that is purely up to the discretion of the head of government, as is the case in Great Britain; it may only be dissolved in particular circumstances and has only been done once.

The Bundestag has several means of holding the chancellor accountable. Beyond the threat of the "constructive no-confidence vote" noted above, the Bundestag has adopted the British institution of the question period. From a modest start in the early years of the republic, the volume of questions has grown steadily. In addition, a group of deputies can generate a debate over a particularly pressing problem, much like the Standing Order Number 20 procedure in the British House of Commons, which also allows a discussion out of order on any developing emergency (such as Thatcher's Invasion of the Falklands). The Bundestag has investigatory powers over government and administrative activity; however, with highly disciplined parties controlled from the top, these powers have not been extensively used. Debate over the government programs itself is a potentially effective means of holding governments to some extent accountable, providing that the debate itself is a lively give-and-take phenomenon that critiques and defends the substance of government policy. Observers of German politics disagree as to the extent to which debate in the Bundestag

may be so characterized; however, they generally agree that it is moving in this direction, especially since the introduction of rules limiting the length of given speeches.

Deputies sit in a semicircular arrangement at desks in a fairly large chamber facing a podium from which the chamber is addressed, the president's chair, and long desks behind that sit members of the government (see Figure 5-1), in contrast to the arrangement in the British House of Commons, described in Chapter 3, in which government and opposition sit on benches facing one another in a much smaller room. The German deputies have traditionally been treated to a series of lengthy speeches that could hardly be characterized as debate until the aforementioned curbs on the length of each presentation were imposed. There has even been some talk of remodeling the Bundestag

FIGURE 5-1   The interior of the Bundeshaus where the West German Bundestag meets. Note the arrangement of seats whereby government and opposition do not face each other. Note also the podium with microphones in front from which speeches are made.

chamber along British lines, but nothing has come of this.

Most of the work of the Bundestag is done in its 20 standing committees, which are the object of a fair amount of interest group activity. The committees, however, do not have the power to "pigeonhole" a bill (refusing to consider it and thereby letting it die), as happens to the vast majority of bills that enter the committee structure of Congress in the United States. The Bundestag as a whole meets for far less time than does the Congress or the British House of Commons. The overall impact of the Bundestag on the policy-making process is hard to gauge. Its influence and prestige have been growing, but it started at a very low level in a nation that, unlike Great Britain, had never allowed the legitimacy of a parliamentary tradition to evolve.

ADMINISTRATION IN GERMAN POLITICS

In a nation that traditionally regards government as a matter more of administrative efficiency than of the articulation of and responsiveness to interests and demands, and that, with the concept of *Beamtenstaat*, sees the bureaucracy as embodying the spirit of the state, it is not surprising that the political role of the higher civil service is well established in Germany, as it is in France.[33] The *Beamtenstaat* concept of the state does not recognize the Anglo-American myth of the neat and effective separation of political and administrative functions.

The German administration had been widely regarded by such eminent students of the administrative process as Ferrel Heady as the epitome of a classical administrative system with a well-developed hierarchy, a well-entrenched routinization based upon a comprehensive set of impersonal rules, re-

cruitment based upon competitive examination and rigorously selective higher education that virtually eliminates the offspring of working-class families, and a widespread sense that these highly advocated people are the best qualified to know the truth, which leads to disdain for and impatience with the uncertainties and inefficiencies of the democratic process.[34] This classical view regards the bureaucrat as the objective expert, neutral and above the political fray, yet, the bureaucracy became completely coopted and corrupted by the state during the Third Reich.

The classical nature of German bureaucracy that some observers had found in the past may be viewed to some extent as a stabilizing response to the constitutional instability and ineffectiveness of the political sector, much as we found in France. This bureaucratic continuity in the face of political instability may have enhanced the political role of the administrative sector, again as we have seen in the French case.

Recognizing the political role of the administrative sector, the West German bureaucracy endured a process of de-Nazification immediately after the war, and more recently a 1972 executive decree, the *Radikalenerlass*, banned radicals from government positions.[35] Specifically the decree banned individuals who have "engaged in activities hostile to the constitutional order" or have even belonged to political parties who oppose that order. It provoked a vigorous public debate in academic, political, and popular media. It also reflects the legalistic German political style, for rather than addressing the causes of a possible growth of radicalism, they formulated a rule banning radicals from government service.

Empirical research frequently has a way of giving lie to conventional wisdom. Research by Robert Putnam on the attitudes of senior civil servants in four European nations contradicts the conventional wisdom that members of West Germany's higher civil service exhibit the attributes of classic bureaucracy outlined above.[36] Putnam found that they instead "displayed great sensistivity to and support for the imperatives of politics in a democracy." This was particularly true of the younger civil servants rather than the older carry-overs from the Third Reich and immediately thereafter. Putnam apparently found a generational difference in attitudes instead of a case of individual civil servants changing their minds. His findings appear to be encouraging for those looking for a move away from the attributes associated with Germany's authoritarian past. Apparently the German public bureaucracy has undergone some of the same cultural transformation toward attitudes and orientations compatible with liberal democracy that we have observed in the general German society, which it seems reasonable to expect.

PARTIES AND THE REPRESENTATION OF INTERESTS

The founding of the Federal Republic was greeted by a reassertion of the old party system fragmentation that had plagued the Weimar Republic. Numerous small parties from the pre-Nazi period reemerged, and some new ones, such as the Refugee Party, representing the thousands who poured in from Communist East Germany before that regime stopped emigration, were founded. That party won 27 seats in 1953 but none only four years later. In the first election of the Bonn republic, no less than 11 parties gained seats in the Bundestag. Within a few years, however, the number of parties that had regular representation in the Bundestag dropped to 3. The West German party system has consequently been characterized as evolving toward a two-party model.[37]

From the early 1960s to the late 1980s, two major parties, the Christian Democratic Union, with its Bavarian affiliate the Christian Social Union (CDU/CSU) on the center right and the Social Democrats (SPD) on the left, controlled around 90 percent of the votes and seats in the Bundestag, while the classical, or "Manchester," liberal Free Democratic Party (FDP) has held around 10 percent of the votes and seats. Only in 1959 did one party win over half of the seats in the Bundestag; hence, the small FDP exercised a political influence far out of proportion to its actual strength. By the early 1990s, however, the Green Party (discussed in Chapter 2) along with a new leftist group, Alliance 90, broke into the Bundestag, while the two major parties controlled just 78 percent of the vote in the 1994 election. The FDP, with a weakened vote total in 1994, was even more indispensable to the ruling CDU/CSU as their leader, chancellor, Helmut Kohl, was reinstalled as head of government in that year by just one vote. The Bundestag must confirm the selection of the Chancellor and Kohl received 338 of the 671 votes, one more than the necessary minimum.

The Germans have guarded against a recurrence of the situation of the Weimar Republic, in which numerous small, antidemocratic parties of both the right and the left received representation in the Reichstag, thus blocking the formation of any stable and effective government, by two legalistic methods—the 5 percent rule and the use of the Anglo-American plurality system to choose half the deputies in the Bundestag. The 5 percent rule stated that a party must win at least 5 percent of the national vote in order to share in the party list system by which the other half of the seats in the Bundestag are distributed, regardless of how many seats it would otherwise have obtained in this proportional distribution. The Germans relied on these legalistic mechanisms to counter the growing electoral support for the ultranationalist National Democratic Party (NDP) during the years of the Grand Coalition of 1966 to 1969. Many of the leaders and supporters of this party were former Nazis, which generated a vigorous debate and some fear as to whether the NDP was a neo-Nazi party. While a fair amount of the growing NDP support came from the elements of society to whom Nazism appealed—small farmer and peasant types and lower-middle-class businesspeople and artisans—some was merely an expression of opposition to the Grand Coalition when no other credible opposition was available, a conclusion borne out by the fact that support for the NDP, which had never exceeded some 8 percent of the electorate, dwindled rapidly, when the Grand Coalition broke up and has not been an electoral factor since. Meanwhile, the 5 percent rule has made it difficult for other new or minor parties to achieve Bundestag representation. However, small parties have not disappeared from Germany. In 1994, the Greens broke the 5 percent barrier with 7.3 percent of the vote, and the former East German Communists—the Party of Democratic Socialism (PDS), or "Red Socks"—placed 30 members in the Bundestag by winning four constituencies in Berlin. The presence of these small parties did not produce a hung parliament, as some had feared, however, and Kohl was reelected as chancellor, as dis-

cussed above.[38] The German political party line-up in 1994 is shown in Table 5-2.

As explained, throughout the 1970s and 1980s, West Germany was blessed with what might be called a modified two-party system, in which the head of government came from one of two parties and in which each of these two major parties had some reasonable chance of winning control of that government. From the founding of the Bonn republic until 1966, the CDU/CSU dominated control of the government, beginning with the long, paternalistic, and virtually unopposable reign of Konrad Adenauer. The SDP, beset with an ideological baggage of orthodox Marxism, was firmly locked into the role of what seemed to be the permanent opposition, with the support of under 40 percent of the electorate, which was apparently nonexpandable.

In the increasingly nonideological milieu of the Federal Republic, the CDU/CSU quickly evolved under Adenauer from a Catholic, centrist party epitomizing what has loosely been called "Christian Democracy," to a broad, centrist, or "catch-all" party. It is so ideologically amorphous that its early espousal of capitalism to appeal to its clientele among industrialists and financiers was tempered to include a strong social welfare component to appeal to its Christian, working-class clientele. As such, and riding the crest of Germany's postwar economic prosperity,

TABLE 5-2   Bundestag Election Results, 1994

Party	1990 Vote (%)	1994 Vote (%)	Seats in Bundestag, 1994	Seats in Bundesrat, 1994
CDU/CSU	43.8	41.5	294	10
FDP	11.0	6.9	47	–
Greens	3.8	7.3	49	–
Alliance 90	1.3			
PDS	2.4	4.4	30	–
SDP	33.5	36.4	239	41

Source: The Economist, vol. 333, no. 7886 (October 22, 1994), p. 47.

the party acquired electoral support from a wide variety of groups and interests, and thereby aggregated a near majority of votes and seats.

The Social Democrats, on the other hand, were the original Marxist party, with a century-old emotional commitment to that ideology. Waving the red flag and singing the anthem of the Socialist International at their annual meetings were part of the essence of their party. The SDP has always had a problem of identity, on the one hand seeing themselves in Marxian terms as a revolutionary movement of the oppressed working class, fighting an irredeemably corrupt system, and on the other hand striving for success in electoral politics, a strategic goal that entailed fostering a public image as the government of all the people and the defender of that system. Sensing a genuine chance to acquire power within the system, it allowed its reformist wing, led by Ferdinand Lassalle, to prevail over the revolutionary Eisenacher faction at the party's beginning, resulting, much to the anger of Marx and his ideologically pure followers, in the nonrevolutionary Gotha Program of 1875.[39] The SDP continued to struggle with what Karl Schorske has called "the Great Schism," the split between its revolutionary and reformist wings.[40] This schism was only temporarily contained by the Erfurt Synthesis of 1891, when a platform was drawn up to combine both a statement of ultimate objectives—especially the overthrow of the capitalist order—and a statement of tactical reformist goals to be attained in the short run. The party over the years has remained deeply split between its revolutionary and reformist wings, sometimes dominated by the one faction, sometimes by the other. As has frequently been the case with other political parties with a working-class electoral clientele in the democratic world, the reformist faction has tended to become dominant when the prospect or reality of attaining

and exercising real political power presented itself. When the SPD found itself in power in World War I, its slogan, "To this system, man and no penny," was replaced by, "In the hour of danger, we will not leave the Fatherland in the lurch."

In the immediate postwar period, the SPD was led by the courageous but doctrinaire Kurt Schumacher, a man who had survived years of torture and imprisonment under the Third Reich with his faith in orthodox Marxism unshaken. This kept the party in permanent opposition until a group of young dissidents within the party, led by Willy Brandt, took power at the Bad Godesburg Convention of 1959. Brandt and his followers pushed through a new Basic Program (equivalent to an American party platform or British party manifesto) that stated, among other things, that "private ownership of the means of production can claim the protection of society just as long as it does not hinder the establishment of social justice."[41] The pursuit of the profit motive and the value of the free market were even sanctioned by this Basic Program, a document that signaled the de facto abandonment of the party's socialist objective. The Bad Godesburg Basic Program was such a revolutionary break with the party's Marxist tradition that Marx himself might have been spinning in his grave in reaction. This strategy earned the party an immediate expansion of middle-class support and brought it into the government with the Grand Coalition of 1966, and into control of the government by 1969 in coalition with the Free Democratic Party.

Although the early SPD pacifism on Cold War matters was seriously modified in the Bad Godesburg Basic Program, the party, first under Willy Brandt and then under Helmut Schmidt, became more accommodationist toward the Warsaw Pact nations and more hopeful of possible reunification with East Germany. Brandt's accommodationist stance toward the Warsaw Pact nations and the USSR was known as *Ostpolitik.*

The 1959 *embourgoisement* of what had been the party of the Marxist and romantic left probably drove many of these leftists out of the electoral arena and contributed to the rise of the revolutionary left underground that became so visible in Germany in the l960s and early 1970s, a movement led by the notorious Baader-Meinhof Gang. With the capture of several of its leaders in 1972, radical left-wing violence substantially subsided, although radical right-wing violence has been on the rise after reunification, in the more economically uncertain 1990s. It is interesting that the leadership of this wave of left-wing radicalism came largely from middle- or professional-class backgrounds, supporting the aforementioned Inglehart thesis of value change as applied to Germany.

As the former East German citizens became voters in the new united Germany, they were even less likely than the voters of the former West Germany to be attracted to an orthodox or classical Marxist appeal, having only recently extricated themselves from a Marxist system. The convincing victory of West German Chancellor Kohl's CDU in the first all-German election in 1990 seemingly corroborated this judgment. However, after the disillusionment of the first few years of a capitalist market economy that left serious unemployment and economic hardship in the East, the PDS almost doubled its 1990 vote in the 1994 election, and the SPD made substantial gains. The high expectations of the East Germans for the material fruits of Western capitalism have resulted in bitter disappointment, while the citizens of the former West Germany are increasingly unhappy with the costs of reunification. The 1994 election clearly shows that while Kohl barely hung on to his job, the center-right coalition lost a significant share of votes and seats. Still, the success of the SPD in the new united Ger-

many would seem to depend on its ability to sell itself as a centrist, catch-all party. Yet, many young people in the party are still attracted by the policies and principles of what is loosely called "the new left," the liberal position on those postmaterialist issues that Baker, Dalton, and Hildebrandt have shown are becoming increasingly salient in German society.[42] As such, they were alienated from the centrist policies of economic austerity of the Schmidt government in the face of Germany's economic difficulties of the 1980s. This continuing relevance of the split between the party's romantic left wing and pragmatic centrist wing, essentially a continuation of Schorske's "Great Schism," will be an ongoing problem for the party as it attempts to aggregate the broad national support needed to govern in Germany's current aggregated party system.

The Free Democratic Party might be best characterized as a party of classical liberalism. This philosophical base is burdened in the German context with the problem that it faces in other contexts—the fact that it is no longer relevant to the salient issues of the postwar world. The lack of a coherent set of principles or programs has led to two distinct wings in the Free Democratic Party: a conservative, nationalist wing tied to business interests and a more left-oriented wing. This split in German liberalism had been expressed in separate parties in the Weimar regime. Essentially, the party is another bourgeois party that does not endorse the religious component of the CDU/CSU.

With the lack of a coherent set of principles and programs, the FDP has never received more than 13 percent of the vote in a federal election and would not have received any seats in a straight Anglo-American, single-member-district, plurality election. All of the FDP's seats have come from the proportional part of the German electoral system. In recent elections, its share of the vote has been encroached upon by the Greens and has hovered under 10 percent. In 1994, the party dropped from its 1990 total of 11 percent of the vote and 79 of the 662 seats to just 6.9 percent of the vote, although it managed to hang on to 47 seats of the total of 672. Still, with Kohl's narrow majority in the Bundestag, he cannot govern without the support of the Free Democrats; hence, they will continue to exercise disproportionate influence as the government's indispensable junior coalition partner.

Because it has frequently been the case that neither of the two major parties, the SPD and the CDU/CSU, has had a majority of the seats in the Bundestag, they have either had to accept the terms of coalition from the Free Democrats or go into opposition; therefore, the FDP was in 13 of the first16 governments of the Bonn republic. Of course, the amorphous ideological baggage of the FDP is a prerequisite to its ability to form coalitions with either the SPD or the CDU/CSU.

Presenting a much more coherent ideological appeal is the rising Green Party (*Die Grünen*). Although its strength declined sharply in the 1990 elections to just 3.8 percent of the vote, it experienced an electoral resurgence in 1994, breaking the 5 percent barrier with 7.3 percent of the vote and 49 seats. Emerging, as the name implies, as basically an ecology and environmentalism movement, the party has evolved into a more generic postmaterialist "new left" party espousing most of the grievances and alienation of the anti-establishment left throughout the Western world. The early 1980s saw the Greens in the forefront of protests against the deployment of American intermediate-range missiles in Europe and the assertion of NATO and U.S. power. The original party leader, the late Petra Kelly, was vocal in expressing support for various revolutionary or anti-Western political movements, such as the Palestinian Liberation Organization and the African National Congress,

which seem to have at best a marginal relationship to environmentalism. The relationship between these causes and the party is a basic animus toward the capitalist and industrialized West that is perceived as a root cause of most of the world's ills.

The party has appealed to a variety of constituencies, including some Marxists and Maoists on the left-wing fringe. Recent research by Hans-Georg Betz indicates a substantial amount of the Greens' electoral support comes from the highly educated but professionally insecure.[43] That is, with the growth of access to education in the postindustrial age, the economy has not continued to expand at a rate sufficient to absorb this increasing corpus of educated talent. Many individuals from this group are either unemployed or employed at jobs whose status is below that for which they were trained. One study found that 47 percent of unemployed university and secondary school graduates preferred the Greens.[44] Supporters of the Greens are frequently people who are more concerned with finding self-fulfilling occupations and avoiding wage-slave work merely to earn a living. In the sense that monetary reward is not their primary motivation in seeking work, many of these Greens may be classified as postmaterialist.

The party actually has two distinct wings— those who advocate ideological purity, regardless of the political costs (*fundis,* for "fundamentalists"), and those who advocate a politically realistic approach (*realos*). The anti-establishment character of the party appears to dominate its essence to the extent that the party appears to try to cultivate an image as an antiparty party. For example, deputies from the Greens not only are expected to turn a high percentage of their official salaries over to the party, but they also are supposed to give their seat to a replacement designated by the party—the so-called rotation principle, which carries the party's antileadership disposition to its *argumentum ad absurdum.* As with those who affect a self-consciously counterculture image in American academia and elsewhere, Green deputies eschew traditional business dress in favor of jeans and sweaters in a chamber where dark suits and white shirts are the norm. The Greens appear to be obsessed with avoiding the pitfalls of Roberto Michels's "iron law of oligarchy," the principle that leadership roles in all large organizations become so specialized that they cannot really be accountable to the rank and file, even in organizations with an egalitarian ideological baggage such as the Greens. The anti-Western doctrine of the Greens is epitomized in a quote by Green activist Rudolph Bahro.

> In the richest, industrially overdeveloped countries of the West, a fundamental opposition is growing. . . . It is reacting to the now clearly and markedly self-destructive, outwardly murderous and inwardly suicidal character of our industrial civilization, and to its institutional system which is geared to continuing in the same old way.[45]

Early indications and expectations are that the new voters absorbed from East Germany tend to be strong anti-Communists. If these voters decide that the left-wing, fringe supporters of the Greens are representative of its nature, the party's prospects in the new united Germany will certainly be diminished. If Betz is correct in arguing that the Greens are still primarily a postmaterialist party, this may also diminish their appeal to the incoming East German voters, who appear to be attracted to the prosperity and consumer goods of the West.

POLICIES AND PROSPECTS IN A NEW UNITED GERMANY

The dramatic diplomatic achievement in July 1990 by West German Chancellor Kohl in securing the acceptance by Soviet President Gorbachev of a united Germany in NATO removed the last serious obstacle to the reunification of Germany. This achievement of a reunited Germany as the dominant power in Europe and one of the major economic powers of the Western world, less than half a century after Germany's utter defeat in World War II and its dismemberment by the victorious Allied powers, constitutes a policy success of unprecedented proportions. The unpredicted reunification was greatly facilitated by factors external to the nation, as, to some extent, was the initial impetus to the enormous resurgence of its economic and industrial capacities in the decades following World War II; nevertheless, the government of West Germany and the political system itself were able to reap considerable credit and legitimacy for these achievements. The success of the system in reaching its once-thought unreachable core foreign policy goal and in providing an overall record of economic growth that was virtually unparalleled in modern Western history has been buttressed by the relatively egalitarian distribution of material well-being through one of the most advanced welfare states in the Western world. That period of economic growth, sometimes called the "economic miracle," was manifested in a growth in real wages that measured 115 percent between 1949 and 1964, and growth rates in the GNP for both the 1950–58 and 1958–64 periods that comfortably exceeded those figures for the other major Western powers—Great Britain, the United States, and even France, with its "thirty glorious years" (see Table 5-3).

The foregoing sanguine picture of German policy successes in the postwar era should be qualified by the acknowledgment of some problems or potential problems that have emerged or are likely to emerge. As Table 5-3 shows, the economy is no longer growing nearly as fast as it was in the immediate postwar period and in relative terms was eclipsed by the growth of the French

TABLE 5-3   GNP Growth Rates Among Western Powers, 1950–79

	1950–58 (%)	1958–64 (%)	1969–79 (%)
West Germany	7.6	5.8	3.3
France	4.4	5.4	4.0
Great Britain	2.4	3.9	2.2
United States	2.9	4.4	2.9

Source: Adapted from Stanley Rothman, *European Society and Politics* (Indianapolis: Bobbs-Merrill, 1970), p. 749; and William Safran, *The French Polity* (New York: Longman, 1985), p. 30.

economy at the end of the period. With the problems and costs of reunification, Germany's GDP was eclipsed even by Britain's by 1994, as shown in Table 3-1. This slowdown in the overall vigor of the economy has prompted a slight retrenchment in the redistributive policies of the welfare state, a system that had been one of the most highly developed in the West. In this system, workers have been extensively protected against the vicissitudes of unemployment, illness, or accidents; parents are financially compensated for the costs of raising children; and access to most forms of health care is virtually guaranteed.

For health care in Germany, a general insurance fund, the *Krankenkasse,* is administered by the state. All working people are required to contribute 12 percent of their income, and employers contribute an equal amount; however, the medical expenses of everyone, employed and unemployed alike, are covered, unless they have private insurance. Some 93 percent of the population is covered by the *Krankenkasse.* Meanwhile, medical care costs are fixed by general consultation with the organized health-care community in a corporatist arrangement. Further cost control is achieved by the rule that all modernization in private hospitals must be approved by the government, a rule that also

slows the pace of modernization. Each patient receives care from a general practice physician registered with the *Krankenkasse.* This physician has a list of specialists to whom the patient can be referred, as is the case in the British National Health Service. The specialists report back to the general practitioner. This gate-keeping role of the general practitioner is another cost-controlling factor, since specialist care tends to be more costly and is frequently unnecessary, as critics of the overspecialization in the American health-care system have argued.

More recently, government-financed social welfare has been trimmed in the new era of economic austerity. For example, the rate of pension increase has been trimmed, and retirees must now pay part of the cost of their health insurance. Hospital patients also now pay part of the costs of their stay. Student grants have been converted to student loans. Child allowances have been cut back. Further cuts, however, are problematic because of the precarious political position of the center-right Kohl government. Not only is the government majority, even with the uncertain cooperation of the Free Democrats, razor thin, but the government must receive the assent of the Bundesrat for most major pieces of legislation, and the Bundesrat is firmly controlled by the more leftist Social Democrats, who have 41 of the 68 seats, while the CDU/CSU has only 10.

All of these cutbacks are similar to those that have been seen in other Western welfare state democracies that have faced similar economic slowdowns beginning in the 1970s, slowdowns that were in large measure a reflection of the increasingly inescapable reality that the world's resources, especially those relating to energy, are finite. The 1980s saw an apparent glut in the world supply of oil following the seeming collapse of OPEC's ability to control production. However, the armed occupation of Kuwait by Iraq in 1990 has apparently once again ushered in an era of an uncertain supply of crude oil that is going to be increasingly expensive, a fact that is especially salient to those Western powers like Germany that are almost totally dependent on imported oil. This invasion also evoked a resurgence of the demand from the United States that Germany and other Western powers should now foot more of the costs of maintaining a deterrent force on or for the European Continent. Germany, which like its defeated Axis ally Japan, was limited by the victorious occupation forces in terms of the size of its armed forces, was able to divert much of what might have been its defense budget to investment in the private sector and thus to economic growth. All of this may now be changing in light of a substantially reduced American military commitment to and presence on the Continent. A smaller segment of the German GNP will henceforth be available for private investment.

Reunification will place an additional strain on the German economy. The free exchange of the almost worthless East German currency for West German Deutschmarks cost the Federal Republic a considerable sum. East Germany was not highly productive, and its subsumption by the West will almost certainly be on balance an economic burden to the Federal Republic. According to a report in *Newsweek,* the East German economy was on the verge of collapse.[46] Massive strikes in the summer of 1990, with a sharply reduced demand for domestically produced goods, threatens the nation with sharply rising levels of unemployment, which some predict may reach as high as 60 percent. Consumer goods in the former East Germany are in short supply, but the prospect of freedom and affiliation with the consumer-oriented West may generate high expectations; hence, it is unlikely that those who were East German citizens will be very

enthusiastic about the austerity measures that the Bonn government has felt necessary to implement in the face of slowed economic growth. The additional demand for material satisfactions will not be balanced by proportionate increases in production. Moreover, the East did not, by virtue of its putative Marxist character, encourage the development of a commercial or capitalist class engaged in the process of capital accumulation and investment for profit that creates the wealth measured by such figures as GNP.

Moreover, the crisis in the Middle East generated by Iraq's invasion of Kuwait constricted the supply of oil to the West with some increases in its cost. Germany, like the rest of Western Europe, is more heavily dependent than the United States on imported oil from this part of the world. Hence, such crises tend to slow economic growth and generate inflation. In any event, some form of continued economic difficulties in the reunified Germany appear likely. We have seen West German democracy thrive in nearly fifty years of unbroken prosperity. We can be less certain about how the system will function in the face of an economic crisis the like of which the system has not as yet encountered.

Noteworthy among the political strains imposed by reunification is the difficult task of reconciling the substantial difference between the former East and West Germanies with respect to the regulation of abortion. The formerly Communist part continues its more liberal policy of not restricting first trimester abortions, while in the former Federal Republic women cannot obtain a legal abortion without permission from a licensed social worker and a doctor. In practice, this permission is often difficult to get. This difference in policy and attitude reflects the influence of the churches in West Germany, especially the Catholic Church in the southern Länder, an influence that was restricted in the officially atheistic and more Protestant eastern territories. Unable to resolve this issue of national abortion policy, the German government is apparently allowing the difference between east and west to remain.

Moreover, the sanguine assurances of scholars such as David Conradt that the remaking of the German culture into a model of stable, effective democracy is now complete[47] rely on data from the Federal Republic that focus upon stated preferences for democracy among West German respondents. The apparent enthusiasm of the former East German citizenry for affiliation with the West may at present have less to do with a commitment to the abstract values of democracy and the open society than with a longing for the consumer goods and material well-being of their neighbor. The data on the growth of democratic orientations in the Federal Republic of course do not consider the unknown cultural attributes of the East Germans. We do know several pertinent facts in this regard, however. First, the socialization into democratic norms was, of course, confined to West Germany. For nearly half a century, the East Germans were actively socializing their youth into values and orientations appropriate to their Soviet-style dictatorship. If the West German democratic orientations are the result of cultural engineering, one can therefore presume that cultural engineering to some extent works and that cultural attributes can be shaped by conscious socialization. One can hardly expect a comparable commitment to such orientations among the former East Germans, who were socialized in the opposite direction. Second, we know that some of the earliest and strongest support for the Nazis in 1932 came from the areas that were part of East Germany. Third, the extreme right violence against foreigners in general (centered, it will be recalled, in Rostock) and Jews in particular in 1992 was concentrated in the former East Germany, reinforcing the suggestion that the citizens of the former "Democratic Republic" are more weakly socialized in and committed to democratic values than are the citizens of the former Federal Republic.

In their analysis of data from the former West Germany, Baker, Dalton, and Hildebrandt document an significant growth in a sense of political efficacy as measured by agreement with four statements at a level as high as that recorded in the rest of Western Europe and comparable to that found in the United States. The statement, "I don't think public officials care much what people like me think," elicited disagreement from 38 percent of the German sample in 1969 and from 47 percent in 1972. The statement, "Voting is the only way that people like me can have any say about how the government runs things," elicited disagreement from a little over 10 percent in 1959, from 25 percent by 1969, and from 31 percent by 1972. The statement, "Sometimes government and politics seem so complicated that a person like me can't really understand what's going on," elicited disagreement from 24 percent in 1969 and from 39 percent in 1972. The statement, "People like me don't have any say about what the government does," elicited disagreement from less than 30 percent in 1959, from 33 percent in 1969, and from 40 percent by 1972. Therefore, there has been a perceptable growth in democratic norms in at least West Germany.[48]

The likelihood of a significant degree of disaffection from the German political system by its citizens in the face of economic difficulties is further reduced by the very substantial credit that has accrued to the system for its achievement of the overriding if frequently unarticulated goal of West German foreign policy since World War II—reunification with East Germany. The short-run euphoria over the new triumph of German nationalism has enabled the reunited system to survive any immediate economic problems.

The longer run may be less certain if economic difficulties persist.

Moreover, in whatever ways the new German nationalism is expressed, a policy of territorial expansion through the use of force, the scenario that Germanophobes fear the most, is not longer as viable an option as it may have been in the late 1930s, given the proliferation of chemical and nuclear capabilites. It does not appear that a united Germany poses an imminent threat to the peace and security of Europe.

The expansion of German national influence over Europe is not a far-fetched prospect, however. Chancellor Kohl has been one of the leading advocates for changing the European Community, at present primarily an economic alliance buttressed by political cooperation among sovereign nation-states, into a genuine federation of Europe in which formerly sovereign nations such as Britain and France would relinquish much of that sovereignty to the parliament and bureaucracy at Brussels. Such a federation would surely be dominated by the government in Bonn through the power of the Bundesbank and thus would favor German interests. This is the fear that has split the British Conservative Party between the Euro-friendly, who are afraid of being left out of an inevitable power federation, and the Euro-skeptics, who see this as the third effort by Germany in the second half of this century to establish hegemony over Europe. (Kohl himself has been referred to in the British press as "Bismarck in a cardigan.") Some measure of greater integration of the nations of Europe has already occurred. One no longer needs to present one's passport when sailing from Britain to France, for instance (although one must show it to British authorities after traveling westward across the Channel). Further integration is probably inevitable. How much sovereignty nations like Britain and France are ultimately willing to relinquish is impossible

to say, but residual distrust of German control, born out of a sense of the past, will certainly slow the rush to a federal state of Europe. Failing to federalize the West, Germany may in the short run turn toward closer ties to the emerging East.

The long-run prospects of reunited Germany are difficult to assess. The pressure from the Allied powers that contributed to the resocialization of West Germans in the post–World War II era will not be present as the nation tries to absorb and assimilate the East German population, whose members have been socialized in a very different context and from a very different perspective. The cultural context of Germany a decade from now is impossible to predict with confidence. The precipitous absorption of an entire nondemocratic population by a nation that itself has only recently been socialized into democratic norms is virtually unprecedented. The world awaits the result with nervous anticipation.

NOTES

1. Ronald Inglehart, "The Silent Revolution in Europe: Intergenerational Change in Post-Industrial Society," *American Poltical Science Review,* vol. 65, no. 4 (December 1971), pp. 991–1017.

2. Quoted in Karl Popper, *The Open Society and Its Enemies* (New York: HarperTorchbooks, 1962), pp. 65, 69.

3. Quoted in William L. Shirer, *The Rise and Fall of the Third Reich* (New York: Simon and Schuster, 1960), p. 99.

4. Quoted in Popper, *The Open Society*, p. 31.

5. Ernst Nolte, *The Three Faces of Fascism* (New York: Holt, Rinehart and Winston, 1966).

6. A. James Gregor, *Interpretations of Fascism* (Morristown, NJ: General Learning Press, 1974), pp. 4–5.

7. A. James Gregor, *Italian Fascism and Developmental Dictatorship* (Princeton: Princeton University Press, 1979).

8. The classic paradigm of totalitarianism is presented in Carl Freidrich and Zbigniew Brzezinski, *Totalitarian Dictatorship and Autocracy* (Cambridge: Harvard University Press, 1956).

9. For a classic and thorough analysis of the historical and philosophical roots of the romantic and anti-intellectual aspects of the Third Reich, see George L. Mosse, *The Crisis of German Ideology: Intellectual Origins of the Third Reich* (New York: Schocken Books, 1981), pt. I.

10. Henry A. Turner, "Fascism and Modernization," *World Politics*, vol. 24, no. 4 (June 1972), pp. 547–64.

11. These themes in the writings of prominent German philosophers are analyzed in Mosse, *The Crisis of German Ideology*.

12. See, for example, Bertram Schaffner, *Fatherland: A Study of Authoritarianism in the German Family* (New York: Columbia University Press, 1948).

13. Gabriel Almond and Sydney Verba, *The Civic Culture* (Boston: Little Brown, 1965), pp. 312 ff. and passim.

14. This theme is most cogently explored in the popular mass psychoanalysis of Central European society— Eric Fromm, *Escape from Freedom* (New York: Avon Books, 1965), esp. chap. 6.

15. Mosse, *The Crisis of German Ideology*, pp. 67–69.

16. Facts on File, 1992. Infobase Holdings Co., p. 739.

17. Ibid.

18. Sidney Verba, "The Remaking of Political Culture," in Lucien Pye and Sidney Verba, eds., *Political Culture and Political Development* (Boston: Little Brown, 1965), p. 139.

19. Karl Deutsch, "The German Federal Republic," in Roy Macridis and Robert Ward, eds., *Modern Political Systems: Europe*, 2nd ed. (Englewood Cliffs, NJ: Prentice Hall, 1968), pp. 351–52.

20. Cited in David Conradt, "Changing German Political Culture," in Gabriel Almond and Sidney Verba, eds., *The Civic Culture Revisited* (Boston: Little Brown, 1980), p. 226.

21. David Conradt, *The German Polity*, 4th ed. (New York: Longman's, 1989), pp. 51–52.

22. Verba, "The Remaking of Political Culture," p. 140. For survey literature showing that in the 1950s only a quarter of the German population valued democracy for its own sake, see Erich Peter Neumann, *Public Opinion in Germany*, 1961 (Allensbach and Bonn: Vewrlag fur Demoskopie), pp. 50–51. See the data supplied in Elizabeth Noelle Neumann and Erich Peter Nuemann, *Jarbuch der Offentlichen Meinung*, vol 1, pp. 125–37, showing that a large proportion of the electorate in the early 1950s approved of the Nazi dictatorship.

23. Kendall Baker, Russell Dalton, and Kai Hildebrandt, *Germany Transformed: Political Culture and the New Politics* (Cambridge: Harvard University Press, 1981), p. 30.

24. David Conradt, *The German Polity*, p. 72.

25. Conradt, "Changing German Political Culture," p. 252.

26. The theme of value change and its implications in West Germany is explored at length in Baker, Dalton, and Hildebrandt, *Germany Transformed*.

27. Conradt, "Changing German Political Culture," pp. 258–59.

28. Almond and Verba, *Civic Culture*, pp. 312–13.

29. Conradt, "Changing German Political Culture," p. 239, Table VII.9.

30. Baker, Dalton, and Hildebrandt, *Germany Transformed*, p. 40, Table 2.1.

31. Nolte, *Three Faces of Fascism*.

32. See the discussion of the congruent and formalistic models of federalism in Lawrence Mayer, "Federalism and Party Behavior in Australia and Canada," *Western Political Quarterly*, vol. 23, no. 4 (December 1970), pp. 795–807.

33. See Gregg O. Kvistad, "Radicals and the State: The Political Demands on West German Civil Servants," in James Caporaso, ed., *The Elusive State: International and Comparative Perspectives* (Newbury Park, CA: Sage Publications, 1989), p. 111, for a discussion of the concept of *Beamtenstaat* and other traditional German conceptualizations of the role of the state and the civil service in society.

34. Ferrel Heady, *Public Administration: A Comparative Perspective* (Englewood Cliffs, NJ: Prentice Hall, 1966), pp. 41–45.

35. See the extended discussion of this decree in Kvistad, "Radicals and the State," pp. 106ff.

36. Robert Putnam, "The Political Attitudes of Senior Civil Servants in Western Europe: A Preliminary Report," paper delivered to the annual meeting of the American Political Science Association, Washington, DC, September 5–9, 1972, and later published in *The British Journal of Political Science*, vol 3, no. 3 (July 1973), pp. 257–90.

37. F. R. Alleman, "Germany's Emerging Two-Party System," *New Leader*, vol. 41, (August 4 and 11, 1958).

38. See *The London Times*, Wednesday, November 16, 1994 p. 11.

39. Karl Marx, *Critique of the Gotha Program* (New York: International Publishers, 1935).

40. Carl E. Schorske, *German Social Democracy, 1905–1917: The Development of the Great Schism* (New York: John Wiley and Sons Science Editions, 1955).

41. *Basic Programme of the Social Democratic Party* (adopted November 13–15, 1959, at Bad Godesberg), p. 11.

42. Baker, Dalton, and Hildebrandt, *Germany Transformed*, pp. 141ff.

43. Hans-Georg Betz, "Value Change and Post-Materialist Politics: The Case of West-Germany," *Comparative Political Studies*, vol. 23, no. 2 (July 1990), p. 244.

44. Ibid.

45. Quoted in Russell Dalton, *The Green Rainbow* (New Haven: Yale University Press, 1994), pp. 48–49.

46. *Newsweek*, August 20, 1990, p. 49. This characteriza-

tion of East Germany as an economic basket case followed an analysis in the same periodical just a month and a half earlier predicting that a united Germay would be "wealthier than ever" (*Newsweek*, July 9, 1990, p. 31).

47. Conradt, "Changing German Culture," p. 263.

48. Baker, Dalton, and Hildebrandt, *Germany Transformed*, pp. 29–29.

6

The Theory and Practice of Modern Dictatorships

There have, of course, been autocratic systems throughout history, taking such forms as empires, tyranny, theocracy, divine-right monarchy, and traditional dictatorships. But two of the most dramatic and significant features of the century in which we live have been the social and economic phenomena of industrialization and modernization and the rise of new political ideologies and institutions in reaction to these socioeconomic developments. Marxism, the philosophical foundation of Communism, was a reaction to and critique of nineteenth-century capitalism and the industrial revolution, and the totalitarian dictatorships of Communism, fascism, and National Socialism (Nazism) have been described as the adaptation of autocratic systems to twentieth-century industrial society, or, as in the case of Nazi Germany, their reactions against it. Beginning with the revolution in Russia in 1917, and epitomized by Hitler's Germany and especially Stalin's Soviet Union, this pattern of government, with its extreme emphasis on the state and state control of most social and individual activities, has been a dominant feature of the entire era. By 1970, however, Samuel Huntington and Clement Moore were already asking whether such authoritarian governments were compatible with modern industrial societies.[1] Although they were writing well before the time of Mikhail Gorbachev, his concepts of *perestroika* (restructuring), *glasnost* (openness), and democratization were in direct response to the needs and problems of a modernizing Soviet Union.

Twenty years later, the question seems even more relevant. Indeed, former National Security Adviser Zbigniew Brzezinski's book on *The Grand Failure* of Communism was only one of a number of such autopsies that have attempted to explain the reasons for the demise of Communist systems around the world.[2] As we entered the last decade of this century, attention turned, in what has been called the beginning of the post-Communist era, to questions of what types of new systems would emerge and how the transition would take place. There have been developments within Communist countries and in their international relations that were not even thought to be possible just a few short years ago. Many of these events came together in the watershed year of 1989, when in the international realm the media in the United States spoke of a new period "beyond the

Cold War," and the leaders of the Soviet Union and the People's Republic of China met for the first time in 30 years and declared that their relations had been "normalized."

Significant as these changes were, they were greatly overshadowed by developments within the countries of the Communist world. The dynamics involved in the visit of General Secretary Gorbachev to China in May of 1989 demonstrate the complexity. The historic meeting, intended to bring an end to the 30-year Sino-Soviet split, became secondary to the dramatic events unfolding in Beijing at the time. Precipitated by the funeral of reform leader Hu Yaobang, demonstrations demanding dialogue with the leadership concerning greater democracy and freedom of expression eventually grew to a million people in Beijing's Tiananmen Square. Protesting students, joined by intellectuals, workers, and others, praised Gorbachev for initiating political reforms in the USSR and called for *glasnost* in China. The continuing massive demonstrations spread to other cities and caused a crisis within the government. When martial law was eventually declared, the military refused to take action to enforce it. The drama of the unfolding events was captured in the observation of a newsman, Bernard Shaw, that they had gone to cover a summit meeting and found themselves in the middle of a revolution.

While events in China were the most dramatic, change was evident in the Soviet Union and Eastern Europe as well. Gorbachev returned home to a rally of thousands of people calling for further reforms during the meeting of the Congress of People's Deputies, which was the culmination of the first multicandidate elections in that country since the time of Lenin. At about the same time, countries such as Czechoslovakia, Hungary, and Poland continued their quiet "velvet" revolutions with experiments in political and economic reform. As these countries moved in the direction of multiparty systems, the Polish trade union Solidarity was perhaps the symbol of the changes taking place. In the early 1980s it had been banned, and its leaders, including Lech Walesa, were arrested or driven underground. In 1989, Solidarity was officially recognized and allowed to run candidates in opposition to the official party, and the following year Walesa ran for the office of president of Poland. In the economic arena, these Eastern European countries joined the USSR and China in experiments moving away from centralized command economies and in the direction of greater emphasis on market forces. In Germany, the Berlin Wall came down in late 1989, ending almost 30 years as the most visible symbol of the differences between political societies. Even more remarkably, less than a year later East Germany ceased to exist when it was merged into a new united Germany, as discussed in Chapter 5.

The point is that the last decade has been one of great change for autocratic Communist systems as they deal with the economic, social, and political needs and demands of increasingly complex societies.

INDUSTRIAL SOCIETY

Since the definition of industrial societies was discussed at some length in Chapter 2, it will be necessary here only to mention certain aspects. Recall that the main indicator used to define them is whether half of the work force is engaged in industrial pursuits, and that it is useful to think in terms of more or less industrial societies rather than an absolute distinction of either industrial or not. As societies mature, an increasing portion of the population moves progressively from primary to secondary to tertiary pursuits. Primary activities are those involving mining and agriculture, secondary ones deal with manufacturing and production, and tertiary work include such things as providing services and information. As most of the population become engaged in tertiary pursuits, a society moves into what is called the postindustrial stage of development.

Using this standard, where can we place the Soviet Union during the Communist era and Russia and the other successor states in the post-Communist period? Even though a much larger proportion of its population was engaged in agriculture-related pursuits than is true in most industrial countries, one of the major factors in bringing down the USSR was its inability to feed its people while at the same time meeting its obligations to client states. In addition, both the quantity and quality of consumer goods and of computer and other information equipment were and are way behind other developed countries. With the collapse of the Soviet Union, it is necessary to acknowledge a wide range of development within its former borders, with European areas like the Baltics at the more advanced end, and those of Central Asia at the other. Similarly, of the former Communist countries in Eastern Europe that are now making the transition from Communism, some (such as Czechoslovakia or the former German Democratic Republic) could be considered as more mature, while others (such as Bulgaria or the former Yugoslavia) are less so. Communist countries outside of Europe, including the People's Republic of China, would have to be put in an earlier stage of the industrializing process. Even in this last group, however, the issues to be dealt with and the style of political leadership are drawing closer to those of more mature systems. This concept of industrialization is an important one, and one of the major interests of contemporary social scientists is in trying to see how this process of industrialization and modernization will affect not only politics but the economic system, societal values, and societies in general.

AUTOCRACY OR DICTATORSHIP?

Although the recent trend has been in the direction of democracy, when one looks at the nations of the world, it is rather clear that democracy is still the exception rather than the rule. Depending on the criteria used, there are only several dozen or so democratic countries as we in the West understand the concept of democracy. As was pointed out in Chapter 2, a core democratic value is accountability. In a democracy, accountability is largely structured through regular, competitive elections that cause the rulers to feel subject to certain constraints. By this standard, most nations would have to be classified as autocratic rather than democratic. Once again, it may be useful to point out that constraint is a matter of degree. No ruler is completely free to do as he or she pleases, but in more autocratic systems the limits are much broader and largely self-imposed rather than from the outside.

It is a testimony of the universal appeal of democracy that one of the interesting characteristics of the systems with which we are concerned has been their use of the language and institutions of democracy. In fact, the system of the Soviet Union was once described as an autocratic one masked in democratic phraseology and incorporating Western democratic forms counterweighted with fundamental controls to prevent them from operating in a truly democratic manner.[3] Perhaps the most conspicuous of these forms is elections. The USSR's claim to democracy rested in part on the holding of regular, secret elections. The key, however, is that until the reforms of 1989 and after, they were not competitive elections. There was only one name on the ballot, and that name was determined in a caucus-like procedure controlled by the Communist Party. When, in response to General Secretary Gorbachev's *glasnost,* an opposition party made an attempt to organize in 1988, it was met with swift repression. When the transition toward pluralism began with the election of the Congress of People's Deputies in 1989, 1,500 of the 2,250 seats were filled by open elections, but the remainder were reserved for and controlled by organizations such as the Communist Party, Komsomol, trade unions, etc.

Interestingly, however, the Communist Party's claim to legitimacy did not rest solely on the fact that leaders were elected, but rather on a mixture of process and ideology. This mixture was found in Jacob Talmon's concept of totalitarian democracy, Jean-Jacques Rousseau's concept of the embodiment of the mystical "general will" in the leader, and Hitler's claim to embody the true values and spirit of the German folk. Thus, autocratic leaders do not see any contradiction between their electoral process and the concept of democracy, because they profess to represent and act on behalf of the people. Until the reforms of 1990, Article 6 of the Constitution of the USSR acknowledged that the Communist Party of the Soviet Union (CPSU) was "the leading and guiding force of Soviet society and the nucleus of its political system." It went on to say that the party existed for and served the people. The rules of the party used almost identical language in describing the party as the "vanguard" of the Soviet people. In such an arrangement, there is no need for competitive elections. The party rules on behalf of the people's best interests, and from time to time the people give their vote of approval and confidence by re-electing the party's candidates.

TOTALITARIAN DICTATORSHIP

Totalitarianism

The concept of totalitarianism arose in large part as a response to the rise and fall of several authoritarian regimes and leaders in the 1930s and 1940s. While Communism under Stalin in the Soviet Union and National Socialism under Hitler in Germany are usually thought of as the prototypes, mention is often made of Fascism under Mussolini in Italy. In fact, the latter two are often grouped together in a comparison of Communism and Fascism. Taken as a group, they were seen as a new or even unique form, and a great deal of attention was devoted to explaining their origin, characteristics, and development.

Definition

As is true of any major concept, significant effort was spent in attempting to define the essential features of totalitarianism and then to discussing their applicability to specific examples. The classic definition, and the starting point for subsequent discussions, is the one formulated by Carl Friedrich and Zbigniew Brzezinski in the 1950s and later modified by them.[4] As originally stated, they saw all totalitarian systems as having six basic features:

1 A totalist ideology, consisting of an official doctrine covering all aspects of life, which everyone is to follow and which projects an eventually perfect state of mankind.
2 A single party, usually led by one person, consisting of a small percentage of the population and dedicated to the ideology.
3 A system of terror (random, arbitrary violence) applied by the party or a secret police using modern scientific methods.
4 Technologically conditioned, nearly complete monopoly control, by the party and govern-

ment of all effective means of mass communication.

5   Similar control of the effective use of all weapons of armed combat.

6   Central control and direction of the entire economy and most other social organizations.

In listing these characteristics, the authors pointed out that they must be considered as a pattern. That is, one cannot identify a system as totalitarian simply because it can be said to have one or more of the traits. There are many dictators and single-party systems, but if they are not acting on the basis of an ideology or mobilizing their population in the direction of some ideal society, they cannot be classed as totalitarian. In a later work, Friedrich suggested that there might even exist a need to maintain a certain balance among the various features of totalitarianism, such as the roles of the party, police, ideology, terror, etc. He also acknowledged that there would be significant variations in systems deemed to fit the general pattern. The form and content of the ideology might differ, for example, or the role of terror or the party.

Modifications or variations of the original definition began with the authors themselves, and continued with countless criticisms and alternatives. Brzezinski put it this way:

> Totalitarianism is a new form of government falling into the general classification of dictatorship, a system in which technologically advanced instruments of political power are wielded without restraint by centralized leadership of an elite movement for the purpose of effecting a total social revolution, including the conditioning of man on the basis of certain arbitrary ideological assumptions, proclaimed by the leadership in an atmosphere of coerced unanimity of the entire population.[5]

Within a decade of offering the original definition, Friedrich reflected on what he called the "change in the theory and practice of to-talitarianism." The most important of these he felt to be the idea that totalitarian dictatorship is a relative rather than an absolute category. Instead of worrying about an "ideal type," he suggested that one think in terms of more or less totalitarian and even of totalitarian trends.[6]

While Friedrich and Brzezinski offered a comprehensive definition of the phenomenon of totalitarianism, others attempted to focus on its "essence." Hannah Arendt, for example, spoke of its total terror, and described such systems as having gone beyond the mere use of terror to the point at which their very essence is terror. Certainly one cannot think of Nazi Germany and Stalin's Soviet Union without features such as concentration and labor camps, arbitrary attempts to eliminate whole groups of people, disregard for due process, and other coercive measures on a massive scale. It is important to distinguish between ordinary repression, which all authoritarian regimes use, and terror. The point of terror is the random, arbitrary, unjustified, and irrational nature of the violence and punishment involved. With terror, individuals might be punished or killed for no apparent reason.

Many commentators have pointed to the totalist element as the key aspect distinguishing totalitarian systems from other autocratic systems as well as from democratic ones. Often described as the politicization of society, this means that everything is to be controlled by those in power. The key is the absence of a distinction between the public sector (concerns that government may deal with) and the private sector (concerns that are none of government's business). Especially in democracies, but even in traditional dictatorships, the scope of political decisions is seen as being limited. Many of the day-to-day activities of groups and individuals are viewed as outside the authority of politics. In democratic societies, the proper sphere and role of government are constantly debated. In fact, some people think of democracy not so much as a system of popular input and participation but rather as one in which individuals and businesses are left to make their own choices with a minimum of government regulations and interference. Even dictators will often let the people go about their daily business as long as there is no challenge to their political authority. But in totalitarian systems, the line between state and society is destroyed, and the state claims the right to direct all aspects of human activity in accordance with its ideology as it proceeds toward the future perfect society.

Some, viewing the terror and totalist elements together, that the essence of life in a totalitarian society is being in a constant state of anxiety. While terror is sometimes a factor, it is usually overshadowed by the demand for conformity. A fear of being perceived as out of step with the program produces the "atomized individual effect," as people are reluctant to join groups or to voice opinions. Especially since the party line may change at any time, anxiety becomes constant and is institutionalized as a feature of the system.

Totalitarianism Versus Democracy

While there are inherent problems in defining such broad concepts as totalitarianism and democracy, it is sometimes helpful to compare some of the features and patterns associated with the two. In fact, Talmon has argued that what is taking place in the twentieth century is a clash of two types of democracy.[7] On the one hand is liberal democracy, and on the other what he calls "totalitarian messianic democracy." Speaking in terms of schools of thought rather than actual political systems, he suggests that both believe in liberty but differ in the manner of attaining it. The liberal finds the essence of freedom in spontaneity and lack of coercion; views poli-

tics as a pragmatic, trial-and-error process; and recognizes that many individual and group activities are essentially outside the realm of politics. The totalitarian approach says that classical liberalism leads to selfish individual activities to the detriment of society as a whole, that true freedom can only be realized when individuals unite to attain an absolute collective purpose, that politics can be defined precisely in terms of an exclusive truth, and that all human thoughts and actions fall within the scope of politics. The ultimate question Talmon poses is what he calls the paradox of freedom: is human freedom compatible with an exclusive pattern of social existence, even if this pattern aims at the maximum of social justice and security? This raises the question of whether there is such a thing as totalitarian liberty.

Talmon is not alone in suggesting the relationship between the two developments. For example, A. James Gregor says that totalitarian ideologies and movements are inconceivable outside the context of mass democracy (and modern technology).[8] The argument is that the breakdown of the classical liberalism of the nineteenth century led to the advent of mass democracy, collectivism, and welfare liberalism. Totalitarian movements, in turn, are seen as a radical form of the planned, collectivist features of modern welfare liberalism.

In many respects, the differences between the two systems seem to revolve around the classic question of the relationship of the individual on the one hand and the state or society on the other. Democracy tends to emphasize the importance of the former, to encourage criticism and the expression of various points of view, and to view the state as an instrument to serve the people. Constitutions are a means to limit the power of the state, and politics will include a variety of political parties and interest groups. Totalitarian systems, by contrast, are characterized by the idea of a vanguard party or group that claims to know what is best for society. This means that there is no need for other parties or groups in the political process, and that a constitution, rather than limiting the state, should provide the mechanism whereby the vanguard can direct the society. The interests of the individual are to be subordinated to those of the society as a whole. This organic concept of the state as having an essence and value beyond the individuals who comprise it, constitutes a whole school of thought in reaction to classical liberalism, which can be traced throughout the nineteenth century and is an important philosophical component of totalitarian thought and structures.

A look at the Soviet Constitution of 1977 will illustrate the difference in emphasis. In contrast to the notion of a constitution limiting governments, one commentary on the Soviet document characterized it as containing burdens that made the citizens of the USSR the most constitutionally bound individuals of modern times. While a description of rights was included, there was great emphasis on the duties and obligations of individuals and on the protection of the interests of society. In the economic realm, property could not be used for "selfish purposes" or to harm the interests of society (Articles 10 and 13), the state regulated individual labor activity in the interests of society (Article 17), and the evasion of socially useful labor was incompatible with the principles of a socialist society (Article 60). It often comes as a surprise to learn that the Soviet constitution contained guarantees of the freedom of speech, press, assembly, conscience, inviolability of the person and home, and the like (Articles 50–58). However, the exercise of these rights could "not injure the interests of society and the state"(Article 39), and had to be in accordance with the goals of Communist construction and for the purpose of strengthening and developing the socialist system.

To return to the definition of totalitarianism, the point is that in a totalitarian society, a vanguard party is directing it toward the ideologically prescribed goal. Apathy and lack of participation of the people are not acceptable. Working, voting, and many other social activities become obligations rather than matters of choice.

Left Versus Right Totalitarianism

The final aspect of the definition to be considered is the distinction between totalitarianism of the left (Communism) and of the right (fascism and National Socialism). In addition to distinguishing totalitarian systems from other types, attempts have been made to draw comparisons among such systems. While the subject of the present study is Communism, a brief consideration of these comparative efforts may aid in understanding the overall concept. In fact, while it is outside the scope of this work, Gregor has suggested that as the first mature national totalitarianism, fascism represents the paridigm for contemporary totalitarianism in an era in which the nation has become the focus of many movements. It must be acknowledged at the outset, however, that comparison is complicated by the fact that the prototype versions of the right lasted only a relatively brief time (partly under wartime conditions) and ended over five decades ago, while Communism in the Soviet Union continued to develop for 75 years, and the Chinese version was born only after Nazi Germany ceased to exist. Of course, now that Communism has ended in the Soviet Union and exists in only a few non-European countries, one of the major questions in comparative politics is what type of system will replace it.

At first glance, one tends to see the similarities of the various forms of totalitarianism, especially between Nazi Germany and the USSR under Stalin. Differences tend to be obscured by the common traits of special police forces, arbitrary arrests, internment camps, and other elements of terror and coercion. Equally striking are the single party, the very strong leader, the lack of genuine elections, and the massive propaganda and mobilization efforts in the name of the ideology. A pattern develops in these systems in which one consideration (class, race, nation) becomes supreme, and all other values and institutions derive from and are subordinate to it. Thus, such things as economics, science, art, personal relationships, and the administration of justice are all explained in terms of class (Communism), race (National Socialism), or nation (fascism).

Closer examination, however, reveals that there are significant differences, especially with regard to ideology and underlying assumptions. While some people would disagree, most consider Communism to be a more coherent, rigorous, and universal ideology than the others, which are often described as parochial and limited collections of standard concepts. One illustration of the contrast is in the basic appeal approach of Communism versus that of National Socialism. The former emphasizes reason and knowledge. Marxism-Leninism claims to be scientific in the sense that everything about the physical and social worlds can be learned and understood rationally. In this approach, there is no place for such things as religion, the supernatural, and intuition. In this type of system, ideology is said to play a central role as a blueprint or master plan to be understood and followed.

National Socialism, on the other hand, was essentially anti-intellectual and mystical, relying on will and intuition rather than reason. Whereas Communism planned to reorder the world on the basis of an objective understanding of history and society, National Socialism would engage in a heroic struggle to reshape those forces in its own subjective

image. Since Germany was also guided by the *Führer* (leader) principle, this meant in practice that the spirit of the folk was manifested in the *Führer* (Hitler) in the same manner as Rousseau's leader embodied the general will. While one must be careful not to overstate the case, the Soviet Union continued to emphasize the role of the ideology and the party rather than the individual leader. The term "cult of personality" has been used to criticize leaders for putting themselves above the party and its program. However, the difficulty of dealing with this dynamic is illustrated by the fact that Stalin, Khrushchev, and Brezhnev have all been accused of doing so by their successors. While it is also true that the ideology is subject to modification and interpretation by the leaders, the fact remains that systems of the left continue to insist on their programmatic nature.

A related point of difference, associated with Henry Ashby Turner, deals with the attitutes of the two types of totalitarianism toward modernization. This thesis suggests that while Marxism was definitely oriented toward a future based on a highly developed, urbanized economy and society, National Socialism had its utopia in the dim past and was in fact a revolt against modernity.

A final consideration with respect to comparisons involves the matter of economic patterns. In the definition of democracy in Chapter 2, it was pointed out that although capitalism may promote democracy, there is no necessary connection between one type of economic system and one type of political system. Property ownership is not necessarily a key distinguishing characteristic among totalitarian systems or between them and democracies. It is possible to have state ownership and planning in a democracy, and totalitarian Italy and Germany both had private property in systems that basically retained capitalist economic structures and principles under the direction of the state. Communist systems provide for a socialist economy with state planning and ownership of the means of production, but probably the greatest variety among such systems has been in the economic realm. China and the countries of Eastern Europe (especially Yugoslavia) experimented with mixed patterns of ownership and planning, and economic restructuring in the direction of mixed forms was a central feature of Gorbachev's *perestroika.*

Critiques of Totalitarianism

Over the last quarter-century, many observers have moved away from using the term *totalitarian*. While it continued to be widely used by politicians to describe countries they did not like, most scholars and academicians found it to be less and less useful, and many eventually spoke of the posttotalitarian period. Criticisms of totalitarianism included those that dealt with the validity of the concept itself and those that questioned the applicability of the definition to actual countries and systems, especially the former Soviet Union. The value of the concept itself is questioned on several grounds. The first of these involves the lack of precision. The definition discussed above is what is known as an "ideal type." That is, the characteristics described are those that would be found in a theoretical, perfect system of that type. Needless to say, there are no perfect systems (totalitarian or democratic), so all cases in the real world will deviate from the ideal to some degree. Once it is acknowledged that none will fit the definition exactly and that their fit is a matter of degree, there are many problems. How much terror or coercion must be present to include a given system in the category? How much control must the party exercise over the society, etc.? As long as the discussion is in terms of varying degrees rather than definable threshold levels, the value of the concept is limited in terms of empirical analysis

and explanation. Recall from Chapter 1 that empirical concepts must refer to an unambiguous category of cases. Other critics feel that lack of precision results from attempting to group the examples of left and right totalitarianism. Were the Communist, Italian Fascist, and National Socialist systems enough alike that they constitute one type, or does one sacrifice precision in trying to fit them into one group?

Yet another limitation on the comparative value of the definition is the charge that it is based on a very small number of examples at a given point in time under extraordinary circumstances. At best, the criticism goes, it is a static description of three examples, two of which covered only a couple of decades. Thus, as soon as circumstances change, the search is on for a new framework. At worst, the concept of totalitarianism is seen as a postwar reaction to Hitler and the Soviet Union, with all of the negative and polemic connotations that involves. In short, the concept is viewed by many as an idealized, imperfect description of a few historical systems that no longer exist. It was too vague in that it tried to lump together systems with significant differences, and too static and rigid in its inability to accommodate the process of change and development.

The element of change is at the heart of the second group of criticisms. Putting aside the concerns just discussed concerning the concept itself, they question the applicability of the definition to contemporary Communist systems because of the changes that took place after the death of Stalin in 1953 and the subsequent de-Stalinization in the Soviet Union and Eastern Europe. Using the standard definitions of totalitarianism as a point of reference, scholars increasingly suggested that they were inadequate and needed to be replaced with a newer, more appropriate framework. It must be pointed out, however, that many of the proposed alternates retained much of the original concept, modified to be more relevant. The classic question is at what point does making changes in the system result in the creation of a different type of system?

How do these criticisms apply in practice to the classic definition of totalitarianism? Many of the concerns involve the degree of control exercised over the society and the changed role of terror, the party, and the ideology.

The question of the role of terror illustrates both types of criticisms mentioned above. Although Arendt and others focused heavily on this element, some even excluded it as an essential aspect on the grounds that even though it may play a prominent role in totalitarian systems, it is also found in others that would not be so classified. Some, such as Allen Kassof, suggested that the terror and "gross irrationality" of the Stalin period had been replaced by administrative and bureaucratic control in what he called "the administered society: totalitarianism without terror."9 But is terror a quantitative or qualitative matter? There is no question that conditions during the later stages of Communist rule in the Soviet Union and Eastern Europe were nothing like those under Hitler or Stalin, in which millions of people were victimized for no apparent reason or solely because of their race, religion, or nationality. While there may still have been some such cases, most punishment seems to have been as a result of opposition to the system—dissent. Much as one might object to such treatment of dissent, it is rational (in the sense that it is predictable and administered with some consistency) and therefore not terror. But, to complicate things, the regime in the Soviet Union was accused of politically abusing psychiatry by punishing some dissidents by placing them in "psycho-prisons" that have been described by those so treated as terrifying.

In summary, is terror an essential ingredient of a totalitarian system? If it is, what does it do to the definition to change from a situation where millions are sent to labor and death camps for unpredictable reasons to one in which thousands are sent to camps, prisons, or exile primarily for opposition to some aspect of the system, while the remainder of the population is kept under control primarily through socialization and bureaucratic administration rather than coercion?

Questions have also arisen concerning the role of ideology. In the early 1960s, there was a debate as to the influence of ideology in industrial societies in general, an issue discussed in more detail in Chapter 2. In this so-called end of ideology discussion, it was argued that the dynamics of the industrial and postindustrial societies (with the increased emphasis on science, education, technology, and bureaucracy) are incompatible with closed ideological systems such as Marxism-Leninism. In discussions of Communist systems, this was once referred to as the "red versus expert" controversy. What are the relative roles of the reds (those following the Marxist ideological blueprint) and the experts (pragmatic bureaucrats and technocrats pursuing efficiency)?

This issue becomes more critical in discussions of Communist systems because they claim to be following an ideological course. Countries such as the United States are based on certain principles but do not claim to have a fixed, closed thought system that provides all the answers to society's needs and questions. It is generally agreed that ideology in the Soviet Union performed the usual functions of communication and (at least to some extent) legitimization. The real question is whether it was the driving, motivating force or mostly a technique used to give theoretical justification to policies arrived at for pragmatic reasons. There is, as one would guess, a difference of opinion as to the answer.

One argument against the end of ideology in the USSR was made by Brzezinski and Huntington.[10] In their view, the ideology becomes institutionalized in the ruling elite, whose organizational interest thus breathes new vitality into it. The ideology becomes embodied in the party bureaucracy, which acquires a vested interest in its perpetuation. Thus, it does play a role in the making and the content of decisions.

The opposite position can be illustrated by the observations of Richard Lowenthal and Milovan Djilas concerning the nature and motivations of the Communist Party leadership.[11] Describing the post-Khrushchev regime as bureaucratic and postrevolutionary, Lowenthal commented on the convictions of the leaders at such a stage. They no longer believed in the possibility of transforming society in accordance with the blueprint, and no longer needed the vision of a revolution to inspire faith and sacrifice. In the place of these concepts was a belief in science, education, and increased productivity, and for what was required of the people at this point, a combination of material incentives and appeals to patriotism would suffice. These were cautious and pragmatic leaders who were "agnostic in everything but their commitment to the greatness of Russia and to the need for orderly procedures." In foreign policy they defined their objectives in terms of the national interest of the nation-state rather than of the worldwide victory of Communism. Djilas, a former Communist vice president of Yugoslavia, came to an even harsher conclusion as he described the leadership of Communist states as a new ruling and exploiting class that no longer needed revolutionaries or dogmatists. The primary consideration in policy making was the interests and aspirations of this new class, whose goal was to increase its power and material privileges rather than to lead a revolutionary movement.

It is, of course, not as simple as whether people do or do not believe in the ideology. As would be true in most cases, there are probably some "true believers," some who are passive and indifferent, and many who are cynical but go through the motions for the sake of such things as material benefits and career advancement. Whatever conclusion one reaches, it seems that serious questions have been raised over whether ideology occupies the totalist, transforming role envisioned in the classic definition or is used mostly to justify and rationalize actions taken for practical or selfish reasons.

Another set of questions, revolving around the role of the party and its degree of control over both the policy process and the society as a whole, has been described in terms of the consensus and conflict models. Those advocating the conflict approach saw the definition of totalitarianism as inaccurate and misleading in its portrayal of the society as atomized, and criticized the consensus approach because of its emphasis on viewing the policy process as totally controlled by a unified party. Such an approach, they objected, ignores conflict and factions within the leadership and completely denies the role of institutional, bureaucratic, and other groups in the political process. This approach does not deny the primary role of the party, but does insist that we be aware that it contains far more infighting and struggle than is conveyed by the picture of a monolithic party led by one person. It also argues that on particular policy questions, such as education reform, economic priorities, and the like, the relevant bureaucracies, specialists, and interests have a role in the process. One study of attitudes held by the party and by "specialist elites" (economic, legal, military, and literary) in the 1960s concluded that the Soviet political system conceived as a monolith was a myth, that relations between the groups were marked by conflicts, and that a new model was needed to incorporate specialist elite participation.[12]

Commenting on this growing pluralism of interests in the postrevolutionary period (and in light of the diminished role of ideology), Lowenthal and others suggested a changed role for the party. Rather than being the driving force imposing a revolutionary transformation of society from above, it should be seen as a mediator or arbiter among the institutional groups that reflect the interests of an increasingly complex society. It was seen as reacting rather than dictating as it tried to keep the evolution of societal developments within acceptable limits. We must be clear that we are not talking about the same interest group dynamic and political process found in democratic systems, but neither are they those of the prototype totalitarian societies. From this viewpoint, the party had not lost its leading position, but there were other players and modified rules.

ALTERNATIVE MODELS

While most politicians and some scholars continued to use the concept of totalitarianism, from the 1960s on these and other perceived shortcomings resulted in a search for a better framework for studying Communist systems. As might be expected, what emerged was a variety of suggested perspectives. Some accepted the basic validity of the concept and called for changes in terminology or modifications to accommodate changes, while others essentially rejected it and proposed entirely different approaches. We must, of course, remind ourselves that the same general criticisms will apply to these suggested alternatives. They are also ideal types with their own shortcomings, but do provide a different way of looking at things.

The most modest calls were simply for a change in terms. There was no denial that the features described were present in Communist countries, but some felt that the word *totalitarian* was so full of negative and Cold War connotations and so associated with Hitler and Stalin that its value was very limited. Others felt that the term had come to be used too loosely as a generic description of any nondemocratic system of which the user (especially politicians) disapproved. In either case, a new terminology might be helpful.

Perhaps the best example of an approach that affirmed the basic nature of totalitarianism from a different perspective was Kassof's "administered society: totalitarianism without terror." Acknowledging the significant changes of the Khrushchev period, he disagreed with those who saw those changes as a liberalization moving away from totalism. On the contrary, he viewed the new phase as streamlining and adapting the past, rather than rejecting it, with the potential for a more advanced form of totalitarianism. The only major difference between the administered society and classic totalitarianism was the absence of the widespread use of terror and coercion usually associated with the latter. There was still a powerful ruling group directing the society from above on the basis of its asserted exclusive understanding of the laws of historical and social development. The elite exercised control by substituting coordination, planning, socialization, propaganda, and the like in place of coercion.

Related to Kassof's approach, in what are sometimes called the *directed society models*, are several that used a corporate or bureaucratic perspective. Alfred G. Meyer defined Communism as "the application of the corporate pattern of entrepreneurship to modernizing countries" and "the corporation writ large." Explicitly rejecting both the open society and totalitarian models, and acknowledging that there are significant differences between Communist and democratic systems, he suggested that the USSR could best be understood as a large, complex bureaucracy comparable in structure and functions to the giant corporations and institutions with which we are all familiar. Although Communism is the corporation "writ large" (that is, the totalist pattern is extended to all areas of life), Meyer also argued that all giant organizations share certain characteristics, such as an authoritarian political structure and the urge to organize not only professional activities but social and individual as well.[13]

This point of view was very much shared by T. H. Rigby, who described the Soviet system as mono-organizational and the dynamic within it as "crypto-politics."[14] A mono-organizational system is one in which there is a single center from which commands can be issued to any level in the society as it seeks to run the whole social life of the society. In using the term "crypto-politics," he was trying to contrast the political dynamic with the open, institutionalized politics of Western democratic societies. If we would understand how Communist systems operate, we must think instead in terms of the covert, behind-the-scenes office or board-room politics practiced in large organizations such as universities or corporations. To succeed in such an environment, one must adopt the corporate patterns of behavior, work up through the ranks, have a mentor, belong to the right clique, etc. The contrast with a democratic style is often quite dramatic. With respect to interest articulation, for instance, Rigby pointed out that it is often vital to avoid articulating interests in public. Rather, one must engage in the intricate, covert maneuvers of bureaucracies. Adoption of a policy is accomplished not through electoral, legislative, or judicial victories, but by persuading the powerful directors of the organization. The struggle will be among organizational hierarchies with shared concerns, with the entire process being mediated through cliques of top officials and their followers.

The real move away from the totalitarian model began in the late 1960s and acceler-

ated as Communist systems evolved. One factor at that point was a growing concern that the totalitarian model focused almost exclusively on outputs (policy results) and gave almost no attention to inputs (the policy process). At the same time, students of the Soviet Union and other Communist systems were attempting to move from an area studies approach into the mainstream of comparative politics and political science. Thus the constant tension of whether to see Communist countries as unique or to apply to them the broader concepts of comparative politics was resolved in favor of the latter.

The major approach used to accomplish this break with the totalitarian model and emphasize a common framework was pluralism, which in its various forms emphasizes the legitimacy of group competition and bargaining. In the pioneering and classic work in this area, H. Gordon Skilling asserted that an approach that excluded group interest and conflict was no longer appropriate, and that it was time for systematic study of "the reality of group politics."[15] Responses to that call produced concepts such as his own "pluralism of elites," Jerry Hough's "institutionalized pluralism,"[16] and Darrell Hammer's "bureaucratic pluralism." Once again, it should be pointed out that everyone using this approach conceded that the group dynamic will not be identical to that of traditional Western democratic societies, but suggested that pluralism could be used as a familiar point of reference. The major benefit is the emphasis on the fact that power is not as concentrated as in the past and that it is necessary to study the new patterns of dispersal.

Skilling suggested a progression of categories into which Communist states might be placed. They range from quasitotalitarian, in which groups outside the leadership are considered illegitimate and are tightly controlled, to democratizing and pluralistic authoritarianism, in which groups endorsed by the leadership play a significant role in policy making. An example of the latter might be the reforms and processes that were taking place in Czechoslovakia in 1968 before the invasion by the USSR and other Warsaw Pact nations. In between these are consultative authoritarianism and quasipluralistic authoritarianism. The consultative type corresponds rather closely to the directed society approach, in which coercion is replaced by administration and specialists are brought into the process under the tight supervision of the party. The quasipluralistic is probably the dominant and most relevant type. Although the party remains the dominant factor, intellectual and opinion groups assert themselves through criticism and policy proposals, and a real conflict takes place. Factional conflict among the top political leaders may heighten this process and give the groups some influence in the policy process.

More recently, the most prominent version of the pluralist approach was Hough's institutionalized pluralism. Describing the policy process as a highly participatory one for both individuals and institutions, he emphasized that such participation must take place within official channels in order to be considered legitimate. People cannot form interest groups or opposition political parties, but their interests can be represented if they work through existing official institutions. Hough explained that his use of the concept was intended to explore the changes perceived to be taking place between the Khrushchev and Brezhnev regimes. Whereas policy outcomes in the former were seen as being dictated or affected mostly by the leader or leaders, under Brezhnev he saw things developing in the direction of the specialized policy complexes that exist in democratic countries and that have been known by various terms such as whirlpools, iron triangles, or subgovernments.

It is at this point that the matter comes closest to the democratic pluralist model and the idea of subgovernments, or groups of executive departments, congressional committees (or their staff), and interest groups that make policy in their particular area of interest. Perhaps the most conspicuous example in U.S. politics is the so-called military-industrial complex composed of defense contractors, the Pentagon, and the relevant congressional committees, but there would be similar "whirlpools" in agriculture, health, education, and virtually any other policy area. The point of this approach is that conflict is not so much between branches of government as it is among the policy complexes representing competing interests. Applied to the former Soviet Union, it suggested that while the leadership retained the power of final decisions, it would more and more follow the advice of the "whirlpools" in their respective areas, while it set overall goals and settled disputes among them. Case studies have been done with respect to the roles of some groups (such as educators, criminologists, economists, and the military) in policy and reforms related to their areas, and Hough seemed to reflect some criticisms of American interest groups when he described his institutionalized pluralism approach to the USSR as one in which defense policy was made by the military and defense industry, health policy by doctors, etc., all in a selfish manner.

It is obvious by now that any one model or approach has both value and shortcomings. In addition to some inherent criticisms of the pluralist approach, there are other dangers of applying it to Communist regimes, but the objective is to compare when possible. While the totalitarian model tended to point out the distinct and different nature of such systems, the "whirlpool" concept focuses on policy areas, invites comparison, and provides a different perspective. By the same token, one of the dangers is that in the attempt to generalize we may read things into Communist or other authoritarian systems that are not there and try to make them too much like other systems. Thus, one of the reactions to the emphasis of the pluralist approach for similar processes and dynamics was a call for a temporary suspension of the passion for comparison and a new focus on the uniqueness of Communist political systems. Since the act of generalizing implies looking for patterns among phenomena that are otherwise different, perhaps the answer is not to give up attempts at comparison, but to take care not to overlook the essentially distinct attributes of the former Soviet Union and other Communist or post-Communist systems.

Corporatism

Toward the end of the Brezhnev era, the use of the concept of corporatism was proposed as a means to deal with criticisms of both the totalitarian and pluralist models by accommodating some elements of each. The term was originally used to describe Mussolini's Italy and then other Fascist-type authoritarian regimes (such as in Latin America), and was subsequently applied on a wide scale to the study of Western European industrial democracies. By about 1980, the term *neo-*, or *liberal, corporatism* (as discussed in Chapter 2), made its way to Communist studies, largely as a result of criticism that such systems were not pluralistic in the same sense that democracies were.

The classic definition is that of Philippe Schmitter:

> Corporatism can be defined as a system of interest representation in which the constituent units are organized into a limited number of singular, compulsory, non-competitive, hierarchically ordered and functionally differentiated categories recognized and licensed (if not created) by the state and granted a deliberate

representational monopoly within their respective categories in exchange for observing certain controls on their selection of leaders and articulation of demands and supports.[17]

Proponents of this approach felt that it came closer to describing the dynamics within Communist systems than did a pluralistic framework. The differences between the two approaches can be seen by examining the political process in terms of two aspects: the relative roles of the state, interest groups, and the general public; and the emphasis on planning and rationality.

Pluralism tends to see all groups as part of the process; to view them as independent, autonomous actors; and to stress conflict and competition among them. This group dynamic is the main element in the political process, and the role of the state is often portrayed as that of a broker, mediator, or referee. The corporatist approach paints the role of the state as a much more active one, sees the groups as less than autonomous, includes functional groups (business, labor, etc.) but not attitudinal ones, and emphasizes cooperation and consensus rather than competition. Of course, as was pointed out in the earlier discussion of European corporatism, the situation may go beyond cooperation to the point at which the key groups are actually "coopted" by the government.

Another major difference is with respect to goals and planning. A successful pluralistic system, it is alleged, cannot plan and has few or no explicit policy goals. The major concern is with maintaining the process, and the assumption is that things will work themselves out as a consequence of the group dynamic. A corporatist system, on the other hand, starts with a set of explicit objectives and emphasizes working together through a planned process in order to reach the goals. The goals may be similar (economic growth, stability, maintenance of the current distribution of power), but the assumptions and process used to attain them are quite different.

These and other characteristics seemed to make this approach useful in understanding Communist systems, and it was discussed and applied particularly during the Brezhnev period. It contains the elements of planning, control, and an active role for the state as well as a degree of participation (at least for the functional types of groups), but to some extent also strikes a deal between elites and masses of exchanging control for security and a certain level of welfare state benefits. The element of planning also seems attractive at a time when all systems, including democratic ones, are experiencing what the Soviets called the "scientific-technical revolution," or STR. The STR is the universal process involving the growing application of science and technology in which technology replaces people in the production process. In order to obtain maximum benefits from these changes, there must be new organizational structures and highly trained specialists to manage the forces at work in this revolutionary new era.

The corporatist approach seems to many to be well suited to deal with these new developments. It envisions an expanding, active role for the state (with or without the single party) as a catalyst and planner in a process that brings together the major functional interests with their specialized knowledge and expertise in the quest for economic growth, stability, and a distribution of power in which all will prosper. Economic growth will allow the leadership to extend to the people more of the material security that the elite has had all along, possibly continuing or restoring the arrangement some feel has existed in which, in exchange for increased material and personal security and well-being, the people accept a certain degree of control and exclusion from the political process.

Modernization and Convergence

Whether one chooses to adopt the corporatist approach, it is clear that the dynamics it attempts to address are the ones that faced the Soviet Union and other Communist or post-Communist societies. These problems, as Richard Lowenthal put it, were those of a postrevolutionary, established, single-party regime in a more or less mature industrial society. What will be the affects of the inevitable process of modernization and the scientific-technical revolution on the authoritarian political and social systems of these countries?

Since the beginning of the Gorbachev era in 1985, it has been precisely these two sets of problems that the Soviet Union and now Russia and the other post-Communist systems have faced. On the economic level, the question is one of how to meet the increased need for efficiency and rationality of a modern industrial society that must compete with other such societies. The related social question is that of how to respond to the increasingly complicated interests of such a modern society, especially the desires of the specialized groups whose knowledge and cooperation are needed to make the economy work.

The concepts of *perestroika* (restructuring) and *glasnost* (openness or public discussion) were direct responses to the two issues. Initiated immediately by the new leader in 1985, and developed and ratified by the Twenty-Seventh Party Congress in 1986, an extraordinary Party Conference in 1988, and the Twenty-Eighth Party Congress in 1990, the proposed reforms were intended to set the society on a new path. Placing the blame for the obvious economic problems on the failure of earlier leaders (especially Brezhnev) to modernize and make necessary changes, Gorbachev called for sweeping economic, social, and (eventually) political reforms.

In the economic realm, the call for radical restructing (*perestroika*) began with efficiency measures such as consolidating ministries, giving more decision-making authority to factory and farm managers, allocating resources to promote the development and application of technology, and instituting a campaign to reduce corruption, alcoholism, and similar practices. But significant results would also require personnel changes. After a Brezhnev regime marked by a lack of such changes, the new leadership proceeded with the massive turnover of economic and political officials in both the party and the government. Older officials were replaced by younger, better-educated technocrats with experience in the technologically advanced sectors of the economy.

The other major reform, *glasnost,* resulted from the realization that it is impossible to revitalize the economy without also making broader social changes in the direction of greater openness. Before changes can take place, there must first be a more open and honest discussion of the problems. People must be free to point out shortcomings and propose solutions. One of the most dramatic developments of the new approach has been the kind of public disagreement that first occurred among the leadership at the 1988 Party Conference concerning the pace of *perestroika* and has continued at virtually all meetings since. To the extent that reform depends on the participation of the people, or at least the intelligentsia, they must be better informed and more involved.

While *glasnost* was originally intended to promote economic reform, the openness eventually went well beyond economic matters. The release of Andrei Sakharov from years of internal exile was the first of many changes in the treatment of dissidents who questioned features of the broader social and political systems. Previously unheard of press conferences became routine symbols of a more public style of politics, public speeches became much more candid in acknowledging problems and resistance to the solution of those problems, sessions of party and government bodies were characterized by open and heated debate, and there were attempts at a more accurate rewriting of the country's history. At a more popular level, the changes were somewhat reminiscent of the "thaw" of the 1950s under Khrushchev, as previously banned books, films, and art were permitted, and restrictions toward emigration and religious activities were modified. The Party Conference even initiated discussion of political reforms such as fixed terms for political leaders, more than one candidate on a ballot, and a modified relationship between the party and government bureaucracies. While the eventual new form of the social, economic, and political systems of the former Soviet Union and other once Communist regimes remains to be seen, there is universal agreement that the extent and pace of change were far greater than anyone anticipated when Gorbachev came to power. Within just one decade, reforms originally intended only to make Communist systems more efficient resulted first in their collapse and then in significant progress toward the transition to democracy, market economics, and the development of civil society.

Convergence Theory

As mentioned in Chapter 2, the idea that advanced industrial democracies and industrial autocracies are coming closer together because of the imperatives and processes of modernization and technology is known as convergence theory. The underlying assumption of the idea of convergence is that the industrial (and postindustrial) way of life has a structuring effect on political, economic, and social life that is stronger than ideology and past structures. That earlier chapter dealt with the industrial democracies in terms of the need for planning, neocorporatism, and the enlarged role of the technocrats and administrative elite.

We have long talked about an evolution of one-party systems from a revolutionary stage where ideology and charismatic leadership are primary to a later one in which technocrats, bureaucrats, and efficiency are the key. With respect to the Soviet Union and Eastern Europe, it has been suggested that the concept of developed socialism may have been a version of convergence. Developed, or mature, socialism was the term used by the Soviet Union in the Brezhnev period to describe the application to the USSR of the universal societal consequences that accompany the scientific-technical revolution. It envisioned an expanded managerial and administrative role for the state and an ever-increasing role for scientists, managers, and all technical experts in the making of economic, social, and political decisions. According to this idea, as the Soviet Union moved into the postindustrial stage of development, the greatest growth would take place in high-technology industries, scientific research, and the sectors of the economy dealing with services and information.

Despite the seeming parallels between Western accounts of industrial and postindustrial society and the Soviet concept of developed socialism, convergence theory has been rejected by many on both sides. While they may agree that there are some similarities in form and process, critics felt that there could be no coming together in the crucial matters of content and essential values. Both sides stressed the incompatible differences of the two types of systems. But, as Jeffrey Hahn has pointed out, both rejections reflected essentially ideological preoccupations with such differences rather than an attempt to explore the industrial society model.[18] Soviet critics focused on the economic dimension,

and concluded (in good Marxist fashion) that capitalism and socialism are anathema and can never converge. Only an end to capitalism could bring the two closer together. In a similar fashion, Western critics stressed the political differences and highlighted the nondemocratic nature of Communist societies. In this view, adoption of Western-style democracy is a precondition of any convergence. Thus, each point of view felt that the basic nature of the other must change to conform to it.

Hahn suggests that both are missing the real point. The issue of convergence theory is not so much whether they are becoming more like us or we are becoming more like them, but rather whether both (in response to the imperatives of modernization) are changing in similar ways into something else.

One person who has not given up on the value of convergence theory is Ronald Inglehart, who has taken a somewhat different approach.[19] As popularly perceived in the 1960s, the convergence was partly one of processes and bureaucracies coping with modernization. For some 20 years, Inglehart has examined the question of cultural changes, focusing on what he called "materialist" and "postmaterialist" values. Materialistic values deal with matters of physical and economic security, such as maintaining law and order and promoting economic growth and stability. Postmaterialism places the emphasis more on the need for self-expression in terms of aesthetic and intellectual needs, the political dimension of which is the desire for free speech and a larger voice in politics. One of his findings, based on data from a large number of studies, is that the emphasis in advanced industrial societies is gradually shifting from materialistic to postmaterialistic values.

While Inglehart concentrates on other countries and systems, he does have some observations about convergence between Communist regimes and the West in several respects. Dealing with classic forms of the theory, he argues that there has been a long-term tendency in both the economic and political realms in recent decades. While government expenditures account for an increasingly larger portion of the gross national product in Western countries, Communist countries began experimenting with ways to move away from centralized control and toward individualized activities. In the political arena, Inglehart focuses on the increased pressures for broader political and social participation in both types of systems. It was only in the last quarter-century that the United States, with its more open society, was forced to come to grips with demands for such participation by African Americans, women, and other groups. When similar pressures developed in Communist countries, they were repressed. But that only created greater problems in the long run, as Gorbachev pointed out and as we have since witnessed in very dramatic form.

Here we come to the core of Inglehart's argument of the cultural shift. The process of restoring the economy will give rise to a dynamic that will lead to demands for participation in both economic and political decision making. Improving the economy requires innovation, initiative, and such technology as computers and communication. Denying their use will eventually lead to economic collapse, yet allowing them will have inevitable social and political consequences. Inglehart acknowledged that many of its problems and concerns seemed to place the Soviet Union more in the materialistic category, and that economic modernization does not make political liberalization inevitable. Having said that, however, he argued that it does make it increasingly difficult to avoid, that the long-term outlook seemed more conducive to convergence than to divergence between Soviet-style and Western societies,

and that a gradual, long-term cultural shift was probably taking place in the Soviet Union. The essence of convergence theory, as we have used it, is the growing importance of the bureaucracy and the technocracy in all modern systems.

THE POST-COMMUNIST ERA

We began this chapter by suggesting that Communism and the other systems described as totalitarian were early twentieth-century reactions to the coming of capitalism and the industrial revolution. We have now had an opportunity to see how both democratic and nondemocratic systems have dealt with and adapted to the social, economic, and political pressures of industrialization and modernization. Marxism and Communism have played large roles during most of the century, but as we approach its end we now speak of the post-Communist era.

On the one hand, the crisis of capitalism that Marx and his followers anticipated has not happened. Much of the appeal of Marxism as an alternative to the injustices and exploitation inherent in capitalism has been undercut by developments in capitalist countries. The bleak economic and social conditions of the nineteenth century have been modified by the implementation of measures such as the welfare state, social security, a mixed economy with varying amounts of government regulation of business and the economy, and the extension of civil rights and liberties.

At the same time, Communism and the other forms of totalitarianism have had their chance and failed. The nature of their problem was illustrated by Lowenthal's assertion that modern Communist-ruled societies that did not evolve toward pluralistic democracy would likely stay below their potential for economic growth and fall victim to recurrent political crises because of the resulting lack of legitimacy (public acceptance). Those recurrent crises caused Eastern Europe to abandon Communism completely, and the Soviet Union and China to struggle with the new arrangements to replace it. As Brzezinski put it in *The Grand Failure,* the central surprise of Communism's confrontation with history was discovering "its manifest irrelevance to modernity." That is, the more advanced the society is, the less politically relevant is the ideology and means of control of the Communist Party.

This collapse of Communism leads to the final question: what will things look like in the post-Communist era? It is far easier to explain why one system failed than it is to replace it with a different one that will succeed. While Marx and others had written of the transition from capitalism to socialism or Communism, there was no guidebook for the return trip from Communism. Even in Eastern Europe, where Communism was imposed from the outside after World War II on countries that had earlier experienced greater economic and political freedom, the economic and political transition has not been an easy one. After the initial celebrating and euphoria, all the countries involved have had to face the hard realities of the social, economic, and political struggle ahead of them. Already, this process has produced frustration, disillusionment, and even civil war. It does appear that pluralist democracy may eventually prevail and that the former Communist-bloc countries will become part of the new Europe, but only after a prolonged and difficult struggle.

In other countries, including the former Soviet Union and the People's Republic of China, the eventual outcome is not so clear. By 1990, the Soviet Union had undertaken momentous political reforms, such as removing the monopoly position of the party, holding multicandidate and even multiparty elec-

tions, and granting religious freedom, but was locked in heated debate about the extent and pace of needed economic reform, with the old, entrenched *"apparat"* doing its best to limit and slow reform. The events following the abortive coup of August 1991 resulted in the discrediting of the Communist Party and an acceleration of the process of change, but it will take years or even decades before the new economic, social, and political forms are established. By way of contrast, China had undertaken far more extensive economic changes, but, in the wake of the prodemocracy demonstrations in Tiananmen Square in the summer of 1989, inflicted severe punishment on the demonstrators and insisted on even greater ideological training and political conformity for the entire population.

Given the dimensions of the economic and social crises facing Russia and the other successor states in the 1990s, a number of possibilities exist. One would be to continue with the reforms set in motion by Gorbachev and implemented by Boris Yeltsin, either individually or perhaps in some form of confederation, emerging eventually on the European path of socialist democracy with genuinely democratic processes and a mixed economy. Gorbachev insisted that his reforms were not an abandonment of socialism, but rather its renewal in the form of a realistic "humane socialism" to replace the failed dogmatic, authoritarian form that he had inherited. The end product of this process would be, as one source has put it, "normal" societies in which citizens know that they are free to come and go as they please and to express themselves as they please, and in which the changes have been made in such a way that they are permanent.[20]

But such normalization is neither guaranteed nor easily achieved. Democracy cannot simply be superimposed from above on a society that has no real experience with or understanding of its dynamics. Democracy has certain cultural requirements, which for the most part are not part of the political culture left over from the Soviet Union. The whole history of the area is one of submission to paternalism and authority. Concepts such as equality, respect for all individuals and political parties, and pluralistic political competition will have to become much more widely accepted.

This process of attempting to instill democratic values and structures is complicated by the heterogeneous nature of the society that the Soviet Union inherited from the Russian Empire and passed on to its Russian and other successors. As was suggested in an earlier chapter, in segmented societies cultural defense in the form of ethnic violence or strife is becoming a major problem around the world. This is certainly true in the former Soviet Union. The problem is that as authoritarian rule has been relaxed, formerly suppressed social forces and strife have risen to the surface. In the less authoritarian atmosphere, various ethnic, nationalist, and chauvinistic groups are able to express their long-held hatred for one another and for their rulers, and both organized crime and common street crime have risen dramatically. Various parts of the former USSR have experienced civil war. On the other side of the coin, there has been a burst of chauvinistic, Russian nationalism against the Jews and other non-Russian groups. It should be obvious that these conditions do not facilitate the kind of mutual respect, compromise, and stability on which democracy is based.

This instability leads to suggestions that pluralistic democracy may not be the outcome anytime soon. Ethnic conflict, coupled with the desperate state of the economy, caused Gorbachev in 1990 to ask for and receive emergency powers. In late 1991, Yeltsin was granted similar powers to suspend elections, demonstrations, and the like. Is it possible that continuing and even deteriorating social and economic conditions might lead to a longing for the "good old days"? After all, things continued to get worse, the argument goes, after Gorbachev instituted and Yeltsin accelerated their economic and political reforms. Communism has lost its appeal, but could the post-Communist era, in a search for stability, produce a traditional form of authoritarianism based on traditional national factors rather than ideology?

From the viewpoint of comparative politics, the "Second Russian Revolution," as the developments following the 1991 failed coup have come to be known, has raised a number of fascinating questions and possibilities. Perhaps most significant are its implications for the perennial issue of the difference between area studies and comparative politics. With the end of the dominance of the Communist Party and ideology, and the eventual collapse of Communist systems, attention can shift to the broader concerns of establishing a pluralistic democratic system and a legal system based on law, dealing with ethnic- and nationality-based social conflict, and instituting the incentives and infrastructure for an economy based more on markets and privatization. While it is true that all of these things must be accomplished in the particular context of the former USSR and other formerly Communist countries, the questions and dynamics involved are familiar to political scientists, economists, sociologists, and others in general. The post-Communist period, therefore, opens up the once more limited field to the possibilities of inquiry and comparative study by a much broader range of disciplines.

THE TRANSITION TO DEMOCRACY

A good many people spent most of this century trying to understand Communist systems. As we approach the beginning of a new century, the end of Communism in the Soviet

Union and Eastern Europe, and then the end of the Soviet Union itself, have resulted in a change in the focus of study toward an effort to understand and assist the transition taking place in those areas from Communism and in the direction of greater political democracy, market economics, and a more open society. But, in fact, the overall surge of democracy since the 1970s, described by some as perhaps *the* political feature of our time, has prompted an even broader area of study. Samuel Huntington, for example, refers to the worldwide process beginning in 1974 as the "third wave" of democratization.[21] The first, long wave, led by the United States, was from 1828 to 1926. A second, short wave was from 1943 to 1962. Interestingly, he reminds us that each wave is followed by a "reverse wave," in which some countries that had begun the transition then revert to nondemocratic rule. This third wave, which did not begin with and is not limited to the formerly Communist systems, involves some very interesting questions for comparative politics. On the one hand, there are attempts to understand the factors and process involved in the collapse. On the other, the questions deal with what kind of institutions and processes will eventually take the place of the old ones and how long this will take. Is there a pattern to the collapse of authoritarian systems? Is there a difference between the collapse of Communist systems and of traditional oligarchies? Once the collapse takes place, are there patterns in attempting to establish and consolidate democracy? What forces are likely to be at work promoting and resisting change? Since the transition from Communist systems toward democracy is uncharted territory, there is great variety in the approaches to the subject.

The range of possible explanations for the collapse of Communist systems in general and the USSR in particular is illustrated by the fact that some were asking how the Soviet Union could have collapsed so quickly and completely, while others asked how it lasted as long as it did. One example of an attempt at a general explanation is that of Sabrina Petra Ramet, who used the term "collapsed authoritarian system syndrome" to suggest that when such systems do collapse, they do so according to a regular pattern.[22] Comparing the Soviet collapse with the Bolshevik Revolution of 1917, the Chinese Revolution of 1911, the overthrow of the Spanish monarchy in the 1930s, and the collapse of post-Tito Yugoslavia in 1989, she suggests certain probabilities and patterns, including: (1) a long process of political decay building over decades; (2) an opposition inspired by hopes of and initial strong impulses toward democracy; (3) serious economic deterioration; (4) regionalization of the country; and (5) foreign intervention (at least in the four earlier cases). Furthermore, in the four earlier cases the collapse led to a period of prolonged internal chaos and civil war.

Taking a different approach, Baohui Zhang examined the capability of various regimes as they were faced with demands for change.[23] If the regime also lost its repressive capability, it just collapsed (East Germany or Czechoslovakia). If it still retained a strong repressive capability, hard-liners in the party, military, etc., attempted to reverse the reform process. If they were successful (as in China), there was a reversion to or continuation of authoritarian rule. If they failed (as in the August 1991 coup in the USSR), the result was collapse. If the regime still had support within the society, it could undertake top-down reforms, as was the case in Hungary. Finally, if the system was still based on personal rule, as in Romania, the likely result was revolution.

While it is important to understand why Communist systems collapsed, there is, understandably, even greater interest in examining what is happening now and what the future may hold. With the tearing down of the Berlin Wall and the subsequent collapse of Communist regimes in Eastern Europe, many assumed that the inevitable consequence would be the development of economic and political processes and institutions along the lines of those found in Western Europe. The years since then have demonstrated that anti-Communism is not necessarily the same as prodemocracy, and that it is difficult to develop the system of market-oriented economics and political democracy that so many take for granted. In earlier chapters we discussed the importance of allowing such factors as democratic institutions and processes to develop over centuries and in the proper sequence. The seemingly impossible task facing the post-Communist systems is, as Alexander Motyl stated in speaking of the Ukraine, to develop the state, the rule of law, civil society, the market, and democracy, and to do it in exactly that order. He argues that a radical, all-at-once approach cannot work, because each stage is a precondition of the next. Democracy can only develop after establishment of the other events have occurred.[24] Although parallels are sometimes drawn with Weimar Germany, it has been suggested that since the rise of democracy, there has seldom, if ever, been an attempt to create democratic systems in such conditions of economic disintegration and social chaos.

Civil Society

Since they are preconditions to the consolidation of democracy, quite a bit of attention has been given to attitudes such as political culture, civic culture, and civil society. While it might be possible to set up democratic institutions without these attitudes, it would be almost impossible to maintain such institutions without them. *Civic culture* is a set of attitudes about government and the people's relationship to it. If you have a sense of civic culture, you feel that you have a duty to participate in political life, that everyone else has a right to do the same, that government has a duty to serve the people, that you can influence government decisions, that decisions are to be made through proper democratic procedures rather than violence, etc. Support for the system is not based solely on performance, and you abide by the results of properly conducted elections, even if your side loses. You have a certain level of trust of both the government and your fellow citizens. *Civil society* is a term often used together with civic culture. It is applied in a variety of ways, but may be defined as "a dense network of nongovernmental associations and groups established for the autonomous pursuit of diverse socioeconomic interests and prepared to rebuff state efforts to take control of these activities."[25] This network includes groups such as the media, churches, labor unions, business and professional organizations, and political parties. In a democracy, these groups institutionalize the values of the civil culture and serve as a counterweight to government efforts to play too large a role in the society in general.

The difficulty in applying the concepts of civic culture and civil society to the post-Communist states takes us back to the earlier discussion of totalitarianism. One person described the situation in the former Soviet Union as a "political void" and a moral and spiritual "wasteland" caused by the fact that the weak civil society that had existed before 1917 was "systematically destroyed" in the Soviet period.[26] Speaking of Czechoslovakia, Vaclav Havel, the dissident playwright who was elected president in 1989, after spending more than five years in prison during the Communist period, described that country as a "foxhole of purely material existence" characterized by despair, apathy, and a gradual erosion of moral standards, with deceit being the norm.[27]

The system developed by Lenin and Stalin, and exported to varying degrees to other Communist countries, aimed at and resulted in an "atomized" society in which autonomous societal institutions were not allowed, and in which individuals were socially isolated and extremely untrusting, suspicious, and cynical not only of the authorities but of one another as well. This, of course, is exactly the opposite of what is needed for development of a civic culture. Even with the changes of the posttotalitarian period (after Mao and Stalin), the organizations that existed are often described as "transmission belts" because their purpose was to mobilize the society on behalf of the regime. The organizations mentioned earlier, such as the media, labor or writers' unions, and youth or women's groups, were auxiliaries of the party rather than autonomous or reflecting societal control and interests. One of the implications of this lack of societal institutions is its impact on the nature of political opposition, which tends to be in the form of broad social movements rather than political organizations, and opposition leaders tend not to have a specific institutional power base. Thus, they must appeal directly to the masses, on the basis of nationalism or a populist opposition to existing leaders and systems. This tends to make political discourse more radical and opens the way for demogogues such as Vladimir Zhirinovsky in Russia. At the opposite extreme, the lack of institutions can result in an excessive number of parties and groups running for office once competitive elections are allowed. According to one source, in the elections of 1990 and 1991, there were 30 such groups in Germany, 65 in Hungary, 61 in Bulgaria, and 90 in Poland (where the Polish Beer Lovers Party won 16 seats in the parliament).[28]

Discussion of the need to reinvent civil society leads to another illustration of the possible differences in approaches to anticipating how things will turn out. In what is sometimes called the political-institutional approach to transitions, one person asked if it is more important to know where these systems are coming from or where they are headed?[29] How much emphasis should be put on the historical context in which choices must now be made, and how much on the ability of the present actors to shape future outcomes, in spite of the past, by their choices and performance? While there is obviously an interplay of context and actors and choices, if performance is important to the consolidation and durability of democracy, how much does such performance depend on the various factors?

CONCLUSION: CHANGE AND COMMUNIST SYSTEMS

In examining the developments in Communist systems in recent decades, one cannot help but be struck by the element of change and reform. Stalin was denounced by Khrushchev for his crimes and repressive rule. Khrushchev attempted to institute reforms and was eventually removed by his colleagues for too much innovation and "hare-brained scheming." The more conservative Brezhnev period eventually resulted in serious economic, social, and political stagnation, and was denounced by Gorbachev, who in the form of *glasnost* and *perestroika* proposed the most far-reaching reforms since the Russian Revolution. The implementation of those reforms, however, produced an almost immediate counterattack by conservative forces, an eventual backing down by Gorbachev, the dramatic "Second Russian Revolution" in 1991, and finally the failure of Communism and the breakup of the Soviet Union. Although the Commonwealth of Independent States (CIS) was established as a nominal successor to the Soviet Union to deal with such matters as trade and security, the Soviet Union has been replaced by 15 independent countries.

The experience of the People's Republic of China has produced even more disruptive swings of policy. Periods of relative stability and progress have been interrupted by radical programs such as the Great Leap Forward, begun in 1958, and the Great Proletarian Cultural Revolution of the late 1960s. The events of the summer of 1989 produced a retreat from some of the reforms and a renewed emphasis on ideological training. Events such as the l968 "Prague Spring" in Czechoslovakia and the Solidarity Movement in Poland were illustrations of the continuing reform in Eastern Europe, which eventually led to the dramatic events of 1989 and 1990 in which all of the countries in that area abandoned the old forms of Communism and the leadership of the Communist Party and began the implemention of varying forms and degrees of political pluralism and economic reform.

With all these changes, it should come as no surprise that observers have used a variety of approaches to try to understand the dynamics of the systems under study. While some conservative members of the public continued to picture the Soviet Union largely in terms of the patterns and institutions of the Stalinist period, and in some cases even insisted that the changes of the late 1980s were just another Communist trick, the totalitarian model was eventually discarded by most academics. While none of the proposed alternatives was perfect, they were intended to provide a fresh perspective for understanding and exploration. Thus, pluralism was intended to draw attention to the input aspect of the political system, and corporatism and the industrial society sought to apply to Communist societies concepts that are used to discuss industrial democracies.

As we look to the future, the challenge is to conceptualize what things will look like in the post-Communist era of the twenty-first century. These formerly Communist countries are in uncharted territory. There is no road map or manual to guide them. No one has ever made the transition from totalitarianism to democracy and market economics. To make things even worse, many are attempting this transition under the most difficult circumstances imaginable. They must transform or create both the institutions of democracy and market economics and the civic culture and civil society that will sustain them. And in many cases they must do this in the midst of chaotic political conditions, economic disintegration, ethnic strife, and even civil war. Will former Communist systems evolve into "normal" pluralistic social democratic systems, into a more traditional type of authoritarianism without the ideology, or into some new hybrid? Subsequent chapters will explore both the nature and development of Communist systems and the changes that are taking place in the post-Communist era as they attempt the difficult transition toward the rule of law, democracy, market economics, and civil society.

NOTES

1. Samuel Huntington and Clement Moore, eds., *Authoritarian Politics in Modern Society* (New York: Basic Books, 1970).
2. Zbigniew Brzezinski, *The Grand Failure: The Birth and Death of Communism in the Twentieth Century* (New York: Charles Scribner's Sons, 1989).
3. See John Hazard, *The Soviet System of Government,* 5th ed. (Chicago: University of Chicago Press, 1980).
4. Carl Friedrich and Zbigniew Brzezinski, *Totalitarian Dictatorship and Autocracy,* rev. ed. (New York: Praeger, 1967).
5. Zbigniew Brzezinski, *Ideology and Power in Soviet Politics* (New York: Praeger, 1967), p. 46.
6. Carl Friedrich, "The Evolving Theory and Practice of Totalitarian Regimes," in Carl Friedrich, Michael Curtis, and Benjamin Barber, *Totalitarianism in Perspective: Three Views* (New York: Praeger, 1969), pp. 123–64.

7. J. L. Talmon, *The Origins of Totalitarian Democracy* (New York: Praeger, 1960). See especially the introduction.

8. A. James Gregor, *Contemporary Radical Ideologies: Totalitarian Thought in the Twentieth Century* (New York: Random House, 1968), pp. 336–47.

9. Allen Kassof, "The Administered Society: Totalitarianism Without Terror," *World Politics,* vol. 16, no. 4 (July 1964), pp. 558–75.

10. Zbigniew Brzezinski and Samuel Huntington, *Political Power: USA/USSR* (New York: Viking Press, 1964), esp. pp. 56–70.

11. Richard Lowenthal, "The Soviet Union in the Post-Revolutionary Era: An Overview," in Alexander Dallin and Thomas Larson eds., *Soviet Politics Since Khrushchev* (Englewood Cliffs, NJ: Prentice-Hall, 1968) pp. 1–22; Milovan Djilas, *The New Class* (New York: Praeger, 1957).

12. Milton C. Lodge, *Soviet Elite Attitudes Since Stalin* (Columbus, OH: Charles Merrill, 1969).

13. Alfred G. Meyer, *The Soviet Political System: An Interpretation* (New York: Random House, 1965).

14. T. H. Rigby, "Politics in the Mono-Organizational Society," in Andrew Janos, ed., *Authoritarian Politics in Communist Europe* (Berkeley, CA: Institute of International Studies, 1976) pp. 31–80.

15. H. Gordon Skilling and Franklyn Griffiths, eds., *Interest Groups in Soviet Politics* (Princeton: Princeton University Press, 1971).

16. Jerry Hough, "Pluralism, Corporatism, and the Soviet Union," in Susan Solomon, ed., *Pluralism in the Soviet Union* (New York: St. Martin's, 1983) pp. 37–60; Darrell Hammer, *The USSR: The Politics of Oligarchy* (Boulder, CO: Westview Press, 1986).

17. As quoted in Valerie Bunce and John M. Echols III, "Soviet Politics in the Brezhnev Era: 'Pluralism' or 'Corporatism'?" in Donald Kelley, ed., *Soviet Politics in the Brezhnev Era* (New York: Praeger, 1980) pp. 1–26. The discussion of the approach is based on this article.

18. Jeffrey Hahn, "Is Developed Socialism a Soviet Version of Convergence?" in Jim Seroka and Maurice Simon, eds., *Developed Socialism in the Soviet Bloc* (Boulder, CO: Westview Press, 1982) pp. 21–36.

19. Ronald Inglehart, *Culture Shift in Advanced Industrial Society* (Princeton: Princeton University Press, 1990), esp. chap. 13.

20. Donald Barry and Carol Barner-Barry, *Contemporary Soviet Politics* (Englewood Cliffs, NJ: Prentice-Hall, 1991).

21. Samuel Huntington, *The Third Wave: Democratization in the Late Twentieth Century* (Norman: University of Oklahoma Press, 1991).

22. Sabrina Petra Ramet, ed., *Adaptation and Transformation in Communist and Post-Communist Systems* (Boulder, CO: Westview Press, 1992), pp. 279ff.

23. Baohui Zhang, "Corporatism, Totalitarianism, and Transitions to Democracy," *Comparative Political Studies,* vol. 27, no. 1 (April 1994), pp. 108–36.

24. Alexander Motyl, *Dilemmas of Independence: Ukraine After Totalitarianism* (New York: Council on Foreign Relations Press, 1993), chap. 2.

25. Karen Dawisha and Bruce Parrott, *Russia and the New States of Eurasia: The Politics of Upheaval* (Cambridge: Cambridge University Press, 1994). Chapter 4 is an excellent survey of the state of civil society in the former Soviet Union.

26. Peter Frank, "Problems of Democracy in Post-Soviet Russia," in Ian Budge and David McKay, eds., *Developing Democracy* (London: Sage Publications, 1994), p. 288.

27. Quoted in ibid., p. 287.

28. See Ronald Hill, "Democracy in Eastern Europe," in Budge and McKay, *Developing Democracy,* p. 272.

29. Gerardo Munck, "Democratic Transitions in Comparative Perspective," *Comparative Politics,* vol. 26, no. 3 (April 1994), pp. 355–75. This is a review article covering Samuel Huntington, *The Third Wave: Democratization in the Late Twentieth Century;* Adam Przeworski, *Democracy and the Market: Political and Economic Reforms in Eastern Europe and Latin America;* and Scott Mainwaring, Guillermo O'Donnell, and J. Samuel Valenzuela, eds., *Issues in Democratic Consolidation: The New South American Democracies in Comparative Perspective.*

7

Russia and the Former Soviet Union

In March 1985, Mikhail Gorbachev became the leader of the Soviet Union and initiated a reform of the system, including economic restructuring (*perestroika*), more open public discussion of issues (*glasnost*), and "new thinking" in dealing with the rest of the world. By December 1991, the Soviet Union had ceased to exist, and the area became a new international subsystem as it was split into 15 independent countries, most of which were loosely aligned in a new entity called the Commonwealth of Independent States (CIS). What had been domestic issues among 15 union republics now became foreign relations between Russia—the dominant center—and what it refers to as the "near abroad" (see Table 7-1).

No area of the world demonstrates more vividly than does the former Soviet Union some of the major themes of this book, such as the changing nature of the world, the rising tide of democracy, the difficulty of the transition to democracy, and the importance of ethnic factors and conflict (cultural defense). The rise and development of Communist systems have been one of the dominant features of the twentieth century. Now, as we approach the end of the century, no development has been more dramatic than

their collapse and the attempt of the successor states to make the transition to either more democratic societies or whatever forms eventually develop. Since this process (which all agree will take decades if not generations) is ongoing, our focus will be on understanding a thousand years of Russian culture and history, about 75 years of the Soviet system, and some sense of the process of transition and the difficult circumstances in which the current transition is taking place. The final outcome, of course, is still to be determined.

Beginning with the first Communist Revolution in Russia in 1917, the Union of Soviet Socialist Republics had the longest experience with that type of system and was to varying degrees the model according to which others patterned themselves or from which they deviated. The question is whether such systems, born in Russia in 1917 and spread to other parts of the world, especially in the period shortly after World War II, could deal with the increasingly complex social, economic, and political dynamics associated with the process of modernization. As was noted in Chapter 6, the dramatic developments of recent years have suggested that the latter part of the twentieth century may be remembered as the period in which the failure of

TABLE 7-1   The New States of the Former Soviet Union

Name	Population (1991)	Percent of Population of USSR	Percent of Area of USSR	Percent of Major Ethnic Groups and Russians
The Slavic States				
Russia	150,000,000	51	76	83% Russian
Belarus	10,000,000	3.6	1	79% Belarussian
				13% Russian
Ukraine	52,000,000	18	2.7	73% Ukrainian
				22% Russian
Baltic States				
Estonia	1,600,000	0.6	0.2	65% Estonian
				28% Russian
Latvia	2,700,000	1	0.3	54% Latvian
				33% Russian
Lithuania	3,700,000	1.3	0.3	80% Lithuanian
				9% Russian
Central Asian States				
Kazakhstan	17,000,000	6	12	40% Kazakh
				41% Russian
Kyrgyzstan	4,500,000	1.5	1	52% Kyrghiz
				22% Russian
Tajikistan	6,000,000	1.8	0.6	65% Tajik
				3% Russian
Turkmenistan	4,000,000	1.2	2.2	73% Turkmen
				10% Russian
Uzbekistan	22,000,000	7	2	71% Uzbek
				8% Russian
Transcaucasus States				
Armenia	4,000,000	1.1	0.1	93% Armenian
				2% Russian
Azerbaijan	7,500,000	2.5	0.4	83% Azerbaijani
				6% Russian
Georgia	5,500,000	2	0.3	70% Georgian
				6% Russian
Other				
Moldova	4,500,000	1.5	0.2	65% Moldovan
				13% Russian

Sources: Rand McNally Update, *The Soviet Union in Transition;* Global Studies, *Russia, The Eurasian Republics, and Central/Eastern Europe,* 5th ed. (Guilford, CN: Dushkin) 1994.

Communism was demonstrated, and that the next century may see an evolution into either social democracy or some other form, perhaps an enlightened one, of autocracy.

With the end of the Communist regimes in Eastern Europe and the Soviet Union, culminating in the breakup of the latter at the end of 1991, the focus has changed to the process of transition facing these ex-Communist systems. As we try to understand the confused present situation and anticipate the future, it is a good idea to remind ourselves that the critical first step is "the need to consider the defining features of the non-democratic regime from which a transition departs, and going even further back, the practices during the period before the origins of the authoritarian regime."[1] Since it was the flagship of the Communist world, we begin our examination of that question with the Soviet Union.

Trying to understand and predict the nature and actions of the Soviet Union was always a risky business. One of the famous quotes in this regard came from former British Prime Minister Sir Winston Churchill. Speaking in 1939 about the Soviet Union's possible foreign policy moves in the context of the rise of Adolf Hitler, he described the country as "a riddle wrapped in a mystery inside an enigma." While we have gained a great deal of knowledge and understanding since then, anyone embarking on such a study would be well advised to heed the often heard caution that there are in the final analysis really no experts on the Soviet Union—there are only varying degrees of ignorance. This point has been reinforced dramatically in recent years as events unfolded so quickly in Eastern Europe and the Soviet Union that the "experts" were repeatedly caught off guard. As things developed after the initiation of the reform process by Mikhail Gorbachev in 1985, it became obvious from his many revisions and changed positions that even he had no idea of the magnitude of the forces he had unleashed in both domestic and foreign policy.

There are many interesting consequences of this difficult attempt to understand what has been going on in Communist countries. For example, whenever a "summit" meeting between the leaders of the United States and the USSR, or some major event in the Soviet Union, would take place, television shows would call on "expert" scholars, diplomats, émigrés, government officials, etc. (The expression in media circles is to "round up the usual suspects.") The problem has always

been that a person listening to the differences in their comments about the motivation and situation of the Soviet Union might wonder if they were even talking about the same country. The diversity of assumptions and predispositions about the nature of Communism and the USSR, combined with a variety of firsthand experiences and knowledge, leads to a variety of differing perspectives about the subject. For several years after Gorbachev's call for significant domestic reforms, and even after he allowed the dramatic changes in Eastern Europe to take place, there were still intense debates as to whether he was really sincere and represented a genuine change or was just the ultimate public relations man trying to fool the rest of the world with the latest Communist trick in a continuing plan to take over the world.

One point on which everyone would agree, however, is the continuing interaction between Communist ideology and institutions on the one hand and Russian history and political culture on the other (see Table 7-2). As is true in any country, one can only understand the current situation and project future developments if there is an awareness of past experiences and of their social, economic, and cultural context. While one may argue as to the degree of influence of factors such as history, geography, and national character, there can be no doubt that they all play some role. Did Communism represent a radical break with the past, or was it essentially just the latest version of centuries of authoritarian rule? Will it be able to evolve into some type of democracy (a form with which there is no historical experience), or will this variation be followed by yet another hybrid, non-Communist form of authoritarianism?

If given a choice, the Bolsheviks would probably not have chosen to begin their great social and political experiment during World War I and in the context of the very hetero-

TABLE 7-2   Selected Chronology

862	Founding of Kievan Run
988	Adoption of Christianity (Eastern Orthodox)
1223	Beginning of Mongol invasions
1480	End of Mongol rule
1547	Ivan IV crowned as first czar
1613	Founding of Romanov dynasty
1700	Peter I, the Great
1861	Emancipation of the serfs
1905	Bloody Sunday; war with Japan
1917	Russian Revolution; end of monarchy
1918–20	War Communism and civil war
1921–28	The New Economic Policy
1922	Establishment of the USSR
1922	Beginning of Stalinist period
1924	Death of Lenin
1934	Beginning of mass terror and purges
1953	Death of Stalin
1953–64	Khrushchev period
1956	Beginning of de-Stalinization
1964	Khrushchev forced to retire
1964–82	Brezhnev period
1982	Death of Brezhnev; succeeded by Andropov
1984	Death of Andropov; succeeded by Chernenko
1985	Death of Chernenko
1985–91	Gorbachev period
1991	December 25—Gorbachev resignation; establishment of Commonwealth of Independent States; end of USSR

geneous and diverse society they had inherited from the Russian Empire. But then again, if it had not been for the war and the chaotic social, economic, and political conditions that accompanied it, there might never have been a Russian and Bolshevik revolution, and the country might have moved increasingly in the direction of increased democratic reforms. The recent attempts to make the transition to political democracy and toward a market economy are made more difficult by both Communist ideology and past experiences. Under the command-type economy that was implemented under the Marxist ideology, basic commodities such as food, rent, and transportation were highly subsidized, and employment was virtually guaranteed. Although people longed for the higher living standards they hoped a move toward market capitalism would produce, when they discovered that the price could include unemployment, layoffs, and a doubling or tripling of prices, their enthusiasm was dampened somewhat. In the cultural realm, as the political authority of the government has diminished and fragmented as a consequence of democratization, there has been a revival of centuries-old ethnic and nationality conflicts, and calls for greater authority and law and order to deal with increasing crime rates and social instability. Thus, before we deal with the more conspicuous political institutions and processes, we must become more familiar with the historical and cultural contexts in which they operate.

POLITICAL HISTORY

Part of the difficulty in understanding and dealing with the Soviet Union lies in the fact that its historical, cultural, philosophical, and political development was so different from that of the industrial democracies of the United States and Europe. In the past, Soviet dissidents, such as Andrei Amalrik, lamented the fact that such fundamental concepts as self-government, equality before the law, and personal freedom "are almost completely incomprehensible to the Russian people," that the very idea of freedom has been seen as synonymous with disorder and danger, and that it is "preposterous to the popular mind" that the human personality should represent any kind of value.[2] While many in the West were most troubled by Marxist-Leninist values such as atheism, opposition to private property, a central, dominating role for the state, and a vanguard monopolistic political party, earlier Russian experiences were also very different from those of most Western countries. Compare, for example, the development of constitutional, limited, representative government in Great Britain, France, and the United States with that of Russia, where the monarchy of the czar was ended only in 1917, and where limited steps in the direction of democratic philosophies, institutions, and processes began only a decade ago with the rise of Gorbachev.

PREREVOLUTIONARY RUSSIA

According to tradition, based on the Chronicle of Ancient Years, the first Russian state dates to 862. Known as Kievan Rus, it was reportedly established when the Slavic people living in the area around present-day Saint Petersburg (formerly Leningrad), probably in response to the threat of invasions, invited or allowed the Varangians (Vikings) from the north to come and set up an orderly government and provide some measure of security. The Rurik dynasty (named for the first ruler) soon expanded to the south, made Kiev its capital, established ties with the Byzantine Empire, experienced the high point of its political and cultural greatness in the middle of the eleventh century, and then declined because of internal conflict and invasion by the Mongols in the thirteenth century.

The most significant legacy of this early period resulted from the extensive ties with the Byzantine Empire (present-day Turkey), the thrust of which was to send Russia in the direction of Eastern rather than Western culture. In 988, the ruler of Kiev adopted Christianity as his personal religion and the official religion of the state, and required everyone to be baptized. The important point, however, is that he chose the Eastern Orthodox version of Christianity rather than the Roman Catholicism of the West, thus align-

ing Russia spiritually and culturally with an Eastern model. The subsequent Mediterranean influence can be seen not only in the religious realm, but also in such forms as the Cyrillic alphabet (any member of a "Greek" campus organization will recognize several of its letters), architecture, and a tradition of centralized and autocratic control.

Although Kievan Rus was already in a state of decline for internal reasons, the beginning of the thirteenth century marked a long period of foreign invasion and domination. The major force involved was the Mongols (the Russians call them Tatars), who stormed out of Central Asia headed for Western Europe. Although they did eventually make it as far as Vienna before withdrawing, the "Golden Horde" captured Kiev in 1240, and for over two hundred years (1240–1480) Russia was forced to submit to the "Tatar yoke." Although they were extremely cruel and violent, they did little in the way of imposing their culture or institutions on their conquered subjects. As long as they received payment or tribute, in the form of money and slaves, they allowed the church and local rulers a certain degree of autonomy. By the time the Tatars were finally defeated in 1480 by forces under the leadership of the prince of Moscow, their domination had produced serious consequences for Russia's development, as local rulers had used the cruel, despotic methods of their conquerors against their own people, thus reinforcing the earlier authoritarian Byzantine traditions.

At least as important were the implications of Tatar rule for Russia's cultural and philosophical development. The long period of Tatar control had isolated Russia from Western Europe at the very time that the latter area was experiencing crucial events such as the Renaissance and Reformation. It is difficult to overstate the importance of this period, which is among the most significant in the history of Western civilization and is considered to mark the beginning of the modern era. As a consequence, Russia never really participated in the ideas and debates concerning such issues as the proper relationship of church and state, the questioning of state and church authority, and the importance and value of the individual.

Russia's experiences at the time of the Mongol invasion can be used to illustrate a feature of the Russian psyche that is still with us—the perceived need for security and protection from invasion, which caused the Soviet Union to want to surround itself with a buffer zone of friendly countries after World War II. While it is also correct to think of Russia as an expansionist power, especially from the sixteenth century on, we should be aware of the other side of the coin. While Kiev was fighting the invaders from the East, several European groups, most notably the Swedes and Germans, seized the opportunity to stage their own attacks. These and other invasions down through the centuries, by Poland, Sweden, France, Germany and others, may help to explain a subsequent Russian feeling of insecurity and a preoccupation with strength, security, and buffer zones.

A final result of Mongol rule, perhaps ironically, is the role it played in the eventual emergence of Moscow as the center of the first unified Russian state. Even though they were all under foreign domination, rivalry continued among the rulers of the various areas such as Kiev, Novgorod, and Moscow. As Moscow eventually gained the upper hand in these conflicts, it was in the interest of the Mongols to support a centralized entity through which it could impose its rule and collect its tribute. At the same time, resistance from the people from whom this tribute was being extracted led to the development of harsher and more efficient measures of collection and control in order to avoid the wrath of the Mongols for nonpayment. Under the leadership of Ivan III

(1462–1505), Moscow was finally able to put an end to the Mongol domination of two and a half centuries, subdue its internal rivals, extend to them its form of autocratic rule, and make Russia for the first time a united political state.

Aiding in this process of national unification was the concept of Moscow as the "third Rome." At about the same time that consolidation was taking place in Russia, the Muslim Turks conquered the city of Constantinople, which was the capital of the Byzantine Empire. In its time, Rome had been the political and religious center of the entire world, but especially of Christianity. With the fall of Rome and the end of the Roman Empire, the Byzantine Empire inherited that position and became the "second Rome." Now, with the fall of Constantinople, the mantle would pass to Moscow. Thus, the newly formed Russian state also had a sense of mission as the repository of the true faith and the defender of Christianity (the Eastern Orthodox version, of course).

For the next several hundred years, Russia continued to develop along lines more or less consistent with the early autocratic pattern. Increasingly, however, that took it in a different direction from Western Europe. While both Russia and the Western European countries were ruled by absolute monarchies and dynasties in the early stages, and while all had to deal with questions such as the position of the nobility and how to govern more efficiently, their approaches and experiences became increasingly divergent. For example, contrast the British pattern of the gradual establishment of practical constitutional and institutional limits on the monarch, on the one hand, with the fact that even at the time of his abdication in 1917, the last czar of Russia was still claiming an absolute right to rule on the basis of divine authority from God. Even in France, whose earlier absolutism is probably closer to the Russian experience, the basis for monarchy changed from divine right to reason, and the concept of the monarchy itself was challenged by those who wanted a republic. When there were attempts at reform and change in Russia, they tended to be imposed from above by the rulers rather than demanded by the aristocracy or the people, and directed toward more efficient government rather than more limited or representative government. Although from time to time the ruler might establish or permit some sort of assembly of nobles or others, those bodies never acquired the kind of bargaining power they eventually did in Great Britain, and they were invariably dissolved if they tried to do anything other than what the rulers intended.

The attempt of Peter the Great (1682–1725) to transform his country provides interesting insights into the dynamic of change. Peter is often considered the founder of modern Russia because of his recognition of the need to modernize through the incorporation of certain Western concepts and techniques. His exposure to the Western community living in Moscow, and eventually to the West itself through his travels, demonstrated the necessity for Russia to adopt certain skills and ideas in order to avoid being left far behind by its neighbors, especially in commercial and military matters. But, notice the dynamic involved. In Europe, modernization was a more or less evolutionary and spontaneous process, resulting from intellectual movements such as the Renaissance and Reformation, and from some degree of interaction and pressure from the nobility and the developing social classes.

Several aspects of the situation facing Peter are useful in illustrating the problems that change and feelings of ambivalence toward the West have posed for Russia, even up to the present time. The difficulty for Peter was that he only wanted to adopt certain aspects of Western culture while rejecting oth-

ers, and that most of the Russian people did not share his view of the necessity and desirability of Westernization and modernization. In fact, many reacted irrationally and violently to this perceived threat to their whole culture and way of life. Because of the manner of its development, change in Russia has almost always had to be imposed on the society from above by the state. Through the selective use of techniques, Peter and his more contemporary successors attempted to make the state stronger or more efficient, while at the same time preserving traditional autocratic social and political structures and values. Earlier in the Communist period, there was the example of the extreme social and economic measures imposed by Stalin in the name of modernization and industrialization, which were understandably resisted by the people at the cost of millions of lives. More recently, of course, we have seen the Gorbachev administration fighting alcoholism and corruption and trying to impose some degree of reform on the economic and political institutions and processes. While some of the opposition understandably came from bureaucrats and others with vested interests in the status quo, the Russian culture has always included a large measure of the type of conservatism that views almost any change, particularly from the outside, as threatening and therefore resists it.

The problems associated with trying to use only certain aspects of the outside culture are also familiar to past and present leaders of Russia, China, and other countries. Much as they would like to do it, it is just not possible to import technology and certain specific concepts without exposing the receiving society to the broader social and intellectual framework that produced the technology. Those who accompanied Peter to Europe, primarily to learn specific skills such as shipbuilding, could not be shielded from other aspects of the cultures they were observing.

During his long time in power, Stalin attempted to follow a policy of economic, political, and cultural autarky (self-sufficiency) in order to avoid the implications, economic and otherwise, of increased interdependence with the West. Both the USSR and the People's Republic of China learned in subsequent years that the acquisition of Western technology and methods involves broader implications. Economic reform does not seem to be possible without the broader exchange of people and ideas, which in turn leads to demands for political and social change.

The process started by Peter took many forms throughout the next two centuries. Although many Western mannerisms were adopted, especially by the aristocracy, the debate raged on as to whether modern Western influences represented progress or ruin. The nineteenth century brought tremendous changes in Europe in the wake of the French Revolution and the Napoleonic Wars, as capitalism and democracy became more important forces. The internal conflict grew more intense as a result of these momentous social and intellectual developments in Europe and especially of the military encounters between Russia and the Western European powers. In the first half of the century, Russians felt understandably proud of defeating Napoleon in 1812, and Czar Nicholas I was known as the "gendarme of Europe" because of his attempts to contain liberalism and nationalism by repeated interventions in the European revolutions resulting from those movements.

Interestingly, however, it was also during the reign of Nicholas I that a true intelligentsia really began to take shape in Russia. One of the divisions within this group, between Slavophiles and Westernizers, was over the continuing question of which path Russia should take. The Slavophiles were essentially nationalists and isolationists who were proud of Russia's past and who, in the legacy of the "third Rome" concept, believed that the Rus-

sian faith and culture were superior to those of the West. For them, the future was not in copying the West but rather in returning to and developing their own grand traditions. The Westernizers, who were not so proud of their past and present, considered this approach to be backward looking and its inevitable result to be the preservation of the worst autocratic and repressive aspects of Russian culture. Praising Peter's efforts of a century earlier, they called for change and progress through the selective incorporation of European institutions and principles such as liberalism's respect for the individual and for human rights. Elements of this debate could still be seen more recently as dissent developed during the Communist regime in the post-Stalin period. Among the groups who objected to the system for a variety of reasons were those nationalists, the best known of whom is probably the writer Alexander Solzhenitsyn, who called for an end to Communism and a return to the "good old days" of prerevolutionary traditional Russian religious and other social values. On the other hand, there were people like Andrei Sakharov, a physicist known as the "father" of the Soviet Union's H-bomb, whose dissent went more in the direction of calling for acceptance of Western liberal philosophical values such as those placing greater emphasis on freedom of thought, more limits on the authority of the state, and greater respect for the individual and for human rights.

The practical nineteenth-century answer to the debate was provided by Russia's defeat in the Crimean War (1854–56) by Great Britain, France, and Turkey, and then by subsequent defeats by Turkey in the 1870s and by Japan in 1905. In spite of Russia's apparent successes earlier in the century, those wars were dramatic demonstrations of internal weaknesses and of the widening gap in areas such as military technology and equipment as well as in basic transportation and communication capability. This shocking loss of prestige and confidence meant that the growing problems of economic and social modernization could no longer be ignored. Interestingly, the Soviet Union's predicament in the 1980s sounds strikingly like that of Russia a hundred years earlier. It grew to be considered a superpower, but in fact was super in only the military dimension. It became increasingly apparent that the USSR still did not have the technological base and overall infrastructure in areas such as transportation and communication to compete with other powers in any aspect other than the military. Thus, under Gorbachev, it had to acknowledge this fundamental economic weakness, attempt to institute internal reforms, and turn to the West for assistance such as technology transfer.

Unfortunately, the events surrounding the eventual revolution in 1917 are evidence that the country's nineteenth-century problems had not been dealt with successfully. The half-century following the Crimean War was characterized by growing social pressure and unrest, the response to which was a repeated pattern of attempted reforms and subsequent crackdowns. For example, although Alexander II (1855–1881) is often called a liberator and reformer because of his attempts to respond in a constructive way to social problems, he never considered giving up the basic autocratic nature of the system.

Alexander's chief reform, the emancipation of the serfs in 1861, is a good example of the complexity of the process. Although subject to a number of variations, serfdom was similar to the American institution of slavery in that serfs were essentially owned by landlords. The need for reform had been recognized for decades, but it is often suggested that when emancipation finally came, it took an unfortunate form and provided about as little real freedom as did the issuing of the

Emancipation Proclamation in the United States at about the same time. While the serfs were no longer owned by landlords, they did not receive either individual freedom or private property. The land was sold by the landlords to communes (groups of peasants) that had the collective ability to regulate daily life. Thus, peasant revolts continued, land reform was still a crucial issue at the time of the revolution, and it has even been suggested that this communal farming was a convenient precedent for the system of collective farms (*kolkhozy*) later imposed by Stalin. For this and other reforms, Alexander was criticized by extremists on the right for weakening the authority of the government and by those on the left for not making enough changes. A repeat of this classic situation was seen most recently when Gorbachev's proposed reform program was met with similar criticism from hard-line conservatives on the right and radical reformers on the left. Eventually, and perhaps ironically, the liberator-reformer Czar Alexander was assassinated by a radical terrorist group.

Predictably, in a pattern of reform and reaction similar to what we have seen in the post-Stalin period, his son (Alexander III) reverted with a vengeance to a conservative, antireformist program. In this case, it took the form of a program emphasizing traditional Russian values, religious and nationality persecution, and in general an autocratic reign of terror against political opposition. The determination of the czars to preserve their prerogatives held true to the very end as Nicholas II, the last czar, proclaimed his intention to follow in his father's autocratic footsteps.

Even in the midst of political repression, however, the imperatives of economic development and modernization remained, and there were continuing attempts at economic reform to deal with the emerging industrial society. In fact, reformers such as Count Sergei Witte and Peter Stolypin have been compared to those in Germany under Bismarck in their common belief in using the bureaucracy of an absolutist government to accomplish industrial and land reform. The idea is to use the authority of the state first to intimidate the populace into a condition of compliance and then to impose reforms. Under Witte's direction, Russia was making progress in establishing the financial and transportation infrastructure necessary for modernization through such measures as railroad construction, the acquisition of foreign capital, and a greater degree of national planning. Under the land reforms, including Stolypin's, the communes (*mir*) established at the time of emancipation were replaced by individual ownership, and the purchase of land and equipment was made easier.

To summarize, how can we characterize Russia as it stood on the verge of the twentieth century and the path it had taken to get to that point? What had started out as the original Kievan Rus was by then a huge, multinational empire. Over the centuries, Russian foreign policy had involved constant expansion, but during the same period Russia had also been the victim of countless invasions from all directions.

In the political realm, what had resulted was a highly centralized, bureaucratic, repressive, autocratic system headed by czars who claimed even into the twentieth century to rule by divine right. While there had been attempts at reform, such as the local councils (*zemstvos*), they were always instituted by the rulers from above and thus could always be rescinded by them. One of the marked differences between Russia and most of the rest of Europe was the absence in the former of prolonged struggle between the monarch and a social elite such as barons or merchants. Unlike countries such as Great Britain or France, there was little or no development by the people or the aristocracy of the forces and institutions that could bring

pressure for change. With little possibility for peaceful, evolutionary change, assassination and political terrorism became more common. But as Hugh Seton-Watson has pointed out, the conflict and violence were usually to decide which individual should rule rather than whether or how power should be shared, divided, or limited.[3]

Culturally, much of the early influence on Russia had come from contacts with the eastern Byzantine Empire and the two-century-long domination by the Mongols. Later, especially from the time of Peter, there was great conflict, such as between Slavophiles and Westernizers, over the necessity or desirability of adopting many of the ideas and institutions of the West. Overall, however, the great European developments of the Renaissance, Reformation, liberalism, capitalism, and democracy exerted little influence on Russian society and institutions.

The relationship of church and state is a good example of the different paths of development. Beginning with the Byzantine tradition of church submission to or cooperation with the state, the czars eventually reduced the power of the church while assuming for themselves the role of defenders of the faith. Much of the time, the church was more interested in liturgy and the soul than politics. In the opinion of Michael Florinsky, when Peter appointed the Holy Synod in 1721, the church lost whatever political power it had had and became little more than a department of the state bureaucracy.[4] This tradition stands in contrast to the classic European confrontations between kings or emperors and popes, and in even sharper contrast to the eventual development in the United States of the concept of separation of church and state.

Socially, perhaps the most conspicuous feature was the lack of development of a middle class. While there were small numbers of urban workers and writers and other intellectuals, the two basic groups were the peasants and the aristocracy. Both were conservative, with the peasants living in abject poverty, and the aristocracy interested primarily in protecting its own dominant position. While the classic Russian writers could critique their society from a philosophical point of view, there were virtually no inventors, capitalists, and entrepreneurs with an economic stake in progress and development. In a pattern reminiscent of Europe a century earlier, the Russian aristocracy became increasingly oblivious of worsening economic and social conditions as it sought to hold back the changes associated with industrialization and modernization.

One cannot help but be struck by some of the similarities between the nineteenth century dynamics and those of the present time. There is still not much of a middle class between the relatively small group of privileged former party and other elite, and the vast majority of workers and farmers with their poor standard of living. The Soviet Union was, and to a lesser extent Russia still is, a military giant without the economic infrastructure to satisfy the agricultural and other material needs of its people. There is still an ambivalence toward the West, whose capital and technology are needed and sought, but whose liberal democratic philosophy and institutions are resisted by many. And there is still the cycle of attempts to reform admitted economic woes followed by conservative reaction and retrenchment.

REVOLUTION

Revolution was an almost inevitable result of the conditions and attitudes described above. Although it is known as the revolution of 1917, that being the date of the end of the czarist dynasty and the eventual seizure of power by the Bolsheviks, the dramatic events of that year were only the culmination of a process that was several decades in the mak-

ing. In a sense, there was a race of sorts going on, pitting modernizing reformers such as Witte and Stolypin against an increasingly revolutionary intelligentsia. In the years right around the turn of the century, the continued lack of responsiveness by the autocratic regime led to the organization by the intelligentsia of revolutionary opposition political parties. Throughout the 1880s, Alexander III had attempted to rescind what remained of earlier reforms as he reduced the influence of governmental bodies such as the judiciary and increased the powers of groups such as the secret police. These political and social developments were complicated by the severe famine at the beginning of the 1890s. This backward-looking unresponsiveness was in the face of growing problems and mounting evidence that change and industrialization were coming even to Russia.

It should come as no surprise that under this set of circumstances, Marxism had a strong appeal to elements of the Russian intelligentsia. Claiming to present a scientific and rational way to understand the process of history and human development on the basis of economic relationships, it addressed itself especially to the problems of the nineteenth century. Much of the attractiveness of this revolutionary philosophy was the way it spoke to the problems of modernization with its promise that a scientifically based and technologically advanced industrial society would produce both economic benefits and social justice in a subsequent stage of development. What was needed was for the people to seize control of the economic and political processes.

There had been uprisings in Russia before, perhaps the best known being the Decembrists in 1825, but they had mostly been "palace revolutions" among the elite. The term the "first people's revolution" is often used to describe the developments of 1905, which began over a decade of political and economic unrest involving much broader segments of the population and which eventually culminated in the historic events of 1917. This process was centered around two interrelated events: an unsuccessful war with Japan and a series of uprisings sparked by the actions of what became known as Bloody Sunday.

At the beginning of 1904, Japan attacked the Russian navy. Beginning with that engagement, and over the next year and a half, Russia lost a series of land and naval battles and eventually the war. The consequences of the defeat went far beyond the cost in money and loss of life, serious though those aspects were. As suggested, this was seen as one more example of the now backward and weak position of the once strong Russian empire and state. But there was a more direct connection between the war and internal events. At the same time that it was at war with a foreign power, the Russian government was having to deal, in terms of both manpower and attention, with an internal uprising. It is interesting to speculate whether the results might have been different if the government or the leaders had been dealing with one or the other, but the combination would prove to be fatal.

Bloody Sunday was one of history's catalytic events. There had been discontent and even violence for some time, but beginning in 1905, they became more widespread and organized, and evoked a response by the authorities. On a Sunday in January of that year, a crowd of several thousand people marched to Palace Square in the capital of Saint Petersburg with a petition asking the czar to take measures to improve their economic conditions. When the response of government forces was to open fire on the unarmed crowd, the lesson was inescapable. Since this autocratic government would not respond to peaceful petitions, the struggle took on a more violent and political character, and the 1905 revolution (later described by Lenin as the "great rehearsal") was under way. As in any revolutionary situation, the various elements involved wanted different things. The demands included a greater share of power for the aristocracy, land reform for the peasants, better wages and working conditions for laborers, and greater autonomy for ethnic minorites. The common element, of course, was the demand for more representative and responsive political institutions through which they might obtain these changes.

In the years that followed, there were various responses by the government. The 1905 October Manifesto acknowledged the unrest, called for establishment of a representative body (*Duma*), and spoke of civil rights and political participation. In addition, and in part due to a recognition of the ultimate importance of the peasantry, there were significant attempts at land reform until 1917. In spite of these developments, however, the passage of time revealed the unchanged fact that the czar would not permit a legislative body that was truly representative or that threatened to place real limitations on his power. As a result, the necessary changes, although hinted at, did not take place. Conditions continued to deteriorate, resulting in greater opposition to the monarchy among the aristocracy and intelligentsia, strikes and demonstrations among the workers, uprisings among the peasants, and assassinations.

The final element in this revolutionary mix was another disastrous and humiliating war. Russia's participation in World War I on the side of the Allies, beginning in 1914, added to the already explosive internal situation and eventually produced the two-stage revolution of 1917. The country, weary and drained from three years of war (with an end nowhere in sight), and experiencing severe food shortages, was slipping rapidly toward chaos and anarchy.

The first stage of the revolution came in

FIGURE 7-1

March, when the members of the *Duma* met in defiance of the czar, formed a provisional government, and demanded and got the abdication of the czar. Notice that the Bolsheviks played little or no role at this point, since the provisional government represented mostly other elements of the intelligentsia. In fact, most of the Bolsheviks were either outside the country or in internal exile in Siberia. They gathered quickly, however, and in the months that followed, their organization and strategy stood in stark contrast to the disunity, indecisiveness, and lack of action by the provisional government, which did little to solve the problems that had led to its formation in the first place.

This was Russia's experiment with democracy. The provisional government, under the eventual leadership of Alexander Kerensky, undertook a number of reforms expanding legal and civil rights and granting amnesty to political prisoners. But they were sensitive to the need to operate in a properly democratic manner, and it was decided that other basic reforms should be considered by a new popularly elected body called the Constituent Assembly. Unfortunately, the decision to postpone the elections several times (they were finally set for November 12) meant that no action would be taken in the meantime on the critical problems of land reform, food shortages, labor unrest, and continued participation in the war. Thinking once again in terms of parallels with the contemporary situation, one is tempted to draw comparisons with the Gorbachev "revolution." While he did initiate significant changes in the direction of democracy in the structure and operation of political institutions, the accusation by those who wanted more change was that he was unable or unwilling to proceed with the radical changes needed to deal with the extreme social and economic problems. Then, as these conditions seemed to get even worse, and as the system appeared once again to be sliding toward chaos and instability, there was a predictable conservative reaction calling for the reimposition of authoritarian controls.

In 1917, the lack of decisiveness created the opening for the Bolsheviks, a very small but very well organized minority, who seized power in a coup on November 7. The next day a Congress of Soviets approved several decrees to deal with the peace and land issues. Several days later, the election to choose delegates to the Constituent Assembly was held as planned, and shortly thereafter the Assembly held its first and last meeting. As expected, the Bolsheviks fell far short of a majority. When the Assembly thus failed to ratify their program at its first meeting, it was dissolved, and the experiment with democracy was over. The next competitive democratic elections would come over 70 years later with the democratization under Gorbachev and the election of the Congress of People's Deputies.

One of the perennial questions involves the extent to which the Bolshevik revolution and regime represented a break with the Russian past. Was the system subsequently established by Lenin and Stalin, which would then serve as one of the prototypes for the concept of totalitarianism, just the latest form of absolutist authoritarianism or something new? While there were certainly differ-ences, most conspicuously the Marxist-Leninist ideology, it has been argued that there were also many similarities and continuities. From the time of the rulers of Moscow around 1450 until very recently, absolutism was the continuing pattern in Russia. Important political, economic, or social changes have come from above through the decrees of rulers rather than through evolutionary processes. Emphasis has always been on the importance of the state or the interests of society collectively rather than of the individual, and debates on the use of power have focused on who should exercise power rather placing limits on it.

In the 75 years since the revolution, there have been several cycles of reform and reaction between what have sometimes been called conservatives and reformers. Until the Gorbachev period, this was a conflict within the leadership between those who favored maintenance of the status quo and others who called for greater efficiency and some change within the basic existing system. Some people have suggested parallels between the initiation of the Gorbachev reforms of the 1980s and the dynamics of the early 1920s, when attempts to initiate radical reform based on Marxist ideology immediately after the revolution had to be abandoned. In both instances, desperate and deteriorating economic and social conditions forced the leaders to resort to pragmatic and expedient measures rather than those supported by the ideology. Lenin himself was forced to initiate the New Economic Policy, a program that included individual ownership of land and other pragmatic measures designed to accomplish economic recovery after the revolution and resulting civil war. More recently, Gorbachev admitted that the existing system was not working, and proposed similar measures away from the type of economic and social organization called for by the ideology and in the direction of practical incentives and market mechanisms designed to improve economic and social conditions.

It was during Stalin's long tenure, however, that most of the basic features of the Soviet system were developed. The term "second revolution" is often used to indicate the fact that although the political revolution took place in 1917, it was not really until the late 1920s and beyond that radical social and economic change was instituted. Once again imposed by the ruler from above through repressive and brutal measures, it reemphasized the role of the state in everyday economic and social activities, and included such policies as the forced collectivization of agriculture.

Stalin's death in 1953 paved the way for a period of de-Stalinization under Nikita Khrushchev, who denounced the terror of the earlier period, granted amnesty or posthumous "rehabilitation" to many of its victims, and in general ushered in a period known as "the thaw." Stalin's policy of "socialism in one country," which involved relative isolationism and economic self-sufficiency, was replaced by a more active international role. In the economic realm, a number of policies were tried in an effort to achieve greater efficiency. Under the policy of "Libermanism," named for a reformist economist, there were moves in the direction of the decentralization of the decision-making process. Greater responsibility, discretion, and incentives were given to local enterprises and managers in an attempt to make them more productive, and a number of regional economic councils (*sovnarkhozy*) were created to deal with the classic problem of an oversized, overcentralized bureaucracy trying to plan and run everything from Moscow.

But these and other changes were too threatening to the conservative bureaucracy, which accused Khrushchev of "harebrained scheming" and eventually ousted him in 1964. The regime that followed, led by Leonid Brezhnev, reversed his reforms, created perhaps an even more centralized process, cracked down on domestic dissent, and emphasized the status quo and lack of changes in policies and personnel to the point that the ultimate result was stagnation. Economic growth declined steadily, life expectancy began to decrease, and infant mortality rates rose. When Brezhnev died in 1982, the stagnation was prolonged by virtue of the fact that the next two leaders lasted only a total of a little over two years. The first, Yuri Andropov, did initiate some reforms, such as an anticorruption campaign, but died after little more than a year in office. When 72-year-old Konstantin Chernenko was chosen to succeed him, it was a clear signal of an intention to preserve the status quo. When he died after a year in power, the new era finally began.

When Gorbachev came to power in 1985, the cycle was repeated. He denounced the Brezhnev regime for allowing social and economic conditions to deteriorate so badly, and launched the far-reaching policies of *glasnost* and *perestroika*. In the classic mold, he began by calling for better results from the existing system by cutting down on corruption, alcoholism, and other inefficient practices, and by once again granting more autonomy to local enterprises and managers to provide the incentive for more individual initiative. Eventually, there were calls for more fundamental reform of the system in the direction of a market economy and greater individual economic activity. Gorbachev seemed to support these calls in the form of the "500-day" plan for radical economic reform prepared by his economic advisers, but when the moment of truth arrived, he refused to back its adoption and settled for a more moderate one. When the president of the Russian republic, Boris Yeltsin, announced that his republic would proceed with the radical version, Gorbachev appeared to be the conservative.

Predictably, much of the opposition to

major reforms came from bureaucrats with vested interests who stood to lose power and control. Perhaps less expected was the reaction of many workers and other members of the public. Proposals to implement a new set of economic principles and structures are bound to produce a great deal of anxiety. Accustomed to the old arrangement, which included a virtual guarantee of job security and a system of subsidized prices, they felt threatened by new procedures that might result in the risk of layoffs, firings, higher prices, and other sources of anxiety. In addition, there was a suspicion among many that whereas the existing system tended to stress treating most people more or less equally, the proposed individual economic activities, rather than benefiting everyone, would allow even more opportunities for a few greedy people to prosper at the expense of everyone else. A country's historical experiences are instrumental in shaping its social and cultural characteristics and attitudes, and it is to those factors that we turn next.

THE SOCIAL AND CULTURAL CONTEXT

While the main focus of this section will be the importance of elements of social stratification such as ethnic and nationality groupings, we begin with a consideration of the attitudes toward authority in the Russian political culture. Recall that in earlier chapters, such attitudes were classified as submissive, deferential, or egalitarian. Historically, the Russian culture has been placed in the submissive category, meaning for the most part unquestioning and unqualified obedience to those in positions of authority. The claim of the czars was that they were all-wise and all-powerful, and that they ruled by divine right. Their position was strengthed by the stand of the Russian Orthodox Church, which, consistent with its Byzantine origins,

taught obedience to the state as well as to the church. After the revolution, the Communist Party made a similar claim to being all-knowing on the basis of its ideology and therefore deserving of the right to direct the activities of society in an authoritative manner.

The standard method for examining attitudes is the use of survey research and questionnaires. This being the case, there has obviously been more difficulty in obtaining direct interviews and information when dealing with the Soviet Union and similar countries than with open and democratic systems. While the changes since the 1980s have opened the way for greater examination of attitudes by both local and outside scholars, we have nothing comparable to *The Civic Culture* and similar works cited in earlier discussions of the cultures of European democratic countries. The exceptions to this general observation in earlier years were two projects undertaken after World War II to examine the opinions of former Soviet citizens who had left their country.[5] While one would expect their positions toward the regimes they had fled to be negative, the surveys were very useful in revealing their basic attitudes toward authority and on other topics. Both studies pointed toward the need and desire for dependence, protection, and security. Authority figures were expected to be stern, demand obedience, and use the measures necessary, including coercion, to ensure compliance. Henry Dicks observed that many of those interviewed spoke of authority in terms of a good but strict father. Alex Inkeles suggested, early in the Khrushchev period, that the new leadership might be able to use this tradition to gain substantial popular support for the continuation of authoritarian institutions and policies by being less harsh and arbitrary and by expressing more fatherly interest in the people.[6] Interestingly, a number of scholars have distinguished between the Stalin and Khrushchev regimes by pointing out that the latter relied on rationality, persuasion, and socialization rather than the irrationality and terror of Stalin.[7] No one doubted, however, that the system remained authoritarian.

The attitudes suggested from those studies were echoed to some extent in the pessimistic, even devastating portrayal of the masses by the Soviet dissident mentioned earlier, Andrei Amalrik. Writing around 1970, he expressed the view that "whether because of historical traditions or some other reason," freedom is perceived in a negative way as giving individuals the opportunity to engage in some type of dangerous behavior. Russia's lack of Europe's humanist tradition, reinforced by official Communist propaganda stressing the collective over the personal, creates a situation in which one can respect authority, strength, or even intellect, but the idea of respecting the rights of an individual as such "simply arouses bewilderment." Even the concepts of justice and equality have negative meanings, amounting to a sense that "nobody should live better than I do," and a hatred of anything that is outstanding and innovative.[8] While perhaps not quite so pessimistic, countless others have echoed Amalrik's characterization of the ordinary citizen in the Soviet Union as deeply conservative and opposed to change.

The events surrounding and following the abortive August 1991 coup did seem to indicate a greater commitment to change and established procedures than many thought existed. When Gorbachev was taken hostage, thousands of people rallied around Yeltsin at the "White House" in Moscow. It was subsequently learned that one reason for the failure of the coup was the refusal of elements of the military and KGB forces to follow orders to crush Yeltsin and his popular support. Others have pointed out that these events took place in Moscow. While attitudes may be changing among the urban intelligentsia,

they argue, much of the population still lives in the countryside or smaller cities, and tends to hold on to the more traditional and conservative patterns. In the context of the social unrest created by severe economic shortages and ethnic strife, there has been no shortage of voices suggesting that the people were not ready for democracy and radical economic change, and calling for law and order to restore the old stability. Conservatives opposed to economic reform have been able to appeal to the anxieties of the people. An economist from the State Planning Committee, opposed to market reform, argued that private property would only "give rise to exploitation of man by man, anarchy, and unemployment."[9] In a television interview in early 1991 dealing with the independence movements in the Baltic republics, political scientist Stephen Cohen expressed the view that outside of those republics, the dissident democratic movement was an island in a sea of antidemocratic traditions.

In short, this view of the Russian personality suggests that one might expect substantial support for a paternalistic type of authoritarian system that is perceived as expressing concern for the people, that is able to meet more of their material needs, and that relies on socialization rather than coercion and repression. Both submissive and deferential types of political cultures hold that some are more fit to rule than others. But one of the key differences is whether decision makers are held accountable to the people. While not matching the standards of Western democratic nations, the Gorbachev reforms initiated more open political debate and more competitive popular elections. Perhaps a greater degree of accountability will eventually become part of that system, and it will move in the direction of a deferential rather than a submissive political culture.

One of the key questions with which political scientists in general and this book in particular are concerned is the extent to which social and cultural dynamics produce political change. As was mentioned in Chapter 6, one school of thought has argued for some time that the processes of modernization and urbanization, with their increased levels of education, communication, etc., make authoritarianism much more difficult in the late twentieth century. One of the most important forms of this approach is Ronald Inglehart's concept of "postmaterialist" values and orientations.[10] The idea is that as people's material needs are more satisfied, modernization leads them to focus less on economic matters and more on values like equality and self-expression. These values in turn facilitate the process of democratization. Writing toward the end of the Soviet period, Inglehart acknowledged that the short-term focus in the Soviet Union would include a heavy emphasis on material needs, but he still felt that postmaterialism might already be related to change in that country. It may also be necessary for us to distinguish between urban and rural patterns. The changes taking place have been concentrated more in the key cities of the Russian federation and the other areas of the former Soviet Union. It will be interesting to see if further research indicates whether and how the traditional conservative attitudes are being affected by modernization and postmaterialism.

SOCIAL STRATIFICATION

Class

The concept of social class is at the heart of Marxist-Leninist ideology, which taught that the central conflict throughout history has been between economically based classes rather than between nations. As people's class consciousness was raised, they would realize that the key question was whether they were part of the exploited proletariat working class or the exploiting capitalist class. This realization and the truly universal nature of the ideology would do away with national antagonisms. Applied to the Soviet Union, the official position was that in the postrevolutionary period, there were friendly groupings such as workers, farmers, and intelligentsia, but that their interests coincided and there were no longer antagonistic classes seeking to exploit one another.

We know, of course, that things did not turn out that way. Consistent with the Marxist dialectic, a new system replaced the old. Contrary to the claim of a classless society, however, in reality the Communist Party became, in the words of the former Communist vice-president of Yugoslavia, Milovan Djilas, "the new class."[11] Rather than producing a classless society, he observed, Communism created a political bureaucracy whose members possess economic and other privileges because they control the administrative processes and machinery of the society. Although they did not own property and thus could not pass it or large amounts of wealth on to their heirs, they enjoyed the material and other benefits that ownership normally brings. This included access to medical care, food, travel, and other privileges not available to the rest of the population. It was not, however, just a matter of whether one belonged to the party or not. There was also a hierarchical system of access based on one's rank and position within the party. In a classic Communist system, there is, therefore, a stratified society based on a person's position within or with respect to the party.

THE NATIONALITY PROBLEM

The study of different types of political systems, whether democratic, Communist, or Third World, reveals the recurring phenomenon of what we have called *cultural defense*—the conflict among different cultural and ethnic groups within a heterogeneous society. Just as Communism's prediction of a classless society was not realized in the Soviet Union, neither was the expectation that national identities and antagonisms would diminish. We suggested in earlier chapters that the political relevance of class is to a large degree dependent on the absence of other important types of divisions within a society. In the wake of the collapse of the Soviet Union, the economic crisis and the nationality question, in the form of separatist and independence movements, have become the dominant issues of the 1990s and beyond. And, as serious as the economic problem is, in many respects it is easier to solve it than it is to deal with the emotions surrounding ethnic disputes.

Because the Soviet Union was the successor to the Russian Empire, it was a very large country containing well over a hundred nationalities speaking over 125 distinct languages. In the imperial phase, the dominant Russian group expanded in all directions and conquered this variety of groups. After the revolution, the decision was made to accommodate the major nationalities by setting up a federal form of government, consisting of the central government and a number of regional units, called union republics, which were analogous to states in the U.S. system. For most of its existence, the USSR was composed of 15 union republics, with the largest and most diverse republics then further divided into smaller units, still based on nationality groupings. In recent years, the organization of these republics (now independent countries) along ethnic lines has had serious implications for social unity. It means that each of the major nationality groups has its own territory and government, arranged with the largest minorities located in relatively compact groups around the edges of the dominant Russian group, which occupies

the central and largest land mass. For the most part, this is a cumulative rather than a cross-cutting pattern. That is, these geographically organized ethnic groups have their own distinct national history, literature, language, religion, and governmental structures, all reinforcing one another rather than promoting identity with the country as a whole.

These cultural distinctions are in some cases emphasized even further by distinct regional differences. While each republic was a separate entity, they were sometimes placed in larger, looser groupings on the basis of certain common features. When the Russian republic (RSFSR), which was by far the largest in terms of both area and population, was combined with the Ukrainian and Belarussian to form a Slavic group, their total population was about 70 percent of the entire country. Until they were granted their independence in 1991, the three Baltic republics constituted a group whose history, religion, and culture were more like those of Western Europe. The Central Asian republics, on the other hand, have almost nothing in common culturally or historically with the dominant Slavic areas. Their language, Muslim religion and history, are completely different. This leaves several republics that are not so easily grouped. Georgia, Azerbaijan, and Armenia share a location, and are thus referred to as Causasian or Transcaucasian, but there are both similarities and differences among them. The main problem is that there are wide cultural differences from one region to another in terms of factors such as urbanization, education, per capita income, and family size.

According to the 1989 census, the Russians constituted just over half of the total population of the then USSR of about 285 million. Because of the difference in birth rates, even if the other republics and groups had remained a part of the Soviet Union, by the beginning of the next century the Russians would no longer have been a majority, as their proportion of the population fell below that psychologicaly important 50 percent mark. But with some 145 million people, they were still by far the largest single group. The other half was fragmented among a hundred different groups, with only about two dozen having more than a million members. The next largest were the Ukrainians (44 million) and then the Uzbeks (17 million), and the smallest ones numbered only in the hundreds or thousands. Even combining all of the Muslim peoples of the Central Asian republics produced a figure comparable to the Ukrainians. But because of the difference in growth rates—an increase of about 30 percent in a decade for the Central Asians compared to less than 10 percent for the Russians and other Slavs—the steadily decreasing numbers for the Russians would have made it ever more difficult for them to maintain their historic cultural domination of the rest of the population, even if the Soviet Union had held together. Of course, now that the 15 former republics have gained complete independence, the conflict has been both among states that are independent and have very little in common as well as within those states, as various minorities have declared and fought for their own independence. Beginning at the very end of 1994 and continuing into 1995, the bloody Russian suppression of Chechnaya's bid for indcpendence is but one of the more publicized of these continuing conflicts.

Until the time of Gorbachev, Soviet authorities had always tried to maintain that the nationality problem had been resolved successfully. While those familiar with the society knew that the feelings of enmity remained, the authoritarian nature of the government, especially under Stalin, tended to keep people from acting out those feelings, and actual conflict remained at a minimum. Although the policies of democratization, *perestroika,* and *glasnost* were initiated primarily to bring about economic reform, one of the consequences (apparently unintended and unanticipated) was the awakening and intensification of ethnic hatred and strife. Once people were allowed to express their feelings under the policy of *glasnost,* which called for or permitted more openness and public discussion, the situation deteriorated rather quicky into demonstrations and then violent clashes. (An even more tragic example of this dynamic is the civil war that broke out in 1991 in Yugoslavia among competing ethnic areas.)

These nationality-related conflicts have taken several forms. One is the relationship between the Russians, who used various policies to maintain their political and cultural dominance, and all of the other groups who made up the non-Russian half of the population, and who naturally resented their subordinate positions and felt that they had been discriminated against. Another is represented by clashes among the non-Russian nationalities in various areas. Of course, a third possibility is created when Russia attempts to maintain its domination of the region by intervening in disputes between two non-Russian factions or countries. In that case, the two can hate both one another and the Russians. With the end of the Soviet Union, there is yet another dynamic. Large numbers of Russians who had lived in the non-Russian republics of the Soviet Union now find that they are the minority in a non-Russian independent country. Russia has naturally felt a special responsibility for these groups, and this creates yet another potential source of conflict.

It is easy to understand the resentment of non-Russians who were made a part of the Russian Empire against their will, who have seen Russians moved to their areas and placed in positions of economic, social, and political control, and who have been discriminated against in various ways. Thus, it is not surprising that by 1990, for this and other reasons, all of the union republics had adopted policies calling for independence or varying degrees of autonomy from the central government. Leading this movement were the Baltic republics of Lithuania, Latvia, and Estonia, whose charges against the Moscow leaders were both territorial and ethnic in nature. While the basic contention was that these then independent areas were annexed to the Soviet Union against their will as part of a Nazi-Soviet agreement in 1939, there was continuing resentment over policies implemented since then to "Russify" them. There were, for instance, demands that the large number of Russians who had settled in those republics should return to the Russian republic. At about the same time, the Estonian republic passed laws, obviously directed at those Russians, making their native language rather than Russian the official language of the republic.

There are several reasons why the Baltic republics continued to be the most dangerous flash point in the struggle between non-Russian republics and the Russian-dominated central government. The first, of course, was the fact that they had been the leaders in calling for complete independence. A complicating factor was the position of the United States and some other countries, who made a distinction between the status of the Baltic republics and other areas of the Soviet Union. The United States never acknowledged the reannexation of the Baltics after World War II, so it treated their calls for independence somewhat differently than those from republics that had been part of the USSR for a longer time and that had become so under different circumstances. Finally, while there had been violence and loss of life in several other parts of the country when the military had intervened in ethnic clashes, there were several instances of deadly intervention by the Soviet military against the Baltic independence movements, including those at the very beginning of 1991, when the storming of the interior ministry and communication facilities by special "black beret" military units caused some 20 deaths. All of these factors led both the outside world and the central government itself to acknowledge the complete independence of the Baltic republics in 1991.

Perhaps less obvious than these calls by non-Russians for independence or greater autonomy is the backlash these movements have created among those who argue that the new policy of openness has paved the way for attacks on the Russian language and culture. The result has been a revival of Russian nationalism. A certain amount of nationalism is necessary and healthy, but social crisis often leads to extreme manifestations. In its positive form, this movement has been championed by such people as Alexander Solzhenitsyn, who denounced the Communist period and called for a return to the religious and other cultural values and institutions of pre-revolutionary Russia. Some of these nationalist positions were reminiscent of the old "Slavophiles versus Westernizers" debate, as they opposed Gorbachev's political and social reforms on the grounds that they would result in true Russian cultural values being replaced by the inferior ones of the West. In its extreme negative form, this reaction is represented by groups such as the neofascist, ultranationalistic, anti-Semitic organization known as Pamyat (Memory), which call for a return to authoritarianism and oppose everything that is not Russian. Unfortunately, as was the case in Germany, Russian nationalism and conservatism go hand in hand with anti-Semitism. Thus, the latter is also on the increase in both subtle forms, such as references to the "other nationalities" who would control a market economy, and not-at-all subtle ones, such as beatings.

The second major type of conflict has come to be symbolized by the dispute between the republics of Armenia and Azerbaijan beginning in the late 1980s over Nagorno-Karabakh, a territory located inside Azerbaijan but with a population that is mostly Armenian. Although the situation had existed since soon after the revolution, once again it was *glasnost* that brought things to the surface. Beginning with demonstrations calling for the incorporation of the territory into Armenia, the situation resulted in riots, reports of the deaths of at least several dozen people, and eventually martial law. Although the central government was eventually forced to intervene with armed force, the conflict was between two non-Russian ethnic groups. Of course, when the Soviet Union came to an end, this conflict shifted from a domestic one to war between two independent countries. Although Nagorno-Karabakh is perhaps the best known, there are similar disputes in all regions of the former USSR. Over the past few years, thousands have been killed and countless more injured in such clashes among ethnic groups themselves and in the subsequent interventions by the military. As mentioned, a federal form of government was established after the revolution to deal with the nationality question. For some 70 years, however, the Union of Soviet Socialist Republics was federal only in form. In reality, it was a highly centralized authoritarian system with virtually all decisions made in Moscow. As the economic and ethnic crises of the late 1980s unfolded, one could only wonder if the leadership in Moscow and the republics were familiar with the events and debates that took place in the United States before the Civil War as to the proper roles of the states and the national government. As some of the Soviet republics declared themselves independent, while others demanded a degree of autonomy or refused to comply with policies with which they did not agree,

one is reminded of the doctrine of John C. Calhoun and others that states could nullify within their boundaries federal laws to which they were opposed. Gorbachev's attempt to deal with these questions through a new union treaty was a major factor leading to the attempted coup by hard-liners seeking to prevent the devolution of power in August 1991. That failed coup, in turn, contributed greatly to the dissolution of the country just four months later. These ethnic conflicts have continued unabated since the breakup of the Soviet Union, as the borders changed but the violence remained and shifted to minority nationality groups within the new independent states. They have yet to determine how far the dynamics of independence and autonomy will go.

THE POLITICAL PARTY SYSTEM

The Role of the Party

Before examining the role of a Communist Party, it might be helpful to point out the varying importance of knowing the political party organization and operation in different types of systems. While it is useful to be familiar with the internal organization of the Republican and Democratic Parties in the United States, it is probably not crucial to an understanding of the overall political process. In Great Britain, with its parliamentary form and more "responsible" political party system, such knowledge is more important. In Communist regimes, because of the party's monopolistic claims and position, it is central to knowing how the process really works. Since decisions were actually made within the party but had to be legitimized and implemented by government agencies, two sets of parallel, overlapping structures developed. Thus, we must examine both party and state, but with more attention to the party than usual. As will be pointed out, however, the role of the party in the Soviet Union was changing drastically as a result of the Gorbachev reforms and the failed coup, even before the USSR collapsed.

The most critical and conspicuous distinction between democratic and authoritarian party systems is that in the latter only one party is officially allowed to exist and to function. Rule by a single monopolistic party, usually headed by one person, is one of the central defining features of totalitarianism in general and of Communist systems in particular. In Communist regimes, the party is given this privileged position by the official ideology on the premise that it alone understands the true needs and interests of society. Given this concept of truth, it is logical that competitive parties are unacceptable, and that political structures and processes are designed to resist spontaneous, special interest claims that might interfere with the directions set by the vanguard elite. In practice, this concept was incorporated in Article 6 of the constitution of the USSR adopted in 1977: "The leading and guiding force of Soviet society and the nucleus of its political system, of all state organizations and all public organizations, is the Communist Party of the Soviet Union." To implement this principle, Communist systems set up parallel structures in the party and state organizations. Policy decisions were made by the party (Politburo), legitimized by the government legislature (Supreme Soviet), implemented by the government cabinet (Council of Ministers), and monitored for compliance by the party (Secretariat and Central Committee). There was never any doubt that party positions and officials were more important, with the most powerful position in the entire political process being that of the general secretary of the Communist Party.

Since there was only one party, and especially since that resulted in only one name on an election ballot, the inclination was to dismiss such parties as unique at best and as a farce at worst. But the "functional" approach to politics caused scholars to ask if many of the same functions might be performed by both single parties and their democratic counterparts, even though the institutions or methods were different. Michael Gehlen, for example, suggested that the role of parties such as the Communist Party of the Soviet Union (CPSU) was basically an integrative one. That is, they are concerned with political recruitment, socialization, and mobilization. However, since the methods and processes seem unfamiliar to us, we may assume that these functions are not being performed.[12]

In a very thought-provoking comparison of certain aspects of British and Soviet politics, Jerome Gilison approached the subject of political party systems by suggesting that the two were similar up to a point in serving as links between people and leaders and in performing such functions as recruitment and socialization. The fundamental difference he saw was that the CPSU went much further by assuming economic and social roles that British parties did not. He was referring, of course, to the claims of the CPSU, as the vanguard, to infiltrate social groups legitimately and to guide and supervise all of the social and economic activites of the society.[13] It is precisely this claim that causes many to maintain that one-party systems are fundamentally different from democratic ones.

However one sees the role of the CPSU up to that point, one of the most dramatic and far-reaching changes contained in the political reforms of 1988 and after was the end of the monopolistic position of the party and the transfer of significant power from the party to the government. Article 6 of the constitution, quoted above, was amended to read: "The Communist Party of the Soviet Union and other political parties, as well as trade unions, youth, and other social organi-zations and mass movements, participate in the formulation of the policy of the Soviet state and in the administration of state and social affairs through their representatives elected to the soviets of people's deputies and in other ways." So much for an officially recognized monopolistic vanguard! Accom-panying this change in the constitution were equally momentous developments within the party. The groundwork was laid at the party conference in 1988, and then the Twenty-Eighth Party Congress in 1990 became "the occasion when the demise of the Party as the supreme political institution was played out in public."[14] Gorbachev called for and got a series of changes designed to bring about a clearer separation betwen party and govern-ment functions and agencies, to introduce greater democracy and openness to party bodies and proceedings, and to effect the transfer of power from the party to the state. After a description of the classic party struc-ture, we will return to these reforms.

In spite of everything just said about the discredited position of the Communist Party and its ideology, it is well to remember sev-eral things. While the party as such may have lost its former position, its legacy lives on in the areas of the former Soviet Union, in fact if not in name. In many of the elections held since independence, especially in Central Asia, those who were in office in the Soviet period have run under another label and been elected. In the Soviet period, key posi-tions were obtained in all aspects of society (education, the media, etc.) through a patronage mechanism called the *nomen-klatura*—a list of positions to be filled by or with the approval of party officials. When the Communist period ended, these people were the ones with the knowledge and experience to run things.

In addition, while the Communist Party is gone, opposition or competing parties in the

Western sense will take a long time to orga-nize and be effective. History also reveals that Russia and then the Soviet Union experi-enced alternating periods of reform and re-action. Perhaps we should remember, with re-spect to judgments about the demise of the influence of the Communist Party, the re-mark attributed to Mark Twain that reports of his death had been greatly exaggerated. In spite of what happened in the Soviet Union, variations of the classic party organization it developed are still used by the small number of surviving Communist countries. Thus, some description of that organization is needed to understand what did go on in the Soviet Union and still exists in a few coun-tries.

Party Structure

Since there were structural changes made by the Party Congress in 1990, we will start with the classic pattern and then describe the changes. The general organizational struc-ture of a Communist party starts with a body called a Congress, which is large and meets infrequently but is formally designated by the party rules as the organ of supreme power. It then selects and delegates power to the Cen-tral Committee, a smaller group that meets more often and is authorized to lead the party between Congresses. It in turn chooses the two smaller, continuously functioning bodies that hold the real power: the Polit-buro and Secretariat.

Although it met more or less frequently in the past, the party rules called for a Congress every five years (roughly coinciding with the five-year economic plans). Some 5,000 dele-gates and observers converged on the Palace of Congresses in the Kremlin in Moscow for about two weeks. Until the Twenty-Eighth Congress in 1990, they literally performed the functions indicated in the party rules: "to hear and approve reports." They would listen to long (three- to five-hour) speeches and reports, applaud at the appropriate times, and vote to approve the policies recommended and "elect" members of the Central Committee. If you have ever watched the national convention of a U.S. political party that is renominating an incumbent president, you have the idea. Everything is carefully planned and scripted and very harmonious.

Even if the Congress had no real power, it still had significance, especially as a platform for policy pronouncements or changes and for the revelation of changes in top personnel. It was at the Twentieth Congress in 1956 that Nikita Khrushchev delivered his "secret speech" that denounced Stalin and began the process of de-Stalinization, and Gorbachev issued his call for radical reform at the Twenty-Seventh Congress in 1986. While leadership changes could be made at any time, and often were, Kremlinologists carefully studied the elections at the end of Congresses to see which individuals and factions seemed to be gaining or losing influence. In addition to the substantive changes adopted, the Twenty-Eighth Congress was important for the innovations in the way the meetings were conducted. In line with the concept of greater public discussion (*glasnost*), there was more in the way of debating and complaining about whether reforms were moving too fast or too slowly. There were even criticisms of General Secretary Gorbachev. Although in the end he was reelected to that position and his desires for changes in personnel and structures were accepted, the criticisms and the departures of Boris Yeltsin and others from the party raised serious questions about its future and influence.

The Central Committee is probably the most difficult body to discuss. Formally, it was given the power to direct the party between Congresses, which meant almost all of the time. While its size of several hundred members was much more workable than a Con-

gress, its infrequent meetings prevented it from really running things. The rules called for meetings at least twice a year (under Gorbachev it was three or four), but since they only lasted a few days, this also is clearly not a continuously functioning, decision-making group. As a gathering of the top several hundred Communists in the country, however, it cannot just be dismissed as of no importance. As it is sometimes put, it is not that you are important because you are a member of the Central Committee, but rather that the Committee is important because of the people who serve on it. It has in rare instances taken action, the potential was there for it to become more important, and it could serve as a recruitment source for members to take the final step to the very top rungs of the party elite. Formally, the functions of the Central Committee included the selection of the members of the two smaller, continuously functioning bodies—the Politburo (now called the Presidium) and the Secretariat—which have been the real holders of power.

Although given somewhat different areas of responsibility, the two overlap in both membership and functions. The party rules said that the Politburo was to direct the work of the party between meetings of the Central Committee and that the Secretariat was to deal with the selection of personnel and the verification of the fulfillment of party decisions. Thus, although it is never possible to separate the two completely, the Politburo was thought of as *the* policy-making body, while the Secretariat was seen as primarily responsible for internal party recruitment and discipline and for supervising government agencies. As with other party bodies, these two had no specified size, but the Politburo usually had about 20 members. The Secretariat was actually a rather large bureaucracy with a number of departments, but was headed by about 10 officials with the general secretary at the very top. Typically, about half of the members of the Secretariat would also sit on the Politburo. Since their meetings were always in private, most of what we know about their manner of operation, such as the fact that they held formal meetings weekly, comes by way of statements from their members or staff.

The composition of the Politburo made it ideally suited to make decisions, since it brought together in one group key officials from the party and the government. While there was never a list of specific positions holding seats on the Politburo, which meant that the holders of some posts might or might not belong, certain patterns did emerge. As mentioned, the central party apparatus was represented by members of the Secretariat, the most important of whom was the general secretary, who presided at the meetings. In addition, there were members from other important geographical regions, such as the party first secretary from the cities of Moscow and Leningrad (Saint Petersburg) or from key republics such as the Ukraine. Then there were their government counterparts. From the central government there were members of the Council of Ministers (cabinet) such as the chairman, ministers of defense and foreign affairs, and perhaps the head of the KGB or the Supreme Soviet (legislature). Finally, there were regional government leaders, such as the heads of the executive and legislative branches of the Russian republic or other key republics. Working together as the Politburo, this relatively small group of people would make the major personnel and policy decisions for both the party and the entire country. They would then resume their roles as party or government officials to see that the decisions were carried out.

The Secretariat, headed by the general secretary, had a number of functions, including serving as a staff resource for the Politburo in preparing reports and recommendations; handling the internal personnel and administrative affairs of the party, such as appointments, discipline, and training; and serving as "keeper of the faith" by interpreting and applying the ideology. But most of its work and staff were organized by departments that paralleled government ministries and whose task it was to see that the government bureaucracy was carrying out the correct policies. Before the Gorbachev reforms, there were probably several hundred thousand people organized into about 20 such departments dealing with areas such as agriculture, defense, economic and social policy, and international affairs.

Party Reforms

The classic organization of the party just described was most applicable to the Soviet Union in the period from Khrushchev to the early years of Gorbachev. Stalin, with his dictatorial rule, which was later criticized as a "cult of personality," tended not to call Party Congresses, to purge or kill high party officials, and in general to ignore rules and structures. Khrushchev's reforms, although eventually opposed by the bureaucracy because they threatened it, did include renewed emphasis on the role of the party and more regular procedures. Reacting in part to those reforms, the Brezhnev period brought a renewed emphasis on centralization, collective leadership, and almost no turnover in the people holding leadership positions. The ultimate result was a conservative, status quo gerontocracy, which left the economy and society in a deteriorating condition. It was these conditions that caused the new leader, Mikhail Gorbachev, to criticize sharply the Brezhnev era and call for "new thinking" and restructuring.

In the beginning, it appeared that Gorbachev thought that progress could be achieved through moderate moves such as a campaign against corruption and ineffi-ciency, accomplished in part through changes in personnel. Accordingly, there was the mas-sive removal of party officials throughout the country. But as time passed, it became in-creasingly evident that the vested interests of the conservative party bureaucracy itself were a major barrier to reform. Thus, during the period from 1988 to 1990, culminating in the Twenty-Eighth Party Congress, there was a major reorganization of the central party ap-paratus.

A number of the changes affected the op-eration of the party as a whole. A major em-phasis was on a clearer division of operations between party and state. The party was to re-tain its overall responsibility for guiding the political, economic, and social systems, but was to do less "micromanaging" of the day-to-day operations of government agencies. In accordance with this goal, the party organiza-tion was to be streamlined and the size of the bureaucracy was to be reduced significantly from top to bottom, largely by ending the ex-isting duplication of party and state agencies. Along the same lines, direct rule by the party was to decrease as a result of a reduction in the use of the *nomenklatura,* the patronage system under the direct control of the party. Intraparty democracy was to be promoted by more open discussion, multicandidate elec-tions, and secret ballots, and all party officials were to be limited to two five-year terms and subject to a mandatory retirement age.

In terms of specific agencies, changes re-lated to the Party Congress were informal and affected its manner of operation rather than its size or formal functions. While the Twenty-Eighth Congress wound up giving Gorbachev most of what he wanted, there was much more open debate and criticism than in previous meetings. Gorbachev's reelection as general secretary, for example, was consid-ered as a separate item of business in open session rather than being done by the previ-

ous method of simply approving a recom-mendation of the Central Committee. Of course, any time changes are made infor-mally, it is that much easier to reverse or alter them without having to go through a formal process.

There was, however, a recommendation to regularize the procedure used to formulate the reforms with respect to the Party Confer-ence. Since it was not close to the time of a Congress when Gorbachev was ready to move on reform, he used the Nineteenth Party Conference in 1988 to propose changes and then the Congress in 1990 to finalize them. He proposed that, since Congresses were scheduled only every five years, Party Confer-ences should be held on a regular basis in the interim to make further policy or leadership changes. It was also decided to cut the size of the Central Committee by about half (to about 200) and to make the smaller group more of a continuously functioning body rather than one following the former pattern of holding only two to four meetings a year.

Since the Politburo and the Secretariat had been the real centers of power, perhaps the most significant of the changes in the shift of power from party to government were related to these bodies. This was especially true with respect to the Politburo, which had been the single most important and powerful decision-making body not only in the party but in the entire Soviet political process. While the size of the Politburo was never spelled out in the party rules, it had around 20 members, all drawn from top party and government leaders from Moscow and from certain key union republics. In the 1990 re-forms, the name was changed to the Presid-ium, and the size was increased to 30, with half of the members being the top party leader from each of the union republics. The other half were to be chosen by the Central Committee, and when the selections were made, only Gorbachev and one other person (the choice for deputy general secretary, Ukrainian party leader Vladimir Ivashko) were retained from the previous membership. In keeping with the theme of the separation of party and state functions, a number of leading government officials lost their posts on this top party body, including the chairman of the Council of Ministers, the ministers of defense and foreign affairs, and the head of the KGB. This change in structure meant that half of its membership would have to gather from all parts of the country, making frequent meetings more difficult. Probably more importantly, its membership would now be larger, with more diversity in party membership but virtually no representation from top government leaders. It is difficult to see the changes in any other way than as an attempt to diminish its power and to limit it to more of an internal party role rather than the central policy-making position it had previously occupied.

The reorganization of the Secretariat, which was carried out in 1988, appeared to be consistent with the overall goals of reform. Its former 20 departments were cut to about half that number and were to serve as the staff for 6 newly created agencies, called commissions and headed by central committee secretaries, that would deal with ideology, social and economic policy, agricultural policy, international policy, legal policy, and personnel. Since most of the central party bureaucracy was within the Secretariat, we can only assume that both its numbers and its day-to-day tasks were reduced and streamlined in this shift of responsibilities from the party to the state. These were the party bureaucrats who were looking over the shoulders of government bureaucrats. If the role of the party was to be made a more general one, there would be less need for so many monitors. In a final symbolic move, the title of the party leader was changed from general secretary to chairman.

Why, you might ask, were there all these political changes to move power from the party to government bodies? Many of the personnel changes were made to shake up and replace the complacent and corruption-ridden apparatus that was left over from the Brezhnev period. Then, as Gorbachev was preparing to initiate his restructuring, he realized that the changes it called for would encounter vigorous opposition from the conservative party bureaucracy, led by people such as Yigor Ligachev, one of the principal opponents of reform. While massive changes in party personnel throughout the country did take place, part of Gorbachev's strategy appears to have been an end run around this party opposition by creating or strengthening state agencies over which he would have more control. While initial assumptions were that Gorbachev's motivation was a sincere belief in "new thinking" (perhaps prompted by economic necessity), the eventual defections of his top political and economic advisers were accompanied by warnings that, regardless of his intentions, he was producing a dictatorship.

The proposed changes produced a classic situation of opposition from both the left and the right. While there was the natural opposition from conservatives who correctly saw a threat to their vested interests and power, others felt that even the changes pushed through by Gorbachev were not enough, and they called for faster and more radical political and economic reform. They still saw the party, the central party and government bureaucracies, and even Gorbachev himself as unwilling or unable to undertake the drastic measures needed to save the country from its deepening economic crisis. Boris Yeltsin became the symbol of this group. Earlier he had been removed from the Politburo for his persistent and outspoken criticism that reform was not proceeding fast enough, and he had even been denied a seat in the new national legislature (Congress of People's Deputies). He then turned to the people, won election to that legislature as a populist candidate running against the central leadership, and eventually was elected president of the Russian republic, the largest of the 15 republics. When he dramatically chose the Party Congress to announce his resignation from the Communist Party, his example was followed by officials of the two largest cities in the country, Moscow and Leningrad (Saint Petersburg), and a number of other progressive reformers. Subsequently, non-Communists were elected to government positions in various parts of the country even before the demise of the Soviet Union. There were also indications that the total membership of the Communist Party, which had risen to about 20 million, had begun to decline as it became increasingly apparent that the party did not have the solutions to the country's problems. The involvement of high party officials in the attempted coup resulted in a ban of party activities in the workplace, the seizure of party buildings and property by government officials, and a complete loss of credibility.

GOVERNMENT STRUCTURES

Until the time of the reforms and other events just discussed, we would have said that while it was necessary to be familiar with the constitution, the federal form of government, and the organization and operation of government agencies in the USSR, they were not nearly as important as those in the Communist Party, and existed mostly to legitimize and facilitate the implementation of party decisions. There was no doubt that the power of party bodies and especially of the general secretary was greater than that of the state and the chief of state. As we have just observed, however, that situation was already changing as state agencies were given more freedom

from supervision by their party counterparts. Then, at the time of the coup, there was the symbol of Yeltsin, popularly elected president of the Russian republic and former member of the Communist Party, coming to rescue Gorbachev from the hands of top central government and party leaders. In this section, therefore, we will take a look at recent constitutional developments, the federal structure of the Soviet Union, the organization of state institutions, and the changes taking place in these areas.

The Constitution

In this day and age, virtually every country has a constitution that, at the very least, normally performs the functions of describing the agencies that exercise power and placing certain limits on that power. Although the USSR had a constitution almost since the revolution, its role was somewhat different because of the ideological assumptions involved. The difference is obvious immediately, as one reads the preamble to the 1977 document, which speaks in narrative and ideological terms of the Communist Party—led victory in the "Great October Socialist Revolution" that began the historic turn from capitalism to socialism, the ultimate goal of which was the building of a classless Communist society.

While Soviet-era constitutions described political institutions and processes such as elections, it has been pointed out that until the very end, the real power was with the party rather than the state. Thus, a description of the government structure did not reveal the actual decision-making process and bodies. For that, one looked to the party. In accordance with the concept of the vanguard role of the party and the claim that the revolution put an end to class conflict, the constitution was intended to facilitate the rule of the party rather than to limit it. Thus, there was no perceived need for a separation of powers in which the branches check one another. Similarly, although there were provisions similar to the U.S. Bill of Rights, those rights were to be exercised (according to Article 50) "in accordance with the interests of the people and in order to strengthen and develop the socialist system." It was the party, of course, that decided if they were being exercised in the proper manner.

Consistent with the Marxist dialectical concept of different stages of development, the Soviet Union had had four constitutions and was talking about a fifth when it came apart. Rather than just amending the existing document, they adopted new ones to mark the revolution (1918), the formation of the USSR (1922), the "second revolution" of the Stalin period (1936), and the post-Stalin era (1977). As a result of widespread agreement that the reforms of the Gorbachev era marked the beginning of yet another new stage, a commission was established to formulate a new document, but the pace of change was so fast that amendments were used in the interim rather than delaying essential reforms until the lengthy process of debating and adopting a new constitution could be completed. Thus, the amendments of 1988 and 1990 were very extensive, changing in varying degrees almost a third of the articles of the existing 1977 document. The elimination of the role of the Communist Party, followed by the changes in the political structures and processes, had occurred before the breakup of the Soviet Union and were in place to some degree when the end came. This inheritance of the newly independent states has put a renewed emphasis on the need to understand constitutional arrangements such as federalism, the electoral process, and the structure and operation of state agencies. Thus, we turn next to an examination of how the government was organized and eventually reformed.

Federalism

A good example of the difference between substance and form when dealing with structures and constitutions is the question of federalism. The very name, Union of Soviet Socialist Republics, indicated, as the constitution said in explicit terms (Article 70), that the country was a federal, multinational state formed as a result of "the free self-determination of nations and the voluntary association of equal Soviet Socialist Republics." As is usually true, a federal form was chosen as a compromise, in this case to accommodate the large number of diverse nationality groups inherited from the Russian Empire. The major ethnic groups (Russian, Ukrainian, Georgian, Uzbek, Lithuanian, etc.) were organized into regional governmental units called union republics. In the provisions that followed, a classic federal arrangement was established in which responsibilities were divided between the republics and the central government. The jurisdiction of the central government was spelled out in a list that included such areas as national security, international relations, the national economy, and the national budget. In matters other than those listed, a union republic "exercises independent authority on its territory." Each republic had its own constitution (conforming to that of the USSR), and in the event of a conflict, the law of the USSR was to prevail. In addition, the constitution gave republics two rather unusual rights that did not get much attention until the Gorbachev period. One was that of entering into relations with other countries, including exchanging diplomats and concluding treaties, and participating in the activities of international organizations. The other (found in Article 72) said that "each union republic shall retain the right freely to secede from the USSR."

Until just before the end, the country was federal in form only. Given the authoritarian nature of the system, virtually all activities, political, economic, and others, were under the control of the central (all-union) level, and decisions were made in Moscow. While other levels of government had their own institutions, everything was highly centralized. As discussed in the section on culture, there were political resentments of Moscow by non-Russians and ill feelings among the various other ethnic groups, but there was little opportunity to express them in such a tightly controlled system.

All that changed with the Gorbachev period, as the Soviet Union became a political laboratory for exploring the concepts of federalism, confederation, and centralized governments. The crisis was precipitated by the Baltic republics, when they took the constitution literally and declared their independence of the Soviet Union, but subsequent calls by every union republic for some degree of greater autonomy from the central government followed. In a move reminiscent of events in the United States before the Civil War, the Estonian Supreme Soviet (legislature) declared its right to nullify any all-union legislation that violated its autonomy, and several other republics followed in asserting that union-republic laws took priority over those of the central government. The most critical point was when the Russian republic, led by Yeltsin, took this step in 1990. Since that republic contained about three-quarters of the land and half the population of the Soviet Union, its challenge, when combined with the earlier ones, threatened to bring about the literal disintegration of the country. Those union republics not declaring their intention to leave seemed to be calling for either a Soviet version of what U.S. leaders have called a "new federalism" or some form of confederation. That is, they wanted a federal arrangement in which the republics were given more authority, or an even looser system in which the republics would deal with

virtually all domestic matters, such as economic and social policy, while the central government concentrated on such things as national security and foreign policy. Many of these measures taken by the union republics were, of course, considered by the central government to be unconstitutional, and the confrontations began.

The response of the central authorities took a number of forms. On the question of secession, the USSR Supreme Soviet in 1990 seemed to concede the right when it passed legislation setting up the procedures a republic must follow in order to secede. The law mandated that rather than a government declaring independence, there must be a referendum in which two-thirds of a republic's citizens vote to leave. If they voted to do so, a waiting period of up to five years was provided in order to work out practical matters such as property settlements, what to do with people (such as Russians) who did not wish to leave, etc. At the same time, however, renewed emphasis on other provisions of the constitution (Articles 74 and 75), which stated that in the event of a conflict USSR law prevailed and declared that the USSR was "a single entity and comprises the territories of the Union Republics," seemed to call into question the right of republics to leave. In an attempt to get the republics to reconsider their decisions to secede, Gorbachev offered to negotiate a new treaty of union that could deal with their concerns and might modify the relationships, but the republic leaders rejected the offer. When Lithuania held a nonbinding referendum on independence in early 1991, in which 90 percent of those voting favored independence, Gorbachev declared that such a vote would be illegal, in part because it was not part of the nationwide vote that he had proposed.

In a further effort to address the problem, the constitutional amendments adopted in 1990 included the establishment of a new

By MIKE PETERS FOR THE DAYTON DAILY NEWS

FIGURE 7-2

Council of the Federation to deal with issues related to federalism and the nationality problem. This Council was made up of the top government official (president) from each of the republics and was headed by the president of the USSR. Its functions included examining questions of compliance with the union treaty, making recommendations for implementing the country's nationalities policy and for dealing with conflicts and disputes among the various ethnic groups, and ensuring the participation of the republics in resolving questions of nationwide significance.

On the other hand, the central government took economic and military measures against the Baltic republics that questioned their intention to allow secession. The response to Lithuania's declaration of independence in 1990 was an economic boycott intended to force the republic to back down. Interestingly, other republics indicated at the time that they would not observe the boycott and would deal directly with the Baltic republics. The most drastic measures involved the use of military forces to intimidate independence leaders or to seize property to inhibit their activities. At the very beginning of 1991, for example, some 20 people were killed when military units moved into Baltic cities to seize police and communication facilities. These incidents had implications well beyond the borders of the Soviet Union as they, along with the war in the Persian Gulf, caused the postponement of a summit meeting between Presidents Bush and Gorbachev.

Dissolution of the USSR in 1991 merely moved the discussion to different levels. On the one hand, the 15 new states were faced with the question of whether to proceed individually or to enter into some new form of arrangement. Eleven of the 15 chose to form a type of confederation called the Commonwealth of Independent States (CIS), which was neither a state nor a supranational government. It did recognize, however, that a number of common interests, such as economic and security arrangements, still existed among them. At the same time, several of these now independent countries were faced by internal demands for independence or greater autonomy by minority ethnic groups within their borders. While Russia's confrontation with Chechnya and civil war in Georgia over independence for Abkhazia and Ossetia are perhaps the most dramatic, similar demands have been faced by virtually all of the new countries. Working out a satisfactory arrangement among themselves and dealing with internal conflicts will remain serious problems for years.

Government Organization and Operation

Just as the nature of the union and of the role and structure of the party had been changing even prior to late 1991, the same was true of the government. As noted, in the Soviet period the role of state agencies was of much less importance than that of the party. With the shift in emphasis and power from the party to the government, and the accompanying changes in structure, there was a renewed importance in understanding how the government was organized and operates. After independence, the new states inherited a hybrid form of the old structures and the Gorbachev reforms.

In discussing the European democracies, we described the parliamentary and presidential types of government. In the presidential form, such as is found in the United States, there is a separation of powers between the executive and legislative branches, and the president and legislature are elected and operate independently of one another. The presidency combines the role of working head of government with the ceremonial role of chief of state. In the parliamentary form, of which Great Britain is the classic example, there is a joining of the branches. Only the members of the legislature are popularly elected. They, in turn, choose from among their membership the leaders of the executive branch, the prime minister and the cabinet. While the prime minister serves as the head of the government, the ceremonial, symbolic functions of the head of state are performed by the monarch.

Prior to the changes that began in 1988, the Soviet Union had a fairly classic version of the parliamentary form. The legislative body, called the Supreme Soviet and described by the constitution as the supreme body of state power, was a popularly elected bicameral body with 750 delegates in each house. The bicameral arrangement was similar to that of the U.S. Congress but with some differences. Somewhat like the U.S. Senate, one chamber, the Soviet of Nationalities, was based on nationality, with each union republic and other national-territorial areas having a certain number of representatives. The other, the Soviet of the Union, like the U.S. House of Representatives, divided the entire population into electoral districts. Each chamber had its own officers and a number of standing committees. The constitution called for the Supreme Soviet to be convened twice a year, and those meetings usually lasted only several days each. So, as we saw with the party, supreme power was placed formally in a large body that met very infrequently. To the extent that seating arrangements provide an indication of the dynamics of a legislature, a word about the Soviet Union and Russia is in order. In Great Britain's House of Commons, the two parties sit on benches facing one another to facilitate the function of debate, with the speaker presiding in the middle. In the U.S. Congress, members sit at desks in a semicircular arrangement with an aisle dividing the two parties. In the old Soviet Union, and now its successors, whether at Party Congresses or meetings of the Supreme Soviet, the leadership sits in several rows on a stage, and the members sit together like an audience in a theater.

Consistent with the party practice, the large Supreme Soviet was to elect two smaller, continuously functioning bodies to act on its behalf in between regular sessions—the Council of Ministers and the Presidium of the Supreme Soviet. In accordance with the parliamentary pattern, the Supreme Soviet named the members of the Council of Ministers, which the constitution called "the supreme executive and administrative body of state power." Its membership included a chairman, the heads of all the ministries, such as defense and agriculture, and the chairmen of state committees, such as the state security committee (KGB) and planning committee (Gosplan). Since the state claimed responsibility for so many more areas of economic and social life, the Council's approximately one hundred members made it much larger than its Western counterparts. The federal principle was reflected by the fact that the chairmen of the Councils of Ministers of each of the 15 union republics were ex-officio members of the USSR Council. Since the position as head of this "cabinet" was similar to that of the prime minister in Western democracies, he was often referred to by that title in the West. Since the chairman of the Council of Ministers directed the entire governmental administrative bureaucracy, he had a significant power base and was one of the most powerful people in the government. The general secretary

of the Communist Party was, however, still the single most powerful individual.

The other body selected by the parliament, the Presidium of the Supreme Soviet, had no close equivalent in the West. Headed by a chairman and consisting of some 40 members, part of its role was as a collective head of state. Since it was given the role and functions of head of state but did not often meet as a group, in practice the chairman acted as the head of state (often called the "president" by Westerners). Since the last five general secretaries of the Communist Party (from Brezhnev to Gorbachev) assumed this position, they combined the posts of head of state and head of the party. The other aspect of the Presidium's functions does not fit the usual parliamentary mold, but grows out of the fact that the Supreme Soviet met for only a few days twice a year. Since it was obviously not a full-time legislature, the Presidium was to act as the "continuously functioning agency of the USSR Supreme Soviet" (Article 119). As such, it could issue decrees with the force of law, ratify treaties, and perform other legislative acts. It could also perform a number of functions that are normally thought of as executive, such as granting pardons and appointing diplomats, and even certain judicial actions, such as interpreting laws.

Thus, as was the pattern with the Communist Party structures, the smaller, permanent agencies had the real power. The Presidium, and especially its chairman, would perform the day-to-day legislative functions of adopting party policies and decisions, the Council of Ministers would direct the government bureaucracy in implementing them, and the full Supreme Soviet would meet periodically to ratify these actions with the same type of unanimous votes that characterized the Party Congresses. In all of these activities, however, the entire state organization was secondary and subordinate to the party, which was the real repository of power.

Government Reforms

Against this backdrop of the old structures, the changes since 1988 have been truly momentous. We have had the rare opportunity to observe an economic, social, and political reform movement attempt to change the overall authoritarian traditions of a thousand years and the Communist pattern of some 75 years. We say *attempt* to change because there has been strong resistance, the changes are still taking place, and it will be some time before the final structures and processes are established. Whether out of conviction or because of the need to fix a failed system, Gorbachev and his supporters launched an effort toward significant democratization of the political process. When the failure of the economic and social policies led to the elimination of the monopolistic position of the party in the policy process, by itself a radical move, a whole new dynamic was created. With no prior experience, the system would have to take on such tasks as setting up competitive multicandidate elections, developing additional political parties, placing limits on terms of office, and turning a rubber-stamp legislature into a truly deliberative one. All of these would have to be done in the context of rising ethnic conflicts and growing economic hardships, either of which by itself might be enough to tear the country apart. In this process, the new reforms changed the structure and nature of all of the government bodies, and transformed the system from a parliamentary type to a presidential one, creating in the process a new strong position of president.

An entirely new layer was added when the old Supreme Soviet was replaced as the "supreme organ of state power" by a new body called the Congress of People's Depu-

ties. Consisting of 2,250 deputies, the Congress was to meet at least once a year and actually met twice in its first year. The process of electing these new deputies is a lesson in the difficulty of the transition from authoritarian to democratic practices. Of the members, 1,500 were to be elected in a manner similar to the old Supreme Soviet. That is, 750 were from election districts based on national-territorial units (union republics, etc.) and 750 from districts based on population. But the distrust of open elections is reflected in the fact that the remaining 750 were to be chosen by "social organizations" such as the Communist Party, trade unions, and others that were controlled by the establishment, giving it a large bloc of votes with which to manipulate the Congress. The elections were very interesting. Unlike the longstanding election system in which there was only one name on the ballot, more than 1,100 of the 1,500 seats up for popular election were contested by two or more candidates. It must be pointed out, however, that the overwhelming number of candidates were Communist Party members. In most cases it was a matter of reform-minded challengers against the establishment. After being removed by the leadership, Boris Yeltsin started his political comeback by winning in his Moscow district. Several top party leaders, the most dramatic being Politburo member and Leningrad (Saint Petersburg) party head Yuri Solovyev, were humiliated when they ran unopposed and lost by failing to get the necessary majority when their names were crossed out on more than half the ballots.

Although the Congress had a long list of functions, including the power to pass laws, amend the constitution, and set the basic guidelines of domestic and foreign policy, the fact that it would meet only once or twice a year for brief periods indicated that while it might be a significant forum, it could not be a full-time legislature. Thus, its most important tasks included the ratification of a number of other officials, including the chairman of the Council of Ministers and the Supreme Court, and the election of the members of a new USSR Supreme Soviet.

This Supreme Soviet, now described as "the permanently operating legislative and monitoring organ of state power," was changed in almost every respect, including method of selection, size, length of sessions, and manner of operation. The new Congress of People's Deputies was the popularly elected legislature, and the new Supreme Soviet was elected by the Congress from among its members. While the arrangement of two equal houses was retained, the size of each was reduced from 750 members to 271. It would still meet twice a year, but now for three to four months each time rather than a few days. The extended sessions bring us to the most intriguing aspects of this process. There appeared to be serious attempts to make this a real legislature rather than one that merely performed the brief, compliant, unanimous rubber-stamping exercises of the past. For the first time, membership in the Supreme Soviet would become a full-time position rather than a trip to Moscow for a few days twice a year. Scholars have long written of the "folkways" and informal processes found in democratic legislatures. All of these would have to be developed, including parliamentary debate, real committee proceedings, and staff support for members, if the new body were to become a genuine part of the political process. The first sessions set a good precedent, as delegates displayed a fair degree of independence. The proceedings, open to television and the press, were characterized by lively debates, criticism, and rejection of some leadership proposals, as well as initiatives from the members.

One example was the function of confirming the membership of the Council of Ministers. In their initial form, the changes followed the parliamentary model, in which one of the functions of the legislature is to choose the government, in this case the Council of Ministers. In the past, collective approval of the members of the Council would have been presented as a recommendation, which the legislature would have accepted without debate. In the first session of the new Supreme Soviet, however, nominees were questioned individually before the entire parliament and, in a few cases, rejected. In a further attempt to make the Council accountable in the classic parliamentary manner, a constitutional amendment provided that the Supreme Soviet could, by a two-thirds vote, "express no confidence in the USSR Government, which entails the latter's resignation."

Just as things seemed to be going well and moving toward a healthier, functioning parliament and a more accountable government, the reforms turned in another direction. Before the changes, the Supreme Soviet named the members of the Presidium of the Supreme Soviet (head of state) and the Council of Ministers (government). While the manner of selection remained the same, the position and role of both were altered by the creation in 1990 of the new office of president of the USSR (to be discussed shortly), which combined the roles of head of state and government. The effect on the Presidium was drastic, changing it from a minilegislature and collective head of state to an administrative body whose task was to "organize the work of the USSR Supreme Soviet" through activities such as coordinating the work of committees, publishing the texts of laws, and leading nationwide discussions of proposed legislative changes. Its former, more significant functions were transferred to the reorganized executive office.

The Council of Ministers retained its role, as the highest administrative body, of directing the government bureaucracy in implementing government policies. Creation of the position of president, however, eventually changed the lines of accountability and eliminated the role of the chairman. The initial changes of the Gorbachev period made the Council accountable to the Congress of People's Deputies and the Supreme Soviet. Then, in the Congress held in December 1990, he pushed through a reorganization of the executive branch that included measures changing the name to the Cabinet of Ministers and establishing a "vertical line of authority" in which it answered directly to him rather than the legislature.

The culmination of all of these changes was the creation of the strong presidency in 1990, which effectively changed the system from parliamentary to presidential and made the president, rather than the general secretary of the party, the single most powerful individual. A number of factors led to this development. This was at the same time that Article 6 of the constitution was being amended to remove the monopoly of the party. Leadership had come from the Politburo, Secretariat, and especially the top post of general secretary. If their roles were to be reduced, who would take their place? The answer to that question was imperative in view of the mounting dual crises of severe economic shortages and ethnic strife, either of which might be sufficient to cause national chaos and collapse. As attempts to implement radical economic reform met continued resistance from party conservatives and entrenched bureaucrats, as coal miners and others went on strike, and as calls for independence and autonomy continued to come from all parts of the country and to grow more violent, more and more segments of the leadership and populace came to see a strong government executive as the solution.

Article 127 of the constitution called for the new president to be popularly elected for no more than two five-year terms. In a transitional compromise opposed by many deputies, Gorbachev had his way and was elected to his first term by the Congress of People's Deputies in March 1990, but the next election was to be by the people. (There is an interesting requirement that the election is valid only if at least 50 percent of voters participate. Such a provision might invalidate a U.S. election!) Further evidence of the trend toward presidential government and the separation of powers was the stipulation that the president could not be a member of any legislative body. This differed from both the old system, in which the chairman of the Presidium of the Soviet was a member of the legislature, and classic parliamentary systems such as the British in which the prime minister must be a member of parliament.

Most of the presidential powers listed were the usual ones for a chief executive. They included such things as representing the country in foreign relations, coordinating the actions of state agencies, nominating officials for top government positions, commanding the armed forces, and declaring martial law. But there were also some broader powers that warrant closer examination. He was to take the "necessary measures" to protect the sovereignty, security, and territorial integrity of the USSR, and he could, in the interests of safeguarding the security of citizens, declare a state of emergency in particular localities, "introduce temporary presidential rule," or "issue decrees that are binding throughout the territory of the country." While these provisions often called for consultation with the Supreme Soviet or union republic officials, in times of economic and ethnic unrest, he was given broad discretionary powers to implement economic reform and maintain law and order. The Supreme Soviet, for example, gave him the specific power to issue emergency decrees to accomplish the transition to a market economy. In the relatively short time he was in power after their establishment, Gorbachev used these powers to issue a number of edicts and decrees dealing with ethnic and economic unrest in the republics. The new Russian constitution, proposed by Yeltsin and approved in a referendum, continues this pattern of similar emergency powers for the executive.

To assist the president in his duties, the new executive arrangement created a Presidential Council and the Council of Federation. The former, whose members were to be appointed by the president and to operate under his direction, was "to elaborate measures" to implement domestic and foreign policy and to ensure the nation's security. Gorbachev's first Council seemed a lot like a replacement for the old party Politburo, as he named a combination of party and government officials and intellectuals. Once again, however, these changes were barely in place when they were replaced by others. When the new Cabinet of Ministers, mentioned above, was created and placed under the president's control, it replaced many of the functions of the Presidential Council.

The Federation Council was an attempt to create an organization at the central government level to deal with a country that was in danger of disintegrating in large part because of the nationality question. Headed by the president, its official members were the top government official (president) from each union republic. The leaders of the other subordinate nationality-based entities and the leaders of the USSR Supreme Soviet, although not members, were entitled to participate in the Council's deliberations. It was given a broad charge to recommend measures to implement the nationality policy, resolve ethnic disputes and conflicts, and ensure that the union republics and the groups they represented had a voice in the political process of the central government. One of the matters with which the Council dealt was Gorbachev's proposed union treaty, which

was an effort to hold the country together by spelling out the areas of responsibility of the republics and the central government. As expected, each side felt that the other wanted too much. The treaty stated that the republics would decide what powers the central government would have, but then proceeded to list more areas than the republics were willing to agree to.

In the process of these major government reorganizations, the long-standing problem of political succession was also addressed. Until recently, as is true in authoritarian systems, there were no formal procedures for naming a successor to the leader. Thus, when the top leader died, there were political struggles of varying length and intensity until the new leadership, and eventually the new leader, emerged. The provisions establishing the new presidency provided that if he were unable to carry out his duties, his powers would be assumed by the chairman of the USSR Supreme Soviet or next by the chairman of the Council of Ministers. In either case, the election of a new president was to take place within three months. Subsequently the position of vice president was established, and in December 1990, the Congress of People's Deputies named Gorbachev's choice, Communist Party official Gennady Yanayev, to that post. Thus, there was for the first time a formal line of succession.

THE SECOND RUSSIAN REVOLUTION

In early 1991, *Moscow News*, a weekly publication representing a reformist viewpoint, printed this banner front-page headline: "*Perestroika* Is Over." Barely a month earlier, on December 20, 1990, Foreign Minister Eduard Shevardnadze had stunned the Congress of People's Deputies by announcing: "I am resigning. Let it be my personal contribution—protest if you will—against dictatorship." "Reformers have gone and hidden in the bushes," he continued. "Dictatorship is coming." Shevardnadze and Gorbachev, friends since their youth, together had developed the foreign policies that had allowed the return of democracy to Eastern Europe, the end of the Cold War, and improved relations with the United States, and the domestic reform policies of *glasnost, perestroika,* and democratization. Thus, his dramatic warning about the concentration of power carried more impact than would have that of any other person. After his speech, however, there were statements by others sharing his concern about the drift toward repression and violence.

In his response, Gorbachev acknowledged that the Soviet Union was dealing with "strong power," but insisted that such actions should not be confused with dictatorship. As events unfolded following the Congress, however, it became increasingly obvious that the conservative elements affected most by the reforms were staging their counterattack. As those factions supporting change argued among themselves and criticized Gorbachev, a right-wing coalition was forming. It included reactionary Russian nationalists who opposed the influx of Western influences, and party hard-liners such as the newly formed Russian Communist Party (not to be confused with the CPSU). Another element was the military-industrial-security complex of the KGB, military leaders whose budgets and influence were being reduced, and the heavy industries related to the military. In fact, the position of the military in the political process appeared to be as strong as ever. The use of special military units earlier to deal with protests in the Georgian capital of Tbilisi had resulted in some 20 deaths. Then, within one week in January of 1991, Soviet elite military "black berets" staged a series of attacks, first on a radio and television center in Lithuania and then on a republic Interior

Ministry building in Latvia. The toll in this crackdown on the independence movements was another 20 people killed, with others wounded. It became increasingly obvious to both reformers and conservatives that the Gorbachev regime seemed to have fallen more and more under the influence of these conservative forces.

As the more open media, which had been spawned by his own policies of greater public discussion, began to criticize him for these and other measures, Gorbachev called for tighter restrictions, including the suspension of recently passed laws on freedom of the press. While the Supreme Soviet did not agree to a formal suspension of the law, a number of popular, alternative news and feature television shows were ended, and greater censorship was imposed. During most of the Gorbachev period, the influence of the military and KGB had been reduced, but faced with growing chaos, separatist movements, and a surge in street crimes, the president issued a series of law and order decrees. For example, the KGB would be allowed to search buildings with fewer restrictions, and members of the military would join militia members (police) in patrolling the streets of major cities.

This turn to the right caused a number of top advisers and key members of the reform movement either to resign or to be forced from their posts. Shevardnadze's dramatic resignation was soon followed by other departures. Former Politburo member Alexander Yakovlev, another of the architects of the original reforms, was dropped from the team, and Interior Minister Vadim Bakatin was forced out by hard-liners when he opposed the crackdowns. The list also contained two of the critical economic planners, including Stanislav Shatalin, the author of the 500-day plan for radical market-oriented reform. Although the Russian republic voted to begin implementing the plan in November 1990,

Gorbachev eventually backed down from it and then let Shatalin go. Gorbachev's top economic planner, Nikolai Petrakov, left in a more dramatic manner after joining other reformers in writing an open letter to *Moscow News,* in which they spoke of "opposing the onslaught of dictatorship and totalitarianism," and described a regime in its death throes, making a last-ditch stand by blocking economic reform, reinstating censorship, reviving demagoguery, and declaring war on the republics. It was this letter that Gorbachev cited in asking the Supreme Soviet to suspend the law on freedom of the press. When the Soviet objected, he did not push the point.

Communist Party conservatives, on the other hand, were encouraged by these developments. Reformers had set up new organizations, first to take advantage of the opening up of the political process and then to protest more recent reversals. For conservatives, the opposite was true. After seemingly losing ground to a liberalization process that downgraded its influence as well as that of groups such as the KGB and military, the party led these forces in a resurgence. In reaction to negative developments in the national party, a more hard-line Russian Communist Party was formed in 1990. At a meeting of national party leaders in the Kremlin in early 1991, the deputy chief of the CPSU, Vladimir Ivashko, declared that *perestroika* had been a setback, that Communists must fight harder against "destructive ideas and actions," and that there should be no more talk of things like a multiparty system.

In August 1991, when Gorbachev and the leaders of various union republics were about to sign the new union treaty transferring significant power from the central government to the republics, the conservative forces with which he had surrounded himself made their move in an attempted takeover of the government. In a development reminiscent of the 1964 removal of Khrushchev, Gorbachev was held hostage while resting in the Crimea. Perceived by many as a desperation move led by the very top officials of the defense, police, military, and party establishments, the coup had far-reaching consequences.

Of course, when the attempt failed, it led to the removal (or in some cases suicide) of the people involved, and the discrediting of the forces and agencies they represented. The minister of defense and the head of the KGB were among the committee that had attempted the takeover, and many others who were not actually involved, such as the foreign minister, "called in sick" the day after rather than opposing the coup. It is inconceivable in the short term that the military or KGB will be allowed to hold the power that they formerly enjoyed. The conspirators were replaced by lower-ranking officials whose primary qualification was that they had spoken out against the failed attempt, but in the years since they have never been punished.

The ultimate winner in the wake of the coup was Yeltsin, who the preceding summer had won popular election as president of the Russian republic. When Gorbachev was taken hostage, it was Yeltsin who became the hero by literally standing on a tank to rally the people and eventually causing the conspirators to back down. When Gorbachev returned to Moscow, he was a much weaker president heading a much weaker central government, and Yeltsin was giving the orders. Understandably, Gorbachev experienced something of a "conversion" as a result of his experience, and when he agreed with Yeltsin that more radical reform was necessary, the two men were able to form something of a partnership (with Yeltsin as the senior partner). Gorbachev's place in history as the man who acknowledged the system's problems and initiated the reform process is secure, but the reform process had passed him by, and the country had entered a new era with new leaders.

Because of the new relationship between the central government and the republics brought about by the failed coup and Gorbachev's rescue by Yeltsin, almost immediately people began to speak of the "former Soviet Union." For several years, the various republics had declared their independence from the USSR or demanded a greater degree of autonomy within a new arrangement of some type. By the end of 1991, the central government had recognized the full independence of the Baltic republics, and was negotiating with the remainder to establish a new set of economic, security, and political arrangements and structures. It became clear almost immediately that the size, functions, and revenue of the central government would be reduced as Yeltsin's Russian republic announced that it would assume many tasks formerly performed at the center and, accordingly, would reduce the amount of revenue that it had sent to that level. Then, as things continued to spin out of control, in December the Soviet Union was dissolved and replaced by 15 independent countries, some of which associated themselves as the new Commonwealth of Independent States.

While it will take years or even decades for the new structures and processes to become established in the former Soviet Union and the former Communist systems of Eastern Europe, political scientists and others have offered a number of observations about the dynamics involved in the collapse. The failed coup attempt and subsequent events produced a good news–bad news situation. On the bad news side was the fact that the central government institutions had failed as a source of resistance to the conspirators. When the heads of the Ministry of Defense, the KGB, and other top agencies staged the takeover, the Supreme Soviet and the heads of other agencies (such as the foreign minister) were either unable or unwilling to oppose them. In spite of the period of *glasnost*,

the media was also silent or silenced for the most part. Thus, the processes of democratization and *glasnost* had not yet progressed to the point at which political and social institutions could or would stand up to such an unconstitutional seizure of power. Perhaps true to the Russian culture, everyone else looked to one strong leader, in this case Boris Yeltsin, to save the day.

But there was also good news. The coup did not succeed in part because when Yeltsin stood up to the attempt, there were public rallies in support of the *popularly elected* president of the Russian republic, and in part because some elements of the military and the KGB refused to follow orders and take the bloody measures necessary to put down Yeltsin and his popular support. Apparently the reform measures initiated by Gorbachev had struck a responsive chord among at least some elements of both the people and the regime. These developments led some to the conclusion that more and more people now want a law-governed democratic society rather than the traditional authoritarian rule by the state or individuals, and that, with time, the prospects for democracy are good in the formerly Communist countries.

After the Soviet Union

The collapse of Communism and the Soviet Union created a whole new dynamic. There was a hope, perhaps even an expectation, that the result would be a fairly rapid transition to a more open society, a market-oriented economy, and a democratic political system. But events in the states of the former Soviet Union, the former Yugoslavia, and elsewhere quickly demonstrated that the process would be difficult and lengthy. Although the Communist systems might have been defeated, that very result raised the possibility of new struggles. The defeat of the antidemocratic Communism did not necessarily mean victory for democracy. The vacuum created might also be filled by the intolerance, civil war, and ethnic conflict that have accompanied a revival of nationalism, or by a return to the non-Communist but nevertheless authoritarian tradition of a thousand years of history. Yeltsin, for example, was successful in establishing the autonomy of the Russian republic from the central government, but when the Chechen-Ingush region (a Muslim area of over a million people) within the Russian federation declared its independence, his response was to declare the action illegal and send in troops. While the challenges facing these new states seem unending, one way to examine them is in terms of five of the major tasks. They must make the transition: (1) from an authoritarian to a democratic political system; (2) from a centralized command economy to a workable market-oriented one; and (3) from a largely closed and atomized society to a civic culture and a civil society. At the same time, they must: (4) find a way to deal with the explosive forces of nationalism and ethnic conflict; and (5) do all of the above in a proper, manageable manner and sequence.

The context in which these challenges must be undertaken is a difficult one. As Alexander Motyl[15] has pointed out, the successor states are having to deal at the same time with the end of totalitarianism and the end of empire. This, in turn, creates two contradictory forces with which they must cope. The collapse of the Russian Empire creates the desire for and possibility of rapid and fundamental change in the direction of new forms of political and socioeconomic systems and organizations. However, the end of totalitarianism reveals a legacy that undermines the ability of the leadership to undertake that radical change and of the population to tolerate it. As discussed in Chapter 6, the goal of such systems is the central control of the entire society and the atomization of society by preventing the type of social organizations that characterize a civil society as it is normally defined. Thus, the irony of the collapse of such systems is that they deny their successors the institutions and resources needed to create a new system and the public support needed to endure the inevitable hardships involved in the transition. The challenge, as Motyl puts it, is not in the transformation of existing social, economic, and political institutions, but in their wholesale creation.

Building Democracy

Timothy Colton has divided the 15 new states created by the breakup of the USSR into what he calls *protodemocracies* and *predemocracies* based primarily on whether they meet the primary procedural conditions of democracy with respect to the holding of fair, honest competitive elections in which all are free to organize and participate.[16] Using this standard, he placed 6 of the 15, containing about three-quarters of the population, in the first group: Russia, Ukraine, Armenia, and the Baltic states of Estonia, Latvia, and Lithuania. To varying degrees, this group met the criteria even under the parliamentary and presidential elections conducted in 1990–91, when the Communists were still a factor, as anti-Communist reform groups formed "popular fronts" and either won the elections outright or at least won a plurality. Although these states are on the right path and setting the pace, they are "incomplete, unstable, and unconsolidated democracies-in-the making" where democracy is still, in Colton's words, "breathtakingly immature."

Incomplete as the protodemocracies are, they are farther along than the predemocracies, which consist of the remaining quarter of the total population, divided among the nine states of Belarus, Moldova, Georgia, Azerbaijan, and the Central Asian areas of Kazakhstan, Kyrgyzstan, Tajikistan, Turkmenistan, and Uzbekistan. While the members of this group have adopted more democratic forms, it would be difficult to describe their elections as fair and competitive. In many cases the former *nomenklatura* officials from the Communist era have had little trouble manipulating the election process and results in order to keep themselves in office and reform elements to a small minority. In some cases, such as Georgia, a state of virtual civil war has made much progress impossible. For these countries, real democracy is probably not in the near future.

The electoral process has always been viewed as the critical test of democracy. Communist countries always held elections, but they were never open or competitive. One definition of a democractic system is one in which parties *lose* elections and abide by the results by relinquishing power. This is in contrast to cases in which elections are held, but people only abide by the results if they win, and the losing side may take to the streets and resort to revolution. Samuel Huntington takes the definition one step further in his "two turnover" test. Under this notion, the process of losing an election and relinquishing power must happen twice. Not only must the original holders of power give it up, but those who defeated them must not simply replace them indefinitely. True consolidation of democracy requires some alternation of office. One difficulty with this standard is the time required to judge the progress of democracy if, for example, presidential elections are only held every four or five years.

Even if they are successful in creating a fair system of elections, these new states have a long way to go to take advantage of them. The Communist Party was the only one with an institutional power base and political skills, so it enters all elections with an organizational advantage. The potential opposition forces must start from scratch. Thus, they tend to be broad social movements rather than organized political parties, and there is a greater possibility that their appeal will be of a more radical, populist, and even demagogic nature, denouncing everything about the current system and leadership. In addition, leaders make their appeal more directly to the masses on a much more personal level, rather than to a political party constituency. Thus extreme nationalistic appeals can be made by people such as Vladimir Zhironovsky. In the December 1993 elections that were a referendum on his leadership, Yeltsin took the position that as president he should remain above partisan politics. Like everything else, it will take time to develop a coherent political party system.

In addition to establishing an open, pluralistic electoral system, democracy involves setting up institutions and building relationships among those institutions and their leaders. The highly centralized, authoritarian nature of the political and economic systems in the Soviet period was a major cause of their downfall. Since the breakup, however, there is a question of whether they have gone from one extreme of powerful agencies like the KGB to the other, in what appears to be disorder and a lack of adequate government control even in basic law enforcement. One evidence of this is increased crime. A by-product of a police state is that ordinary citizens are relatively safe from ordinary street crimes. In recent years, however, that has not been the case in the former USSR. Increasingly, the question is raised whether economic activity is under the control of the government or of organized crime (the *mafiya*). The *Washington Post* in early 1995 quoted President Yeltsin as telling the parliament that "the overwhelming majority of Russians are haunted by an oppressive feeling of defenselessness before criminals," and the Russian Security Council as reporting that "the lack of tangible results from the battle against organized crime is discrediting state powers

... and, as a result, threatening the security of Russia."[17] The situation in the Caucasus area of Georgia has been described as a culture of violence, as an elected president was forced from office by warfare, and civil war has become the norm.

In addition to this question of whether there is enough government control, both political and economic power continue to be increasingly fragmented and regional. The centrifugal forces that led to the disintegration of the Soviet Union still seem to be at work. The Russian Federation, as its name indicates, has all the problems of federalism. With the few but conspicuous exceptions of areas such as Tatarstan and Chechnya, its 89 regional subdivisions are not seeking independence from Russia. They are, however, demanding greater autonomy with respect to Moscow. The 1993 Russian constitution did not grant them much of this autonomy, but this will be a continuing problem to be resolved.

As it is in any political system, a critical dimension of the political dynamic will be working out a satisfactory relationship between the president and the legislature of the various successor states. This is a difficult challenge even in long-established democracies. France, for example, has alternated between periods of strong executive dominance and periods in which the parliament has played a larger role. In the Soviet era, legislatures were little more than rubber stamps controlled by the party. Since the Gorbachev reforms, they have become multiparty, and have, to widely varying degrees, gained some power to deliberate and make policy. A pattern has emerged, especially in Russia and Ukraine, of the president pushing reform (especially economic) and the legislature resisting.

Consider, for example, the confrontation in 1993 between Yeltsin and the Congress of People's Deputies, led by Ruslan Khasbulatov. When the hard-line Congress continued to obstruct his attempts at economic reform, he eventually tried to dissolve both it and the smaller Supreme Soviet; he also suspended the constitution as well as Khasbulatov's ally, Vice President Alexander Rutskoi. The legislature in turn declared that Yeltsin was no longer president and replaced him with the vice president. After about a two-week standoff, the parliamentary leaders urged their followers to resort to violence to overthrow Yeltsin. In an incident seen on live television around the world, Yeltsin called in the military, and tanks fired on the parliament building (known as the White House), leaving it on fire and its leaders defeated and in jail. Yeltsin himself ran the government for about three months, until elections were held to choose a new legislature and approve a new constitution. (During the election, Yeltsin declared that the media could discuss the proposed constitution as long as they were not critical of it!) The constitution, which was approved, reminded many of the French pattern. It set up an executive-oriented system, giving the president power to declare a state of emergency and to dissolve the state *duma* (legislature) created in the new system. The point, of course, is that democracy involves bargaining, compromise, and a give-and-take process, not the violent confrontation (and even civil war) often found in the states under consideration. In the 1993 parliamentary election, opposition groups, such as the hard-line former Communists and extreme nationalists such as Zhironovsky, got almost as many votes as those backing Yeltsin and reform.

A similar institutional executive-legislative confrontation took place in Ukraine in 1994. Leonid Kravchuk was president and Leonid Kuchma was prime minister—both elected back in the Soviet period. In this case, Kuchma was the economic reformer, and Kravchuk, a former Communist ideological leader, and the legislature were in favor of only slow change. In the midst of near economic collapse and pressure from striking coal miners, new elections were held. Once again, there was a mixed result. Kuchma, the reformer, was elected president (a turnover of power by the more conservative Kravchuk), but the new parliament was dominated by conservatives. Thus, while there are very critical policy issues to be dealt with, these systems are still engaged primarily in an institutional struggle for power.

Economic Transition

You may have noticed that the institutional conflict discussed in the last section centered on the issue of economic reform. With no tradition to fall back on, the attempt to establish political democracy would be difficult under the best of circumstances. Unfortunately, the states of the former Soviet Union have the worst of circumstances. Democracy must be developed under conditions of a deteriorating economy and increasing nationalism and ethnic conflict.

Poor and declining economic performance was one of the major contributors to the end of the USSR. Khrushchev had undertaken reform measures earlier, and Gorbachev undertook *perestroika* in an effort to rescue the economy from the stagnation he had inherited. When conditions continued to go downhill, he eventually was less popular in his own country than he was when he visited other parts of the world. With the end of the Communist system, there was once again hope that the economy would improve. However, "two years after the breakup of the Soviet Union, none of its former republics had achieved positive economic growth."[18] By the usual measures, such as gross domestic product, economic activity continued to decline. Some of them experienced hyperinflation, with inflation rates of over 1,000 percent a year not unusual. In early 1995, the Russian government reported with pride that the monthly inflation rate was down from 15 to 10 percent. We will examine briefly some of the features of the old system inherited by the new states, and then some of the problems and prospects facing them.

Marxism-Leninism, the ideology on which the Soviet Union was based, placed economic factors and relationships at the core of all elements of society. Thus, when the system failed, it was as much an economic failure as anything. As was true in the political realm, old practices and institutions would have to be replaced by entirely new ones. The Soviet Union had what is known as a command economy, rather than a market economy. In essence, this meant that all decisions about planning, prices, wages, currency value, etc., would be made arbitrarily by order of the central authorities rather than by market forces. A state planning agency (Gosplan) would draw up a five-year plan directing what the various sectors of the economy were to produce. The price of such items as public transportation, basic foodstuffs, and housing were kept artificially low through subsidies. The unit of currency (ruble) was made nonconvertible. That is, rather than having its value set in relation to other currencies on the international market, the ruble was worth what the government said it was worth, and no one could bring rubles into the country or take them out. Inefficient factories and businesses were allowed to operate so that everyone would have the security of a job. According to the ideology, the root of exploitation is ownership of private property. Thus, individuals could only own personal and household property. Factories, farms, real estate, etc., were to be owned and operated in common (such as collective farms) or by the state. That way all would benefit, and no one would be in a position to exploit others through employer-employee or landlord-tenant relationships.

It is not difficult to see the radical and traumatic measures required to move from this type of system to a market-oriented one with private property. Subsidies must be lifted, prices allowed to rise, inefficient enterprises shut down with the resulting unemployment, businesses put into private hands, greater competition introduced, and decision making decentralized. The Soviet system was inefficient, but the emphasis was on economic security. The quality and amount of housing and food might not be great, but most people's basic needs were being met, and they were protected from risks. Everyone had access to a job, even if it meant substantial underemployment and waste. Starting the transition to a market economy could mean greater opportunity or loss of a job and housing and higher prices. To date, the consensus seems to be that while some entrepreneurs who know how to use the changes have gained from them, more people are disillusioned and worse off than before the reforms. While those of us who have grown up in a market economy see the opportunity aspect of the market, those who have known only the Communist system may see the new conditions as threatening their former security and allowing others to take advantage of them.

There have been several approaches proposed to make the economic transition. The critical factors are sequence and timing. The method proposed in the Gorbachev period, known as the Shatalin, or 500-day, plan, laid out a specific sequence of steps to be completed within 500 days. This included a massive sale of state holdings and assets, followed by a gradual lifting of price controls on all but the most essential goods, decentralized decision making, gradual privatization of much of the economy, reform of tax and banking systems, etc. Both Gorbachev and Yeltsin initially endorsed the Shatalin plan, but both subsequently backed down because

of the political instability of the period. In contrast to the sequential approach of the 500-day plan, Yegor Gaidar advocated what is known as the "big bang" or "shock therapy" approach, which called for putting into effect the full range of reforms immediately and simultaneously. He argued that a piecemeal approach would not work because the time in between the various steps would cause them to lose their effect. Privatization, price decontrol, currency and banking reform, etc., all must be done together.

Which approach to use poses a dilemma for policy makers. If they follow the path of radical economic reform, as Russia has attempted to do for the most part, it may very well lead to massive social and political discontent made possible by the simultaneous effort to create a more open and democratic society. Anticipating this reaction, the other choice is to seek to preserve social and political stability by slowing economic reform. This path, chosen to a greater extent by Ukraine, may well result in continued deterioration of the economy. The dilemma is caused to some extent by the need for both political and economic reform. Stability in either area would make subsequent reform of the other much easier.

As is true for the political realm, the results so far have been mixed, with some states making beter progress than others. There is still a great need to build the legal and financial infrastructures required to support a stable economy. Private property rights and contracts must have greater protection, and the banking and currency systems leave much to be desired. In the physical realm, plants and machinery are often obsolete, and all of the former Communist countries are ecological disasters. Environmental protection normally increases costs, and since there was such an emphasis on increasing production with relatively scarce resources, environmental considerations were completely ignored. There has been significant privatization, but the term "quasiprivatization" has been used to indicate that in many cases the benefits have gone not to ordinary people but to members of the elite who managed things under the old system. Paralleling the political trend, there has been a decrease in overall economic activity and production, and the decline in and fragmentation of central political authority has been accompanied by a similar regionalization of economic power. In Russia, for example, areas such as Tatarstan have set up tariffs, asserted some degree of local control over their natural resources, and attempted to withhold revenues from the central government.

Creating a Civic Culture and a Civil Society

Underlying the effort to develop the institutions of democracy and market economics, and vital to its success, is the question of attitudes. As Sabrina Petra Ramet puts it, the political coloration of the old or new order is not as critical in the process as is the need for social consensus, and the legacy of decaying systems is a breakdown of the consensus concerning values.[19] Neither prerevolutionary Russia nor the Soviet Union had a tradition of values such as pluralism, tolerance, trust, compromise, and participation, which lead to and support democracy. In the Soviet period, there was an attempt to remake the traditional Russian culture in accordance with the principles of Communism and Marxism-Leninism. When that system failed, there was a vacuum of sorts for many people. Unfortunately, the collapse of the old order does not necessarily mean the emergence of a new consensus. In fact, the end of an authoritarian regime has seemed to lead to an identity crisis and to have opened the door for a free-for-all among Communists, democrats, extreme nationalists, neofascists, and others. Some, such as Alexander Solzhenitsyn, call

for a return to traditional Russian culture and values (which were never very democratic); others call for a restoration of the Russian Empire (by force if necessary); while still others look more to emulate Western ideas and institutions.

What is needed for democracy is the establishment of what is known as a civic culture, a certain pattern of attitudes and behavior.[20] In the ideal civic culture, there is a level of involvement and activity by citizens, but it is balanced by a degree of noninvolvement and passivity. The citizens' commitment and support (or lack thereof) are based not only on the actual performance of a particular leader or government, but go beyond to support the system itself, independent of performance (sometimes known as diffuse support). Attitudes toward the political system are supplemented by a level of trust in the broader society and its organizations. There is, thus, a supportive spirit that includes participation based on the belief that one can make a difference, a certain level of trust in government and other people, and an expectation that government will serve society's interests.

The development of a civic culture is tied to the development of civil society, which has been defined as "a dense network of nongovernmental associations and groups established for the autonomous pursuit of diverse socioeconomic interests and prepared to rebuff state efforts to take control of these activities."[21] Such groups include labor unions, business and professional organizations, the media, churches, and political parties, which serve as a counterweight to government and that institutionalize the civic culture.

This is where the Soviet Union's authoritarian, totalitarian history becomes relevant. One result of that system is the lack of autonomous societal institutions and the attitudes that support them. The Communist Party claimed a monopoly on societal representation and the political system. Although there were various types of organizations, such as trade and writers unions, youth and women's groups, and scientific academies, they were little more than auxiliary arms of the party. They served as "transmission belts" to mobilize the people to do the party's will, but not to operate in their own right. Thus, the legacy of the old system is a lack of the institutional preconditions of democracy. Democracy and market economics involve bargaining and negotiation between the government and supportive nongovernmental organizations and among these organizations. In their absence, there tends to be continued personal rule by an elite, and the public feels excluded and alienated. So, once again, there is a need to create the attitudes and institutions conducive to democracy. As was indicated in Chapter 5, the lesson from Germany seems to suggest that such changes in attitude are generational. In this case, it may mean that the older portion of the population living away from the major urban centers may have the hardest time adapting, while the younger, more urban segment may make the transition more easily.

In earlier chapters we have spoken of corporatism and in particular of whether that approach had relevance to understanding the political dynamics of the former USSR. Bao-hui Zhang has suggested that corporatist authoritarian regimes, such as Brazil or Spain, have a distinct advantage over totalitarian ones, such as the former Soviet Union or China, in an attempted move toward democracy.[22] While corporatist institutions are not autonomous, Zhang describes them as "semi-official and semi-societal," which means that they do provide a mechanism to negotiate the necessary political pacts among societal interests that totalitarian systems were not willing to form. Colton predicts that we will see more of the form of corporatism exhibited already in Russia—the government conducting privileged negotiations with established, but not necessarily representative or democratic, groups about how to allocate resources and implement economic reforms.[23]

NATIONALISM AND ETHNIC CONFLICT

As if all of the challenges already mentioned did not create enough of a challenge, they must be accomplished in the highly charged atmosphere of national and ethnic tensions. Russia and the Soviet Union were diverse empires, but the ethnic strife was kept in check to a large extent by the authoritarian nature of their social and political systems. It is often suggested, as well, that there was an implicit social agreement. In exchange for the regime providing an acceptable level of security and material well-being, there was a relative silence of ethnic and other opposition. The virtual disintegration of central authority and economic production has created a whole new dynamic in which nationalism has come to the fore, and ancient ethnic quarrels and hatreds are being acted out. The various newly independent states involved must discover their new identities.

A certain amount of national pride and identity are necessary and healthy, but too much or too little is a problem. Some Russians cannot accept Russia as less than an empire—or at least one including Ukraine and Belarus. Others display extreme chauvinism, seeing the "real" Russia as being destroyed by contact with the values of the West. Nationalism can be inclusive or exclusive. Ukraine is an excellent example of the former. In the Soviet period, there were many ethnic Russians living in the non-Russian areas for the purpose of maintaining Russian control. With the end of the USSR, these Russians are now ethnic minorities living in a foreign country. About a fifth of the population of Ukraine is composed of ethnic Russians. How should they now be treated by those they formerly dominated? Over the objections of some nationalist elements, Ukraine has taken the inclusive approach of emphasizing territory rather than ethnicity, referring to all residents as "People of Ukraine," and guaranteeing equal political rights to all, regardless of ethnic origin. The Baltic states of Estonia and Latvia have taken a more exclusive approach. Automatic citizenship is granted only to those who had lived in those countries before World War II and the Soviet takeover. All others must apply for naturalized citizenship, which includes a residency requirement and may be refused for political reasons related to the Soviet period.

In other parts of the former Soviet Union, the question is not so much that of inclusive or exclusive nationalism, but whether there is a sense of nationalism at all. In Central Asia, which is the least modernized and urbanized area, identity and loyalty may be to something higher than or less than the nation-state. Higher, or supranational, identities may stress their pan-Turkic cultural or Islamic religious ties, both of which transcend political boundaries. At the other extreme are lower, or subnational, feelings. The sense of national consciousness may be weak because of a greater loyalty to such groups as clan, tribe, family, or region. The Caucasus area has been a lesson in how national governments have been drawn into sub- or supranational conflicts, as the sense of nationalism has been overwhelmed by civil war in Georgia, and by war between Armenia and Azerbaijan over the ethnic-religious question of Nagorno-Karabakh.

THE QUESTION OF TIMING

We have mentioned in earlier chapters the importance of timing in establishing the legitimacy of a system and in dealing with soci-etal problems. These formerly Communist regimes have the worst of all possible situations. The process of converting from authoritarianism to democracy and from a command economy to a market economy would be difficult under the best of circumstances. But the very reason the conversion is taking place at all is the terrible circumstances surrounding the collapse of one type of system. A well-established regime would have great difficulty solving the economic and ethnic problems that now exist. The conflict produces some interesting dilemmas. To attempt to deal effectively with the economic and ethnic crises, Yeltsin asked for and received emergency powers to suspend temporarily some of the aspects of democracy (such as elections and demonstrations). In another case, the power to make decisions regarding the export of certain commodities was transferred from a government ministry to a private agency. When it was alleged that the new agency was exporting too much and short-changing Russians, however, the government ministry was put back in charge. There also continue to be indications that while we in the United States admire capitalist success stories, there is still great popular resentment in the Soviet Union and the People's Republic of China against the economic success of managers and entrepreneurs.

As if the magnitude of the tasks facing these countries is not enough, if Alexander Motyl is right, they must be done in a certain, necessary order. Democracy, he suggests, is the final step in the process. First must come the political development of a strong, healthy state in which the rule of law prevails. Then comes the establishment of civil society, a network of autonomous social organizations acting as a counterweight to the state, with both operating under the rules and regulations set up by the rule of law. The rule of law and civil society make possible the development and operation of a modern market economy.

While the institutions and facade of democracy can be set up anytime, the argument is that genuine democracy can only be consolidated after all of the above have been accomplished. The difficulty, as we have suggested, is that in many cases the countries involved are starting from scratch—political, social, and economic institutions and patterns must be created, and the entire process will take decades if not generations. In the meantime, both the people affected and outside observers like the West may be expecting and even demanding immediate democracy and market economics.

CONCLUSION: A LOOK BACK AND AHEAD

We began the chapter by asking whether authoritarian Communist systems could cope with the increasingly complex dynamics of modernization. At the time of the Russian revolution in 1917, there were great hopes for this grand social and political experiment. Seventy-five years later, the experiment had failed, the Soviet Union had disintegrated, and the focus of study is on the period and process of transition to whatever will succeed Communism. Against a background of a thousand years of historical and cultural development, and a 75 year experimentation with Communism, Russia and the other new states of the former Soviet Union offer a veritable laboratory in which political scientists and others can examine many of the classic questions, such as how transitions to democracy are accomplished.

Some historians and others like to speak of history as moving in cycles. In a sense, that was the experience of the Soviet Union. One can speak of conservatives and reformers or in other terms, but there seem to have been alternating periods. The repressive, inward-looking "socialism in one country" approach

of Stalin was followed by "the thaw" and innovations of the Khrushchev years. Khrushchev, in turn, was accused of "harebrained scheming," and ousted by a group of conservative bureaucrats and party hacks who made an art of corruption, growing old together in office, and stagnation. After the passing of this old guard, it was Mikhail Gorbachev who stepped up to center stage in 1985, and declared that the system was in serious trouble and needed restructuring and "new thinking."

The early focus of the Gorbachev reforms was the disastrous economic state in which the country found itself. To deal with the economic crisis, Gorbachev introduced his restructuring measures. The classic method used in the Soviet Union to increase productivity was to add more capital or workers. Gorbachev took a somewhat different direction in placing the initial emphasis on making better use of the existing resources by fighting the corruption, alcoholism, and inefficiency that had become an integral part of the system. When things actually got worse rather than better, he and other reformers were forced in the direction of reforming the basic features of the system itself. Proposals were developed such as Stanislav Shatalin's 500-day plan for making the transition from a command to a market economy, but when the moment of truth came, the conservatives were not willing to adopt it, and Gorbachev compromised. As a consequence, the economic crisis grew even worse. The shortages became so severe that nearly all food items, including basic commodities such as tobacco, sugar, grain, and meat, had to be rationed. Although Moscow was exempted for as long as possible, widespread rationing was imposed on the capital in early 1991.

As we saw in Tiananmen Square in the summer of 1989, it is difficult to separate economic reform from its political component. Since the Communist Party had claimed a privileged position in leading society, when the system did not perform, the party began to lose its credibility. When the party apparatus was then perceived as resisting the changes proposed to remedy the economic problems, it was further discredited. In response, Gorbachev initiated basic changes in the political process. First there was massive turnover in party officials in an attempt to make them more responsive. When that failed, the role of the party in the directing of the society was downgraded, and power was transferred to government agencies. Elections were changed from the former single-candidate arrangement to multicandidate, limited fixed terms of office were established, and party and government meetings were opened to public debate and criticism. Of course, it is one thing to establish more open democratic procedures, and quite another really to implement them in a culture that has no experience with the dynamics of democracy. In a final move that some saw as necessary, and others as ominous, a new office of president was created and given extraordinary powers to deal with the economic crisis and social instability.

While Gorbachev was concentrating on the economic restructuring and the changes in the political process necessary to effect economic change, his policy of encouraging freer and more open discussion facilitated the creation of the other major crisis. The nationality problem, in the form of ethnic conflicts and independence movements, literally tore the country apart. Led by the successful demand of the Lithuanian, Latvian, and Estonian republics for complete independence, all of the republics called for some change in their relationship with the central government. Responses to that problem included economic sanctions, military intervention, discussion, and negotiation within the framework of the Council of Federation, referendums by the central government and union republics on whether to preserve the union, and extensive negotiations on a new treaty of union to establish new and creative economic and political arrangements among the republics and between them and the central government. When Gorbachev and the central government refused to undertake radical economic reform on a nationwide basis, President Yeltsin of Russia announced that the largest and most populous republic would proceed on its own, and suggested that the republics should by-pass Moscow and deal with one another directly.

By the end of 1990, all of these manifestations of modernization and nationalism had taken the Soviet Union to the brink of disaster. Five years of *perestroika* had introduced a number of political and social changes, but Gorbachev stopped half-way when he refused to adopt radical economic changes in the direction of a market-oriented system. As a resuslt, living standards grew worse, and the worst food rationing since World War II was imposed throughout the country. The accompanying policy of greater openness and public discussion had unleashed longstanding feelings of extreme Russian nationalism, anti-Semitism, and interethnic hatred, the eventual result of which was violent clashes. In addition, there was the matter of law and order in general. One of the consolations of an authoritarian system is that the rate of violent crime is generally low. A further indication that the whole system was drifting toward chaos was the generally acknowleged dramatic increase in violent street crimes. On a personal level, a curious situation developed with respect to Gorbachev. While his popularity within the Soviet Union fell to almost nothing as the people blamed his reforms for the worsening conditions, he retained such respect in the outside world that he was awarded the Nobel Peace Prize for foreign policy moves such as the liberation of Eastern Europe and progress on arms limitations.

In the midst of these deteriorating economic and social conditions, it was not surprising that the emphasis shifted from reform to the restoration of stability, the preservation of law and order, and the survival of the country. Unfortunately, those issues played right into the hands of the conservatives, and the Soviet Union made a turn to the political right, which resulted in the failed coup in August 1991. For years, discussions of the eventual outcome of developments in the Soviet Union posed three main possibilities. It could go in the direction of reverting to a greater degree of central authority, coercion, and repression; choose the path leading to some form of pluralist socialist democracy; or continue to muddle through.

The critical and worsening economic and social conditions, Gorbachev's response to them in the reforms of *perestroika, glasnost,* and *democratization,* and the eventual coup attempt of the conservatives in response to his changes eliminated the muddling-through option. At least as far as the Soviet Union and Eastern Europe are concerned, Communism failed and collapsed. That makes the question one of whether the next stage and the eventual outcome will be some creative new version of authoritarianism or a move in the direction of pluralist democracy.

With the breakup of the Soviet Union, 15 independent countries must deal with the old questions of political and economic reform, ethnic conflict, etc., while at the same time working out a new dynamic among themselves. Russia is the key, and there is a degree of interdependence, but each has its distinct set of circumstances. In general, the Baltic states, with more favorable internal factors and a more sympathetic reception from the European democracies, are considered as having the best chance at a successful outcome. At the other end of the path are the Central Asian countries. They are the poorest, least modern and developed predemocracies, and their reform has been the slowest. Military conflict in the Caucasus area has tended to overshadow everything else, making political, economic, or social reform very difficult. For obvious reasons, much attention has been focused on Russia as it attempts the transition. While everyone agrees that there will not be a return to Communism, there are varying degrees of optimism and pessimism about the eventual outcome. Stable democracy requires a certain level of economic performance and social stability (civic culture and civil society), which Russia does not yet have. The fear is that continued delay, political fragmentation and conflict between president and parliament, declining economic production, and increased social disorder in the form of crime and ethnic conflict all will lead to the authoritarian temptation. Opposition leaders such as Vladimir Zhirinovski thrive on conditions that allow them to tap into fear and anxiety and to appeal to extreme nationalism and a need to return to law and order and security through a strong ruler.

The Case of Chechnya

In many ways the tragic case of Chechnya is a microcosm of many of the problems facing Russia and the other new states of the former Soviet Union. Located in a hotbed of ethnic unrest in the southwestern part of Russia, in the northern Caucasus, it has a Muslim population of about a million. As the Soviet Union was breaking up, the centrifugal forces of nationalism continued as a number of smaller ethnic areas declared their sovereignty and independence of both the Soviet Union and Russia. When Chechnya did so in 1991, President Yeltsin (who himself had led the drive for Russia's independence of the USSR) declared a state of emergency in the area and threatened the use of troops. This provoked a confrontation with the Russian legislature (led by Ruslan Khasbulatov-a Chechen), which opposed such use of force, and Yeltsin settled for negotiations. In 1992, after the formal dissolution of the USSR, Yeltsin proposed a new federal treaty to define the relationship between Russia's central government and its constituent units. Chechnya, along with several others, reaffirmed its independence and refused to sign. Together with several other areas, it also announced plans to implement its own local currency and taxes, and to control its own natural resources, in this case petroleum.

This stalemate continued until the end of 1994, when Yeltsin decided it could no longer be tolerated and ordered a military invasion to put down the rebellion. The main confrontation lasted for months, left the city of Grozny a wasteland, and cost thousands of lives. A guerrilla-type resistance is likely to last for years. The fallout from this decision has been endless. Internally, it cost Yeltsin the political support of many groups, such as the Civic Union, that had previously backed him, and confirmed for many the suspicion that he was no democrat and would continue to settle issues in an autocratic and military manner. The invasion also rallied Chechnya's neighbors and worried ethnic groups throughout the former Soviet Union as to their treatment by Russia. Given the state of its economy, the last thing Russia needs to do is engage in civil war. Questions were also raised about the influence of the military on policy making and the status of the military overall. There were reports at the time that one source of guns for the Chechnyans was members of the Russian army who, at the end of their tour of duty, would sell their weapons to the rebels.

This resort to the use of force also had international implications. It will be very difficult for Russia and the other new states to solve their economic problems without help from international economic organizations and bilateral aid. Russia has sought a role in world affairs through eventual membership in security arrangements such as NATO, and economic representation in the meetings and decisions of the "group of seven" leading industrial countries. Those responsible for such help reacted very negatively to the events in Chechnya. As a result of the level of violence, President Clinton threatened to cancel a planned summit meeting, and opponents of aid to Russia were able to call into question the fundamental intentions and direction of developments in that country.

The changes in the last decade with respect to the failure of Communism and the disintegration of the Soviet Union have been absolutely breath-taking. The new states are engaged in what will be a lengthy and difficult transition to a new era. For those involved it is a very challenging and trying time, with varying prospects for success. For those of us looking on, it is a fascinating opportunity to observe how they create new social, economic, and political institutions and attitudes and handle issues such as nationalism and ethnic conflict.

NOTES

1. Gerardo Munck, "Democratic Transitions in Comparative Perspective," *Comparative Politics*, vol. 26, no. 3 (April 1994), pp. 355–75.
2. Andrei Amalrik, *Will the Soviet Union Survive Until 1984?* (New York: Harper & Row, 1970), pp. 32–33.
3. Hugh Seton-Watson, *The Russian Empire, 1801–1917* (London: Oxford University Press, 1967), p. 10.
4. Michael Florinsky, *Russia: A History and an Interpretation* (New York: The Macmillan Company, 1953), p. 415.
5. Alex Inkeles, *Social Change in Soviet Russia* (New York: Simon and Schuster, 1968); Henry Dicks, "Observations on Contemporary Russian Behavior," *Human Relations*, vol. 5, no. 2 (1952), pp. 111–75.
6. Inkeles, *Social Change*, p. 127.
7. See, for example, Allen Kassof, "The Administered Society: Totalitarianism Without Terror," *World Politics*, vol. 16 (July 1964), p. 559.

8. Amalrik, *Will the Soviet Union Survive?* p. 33.

9. Quoted in *Newsweek*, February 12, 1990, p. 37.

10. Ronald Inglehart, *Culture Shift in Advanced Industrial Societies* (Princeton: Princeton University Press, 1990).

11. Milovan Djilas, *The New Class* (New York: Praeger Publishers, 1957), esp. chap. 3.

12. Michael Gehlen, *The Communist Party of the Soviet Union: A Functional Analysis* (Bloomington: Indiana University Press, 1969), esp. chap. 1.

13. Jerome Gilison, *British and Soviet Politics* (Baltimore: The Johns Hopkins University Press, 1972).

14. Donald Barry and Carol Barner-Barry, *Contemporary Soviet Politics: An Introduction* (Englewood Cliffs, NJ: Prentice Hall, 1991), p. 125.

15. Alexander Motyl, *Dilemmas of Independence: Ukraine After Totalitarianism* (New York: Council on Foreign Relations, 1993), esp. chap. 2.

16. Timothy Colton, "Politics," in Timothy Colton and Robert Legvold, eds., *After the Soviet Union: From Empire to Nations* (New York: W. W. Norton & Company, 1992), pp. 17–48.

17. *The Washington Post Weekly Edition,* March 20–26, 1995, pp. 4, 6ff.

18. Carol Barner-Barry and Cynthia Hody, *The Politics of Change: The Transformation of the Former Soviet Union* (New York: St. Martin's Press, 1995), p. 196.

19. Sabrina Petra Ramet, ed., *Adaptation and Transformation in Communist and Post-Communist Systems* (Boulder, CO: Westview Press, 1992), chap. 10.

20. For a fuller discussion of the concept, see Gabriel Almond and Sidney Verba, *The Civic Culture: Political Attitudes and Democracy in Five Nations* (Boston: Little, Brown and Company, 1965).

21. Karen Dawisha and Bruce Parrott, *Russia and the New States of Eurasia: The Politics of Upheaval* (Cambridge: Cambridge University Press, 1994), p. 125.

22. Baohui Zhang, "Corporatism, Totalitarianism, and Transitions to Democracy," *Comparative Political Studies*, vol. 27, no. 1 (April 1994), pp. 108–36.

23. Colton, "Politics," p. 46–47.

8

The Nature of Political Development in The People's Republic of China

POLITICAL CULTURE AND HISTORY: THE SOCIOCULTURAL CONTEXT OF CHINA'S POLICIES AND INSTITUTIONS

In the era of Chinese Communist Party rule (1949 to the present), China's culture has been a critical force in shaping the country's policies, problems, and developmental issues. Most modernized states have seen their cultures reshaped in an evolutionary, incremental way over 100 years or more (even if perhaps pockmarked with revolutionary bursts), and most have, in fact, consciously participated in the restructuring of their cultures. But China's traditional culture remained remarkably coherent and untouched, even as the forces of modernization pounded on its doors. When China's rulers conceded the need for development in the late nineteenth century, its traditional culture proved unusually resistant to change. To this day, most of its values and beliefs persist. Even as China's culture undergoes repeated assaults from foreign values and rapid social and economic change, it remains recognizably and definably "Chinese."[1] In the face of major social, economic, and political up-

heaval, and the nearly complete erosion of Marxism-Leninism-Mao Zedong Thought as the political text that defined the society's ideals, its culture may, in fact, be the critical element holding China together today.

REBELLION AND AUTHORITARIANISM

This is stunning testimony to the strength of Chinese culture, for at many times in its more than 2,000-year documented history, and certainly for more than 100 years preceding the Chinese Communist victory in 1949, China had been a seething, boiling pot of discontent, anger, chaos, revolution, and war. Beneath it all, and perhaps underlying China's inability to cope either with the outside world or with the internal issues of development that would have mitigated the revolutionary impulse, was the deep-rooted, change-resistant tradition of China.

Yet that very same tradition—which is so rich and complex that it would require volumes to address its substantial repertoire of culturally acceptable themes and attitudes—has provided a powerful glue for holding

China together against centrifugal forces. Chinese culture has, moreover, been flexible enough to allow its core themes and values to be interpreted in ways that are compatible with the modern pulse. Ironically, it appears that when the Chinese rebelled, they were not consciously rebelling against their various traditions of authoritarianism, which included the following:

- the absolutism of emperors who ruled with the "mandate of heaven"
- hierarchical values of superior-inferior, subordination, loyalty, and obedience
- the power of officials over ordinary people
- the administration by bureaucrats steeped in little other than Confucian morality, language, the classics, and poetry
- the lack of a critical outside role for intellectuals, who were mere servants of the state and were, in fact, absorbed into the official ruling class rather than serving an independent role
- general illiteracy caused by the inaccessibility of education to all but the wealthy (or the singularly lucky boy chosen and supported by his clan)
- an historical predisposition toward secrecy and, with it, a lack of accountability
- the isolationist, antiforeign, and centralized ruler-centered society

Rather, they were rebelling against the *results* of the system that arose out of Chinese culture and tradition characterized by

- the subordination and oppression of the masses by gentry-officials
- the corruption that flourished from the lack of accountability and from the inability of the people to get what they needed without the involvement of officials
- the economic stagnation that resulted in massive hunger
- the semicolonization of a weak China by foreign countries
- the inability of China to generate wealth

Thus, rebellion was merely a means to change *who ruled,* not the structures, values,

principles, or culture responsible for these unhappy results. These continued, largely unchallenged, until the last years of the 19th century.

Historically, the Chinese people have been known to "eat bitterness," to accept their fate stoically until conditions became so intolerable that they would organize a rebellion. Such conditions led to major rebellions in the first part of the nineteenth century, but it was not until the twentieth century that the Chinese people seriously questioned the authoritarian tradition, and imperial system. Even then, the 1911 Revolution only led to the replacement of the imperial monarchical system with the structures and institutions, not the processes and values, of a republic. Apart from their hatred of China's Manchu rulers (1644–1911), the Chinese rebelled largely because they thought this would bring them wealth and power. Their attempt to turn away from a centralized authoritarian system owed little to a belief that a more representative democratic system had merit in its own right. Such democratic values as the rights of the individual against the state, the equality of all (at least in the eyes of the law), and competition for elected office were not seen as obviously superior to the values the Chinese had always known. Further, such values did not make intuitive sense to a people whose history had shown that chaos inevitably followed in the wake of the disintegration of centralized authoritarian control.[2]

The initial introduction of democracy in the twentieth century was accomplished by the revolutionary overthrow of a 2,000-year-old imperial system of rule.[3] The extraordinarily intricate institutions and processes of democracy that had developed in the West were supposed to take root in a heretofore monarchical, illiterate, war-torn society absorbed in the daily misery of life and rooted in Confucian values, but for the wretchedly poor majority of Chinese, the only realities that mattered were food, shelter, and safety. They were ill prepared for functioning effectively in the abruptly introduced Republic of China. Their heritage offered them little in the way of either the experience or the ideology of democracy.

Communism appeared in the same revolutionary way.[4] Following decades of bitter conflict after the establishment of the Chinese Communist Party (CCP) in 1921, the Communists managed to defeat the Nationalist Party (Kuomintang) rulers in 1949. They replaced the authoritarian system of the Nationalists (who in the *name* of a republic had replaced the authoritarianism of imperial China with the authoritarianism of nationalism). The Communists, in turn, only modified some aspects of Chinese culture: they permitted women to divorce their husbands; promoted literacy more than the Nationalists had; divided wealth more equally; and encouraged workers and peasants to stand up against the old ruling class—the landlords, rich peasants, and certain types of "capitalists."[5] Yet they drew the line when anyone challenged the authority of the CCP regime. The authoritarian tradition of China thus continued under CCP rule, with change being introduced from the top down, and with extreme shifts of policies, rather than the accretion of practices or a regularized process of trial and error, providing the norm.

In short, at the same time that the CCP endorsed egalitarian, Communist values,[6] it also retained the hierarchical, elitist values of its authoritarian predecessors.[7] Herein lies another aspect of Chinese culture that has fed into and been built upon by Communism: by insisting on unquestioning obedience to authority, the CCP leaders have neither been responsive to the public nor accountable for their actions. They have unilaterally determined the content of absolute truth, and the meaning of the public interest (usually defined as being synonymous with maintaining their own power).[8]

CHINESE COMMUNIST PARTY REGIME NOT TOTALITARIAN

Since taking power in 1949, the CCP regime has been decidedly *authoritarian*, but it really does not fit the definition of a *totalitarian* regime. It is true that, at least until the mid-1980s, one centrally directed party managed to control most policy implementation through a well-organized party network of some 5 percent of the population—but only if the population in general, and the middle and lower level cadres in particular, were in agreement with the policies they were being asked to follow. When they opposed mandated policies, the limited power of the CCP-led government became all too evident. The major reforms of the 1980s and 1990s, of course, eroded the centralized power of the CCP still further.

RESISTANCE TO POLICIES

In the period of CCP rule, there are well-documented instances of both the ability and willingness of people at the local level to resist implementing centrally mandated policies. Consider, for example, the peasants' resistance to eating in communal mess halls in 1958, which broke the back of the Great Leap Forward policy of moving all peasants into communes; the pervasive refusal of the people by the 1970s to attend meetings called by local CCP leaders; or their unwillingness to participate in a witch hunt within their work units and among their friends to ferret out the leaders and participants in the Tiananmen Square protest movement in 1989. Indeed, the effect of the Great Proletarian Cultural Revolution, which destroyed much of the societal cohesion so carefully cultivated since 1949, undermined the power of individuals in authority, such as teachers[9] and CCP leaders, who would normally have commanded respect and obedience.

Considerable dissent *within* the central CCP leadership, moreover, undercuts centralized totalitarian control. Factions have plagued the leadership since the late 1950s, and rapid shifts in policy occur when a new faction wins out against the formerly predominant one.[10] Such factors allow local leaders, and the people, to stonewall until a policy collapses or is abandoned.

An additional factor contributing to the CCP's inability to control China in a totalistic way is China's size and diversity.[11] Regional and even provincial interests are repeatedly asserted at the expense of a centrally mandated policy. For example, the southern province of Guangdong (which is contiguous with Hong Kong) has taken advantage of the reforms decentralizing economic control in the 1980s and 1990s to adopt policies far in advance of Beijing's centrally approved free market policies.[12] Since the late 1980s, in fact, the central government has found itself confronted by provinces that refuse to go along with economic policies to recentralize authority over provincial production and over fiscal and taxation policies. To wit, entrepreneurs in the burgeoning private/collective sector are increasingly difficult to control. Unlike the technologically advanced industrial democracies of Japan and the West, the Chinese government lacks the means to keep track of the earnings of millions of independent entrepreneurs who do not receive wages from the state sector. As they work for themselves, and without the assistance of computers, cash registers, or receipts, the government simply has no idea how much they earn or what part of their earnings should be paid in taxes to the state.

In short, the lack of advanced technology and comprehensive legal and commercial codes has hindered the CCP's efforts to exert totalitarian control in a more Orwellian way.

RESPECT FOR EDUCATION

Chinese culture did not uniformly resist modernization. Indeed, once China's rulers decided that modernization was something they wanted, certain aspects of that culture provided a strong source of support for it. Most notably, the same reverence for education that in imperial China put educated individuals at the very pinnacle of power as members of the scholar-gentry-official class carried over into the post-1949 Communist era. China is one of the few countries in the world that has a long history of recruitment into a civil service based on educational achievement, an important element for modernization.[13]

Although the CCP leadership has repeatedly disrupted this pattern in favor of promoting those with politically reliable credentials to positions of power,[14] efforts of the CCP regime to diminish the people's reverence for the educated class by favoring "redness" (that is, political qualities and activism) over "expertise" have failed. The Chinese continue to revere the educated, especially the university educated. This has given China's intellectuals—when they have dared to speak—influence far greater than that of the ruling CCP, and this is precisely why the leadership acts so quickly to silence intellectuals when they publicly challenge CCP rule. In any event, campaigns to undercut the power of China's educated individuals have inevitably been abandoned (albeit after doing considerable damage), and the value of education for China's leaders reaffirmed. Today, with the power of the market driving the way in which leaders are chosen, competence matters more than the political criteria of "redness" and devotion to Communist principles. Even at the very center of power, competence is now critical, whereas in the past, a leader's political pedigree and factional alliance would have weighed more heavily. Thus, the importance of education is being reaffirmed in the recruitment of China's officials and civil servants.

XENOPHOBIA

Another cultural issue is whether China's traditional xenophobia (fear, suspicion, and disdain for foreigners), which continues to this day, may have closed it to the possibilities the rest of the world offered—trade, the transfer of science and technology, and ideas about how to develop China. How did China become so xenophobic? One explanation is that, as a continental country surrounded on three sides by potential enemies, China's rulers developed a defensive mentality early on. Much of their energy was devoted to limiting penetration by "barbarians," which led to such monumental productions as the Great Wall. The Chinese also invented passports, another way to control the movements of foreigners in and out of China. China's defensive mentality, combined with sheer arrogance about the superiority of Chinese culture, made its rulers less inclined to think about major expeditions outside of China to learn about other peoples' accomplishments and values. Their concern for security was a concern for the security of Chinese *culture,* and throughout the more than 2,000 years of a unified China, the name "China" was coterminous with the reach of Chinese culture. The term for "China" (*Zhongguo*) meant "the central kingdom," that is, the center of world culture,[15] and China's emperors ruled by dint of a heavenly mandate.

Thus, China's boundaries expanded and contracted as acceptance of Chinese culture by neighboring peoples expanded and contracted. Since China's historical experience was that Chinese culture overpowered "barbarian" cultures, they concluded that Chinese culture must indeed be superior. Therefore, when confronted with the West and its mighty industrial revolution in the nineteenth century, the Chinese wrote off the West as just one more group of "barbarians." They saw nothing of value to be learned from the West, nor did they wish to acquire the technology or the products of the industrial revolution. From the time of the Opium Wars (1839–42), the Chinese suffered one humiliating defeat after another at the hands of the industrial Leviathans of the world. Yet they thought they had negotiated satisfactory settlements of these conflicts when they agreed merely to open up China for trade with the West through "treaty ports." From the Chinese perspective, the designation of treaty ports was an excellent way to contain the new foreign barbarians within geographically delimited areas.[16] Little did they realize how important these ports would become for the West's continued cultural, military, and economic incursions into China.

By the late nineteenth century, the West had overwhelmed the Chinese with its superior military and industrial power. Yet initially even defeat only provoked the Chinese to wonder if they could gain *useful* things from the West, while holding at bay the ideas and values that had made the Western industrial revolution possible. In the late nineteenth century and then in greater numbers in the twentieth century, many of China's intellectuals realized the error and began to ask which Western values might be useful to China's modernization and to the creation of a powerful, wealthy, and democratic state.[17]

China's hesitancy in becoming more fully integrated into the international system continued into the Communist-led period after

1949. For example, the Chinese matched the U.S. Cold War policy to isolate and contain China, lasting from 1950 (the Korean War) to 1972 (President Richard Nixon's visit), with policies of self-reliance and self-imposed isolation. The Great Leap Forward of 1958, an effort to make China self-reliant that went to horrifying excesses, led to the starvation of an estimated 20 to 30 million Chinese, the withdrawal of Soviet aid, and the eventual severing of relations with the Soviet Union.[18] China's withdrawal from the world went to extremes during the Cultural Revolution that began in 1966, when the government shut down its embassies throughout the world and brought diplomatic personnel home; when China's workers wrote textbooks and scientific manuals based on their limited education instead of relying on more advanced books from abroad; and when individuals who had even the most distant foreign connection (e.g., a cousin they had never seen who lived in Taiwan or the United States, or a trip abroad as far back as the 1920s) were hounded by "the masses" during "mass movements" and "criticism/self-criticism sessions."[19]

Although the post–Cultural Revolution leadership recognized the damage caused by such excesses, it nevertheless continued in the 1980s to use mass campaigns to halt the "spiritual pollution" caused by the onslaught of foreign values.[20] In 1989, the CCP leadership, which badly misjudged the international reaction to the military crackdown on Tiananmen demonstrators in 1989, once again responded with antiforeignism at home and the pretense of smug indifference to being included in the international system.

Of course, a China isolated from the international community did not benefit from the opportunities to develop within the context of the world scientific, technological, trade, and financial systems. Yet at many levels, the psychology of autarky and self-reliance—that we can do it ourselves—could be seen as having had some positive effects on China's development. As a consequence of its isolation, China has never developed a mentality of dependency on other countries to develop China for the Chinese. Its policies of self-reliance may also have protected China from exploitation by developed countries, a phenomenon suffered by so many developing countries. Thus, as China has become more integrated within the international community, it has for the most part been able to stand independently within it, and to act in some sense as an equal of other, more developed states because it has developed so much internal strength of its own; it has also repeatedly demonstrated its willingness to attempt the self-reliant road if the demands of other states become unacceptable.

In the 1990s, China has made a concerted effort to regain the respect of the international community it lost because of the use of force against demonstrators in Tiananmen 1989—a recognition by China's leaders of how much the country could lose by being shut out of international activities.[21] Caught up by the desire to benefit from foreign investment and greater involvement in the international commercial, financial, and scientific communities, China's leadership has grown more responsive to foreign pressures to curb repressive behavior, and more constrained in the measures it takes to filter out foreign values that accompany trade and investment. Yet, China still feels that every step taken toward international integration risks its sovereign control over its own affairs, and that foreign values and ideas "pollute" Chinese culture. Thus, China's policies attempt, as they have since the nineteenth century, to isolate valuable foreign technology from foreign values that might threaten Chinese culture, Chinese national sovereignty, or CCP rule. But, given the huge amount of foreign capital, the large number of foreigners doing business in China, and the exponential growth of the mass media, the ability of the CCP to filter out unacceptable values is considerably diminished.

A SECULAR WORLD VIEW

One other aspect of Chinese tradition, the secular world view offered by Confucianism, has given China an advantage over other traditional societies attempting to modernize. The very same Confucianism that emphasized patriarchy, inequality, hierarchy, and authority was also practical, concerned with relationships between human beings, and oriented to the here and now. Unlike such organized religions as Christianity, Hinduism, Islam, and Buddhism, it was not concerned with salvation, the creation, the relationship of the individual to God, or life after death, and Confucianism lacked an organized priesthood that took money from the people in exchange for promises of salvation. Confucianism's world view made the Chinese people resistant to the appeals of Christian missionaries in the nineteenth and twentieth centuries; it also made atheistic Communism less objectionable to the Chinese than it proved to be for more deeply religious peoples.

Still, few Chinese were without their folk religious beliefs and superstitions. The reverence for ancestors encouraged by Confucianism became ancestor worship, a costly practice that focused on appeasing ancestors whose spirits would otherwise come back to haunt them as ghosts. Countless shamans and others claiming supernatural powers would, for a price, attempt to cure illness or to rid a family, a building, an animal, or the land of ghosts. Often through clever schemes of entrapment of an unsuspecting male, they would marry young men to deceased "brides"

to avert disaster for a clan, and they promised prosperity, health, or happiness to those who made offerings. Animism, the belief that all objects in nature possess a soul, flourished alongside the belief in the supernatural and ancestor worship.[22]

Because Marxism viewed religion as the "opiate of the masses" and condemned superstition for draining people's energies away from positive actions to change their own lives, the Chinese Communists committed themselves to eradicating superstitious practices. Superficial evidence indicated that they had succeeded in doing so. Yet, under the more liberal political policies that emerged after 1979, including greater tolerance of religious practices, ancestor worship and animism quickly reemerged from their sequestered status. China's countryside is once again alive with temples and religious festivals and practices.[23] It now appears that the Chinese had actually continued these practices, often with the full knowledge of local officials, for the 30 years they were prohibited.[24] Perhaps most striking is the importance these religious activities seem to have assumed in supplying values to the hundreds of millions of Chinese for whom Communism no longer functions as a guiding ideology.

LACK OF INSTITUTIONALIZED CHANNELS FOR CHANGE

Countries that are able to deal with issues sequentially over time, rather than all at once, are likely to be more successful in finding solutions to controversial issues facing modern states. But the Chinese Communists rarely dealt with issues sequentially. First, the CCP did not institutionalize channels for dissent and change that would encourage adjusting policies over time to respond to criticisms; and second, like Chinese governments before them, the CCP looked for total solutions, panaceas in the form of an all-encompassing ideology. Rather than relying on a trial-and-error process that would permit readjustment and tinkering with policies so that they could evolve over time, until the more pragmatic 1980s the CCP leadership tended to focus on ideological consistency and be guided by an arbitrarily defined truth. The government adopted an all-encompassing ideology from which a policy was permitted to deviate only if it still *sounded* as if the ideology was being followed. A concern with the actual impact of the policy frequently seemed to have been of secondary importance.

In imperial times, loyal retainers who offered criticisms of policy to the emperor were often either dismissed or executed. After 1949, the CCP viewed dissent, even within the leadership itself, not as useful for fine-tuning and adjusting policy but as seditious, a potential threat to its continued rule. Rather than listening to criticism and responding to it in a proactive manner, the CCP impugned the motives of the dissenters and thereby dismissed the critiques. In the process of losing the benefit of valuable critiques, they alienated those who had valid grievances or reasons for questioning certain policies. Because of the CCP's refusal to respond to criticism, problems tended to reach crisis proportions, eventuating in massive reversals of policies.

In recent years, however, the leadership has grown increasingly responsive to public anger, and has done much to institutionalize processes that respond to private citizens whose problems are created by bad policies or who are confronted with nonresponsiveness from the appropriate officials. It appears that the risk of being punished for criticizing officials is low enough not to discourage people from complaining. Indeed, the leadership is encouraging citizens to report official corruption and follows up many such reports

with investigations. When official corruption is verified, the government (or Chinese Communist Party) may well deal with the officials harshly. The government has not, however, been consistent, and for this reason, those officials with the right sort of protection from higher levels continue being corrupt with impunity.

Finally, by the mid-1990s, the leadership appeared far more able to tolerate, or maybe simply less able to prevent, the rapid development of groups that represent special interests. At the moment, the vast majority of these groups represent commercial and economic issues, but citizens have also formed groups concerned with pollution, environmental degradation, unplanned urbanization, unsanitary working conditions, juvenile crime, and with the vast numbers of unemployed rural inhabitants who have flooded the cities.

SOCIAL STRATIFICATION

Traditional Values

Traditional Chinese culture, based on Confucian principles of social order, provided the rationale for institutionalizing hierarchical principles of social stratification. Of the five Confucian relationships (ruler/subject, father/son, husband/wife, older brother/younger brother, and friend/friend), only the last was egalitarian. The rest were between superiors and subordinates, and if conflict arose, society and the law usually favored the person in the superior position. Among China's "subjects," the peasantry ranked at the top, and merchants and soldiers at the bottom. Likewise, among China's scholar-officials, ranking was according to an elaborate set of criteria, the major one being the level of achievement on civil service examinations.

In short, China's tradition embraced a

ranking of its people that was based on a variety of factors: ascribed characteristics (as in father/son, older brother/younger brother); achievement (scholar-officials); or functional characteristics (peasants, merchants, soldiers). The ramifications of social stratification were cosmic. It affected not only how individuals related to each other at a human level (resulting, for example, in the common people cultivating the good will of officials through gift giving and obeying official orders regardless of their unfairness), but also the distribution of opportunities and therefore decisions that individuals made about how to structure their lives. For example, since the merchant class ranked so low, those who became wealthy through commerce would usually invest their money in buying land so they could become landed gentry, and in educating their sons to become scholar officials. As a result, China's merchant class lacked a social or cultural incentive to develop commerce.

Leninist Principles

With this as their cultural heritage, it is no surprise that after the Communist victory in 1949, the Leninist principles of hierarchical ordering and governance ensured that the authority of those at the center took precedence over egalitarian Marxist principles. Hierarchical principles pervade all of China's institutions—the military, the party and governmental bureaucracies, academic and research institutions, and work units. Decisions are made at the center, and each level of cadres has power over the layer of cadres immediately below it. This hierarchical authority structure allows individuals in higher ranks to control the resources and opportunities available to those in lower ranks. The latter are therefore beholden to the former.[25]

The Chinese Communists believe that the hierarchy of authority embodied in "democratic centralism" provides for obedience to superiors, but it also angers those who suffer from their superiors' arbitrary abuse of power. The willingness of so many individuals to participate eagerly in the initial stages of the Cultural Revolution in the 1960s may partly be understood in terms of the hope of those in the lower ranks of officialdom or lower work grades (as within research institutions or industrial/commercial enterprises)—as well as those without *any* power or access to resources and opportunities—to retaliate against their superiors. Democratic centralism is a principle of rulership and organization that permits the CCP to rule in an orderly way by allowing those at higher levels to control those at lower levels. It does not encourage a democratic process.

In a scarcity society with a centrally controlled economy and a fairly equal distribution of wages, opportunities and access matter more than wages. Among the ranks of officialdom, privileges (such as access to foreign newspapers or to the work unit's car), opportunities (such as a chance to study abroad, to gain admission to overnight nurseries and the best schools, or to have contact with foreigners), and scarce resources (such as larger apartments) are distributed according to rank. Only officials of a certain rank may read foreign press reports, specified government documents, or even novels, plays, and poetry that the CCP leaders, for whatever reasons, find threatening or immoral according to Marxist or Chinese values. Officials at lower ranks, and certainly the common people, are not to be trusted with such information. All such potentially seditious materials are marked "internal" (*neibu*) down to a certain rank of cadre. Anyone who discusses such material with or circulates such information to those who are not of equal rank may be found guilty of giving away "state secrets" and punished as a criminal.

There is, however, more to the story of social stratification in China than this. Although the repeated class-struggle campaigns after the Chinese Communist victory in 1949 had the intention of equalizing citizens, first according to the amount of property they possessed and, later, according to how much power they had (determined largely by their position in the workplace or in the party bureaucracy), these campaigns only partially succeeded. To a degree this was because, at the same time that the Communists eliminated one inequality, they would establish another. For example, in the early 1950s, the CCP eliminated economically defined class distinctions by redistributing property, but they then set up work-grade categories to differentiate among workers and cadre ranks to distinguish among officials. Tens of dozens of work-grade and cadre levels, as well as ranks for soldiers, professors, researchers, writers—everyone, combined with other complicated family and political background factors to form a complex jigsaw puzzle of class labels and social status. Depending on which leadership faction was in power, one aspect or another of class background would be used to justify attacking the adherents of a contending faction. Just who in the central CCP leadership had adequate power to orchestrate a new round of class struggle determined whether "the enemy" would be labeled "rightists," "ultrarightists," "ultraleftists," "die-hard rightists," "bad elements," "revisionists," "counterrevolutionaries," "new-born bourgeois elements," or even "Confucianists,"[26] to mention but a few.

What consequences were there for those who fell into the wrong category? The goods valued in a scarcity society without a market economy, such as access to good schools, membership in the CCP, a good job, and the right to serve in the People's Liberation Army, could be, and were, denied to those who suddenly found themselves classified in the wrong group. At the personal level, those villified because of their class labels were socially ostracized to an extent usually unknown in the West. The targets of intense class struggle would discover that no one would speak to them—even look at them—in the workplace or in their living unit, and marriage became far more difficult with a bad label attached to one's name. Family members frequently tried to distance themselves from the targeted person (sometimes divorcing their spouses) in hopes of avoiding the spread of the opprobrium to themselves.[27]

Further, those who as of the late 1940s hailed from wealthier backgrounds (such as rich peasants and landlords in the countryside, and the bourgeoisie of whatever gradation in the cities) retained evidence of their "bloodlines" (and their pejorative labels) in their dossiers and local police records for the indefinite future. Later, this information was used against them. For example, in the Anti-Rightist Campaign of 1957, Mao Zedong, stunned and enraged by the harsh criticism intellectuals made of socialism and the CCP's policies, decided that the elimination of property distinctions had not eliminated the exploitative mentality of the capitalist class (the bourgeoisie). Since most of China's intellectuals came from a capitalist background, Mao concluded that class struggle should continue not between property-based classes but between class ideologies.[28] Class struggle was, in Mao's view, the best method for instilling a new class viewpoint. Marx, after all, had not been raised in the working class; and Mao had grown up in a rich peasant's family. Thus, a revolutionary class viewpoint could be acquired.[29]

This perspective—that it was possible to change an individual's attitudes and thoughts—was firmly grounded on traditional Confucian views. What people in the West might call "brainwashing" was, in China, considered a normal and acceptable aspect of "education." The numerous "rectifications," "purges," mass campaigns, and struggle sessions in China take a different form, then, than they did in such places as the Soviet Union. In China, those leaders, officials, intellectuals, or ordinary people who are believed to have thought the wrong thoughts or abused their power are not *executed*. Instead, they are "reeducated" through the use of intensive "thought reform" (including hard labor). When they show evidence of having changed their viewpoint, have admitted to the evil that lay within them, and then embrace the most recent party perspective, they are usually permitted to return to their old jobs—and face their former tormentors.[30] It is important to realize that many victims of these endless class struggles or mass campaigns did in fact *believe* that they had done something wrong, and worked very hard to eradicate their shortcomings and wrong attitudes, as defined by others.[31]

The CCP has also used class labels to distinguish between "the enemy" and "the people," between "the exploiter" and "the exploited." If individuals failed to participate in class struggle campaigns, they would be under suspicion. Individuals proved their goodness by struggling against those who suddenly found themselves in "the enemy" class, however defined. And, as the definition of class changed repeatedly, people could never be sure that those they struggled against today would not be reclassified tomorrow—and get revenge against those who had victimized them in struggle sessions.

Nor could they be certain that they themselves would not fall into a newly formed bad class category, as happened in the 1960s to the party vanguard. This was because, once distinctions based on property were minimized, other, noneconomic categories of class surfaced. For example, Mao redefined class in a way that referred to those within the state or government bureaucracies who used

their power as "capitalists," and denounced them as members of a new bureaucratic class. These "capitalist roaders" had been the creators, and the inheritors, of the CCP victory in 1949. The state and party bureaucracies formed after that victory thus gave rise to a new sort of bourgeoisie, whose unequal access to power and opportunities led to new social stratifications based on exploitation.

In deference to Marxism, however, Mao Zedong continued to use the terminology of class to justify what many consider to have been nothing more than a brutal struggle for power. This struggle arose because of a rather common problem: bureaucratization of the party and state apparatus, which Mao interpreted as a trend that would undo the achievements of the Communist revolution. But he framed it in class terms: the new bureaucratic class used institutional power the way the capitalists used money—to exploit others. For this reason, he resorted to the wrong techniques—class struggle and mass movements—to address very serious problems arising from bureaucratization that might better have been addressed by more relevant, less shattering means.

Repeated class struggle after 1949 profoundly damaged the fabric of Chinese society by generating tension and intense hatred. Colleagues, friends, and relatives turned against each other in an effort to prove their own revolutionary ardor. Few Chinese who lived in the period from 1949 to 1976 were not victimized in some way by the shifting interpretations of class. In fact, the repeated use of class struggle to eliminate the inevitable distinctions that arise among people has probably done more harm to China's societal cohesiveness than any other single policy the CCP adopted after 1949. In the process, it also undermined the people's faith in the CCP's ability, and right, to lead; for if the CCP could not establish reliable and consistent standards for defining class enemies, and if new class enemies inexorably appeared, how could it be trusted to lead China?

In the decade following Deng Xiaoping's rise to power in late 1978, only empty expressions of class struggle remained. The CCP eliminated the class labels of "landlords" and "rich peasants," labels which were still causing anxiety, suffering, and deprivation to more than 4 million people in the countryside 30 years after they had been imposed. The CCP eliminated behavioral and attitudinal criteria for determining class and stated that "bureaucrats *could not* form a class because they were paid wages by the state, and they owned none of the means of production."[32] The Marxist economic yardstick, which measured the amount of property owned, again became the means for defining class, thereby causing many to hesitate to "get rich."

Nevertheless, as the opportunities for economic gain continued to beckon against a background of policies that abjured class struggle, most did not hesitate to seek greater wealth, for Deng's "get rich" policies stressed development, not class struggle. The result was the decade of rapid economic growth from 1979 to 1988—and the simultaneous emergence of an enormous gap in wealth between the wealthiest and poorest Chinese. The renewed emphasis on class struggle that began in the wake of the Tiananmen demonstrations in 1989 was not directed against these newly rich, who form a true economic class, but ironically, against those who attacked the CCP leadership. The conservative wing of the CCP leadership faction thereby implicitly supported the continued development of real economic class divisions, arguing instead that opposition to CCP rule ("political liberalism") was a sign that "bad class elements" still existed. For the first time since 1949, however, the Chinese people refused to participate in this renewal of class struggle, thus ensuring its demise. Yet the rhetoric of

"vigilance against class enemies" and of decrying Western influence that sees China's "peaceful evolution" away from Communism as an insidious class plot continued.

The desire to do whatever is necessary to distinguish oneself from others in a way that will lend a greater sense of status, power, or privilege seems endemic in China. Whether it is due to the insistence of Communist ideology on equality, which infuriates individuals who, as human beings, necessarily want to discover what is unique about themselves in order to have value, or to the continuation of a powerful cultural heritage that insists on a hierarchically ordered society, the fact is that the Chinese continue to view distinctions of status, power, and wealth as important to their lives, and crucial to how they relate to others. Their relentless pursuit of these goals into the mid-1990s has left China considerably wealthier, but also plagued by all the problems attendant on a serious polarization of wealth. It is a situation that, at least in this one very important respect, mirrors the class divisions and class exploitation of republican China, a situation that ultimately led to the Communist revolution of 1949.

POLITICAL STRUCTURE

The CCP's Penetration of Administrative Structures

The Chinese Communist Party is the vanguard of the proletariat, and it thereby lays claim to the leadership of China. Although not all CCP members are cadres (*ganbu*), the vast majority of the CCP's 50 million-strong membership do hold leadership positions at one level or another. The CCP leadership determines which values will guide policy. This framework for policy making is stated in the CCP's general line. The government, in turn, implements these values in its policies concerning the economy, culture, education, the military, and so on.

In theory, the government administration is a completely separate structure with separate personnel, who need not be party members. In reality, however, as cadres move up to the higher levels of the government's administrative bureaucracy, virtually all are party members.[33] Further, although the CCP in its role as ideological policeman is responsible only for ensuring that policy conforms to the framework established by the general line, over time the CCP has become more and more deeply involved in structuring the form that policy would take at the middle and lower levels—down through the provincial, county, city, and township (district) levels, and including the enterprise level. As the relationship evolved, then, it moved away from one of the CCP leading the government to one of the CCP controlling the government administrative apparatus. The CCP, in fact, became so invasive, so thoroughly integrated into the administrative structure, that by the 1960s the party and the government had grown to become virtually one and the same.

In spite of serious reforms to separate government and party structures and personnel, little progress occurred. Worse, in the aftermath of the CCP's crackdown on the 1989 Tiananmen protests, the conservative wing of the CCP leadership insisted that CCP control over the government bureaucracies (many of whose own personnel participated in the protests) be strengthened so that such challenges to the authority of the CCP would not happen again. Overnight, much of the progress that had been made in separating the functions of the CCP and government was undone. Since Deng Xiaoping's decision in 1992 to return primacy to China's modernization, however, the role of the CCP has again been marginalized in favor of competent administrators in many sectors of the economy and society.

Hierarchical Principles

Both the government and the CCP are organized along Leninist, hierarchical principles, with the elite corps of policy makers or innovators at the center, and the policy managers or bureaucrats at lower levels.[34] The principle of democratic centralism governs: the central leadership solicits lower levels for ideas and input, but once the center makes a decision, no further questioning of its decision is permitted. The 1982 Constitution, in fact, specifically prohibits lower-level CCP organizations from voicing differences of opinion in public (Article 15). Middle- and lower-level cadres are to obey whatever instructions higher levels give them, although exactly how they interpret and implement these instructions varies according to local conditions.

These cadres are crucial to the success of the central CCP's policies, for they may choose to implement, modify, obstruct, or torpedo policy at will. Given the vastness of China, the diversity of local conditions, and the recurrent inability of the CCP to control the millions of officials at the middle and lower levels, these officials have often succeeded in doing things as they chose, not as they were told. Of course, to hinder policy from being correctly implemented without ruining one's own career demands considerable skill. But the history of policy failures since 1949, for which the central leadership itself has frequently blamed these middle- and lower-level bureaucrats, suggests that cadres' ability to resist centrally mandated policies is a skill many have acquired.[35]

Although the continuing power of the government and the CCP must not be understated, an ever-increasing number of economic, commercial, and cultural decisions are being made outside of the government and party hierarchies. Joint ventures with foreigners and the privatization of commerce and of many factories, businesses, educational and medical institutions, and even many publishing houses and newspapers—which must now rely on their own funds and profits to survive—are carving out their own sphere. In this new sphere, the role of government and party cadres is largely confined to making sure that the activities of these enterprises conform to government regulations and China's laws. For the most part, cadres are no longer the managers, and they no longer are able to control policies within these enterprises and institutions, much less the ideological perspective of their workers.

Resistance to Central Policies

Why might middle- and lower-level cadres in the state-controlled sector resist centrally mandated policies? The reasons are diverse. Some cadres believe that centrally determined policies will actually harm the interests of whatever work unit or community they represent (as with policies to collectivize property, and later, to decollectivize property). Other cadres believe the policies will interfere with their own ambitions, careers, or life style (as with policies that attempt to end corruption through procedural and structural changes, such as free elections).

What does the central CCP leadership do when it is faced with policy failures that it believes arise from recalcitrant cadres at middle and lower levels? In the past it used any one of a number of measures to discipline or purge them from the system: rectification campaigns that remove them from their positions, party consolidation that withdraws their party membership, a "sending down" that assigns them to lower levels of the bureaucracy, consignment to manual labor, criticism/self-criticism sessions or political study group sessions in which participants study "correct" political thought and then discuss how to apply it to their own work.[36] Today, these methods of control have largely been

abandoned. It is increasingly the case that, if local cadres have popular support, there is little the center can do to punish them. Thus, the center is more likely to use positive tactics to encourage obedience rather than negative sanctions.

The Organizational Chart of Leadership

How realistic is an organizational chart of the CCP or government leadership? As was the case for most of the 2,000 years preceding the Communist takeover in 1949, power in China tends to reside in individuals, not institutions. Thus an organizational chart provides only a rough guide to who is really in charge. Of course, the most powerful individuals do tend to take over the most powerful positions and institutions, but sometimes leaders have remained in seemingly insignificant positions yet exercised enormous power. This is easier in an authoritarian system than in a democratic one, for in the former, the public has virtually no way of protesting the accretion of power in a particular individual or institution. A good example of this is the case of Hua Guofeng: from 1977 to 1980, Hua simultaneously held the three most powerful institutional positions in China (CCP Chairman, Premier of the State, and CCP's Chairman of the Military Affairs Commission), whereas Deng Xiaoping held the position of a mere Vice-Premier. Yet by 1979, Deng exercised far greater power than Hua, and was even able to shift the locus of power away from the CCP Chairman (a position Deng was powerful enough to abolish) to the CCP's General Secretary, who at that point was a long-time ally of Deng's.

Similarly, although the Standing Committee of the Politburo (whose role is to direct the CCP's work) is supposed to be the CCP's highest policy-making body, by the early 1980s the CCP's General Secretariat had assumed its functions, for the largely octogenarian members of the Standing Committee, even with their nurses in attendance, were too old and feeble to meet for more than a few hours for one afternoon a week. Today, a rejuvenated Politburo Standing Committee has regained much of its former power, but the General Secretariat continues to direct ideology and propaganda, as well as to organize, direct, and discipline the Chinese Communist Party.

THE INTERACTION OF CHINESE CULTURE WITH SOCIALIST IDEOLOGY

Since 1949, the Chinese Communist Party has tried to carry out socialist policies, but, although its ideology has been highly flexible in its application,[37] the CCP has had to apply it within the context of Chinese culture (that is, those aspects of Chinese culture that the CCP was either unable or unwilling to eliminate after 1949). In many cases, the CCP purposefully built on Chinese culture or manipulated cultural predispositions to achieve its own objectives—objectives, incidentally, that were not necessarily in accord with political and economic development. In other cases, however, it has discovered that some of the aspects of Chinese culture it was unable to eliminate have actually distorted socialist values and objectives.

The source of the CCP leadership's major dilemma concerning Chinese traditional culture is this: the CCP wants the people to challenge authority, but not *its* authority. From its beginning, the CCP viewed the Chinese people's unwillingness to challenge authority (because of the cultural assumption that the ordinary person is powerless to change the system) as the cause of their oppression. During the land reform campaign from 1947 to 1952, the CCP used "speak bitterness" and class struggle campaigns as tactics to force the oppressed, cowering masses to stand up

to individuals in authority. (Landlords were the primary target at that time.) Not only was this meant to create a more egalitarian society, in which formerly impoverished peasants would now treat landlords as their equals, but it was also seen as a method to ensure that officials did not abuse their power.

But the desired objectives did not result. The average person continued to believe that the only way to survive, much less get ahead, was through a complex, expensive system of "gift giving"—that is, bribing officials.[38] As the socialist system that the CCP tried to implement was unable to guarantee fair and equal treatment of all, and as officials still held power over the ordinary person (officials who were in turn beholden to officials higher than themselves), officials encouraged corruption. The practice of setting up relationships through the exchange of favors, which frequently shaded into outright bribery, led to an increasingly corrupt society.

The major reason that the ideal egalitarian system did not appear in China is, then, that the CCP wanted people to challenge authority, but stopped short of allowing them to challenge the authority of the one institution in a position that most invited corruption—the CCP itself. Since the CCP laid claim to absolute truth, it simply was not possible for anyone to question its values and policies. In the name of party policy and values, party cadres did not permit ordinary people to challenge what they said or did:

> the context of the culture in Maoist China was in many ways new, but the idea that China required a uniform culture to survive as a nation and that the authorities should enforce an orthodoxy to maintain cultural, and thus political, cohesion was very old. [Mao's] Marxist-Leninist convictions in this instance reinforced traditional Chinese assumptions. Socialism entails central planning and regulation, not only of economic production but also of all social life, including culture and values. . . . There is

one correct way for society to be organized, and cultural unity and officially imposed ideology play central roles in maintaining social cohesion. Allowing alternative values and cultural practices would hinder the pursuit of socialism and Communism and foster political disunity.[39]

Since CCP cadres have the power to make life miserable for those in their work units or housing units, China's citizens have rarely been so bold as to question their authority. Only when Mao Zedong himself, as chairman of the CCP, called on the people during the Cultural Revolution to challenge authority, did the people have the requisite support of a key central figure to provide an adequate justification for questioning the horribly corrupt cadres who controlled their lives.

The protests at Tiananmen in 1989 are, then, an example of the dilemma the CCP leadership faces: although the CCP leaders concurred with the protestors' demand to eliminate official corruption, they would not permit the protestors to challenge the CCP's own authority—precisely the rubric under which officials could continue to be corrupt.[40] Thus one could argue that socialism's objective of achieving equality in status has been undercut by the continuation of traditional Confucian attitudes that emphasize the authoritarian superior-subordinate relationships between officials and ordinary people, and between higher and lower ranks of officials.

SECRECY

The lack of accountability endemic in China's authoritarian traditional culture also meshed well with the typical desire of an authoritarian party to exercise greater control through secrecy. By using such methods as maintaining dossiers on all adult citizens (who have no access to the dossier nor ability to refute what is in it),[41] which allow the regime to control the population through secrecy on the one hand, and by denying the public access to important information on the other hand, the CCP gives itself greater lattitude in making decisions on the basis of factors other than what is in the public interest. These would include such matters as power considerations, factional ties, and personal relationships. To the extent the CCP exercises adequate power to dictate policy to the people, regardless of whether it is a beneficial policy or not, it can get away with a secretive, nonaccountable decision-making process.

The problem is that, without adequate input from the people whose lives will be affected by policies, the wrong decisions can be—and have been—made. Examples are the agricultural and industrial policies pursued during the Great Leap Forward in 1958, and during the Ten Bad Years from 1966 to 1976, of which the Cultural Revolution was a part. Had farmers or workers been listened to, for example, cadres could have warned the central leadership that policies of growing three crops per year in traditional two-crop areas, close planting, deep ploughing, and growing grain where conditions are unfavorable would not work; nor would backyard furnaces constructed by peasants throughout the countryside to smelt a hodgepodge of metals into steel, or efforts to increase industrial production by accelerating the speed of conveyor belts or intensifying steam pressure.

In the case of the Great Leap Forward, instead of listening to the people, cadres—fearing for their positions and hoping for advancement—simply carried out the centrally mandated policies, and then in the face of unprecedented disaster, pretended they had succeeded. This resulted in the Big Lie—lower- and middle-level cadres, who were (incorrectly) told by the center that other collectives that had been consolidated into the larger commune structure had succeeded in doubling production, felt pressured to say they had at least doubled production. This, in turn, put pressure on still other cadres to pretend to have done at least as much. And, in turn, the central leadership, who now read these falsified reports from intimidated cadres at lower levels, believed that they were true and made policy accordingly.

The leadership's reliance on secrecy thus points to another important aspect of how Chinese traditional political culture has affected today's system of social stratification. By maintaining a monopoly on information, China's rulers have been able to rule in an absolutist way. There is no need for them to be responsive to criticisms of their policies, because so little information is available upon which to make a case against the leadership's policies.

Until the explosion of information sources in the 1990s, the revelation of *any* information about the government, the CCP, or the country was considered a state secret unless the leadership itself announced it. (Even now, many topics about China's leadership, the military, and the government are prohibited.) For example, the excuse the regime used during the democracy movement of 1979 to sentence a worker named Wei Jingshen to 15 years in prison for revealing to a foreign correspondent the name of the commander of Chinese troops who invaded Vietnam was that it was a state secret.[42] Similarly, in May 1989 Party General Secretary Zhao Ziyang made a statement to visiting Soviet President Mikhail Gorbachev (in front of the international press and during the demonstrations in Tiananmen Square) that any important decision by the CCP Politburo must have the approval of the retired leader Deng Xiaoping. Everyone knew this, but no one was permitted to say it publicly. Zhao's public exposure of this information was considered the equivalent of revealing a state secret and

grounds for his dismissal. And Harry Wu, a Chinese who had served 19 years in Chinese prisons and left in 1985 (later becoming a U.S. citizen) was arrested in 1995 as he crossed over the border into China for having taken state secrets (prison documents) out of China on earlier trips.

The point of this tight control of information, opportunities, access, and power is that it allows for a strict authoritarian structure. It also allows the more dominant factions of the leadership to manipulate and even control the less powerful factions. But as of the mid-1990s, China is step by step becoming part of the information superhighway. With the proliferation of satellite dishes, telephones, fax machines, photocopiers, and computers, and growing access to the Internet, controlling information—whether it originates inside or outside of China—is virtually impossible. The Orwellian vision of a technological society that permits a government nearly complete control over its population seems thus far to have been quite inaccurate. Instead, the growth of information technology has allowed the Chinese people far greater information and freedom of communication.

THE LEGAL SYSTEM

The interplay of cultural and ideological factors has also constrained the development of China's legal system, an important component of China's political system.[43] The Chinese have historically had a distaste for lawyers and for resorting to law to settle disputes.[44] The CCP took advantage of this aspect of Chinese traditional political culture to serve its own objectives, for it meshed well with the leadership's preference for having the CCP rather than the legal system and political values rather than legal values determine what was right and wrong. The legal realm has, in fact, been a part of the moral-political realm defined by Confucianism since imperial times, so the CCP merely built upon that tradition when it merged the legal and political realms within the context of Communist morality.

Mediation

China's leaders were, in any event, predisposed to construct a minimalist formal legal system. Having inherited the informal mediation system that the Chinese had historically preferred, after 1949, the CCP further developed it. CCP members frequently sit on mediation committees or oversee their operation. The informal system fits well with the ordinary person's view of the law. First, resorting to the formal legal system often leads to a loss of face, for it indicates a person is unable to settle problems through compromise, which reflects poorly on the individual. Second, once the formal legal system becomes involved, the case may become bogged down in the system, and the results are unpredictable. Third, China has so few courts and lawyers that mediation is more expeditious.

Lawyers

Further, in China, most lawyers are still state employees appointed by the state on behalf of the client, not advocates for their clients. Lawyers, like the law, must serve the collective interests of society. In criminal cases, for example, the most a lawyer is likely to do for their clients is, after encouraging them to confess to their crimes and to appear contrite in court, to ask the judge for a reduced sentence. The array of adversarial tactics that lawyers in Western democratic systems might use, such as efforts to confuse the judge or jury, or to have the court dismiss a case on technicalities (even when the lawyer knows the client is guilty), is not available to Chinese lawyers. A lawyer may be liable to punishment for not representing the interest of the state rather than that of the client.

Law as a Tool of the State

In short, while in the American legal system the emphasis is on process, in China it is on serving the state and society. Murderers must be executed, regardless of how evidence was acquired, because the protection of societal interests takes precedence over the rights of any single individual. In civil cases, when an entrepreneur might wish to sue the state for nonperformance of a contract that led to losses for the entrepreneur (such as not providing contracted resources to the entrepreneur on time), a lawyer is caught in a bind between representing the legitimate interests of the client and protecting the interests of the state. China's laws regarding the economy and commerce have developed rapidly in the last 15 years, however, largely in response to foreign investors who refused to invest without greater legal protection.

One problem with law serving as a tool of the state is that its interests are identical with those of the CCP. As a result, "socialist legality" and "socialist justice" often become confused with the CCP's political objectives, which are arbitrary and capricious. As the arresting and sentencing of protestors during the Tiananmen demonstrations in 1989 for their "criminal" activities indicate,[45] the CCP will continue to determine when a crime has been committed and how the perpetrators will be punished. There is still little protection for the individual who dares to criticize the CCP central leadership in a way that threatens continued CCP rule.[46] Court decisions that challenge existing policies are, moreover, still likely to result in the CCP intervening to reverse the court's ruling. Thus, China cannot yet claim to have an independent judiciary. This is not to say that fair trials never occur, but rather that China's citizens have no certainty that they will receive a fair hearing by the bench under the norms of an impartial law.

The Institutionalization of Law and Legal Procedure

China has been slow to institutionalize law and legal procedure. Indeed, it was not until the new Criminal Law and Law of Criminal Procedure were adopted in 1979 that mass campaigns were no longer considered an acceptable method for investigating crime and determining punishment for the accused. The "Ten Bad Years" from 1966 to 1976 witnessed the complete collapse of the legal system. During this period, the training of lawyers and judicial personnel came to a virtual halt, the party interfered at will in the legal process, and law was condemned as a "bourgeois restraint" on the "revolutionary masses."

The gradual opening to the West and Japan that began in the 1970s provided a stimulus to reshape the legal system and formulate new laws, for the foreign businesspeople whom the Chinese wanted to attract to invest were reluctant to do so without a more fully developed legal system. Foreign pressure has, then, been a major catalyst to China's leadership to codify a more complete legal system and to train more lawyers and judicial personnel. Apart from the new Criminal Law and Law of Criminal Procedure, the bulk of the new laws are in the area of contract law, civil law, commercial law, property law, and environmental law.[47] The plethora of new laws since 1979 may eventually wrap individual Chinese in a protective security blanket that ensures an independent judiciary and keeps the CCP at arm's length.

Yet China's legal system is still characterized by an ex post facto rationalization of Chinese Communist Party policy. Rather than an independent judiciary with the abil-

ity to develop legal concepts that will serve as a guide for and constraint on policy the CCP's policies still guide legal development. In other words, when the CCP makes a policy, lawyers scurry to write laws to support it—even if this means undoing previously accepted laws. Whether these new laws conform to Marxist doctrine is less important than that they serve the needs of the state and the objectives of the CCP. In reality, laws flow from the pens of China's central party leadership, not from an independent judiciary, much less an independent legislature.

The lack of the concept of judicial precedent further inhibits the development of a predictable and stable legal system in China, as well as a theory of law. Decisions made in one court are in no way binding on other courts in any particular district, nor, indeed, on subsequent decisions made in the *same* court. Today the punishment for embezzlement of 35,000 *yuan* in state funds may be three years in jail; tomorrow—execution.

This lack of judicial precedent leaves the system of socialist legality wide open to political interference and the arbitrary handling of cases. When the lack of judicial precedence is combined with the inclination of party and government organs and officials to use bribery, the "back door," or the political power to suppress evidence or intimidate those who might challenge them in court, it further undermines the rule by law and the predictability of law in China.

SOCIALIST DEMOCRACY

A final aspect of the Chinese political system warranting analysis for comparative purposes is the development of its democratic component, or the degree to which people have power vis-à-vis the state, its policies, and its personnel. For the Chinese, the term *democracy* conveys a completely different set of suppositions than it does in the West. Democracy in China means socialist democracy, one committed to serving the interests of the workers and peasants. Embedded in the socialist understanding of democracy is the concept of economic equality. Political equality and equality before the law are not part of the Chinese Communist definition of the term. It contains no commitment to the idea of "one person, one vote," nor to majority rule. Nor has the Chinese leadership interpreted socialist democracy to mean institutionalized channels for the free expression of opinion. Instead, the CCP leads a "democratic dictatorship," and it is the CCP that confers and removes democratic rights at will.

The spread of democratic practices since the 1980s has not, then, been in response to popular demands, but rather results from the reform leadership's decision that democratization would serve its twin objectives of eliminating the power of the remaining leftist leaders throughout the system and accelerating economic modernization. When democratization moved beyond these two objectives to criticize the CCP regime, as in the Tiananmen protests of 1989, the leadership peremptorily removed the democratic rights it had previously conferred.

Rural Practices

This is not to deny that far more democratic practices exist today under the CCP regime than existed before Communist rule began in 1949. For example, before 1949, most of the decisions now made by the peasants either independently or in consultation with local cadres were made by landlords. In the countryside, where some 75 percent of China's population still lives, the "household responsibility system" has given individual peasant households nearly complete control over decisions that affect their daily lives. Even before the reforms of the late 1970s and

1980s introduced the household responsibility system, the environmental and ecological diversity of China meant that any centrally mandated policy took on a variety of concrete forms as it is applied to local conditions. Most of the time, local cadres have involved the peasants in determining the specifics of implementation. When they have not done so, the peasantry has often sabotaged policy.

The introduction of significant electoral reforms in the 1980s and the formation of "villagers' groups" have considerably advanced democracy at the village level in rural China. Multiple candidates may run for any post, although no one may espouse a platform that runs against CCP policy. For those still living in the countryside, these elections have guaranteed that they will have a voice in deciding who will determine economic policies and give them the right to remove from office anyone who does not perform up to expectations.

Urban Practices

In urban work units, however, trade unions are hardly advocates for workers' rights and better working conditions.[48] The assumption in China, as in other former Communist polities (until Poland's Solidarity challenged it), is that the Communist Party represents the interests of the working class, and that trade unions therefore have no need to do so independently. As the CCP controls management, the workers do not need an independent representative of their interests vis-à-vis management. As a result, the key role of a trade union in China has been to provide a social club for its members—organizing recreational and social activities, and perhaps even starting night schools. Trade unions cannot interfere in political affairs or make demands for higher pay, shorter work hours, longer vacations, or improved safety, much less go on strike.

In the charged international atmosphere of the late 1980s and 1990s, however, some of China's trade unions have shown a hankering for power and a desire to follow in the steps of Solidarity to gain greater rights for workers. This explains why the CCP regime has been so brutal in its response to any efforts by trade unions to challenge its authority, summarily quashing them at the first signs of efforts to protest publicly or strike. During the Tiananmen protests of 1989, the CCP leadership showed less fear of the students' participation than of the workers. The regime wanted to thwart any worker movement backed by trade union support for the purpose of empowering workers against state/party-run management. Evidence to date suggests that virtually all those executed for their role in the Tiananmen protests were workers, not students or intellectuals, and that the harshest treatment in prisons and labor camps was reserved for the workers.

In the 1990s, moreover, industrial actions, if not strikes, have become increasingly common in protest against appalling working conditions and exploitative practices. But it should be noted that most of these actions are against employers in the collective and private sectors, where labor unions are not likely to exist, and where laborers are not protected against exploitation by China's labor laws as well as they are in the state-run sector. Thus, although wages in the state-run sector may be low, workers there have guaranteed employment, health and housing benefits, and many other prerogatives unavailable to those in the nonstate sector.

Political Freedom

Do the Chinese long for greater political freedom? This is really the wrong question. The question is, do the Chinese long for greater political freedom if it might mean chaos and insecurity, and/or if it might endanger economic growth? Historically, China's relatively short-lived experiments with democracy have been bitter. When the center has lost power, chaos has resulted, and the people have suffered. Whether those who hold power at the center possess too much authority seems to matter less to the ordinary Chinese than that the center be able to maintain order and stability. Indeed, the CCP leadership used this rationale to justify its brutal crackdown on Tiananmen Square protestors, and evidence to date seems to suggest that many Chinese agreed with this point of view, even if they did not approve of the government's use of force to regain order. Who, after all, would have led China if the CCP regime had been overthrown in 1989? At the time of the military crackdown on the protestors, there was no group of individuals or political party in favor of democratic reforms standing in the wings, ready to take charge.

Thus it is hard to know to what degree such protests as those in 1978–79, 1986, and 1989 are indicative of a deep and widespread desire on the part of most Chinese to exercise greater freedom, or whether they simply reflect the anger and frustration with the CCP regime of an articulate and politically conscious urban group of fairly well-educated individuals, including workers, students, and intellectuals. If the former is true, then the subsidiary question arises as to which freedoms the Chinese would like to have. In 1989, freedom of the press was the major freedom that protestors demanded.

All other things being equal, most people would prefer more freedom in all aspects of their lives. But in China's case, the people's greatest fear is still that all other things will not be equal. In any event, Western concepts of individual freedom, and the rights of the individual against the state, lack a strong historical or cultural grounding in China. Only a few of those who protested for greater democracy in 1989 indicated an awareness that greater responsibility accompanies greater freedom.[49]

If, however, the protests, as in 1989, were not primarily for the purpose of demanding greater freedom or political pluralism, but rather for demanding that the CCP regime reform its ways or else relinquish power, this would confirm the view that what the Chinese still want is a strong centralized authority, but one that maintains high moral standards. In short, it appears that what the Chinese people most want is an end to the official corruption that is corroding the fabric of Chinese society.

Those Chinese who have thought and written about democracy do not agree on what democracy within a Chinese, and socialist, context would resemble. Many of them have, however, voiced agreement on three changes that would make China more democratic. First, a separation of powers—but in China's case initially meaning not the separation of judicial, legislative, and executive powers, but rather, the separation of the powers of the CCP from those of the government; second, institutionalized procedures (notably, regularized elections) for getting rid of incompetent or corrupt leaders at all levels, including the center; and third, equality before the law and rule by law rather than by the whim of CCP officials.[50] Even these changes will not be easy in the context of a 2,000-year-old authoritarian culture and an authoritarian Communist Party that continues to lay claim to absolute truth, a "fact" that brooks no questioning.

Yet forces for pluralization are already cutting away at China's authoritarianism. As China becomes more fully integrated into the international community, it will be increasingly difficult for the CCP to resist democratizing impulses. More and more Chinese are being exposed to international forces for democracy, and, moreover, the Chinese must now act as equals, not as holders of absolute truth, when engaged in political negotiations and commercial relationships with other states.

Finally, as China continues to modernize and becomes a more complex economy, the society is reflecting this complexity. Although the CCP leadership is trying to keep a tight rein on democratic forces, the emergence of a middle class, an information revolution, the internationalization of the commercial and financial sectors, an environmental movement,[51] and a broad range of groups promoting and defending their own economic interests are forcing China's leaders to be more responsive to its citizenry. China's political system may never resemble a Western liberal democratic system, but it has already moved a considerable distance away from its earlier authoritarian practices.

NOTES

1. For several key works on the importance of political culture in China today, see Lucian W. Pye and Mary W. Pye, *Asian Power and Politics: The Cultural Dimensions of Authority* (Cambridge: Belknap Press of Harvard University Press, 1985); Lucian W. Pye, *The Spirit of Chinese Politics* new edition (Cambridge: Harvard University Press, 1992); Richard H. Solomon, *Mao's Revolution and the Chinese Political Culture* (Berkeley: University of California Press, 1971); and Weiming Tu (ed.), *The Living Tree: The Changing Meaning of Being Chinese Today* (Stanford: Stanford University Press, 1995).

2. For the views of Sun Yat-sen, whose thoughts and actions inspired the Chinese to overthrow imperial rule in favor of a republic, see Lyon Sharman, *Sun Yat-sen: His Life and Its Meaning* (Stanford: Stanford University Press, 1968); and Harold Z. Schiffrin, *Sun Yat-sen and the Origins of the Chinese Revolution* (Berkeley: University of California Press, 1970).

3. On the revolutionary introduction of democratic institutions, the difficulties they faced, and their failure, see Mary Clabaugh Wright, ed., *China in Revolution: The First Phase, 1900–1913* (New Haven: Yale University Press, 1968); Harold R. Isaacs, *The Tragedy of the Chinese Revolution*, 2nd rev. ed. (Stanford: Stanford University Press, 1961); and Edward Friedman, *Backward Toward Revolution: The Chinese Revolutionary*

Party (Ann Arbor: Center for Chinese Studies, University of Michigan, 1974).

4. Arif Dirlik, *The Origins of Chinese Communism* (Oxford: Oxford University Press, 1989).

5. For a gripping description of the process of dividing up property in the countryside and engendering class hatred, see William Hinton, *Fanshen: A Documentary of Revolution in a Chinese Village* (New York: Vintage, 1966).

6. On the use of class conflict to create an "egalitarian" society, see Richard C. Kraus, *Class Conflict in Chinese Socialism* (New York: Columbia University Press, 1981).

7. Lucian W. Pye, *The Spirit of Chinese Politics: A Psychocultural Study of the Authoritarian Crisis in Political Development* new edition (Cambridge: Harvard University Press, 1992); Pye and Pye, *Asian Power and Politics.*

8. For example, the CCP regime justified military intervention to halt the Tiananmen Square demonstrations in 1989 on the grounds that they were endangering China's stability. Martial law and the subsequent brutal crackdown were deemed essential to restoring law and order.

9. See Martin Schoenhals, *The Paradox of Power: In a People's Republic of China Middle School* (Armonk, N.Y., M. E. Sharpe, Inc., 1993), in which he documents the refusal of students to listen quietly to teachers whom they do not respect (or who are dull).

10. For an excellent analysis of factions, see Lucian W. Pye, *The Dynamics of Factions and Consensus in Chinese Politics* (Santa Monica, CA: Rand Corporation, 1980).

11. For the importance of geography in China's historical development, see the works of Rhodes Murphy; and Robert Dernberger et al., eds., *The Chinese: Adapting the Past, Facing the Future,* 2nd ed. (Ann Arbor: Center for Chinese Studies, University of Michigan, 1951), pp. 3–150.

12. Ezra F. Vogel, *One Step Ahead in China: Guangdong Under Reform* (Cambridge: Harvard University Press, 1989).

13. Ping-ti Ho, *The Ladder of Success in Imperial China* (New York: John Wiley & Sons, 1964); Robert M. Marsh, *The Mandarins: The Circulation of Elites in China, 1600–1900* (Glencoe, IL: Free Press of Glencoe, 1961).

14. Susan L. Shirk, *Competitive Comrades: Career Incentives and Student Strategies in China* (Berkeley: University of California Press, 1982); Jonathan Unger, *Education Under Mao: Class and Competition in Canton Schools, 1960–1980* (New York: Columbia University Press, 1982).

15. See the many articles and books by John K. Fairbank on the concept of China as "the central kingdom," the tributary system, and China's xenophobia. Note in particular John K. Fairbank, *The Chinese World Order: Traditional China's Foreign Relations* (Cambridge: Harvard University Press, 1968).

16. John K. Fairbank, *Trade and Diplomacy on the China Coast: The Opening of the Treaty Ports, 1842–1854* (Stanford: Stanford University Press, 1969); Fairbank, *The Chinese World Order.*

17. For notable individuals asking how China might also become wealthy and powerful, see Benjamin I. Schwartz, *In Search of Wealth and Power: Yen Fu and the West* (New York: Harper & Row, 1968); and Roger V. Des Forges, *Hsi-liang and the Chinese National Revolution* (New Haven: Yale University Press, 1973).

18. Bevin Alexander, *The Strange Connection: US Intervention in China, 1944–72* (New York: Greenwood Press, 1992); Gordon H. Chang, *Friends and Enemies: The United States, China, and the Soviet Union, 1948–1972* (Stanford: Stanford University Press, 1990).

19. For one extraordinary story of persecution because of foreign connections (in this case fairly substantial ones), see Nien Cheng, *Life and Death in Shanghai* (New York: Grove Press, 1987).

20. China's insistence on remaining isolated and aloof from the world even in the 1980s led Su Xiaokang and Wang Luxiang to write the television documentary series *River Elegy,* which was filmed and shown on national television in China during the summer of 1988. In the series, the authors focus on the combination of China's authoritarian traditions and notions of cultural superiority as the reason China has fallen behind other formerly great civilizations in terms of development.

21. Nevertheless, the Chinese, still sensitive to slights at the hands of formerly rapacious powers, will rail at foreign countries demanding concessions from China, even if the exchange is more than fair.

22. David K. Jordan, *Gods, Ghosts, and Ancestors* (Berkeley: University of California, 1972); Arthur P. Wolf, ed., *Religion and Ritual in Chinese Society* (Stanford: Stanford University Press, 1974); Ching-kun Yang, *Religion in Chinese Society* (Berkeley: University of California Press, 1967).

23. It should be noted, however, that throughout the period of Communist rule in the People's Republic, ancestor worship and animistic practices have *flourished* in both Hong Kong and Taiwan—two places thoroughly Chinese in culture that have modernized quite rapidly. As is evident from studies of religion in other countries and other times, superstitious practices and religious beliefs need not be detrimental for development. Indeed, they can be a positive force.

24. Donald E. MacInnis, *Religion in China Today: Policy and Practice* (Maryknoll, NY: Orbin Books, 1989); Robert P. Weller, *Resistance, Chaos and Control in China: Taiping Rebels, Taiwanese Ghosts and Tiananmen* (London: MacMillan, 1993).

25. Lucian W. Pye, *The Mandarin and the Cadre: China's*

Political Cultures (Ann Arbor: Center for Chinese Studies, University of Michigan, 1988).

26. For a classic example of how during the Ten Bad Years (1966 to 1976), a label was chosen to villify whole groups of people, in this case how individuals previously associated with the extreme "leftist" position of the former Defense Minister Lin Biao were now revealed to be "closet Confucianists" or "rightists," see Jung-kuo Yang, *Confucius, "Sage" of the Reactionary Classes* (Beijing: Foreign Languages Press, 1974).

27. See, for example, Liang Heng's autobiographical account, written with Judith Shapiro, *Son of the Revolution* (New York: Vintage Books, 1983).

28. For the Anti-Rightist Campaign, see Roderick MacFarquhar, *The Origins of the Cultural Revolution* (New York: Columbia University Press, 1974). Vol. 1 covers 1956–60.

29. Richard C. Kraus, *Class Conflict in Chinese Socialism* (New York: Columbia University Press, 1981), p. 21.

30. Liu Binyan, one of China's leading journalists, wrote a poignant story about just this situation. See Liu Binyan, "The Fifth Man in the Overcoat," in Perry Link, ed., *People or Monsters* (Bloomington: Indiana University Press, 1983), pp. 79–97.

31. This comes out repeatedly in talks with Chinese scholars, party members, and officials who were victimized during the Twenty Bad Years from 1957 to 1976. Also touching on this is Ann F. Thurston, *Enemies of the People* (Cambridge: Harvard University Press, 1987).

32. Suzanne Ogden, *China's Unresolved Issues: Politics, Development, and Culture*, 3rd ed. (Englewood Cliffs, NJ: Prentice Hall, 1995), p. 234.

33. For greater detail on party bureaucrats and technocrats, see Hong Yung Lee, *From Revolutionary Cadres to Party Technocrats in Socialist China* (Berkeley: University of California, 1991).

34. Much of the following material is drawn from Chapter 4, "Leadership and Reform," in Ogden, *China's Unresolved Issues*.

35. Of course, some policies failed because they were poorly formed or because the problems they attempted to address were intractable. The leadership, which refused to recognize these possibilities, inevitably blamed middle- and lower-level cadres for their failure.

36. See Hong Yung Lee, *From Revolutionary Cadres*, pts. 2 and 3.

37. One scholar would argue that China's ideology is "adaptive to circumstances" because the depth of knowledge of Marxist-Leninist canon in China is limited, as are the number of people who have such knowledge, and "more to the point, no one has the authority to construe it but the Party." See Lowell Dittmer, "Beyond Revolution: Political Development in the PRC," in Joyce K. Kallgren, ed., *Building a Na-tion-State: China After Forty Years* (Berkeley: Center for Chinese Studies, University of California Press, 1990), p. 42.

38. For an excellent work on corruption, especially in the countryside, see Jean Oi, *State and Peasant in Contemporary China* (Berkeley: University of California Press, 1989); Jean Oi, and articles, "Commercializing China's Rural Cadres," *Problems of Communism* (September–October 1986), pp. 1–15; and Gong Ting, *The Politics of Corruption in Contemporary China: An Analysis of Policy Outcomes* (Westport, CT: Praeger, 1994).

39. Martin K. Whyte, "Evolutionary Changes in Chinese Culture," in Robert Dernberger et al., eds., *The Chinese: Adapting the Past, Facing the Future*, 2nd ed. (Ann Arbor: Center for Chinese Studies, University of Michigan, 1991), p. 715.

40. For a collection of official documents that indicate this, see Michel Oksenberg, Lawrence R. Sullivan, and Marc Lambert, eds., *Beijing Spring, 1989: Confrontation and Conflict, the Basic Documents* (Armonk, NY: M. E. Sharpe, Inc., 1990).

41. The CCP's keeping of dossiers on people is one of the most hated aspects of Communist rule in China. False information may be entered without the individual having any way of knowing it, and therefore a person's enemies have a perfect means of causing harm by writing "unsolicited letters" that are then placed in the dossier. The maintenance of dossiers is still an issue today, but at this point, most people are concerned that protesting the dossiers might be seen as a sign of disloyalty to the regime. Thus, the dossiers, which follow individuals from one workplace to another, remain in tact. For excellent detail on dossiers, see Hong Yung Lee, op. *From Revolutionary Cadres*, pp. 329–51.

42. The real reason the authorities wanted to arrest him was that he had published and distributed a magazine criticizing the CCP leadership.

43. For a far more complete analysis of China's legal system, see Chapter 6, "Socialist Legality and Social Control," in Ogden, *China's Unresolved Issues*.

44. See Victor H. Li, *Law Without Lawyers: A Comparative View of Law in China and the United States* (Boulder, CO: Westview, 1978).

45. They were criminal because they were counterrevolutionary, and counterrevolutionary because they questioned the legitimacy of a corrupt CCP leadership and publicly demanded that Deng Xiaoping and Li Peng step down from power.

46. For the issues that Chinese treatment of political criticism raise for human rights, see Asia Watch, *Punishment Season: Human Rights in China After Martial Law* (New York: Human Rights Watch, 1990); Asia Watch, *Repression in China Since June 4, 1989: Cumulative Data* (New York: Human Rights Watch, January 1991); and Asia Watch, *Rough Justice in Beijing: Pun-*

ishing the Black Hands of Tiananmen Square (New York: Human Rights Watch, January 1991). Also see Ann Kent, *Between Freedom and Subsistance: China and Human Rights* (NY: Oxford University Press, 1993).

47. William Alford, *To Steal a Book is an Elegant Offense* (Stanford: Stanford University Press, 1995); and Pitman Potter, ed., *Domestic Law Reforms in Post-Mao China* (Armonk, NY: M. E. Sharpe, 1994).

48. Andrew Walder, *Communist Neotraditionalism: Work and Authority in Chinese Industry* (Berkeley: University of California Press), 1986; and Chris Smith and Paul Thompson (eds.), *Transition: The Labour Process in Eastern Europe and China* (NY: Routledge, 1992).

49. See the posters, handbills, and speeches from the time of the 1989 Tiananmen demonstrations, as collected, edited, and analyzed in Suzanne Ogden, Kathleen Hartford, Lawrence R. Sullivan, and David Zweig, eds., *China's Search for Democracy: The Student and Mass Movement of 1989* (Armonk, NY: M. E.

Sharpe, Inc., 1992); and Craig Calhoun, *Neither Gods Nor Emperors: Students and the Struggle for Democracy in China* (Berkeley: University of California Press, 1994).

50. For perspectives on democracy by two of China's leading intellectuals, both of whom, because of the roles they are *believed* to have played in fomenting student protests that resulted in the massive Tiananmen demonstrations in 1989, were considered "black hands," hence counterrevolutionaries see Yan Jiaqi ed. and trans. *Yan Jiaqi and China's Struggle for Democracy*, David Bachman and Dali L. Yang (Armonk, NY: M. E. Sharpe, Inc., 1991); and Fang Lizhi, *Bringing Down the Great Wall: Writings on Science, Culture, and Democracy in China* (New York: Alfred A. Knopf, 1991).

51. Richard Louis Edmunds, *Patterns of China's Lost Harmony: A Survey of the Country's Environmental Degradation and Protection* (NY: Routledge, 1994).

9

The Third World and Political Development

"Everything is in flux. . . . You cannot step twice in the same river."

Heraclitus

Scholars of comparative politics have categorized the world into three groups of nations: the industrial democracies, mostly consisting of the Anglo-American and European nations; the Communist-bloc autocracies; and the remainder of the nations, generally less interested in the conflict between the first two blocs and therefore frequently referred to as the Third World. This third group of nations has been variously labeled: some use the term *less developed nations,* or LDCs; some call them the *developing areas;* some call them *non-Western systems;* while others, using the concept of a world economic system, refer to these nations as the *periphery,* as opposed to the industrial core. While problems abound with respect to defining this category precisely and then categorizing all of the nations of the world in this tripartite scheme, there is nevertheless a wide consensus that for the most part the *Third World* refers to the less industrialized nations of Asia, Africa, and Latin America.

The burgeoning interest in this third group of nations was to a large extent a product of the post–World War II breakdown of the colonial empires of European nations and the emergence of legally sovereign and independent nations in their place. When the United Nations Charter was signed in 1945, there were only 51 nations available to sign that document. By 1960, the number of members had almost doubled to nearly 100, and by 1995 had reached 185 member states. Hence, the number of states in the postwar world has more than tripled.

The Third World nations have widely divergent social, economic, and political attributes. Traditional society, rather than being rigorously conceptualized in its own right and thereby giving traditional nations something in common by definition, is treated as residual category. That is, any society that is not modern is called traditional. This creates a diverse category of systems that do not necessarily share anything other than the fact that they do not belong to the other category. It is not clear that these nations have enough in common to justify treating them as a single analytic category. Clearly, by economic, political, and social criteria, there is a vast gulf between the "more developed" Third World nations, such as South Korea or Argentina, and Sahara-belt African nations such as Chad, Mauritania, Mali, or Ethiopia; in fact, the former group have much more in common with such First World nations such as Italy—especially its southern half—than they do with the least developed Third World nations. Indeed, some scholars have suggested that this latter group of nations, lacking the resources or technology to provide even the minimal level of necessities for the sustenance of their respective populations, might well be considered as a separate category—the Fourth World.

CONCEPTUALIZING DEVELOPMENT: ECONOMIC, SOCIAL, AND POLITICAL DIMENSIONS

The foregoing suggests that one of the main difficulties in theorizing about Third World nations is the lack of agreement and precision with respect to the attributes that define the category. In other words, by what criteria are nations assigned to this category? Much of the literature fails to distinguish the social, economic, and political dimensions of modernity.[1] It is not only a possibility but a reality that nations operate with political forms associated with the absence of modernity (i.e., noninstitutionalized, charismatic forms of authority) while possessing a modern industrial plant and advanced technology. We will see below how scholars such as Samuel Huntington raise the question of the consequences of combining the modern attributes of mass communication, literacy, and geometric increases in the rates of political participation with traditional political institutions that are incapable of resolving the issues generated by such high rates of participation.[2] Some scholars have argued that modern political institutions involve some conception of equality in the sense of equal-

ity under law and in the sense of achievement rather than ascriptive bases of assigning rewards.[3] Others suggest that this is a Western and hence ethnocentric view of modernity. The famous German sociologist of the early twentieth century Max Weber was the progenitor of the idea that modernization consisted of a progressive rationalization of institutions and authority forms.[4] Traditional societies legitimate the authority of their elites by tradition or charisma, while modern societies have a rational, legal basis of legitimating authority (such as elections). Rationalization implies a kind of demythologizing of society, a secularization in the sense of the declining salience of closed thought systems. Yet, not all would identify secularization with modernity.

A second difficulty in theorizing about the Third World is the imperfect validity of the assumption that any or all of these dimensions constitute mutually exclusive dichotomies in the sense that nations are either purely modern or purely traditional by one of these criteria. Rather, it is clear that all nations possess some elements of traditionalism and some elements of modernity by any of these criteria, and are more modern along some dimensions than along others. For example, we have seen how traditional societies supposedly have a charismatic basis of legitimating the authority of their leaders. Yet, many of the leaders of our most advanced Western societies, such as Winston Churchill, Franklin Roosevelt, Charles de Gaulle, and Ronald Reagan, have derived much of their authority from their undoubted charisma. Similarly, it has been suggested that traditional societies are characterized by the lack of integration and of a unified communications system.[5] Yet, we have seen in Chapter 2 how sociopolitical segmentation characterizes a number of Western systems, such as Belgium and Canada. Moreover, the process of assimilation into a general culture is imperfect in any system, even that of the United States, as Michael Novack has noted when he wrote about the "unmeltable ethnics."[6] It is further asserted that traditional systems have a more ideological political style; yet, we have seen that a degree of ideologism characterizes the First World nations to a greater or lesser extent. In fact, almost all nations are mixtures of putatively modern and traditional elements. Moreover, rather than the dichotomy of modern versus traditional, more scholars prefer to think of this dimension as a continuum of more or less modern.

A third difficulty is the confusion created by the distinct yet related dimensions of the development process. While it is difficult to dispute the conclusion of Vicky Randall and Robin Theobald that the distinction between development and modernization is difficult to justify,[7] the distinctions between political development or modernization, social development, and economic development are important.

Economic development refers to industrialization and the development of modern technology and productive structures to sustain that technology (such as a factory system, instruments of mass production, and a supply of capital). It is measured by such indicators as the growth of gross national product, per capita caloric consumption, and the percentage of the work force in secondary economic pursuits (production or manufacturing) or tertiary economic pursuits (service or informational), as opposed to primary economic pursuits (agriculture or the raising and herding of livestock).

Social modernization refers to the development of a social context that could develop and would support a modern economy and technology. It entails a degree of social complexity—that is, a specialization of roles and division of labor, and a degree of mobilization into and identification with the broader social system. This last factor in turn entails a

broadening of the intellectual horizons of the average individual to an awareness of relevant life beyond the confines of one's village or even one's tribe to the wider, more abstract concept of nationhood, as discussed by Daniel Lerner.[8] This factor also entails a rapid expansion in the politically relevant segments of the population, those people of whom a government somehow needs to take account. Among the indicators of social modernization thus conceptualized are literacy rates, the spread and average duration of formal education, media exposure, and various measures of political participation.[9]

It is possible to imagine a modern society largely composed of individuals who are literate, skilled, and oriented toward a sense of belonging to a broader social system, a society composed of a complex or specialized role structure that is governed by set of political structures that contradict our sense of what a modern political system should be. Scholars have in fact attempted to delineate the attributes of a modern political system as distinct from the attributes of a modern social system outlined in the preceding paragraph. By the *political system* as distinct from the social system, we accept the now classic definition offered by Easton in 1951—those structures and processes that authoritatively (legitimately and backed by sanction) allocate those things that society values.[10] This is a broader conceptualization than the traditional one of confining the political system to the constitutionally designated institutions and processes without a concern for which structures and processes actually resolve issues and render authoritative decisions.

The characteristics of a modern political system, Gabriel Almond and others have suggested, might usefully be conceptualized in terms of its capabilities. Almond and G. Bingham Powell list five capabilities of a political system—regulative, extractive, distributive, symbolic, and responsive—with the implication that to the extent that systems have lowered capabilities on one or more of these five dimensions, they would be less modern.[11] The responsive capability does not necessarily imply democracy; the Chinese repression of the student uprising in the summer of 1989 may be considered a "response" to the demands of that movement. Other scholars have suggested somewhat different list, but there is a consensus that a modern political system has a greater ability to perform those functions any political system ideally is expected to perform, and to resolve successfully a greater volume and complexity of issues arising from the context of a changing and modernizing society.

This idea of system capability is related to the institutional school, best articulated by Huntington.[12] Institutions are complex and recurring patterns of behavior and interaction that have acquired a degree of legitimacy. When they have acquired a degree of complexity and legitimacy to process a growing volume of increasingly complicated and controversial issues without becoming issues themselves, they have added to the capabilities of a political system.

Social modernization involves mobilization, the induction of the masses into the political process, which thereby increases the politically relevant segment of the population. When these previously inert masses become thus politicized, they acquire an awareness of new horizons or possibilities for the quality of life. This changed awareness, associated with Daniel Lerner and his followers, begins with the process of urbanization, the induction of peasants into urban life. An increase in education and literacy follows and leads to increased media exposure and increased participation. Lerner's model is represented as follows: urbanization → literacy → media exposure → participation.[13] This mobilization generates a qualitative and quanti-

tative increase in expectations and demands, which places great stress on the political system.

The mobilizationists assume that political systems will necessarily adapt to the stress by generating an increased capability to process issues. Huntington argues if that such mobilization precedes an increased capacity of the system to process the issues thus generated, the system will break down or decay.

The emphasis or concern of institutionalists like Huntington is the maintenance of order and stability in the face of the pressures for social change generated by an increasingly mobilized and politicized population. Such scholars are less concerned with various criteria of social justice such as conceptualizations of equality. As such, Huntington and his followers are primarily thought of as relatively conservative on the political spectrum. Dependency theory, discussed below, focuses primarily on the existing level or inequality between the industrialized nations of the West, or the First World, and the less developed nations of the Third World. While they proclaim to offer a theoretical explanation for this inequality, it will be argued that many of them are normatively condeming it and would not mind generating a measure of destabilization in the existing order in order to effect the desired socioeconomic change.

Huntington's concept of institutionalization is one way of conceptualizing *political development* as distinguished from social development or modernization. By conceptually distinguishing the various aspects of modernization, scholars leave open the question of the relationship between them. The mobilization of society may or may not lead to an increased capability of political institutions, and the modernization of the social or political sectors may or may not be a prerequisite for sustained industrialization and technological modernization; however, these are questions best answered through inquiry rather than settled by definition.

In a similar vein to institutionalization, political development was equated by Max Weber with the idea of progressive rationalization, a concept that connotes greater efficiency in the implementation of the functions of government.[14] This rationalization involves a movement from charismatic and traditional to rational, legal bases of authority, as noted above. It also suggests an increasing pervasiveness of the bureaucratic form of organization, which is uniquely equipped to handle the imperatives of modern technology, as discussed in Chapter 2.

Yet, despite the observation of numerous scholars that to equate the political development of modernization with the evolution toward the liberal democratic model would constitute the most egregious ethnocentrism, the suggestion that political development entails movement toward that model still emanates from prominent figures in the field. David Apter, for example, blatantly states that political development involves "greater participation and elite accountability."[15] Despite the fact that this is an oversimplification of Apter's complex and provocative ideas about development, he does make a case for the association of at least some aspects of the democratic model with a modern political system. For example, he argues that what he calls "a reconciliation system," roughly, pluralism in which conflicts of actual interests are resolved through bargaining, is better suited to the later stages of the modernization process with the imperatives of advanced technology than a "mobilization system" based on a single legitimate set of "consumatory" values, because the former is a more open system, tolerant of the exchange of ideas and information on which the development of modern science and technology depends.

In contrast to those scholars who associate some attributes of democratization with political modernity, Huntington has argued that political modernization discouraged the evolution of democratic values in a political system.[16] For Huntington, modernization entails the centralization of authority, the penetration of society by the legitimate power of the state, and the consequent subordination or destruction of competing institutions such as churches, aristocracies, or feudalism. The idea of popular sovereignty, the idea that the ultimate political power in a political system resides with the masses—which as we saw in Chapter 4 was given wide currency through the writings of Jean-Jacques Rousseau and spread through the Napoleonic Wars—is also associated with the modern era. Yet, all of these developments are negatively related to the development of democratic values such as accountability and the constraint of political power. Modernity is associated with the development among people of a sense of control over their own destiny. Such a liberal and expansive sense of competence leads to a demand for a state that has the power to implement policies to achieve goals; yet, democratic values entail control over the exercise of power and safeguard against its abuse. Hence, a modern and therefore more effective state may be necessarily a less democratic one by this train of thought. This points up the confusion about which attributes are included in our conception of a modern political system (not to mention modernity in general). While some scholars suggest that certain conceptualizations of democratization should be included in the idea of a modern political system, others so conceptualize modernity that those systems that achieved modernity earliest and most completely were less able or took longer to evolve toward democratic values. More modern political institutions, such as the centralized and efficient monarchies of sixteenth- and seventeenth-century Europe, may have acted to impede the evolution toward other aspects of modernization, such as the expansion of effective political participation.

It may be thus reported that the mainstream of scholarship in the field of political development or non-Western politics rejects the "compatibility assumption" that the various components of modernization are interrelated such that the modernization of one aspect of the whole system, say the political format, cannot be sustained without a corresponding modernization of the other aspects, such as society, culture, economy, and industrial system. In line with this rejection, many Third World leaders covet some aspects of modernization, especially the technology that underlies the industrial capacity to produce an effective military and an abundance of consumer goods, while rejecting other aspects of what has been identified as modernity, especially cultural aspects of Western society. Yet, it is not self-evident that modern technology, based as it is on the development of modern science, can be maintained in a closed cultural context, such as the Islamic fundamentalist regime of the late Ayatollah Khomeini, that represses the very information and idea exchange on which modern science depends, or that it can be developed without the complex role structure that allows for specialization of function.

The foregoing suggests a lack of agreement among scholars on the meaning of modernization and development (or even on whether those terms ought to be distinguished) and the implications of those meanings for inquiry into Third World politics. This lack of consensus may be conveniently summarized in three major issues. The first is whether it is useful to dichotomize the world by using one category of political systems, variously labeled by terms such as non-Western, Third World, or less developed, that is

precisely definable and clearly distinguishable from the opposite category of Western systems. After a brief flirtation with this idea, serious scholarship has abandonned it for the reasons discussed above.

Second, while some scholars have treated the underdevelopment of the Third World as a state of being, others treat it as a process of moving from one state to another. Thus, while some have focused on development or modernization, others preferred merely to talk about the nature and implications of rapid change.[17] This reflects a third source of disagreement—whether this process of change is a linear process of inexorably becoming more Western. For example, the now largely discredited manifestations of stage theory were based on the assumption that all political or social systems evolve through the same stages, albeit at different speeds, and arrive at the same end of the evolutionary process.[18] This is an application of what Karl Popper called "historicism," the idea that history unfolds inexorably through impersonal forces, irrespective of human will.[19] Moreover, it is assumed by this school of thought that the process is linear, and that all of the system change is in the same direction from traditional or less modern to more modern and thus more like the Western democratic model. Reflected in this disagreement is the related question of whether the Western model of liberal democracy constitutes an outcome that would be desired by the leaders of many Third World nations.

The postwar optimism about the inevitable popularity of the liberal democratic model among newly emergent nations was dashed as the powerful force of nationalism in such nations found a short-term alliance with and was frequently coopted by Marxism, and various forms of authoritarian government became the rule in the Third World. More recent findings of an emerging popularity of democratic government do not negate the reality that Western-style democracy not only remains an exception in the Third World but that numerous cases can be cited of nations moving away from rather than toward that model. Certainly the Islamic revolution in Iran constitutes a move away from aspects of the Western model.

It is thus evident that change does not entail the notion of development insofar as that concept implies progress toward the model of industrialized liberal democracy. It is not even consensually evident that change itself is inevitable among Third World nations. Fred Riggs argued that less developed nations tend to be dominated by their bureaucracies in the face of weakly developed representative or political structures.[20] Since bureaucracy as an organizational form is designed to maximize the administrative values of predictability, efficiency, and technocratic expertise, it is not suited for promoting the political values of flexibility, creativity, adaptability, and responsiveness. Hence, Third World systems combining "the heavy weight of bureaucratic power" with poorly developed representative institutions may tend to stagnate rather than develop and adapt. Riggs's model of such systems suggests that they are neither traditional nor modern, but that they combine a particular hybrid of elements from both worlds that impedes the development process.

Thus, while the literature on Third World systems freely uses the concepts of development, political development, and modernization, it does not reveal any widespread agreement on what these terms mean. This prevents us from reaching an agreement on the categorization of particular systems as developed, modern, or otherwise. Without such agreement, comparative politics as a field cannot confidently resolve the question of what attributes are regularly associated with developed systems or with change in the direction of such development. Otherwise put, we cannot explain development unless we can precisely state what it is.

POLITICAL DEVELOPMENT AND DEMOCRATIZATION

The foregoing suggests that political development should be defined independently of democratization. Earlier gropings with the concept of political development that held Western liberal democracies as the model of a "developed" political system have been widely rejected as ethnocentric.[21] Subsequently, leading scholars have been strongly pessimistic about the prospects for democratization among the Afro-Asian and Latin American nations that we have for convenience been labeling as Third World. Indeed, Samuel Huntington published one of the leading expressions of such pessimism, which is ironic since he has more recently written the most widely cited analyses of the wave of democratizations that has in fact occurred among Third World nations.[22]

The basis of such pessimism with respect to the prospects of democracy in the Third World is the literature on the cultural and social requisites of democracy discussed at length in Chapter 2. After the seminal work of Ronald Inglehart, cited in numerous places in this book, the concept of political culture has again been placed at the cutting edge of this discipline. It was widely concluded that democracy was unlikely to become institutionalized or legitimated in a sociocultural context in which the population was not literate, open-minded or tolerant of diversity, and egalitarian in their attitudes toward authority and their fellow human beings, and in which a strong middle class had not evolved.

Yet, the "third wave" of democratization has in fact occurred since about the middle to late 1980s to the early 1990s, largely in places where the literature on the sociocultural requisites of democracy would have predicted such a transition to be highly unlikely—in Catholic Third World and Communist-bloc nations. For example, Seymour Lipset and others have said that the Western democracies evolved in Protestant nations because, in their view, the closed-minded authoritarianism of the Catholic Church was inimical to democratic values. Yet, as is discussed in some detail in Chapter 11, most of the Third World nations that have adopted a democratic format in this "third wave" are Catholic. This "third wave" has thus provoked a reassessment of classical theorizing on the preconditions of democracy.

There are several possible explanations for this phenomenon. One is that democracy is the political format of the future because it is the only one in which ordinary people can lead a decent and humane life reasonably free from fear and anxiety. Thus, as Edward Friedman argues, since democracy is "humanly attractive and dictatorship inhumanly repellent," scholars who stressed the sociocultural requisites of democracy underestimated the "universal attractiveness of democracy and human rights."[23] If democracy is indeed the wave of the future, it was precisely in those nations lacking the putative sociocultural requisites where the transitions to democracy had to occur, for these were the nations that were not yet democratic.

Second, in assessing the prospects for democracy in Pacific Rim states such as Japan and China, which, of course, lack the Western cultural attributes held up as the requisites of democracy, Friedman forcibly argues that these so-called requisites may not be an explanatory factor for democracy after all. Friedman, Giuseppe Di Palma, and Terry Karl are among a growing chorus of scholars

rejecting the "determinism" of the earlier literature for not placing enough emphasis on the bargaining, coalition-building strategies, and other strategic political choices of the actors involved in a particular situation.[24] Such writers come close to an eschewal of the basic social science and comparative politics approach of generalizing from the patterns of the past to derive expectations of the future.

Third, democracy swept the Catholic nations in the wake of the major changes in the church in the Vatican II conference of 1963 and the liberalizing reign of Pope John XXIII. The "third wave" of democratization in the Catholic world may not be so much a denial of the impact of Catholicism in the modernization of the West but a testament to the fundamental changes in the orientation and impact of the church. Friedman is certainly correct in claiming that Catholicism is not necessarily a barrier to democratization; however, Seymour Lipset may have had a basis in asserting that the church, *as it existed from the beginnings of the modern age to the 1960s,* was not conducive to the establishment and consolidation of democratic institutions and values.[25]

Friedman's assertion that political choices provide part of the explanation for the establishment or legitimation of democracy in any given situation balances the overreliance on cultural or other contextual explanations. However, he goes too far in completely rejecting the impact of cultural factors on the likelihood of the successful establishment and consolidation of democracy.

Democratization has clearly been a major story in the recent history of Latin America, as we will see in Chapter 11. It has made significant inroads in Asia as well. Despite the hegemony, until recently, of the Liberal Democratic Party in Japan, that nation is certainly a democracy in the sense that term was conceptualized in Chapter 2. Recall that the critical factor is not the alternation of elites but the fact that the opposition is not suppressed. The means of selecting the elites in Japan provides a measure of accountability, as attested by the resignation of Japanese prime ministers in the wake of corruption scandals to avoid electoral disaster for the governing party and by the eventual end of Liberal Democratic Party rule. The failure of the democracy movement in China at Tiananmen Square in 1989 did not end popular sentiment for democratic reforms in that nation. A dozen Latin American nations have made the transition to democracy since the 1970s. However, this is not necessarily the end of the story. As we will see in Chapter 11, the fact that power is currently in civilian hands does not obviate the continuing power and influence of the military in those praetorian societies in which the military has moved in and out of power virtually at will. Democracy established is a long way from democracy consolidated. It may be a bit premature to reach a final judgment on the impact of any contextual factors on the ability of democratic institutions to flourish over time.

EXPLAINING UNDERDEVELOPMENT: LENINISM AND DEPENDENCY

The massive level of inequality with respect to almost any index of material well-being between the major industrial powers of the First World and the less developed nations of the Third World is an inescapable fact of central concern to all students of Third World politics. For example, "the 'Big Seven' democracies (United States, United Kingdom, West Germany, France, Italy, Canada, and Japan) constitute less than 14 percent of the world's population; yet, they consume 42 percent of its energy, generate 51 percent of its exports, and enjoy 53 percent of it goods and services."[26] In contrast to the relatively affluent and comfortable life style of the people who

live in these industrial democracies, people in Third World nations endure a standard of living at or near the subsistence level, are not only uneducated but largely illiterate, and are beset with diseases that have virtually disappeared among Western democracies. The question is whether this massive inequality is a self-evident injustice or a just reward for superior achievement.

The fact of this gap in the level of material well-being between nations of the industrial West and the Afro-Asian and, to a lesser extent, Latin nations of the less developed and more agrarian Third World offends the essentially egalitarian values espoused by many scholars; hence, one aim of such scholars is to identify and recommend effective means for reducing this gap. The first step in this enterprise is the explanation of this inequality and the underdevelopment of the Third World. To recommend cures, one must first diagnose the cause.

Explanations of underdevelopment may be classified as one of two types: explanations that focus on causes in the attributes of the nations themselves or on the behavior patterns of their citizens, and explanations that focus on the impact of the world economic and political system and the behaviors of the other nations. Internal explanations focus on cultural attributes, demographics, and policy choices made by the elites of the societies in question. These internal explanations may be subdivided into those that are people-centered (such as cultural) and those that are state-centered (such as policies). External explanations presume a world economic system, and focus on the asymmetrical economic relations between the industrial core nations and the nations of the Third World.

In recent years, external explanations have been favored by leading scholars, and internal explanations have been relatively neglected. Normative considerations may underlie some of this preoccupation with external explanations to the neglect of internal ones. The assignment of the cause of under-development to the developed world relieves the less developed nations from some of the stigma attached to being perceived as less modern or even backward. Furthermore, as we will see, the Marxist-Leninist foundation of dependency theory, the most *au courant* external explanation, affords a prediction of the inevitable triumph and redemption of the downtrodden, a prediction that affords a ray of hope to those nations whose situation appears otherwise dire if not hopeless.

The various external explanations of un-derdevelopment are based upon the idea that the underdeveloped world has been ex-ploited by the industrial West. This wide-spread assumption of an exploitative rela-tionship between the First and Third Worlds emanates in large part from the fact that the relationship between these two parts of the world began chiefly with the outright politi-cal subjugation of much of the Third World by the industrial West through colonialism. The colonial experience therefore affects a great deal of the thinking of both Third World elites and scholars concerned with those nations.

The Colonial Experience

Colonialism, as that term has been commonly understood, refers to the political subjuga-tion and control of one political system by an-other, such that the former is deprived of sov-ereign power in both theory and practice. Colonialism does not conventionally refer to the mere influence of external forces in the decision-making processes of a nation such as might be achieved by the rewards and pun-ishments of superior economic resources, al-though some scholars, such as John Kautsky, choose to define it that way, but rather to a situation in which a nation exercises ultimate political authority over another political sys-

tem.[27] The exercise by a more powerful po-litical system of influence in the political process of a weaker political system without the former system exercising formal political control over the latter is sometimes referred to as *neocolonialism.*

Neocolonialism is a term that has come into vogue in recent decades as a device for continuing to assert that an exploitative rela-tionship exists between the industrial and Third Worlds despite the obvious demise of Western colonial empires as we have under-stood that concept. Colonialism is a term that has acquired a significant pejorative implica-tion; hence, the continued use of that con-cept is means for normatively indicting the West for the enormous gap in material well-being between the First and Third Worlds under the guise of scholarly objectivity. *Neo,* as was pointed out in an earlier chapter, is a prefix that allows one to apply a concept to a situation in which it clearly does not apply. In this way, the difficulties experienced by Third World systems may still be blamed on colo-nialism, even though Western colonialism, as we have understood it, has now for all intents and purposes disappeared.

The West has been in the business of colo-nizing the Afro-Asian and Latin parts of the world for over 500 years. However, much of the empires of the European powers was ac-quired in the late nineteenth century, so the most extensive operation of European colo-nialism lasted less than a hundred years.

The impact of colonialism varied a great deal with the internal attributes of the land being colonized and with the type of colonial administration imposed. With regard to the latter, scholars have found it useful to distin-guish between the *direct* and *indirect* adminis-tration of their colonies.[28] In the former style, found in many of the French colonies, especially Indochina, Europeans occupied offical posts down to the lowest level, leaving the native population little opportunity for acquiring experience in official roles. In the latter style, epitomized by the British administration of India, the imperial power cultivated a significant native role in the administrative and police sectors of the colony, leaving a trained officialdom to perform effectively essential functions upon the achievement of independence. The British varied in the way they administered their colonies, however, resorting to more direct rule in other parts of their empire. The percentage of native administrators was quite low in the British possessions of Uganda and Ghana, for example. The Belgians were even more remiss in integrating Africans into official roles in the Belgian Congo. Moreover, more recent thinking is much more skeptical about the causal impact of the choice between direct and indirect administration of colonies on the eventual stability and success of newly independent nations.

In addition, the resistance of traditional institutions to the impact of modern technologies and the values that support those technologies was clearly greater in some colonial possessions than in others. The tendency of Islamic nations in the Middle East, for example, has been to cling to tradition despite the history of a considerable British presence.

Colonialism has affected the experience of the new nations in one additional way, for the means by which independence was achieved appears to have an impact on the politics of the emerging independent nation. Specifically, if the inevitability of independence was accepted by the colonial nation, the politics of the emerging nation was more likely to be moderate and relatively stable. When the nationalist aspirations of the colony were repressed by the colonial power, the elites of the emerging nation tended to be more extremist and anti-Western, and the politics of such nations has tended to be more violent and unstable. French Indochina is a case in point. Moderate, non-Communist nationalism was repressed by the French by every means, which exacerbated the subsumption of the nationalist front by the Communists.[29]

Dependency Theory

As noted, dependency theory, called *dependencia* by it authors among the Latin Americanists, has become the dominant and most widely accepted explanation of underdevelopment among politically left-leaning students of the Third World. Although the theory is distinguishable in important respects from its Leninist roots, as will be explained in detail below, its logic draws heavily on the Leninist view of the world economic system to the point that it is no accident that the leading proponents of dependency theory have a tendency to be Marxists and/or to propose socialist solutions to the problem of underdevelopment. Accordingly, because the logic of *dependencia* is derived from the Marxist analysis of capitalism and its requirements (and more particularly the Leninist exegesis of Marxism), and because Marxist theory itself retains a considerable following among intellectuals, it is useful to preface our review of dependency theory with a summary and discussion of the Marxist-Leninist analysis of underdevelopment.

Marx predicted that mature capitalism would collapse from the inevitable recurring crises of overproduction, a conclusion that derives from the assumed labor theory of value that Marx lifted uncritically from the economist David Ricardo's assumptions about the economic system and labor force that may be less valid in the postindustrial age than they were in the early stages of industrialization. The labor theory of value holds that the value of a product is equal to the labor put into it. The entrepreneurs (in Marxist jargon, the bourgeoisie), who merely provide the capital, extract profits from the workers (in Marxist language, the proletariat), to whom legitimately belong the fruits of their labor. Since laborers have no bargaining position, due to a reserve army of the unemployed and the interchangeability of essentially unskilled workers, entrepreneurs compel workers to produce additional goods without additional compensation. Since the worker is increasingly unable to purchase that which he or she has produced, the problem of overproduction becomes inevitable, as does a growing supply of capital without opportunities for investment. These problems, in turn, generate a recurring and increasingly severe series of economic crises in which more of the bourgeoisie fall into the ranks of the proletariat, leaving a very few exploiters vainly striving to maintain their oppression of a vast and growing army of the exploited motivated by a naturally growing class consciousness. This system, Marx expected, must necessarily collapse of its own weight as capitalism grows through its natural cycle and reaches a mature stage.

Lenin's ideas may be viewed, among other ways, as an attempt to explain and justify the obvious discrepency between Marx's prediction of the collapse of capitalism in advanced Western nations and the obvious reality of the failure of that prediction in terms of such phenomena as the growing prosperity of the working class and the growing bourgeoisie, as well as the apparent persistence of Western capitalism itself. Borrowing heavily from J. A. Hobson's theory of imperialism,[30] Lenin argued that the colonial empires of the Western capitalist powers were able to stave off the otherwise inexorable demise of these capitalist powers by siphoning their surplus value into captive markets, which also provided outlets for their accumulated investment capital and cheap sources of raw material. Because capitalism now needs imperialism to survive, the strategy for bringing

about the downfall of capitalism becomes the cause of anti-imperialism. *Anti-imperialism* in this context is understood as the political and economic independence of African, Asian, and Latin nations from the Western capitalist democracies. The Communist revolution now becomes a two-stage movement; first, help the forces of nationalism in their struggle against imperialism, and second, coopt the non-Communist nationalists in the cause of Communism. To a large extent, this is what happened in Indochina. Ho Chi Minh first headed a broad front of both Communists and non-Communist nationalists in an organization whose ostensible purpose was national independence, *Viet Nam Doc Lap Dong Minh Hoi.* (*Doc Lap* means "independence.") Clearly, the Communists were able to coopt the movement for their own purposes.

Clearly Marx's original vision of the class struggle has now been transformed in this Leninst perspective. The Western world as a whole, including the industrial labor force that constituted Marx's heroes, the proletariet, now becomes the oppressor, and the Third World as a whole, rich and poor alike, becomes the oppressed.

This convoluted application of Marxism to a context to which it was never intended to apply serves three important purposes. First, the historicist Marxist claim to have discovered the inexorable laws of history through the "dialectic" entails the conclusion that the triumph of the oppressed and the achievement of social justice from a Third World perspective is inevitable. This prediction of inexorable redemption to peoples whose situation otherwise appears hopeless is enormously appealing. Moreover, this redemption is in material terms; Marx's theory is known as "dialectical materialism." To Third World peoples living at a subsistence level if not at the verge of starvation, the value of material well-being takes precedent over the more abstract, or "higher," values of civil liberties or individualism offered by the liberal democracies of the West. Second, this perspective places the responsibility for the less developed state of the Third World on Western capitalist exploitation, thereby removing much Third World guilt for the less developed condition of those societies. Third, the Soviet model epitomized the transformation of an essentially peasant society into a great power in a generation, as opposed to the Western model in which such development unfolded over centuries. To Third World leaders who would like to experience these changes in their own lifetimes, the Soviet model of development has had enormous appeal.

These purposes, together with the short-run convergence of interests between Leninists and Third World nationalists, explain the wide appeal of Marxism-Leninism once had in competition with the liberal democratic model among the newly emergent nations. However, the wave of democratization discussed above that has occurred along with and since the collapse of the Soviet Union suggests that the Leninist model may no longer have a widespread appeal among Third World elites. Some Third World nations, such as in India, Uruguay, and perhaps the Philippines, have had a fairly well established democratic tradition. In each of these nations, however, one might find reasons to qualify the democratic label. Other nations have experimented with a democratic format for periods of time interspersed with periods of authoritarian retrenchment, often of a praetorian nature. Brazil returned to civilian rule in the mid-1980s; Paraguay in 1989. Latin America has experienced nine transitions to democratic rule since 1979, after having experienced numerous retrenchments to authoritarian or military rule in the 1960s. Nigeria has similarly experienced periods of civilian politics with a more or less competitive party system but has been ruled by military juntas for most of its independent existence.

Both dependency theory and Leninism thus argue that the industrialized West keeps the Third World (or the core keeps the periphery) in a state of economic dependence because the emerging nations of the Third World serve the economic needs of the capitalist West. The West accomplishes this task by creating what dependency theorists call an "infrastructure of dependency."[31] This infrastructure putatively consists of structuring economic institutions and roles in a way that serves the needs of the West and that installs native elites, whose role it is to control their nations to meet the needs of the West, and who depend on Western support to stay in power. Thus a class of native "middlemen," called *compradores* in Brazil, has developed. Their role is to engage in the trade of Third World resources for Western manufactured products, minus a profit. These middlemen, who clearly have an interest in maintaining the dependent relationship from which they make their living, frequently control their own governments with western support. Pro-Western dictators of Latin American nations, such as Fulgencio E Batista y Zaldivar of Cuba, Anastasio Somoza Debayle of Nicaragua, Rafael Leonidas Molina Trujillo of the Dominican Republic, who oppressed their own people but rendered their countries as fertile ground for the investment of Western capital in return for Western military and economic support, also exemplify native elites that comprise part of the infrastructure of dependency. American support of such manifestly nondemocratic and frequently brutal and oppressive governments is perceived by liberal critics of American foreign policy as the cynical support of the forces of reaction in the interests of the plutocratic multinational corporations that such critics believe shape U.S. foreign policy in contradiction with the egalitarian and democratic principles for which the country purports to stand.

This infrastructure also consists of economic arrangements designed to serve the imperatives of Western capitalism rather than to promote the economic development of the Third World nations. For example, Western capital is invested in ways that shape the energies and skill development of the Third World countries into extractive enterprises (the mining and harvesting of raw materials for shipment to the West) instead of promoting native productive capabilities. Roads and rail lines are located to facilitate the transportation of raw materials to seaports for shipment to the West rather than to facilitate the development of native productive enterprises.

In this perspective, the profits, extracted by the West for turning Third World resources into finished products, are illegitimate and a form of exploitation. These resources did belong to the Third World country in the first place; hence, the benefits they offer should legitimately belong to that country. Moreover, the technology necessary to engage in the secondary enterprises of turning raw materials into finished products is kept hidden in the West by patent laws, thus preserving the strucure of dependency. Dependency theorists apparently assume that technology ought to be community property available for use on the basis of need or for the widest possible benefit, rather than the property of its creators. The asymmetrical nature of the trade relations, whereby the value accruing to the West in the form of raw materials plus profits always exceeds the value accruing to the native country in the form of payment for raw materials, is presented as evidence of the exploitative nature of the dependency relationship. Independence, in the dependency perspective, connotes not only political sovereignty but economic self-sufficiency as well.

The Leninist foundation of the dependency argument should be apparent from the foregoing. The dependency theory, however, takes the Leninist analysis a step further in blaming Western capitalism for the underdeveloped state of the Third World. In the Leninist perspective, the wealth and development of Western capitalism grew out of some positive attributes of that system, but the capitalist system is maintained and protected from its inevitable demise by imperialism. In the dependency perspective, however, the wealth and development of Western capitalism grew out of the same exploitative processs that created underdevelopment in the Third World. Thus while the Leninists would argue that capitalist imperialism *perpetuates* underdevelopment, the dependency theorists would argue that capitalism *developed* by creating underdevelopment. This dependency perspective rejects the widely held assumption that the Third World nations were underdeveloped prior to the development of the world capitalist system.

The Dependency Perspective Critiqued

Dependency theory constitutes both a putative explanation of underdevelopment and a normative indictment of world capitalism that is widely popular among students of Third World politics and has practically become an article of faith among many students of Latin American politics. The popularity of dependency theory as an explanation of underdevelopment is, however, concentrated among those who are on the political left, who tend to be critical of capitalism and other Western values, and who are rather still impressed by the Marxist perspective on world events. Scholars who are more to the center and right on the political spectrum and who tend to be more pro-Western and less Marxist are increasingly critical of the dependency explanation of underdevelopment.

The criticisms of dependency theory may be conveniently thought of as falling on one or more of three distinguishable dimensions: the logic and internal plausiblity of the theory, the fit of the logical entailments of the theory with the real world, and the presence of alternative and in some ways preferable explanations of the same thing.

Dependency theory is immediately flawed in the minds of some critics in that it offers a simple, single factor explanation—the economic imperatives of capitalism—for an exceedingly complex phenomenon—the state of social and economic modernization of a nation. As a general rule, simple explanations of complex social phenomena might be regarded with suspicion. The argument that the state of development or underdevelopment is simply a function of capitalist exploitation and is utterly unaffected by the cultural, historical, social, or geographic attributes of a nation strikes these critics as unrealistic. Moreover, the theory assumes that the entire infrastructure of a society's economy is determined by the incentive from capital investment by the industrialized and exploitative system. Yet, the level of Western investment in most of these societies is simply not great enough to have plausibly caused a restructuring of their entire infrastructure. For instance, in all of Latin America, the focus of many of the leading dependency theorists, the total foreign investment in 1994 was $19 billion, of which about 65 percent or 12.3 billions came from the U.S. or only about $35.14 per capita, hardly a sufficient sum to have plausibly determined the socioeconomic structure of those systems.[32]

There is a further flaw in the logic of dependency theory in the perspective of its pro-capitalist critics in that it adopts the Marxist perspective toward the value of capital investment and profit. This perspective, adopting the economist David Ricardo's "labor theory of value," regards the extraction of profits from either capital investment or the processing of raw materials into finished products as an illegitimate form of exploitation. Much of the support for the indictment of capitalist exploitation is data that show that the money paid for the raw materials and resources of the less developed nations is far less than the cost of the manufactured products made from those materials and sold back to the less developed nation. This creates a trade imbalance in favor of the industrialized nations and a long-term deepening debt crisis for the less developed world. Yet, critics of dependency argue that value is in fact added to the raw materials by the manufacturing process and that the technology utilized in that process is ethically the property of its creators. Thus, the critics reject the dependency assumption that technology ought legitimately to be regarded as community property, an assumption that underlies the dependency criticism of patent laws.[33] Critics of dependency theory implicitly assume that economic incentive plays a major role in creativity and productivity; hence, unless the rewards for technological innovation are protected by patent laws, the rate of technological innovation itself will be significantly slowed.

Moreover, the profits earned from the mere investment of capital are regarded by the critics of dependency theory as not only legitimate but essential. Capital is invested at a risk in order to transform raw materials into usable consumer goods, a risk that will not be taken if the hope of profits is removed. While raw materials are the property of the less developed nations from which they are extracted, these materials have no value to anyone unless they are transformed by Western technology and Western capital into consumer goods. Middle Eastern oil, for example, is of value largely because of the network of industries built around the technology of the motor car and the ability of oil companies to transform crude petroleum into fuel for automobiles.

Beyond the internal flaws of dependency theory, critics argue that the predictions logically derived from the theory do not conform to the real world. Since dependency theorists maintain that underdevelopment was created out of the exploitative relationship between the Third World and the West, those Third World nations that had the closest and most extensive relationships with the West should be the most underdeveloped, while conversely those few Third World nations that have had minimal contact with the West should be the most developed. In fact, the opposite is closer to reality. Chief among the few Third World nations that were never colonies and that had only minimal contact with the industrialized West are those paragons of industrialization and prosperity, Ethiopia and Liberia. Meanwhile, some of the former colonies that have had very close contact with their colonizer both before and since independence have been the beneficiaries of technology transfers and now are among the most industrialized and prosperous Third World countries. Hong Kong and India may exemplify such states. Clearly, the relationship of Third World societies with the industrialized West has yielded a mixture of negative consequences deriving from exploitation and paternalism, and positive consequences involving technology transfer and the dissemination of modern scientific knowledge.

The major reservation voiced by critics of dependency theory involves the inability of dependency theorists to confront alternative explanations of underdevelopment that may be equally plausible yet flawed by fewer empirical contradictions and fewer questions about the basic assumptions and internal logic of the theory. In order to take seriously the claim of the dependency theorists that they have the one best explanation of underdevelopment, one would have to show that

alternative explanations of underdevelopment are either nonexistent, flawed, or less adequate in accounting for the facts. Yet, serious scholars have offered alternative explanations that are not only equally plausible but that seem to account more adequately for more of the relevant facts.

ALTERNATIVE EXPLANATIONS OF UNDERDEVELOPMENT

In contrast to the external explanations of underdevelopment epitomized by Leninism and dependency theory, internal explanations focus on various attributes common to many Third World nations. At the risk of contradicting our earlier assertions about the range and variablity of attributes among Third World nations, we are suggesting that certain attributes have been widely identified as occurring significantly more commonly in these nations than in those commonly classified as industrial democracies or industrial autocracies. These attributes, which are internal to the nature of these less developed societies, may be logically suggested to create an impediment to the modernization process, independently of the nature or policies of the industrially advanced capitalist nations. Among these attributes are rapid population growth; the prevalence of value systems or ideologies less conducive to modernization as it is understood in the West; the heavy weight of bureaucratic power and of the influence of the military, a phenomenon known as *praetorianism;* and the weakness of legitimate political institutions buttressed by tribalism, regionalism, and clientelism.

Population Growth

One of the principal alternative explanations for much of the persistence of Third World underdevelopment is the geometric population growth in many of these nations, at the least, a population growth that exceeds their ability to maintain the existing populations on a subsistence standard. It will not do, for instance, as dependency advocate Michael Parenti claims to do, to use Ethiopia to disprove the proposition that underdevelopment is maintained and exacerbated by excessive population growth. For the nations on the rim of the increasingly encroaching Sahara Desert beset by chronic drought and crop failure of the most egregious degree, what constitutes excessive population growth may be a lower figure than what would be true in more fertile lands.

In fact, in much of the postwar era, there was a very rapid population growth in much of the Third World and especially in Latin America, the area of focus for most of the leading advocates of dependency theory, while the population of the industrialized world grew at a much slower rate. For example, between 1960 and 1975, the population of the United States grew from about 181 million to around 214 million, an increase of nearly 19 percent, while in the same period, the population of Mexico grew from some 36 million to some 59 million, an increase of 64 percent. Thus, Mexico's population grew at over three times the rate of that in the United States in that brief period. While a number of European nations have achieved zero population growth, the growth rate of the Mexican population was at 2.2 percent as of 1994, a rate that would cause that population to double in about 30 years.[34] Although the growth rate of South America has slowed significantly from a previous high of 3 percent to around 2 percent by the early 1990s, it is still significantly higher than in the nations of the West. The high birth rate in many Third World nations has been an attribute of these systems for a long time, if not always. What is recent in the postwar era is the sharply lowered rate of infant mortality with the introduction of basic Western hygiene, sanitation, and medical technology. While previously families in these nations had many children but few who survived infancy, today many or most may survive.

Yet, it should be noted that the relationship between population growth and development is complex. The data do *not* support a thesis that high birth rates are a necessary or sufficient cause of the level of per capita income. The Philippines, India, Peru, and Mexico, with similarly high birth rates, have widely varying levels of per capita income. Thus, while high birth rates constitute one factor that has a dysfunctional impact on economic growth, the impact of any one such factor can be neutralized or overcome by the impact of other relevant factors.

The significance of rapid population growth for development is that resources that could be used for capital are diverted to consumption. Development, of course, involves the accumulation of capital to be invested in new technologies or in the industrial capabilities for expanded production—steel mills, refineries, transportation, etc. Clearly, the more mouths to feed, the more scarce resources are going to be consumed rather than invested. Moreover, when the population is growing rapidly, a greater percentage of the people are minors and nonproducing consumers. If a husband and wife have two children, the wife may work outside the home, in which case there would be two producers out of four consumers. If a couple has eight children, the wife will almost certainly not work outside the home, and only 10 percent of these consumers will also produce and contribute to the gross national product, while 90 percent are purely consumers. In this way, a national disposition to large families becomes devastatingly dysfunctional for economic growth and development. In light of these considerations, it is hard to see how a less developed nation with the kind of rapid population growth experienced by Mexico can possibly accumulate the capital for substantial investment into capital goods industries, even if exploitation by the core industrial nations was completely nonexistent.

Although the Catholic Church has received more than its share of the blame for excessive population growth because of its position on birth control and abortion, the problem seems to be essentially cultural rather than one of religion in and of itself. Culture as used here, while encompassing religion, is a broader concept including other phenomena as well. While Mexico had the population explosion noted above, quintessentially Catholic Italy experienced a growth of only 8.7 percent. Moreover, many non-Catholic nations in the Third World, such as China and India, are also disposed toward large families and experience destructive rates of population growth. Among the kinds of cultural factors that might account for the high birth rate among Third World nations is the much discussed Latin trait of *machismo* (discussed in Chapter 11)—a kind of swaggering assertion of masculinity that is manifested, among other ways, in proving one's "manliness" by siring as many children as possible. Agricultural traditions of recently agrarian economies may value large numbers of children as useful field hands. Whatever the causes, Third World nations are disposed to much larger families and, in the absence of high infant mortality rates, rapid rates of population growth that in themselves could perpetuate underdevelopment.

Cultural Factors in Underdevelopment

Apart from its indirect impact on development through its effect on population growth, culture, despite the protestations of scholars like Edward Friedman, discussed above, may have a direct influence on development. The argument that the Protestant religion was more conducive to the growth of commerce and capitalism than the previously dominant Catholic faith is now classic. As propounded by Max Weber and R. H. Tawney, the argument is that Catholicism, in its medieval manifestation in Europe, impeded the growth of commerce and capitalist entrepreneurship in several ways: it was anti-material acquisition in its glorification of ascetism; it was other worldly in its emphasis on salvation and the afterlife; and it banned the use of money to make money, as in the charging of interest on loans or as in what we call capital gains, clearly the key function in a capitalist system.[35] Protestantism, on the other hand, placed a positive moral value on competitive success and material acquisition. Such success was deemed to be an indication that one was one of the "elect" destined for salvation. The early versions of Protestantism—Lutheranism and Calvinism—were dour religions, as inhospitable to worldly pleasure as was Catholicism. Some manifestations of early Protestantism, such as the early Anglican Church, had an authoritarian structure, and early Puritanism in the United States certainly did not preach individualism and tolerance, as any reader of Nathaniel Hawthorne can attest. However, because competitive material success now had a positive moral value and the banking and financier functions were now acceptable, Protestantism was much more conducive to the development of the "spirit of capitalism," according to Weber and Tawney.

Ronald Inglehart has presented evidence that this putative relationship between religion and development is but one aspect of a broader relationship between cultural factors and both development and stable democracy.[36] Thus, while concurring with criticisms of asserting an immutable relationship between Protestantism and development in light of the economic development of modern Catholic countries, Inglehart suggests that Weber did not intend to propose such a relationship. Rather, he was asserting that Protestantism at a particular point in history epitomized and promoted certain values and cultural traits that can be shown to be positively associated with development. For example, he shows that a prevailing sense of interpersonal trust in a society has a moderately strong relationship ($r = .53$) with a 1984 measure of gross national product per capita, and that this same economic indicator is even more strongly related ($r = .63$) to a measure of the materialist character of a nation's values (see Figures 9-1 and 9-2). Clearly, the nature of Catholicism has evolved over time; the church of the present day is a far cry from the Church of early modern times. The imperatives of the church that were dysfunctional for development then do not describe the contemporary church. Inglehart shows that the relationship between Protestantism and economic growth was more apparent even at the beginning of the nineteenth century compared to the present time (see Table 9-1).

The point is that the industrial and economic systems associated with modernity are positively associated with certain basic value systems and cultural attributes, and negatively associated with others. There is no imputation that Protestantism is somehow "better" than the Catholicism it replaced, only that Protestantism as it existed at a particular point in history encouraged the development of capitalism and that Catholicism discouraged it. Similarly, Confusionism, freed by Western influence from its doctrinal rigidity and combined with elements of Buddhism and Shintoism, provided a "functional equivalent" to the Protestant ethic for Japan by producing a value system that encouraged economic modernization in that nation.

Other aspects of modernity also seem to be associated with and encouraged by certain

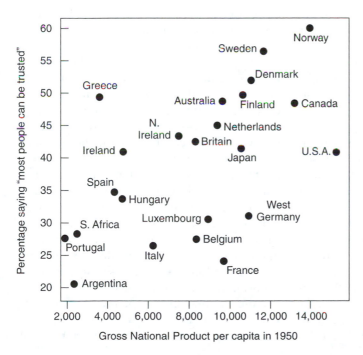

FIGURE 9-1 Economic development and interpersonal trust. Trust levels based on data from World Value survey 1981–1984, and from Euro-Barometer survey 25 (April 1986) for Greece, Portugal, and Luxembourg. $r = .53$. *Source:* Ronald Inglehart, Culture Shift in Advanced Industrial Societies (Princeton: Princeton Univ. Press, 1990), pp. 53 and 58 by permission of the publisher.

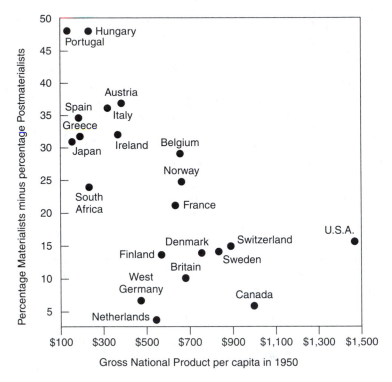

FIGURE 9-2 Economic development and the decline of Materialistic values. *r* = .63. Value priorities data from World Values survey, 1981; Euro-Barometer surveys 19–25 (1982–1986); and Political Action, 1974. Gross National Product per capita calculated from *U.N. Statistical Yearbook, 1958* (New York: 1959). *Source:* Ronald Inglehart, Culture Shift in Advanced Industrial Societies (Princeton: Princeton Univ. Press, 1990), pp. 53 and 58 by permission of publisher.

kinds of values or cultural attributes. The development of the scientific method and hence of modern technology that emanated from the application of that method was facilitated by the breakdown of closed thought systems that, by proclaiming to know all the answers, discouraged the critical inquiry and skeptical mental disposition that is at the heart of the scientific method. It is no coincidence that the development of modern science followed the end of the *Pax Christiana* and the dominance of a single, closed thought system in the Western world.

Beyond the impact of the Latin American version of Catholicism on population growth and the closed, comprehensive nature of many Third World religions, some of the religious and philosophical perspectives characteristic of the Third World may be further dysfunctional to modernization by promoting an attitude of fatalism, a belief that the

events of the world are determined by impersonal forces beyond human capacity to control and that events are predestined, or "in the stars." The importance of fatalism in Islam was humorously used as the basis of the famous musical play *Kismet*. Some scholars have argued that the development of a sense of competence—a belief that the events of the world have causes that can be humanly controlled—is a first step to gaining such control through the development of modern science and technology. One will not inquire into causes until one perceives that controllable causes exist. This sense that knowable causes exist for the events of the world developed in the West with the Renaissance and the "Age of Reason" that closely followed the Reformation and the consequent eventual decline of the salience of religion in many parts of the West.

By contrast, much of the Third World is

TABLE 9-1   Economic Growth Rates in Protestant Countries, as Compared with Catholic Countries and Japan, 1980–1984

Rank	1870–1913	1913–1938	1949–1965	1965–1984
1.	U.S. (P)	Japan (B)	Japan (B)	Japan (B)
2.	Canada (P)	Norway (P)	W. Germany (P)	Norway (P)
3.	Denmark (P)	Neth. (P)	Italy (C)	France (C)
4.	Sweden (P)	U.S. (P)	France (C)	Belgium (C)
5.	Germany (P)	Switz. (P)	Switz. (P)	Italy (C)
6.	Belgium (C)	Denmark (P)	Neth. (P)	W. Germany (P)
7.	Switz. (P)	Sweden (P)	Canada (P)	Canada (P)
8.	Japan (B)	Italy (C)	Denmark (P)	Neth. (P)
9.	Norway (P)	Canada (P)	Norway (P)	Denmark (P)
10.	Gt. Britain (P)	Germany (P)	Sweden (P)	Sweden (P)
11.	Netherlands (P)	Gt. Britain (P)	U.S. (P)	U.S. (P)
12.	France (C)	France (C)	Belgium (C)	Gt. Britain (P)
13.	Italy (C)	Belgium (C)	Gt. Britain (P)	Switz. (P)

Mean economic growth rate in Protestant countries, as a percentage of mean economic growth rate in Catholic countries:

152%	120%	98%	72%

Sources: 1870–1965 rankings calculated from data in A. Maddison, *Economic Growth in Japan and the U.S.S.R.* (London: Allen and Unwin, 1969), 148–149; 1965–1984 rankings calculated from data in *World Development Report, 1986* (Washington, D.C.: World Bank, 1986).

Note: (P) indicates countries in which a majority of the population was Protestant in 1900; (C) indicates countries having a Roman Catholic majority in 1900; (B) indicates countries having a Buddhist majority in 1900.

Source: Ronald Inglehart, *Culture Shift in Advanced Industrial Societies* (Princeton: Princeton University Press, 1990), p. 60 by permission of Princeton University Press.

still in the grip of similar closed religious and philosophical thought systems, placing much of that world in an equivalent to what for the West was the "Dark Ages." As Eric Fromm and his followers have forcefully argued, the breakdown of the institutions and constraints of the Middle Ages was psychologically threatening to many individuals;[37] yet, this process of secularization at the same time created the opportunity for the acceptance of scientific canons of inquiry. It is therefore not clear that sociopolitical systems defined and controlled by a militant, comprehensive, and closed ideology, such as Islamic fundamentalist states or unreformed Marxist regimes, can sustain let alone develop modern technology and the goods and services that emanate from that technology. Moreover, the rising fundamentalism in the Islamic world is especially characterized by a clear hostility to the West and its values, values under which the West achieved modernization. If an alternative path to modernization exists under a different set of values, that path has never been demonstrated.

The Weber-Tawney thesis about the relationship between the Protestant Reformation and the development of capitalism has been questioned and qualified by the research of David McClelland and his associates, who, supported by content analysis at both the individual and aggregate data levels, posited the thesis that a personality factor, an orientation toward achievement and competitive success, explains both individual achievement and differences among societies with respect to economic growth and development.[38] McClelland argues that this personality orientation to achieve is deep-seated and relatively permanent, having been acquired through early patterns of parent-child relations on an individual level and through the socialization of children at the societal level. Individuals with an "achieving personality" occur in some societies with sufficient frequency that they may be said to typify that society and become an attribute of its culture. Although rejecting the Weberian Protestant ethic explanation of modernization as such, this research does strongly support the thesis that there is a cultural component to the variation in modernization among states.[39] To the extent that culture does explain that variation, the Leninist and dependency explanations of underdevelopment are weakened. The development of this personality or cultural factor is clearly impeded by persistence and dominance of various Third World institutions, such as the aforementioned religions, ideologism, tribalism, fatalism, etc.

The point is that the breakdown of institutions dysfunctional to modernization, which occurred in the West with the close of the Middle Ages, has not occured in much of the Third World. Hence, the cultural attributes that kept the West in the Dark Ages still characterize much of the Third World, and these cultural factors, not external exploitation, are widely regarded by non-Marxists and more conservative scholars as the most plausible explanation of the underdevelopement of the Third World.

Thus, many scholars have argued that the essence of the modernization process may be found in changes in the state of mind of individuals. Daniel Lerner argued as much in his now classic thesis that the process of urbanization and the consequent development of literacy, education, and new communication grids generate a broader, more cosmopolitan perspective for the formerly parochial, superstitious, traditional individual.[40] Lucien Pye contributed another classic study of the problems that personality factors presented in the modernization process in Burma, especially the difficulty that Burmese leaders have had in their quest for a sense of identity that reconciles their traditional roles with the modern roles with which they are now confronted.[41] This difficulty, which Pye traced to the Burmese child-rearing process, is manifested in the traditional Burmese dispositions through which the new modern roles are interpreted.

Despite the variety of psychological and cultural explanations of underdevelopment, which suggest a lack of consensus on any given microlevel explanation, serious scholars are increasingly inclined to regard cultural factors as part of any reasonably complete explanation of underdevelopment. The Inglehart study cited above, as well as his subsequent book, *Culture Shift*, present empirical evidence of enduring cultural attributes that are related to various indexes of development. To the extent that this is true, it is grim news for the developmental hopes of Third World peoples, since cultural and psychological attributes are the most difficult ones for a government to alter through public policy. The evidence from the research of Inglehart is that new cultural orientations tend to result from a new generation maturing under different circumstances.[42]

Tribalism, Regionalism, and National Legitimacy

The goal of building modern, effective nation-states presumes the goal of establishing a legitimate national political process. Legitimacy refers to the widespread acceptance of the government as the proper governing authority, an identification with the political system as "we" rather than "them," and a general feeling that one has a stake in the well-being of the political system. Legitimate governments are by and large able to impose allocative decisions and have them accepted without coercion by winners and losers alike. The development of such legitimacy on the national level and of an identification of oneself as a citizen of the wider nation-state is further impeded by the persistence of the phenomenon of what may be called *tribalism* in much the Third World, which will be amply illustrated in the chapter on Nigeria (Chapter 10). This phenomenon refers to the loyalties to ethnic, regional, or tribal groups below the level of the nation-state that interfere with the development of a sense of belonging to the nation at large. This problem is related to Western colonialism in that colonial possessions were carved up without regard to existing identifications and loyalties of the native populations. When these former colonies sought and achieved political independence, the boundaries of the new nations often cut across tribal or ethnic lines, and often grouped formerly bitter tribal or ethnic enemies in the same political system.

A manifestation of this phenomenon was the bitter violence among South African blacks in 1990, stemming from the long-standing rivalry between the Zulu tribe, with their Inkatha political wing, and the Xhosas, who make up the bulk of the African National Congress faction, along with the Sothos, Tswanas, and other tribes. This emergence of tribalism, of course, rendered the task of national integration enormously more difficult than it was in the West. The perceived monolithic character of South African blacks was based upon their common status as victims of apartheid. Once the repressive policies of the Afrikaner regime were relaxed, the tribal differences that had really

been there all the time emerged. This may be compared to the emergence of nationalities in the Soviet Union once the repression of that regime was relaxed under the policies of *perestroika,* as we saw in Chapter 7. Thus, the relaxation of repression in a complex society may actually generate increased conflict as formerly suppressed national, tribal, religious, or ethnic rivalries are permitted to emerge and assert their own distinctive attributes and interests.

Of course, this problem is not endemic to all of the Third World nations. It is particularly apparent in some of the African nations, since tribalism was a characteristic of the traditional societies on much of that continent. A version of this problem may also be said to have characterized India with its multiplicity of dialects, tradition of parochial fiefdoms ruled by maharajahs and other parochial elites, and built-in religious conflicts between the Hindus, Sikhs, and Muslims. The language problem alone would seem to make the problem of national integration in India almost insurmountable. Less than half the population speaks a form of Hindi, and those forms may even be mutually unintelligible. In 1960, Myron Weiner listed 10 distinct linguistic groupings in India, counting the several forms of Hindi as one.[43] Clearly, such a situation would impede the development of a common set of communication grids, a common set of symbols with which one identifies, a common sense of the past, and a common set of values, all of which are prerequisites to the development of the sense of community that characterizes those modern nations that have effectively solved the problem of national integration.

Not all Western nations have effectively managed the problem of national integration. As was made clear in the chapter on Western democracies (Chapter 2), several of those nations are segmented societies that in no sense possess a shared sense of community. Belgium and Canada were among the most egregious examples of this kind of segmentation among Western democracies. Similarly, the Soviet Union promoted Russian ethnicity at the expense of such competing ethnicities as the Georgians and Armenians, just as the African National Congress promoted Xhosa tribalism at the expense of such competing tribes as the Zulus. One could say as a matter of definition that these are examples of the portion of traditional elements that one finds in modern societies, which Almond called "cultural dualism,"[44] or one could deny that national integration is an attribute of modernity. Nevertheless, the problem of a lack of national integration is more pervasive and generally more critical in Third World nations than it is among Western nations, although the existence of severely segmented Western democracies suggests that such segmentation is not an insuperable barrier to modernization or a sufficient explanation of the absence of modernization.

PRAETORIANISM AND MODERNIZATION

A praetorian society is one in which the military plays a disproportionately large political role, such that the military has a greater tendency than is found in the Western democracies to intervene in politics and to dominate the executive when it is not in fact running the country, as through a junta.[45] Such a role for the military in Third World societies is a function of the weak level of development of the civilian political institutions that normally would subordinate the military to civilian purposes.[46] The role of the military in developing societies, however, can have both positive as well as dysfunctional aspects.

Among the positive impacts of the military on development is the fact that the military is frequently the only force with the organiza-

tion and institutionalization necessary to mobilize human and capital resources for the purposes of modernization. Furthermore, the military is generally oriented toward modernity, because military hardware presumes modern technology. The military in a Third World nation is oriented toward the technology of potential military competition, which frequently possesses modern armaments; hence, they tend to accept the modern technology and industrial society that such weapons systems require. Because the military represents the interest and security of the nation as a whole, it tends to have more of a sense of being a citizen of that nation and to be less parochial than the stereotypical villager of traditional society. Recall that the breakdown of such parochial orientations and the integration of people into wider, more effective political groupings, especially into the abstract concept of the nation-state, are among the attributes of modernity, as elaborated in Lerner's classic *The Passing of Traditional Society*. By socializing its members into the wider esprit de corps of the military service, the military is thought to be able to rise above the strife and disorders stemming from what we have called tribalism, the persistence of deep loyalties to narrower tribal, regional, village, or other structures more parochial than that of the nation-state.

As a command structure in which discipline is emphasized, the military is thought to have the capacity to rise above the bickering, indecision, and stalemate of ordinary political life and to offer the power to act decisively. Since, as we will discuss below, modernization frequently involves an unsettling process that produces more losers than winners in the short run, the ability to command and mobilize is necessary to enable the system to elicit short-term sacrifices of individual interests to long-term societal purposes. This command structure and the ability to impose discipline are thought to be important forces in overcoming the destabilizing impact of the modernization process. Finally, the military is organized according to the classic Weberian model of bureaucracy (discussed in Chapter 3) that supposedly epitomizes rational efficiency in the execution of given tasks and the implementation of policy.

Despite the foregoing bases of identifying the military as an agent of modernization, the evidence is that praetorian governments in the Third World do not have a significantly better record in providing stable economic growth and modernization than do civilian governments.[47] Given this empirical reality, scholars more recently have sought to explain these data by showing how praetorianism may actually be dysfunctional for the goal of stable modernization.

In the first place, the military is, in essence, a bureaucracy. Chapter 3 discussed at length how the heavy weight of bureaucratic power in Western democracies discourages the kind of innovation, creativity, and initiative that promotes economic growth. Bureaucracy as an organization oriented to routinization, predictability, and the preservation of the status quo is surely a poor choice to manage the process of development.

In the second place, as Randall and Theobald point out, the capacity of the military to rise above the tribalism and political strife of the society in which it is situated has been greatly exaggerated. The military, like any other institution, tends to reflect the social context in which it operates. Hence, we will see in Chapter 10 how the regional and ethnic conflicts in Nigeria were reflected and even exacerbated through the military. Randall and Theobald recount how a similar situation pertained in Uganda.[48] Worse than merely reflecting social, ethnic, or tribal conflict, the military has been used in some cases by a dominant groups to suppress a rising discontent and strength among heretofore subordinate groups, thus exacerbating feelings of alienation from the system among such repressed groups and forestalling the adaptation of the system to new political realities.

Third, military leaders may be disposed to try to fulfill the function for which they were essentially trained—to fight wars. Therefore, states whose governments are dominated by military men may be more inclined toward military adventurism. Such forays, in that they channel vital resources away from the capital accumulation requisite for economic growth, are necessarily dysfunctional for economic and industrial development. Saddam Hussein of Iraq, for example, a president who came into power on the back of military support and who usually affects military garb, drained away the vital resources of his nation in a fruitless seven-year war with Iran and within a year after the termination of that conflict in 1990, attacked neighboring Kuwait, provoking a political crisis of global proportions. Clearly, the availability of resources for internal devlopment in Iraq were curtailed by these events.

KINSHIP RELATIONSHIPS AND CLIENTELISM IN NEW STATES

The extended family, a phenomenon that is becoming increasingly rare and unimportant in the mobile and individualistic societies of the advanced industrial democracies, remains prevalent among Third World societies. The extended family performs educational and socialization functions in traditional societies that must be assumed by a viable and effective nation-state as the modernization process with its role differentiation begins to develop. Kinship relations based upon the extended family also fulfill other social functions, such as care of the elderly and others unable to care for themselves. Thus, the kinship relations that remain highly salient in traditional societies are in a sense in competition with the citizen role in a modern nation-state.

It is only with the breakdown or at least weakening of these highly resilient kinship units that a modern state is able to emerge and to assume its function as the primary agency for meeting the needs of individuals. Such extended family units weakened slowly in the West over a long period. They were still highly salient in the United States through the nineteenth century and remain important in some of the less "developed" parts of the First World, such as southern Italy. They constitute one of the internal structures that continue to impede the modernization of most of the less developed parts of the world.

Patron-client relationships constitute another structure that continues to characterize the social structure of much of Third World society, impeding the modernization process. *Clientelism* emerges when individuals or groups, perceiving that kinship relations cannot guarantee them the security and other basic necessities they require, attach themselves to a stronger, more prosperous, or more influential patron who, in return for service and loyalty, can provide security and resources. This relationship, although based upon bargaining and mutual interests, is clearly an unequal one, with the patron having by far the superior bargaining position. As Randall and Theobald argue, the basic feature of the relationship between the peasant and the outside world is one of exploitation, which causes the low level of trust in others that, as we have seen in earlier chapters, is an important aspect of the "civic culture" that underlies Western liberal democracy.[49] There are societies such as Japan that have attained a high degree of economic modernization with a significant degree of clientelism in their societies; however, clientelism is logically incompatible with and therefore dysfunctional for such Western liberal principles as equality under law. Japan is

clearly a modern society, but it is modern along different lines than the advanced nations of the Western world.

As the institutions of the traditional world such as the extended family and pervasive religious institutions begin to break down, the ordinary individual feels alone and threatened in dealing with powerful forces he or she does not fully comprehend. Eric Fromm has written persuasively about how the breakdown of the society of the Middle Ages and the emergence of individual freedom and choice were psychologically threatening to the peasants of the West.[50] Peasants, as Randall and Theobald point out, have learned to perceive of their relationship with such outside forces as one of exploitation. They prefer to deal with these forces through someone who they see as having more influence and understanding. Randall and Theobald also suggest that an apt analogy for understanding the operation of this kind of relationship is provided by the model of a political machine in the large American cities in the nineteenth and early twentieth centuries, in which lower party officials insured basic support services, such as a place on the public payroll when a private sector job was unavailable or food for the needy, in return for votes and political loyalty.[51]

Patron-client relationships fulfill the role performed by public officials in a modern political system. To the extent that the political system modernizes and expands its role in a society, more of the functions performed by the patron-client system will be taken over by public officials, as the development of the modern welfare state in the United States subsumed the functions of its political machines. It is unclear whether the pervasiveness of clientelism in the Third World as an alternative structure for performing the functions of a modern state actually impedes the emergence of such a state in some circumstances.

The foregoing suggests that a variety of explanations of underdevelopment exists, no one of which has the consensual support of scholars. The choice of explanations does not seem to depend as much on systematic and intersubjective tests against empirical data as upon one's political orientation. Left-leaning scholars who view the world through a perspective informed by Marxism, Leninism, or some variant thereof tend to accept the external explanation that underdevelopment is the result of the exploitation by the Western industrial world, an exploitation that is inherent in the imperatives of capitalism. Centrist and more conservative scholars tend to place more stress on factors internal to the nature of each system. One does not have to deny the impact of the exploitation of Third World nations by powerful forces in the industrial world to suggest that dependency theory's claim to be the sole explanation of underdevelopment is an overly simplistic explanation of a complex process.

INSTABILITY AND VIOLENCE AS PRODUCTS OF RAPID CHANGE

Despite the hopes that the demise of colonialism and the achievement of national independence in the post–World War II era would issue in a period of prosperity, economic and political equality with the established nations of the industrial world, and stable, effective government, the experience of the emerging states dashed most of those hopes. The preceding section discussed how neocolonialism and economic dependence have helped forestall the achievement of equality with and autonomy from the industrial world. Especially disappointing is the record of instability and political violence that seems to have become a concomitant attribute of the process of rapid social and political change.

This record contradicts the postwar con-

ventional wisdom that the way to avoid revolution and instability was to stimulate development and industrialization, since political violence grows out of the frustration that accompanies the misery, hunger, and privation that characterize so much of the Third World population. Accordingly, under various plans such as Truman's Four Point Plan and the Alliance for Progress in Latin America, U.S. money, technology, and organizational skills were made available to Third World peoples to foster modernization and industrialization.

Paradoxically, a substantial body of empirical research and theorizing now tells us that, whatever the long-term benefits of such modernization, the short-run impact has tended to be more instability and violence, not less. This research suggests that violence and instability are most likely to occur during a period of rapid change.

The historian Crane Brinton suggested as much a generation ago in his now classic treatise *The Anatomy of Revolution*, when he discerned a pattern among the four great revolutions he surveyed, with each occurring in a period of rising prosperity and of improvement in the conditions that were the focus of the revolutionaries' grievances.[52] At the time of the storming of the Bastille, the French peasants were materially better off than they had ever been. Many concessions had been given to the American revolutionaries by the British government just prior to 1776. The explanation for this apparent contradiction to what one might logically expect was perhaps delineated most succinctly by James Davies in his famous "J-Curve" hypothesis.[53] When the satisfactions produced by an industrializing economy and society begin to increase, the expectations of the population also begin to increase. There are limits to how much and how long the material outputs and satisfactions produced by any regime can continue to increase, limits imposed by the scarcity of resources or by cultural factors, among other reasons. Eventually the increase in material outputs begins to level off, while expectations continue to rise at a rapid rate. Around this point, where the gap between expectations and satisfactions is the greatest, the likelihood of political violence is held by Davies to be the highest.

The creative thinking of scholars like Davies and Brinton was entirely speculative and impressionistic. It remained for others, such as Ivo and Rosalind Feierabend, to subject these ideas to systematic empirical testing. Using inferential measures based on aggregate data, the Feierabends and Betty Nesvold created the concept of *systemic frustration* to refer to a feeling of frustration among the individuals in a polity, as measured by a ratio between indicators of the formation of wants and want satisfactions, as expressed in the following equation: low want satisfaction/high want formation = high frustration.[54] High want satisfaction would produce low frustration, regardless of whether the want formation was high or low. Low want formation would also result in low frustration, irrespective of the level of want satisfaction. Want satisfaction was measured by various indicators of material well-being such as caloric intake per capita, per capita income, and number of physicians per unit of population. Want formation was measured by indicators of exposure to the realm of possibilities such as literacy rates, newpapers per unit of population, and urbanization. The relationship between this indirect measure of systemic frustration and political violence was moderately strong across nearly a hundred polities, supporting the propositions that the gap between wants and satisfactions produces systemic frustration and that systemic frustration increases the likelihood of violence.

The idea that violence is produced by a widespread feeling that the political system is reponding to a growing level of demands and expectations was further pursued by Ted Gurr, whose concept of *relative deprivation* may be viewed as a refinement of the Feierabends' concept of systemic frustration.[55] Gurr's concept consists of a ratio between what people think they deserve and what they expect to obtain in the foreseeable future. This idea of distinguishing what people merely want and what people think they deserve implicitly introduces the concept of injustice into the equation, a concept without which, Brinton argues, revolutions cannot develop.

Despite an elaborate effort to devise indicators for his concept of relative deprivation, Gurr's data did not support an inference that this concept directly explains much of the variation in political violence. Rather, he found that the two variables that explained more of this variation than other concepts were what he called *structural facilitation* and legitimacy. The former refers to such things as the presence of organizations capable of mobilizing discontent into action, such as an antisystem or radical political parties. These and other studies support Davies and Brinton's implicit proposition that the mobilization of demands inherent in the process of modernization will probably generate more instability and violence than stable underdevelopment and poverty.

Rapid modernization is now thought to be inherently destabilizing for a number of reasons, as summarized by Mancur Olsen.[56] In the first place, Olsen points out, industrialization requires savings and the accumulation of capital. Capital consists of resources diverted from consumption. The poorest classes devote most of their resources to consumption and have virtually nothing left for savings; hence, for them capital accumulation necessarily involves a short-run cutback in their standard of well-being. Secondly, in periods of rapid growth, the losers tend to outnumber the winners as inequality tends to increase. New technologies make their creators and a few large entrepreneurs very wealthy but render much of the work force structurally unemployable (meaning they lack the basic skills required by the economy at that state of technology). Moreover, rapid modernization creates a situation where even those who have succeeded in economic terms are frustrated because their social status has not kept pace with their economic prosperity, thus creating the difference between old money and new money. These *nouveaux riches* now are as wealthy as the old elites, but they still cannot get into the country club, and their children still cannot court the old aristocracy's children. These individuals, says Olsen, are déclassé in that their new wealth weakens their bonds to their old caste or class, while the rigidities of social status prevent them from bonding to a new caste or class.

In general, modernization entails a breaking down of the institutions of the old order. Many of these institutional ties, such as religions, feudal relationships, clientelism, or a caste system, served to deflect discontent over one's actual state of material well-being and to give individuals a sense of belonging to a larger institutional setting that gave them a sense of purpose, of knowing one's place in the order of things. The isolation of atomized individuals that characterized the breakdown of such traditional orders has been argued by prominent social psychologists to render these individuals susceptible of being mobilized for various radical causes.[57]

Modernization clearly renders some people worse off than they had been in the more traditional societies. Early modernization is accompanied by rapid urbanization, which breeds overcrowding, slum neighborhoods, and the spread of disease. With the breakdown of barter and agrarian subsistence economic systems, the phenomenon of unemployment among industrial workers appears. Clearly, the peasant is better off behind his wooden plow, growing just enough to feed

his family, than he is unemployed in an overcrowded urban slum.

In addition, modernization renders some socioeconomic roles atavistic. Peasants, unskilled labor, and the lower middle class (clerks, small shopkeepers, etc.) are among the groups whose economic roles are displaced by the processes of modernization and who are therefore susceptible for mobilization against the very process of modernization and against the elites or systems that promote it. Peasants, the unskilled unemployed, and the lower middle class were among the earliest and strongest supporters of Nazism in Germany, a movement that was characterized by Henry Ashby Turner as a revolt against modernity.[58]

It now becomes increasingly clear that American policy in the early postwar years to stave off revolution and instability by promoting the modernization of traditional economies and societies in the Third World was naïve and undoubtedly generated more violence than would have occurred had these societies remained in a state of stable poverty and underdevelopment. It is for this reason that the preservation of some measure of order became a central concern with many of the scholars concerned with rapid socioeconomic change, such as Samuel Huntington and those of the institutionalist school. Order thus becomes a value that may come into conflict with some conceptualizations of social justice, with democracy, and with the value of modernity itself.

CONCLUSION: THE DISTORTION OF WESTERN MODELS IN THIRD WORLD SETTINGS

Terms such as *democracy, fascism, Marxism,* and *socialism* have found their way into the lexicon of words used to describe the unsettling processes of rapid change in the Third

World. Students and scholars in the West attempting to comprehend the sudden salience of new types of societies and systems of which we were heretofore only dimly aware and the bewildering rate and processes of change in these societies have tended to resort to the Western models with which we are most familiar. As with the application of so many concepts in unfamiliar contexts, the concepts become distorted from their understood meanings as they are implemented in Third World settings.

For example, the idea of democracy, as that term is understood in the West to entail the accountability of leadership to the governed, evolved over centuries of political thought that is completely alien to most of the Third World. Thus, when Sékou Touré of Guinea used the term "tutelary democracy," he was referring to something very different than what people in the West understand by the term *democracy*. As democracy evolved in places like East Asia, as Friedman argues, its precise definition may require adjustment to the realities of the non-Western experience. Hence, he argues that Japan should be considered democratic despite the hegemonic rule of the Liberal Democratic Party.

Similarly, in most Third World settings the term *party* refers to a structure or set of structures that function to mobilize power and resources and to implement policies or that are virtually coterminous with the political system itself, often overriding and subordinating the formal state. We will see how parties in Latin America are frequently instruments to mobilize support for a charismatic ruler and stand for little else in the way of program or principle. This is in contrast with the role of political parties in the West that function largely as a linkage between the government and the public. While Western parties are expected to structure political competition, such competition in Third World settings is frequently not regarded as legitimate.

Hence, although the same terminology is generally used to describe political phenomena in both the industrialized and Third Worlds, we have seen that the nature of politics and the structure of society and of the political arena are very different in the two settings. This realization forces us to reconsider our conceptualization of political development and modernization. It is increasingly clear that it is not even probable, let alone inevitable, that Third World nations are merely on the way to becoming increasingly like us. It is therefore increasingly ethnocentric to conceptualize political modernity as the degree to which a system fits the model of Western industrial democracies.

As we stressed in earlier parts of the book, the nature of politics and institutions in any political system is to a large extent a product of its cultural and social setting.[59] The values, ideas, and attitudes of Third World nations are very different from those of the West. Even such a rock of apparent consistency as the Catholic Church takes on a very different manifestation in Latin America, where, combined with the cultural attitude of *machismo,* it produces an imperative toward a high birth rate.

Moreover, as we have seen in the discussion of dependency theory, the international position of Third World nations is very different from that of Western nations. The asymmetrical economic relationship between the less developed nations of the Third World and the industrialized nations of the West diminishes the actual independence of the policy-making process of the former class of nations. While we have questioned the extent to which the less modern state of Third World nations can be fully or even largely explained by this asymmetrical economic relationship or whether one can even ascribe the normatively pejorative label of exploitation to the profit taking of Western investment, it is unarguable that the probable course of economic development in the Third World is affected by its relationship with the industrialized West. Given the interdependent state of the world economic system, it may not be possible to avoid this relationship between the First and Third Worlds.

For example, the enormous debt of Third World nations (around a trillion dollars) to sources (essentially banks and governments) within the industrialized world, which drains off scarce capital that could otherwise go for investment, clearly constrains their economic options and potential and perpetuates their economic dependency (see Table 9-1). Lacking capital in the first place, Third World nations began their economic histories by borrowing heavily to finance development schemes that were often out of touch with reality and that did not pay off in real growth.[60] Not all heavy borrowers in the Third World generated a debt crisis; some, like South Korea, invested wisely and were able to generate economic growth with their borrowed capital. The key here seems to be the unwise and sometimes profligate use of borrowed funds on such things as elaborate ceremonies, buildings, monuments, or even whole new cities such as Brasília, rather than investing the funds in a new or expanded industrial infrastructure. The former kind of frivolous spending generates no economic growth and therefore produces an unmanageable debt for many Third World or newly industrialized countries (NICs). A large portion of the scarce resources of NICs goes just to service the interest on their huge debt, further drawing those resources away from being used as capital for investment in growth-generating projects.

Moreover, when the price of energy increased exponentially in the 1970s, the consequent financial difficulties of non-oil-producing Third World states were exacerbated proportionally. However, the debt problems of some oil-producing states, such as Mexico

or Venezuela, were not substantially better. These states had gone heavily into debt with major development aspirations in the boom of the 1970s, when the monopoly of OPEC (Organization of Petroleum Exporting Countries) seemed to be driving up the price of petroleum exponentially. These accumulated debts could not be serviced when the anticipated oil revenues did not materialize in the face of the OPEC collapse and the worldwide depression of the early 1980s. The need for additional loans to service the enormous debt became acute in the face of an increasingly scarce supply of capital.

The major source of such loans was an international consortium of banks known as the International Monetary Fund (IMF). As preconditions for granting loans, the IMF began to make demands on Third World countries with respect to economic and social policies, such as reductions in social welfare expenditures and the excessive size of the bureaucracies that had grown to administer those expenditures. These demands threatened the economic interests of many Third World peoples and elites, and appeared to support the dependency perspective that had become an article of faith for so many Third World leaders. A threat by some Third World leaders to default on their debts was widely perceived as a rebellion against their dependency relationship to Western plutocrats. Thus, while some scholars in the Western world increasingly believe that underdevelopment in the Third World is perpetuated by cultural and other internal factors, the debt crisis has reinforced the persisting faith in the dependency explanation by many Third World Intellectuals and their supporters on the political left in the West.

Finally, as we suggested in Chapter 3 when discussing industrial democracies, the nature of a nation's development and the character that nation assumes are affected by the state of world technology during its formative period. For example, at the present state of world technolgy, the politicization of the masses is both more rapid and inevitable compared to the experience of the most stable and successful Western nations. It is difficult to see how Huntington's implicit prescription of postponing mobilization until institutionalization is accomplished can realistically be followed in the Third World, especially in light of the wave of transitions to democracy among those nations.

The problems and prospects of the Third World may be therefore such that the Western model is of limited utility for understanding these problems and assessing these prospects. Marxism, for example, grew out of a well-founded concern about ameliorating and redressing the social dislocations and massive inequities that were generated by the early stages of industrialization and urbanization in England and Europe. It is primarily about the distribution of the products and benefits of that industrialization. Therefore, Marxism, in its classic formulations, would seem to be of little relevance to systems that have not experienced a significant degree of either industrialization or urbanization. Redistribution is of questionable value to systems that have little to distribute. The problem such systems face with regard to improving their peoples' material well-being might be one of how to generate economic growth in a sociocultural environment that inhibits such growth. Yet, Marxism or its convoluted Leninist and Maoist reformulations have remained popular among Third World regimes that not only lack the urban and industrial base presumed by classical Marxism but also operate in a society characterized by religious commitments such as Islam that are incompatible with Marxist principles. The mesmerization with the Soviet or Chinese model of modernization remains strong among some Third World elites, even in the face of the collapse of that commitment in

Eastern Europe and perhaps even in outlying parts of the Soviet Union itself. (See Part two for a full and expansive analysis of that collapse.)

However, as discussed above, the idea of democracy is now more popular than the Marxist model among Third World elites. Democratic formats have installed 12 Latin American nations since 1979, and, according to estimates by Samuel Huntington, in the 129 nations with populations of over 1 million, the percentage of those with a democratic format increased from just under 25 percent in 1973 to 45 percent in 1990.[61] However, as we will see in Chapters 10 and 11, many of these nation-states that are adopting democratic formats do not possess many of the sociocultural attributes that are widely regarded as conducive to the maintenance and effective functioning of democracy. Thus, despite enthusiasm for the transition from authoritarian or praetorian regimes in so many countries, it is wise to recall that it is one thing to install a democratic format and quite another to consolidate and legitimize that format so that it will last over time and through the inevitable crises that nations face, as the tragic example of Germany's Weimar Republic should remind us.

Many developing areas may be beset with an ideological political style that is dysfunctional for the related goals of industrialization, urbanization, and greater material well-being for their citizens. This ideological style is in the sense of that term developed by Herbert Spiro, and refers to a disposition to make choices by the criterion of their consistency with a set of a priori principles rather than to adjust choices continually in view of observed results on a step-by-step basis.[62] This latter style, variously labled *pragmatism* or *incrementalism,* was seen in Chapter 3 to have characterized Great Britain for much of its history.

The precise form of development that will

work in a particular setting is something that must be resolved incrementally on trial-and-error basis. It is impossible therefore to say with confidence and precision what form development must or will take in any Third World setting, let alone in the Third World as a whole. A survey of the experience of these areas does suggest that First and Second World models do not offer the panaceas or even that reliable guides to the development process, as was once supposed, and that grand theoretical schemes, whether Marxism, classical market capitalism, or their various offshoots are of dubious value as guides to the social and political changes that seem to be endemic to these parts of the world.[63]

NOTES

1. E.g., Lucien Pye, "The Non-Western Political Process," *Journal of Politics*, vol. 20, no. 3 (August 1958), pp. 468–86.

2. Samuel Huntington, *Political Order in Changing Societies* (New Haven: Yale University Press, 1968), esp. chap. 1.

3. E.g., Lucien Pye, *Aspects of Political Development* (Boston: Little Brown, 1966), pp. 45–46.

4. Max Weber, *The Theory of Social and Economic Organization*, ed. Talcott Parsons (New York: The Free Press, 1947), p. 328; H. Gerth and C. Wright Mills, eds. *From Max Weber: Essays in Sociology* (New York: Oxford University Press Galaxy Editions, 1958), pp. 51–55.

5. Pye, "The Non-Western Political Process."

6. Michael Novack, *The Rise of the Unmeltable Ethnics* (New York: Macmillan, 1972).

7. Vicky Randall and Robin Theobald, *Political Change and Underdevelopment: A Critical Introduction to Third World Politics* (Durham, NC: Duke University Press, 1985), p. 30.

8. Daniel Lerner, *The Passing of Traditional Society* (Glencoe, IL: The Free Press of Glencoe, 1958).

9. Karl Deutsch, "Social Mobilization and Political Development," *American Political Science Review*, vol. 55, no. 3 (September 1961), pp. 393–514.

10. David Easton, *The Political System* (NY: Knopf, 1951), p. 129.

11. Gabriel Almond, "A Developmental Approach to Political Systems," *World Politics*, vol. 17, no. 2 (January 1965), pp. 183–214. See also Almond & G. Bingham Powell, Comparative Politics: A Developmental Approach (Boston: Little Brown, 1966), chap. 8.

12. Huntington, *Political Order;* Samuel Huntington, "Political Development and Political Decay," *World Politics*, vol. 17, no. 3 (April 1965), pp. 386–430.

13. Lerner, *The Passing of Traditional Society.*

14. Weber, *Theory;* Gerth and Mills, *From Max Weber.*

15. David Apter, *Rethinking Development* (Newbury Park, CA: Sage Publications, 1989), p. 18. Cf. his formulations about "reconciliation systems" and "mobilization systems" in David Apter, *The Politics of Modernization* (Chicago: University of Chicago Press, 1965), pp. 22ff.

16. Huntington, *Political Order,* chap. 2, esp. pp. 94–95.

17. For example, scholars concerned with the destabilizing impact of modernization sometimes suggest that rapid change itself has this impact rather than the specific attributes of modernity. See, for example, Mancur Olsen, "Rapid Growth as a Destabilizing Force," *Journal of Economic History*, vol. 3, no. 4 (December 1963), pp. 529–52. Cf. Bernard Grofman and Edward Muller, "The Strange Case of Relative Gratification and Potential for Political Violence: The V Curve Hypothesis," *American Political Science Review*, vol. 67, no. 2 (June 1973), pp. 514–39, for the argument that change for the better or for the worse increases one's potential for political violence.

18. Walt Whitman Rostow, *The Stages of Economic Growth* (London: Cambridge University Press, 1960); Kenneth Organski, *The Stages of Political Development* (New York: Alfred Knopf, 1965). C. E. Black, *The Dynamics of Modernization: A Study in Comparative History* (New York: Harper and Row, 1966), pp. 67–89, identifies the "phases" of modernization based on "critical problems that *all* modernizing societies must face" (emphasis added).

19. Karl Popper, *The Open Society and Its Enemies,* 2 vols. (NY: Harper Torchbooks, 1966).

20. Fred Riggs, *Administration in Developing Countries: The Theory of the Prismatic Society* (Boston: Houghton-Mifflin, 1964), p. 268.

21. Among these earlier groupings are Pye, "The Non-Western Political Process"; and Gabriel Almond, "A Functional Approach to Comparative Politics," in Gabriel Almond and James Coleman, eds., *The Politics of the Developing Areas* (Princeton: Princeton University Press, 1960). Among the early critiques of this approach are Alfred Diamant, "Is There a Non-Western Political Process," *Journal of Politics*, vol. 21, no. 1 (February 1959), pp. 123–27; and Theda Skocpol, *States and Social Revolutions* (New York: Cambridge University Press, 1979), p. 19.

22. Samuel Huntington, "Will More Countries Become Democratic," *Political Science Quarterly*, vol. 99, no. 2 (Summer 1984). His seminal disquisition on the negation of his earlier prediction is *The Third Wave:*

Democratization in the Late Twentieth Century (Norman: University of Oklahoma Press, 1991).

23. Edward Friedman, "Democratization: Generalizing the East Asian Experience," in Edward Friedman, ed., *The Politics of Democratization: Generalizing the East Asian Experience* (Boulder, CO: Westview Press, 1994), p. 34. Friedman's work is one of the most forceful rejections of the classical tendency to generalize from the Western experience about the sociocultural determinants of democracy.

24. Giuseppe Di Palma, *To Craft Democracies* (Berkeley: University of California Press, 1990); Terry Karl, "Dilemmas of Democratization in Latin American Politics," *Comparative Politics* (October 1990).

25. Seymour Lipset, *Political Man* (New York: Doubleday Anchor Books, 1963), p. 73n.

26. Cited in Monte Palmer, *Dilemmas of Political Development*, 4th ed. (Ithaca, IL: Peacock Publishers, 1989), pp. 2–3.

27. John Kautsky, *The Political Consequences of Modernization* (New York: John Wiley, 1972), p. 60.

28. E.g., J. G. Furnivall, *Colonial Policy and Practice* (New York: New York University Press, 1956).

29. Perhaps the most readable and complete account of the historical roots of this tragedy is Bernard Fall, *The Two Vietnams* (New York: Praeger, 1963). See also Milton Sacks, "The Strategy of Communism in Southeast Asia," *Public Affairs*, vol. 23 (September 1950), pp. 227–47. The best generic essay on the relationship between Communism and nationalism is found in John Kautsky, "An Essay on the Politics of Development," in John Kautsky, ed., *Political Change in Underdeveloped Countries: Nationalism and Communism* (New York: John Wiley, 1962), pp. 3–122.

30. J. A. Hobson, *Imperialism: A Theory* (London: George Allen and Unwin Ltd., 1905).

31. Susan Bodenheimer, "Dependency and Imperialism: The Roots of Underdevelopment," in K. T. Fann and Donald Hodges, eds., *Readings in U.S. Imperialism* (Boston: Porter Sargeant, 1971).

32. These data are from United Nations Comisión Económica para América Latin y el Caribe, "Foreign Investment in Transnational Corporations in Latin America, no 576/577 (June, 1995).

33. See P. T. Bauer, *Dissent on Development* (Cambridge: Harvard University Press, 1976), for a vigorous exposition of some of these critiques of the dependency perspective. Cf. also Charles Doran, George Modelski, and Colin Clarke, eds., *Studies in Dependency Reversal* (New York: Praeger, 1963).

34. Population Reference Bureau, *World Population Data Sheet*, 1994.

35. Max Weber, *The Protestant Ethic and the Spirit of Capitalism*, trans. Talcott Parsons (1904; reprint, New York: Charles Scribner, 1930); R. H. Tawney, *Religion and the Rise of Capitalism* (New York: Harcourt Brace, 1937).

36. Ronald Inglehart, "The Renaissance of Political Culture," *The American Political Science Review*, vol. 84, no. 4 (December, 1985), pp. 1203–30, esp. p. 1226; Ronald Inglehart, *Culture Shift* (Princeton: Princeton University Press, 1990), pp. 37, 58–59.

37. Eric Fromm, *Escape from Freedom* (New York: Avon Books, 1965).

38. David McClelland, *The Achieving Society* (New York: The Free Press, 1961).

39. Cf. Inglehart, "The Renaissance of Political Culture," for empirical evidence of the association of enduring cultural attributes and indicators of development.

40. Lerner, *Passing of Traditional Society.*

41. Lucien Pye, *Politics, Personality, and Nation Building: Burma's Search for Identity* (New Haven: Yale University Press, 1960), p. 158.

42. Inglehart, *Culture Shift*, chap. 2.

43. Myron Weiner, "South Asia," in Almond and Coleman, eds., *The Politics of the Developing Areas*, p. 158.

44. Almond, "A Functional Approach to Comparative Politics," p. 23.

45. Cf. the definition by Amos Perlmutter, "The Praetorian State and the Praetorian Army: Toward a Taxonomy of Civil-Military Relations in Developing Countries," *Comparative Politics*, vol. 1 (April 1969), pp. 382–404.

46. Morris Janowitz, *The Military in the Development of New States* (Chicago: University of Chicago Press, 1964); Lucien Pye, "Armies and Political Modernization," in J. J. Johnson, ed., *The Role of the Military in Underdeveloped Countries* (Princeton: Princeton University Press, 1962), pp. 68–89.

47. Randall and Theobald, *Political Change*, pp. 74–75.

48. Ibid., p. 75.

49. Ibid., p. 55.

50. Fromm, *Escape from Freedom.*

51. Randall and Theobald, *Political Change*, p. 52.

52. Crane Brinton, *The Anatomy of Revolution* (Englewood Cliffs: Prentice Hall, 1952). For a more recent foray into grand theorizing about the great revolutions, see Theda Skocpol, *Social Revolutions in the Modern World* (New York and Cambridge: Cambridge University Press, 1994).

53. James Davies, "Toward a Theory of Revolution," *American Sociological Review*, vol. 27, No. 1 (February 1962), pp. 5–19.

54. Ivo Feierabend, Rosalind Feierabend, and Betty Nesvold, "Systemic Conditions of Political Violence: An Application of the Frustration-Aggression Theory," *Journal of Conflict Resolution*, vol. 10, no. 3 (September 1966), pp. 249–71.

55. Ted Gurr, "A Causal Model of Civil Strife: A Comparative Analysis Using New Indices," *American Political Science Review*, vol. 62, no. 4 (December 1968), pp. 1104–24.

56. Mancur Olsen, "Rapid Growth as a Destabilizing Force," *Journal of Economic History,* vol. 3, no. 4 (December 1963), pp. 529–52.

57. Fromm, *Escape from Freedom.* Cf. William Kornhouser, *The Politics of Mass Society* (New York: The Free Press, 1959), for a classic analysis of the susceptibility of atomized masses to mobilization from above.

58. Henry Ashby Turner, "Fascism and Modernization," *World Politics,* vol. 24, no. 4 (June, 1972), pp. 547–64.

59. Inglehart, "The Renaissance of Political Culture."

60. This discussion of the debt crisis has been drawn from the excellent examination of that crisis in Palmer, *Dilemmas of Political Development,* pp. 288–89.

61. Huntington, *The Third Wave,* p. 26.

62. Herbert Spiro, *Government by Constitution* (New York: Random House, 1959), pp. 178–238.

63. See Skocpol, *Social Revolutions in the Modern World,* for a discussion of the relevance of the Western experience in understanding social revolutions in the Third World.

Nigeria: Tribalism and Cultural Diversity

"The one absolutely certain way of bringing this nation to ruin, of preventing all possibility of its continuing to be a nation at all, would be to permit it to become a tangle of squabbling nationalities."

Theodore Roosevelt, October 12, 1915

When Western nations carved out the colonial entities in the Afro-Asian world, entities that would become the new nations of the postwar era, they frequently did so without regard to the congruency of the borders of these entities with the tribal and linguistic divisions, whose historical roots are much deeper than those of the emerging nations. As these colonial entities emerged into nationhood, they found themselves lacking that sense of common cultural orientations, shared values, and integrated system of communication and interaction that is entailed by the concept of a community. We have seen in earlier chapters that this absence of community is not confined to the Third World. Segmented societies such as Belgium, the Netherlands, and Canada exemplify the phenomena of cultural and/or linguistic distinctiveness and isolation of subcultures. In general, segmented societies such as these have had more difficulties than others in functioning as integrated nations. Belgium, for example, essentially became a confederacy in 1970, when a constitutional change gave autonomous status to its two culturally and linguistically distinct subcultures—the Flemish and the Walloons (with the French-speaking and Wallonian-oriented citizens of Brussels, located within Flanders, forming what is technically a third independent grouping). Canada has repeatedly faced the prospect of the secession of the perpetually alienated French Canadian community located largely in the province of Quebec. The most recent crisis, the threat of secession with the broader Canadian rejection (particularly in the provinces of Newfoundland and Manitoba) of the so-called Meech Lake Accords, an agreement granting special status to the French Canadians, occurred in the summer of 1990 and with the rejection of the Charlotte-town Accords in 1992.

Nigeria constitutes a quintessential manifestation of such a culturally and linguistically divided society. The centrifugal forces and impediments to the development of a sense of national community appear to be far more acute in Nigeria than in any of the aforementioned Western nations. Thus, if one considers that the Belgian political format, after a century and a half of trying to solidify

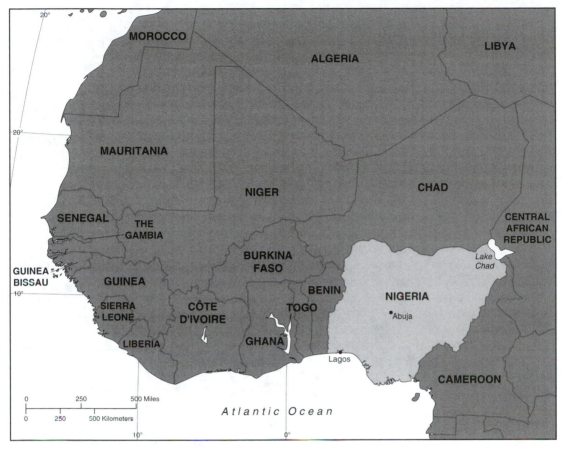

FIGURE 10-1   West Africa

its legitimacy and coping with two distinct linguistic groupings, could not withstand the stress of segmentation, consider the prospects of any Nigerian format, with virtually no accumulated legitimacy and between 200 and over 300 distinct and mutually unintelligible languages (depending of the source one consults), buttressed by geographically defined religious and cultural diversity (see Figures 10-1 and 10-2). The social and cultural segmentation of Nigerian society has resulted in a history of the failure of civilian, not to mention democratic, governments to rule the country effectively. Hence, the history of postindependence Nigeria is one of a series of coups bringing down other juntas or bringing down abortive attempts at civilian democracy and bringing in military rule. These are denoted in Table 10-1. Nigeria may therefore be said to be an almost stereotypical model of the enormous nation-building problems faced by the new nations of the Afro-Asian world. An analysis of the origins of such problems, their scope, and how Nigeria is coping with them may thus provide insights into the problems and prospects of many troubled Third World systems.

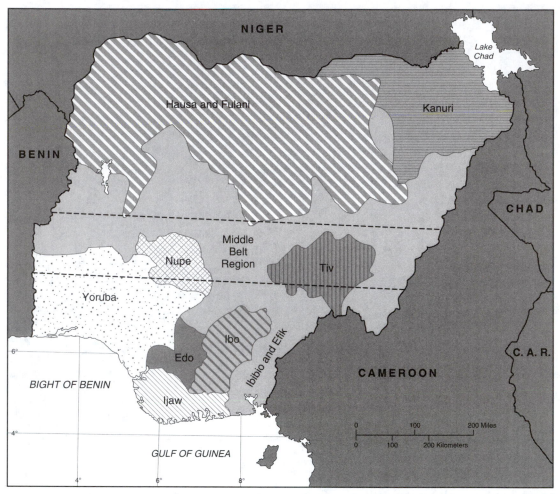

FIGURE 10-2   Major ethnic divisions of Nigeria

THE ROOTS OF NIGERIAN REGIONALISM AND THE HERITAGE OF ITS COLONIAL PAST

Before the coming of the British, what is now Nigeria was occupied by various tribes that developed the aforementioned distinct language groups and autonomous political and social institutions ranging from feudalism in parts of the north to monarchies in the south. These independent tribal roots go back a millennium or more in some cases, compared to the few years of Nigeria's existence as a single political entity. Among the main tribal groupings were the Hausa/Fulani and Kanuri in the north, the Ibo in the southeast, the Yoruba in the southwest, and Tiv in the "Middle Belt." The Ibo and Yoruba provided the overwhelming preponderance of the Western-educated elite that led the struggle for independence. The British practiced a policy of indirect rule in the north, that is,

TABLE 10-1   Regime Changes in Nigeria

Period	Head of State	Type of Regime	How Ended
1914–60	(British colony)	Single colonial system	Independence
1960–66	Balewa	Parliamentary democracy	Coup, assassination
1966	Ironsi	Military junta	Coup, assassination
1966–75[1]	Gowon	Military junta	Coup
1975–76	Muhammed	Military junta	Coup, assassination
1976–79	Obasanjo	Military junta	Elections
1979–83	Shagari	Presidential democracy	Coup
1984–85	Buhari/Idiagbon	Military junta	Coup
1985–93	Babangida	Military junta	Annulled elections[2]
1993	Shonekan	Appointed caretaker	Coup
1993– ?	Abacha	Military junta	

[1] 1967–70 there was also an independent state of Biafra, which was brought back into the nation by civil war.

[2] Bashrun Abiola won the election over Alhaji Tofa.

Source: Adapted and updated from Stephen Wright, "The Government of Nigeria," in Michael Curtis, ed. *Introduction to Comparative Government* (New York: Harper and Row, 1990), p. 572.

of ruling through native social institutions and leaving them more or less intact along with a more traditional orientation.[1] Meanwhile, the peoples of the south and southwest were more highly educated than the northerners in a Western sense, exacerbating the feelings of ethnic differences between the northern and southern tribes. Virtually all of the Nigerian elites who studied in either the United States or Great Britain came from either the Ibo or Yoruba tribes. These Western-educated Nigerians were socialized into a predominantly Christian tradition with Western values, while the northerners either received little or no formal education or were educated into a more conservative Muslim tradition. The early Christian missionaries came by the sea; thus, their first contact with the indigenous population was with the Ibo and the Yoruba, who controlled the major port cities. These groups therefore became the beneficiaries of Western education and culture. Hence, the cultural and linguistic factors that prevented the development of a sense of community among Nigerians were buttressed by fundamental religious differences, creating a deeply segmented society.

Because a disproportionate number of the educated Nigerians were from the southern and southwestern parts of the country, a disproportionate number of government jobs were held by people from these areas. Thus, as late as 1953, southerners held some 82 percent of the civil service jobs in the north, generating a great deal of resentment on the part of northern leaders, who felt that their territory was being invaded and run by southerners. In fact, some northerner sources of opinion, such as the Hausa-based newspaper *Gaskiya Ta Fi Kwabo* and the statesman and Prime Minister Tafawa Balewa, expressed the view that the southerners were replacing the British as aliens controlling what the northerners regarded as their territory.[2] Some northerners were so concerned about the prospect of being dominated by the southerners that they were even skeptical of the wisdom of moving to independence as a single nation.

These social and cultural imperatives toward regionalism and the segmentation of

Nigerian society were exacerbated by some of the policies of the British colonial administration. By 1939, the colonial authority had formally established three distinct regions, a division that was consolidated by 1951, when the McPherson Constitution gave regional assemblies in the north, east, and west (established some five years earlier) permission to make their own laws and to choose their own elites. The Lyttleton Constitution of 1954 formally set up a federal structure for Nigeria, dividing powers between a national government and the three regional governments, and ensuring a proportionate representation of each region in the national legislature.

The establishment of political subunits whose boundaries are more or less congruent with geographically defined cultural, linguistic, and religious diversities, and that were led by elites whose raison d'être was to perpetuate the distinctiveness of these diversities, constitutes an institutional impediment to the formation of the kind of pan-national loyalties that are implied by the nation-state as conceptualized by such gurus of nationalism as Hans Kohn.[3] Federal structures in which the political subunits are congruent with the boundaries of such deep-seated, geographically defined diversities as are found in Nigeria may be contrasted with federal systems, such as Australia, in which the boundaries of the political subunits are not congruent with cultural, religious, or linguistic diversities. The former type has been shown by the present author, among others, to have been a vehicle for the generation of the issue of cultural defense in Canada and Belgium to the point at which it detracts from the sense of identification with common symbols of nationhood essential for the long-term legitimacy of the system itself.[4] As noted, Belgium effectively became a confederation in 1970, and separatist sentiment in Canada experienced another resurgence in 1990 in the face of the failure of the Meech Lake Accords. In

the chapter on Russia, we learned how the emergence of the cultural defense issue among its constituent republics led to the collapse of the Soviet Union as a coherent system.

This impact of the congruent model of federalism on the national integrity and effectiveness of what had been stable and effective Western systems suggests a pessimistic prognosis for the ability of an emerging nation such as Nigeria to develop the sense of legitimacy and trust on the part of its citizenry that political scientists believe is a requisite for the political health of the nation. While loyalty to the constituent tribes and ethnic communities goes back to time immemorial, Nigeria became an independent nation in 1960 and had been a British colony for less than a century before that. The tribes and regions were arbitrarily grouped into a single political entity in 1914 by the British colonial administration. Prior to 1960, no Nigerians or group of Nigerians had ever governed the entire country, as contrasted with Indochina, which had a long tradition as an independent and united political entity prior to its colonization by the French. A.H.M. Kirk-Greene has analyzed Nigeria's problems and concluded they are rooted in the nation's history, a topic that we are about to examine.[5] The task of Nigeria is to build a common sense of citizenship and community—a common political culture—without the tools of a common set of symbols and values, a common language, a common sense of the past, or any other basis for communication and understanding among all Nigerians.

The one advantage that Nigeria has from its precolonial history is an absence of deep-seated, historic grievances between the tribes, although Nigeria as a coherent community really had no precolonial existence. This may be contrasted with the aforementioned Canadian analogy, in which the French have long held a sense of being a conquered people, a superior and suppressed island of religious truth and cultural superiority in a sea of Anglo-Saxon godlessness and inferiority. However, a Fulani Empire, carved out of Muslim holy war, or *jihad,* in the early nineteenth century, has left the northerners with a sense of pride in their past and traditions that in turn led to some resentment at the predominance of the Western-educated Ibos and Yorubas in the Nigerian government in the early years of independence.

British colonial administration, while in some respects institutionalizing and aggravating the segmentation of Nigerian society by establishing regional governments, provided the country with what measure of unity it did have and established and preserved peace among the tribes. Actually, the British were not there all that long. Although they conquered Lagos in the middle of the nineteenth century, they only ruled Nigeria as a whole for around 50 years. During that period, they built roads and established communications that at least provided the cybernetic structure for the unification of the nation. This refers to the development of communication grids that Karl Deutsch and others have hypothesized constitute an essential factor in the development of nations.[6] Admittedly, the British did more to integrate the country economically rather than politically or socially. Unlike the situations in Rhodesia and South Africa, the British did not leave a coterie of white settlers in Nigeria to oppose the building of black African nationhood. This was, in large part, due to the extremely unhealthy milieu that Nigeria provided for whites in the nineteenth and early twentieth century. For example, of the 48 Europeans who went up the Niger to trade and proselytize in 1832, 38 died of malaria, and of the 150 young Europeans who settled in Lagos around the turn of the century, 28 died within a few months. Because of the benefits of not having a white settler contingent, some Nigerians have suggested that the mosquito be accorded the status of a national hero.[7]

The pattern of economic activity and development fostered by the British might seem to support the dependency model discussed in Chapter 9. They built roads and railways running between north and south, to and from the ocean, without comparable routes between east and west. These routes thus served the export and import trade rather than internal trade. Moreover, Nigeria's economy relies primarily on agricultural and extractive activities, with very little in the way of indigenous manufacturing.[8]

Despite the negative impacts of British colonial administration, the British shaped modern Nigeria in a variety of other ways, some of them positive. The British influence in Nigeria is apparent in many of the formal or stylistic practices in Nigerian society and government; for example, barristers and solicitors wear white wigs in courts; until the early 1970s, people drove on the left side of the road, and government and opposition benches face one another in the Nigerian Parliament. The British policy of indirect rule, especially in the northern parts of Nigeria, fostered a set of native institutions and officials, which allowed a legitimate and competent set of rulers to step in and assume some of the day-to-day tasks of governing upon the departure of the Europeans. Thus, they ruled through the emirs in Hausa territory, toning down some of the more "barbaric" (by Western standards) practices of the emirates while retaining their authority and ability to collect taxes.

Most importantly, the British left the heritage of a common language with which these mutually unintelligible language groupings can communicate with one another, clearly the first requisite to building any sense of a Nigerian community. English is the official language of the Nigerian Federal Parliament as well as of the various regional legislatures, of the Nigerian civil service, of the courts, of the major newspapers, and of all secondary schools. Nigerian elites, therefore, acquire considerable proficiency in English and can easily use it to communicate with one another. The problem is that most of the masses do not share in this English proficiency (only about 10 percent are officially literate in English); hence, only those members of the elite who speak the native language of the masses in question can easily communicate with them. The "lingua franca" by which Nigerian elites communicate with the masses is a form of "broken English."

FROM COLONY TO NATION

As was the case of the fall of French Indo-China, the early defeats of the Allied forces by the Japanese in World War II dealt a crippling blow to the image of the European colonial masters as supreme beings, one of the foundations of the shaky legitimacy of colonial regimes. The success of nationalist struggles in other British possessions, such as India, further raised the hopes of Nigerian nationalists.

As with many other Third World nations, the leaders of the Nigerian nationalist movement had received a Western education from which they acquired the idea of the nation-state, the idea of Western imperialism, and concepts such as justice, equality, and self-determination that caused them to question the rightness and inevitability of European control of their homeland. Many of the early Nigerian nationalist leaders were Ibo and Yoruba, the groups that produced the greatest proportion of Western-educated elites. Typical among them and one of the leading nationalists was an Ibo, Nmamdi Azikiwe, who earned a graduate degree in political science at Lincoln University in Pennsylvania, the alma mater of Kwame Nkrumah, who led the nationalist movement in Ghana. Like many other Third World nationalist leaders, Azikiwe was frustrated in the professional aspirations for which he was trained (to teach); hence, he became a militant newspaper editor, mobilizing sentiment against the system that repressed his dreams. In the 1930s, Azikiwe helped found the National Council for Nigeria and the Cameroons (NCNC) with Herbert Macaulay, who became its first president. Based in Lagos, this group was challenged for leadership by the Nigerian Youth Movement (NYM). However, the NCNC split, leaving the NYM with an almost exclusively Yoruba membership. Meanwhile, the Northern People's Congress (NPC) was organized in the late 1940s with a membership consisting of Hausa and Fulani of the northern, mostly Muslim tribes. Hence, the nationalist movement was divided by the end of World War II along ethnic and tribal lines. Moreover, it was further fragmented by the rise of various radical groups that splintered off from the main groupings, such as the Zikists, who took their name from Azikiwe, although he withheld his unqualified support. The Zikists advocated revolution, but Azikiwe was apparently convinced that the British had decided to grant independence to Nigeria eventually without bloodshed. After inciting repeated riots, the movement was declared illegal.

In one sense, Nigerian politics during the period leading up to independence may be viewed as a struggle between the north, with its Hausa/Fulani base, and the south, including the Ibo in the south and the Yoruba in the southwest. With their fear of penetration and control by the better-educated Yoruba and then also by the Ibo, the northerners were less enthusiastic about immediate independence than their southern counterparts. In order to assuage this fear and to get northern support for the drive to independence, a northern demand was granted for a guarantee of at least half the seats in the Nigerian Central House of Representatives at the General Conference for review of the constitution held at Ibadan in 1950. The role of the emirs, the traditional rulers left in place by the British policy of indirect rule in the north only, was another source of conflict between the north and the south. The northerners wished to preserve a continued role for them, while as one easterner, Eyo Ita, put it, "We are out to abolish feudalism, not reform it. We must leave the archaic in limbo."[9]

Although the north-south conflict seemed to structure the politics of Nigeria leading up to independence, one should not get the impression that the south was a united and monolithic entity. In fact, conflict between the Yoruba in the southwest and the Ibo in the southeast was serious and well established. The Yoruba had been exposed to Western education much earlier than the Ibo, although the gap had significantly narrowed by the time of independence. These Yoruba were Western educated, mostly in the law and economics, while most of the Ibo were educated in the technical and scientific fields as well as in military matters. The Ibo were overcrowded in their traditional geographic base in the southeast, and they began to spread into other areas. Hence, their number in Lagos, a major Nigerian cultural center located in Yoruba territory, increased from 264 in 1911 to over 26,000 by 1951. Azikiwe emerged as the head of the Ibo State Union while Obafemi Awolowo emerged as the spokesperson of Yoruba nationalism. Hence, each of the several cultural and linguistic segments of Nigerian society had its parochial elites whose role was to emphasize and perpetuate the autonomy and distinctiveness of these subcultural segments.

In this atmosphere of an already segmented society marked by a tradition of tribal conflict, an election was to be held in 1959 for the Federal House of Representatives that would form the first government of an independent Nigeria. The British had promised that independence would be granted on October 1, 1960. The electoral competition was basically among the three regionally based parties: the NPC from the north, the NCNC from the Ibo-dominated south, and the Action Group from the Yoruba-dominated southwest. The west-east conflict seemed to override the north-south conflict as the NPC and the NCNC seemed to regard the Action Group as their common enemy, and in fact the NPC and the NCNC formed a governing coalition after the election with the Action Group forming the principal opposition. The election underscored the regional nature of Nigerian politics—134 of the 148 NPC seats came from the north, the NCNC won only 8 of 89 seats from the north, and the Action Group won 33 of its 75 seats in the west and some 25 from the north, with most of these coming from the Middle Belt area. The Action Group won 30 of the 35 Yoruba seats, and the NCNC won all 51 of the Ibo seats. The NPC did not even permit southerners to join; it made no pretense at being a national party. The ability of the Action Group and the NCNC to win some northern seats stems from the fact that there are some Christian enclaves in the predominantly Muslim north, and these non-Muslims are concerned about being swallowed up or dominated by the Muslim majority.

THE CULTURAL BASIS OF NIGERIAN POLITICS

The segmentation of Nigerian society that is based on its historical background renders it difficult to generalize with confidence about the cultural basis of Nigeria as a whole. Almost by definition, cultural attributes will differ significantly from one segment to another, and this is surely true of Nigeria.

For example, first the Yoruba and then the Ibo acquired substantial amounts of Western education, from which they learned and adopted many Western values, including tolerance, secularism and/or Christianity, and a measure of egalitarianism and individualism. On the other hand, the north was relatively insulated from Western influence, being under the control of native emirates during British indirect rule. The Yoruba *obas* of Western Nigeria also came into this category of native notables whose role was to some extent protected by the policy of indirect rule. Such policies served to preserve traditional institutions whose breakdown Lerner and others have said are a prerequisite for effective modernization.

Western education has been much more rare among the northerners; hence, the values imparted by Western education were similarly more rare in the north. Moreover, the dominant Muslim religion of the north entails a number of non-Western values, such as a hierarchic and authoritarian view of society, polygamy and the subordination of women, and the view of the state as an instrument to advance and defend the faith, as opposed to the Western concept—extending at least as far back as Pope Gelasius' doctrine of the two swords—of the separation of church and state. Acceptance by the Muslim north of any political format that may result in Christian (or any non-Muslim) control of the government is unthinkable, as is acceptance by the Westernized Christians of the southwest and southeast of continued northern domination. Hence the northern and southern parts of the country did not just differ on some specific policy-relevant values, as between the former Confederacy and the North in the United States. Rather, northern and southern Nigeria have completely irreconcilable world views, or *Weltanschauungen,* that are buttressed and perpetuated by the differences in religion and language. The predom-

inantly Muslim northerners are somewhat more likely to be literate in Arabic than in English, for example.

Northern elites, especially the NPC leaders, have had difficulty adjusting to the Western notion of toleration of political and social opposition. This may be one of the factors at the heart of Nigeria's political problems. Professor Leo Dare reports that the NPC employed a variety of means to suppress and harass the Action Group, the principal opposition force in the House of Representatives elected in 1959. However, it cannot be said that the Action Group behaved in the role of "loyal opposition," as the term has been understood in the British context. After the 1959 election, it turned to radical politics in an attempt to appeal to radical opinion in both domestic and foreign policy. Moreover, an internal split between the leader of the Action Group, Chief Awolowo, and the deputy leader and premier of the western region, the less radical Chief Akintola, led to actual fist fights between the two in the Western Region House of Assembly in May 1962. Although one might point out that physical violence has also appeared in the British House of Commons as late as the end of the nineteenth century, such fisticuffs would be unthinkable today and clearly do not constitute a manifestation of a "civic culture" in Nigeria, a cultural model that stresses a tolerant attitude toward political opposition. In addition, the NPC-NCNC federal government proceeded to prosecute and very possibly frame Awolowo for plotting to overthrow the federal government in a trial that was suspect for a number of reasons. Awolowo was denied the counsel of his choice, and witnesses against him were suspected of being political enemies or opportunists. He was convicted and replaced by the more moderate and less threatening Akintola as leader of the Action Group. Of course, engineering the imprisonment of one's political opposition is an extreme manifestation of lack of tolerance and shows minimal commitment to the democratic rules of the game that we outlined in Chapter 2.

The regionalism and segmentation of Nigerian society and the problems of the Nigerian system in general are buttressed by geographical and demographic factors. First among these is the fact that Nigeria is easily the most populous nation in Africa, with estimates that have grown from 35 million in 1959 to over 50 million in the mid-1960s to currently over 100 million, in a nation that is far from the largest in terms of geographical area. (As with other Third World systems, population figures in Nigeria are less precise than in the industrialized West.) Hence, Nigeria's population is both large and expanding rapidly. We have seen in Chapter 9 how excessive population growth can consume scarce capital available for investment in economic growth. This geometric rate of growth is undoubtedly one of the factors explaining Nigeria's economic difficulties despite the fact that Nigeria possesses considerable oil reserves. Moreover, this population density is not distributed evenly in the nation. The northern region, closer to the expanding Sahara, is more desert-like and more sparsely populated. With over three-fourths of Nigeria's geographical area, the northern area has around half of its people, or less than 70 people per square mile. By contrast, the Ibo region in the southeast is the most densely populated, with over 250 people per square mile in a thickly forested environment. This population density has motivated many Ibo to relocate, generating resentment by people in these other areas against the intrusion of the Ibo minorities.

We have noted how federalism can exacerbate the centrifugal forces of segmented regionalism by establishing parochial elites, whose job it is to represent, magnify, and perpetuate these geographically defined diversities. To the extent that the subsystem boundaries in a federal system are more or less congruent with these geographically defined linguistic, cultural, religious, or other diversities, a federal system will tend to intensify the importance of issues related to the goal of cultural defense. This shows up rather clearly in the Nigerian case with respect to the educational system, which the 1960 federal constitution has explicitly placed under regional control, a move that prevented the socialization of Nigerian children into a sense of Nigerian citizenship and community.

THE NIGERIAN PARTY SYSTEM THROUGH THE 1964 ELECTIONS

We have seen that Nigeria has failed to produce political parties whose support to a significant extent transcends the tribal and regional loyalties that have dominated Nigerian society. There is, in fact, no genuine Nigerian party system in the sense of the British, German, or French systems, whose parties draw significant blocs of support from numerous groups and regions in their respective nations. Rather, Nigeria has been characterized by a set of regionally based one-party systems. The founding of the country saw the NPC appealing to a clientele that was almost exclusively northern Muslim, the NCNC appealing to the Ibo in the southeast, and the Action Group appealing to the Yoruba in the southwest. After the rift between Yoruba leader Awolowo and his deputy, Akintola, leading to the conviction of the former, the radical positions of the Action Group were replaced by a new party claiming to represent the Yoruba in the western region, the Nigerian National Democratic Party (NNDP), which was an amalgam of Akintola's United People's Party and some former NCNC members of the Western House. This group was concerned with, among other things, the intrusion and overrepresentation of Ibo, especially in federal service jobs. Since the Ibo were supported by the NCNC, the NNDP formed an alliance with the NDP against Ibo and NCNC influence. This new alliance was known as the Nigerian National Alliance (NNA).

Meanwhile, the NCNC countered with an alliance with the former Action Group members who did not go along with Akintola's NNDP, an alliance known as the United Progressive Grand Alliance (UPGA). Concerned with the domination by the northerners by constitutional fiat as well as by political and demographic realities of the federal government, the UPGA came out in favor of the creation of additional states, a proposal of course opposed by the NNA. The UPGA was decidedly the leftist force in Nigeria, blaming Nigeria's economic and developmental woes on neocolonialism, as in the dependency tradition discussed in Chapter 9. The UPGA further bought into leftist economic rhetoric with statements such as that Nigeria "should not go backward to the exploitation and corruption of the dying capitalist society" but rather should move "forward with progressive forces all over the world . . . to build a socialist society."[10] The NPC, now in alliance with the NNDP in the NNA, remained the main conservative force in the Nigerian party system.

In a system beset with the cultural, tribal, and linguistic segmentation that we have described, it is not surprising that the idea of secession was raised. Northerners talked of secession in 1966, just after the January coup and also after the countercoup in July, in which more than 30,000 Ibo and other easterners living in the north were slaughtered in a well-orchestrated pogrom by the northern-controlled Nigerian military and police. However, believing that the federal system was controlled by the northern region, especially by its Muslim citizens, and buoyed by substantial oil strikes in their region, which improved their prospect of financial inde-

pendence, some perceived that the Ibo were talking of secession from the Nigerian federation. Other Ibo deny this account. In any event, the UPGA called for a boycott of the election. This move strengthened the electoral showing of the NNA, meaning, in effect, the NPC and the NNDP. Accordingly, President Azikiwe had no choice but to ask Abubakar Tafawa Balewa of the NPC to form a government. He did so reluctantly, however, after several days of hesitation on the grounds that he felt the elections contained irregularities and were unfair. This democratic government rested on a narrow, parochial base of support that would not be able to withstand the deep communal segmentation of Nigeria. The Ibo population felt that they had been outmaneuvered by the Northern Region and they had little respect for the Balewa government. Thus, Paul Anber argues, the Ibo, who had been among the earliest and strongest nationalists (in the sense of being anticolonialists), became increasingly tribally oriented.[11] This means that they became alienated from an identification with the broader Nigerian nation and moved toward a more parochial identification with their tribe. This alienation, he argues, was exacerbated by the fact that the Ibo, more receptive than the northerners to Western education (as was discussed above), were more modern than the Muslim northerners and resented being ruled by them. The Balewa government in fact lasted less than two years.

MILITARY COUP AND CIVIL WAR

The preceding section discussed the distrust by the Ibo in particular and other non-northerners in general of the new government in Lagos, a distrust that culminated in a military coup led by a middle western general, T. U. Aguiyi-Ironsi and Ibo Major Chukwuma Nzeogwu. Actually, Ironsi was not one of the original plotters of the coup. He took over from Nzeogwu when the original group appeared to be in disarray. This coup was accompanied by a considerable amount of bloodshed, significantly including the deaths of the northern-based prime minister, Sir Abubakar Balewa; Samuel Akintola, who had supplanted Obafemi Awolowo as leader of the Western Region; and other northern military leaders, including Brigadier Maimafari, Lieutenant Colonels Langema and Poini. In fact, a disproportionate number of those killed were northerners. The coup had in part been motivated by its perpetrators' loss of patience with the endless regionally based parochialism and interregional squabbling, especially in the west; hence, the Ironsi regime proceeded with a centralizing agenda that northerners saw as a threat to their cultural, religious, and administative autonomy and defense. The Ironsi military junta never had a prayer of possessing legitimacy in the Northern Region, despite an attempt at a veneer of representation of different tribal interests by making such appointments as naming Yakubu Gowon, a senior officer from the Middle Belt, his chief of staff.

In the late spring of 1966, northern soldiers went on a rampage of violence against Ibo in the Northern Region, especially against Ibo soldiers. Thousands of Ibo were slain, including hundreds of high-ranking Ibo officers. Ironsi himself was among those killed that July. The anti-Ibo violence continued into the fall with appalling ferocity. Estimates of the numbers of Ibo victims vary, but the number was certainly enormous. Perhaps as many as 30,000 to 50,000 Ibo were either killed, mutilated, or wounded by November 1966. The carnage was so great that some writers have used the term genocide to describe it. Many Ibo felt that the northerners, especially the Hausa, were intent on their extermination; hence, accepting their rule became impossible.[12]

As a consequence of this wanton destruction of Ibo lives and property in the Northern Region, the military governor of the Eastern Region, Lieutenant Colonel Odumegwu Ojukwu, led a secession of the Eastern Region out of the Nigerian federation and the establishment of the Ibo-dominated state of Biafra. (Biafra also contained other less numerous ethnic groups such as the Ibibio, Efik, etc.) Thus began a long and bitter civil war in July 1967 that was to last some three years. Because of their superior levels of education relative to other Nigerians, many of the leaders of the Nigerian officer corps were Ibo, and this leadership may account for some early Ibo successes against the Nigerian army. The Biafrans were mobilized into intransigent resistance by the belief that the alternative was genocide, a belief that was based upon the large-scale slaughter of Biafrans immediately preceding the war. It was later claimed, however, that many Ibo were living in northern-controlled territory without being molested. The willingness to accept the belief about genocide indicates the depth of antipathy and distrust among the peoples that were supposedly to become common citizens of Nigeria. Although Biafra received substantial support from the Soviet Union and Great Britain, the Gowon forces finally literally starved the landlocked Biafrans into defeat and eventually restored the Nigerian federation.

Since the end of the civil war in 1970, the Ibo have featured less prominently in the national government except for the token Ibo, Alex Ekwueme, who was vice president in the Shagari administration. With the aid of some rehabilitation and reconstruction programs instituted after the war (1979–83), the Ibo have struggled to recover lost ground. However, the antipathy of the northern-dominated system to the Ibo appears to continue. The Ibo heartland has been split into four small states, and Ibo territories were ceded to neighboring states, which left the Ibo cut off from access to the sea. With this continued marginality in national politics, the Ibo have apparently developed a sense of alienation from that system, manifested by a passive willingness to allow other ethnic groups to sort out Nigeria's problems. It seems fair to say that their sense of self-definition as an Ibo now supersedes any sense of self-identification as a Nigerian. This sense of alienation is to some extent shared by other minority ethnic groups of the east, such as the Efik, Ibibio, and Ijaw of the Niger Delta, as well as by the Edo and the Ik-Ibo of the Middle Belt region.

Moreover, Ibo suffered a leadership crisis when the venerated Ibo, Nnamdi Azikwe suddenly abandoned Biafra and fled to the northern-led government at the height of the civil war. On a psychological level, Zik's shocking and inexplicable action led to a general distrust of political leadership among the Ibo and their alienation from the world of politics. It may have undermined the Ibo will to prosecute the war successfully and have led to the collapse of Biafra. This leadership crisis for the Ibo was exacerbated when General Chukwuemeka Odumegwu Ojukwu, a former leader of the Biafran revolution, returned to Nigeria during the Shagari regime and became a senatorial candidate for the National Party of Nigeria (NPN), a party viewed among the Ibo as thoroughly corrupt. Hence, the legitimacy and credibility of a potential leader among the Ibo were fatally eroded, and the alienation of the Ibo and many other southeastern Nigerians from the nation remains deep.

Some prominent students of Nigerian history suggest that the roots of its civil war was the Lugard decision of 1914, when the British attempted to weld the disparate tribes and regions into a single political entity.[13] Surely, there was no cultural or social basis for this decision, and it could be argued that

given the geographically defined linguistic and cultural diversities, it was never possible for a pan-national sense of community to develop in Nigeria.

POSTWAR NIGERIA AND THE STRUGGLE FOR CIVILIAN RULE

General Gowon disappointed hopes for a return to democratic government upon the conclusion of the war in 1970, when he announced that the return to civilian rule would have to wait until 1976. He claimed the intervening time would be used for reconstruction and reconciliation. This disappointment was exacerbated by his announcement in 1974 that the 1976 target date for returning to civilian rule was no longer "realistic." In fairness, it should be pointed out that Gowon's government did engage in several conciliatory gestures toward the defeated Biafrans. Biafran houses and property in the Northern Region had been protected and were returned to their original owners when possible. Former Ibo civil servants were invited to return to their jobs. Moreover, the administrative reorganization of the nation into 12 new states made the Northern Region into 6 states. This seemed to break up the Hausa-Fulani political base that had been used to dominate or threaten to dominate the rest of Nigeria.

The hope for relegating the Nigerian military to the status of a tool of a civilian government was compromised by the power and affluence of the military by the end of the war. The military had grown geometrically from some 11,000 personnel in 1966 to a quarter of a million by 1970, with a pay scale that was some eight times the average per capita income. The military had no wish to relinquish its power, and its men had no wish to be demobilized. We have seen in Chapter 9 how praetorianism—the failure to establish civilian control of the military—is a common problem among less developed systems. Hence, Nigeria was now faced with this problem of the disproportionate influence of military power. A military junta voluntarily handing over power to a civilian government is not a common occurrence anywhere, but the problem of praetorianism in Nigeria is rendered more insoluble by the virtual absence of civilian institutions with pan-national legitimacy.

Despite his best intentions, the junta under General Gowon was unable to control the widespread corruption that has characterized so many Third World Nations, corruption that was fueled by rising revenues from Nigerian oil reserves. These revenues also helped fuel a rising level of inflation and exacerbate the economic inequality. These factors, plus the dashed expectations when Gowon postponed the scheduled return to civilian rule, led to another coup in 1975 that overthrew him. This coup, led by General Murtala Muhammed, assumed power in a fit of reformist zeal that inevitably threatened some entrenched interests. Muhammed's crusade did not last long; he was assassinated in 1976 in an abortive coup attempt by a group of fellow officers, and one General Olusegun Obasanjo assumed the role of head of state. Obasanjo went ahead with plans to return the country to civilian rule; eventually elections were scheduled for 1979, and the 12-year military ban on political parties was lifted.

A period of reformation of the party system followed, and five parties were accredited for the 1979 elections under a constitution drafted in 1977. Not surprisingly, the parties formed primarily along ethnic lines again. Obafemi Awolowo reappeared at age 70 to head the Yoruba-based United Party of Nigeria, and Nmamdi Azikiwe was unearthed at age 79 to head the Ibo-based Nigerian People's Party. There were three accredited par-

ties from the north: the moderately conservative National Party of Nigeria, led by Shehu Shagari; the Great People's Party, led by the wealthy Alhaji Ibrahim; and a socialist-oriented People's Redemption Party. The National Party of Nigeria dominated the congressional elections, and its leader, Shagari, was elected president in 1979. The NPN again won the elections of 1983 amidst charges of widespread election malpractices.

The 1983 government was extremely short-lived, as once again the military overthrew the civilian government. The coup was led by General Buhari, who in turn was overthrown by General Ibrahim Babangida in 1985. The regime of President Babangida ruled Nigeria from 1985 to 1993, despite a failed coup attempt by Major Gideon Orkar in April 1990. Having experienced so many coup attempts in their short history, ordinary people greeted Orkar's assault on the Dodan Barracks with remarkable indifference, going about their personal business in the city much as if nothing unusual was happening. In the wake of the failed coup, Orkar and over 70 of his fellow conspirators were executed in the summer of 1990.

The Orkar coup was another example of the resurgent tribalism from which Nigeria apparently cannot escape. Orkar claimed his coup was on behalf of "the oppressed and enslaved people of the middle belt and south."[14] Orkar, who came from the Middle Belt, had proposed to expel the five northern states from the federation, illustrating that his operation was another manifestation of Middle Belt, southeastern, and/or southwestern (read Ibo and Yoruba, respectively) resentment of the perennial northern domination. (Ironically, the mostly Christian Middle Belt had sided with the Northern Region in the civil war; however, more recently they have been increasingly siding with the southeast and west.) The Muslim north, fearful of being dominated by the more educated and more modern Ibo and Yoruba to the southeast and southwest, has continually insisted upon being guaranteed a dominating position in the government of the federation that they initially opposed because of that same fear. The Yoruba and Ibo populations, looking down upon and fearing domination by the less educated and less modern northerners, have never accepted that condition. Without some means of changing the basic sense of loyalties, or, in Gabriel Almond's terms, the "system affect" (the sense of belonging to and identifying with a political system), from a primary loyalty to one's tribal, ethnic, and linguistic group to a broader sense of Nigerian community, it is hard to envisage the basis for stable democratic politics in Nigeria.

PRAETORIANISM AND THE FACTIONALIZATION OF THE MILITARY

For much of its political history as an independent nation, Nigeria has been ruled by a factionalized military apparatus. Although lacking in the political art of governorship, the military has been able to legitimize its political impact by engaging in a political strategy of sharing administrative functions with civilian employees while retaining ultimate control. This is the essence of what was called a *praetorian society* in Chapter 9. The periodic incursions of the Nigerian military into the political leadership was not simply driven by individual lust for power but rather was a product of the conflict, riddled with intrigue and conspiracy, between the two major elite groups that emerged in the Nigerian military at the close of the civil war—the northern faction, led by the "Kaduna Mafia," and the Middle Belt wing, led by the Langtang faction. The major military coups in Nigeria have emanated from one or the other of these two factions. For instance, while the Gowon-led countercoup of July 1966 was meant to reassert northern control of the country, Gowon, a Middle Belt Christian, was never accepted by the mainstream Hausa-Fulani oligarchy of the north. Hence, the Murlata Muhammed coup of August 1975 was intended to remove any lingering ambivalence about northern control. The failed Dimka-Bisalla coup of February 1976 that led to the death of Muhammed may be seen as a desperate attempt by the military wing of the Langtang faction to reassert lost control of the military and of the country as a whole. Gowon, who was implicated in the coup, was exiled to Britain, and Lieutenant Colonel Dimka, Major General Bisalla, Police Commissioner David Gomwalk, and other military leaders from the Middle Belt Langtang faction were executed. The Langtang faction has not recovered from this decimation of its leadership.

The Buhari-Idiagbon regime that came to power in December 1983 seemed to be an exception to the usual military escapade into national politics in that it made some attempt to address the rampant corruption and ineptitude of the Shagari regime that it overthrew. The northern-based Kaduna faction feared, however, that the Buhari-Idiagbon regime threatened northern control of the nation and engineered the Babangida coup that overthrew Buhari in August 1985.

During the Babangida regime, a new "progressive" faction emerged within the military made up of fringe elements from the Kaduna faction, noncommissioned officers from the Middle Belt (Plateau and Benue States), and an ideological group from the midwest (the Edo Clan). This faction twice attempted to overthrow the Babangida regime, first in December 1985 under the soldier-poet General Mamman Vatsa, and next in April 1990 under the charismatic Major Gideon Orkar. Both coup attempts failed and resulted in the execution of their leaders. This purge of the coup leaders once again took a devastating toll on the Langtang faction from the Middle Belt.

In the final analysis, history will record that the Nigerian military has been one of its own worst enemies with a high propensity to self-destruct. The numerous coups in Nigeria, more than any other factor, have depleted the nation of its finest military talents.

POLITICAL INSTITUTIONS IN NIGERIA

Although Nigeria is frequentlly thought of as one of Africa's democracies, it has been governed mostly by military juntas since independence. It has had two fairly short-lived republics, the first lasting 6 years and the second lasting 4 years, interspersed among its 20 years of military rule. Hence it has been ruled by junta for two-thirds of its existence. A third republic was scheduled to begin in 1992, according to the promise of the head of government, General Babangida. Under Western pressure, General Babangida turned the presidency over to a "caretaker" government headed by a President Shohehan. He was quickly displaced by General Sani Abacha who, as of May 1995 had the delegates to the constitutional conference drop January 1, 1996 as a deadline for transferring power to a civilian ruler. However, if the military does not voluntarily turn over power to civilian rule when they promise to do so, it would not be the first time that a military ruler or dictator has failed to live up to such a promise.

The First Republic, lasting from independence until 1966, reflected the British legacy in Nigeria. The head of government was a prime minister who was named to that post as a result of being the head of the largest party in the Federal House of Representatives. The role of president, first occupied by the popu-

lar Nmamdi Azikiwe, was largely the ceremonial and symbolic one of head of state. In fact, the Queen of England, through her governor-general, was the head of state until Azikiwe assumed the office of president in 1963. Although nominally bicameral, the upper house, or Federal Senate, was an impotent institution consisting of sinecure roles for some 48 traditional chiefs and elders. The lower house, as is generally true in a parliamentary arrangement, was the only potentially significant house. However, the extent to which the Federal House of Representatives actually held the government accountable to it must be assessed in light of the fact that the government did not lose a single division during the entire First Republic. The House never met for more than 30 days in any one year, a fact that indicates its insignificant policy-making role. Actually, as one might expect in such a regionally divided system, a great deal of the power to make policy remained in the hands of the several regional houses of assembly. This relative weakness of the national government is indicated by the fact that the federal prime minister of the First Republic, Tafawa Balewa, was only the deputy leader of the plurality party, the NPC. The head of that party, Sir Alhaji Ahmadu Bello, chose to be premier of the Northern Region. (Could you imagine a politician in the United States choosing to be a governor of a state when he or she could have been president?)

The Second Republic resembled the United States more than Britain in constitutional format. The actual head of government was in the role of the president, who was to be directly elected by a national vote. To avoid the possible perception that any one region would feel that a presidency was imposed upon it by other regions, the constitution provided that a president had to carry at least a quarter of the vote in at least two-thirds of the states in addition to winning the overall plurality of votes in the country. As is consistent with an American-style format with its mandated separation of powers, the president was forbidden to hold a seat in the National Assembly.

The projected format of the Third Republic, slated to begin operation in 1992, is also that of a presidential system with the separation of powers, according to a July 1987 White Paper. In addition, further emulating the American model, the White Paper stipulated that the military will only authorize two political parties to contest elections. The 1992 constitution is clearly influenced by the Babangida military junta in power. Certain topics or options have been foreclosed by fiat of the junta. For example, both the role of the presidency, and the federal structure of Nigeria have been eliminated as topics that the constitutional convention may address.

As noted, however, the nation has been under military government for 25 of the 35 years since its independence from Britain (1960), during which decisions were issued by decree, political parties were banned, and criticism of the government was circumscribed to a considerable extent. In fact, General Murtala Muhammed (leader from 1975 to 1976) established a National Security Organization (NSO) to control opposition to the regime. Many innocent people were victimized by the zeal of the NSO to suppress opposition under the Buhari regime. Under the current leader, General Babangida, the NSO was divided into a Defence Intelligence Agency, a National Intelligence Agency (to gather overseas intelligence), and the State Security Services (to oversee domestic activities). Decrees were issued from a Supreme Military Council—whose name was changed under General Babangida to the Armed Forces Ruling Council—comprised of the top officers associated with the leader.

In each junta, however, one figure remained dominant, and the various institutions remained tools by which the leader exercised control rather than structures that could constrain the leader or hold him accountable. Thus, the institutional structure of the several juntas has been quite simple compared to that of the two republics. The fact that federalism remained intact during these juntas is a testament to the strength of regional sentiment in Nigeria. Ironsi attempted but failed to impose a unitary structure on Nigeria and his attempt may have contributed to his overthrow.

PUBLIC POLICY IN NIGERIA: OIL AND CORRUPTION

It seems strange to those of us in oil-importing nations, faced with uncertain supplies and prices geometrically higher than they were in the early 1970s, to hear of oil-rich nations faced with severe economic difficulties. Yet that is precisely what has happened in Nigeria and in Mexico in the 1980s. During the oil boom brought on by the OPEC cartel in the mid-1970s, the oil income of Nigeria boomed, rising at the rate of around 30 percent per year—from $400 million to nearly $25 billion per year by 1980. After that, oil production and oil revenue declined steadily throughout the 1980s. By 1989, oil revenue was only $4.22 billion. By the mid-1980s, Nigeria was using 44 percent of its foreign exchange earnings to service its debt.

During the period of rapidly rising oil revenue, Nigeria did two things that would render its economy especially vulnerable to the drop in oil revenues in the 1980s. First, it undertook or initiated numerous expensive projects in which the country incurred considerable indebtedness against future oil revenues that never fully materialized. Many of these projects contributed little or nothing to the economic development of Nigeria. Examples include the construction of a new federal capital city at Abuja, a new airport, and new television stations. An immediate 60 percent salary increase was instituted for government workers, clearly not an expenditure designed to produce development or productivity. By 1989, Nigeria had accumulated $30 billion in external indebtedness, the second highest in Africa, contributing to a poor credit rating for the nation.

Second, Nigeria neglected other sectors of the economy in the belief that oil would provide for all its needs. Not realizing that oil markets, as with the market for anything else, eventually fluctuate, the Nigerians regarded their oil reserves as a panacea for all of their economic and developmental woes. As oil revenues rose somewhat in the fall of 1990, a debate arose as to how best to use the oil windfall. Some argued that it should be used to service Nigeria's enormous debt, but opponents argued that a better credit rating would only provoke Nigeria into more irresponsible borrowing. Others argued that the revenue should be spent on developmental goals.

The economic woes of Nigeria had reached such a level that the budget deficits of 1988 were expected to reach 10 percent of the 1987 GNP. The currency, the *naira*, was devalued, with some negative impact on the economic well-being of the domestic population. The most serious domestic impact was the result of an attempt by the government to restructure the economy into one that is more self-sufficient, through a policy known as the Structural Adjustment Programme (SAP) of 1988 and 1989. As the resources of the nation were being diverted into capital goods and investment, there would be some reduction in the resources directed toward current levels of consumption. This short-term deprivation generated a wave of student riots in Lagos beginning May 31, 1989, which were met with severe police repression. A number of people were killed, wounded, or arrested and disappeared, many of whom were not direct participants in the riots. The severe police reaction to the riots increased the resentment against the government. Showing little sensitivity to the growing impatience with the immediate economic consequences of his SAP, President Babangida, in an interview in the *African Concord,* defended his program in terms of its long-term goals.[15]

As of mid-1994, Nigeria's external debt is $28 billion, with repayment arrears due to reach $8 billion by the end of 1994; these economic difficulties have been compounded by the loss of oil revenues due to the collapse of OPEC unity and consequent overproduction. The Nigerian minister of finance, Dr. Klu Idika Kalu, attempted to negotiate a rescheduling of Nigeria's debt; however, given the nation's economic situation, this proved impossible. Hence, the debt and interest payments will continue to drain off scarce capital from investment and to restrain economic growth from attaining a level able to support stable democracy.[16] Meanwhile Kalu has been dismissed as a scapegoat to Nigeria's continuing troubles.

The bankruptcy of the Nigerian government has undoubtedly been exacerbated by a very high level of graft and corruption. To get any public official to perform any duty, that official would probably have to be "dashed," that is, given a payoff. While there is a literature advancing the plausible argument that some amount of what Boss Plunkett of New York's Tammany Hall machine called "honest graft" served the positive function of mobilizing enough unity of purpose and political support to allow the formally fragmented system to function, the level of corruption in Nigeria seems to have exceeded the amount that could have a positive function, although a high level of corruption is not uncommon among civil servants in Third World systems. When enormous personal enrichment becomes the primary goal of public officials (as was clearly the case in the Philippines under Ferdinand Marcos), corruption becomes destructive. The extent of the corruption in Nigeria was enhanced by the low level of system affect among public officials—a low sense of belonging to and having a stake in the well-being of the Nigerian political system—which in turn has been a function of the lack of development of a sense of a Nigerian community. Officials who do not care about the system have no other goal from the conduct of their office than personal enrichment. Furthermore, some of these officials may have had a relatively low sense of self-esteem relative to the Western businesspeople with whom they frequently dealt, for which they may have been partially compensating by delaying their applications and insisting on "dash."

CONCLUSION: THE SEARCH FOR ELUSIVE DEMOCRACY IN A SEGMENTED SOCIETY

The dilemma of the Nigerian national experience becomes more manifest in each attempt to attain democratic rule. One is always confronted with the image of a nation in crisis and in a continuous search for its "soul"— for the essence of the Nigerian *community.* The oft-noted north-south dichotomy may be an oversimplified impression of Nigerian society. The north is split between the Kanuri of the northeast and the Hausa/Fulani faction of the northwest. The Middle Belt, which has been viewed as part of the greater north, has become more assertive in its resentment at being absorbed in an all-embracing north controlled by the Sokoto Emirate. The east is divided between the aspirations of the dominant Ibo, and the singular aspirations of each of the peripheral ethnic groups: Efik, Ibibio, and Ijaw. The west and midwest are also divided among the Yoruba, Edo, Urhobo, and

Ika-Ibo. Overall, the most persistent problem of national unity is the lack of a sense of national community (which, it will be recalled from Chapter 1, is an aggregate or collection of individuals defined by a set of shared values and principles). This sense of community has remained all the more elusive for Nigeria as the country embarks on its third democratic experiment.

A presidential election was held on June 12, 1993, for a return to civilian rule, an election reluctantly authorized by the Babangida regime in the face of severe national and international pressures to live up to a promise he had made to step down by 1992.[17] The military took applications from groups to be certified as political parties allowed to run candidates in the elections for the new government. Some 15 groups applied and only 2 were certified; hence, a two-party system was imposed by military fiat rather than by a cultural propensity to compromise and an ability to consolidate political differences. This presumed that the culture allows enough common ground among the numerous factions to bifurcate political conflict effectively without some strongly felt interests and perspectives perceiving that they have been unjustly or arbitrarily excluded from the political arena. The cultural basis of an essentially dichotomized political conflict buttressed by the tyranny of the electoral system underlies the consolidated, almost two-party systems in those Anglo-American democracies that Nigeria is apparently attempting to emulate.

Fragmented party systems emerge in culturally fragmented societies in which the diversities are perceived with such passion or intensity that they cannot be effectively aggregated into larger groupings. As late as March 1987, substantial religious-based violence erupted between Christians and Muslims in the northern state of Kaduna, indicating that deep hostility between these two religious groups is far from resolved and that the end of the civil war has not meant an end to the communal violence in the nation.[18] The claims of these diverse social, economic, or political interests have to be addressed. They cannot be eliminated by administrative fiat. As discussed in Chapter 2, if a plurality electoral system were to be imposed on such a fragmented social system, there would be enormous pressure to change the electoral system.

In any event, only two questionable and politically naïve candidates were mustered for the June 12, 1993, election: Bashorun M.K.O. Abiola of the Social Democratic Party and Alhaji Bashir Tofa of the National Republican convention. The candidate selection process was subjected to the ethnoreligious conflict that has been the bane of Nigerian politics. Abiola, who is a Yoruba Muslim from the state of Ogun in the west, chose a northern Muslim, Alhaji Bana Kingibe, as his vice presidential candidate and running mate. This ticket was hard to sell in the east and south because it did not include a Christian. Alhaji Tofa, a Kanuri Muslim from the North, chose an eastern Ibo, Dr. Sylvester Ugo, as his running mate; however, the reckless political utterances of Tofa prevented the ticket from receiving much support in the south. Tofa was quoted as having called for a *jihad,* or holy war, against Christians. The Hausa/Fulani oligarchy of President Babangida was not represented on either ticket and therefore felt alienated from the entire process. Unofficial results showed that Abiola won the election, carrying 19 states to Tofa's 11.

Before the election, Abimbola Davis, representing an organization called the Association for Better Nigeria, asked the court to enjoin the conduct of the election, citing electoral malpractice, but the National Election Commission ordered the election to continue. However, on June 23, 1993, President Babangida annulled the June 12 election. He claimed to have stepped in to end judicial proceedings regarding the election and thus to redeem the judiciary from further ridicule. The military then suspended the National Election Commission and the Transition to Civilian Rule Decree. In response to an international outcry at the suspension of the election, General Babangida handed over the power and role of the presidency to Ernest Shonekan, who headed an interim national government for 82 days.

Shonekan's administration quickly incurred the wrath of the powerful Nigerian Labor Congress (NCL) and much of the public, especially for raising the price of petrol some 700 percent, which was exacerbated by Shonekan's uninspiring image as a leader. The NLC called for a general strike, and riots ensued throughout the country. In this atmosphere, in which the election, having been won by a southerner, was annulled by a general from the north, the intensity of intertribal and interregional animosities was very high. The rest of the country began to perceive that the north intended to retain perpetual hegemonic control of the nation.

In November 1993 the Shonekan administration, which had never had much legitimacy in the nation, was declared illegal in a Lagos high court, leaving the country in effect without a legal government. Into this breach stepped General Sani Abacha, the secretary of defense in the interim government, who on November 17 overthrew Shonekan and took over as head of state, once again exposing the essentially praetorian nature of Nigeria—the unrelenting military appetite for civilian power.

When Abacha became head of state, internal purges were launched to weed out Babangida loyalists, purges that heavily hit the Langtang faction from the Middle Belt. Officers either retired under pressure or were reassigned abroad or to low-responsibility posts.

Abacha next initiated a constitutional conference to determine the future constitutional structure of the nation. The 19-member Constitutional Conference Commission was formed on January 14, 1994; however, the idea of the conference was opposed by the Hausa/Fulani faction on the grounds that it would lead to a disintegration of the country. Actually, many believe that this faction was concerned that constitutional government would end its hegemony over the Nigerian state through the vehicle of military coups. For example, one of the most vehement opponents of constitutional government was Alhaji Umari Dikko, a former minister in the Shagari administration who was one of those accused of having looted Nigeria's treasury to the tune of some $5 billion and who had fled to Britain after the Buhari/Idiagbon coup of December 1983. (An attempt by agents of the Buhari regime to kidnap Dikko and bring him back to Nigeria to face charges of embezzlement was foiled by British security agents.)

The northern opposition to the constitutional conference has put it in abeyance, adding to the political stalemate that has beset Nigeria. The current head of state, Abacha, has not convinced much of the nation of his independence from the Babangida junta that placed him in his position; consequently, the nation is without a government with broad legitimacy.

Nigeria is a culturally, religiously, and linguistically fragmented society with very little understanding or social interaction between people of the different cultural, religious, linguistic groups; in other words, it is *a segmented society*. The history of that nation attests to the inability of the representatives of the various groupings to form stable coalitions and to work effectively with one another. Hence, it is not likely that the elites from these respective segments will be able to cooperate effectively with one another in

what Arend Lijphart called his *consociational model*.[19] This concept, developed in a study of the Netherlands, refers to a segmented society that is nevertheless effectively governed by cooperation at the overarching elite level. This model seems inapplicable to the strength of the segmentation in the Nigerian case. An imposed two-party system in Nigeria would inevitably result in significant cultural, religious, or linguistic groups feeling that they have been arbitrarily excluded from the political process. A growing sense of alienation among the members of such excluded groups toward the national political system, with all of its attendant political consequences, seems inevitable.[20]

It has been shown that Nigeria, an entity artificially and arbitrarily contrived by the Lugard Decision of 1914, has made little progress toward developing a sense of national community, which refers to a set of shared fundamental values and assumptions that define the nature of the system. Unless such values are shared, they are not taken for granted. Consequently, they are on the political agenda. When the fundamentals of a society are on the agenda, too much is at stake in political conflict for the electoral process to work. Democratic elections, let us recall, can only work when the leading actors perceive that adhering to the rules of the electoral game is more important than the electoral outcome.

Recall from Chapter 2 that the electoral process requires that the participants be able to accept the prospect of their electoral defeat. The level of suspicion and hostility that has been shown in this chapter to exist between the regional groupings in Nigeria, groupings in which the antipathy emanating from deep tribal differences generally culminates with the partisanship of religious, linguistic, and even socioeconomic diversity, precludes the acceptance of the outcome of interparty competition. The party elites speak not only for differences of political orientations and of interests, as has generally been the case in the West, but also for geographically defined, irreconcilable conflicts of primordial loyalties and fundamental values. The six coups in 30 years of independent political life should not have been unexpected. They are a manifestation of the impossiblity of the losers accepting the result of a national election.

The Western-educated Christian and generally more Westernized peoples of the east and west could never accept domination from the less educated, less Westernized Muslims of the north. The economic success of the Western-educated Ibo and Yoruba population, especially the high overrepresentation of the Ibo in the government service, has always been perceived as a threat by the north. The Muslims of the north, as with devout Muslims elsewhere, have difficulty with the concept of being politically dominated by non-Muslims. Moreover, as noted, Islam may be fundamentally incompatible with a multi-religious society based upon the principle of equal status of the diverse sects. Islam, it will be recalled, regards the state as an instrument to serve the faith. Therefore, Muslims are naturally insistent that any predominantly Muslim population be controlled by a Muslim-dominated government. It is this principle that in part drives the Arab resistance to a Jewish state in the Middle East. It is therefore difficult to imagine Hausa/Fulani acceptance of any democratic arrangement that entails the possibility of Ibo or Yoruba and therefore Christian control of the country. Thus, the religious divisions alone may be too intense for reconciliation by the democratic process. The outcomes of religiously driven politics in Nigeria will always be more important than the rules of the democratic game.

None of the political parties that have been active up to this point have come close to attracting anything vaguely resembling a national constituency. Each has been primarily an advocate of the parochial interests of an ethnic, tribal, or linguistic region and an advocate of the defense of that subcultural segment against absorption into a broader Nigerian community. The raison d'être of Nigerian elites has largely been the role of subcultural defense.

Without that minimal sense of community—a sense of shared values, a common past, and shared symbols and loyalties—it is hard to imagine how any regime purporting to govern Nigeria could hope to acquire widespread legitimacy. Recall that legitimacy has been theorized as a *sine qua non* for long-term political survival. The massive and widespread corruption, discussed above, is a manifestation of the weak commitment and loyalty of public officials to the system, of their lack of a sense of a Nigerian community. It is harder to see how that sense of community could develop without the basic communication grids emanating from a lingua franca widely shared among the masses as well as elites. Mass fluency in English—or even "pidgin English"—could one day evolve to perform this function, but that eventuality is not imminent. Moreover, it is hard to imagine how the prospective elections for posts in the new civilian government could be meaningful if, given the absence of democratic politics since 1983, few of the 5,000 candidates are known to the public or have any kind of track record in public life.

Difficult economic issues loom on Nigeria's horizon. The oil revenues have been depleted without a legacy of long-term economic development, and the short-term prospects of the SAP are for serious domestic deprivations. These divisive issues will continue to be argued in terms of which region should dominate the others and in terms of the question of regime. It is hard to envision any civilian regime, especially a democratic one tolerant of domestic opposition, acquiring the minimal level of legitimacy necessary to govern effectively over time. In these difficulties, Nigeria epitomizes the problems endemic to the newly emerging nations referred to as the Third World; in many respects, these problems are present in a heightened degree in Nigeria. The country's prospects for stable democratic development are bleak indeed.

NOTES

1. See C. L. Temple, *Native Races and Their Rulers* (London: Frank Cass, 1918).

2. Frederick O. Schwarz, Jr., *Nigeria: The Tribes, the Nation, or the Race—The Politics of Independence* (Cambridge: MIT Press, 1965), p. 72. See also Walter Schwarz, *Nigeria* (New York: Praeger, 1968).

3. Hans Kohn, *Nationalism: Its Meaning and History* (Princeton: Van Nostrand, 1955).

4. Lawrence Mayer, "Federalism and Party Behavior in Australia and Canada," *Western Political Quarterly,* vol. 23, no. 4 (December 1970), pp. 795–807.

5. A.H.M. Kirk-Greene, *Crisis and Conflict in Nigeria,* vol. 1 (Oxford: Oxford University Press, 1976).

6. Karl Deutsch, *The Nerves of Government* (New York: The Free Press, 1966).

7. Schwarz, *Nigeria,* pp. 35–36.

8. Ibrahim A. Gambari, "British Colonial Administration," in Richard Olaniyan, ed., *Nigerian History and Culture* (London: Longman Group Ltd., 1985), pp. 163–64.

9. Quoted in Schwarz, *Nigeria,* pp. 35–36.

10. Ibid., p. 144.

11. Paul Anber, "Modernization and Political Disintegration: Nigeria and the Ibos," *Journal of Modern African Studies,* vol. 5 (1967), pp. 163–79.

12. This is the interpretation of Okwubida Nwoli, "The Nigerian-Biafran Conflict," in Joseph Okpaku, ed., *Nigeria: The Dilemma of Nationhood* (Westport, CT: Greenwood Publishing Co., 1972), p. 123.

13. This interpretation may be found in John Hatch, *The Seeds of Disaster* (Chicago: Henry Regnery Co., 1970), pp. 240 ff.

14. Quoted in *African Concord,* vol. 5 (May 7, 1990), pp. 23–27.

15. *African Concord,* vol. 4 (May 1989), p. 40.

16. See the discussion of the economic barriers to democratization in Samuel Huntington, *The Third Wave* (Norman: University of Oklahoma Press, 1991), pp. 311–14.

17. *African Concord,* vol. 4 (December 11, 1989), pp. 14–15. See also the analysis of the prospects of Nigerian democracy in Celestine O. Bassey, "Retrospects and Prospects of Political Stability in Nigeria," *African Studies Review,* vol. 34, no. 1 (April 1989), pp. 97–113.

18. See the summary of these events in *West Africa* (December 7, 1987), p. 2379.

19. Arend Lijphart, *The Politics of Accommodation: Pluralism and Democracy in the Netherlands* (Berkeley: University of California Press, 1968); and Arend Lijphart, "Consociational Democracy," *World Politics,* vol. 21, no. 2 (January 1969), pp. 207–25.

20. See *West Africa,* no. 3987 (February 28–March 6, 1994), for a detailed summary of the events surrounding the election and its nullification.

11

Modernization and Democratization in Latin America

"The greatest challenge to democracy in Latin America . . . is to prove that democracy works. We don't want to arrive at the end of the century with new dictators. But democracy must deliver the goods."

Oscar Arias (Sanchez), former president of Costa Rica

Scholars are divided as to whether it makes sense to speak of Latin America as a single, coherent cultural and political entity. Clearly the diversity of the area—which includes the continent of South America plus Central America and the island nations of the Caribbean—is undeniable with respect to cultural factors, political history, geographical context, and current social and political issues. Distinguished Latin American scholar Lawrence Graham is one of the leading voices presenting the view that it is not tenable to generalize about Latin America as a coherent region.[1] There are relatively modernized societies with cosmopolitan cities, such as Brazil and Argentina, that contrast with far less modernized societies such as Paraguay and Uruguay, and even within nations the gleaming modernity of Mexico City contrasts sharply with the dusty villages in rural Mexico, and the cosmopolitan Rio de Janeiro is another cultural and geographic world from the Amazon Valley of Brazil. Yet, most scholars, such as Howard Wiarda and Harvey Kline, claim that there are sufficient shared attributes among the nations of what we call Latin America to talk meaningfully about that region as a coherent entity.[2] More-over, the residents of Latin America tend to regard it as a coherent region; hence, that is the position that will be assumed in this chapter.

Our approach will be to discuss those common attributes that define Latin America while maintaining our awareness of the rich range of diversity within the region. Accordingly, we will discuss Latin America in general and then proceed to consider the political systems of three of the largest and most powerful nations within the region. This latter discussion, in the spirit of the comparative enterprise that is the raison d'être of this volume, will address both the patterns that these three nations share and the differences that make them unique as well as sovereign nation-states.

Latin America constitutes an important example of our theme of a changing world in several ways. First, while the level of development varies widely throughout Latin America, the level of industrialization and modernization, as that term was conceptualized in Chapter 9, is on the average far greater in Latin America than in Asia or Africa. Hence, Latin America has experienced the modernization process longer and to a greater extent than those other two continents that comprise what we loosely call the "Third World." Second, Samuel Huntington's "third wave" of democratization has manifested itself more in Latin America than in any other area.[3] Since the 1970s, 12 Latin American countries have undergone the so-called transition to democracy, and another, Mexico, while still under the control of the one party that has maintained an authoritarian hegemony of power since it was founded in 1929, has made strides toward the tolerance of political opposition.

When one speaks of Latin America, one is usually referring to the more than 30 sovereign nations of both South and Central America and the Caribbean. There are 18 former Spanish colonies, the large former Portuguese possession of Brazil, the former French colony of Haiti, six former British colonies, a former Dutch colony, and a host of tiny island nations and colonized possessions in the Caribbean. The principal coherence of this diverse group of nations stems from the Iberian heritage that is shared by most of them. Accordingly, for many scholars, *Latin* America refers to those nations with Iberian roots (colonized by either Spain or Portugal, both from the Iberian Peninsula), people who speak either Spanish or Portuguese. It is to these nations that the cultural and other contextual generalizations we shall make about Latin America generally apply. Hence, Suriname, a tiny republic whose principal spoken languages are Dutch, English, some Hindustani, and indigenous dialects, would not be included in such generalizations, although it is located on the South American land mass. Whether one still wants to call places like Suriname and Belize part of Latin America is ultimately a matter of definition; there is no official list of which nations are included.

Change and democratization are the themes of this volume. They are also processes that have strongly characterized the nations of Latin America in the postwar era; hence, an examination of Latin America is important for this volume and for American students. It has been argued that the United States has vital interests in the affairs of our neighbors in the Western Hemisphere, interests that are rendered even more striking by our contiguous, largely unmanned border with Mexico. The United States' legitimate special interest in the affairs of the Americas—an interest conceptualized in international relations by the term *spheres of influence*—was further delineated in the Monroe Doctrine.

The changes that have characterized Latin America, especially the modernization process, have come unevenly to the various nations, adding to the diversity discussed above. Table 11-1 shows the great range among the nations of this region with respect to modernization and size. It will be recalled from Chapter 9 that the percentage of the work force in agriculture serves as a widely recognized indicator delineating the boundary between agrarian and industrial societies, while percent of the work force in the service sector of the economy has served to distinguish industrial from postindustrial societies. It should be noted that in this table there is no relationship between size as measured by area or population and modernity as measured by percentage of the work force in agriculture or services. Brazil, the largest of the nations under consideration, has one of the larger percentages of the work force in the primary sector, and Mexico, the second most populous nation, has over a third of its work force in agricultural pursuits, while Uruguay, with only 3 million people—$1/30$ the population of Mexico and $1/55$ that of Brazil—has only 12 percent of its work force in agriculture and 56 percent in the service sector.

TABLE 11-1   The Diversity of Latin America: Size and Modernity

Nation	Percent in Agriculture	Percent in Service	Area (Square Miles)	Population
South America				
Argentina	14	52	1,072,070	32,664,000
Bolivia	51	26	424,163	7,157,000
Brazil	42	38	3,284,426	155,356,000
Chile	21	52	292,257	13,287,000
Colombia	31	46	439,513	33,778,000
Ecuador	47	29	109,483	10,752,000
Guyana	—	—	83,000	750,000
Paraguay	51	30	157,047	4,799,000
Peru	40	40	496,000	22,362,000
Suriname	—	—	55,144	402,000
Uruguay	12	56	72,172	3,121,000
Venezuela	21	52	352,143	20,189,000
Central America				
Belize	—	—	8,880	186,000
Costa Rica	30	41	19,575	3,911,000
El Salvador	47	38	8,260	5,419,000
Guatemala	57	24	42,042	9,266,000
Honduras	63	22	43,277	4,949,000
Mexico	34	47	761,601	90,007,000
Nicaragua	44	42	45,698	3,752,000
Panama	30	52	183,540	3,913,000
Caribbean				
Cuba	26	43	44,206	10,732,000
Dominican Republic	58	26	18,704	7,385,000
Haiti	40	22	10,694	6,287,000

Sources: Comparative World Atlas (Maplewood, NJ: Hammond Corporation, 1993), pp. 4–5; Charles L. Taylor and David A. Jodice, *World Handbook of Social and Political Indicators,* 3rd ed., vol. 1 (New Haven: Yale University Press, 1983), pp. 208–16.

THE HISTORICAL EMERGENCE OF MODERN LATIN AMERICA

Despite a number of trappings of the modern world, such as cosmopolitan cities and a steadily diminishing portion of its work force in agriculture, Latin America remains different from the industrialized nations of the West in several respects. The economic system of the Iberian colonizers centered around the development of great estates, called *haciendas,* surrounded by the abject poverty of a peasantry, which meant that an essentially two-class social structure emerged from the colonial period and lasted well into the modern era of industrialization. Recall from Chapter 2 Barrington Moore's thesis that the development of a middle class is a necessary precondition for the functioning of democratic institutions. In some places, the native populations that the Iberian colonizers encountered were much larger than those spread out over the North American continent; hence, they could not be easily assimilated and therefore made up a permanent underclass. However, middle classes also failed to form in Cuba, Argentina, and the Dominican Republic, where pre-Columbian populations were small or died out quickly. Therefore, the Iberian authoritarian tradition probably had much to do with the failure to develop a middle class in modernizing Latin America.

Second, the Iberian heritage left the legacy of a conservative Catholic Church that dominated Latin society and that, until recent decades, sided with the forces of authority and privilege. The church, unlike the individualist heritage of the American Protestant tradition that was frequently at odds with political authority, tended to reinforce and legitimate the hierarchical authority structure of the region. We will see below that in recent decades, however, a radical wing of the church has emerged, concerned with the empowerment of the poor. The Spanish church—the church of the infamous Inquisition—in particular, from the background of its long fight against the Muslims, was even more absolutist and intolerant than its other European counterparts.[4] Until recent decades, the leaders of the church were largely those from upper-class backgrounds who had a psychological and socioeconomic interest in the preservation of the status quo. Moreover, the strength of the influence of the church as well as its hierarchical structure helped delay the process of secularization that characterized the Western societies discussed in Chapter 2, a process that supported the modernization and democratization of the West. Later, we will examine the transformation of the Latin American church, but its historical legacy was unequivocally against democratization and modernity.

In addition to the church that the Iberians brought to the Americas, Spanish and Portuguese colonialism was itself a force against democratization and modernization. Spain and Portugal at the time of their imperial conquests in the fifteenth and sixteenth centuries were much more feudal in socioeconomic structure and authoritarian in political structure than were the British, who colonized North America a full century later, by which time the British were experiencing successful challenges to royal authority, as we have seen in Chapter 3. So powerful was the Spanish colonial influence against democratization and modernization that Wiarda & Kline find that "the possibilities for national development and democratization in Latin America have been generally inversely proportional to the degree of Spanish colonial heritage experienced."[5] Thus, the possibilities for such development have been greater in places like Costa Rica, Argentina, Chile (in pre-Allende times), and Uruguay, where the absence of the lure of gold did not attract strong Spanish control (although, for other reasons, Argentina was hardly a sterling example of democracy). However, this alleged authoritarian influence of the Iberian heritage is an interpretation that is not accepted by some Latin American scholars, such as Martin Needler.[6] Needler argues that there were libertarian and egalitarian elements in the Spanish culture of the time and indeed even within the "missionary church," which had its individual "apostles of freedom and peace like Bishop Bartolomé de las Casas, who defended the rights of the native population."

Spanish and Portuguese colonialism, perpetuated in the quest of gold for the mother country to feed a mercantilist policy, was more direct and, in the view of some, more brutal than the British conquest of North America. Hence, Iberian colonialism more strongly corroborated the Leninist perpective of colonialism as purely exploitive of the raw materials and riches of the dependent peoples; therefore, it is not suprising that scholars concentrating on Latin America, such as James Petras and Susan Bodenheimer, are among the leading proponents of the dependency theory discussed in Chapter 9.[7]

The rigidity of the two-tiered society of colonial Latin America, with a small European elite possessing huge masses of land, was exacerbated by the racial factor; the peasants and slaves working the land were Native Americans, reinforced by African slaves, all of whom were kept illiterate. Social mobility was virtually nonexistent.

The wars of independence from Spain occurred largely in the first two decades of the nineteenth century, with the exception of Cuba, which remained a Spanish colony until the Spanish American War of 1898. Brazil's independence from Portugal, by contrast, came about peacefully, when Pedro, the son of the king of Portugal, decided he would rather remain in Brazil than return to Portugal with his father when the French were driven out of the country in 1821. Pedro assumed the role of king of Brazil as it became an independent monarchy in 1822. This peaceful transition enabled Brazil to have a more stable experience in the early years of its independent existence in contrast to the chaotic situation that characterized the rest of the continent.

Meanwhile, armed struggles for independence broke out throughout Latin America against a Spain weakened by the Napoleonic Wars. Partly because the military played such a major role in the violent attainment of independence, and partly because of the weak legitimacy of alternative civilian institutions following independence, the military acquired a powerful role in Latin society and politics, and was to remain a threat to the stability of civilian regimes for the next two centuries. Latin American societies therefore took on the attributes of praetorianism, as that concept was discussed in Chapter 9. While the dominating influence of the military in civilian affairs did not occur evenly throughout Latin America, it was pervasive

enough to produce an image of a Latin America dominated by generals almost to the point of caricature.[8]

The chaotic sociopolitical context and the consequent need for stability and order promoted a recurring search for the strong figure who could ride in and protect the public safety. Into this void rode a figure in some respects unique to the Latin tradition, the *caudillo*—"the man on horseback." In Latin American culture, this connotes a strong, authoritarian leader. Strong leaders are not unique to Latin America, however. The caudillo has been more than this. Emerging in the frontier context of the early years of independence, the caudillos were rural-based, charismatic leaders of the masses who, Michael Coniff finds, were in a sense forefunners of the more modern urban-based populists so prevalent in Latin American politics, such as Juan and Eva Perón and Luis Echeverria (discussed below).[9] Populism is an appeal to a mass following that includes the following attributes: a romantic faith in the essential goodness and common sense of the masses; a distrust of education, science, and other trappings of modernity that is manifested in anti-intellectualism; a conspiratorial view of the world; a sense that society is a coherent and organic entity, a community, defined by knowable values and attributes; and a belief that the populist leader somehow embodies these values in a charismatic fashion. From the early caudillos to the later populist leaders such as the Peróns, Echeverria, or Getúlio Vargas, charismatic leadership, perhaps in the context of the weakness of institutional bases of legitimacy, has been an important factor in Latin American politics. While many caudillos were little more the local war lords with paid followers, some of the early independence period, such as Emeliano Zapata and Francisco "Pancho" Villa, who mobilized the rural peasantry, in many ways epitomized the attributes of populism.

While caudilloism reflected a society that after years of armed struggle had become inured to the use of force to solve social problems, it differed from the military that dominated much of Latin American politics from the mid- to late nineteenth century until almost the present day. Caudilloism was a rural-based populism and often involved local landowners with private armies in an almost feudal arrangement, whereas later military elites were trained, well-educated officers with an urban populist base, a phenomenon that may be characterized as the professionalization of the military. The heavy role of the military in Latin politics has almost become a cliché. One saying has it that "the last step in a military career is the presidency of the republic."[10] In 1954, 13 Latin American republics were ruled by military men. In Argentina, from 1930 to 1957, 8 of the 10 presidents were generals or colonels.[11] To date, 13 Argentine presidents have been removed from office by force, and only two civilian presidents, Raúl Alfonsin (1984–90) and Carlos Menem (began 1990) have been permitted to serve out a full term of office.[12]

This strong military influence in Latin American politics has taken several forms. Its most extreme manifestation is the coup, in which the military uses force to unseat the reigning head of government, an event that has occurred all too frequently throughout the region. However, it has been much more common in some systems, such as Bolivia, which has had almost 200 coups since independence, than in others. Second, military men are frequently elected to the presidency of their nations in Latin America. It should be noted that choosing a career military man to lead the country is certainly not unique to Latin America. The United States has chosen its leading general as president following every major war in its history except World War I. Third, the military may participate with civilian forces in a coalition government.

Fourth, the military may be in a position to exercise a great deal of influence on a civilian government, even to the point of wielding a veto over national policy.

As noted in Chapter 9, the military generally has an interest in modernization; hence, the praetorianism of Latin America has probably been a factor in promoting modernization.[13] Yet, the military is by nature an authoritarian institution and therefore necessarily impedes the development of democratic government. Moreover, it is not clear that the economic performance of military juntas is superior to that of the civilian governments they have replaced. Martin Needler suggests that the "economic policies of recent military regimes have varied from poor to disastrous."[14] Not surprisingly, military regimes are more likely to see that the economic "wish lists" of the military establishments are fulfilled. Military hardware in the modern age is extremely expensive; hence, far less money is available for investment in productive enterprises. Economic growth is thwarted by this diminished level of investment.

The pattern of bureaucratic authoritarianism and military-dominated governments that dominated Latin American politics in the early years of independence right through the middle 1970s gave way in country after country to attempts to institute political democracy. Between 1979 and 1985, military-dominated regimes were replaced by elected civilian rulers in Argentina, Brazil, Bolivia, Chile, Ecuador, El Salvador, Guatemala, Honduras, Paraguay, Peru, and Uruguay (see Table 11-2). Ecuador, moreover, effectively extended the suffrage to the great mass of its population of Indian heritage by abolishing its literacy requirement for voting. Even General Alfredo Stroessner was ousted from his dictatorship in Paraguay, although, with the successor president being his son-in-law, it is difficult to say how truly democratic

TABLE 11-2   Transitions to Democracy in Latin America after 1979

1979	Ecuador adopts a new constitution and elects a civilian government
1980	Peru elects a civilian president and adopts a new constitution
1982	Bolivia elects a civilian president after military withdrawal in 1978
1982	Honduras elects a civilian president
1983	Argentina elects a civilian president after the military government is discredited by the Falklands War
1984	Uruguay elects a civilian president
1984	El Salvador elects a civilian president
1985	Guatemala elects a civilian president
1989	Paraguay's dictator Alfredo Stroessner ousted by coup; General Andrés Rodriguez elected president

Source: Adapted from Samuel Huntington, *The Third Wave: Democratization in the Late Twentieth Century* (Norman: University of Oklahoma Press, 1991), pp. 22–23.

the regime has become. This may be seen as part of the worldwide movement toward democracy in the 1980s, so eloquently documented by Professor Huntington.[15] Gordon Richards presents research to support his claim that the breakdown of these military authoritarian regimes was largely a function of the external debt crisis of the 1980s undermining their legitimacy, a conclusion that Huntington seems to support essentially.[16] The question is whether these countries have developed the economic, social, and cultural prerequisites to sustain their attempts to resuscitate democratic political formats. It is to this topic that we now turn.

THE SOCIAL AND CULTURAL CONTEXT OF LATIN AMERICAN POLITICS

If the Iberian heritage is what gave Latin America a measure of coherence, it must be in the attributes of that heritage that we find common cultural and social factors for the region. The Iberian heritage left an authoritarian attitude toward authority and a strong, conservative Catholic Church that has been a powerful force since the conquest. Latin America was the most solidly Catholic region in the world throughout its developmental

period. The significant inroads that Protestantism has made in some parts of Latin America in recent decades does not fundamentally alter the basic impact of the Catholic Church on the Latin culture. The church fostered a hierarchical view of society and sided with the established order. It is possible, however, to attribute too much to the church itself. The church manifests itself in different ways in different sociocultural settings. For example, as has been noted in previous chapters, the high birth rate that has plagued some Latin American nations does not characterize other Catholic nations, such as Italy, despite the papal stand against birth control and abortion. Similarly, while population growth for Latin America as a whole has been high, particularly compared to Western industrialized nations, the rate has slowed somewhat in recent decades. Thus, while we will see that the rate of population growth for Mexico from 1970 to 1980 was 3.6 percent, by 1994 it was down to 2.2 percent. The growth rate for South America as a whole in 1994 was 1.9 percent compared to 0.7 percent for the United States and Canada and 0.1 percent for Western Europe.[17] The impact of the church on population growth varies a great deal in the region. The growth rate in Mexico, for example, was just under three times the rate of Uruguay, and the birth rate per thousand varies from 37 and 42 in Nicaragua and Haiti, respectively, to 4 in Costa Rica. The impact of the church on fecundity is to a large extent a function of whether it combines with another almost uniquely Latin cultural tradition, *machismo,* discussed below.

The church in Latin America has generally been on the side of established authority. In the years leading to the wars of independence, the church was solidly on the side of imperial Spain and Portugal. When the Spanish were driven out, the church sided with the national elites. For example, the Cristero Revolt in Mexico in the 1920s was a three-year revolt inspired by the Catholic Church. Being concerned with preserving respect for authority and traditional values, the church remained a distinctly conservative force in Latin America until well into the post–World War II era. Many of the leading members of the clergy came from educated and relatively well-to-do families, thereby adding to the conservativism of the church.

In more recent decades, however, the church has seemed to change this conservative orientation fundamentally with the adoption of "Liberation Theology." The beginning of this change was a gradual diminishing of the authority and influence of the church in some countries and in some areas with the urbanization and secularization of Latin America as a modernizing society. The change in the Latin American church was encouraged by the transformation of the Roman Catholic Church as a world organization, most notably the Vatican II Conference of 1963 and the reign of Pope John XXIII. These changes were furthered by changes in the clergy itself. The influx of many foreign-born priests, especially of European origin, weakened the hold of the upper classes on the priesthood. The application of the new orientation of the church toward the social problems of Latin America was delineated in the Latin American Bishops Conference held at Medellín, Colombia, in 1968. The documents emanating from this conference have been called "the Magna Carta of Liberation Theology." Priests and nuns who believe in Liberation Theology subscribe to the idea that a principal function of the church is to strive for what they see as social justice in this world as opposed to being merely concerned with salvation in the next.[18] Further, clerics of this school are more concerned with the well-being of their flock and with the empowerment of the poor and the marginalized Latin society than with protecting the property and authority of the church hierarchy. In this way, its supporters claim that Liberation Theology gets the church back to the essential message of Jesus in the Sermon on the Mount and away from its institutional emphasis on preserving its authority and property. With the advent of Liberation Theology, found more in the urban centers than in the villages and countryside, priests and nuns were frequently active in supporting the political left, sometimes even to the point of supporting radical movements against their governments. The empowerment of the masses was to be accomplished through the growth of Christian Base Communities (*communidades eclesiales de base*) (CEBs), a form of grass-roots Christian organization strongly encouraged by the documents from Medellín.[19] However, Daniel Levine found that these organizations tended to develop vertical linkages to a church hierarchy less than fully sympathetic to the values of Liberation Theology. The hierarchy coopted the energies of the CEBs, hindered the development of organizational skills, and tightly controlled grass-roots activity.[20]

There really are two Catholicisms in Latin America—a traditional, conservative Catholicism of the peasants and other residents of the rural areas, and a progressive religion

FIGURE 11-1   The poverty of the countryside in much of Latin America contrasts with fully modern cities and impressive governmental buildings. Shown here is Guatemala City and its presidential palace.

stressing social justice and political change found in the urban centers (see Figure 11–1). It is in the latter areas, however, that the hold of religion in general has weakened, and where the processes of secularization that, as we noted in Chapter 9, are associated with modernization in general have had their greatest effect. The hold of Catholicism in Latin America has been weakened not only by secularization but by the growth of Protestantism. For example, fundamentalist Protestant sects have enjoyed significant growth among Brazil's urban poor, significant numbers of Lutherans may be found in Chile, and Guatemala's expanding Protestant community was rewarded with a Pentacostalist president, General Efraín Ríos Montt (1982–83).

As stated, whatever impact Catholicism has had on the high birth rate in Latin America has occurred in conjunction with a unique cultural attribute of Latin America, *machismo*, the aggressive assertion of one's masculinity. Among the behaviors associated with this almost obsessive attitude among many Latin American men are the attempts to dominate women—an extreme antithesis of feminism —and to sire as many children as possible. Although violence against women is certainly not unique to Latin America, there seems to

have been a more widespread public and even official tolerance of it in some Latin American nations than is found elsewhere. In Brazil, for example, it has been difficult to obtain convictions of men who did not deny that they beat and even killed their wives and lovers for "disobedience." Evidence of the continuing problem with regard to the status of women in Latin America's machismo environment is the finding of Peggy Lovell that, when measured by the criterion of wage distribution, gender inequality is significantly greater than racial inequality in Brazil, despite that nation's large black population and, in some places, very traditional Indian population.[21] In the context of such blatant disrespect for the basic rights of half of the population, the ideals of democracy must be modified when applied to the Latin American case. Moreover, to the extent that machismo remains a force in Latin American society, that society will have a difficult time making significant inroads on the problem of excessive population growth, which becomes not a matter of the availability of information and technology but the willingness to use them. Population growth, we have pointed out in Chapter 9, is a major factor in impeding the process of industrialization and economic growth in a number of countries in the region. While the rate varies among the nations of Latin America, it has been as high as around 3 percent per year, although by 1994 it had fallen to 1.9 percent for South America and 1.5 percent for the Caribbean, while it is still up at 2.4 percent for Central America (see Table 11-3). While significantly lower than a decade ago, these rates are still significantly higher than those found in the West. Thus, while Argentina and Uruguay have rates comparable to those of the industrial nations of the West, at the current rate the population of Mexico will double every three decades.[22] Such population growth means that the nation's resources go to consumption rather than savings and investment. Without savings, investment is impossible, and without investment, economic growth and industrialization are impossible. While, as we will see below, population growth is far from the only reason for Mex-

ico's current financial crisis, it has played a significant role. Therefore, even with Alliance for Progress funds and oil revenues, Mexico could not generate enough growth even to maintain existing levels of poverty and unemployment, let alone reduce them. Therefore, sources of foreign capital often insisted on a program of family planning as a precondition for loaning and investing funds in Latin nations; yet, those requirements fly in the face of the dispositions of the conservative Catholicism shaped by residual machismo in these nations.

Along with other traditional aspects of Latin culture, machismo is waning, especially among the better educated portions of the population and people in urban centers. It has not disappeared, however, especially among the rural peasantry and lower classes, and is still a factor leading to higher rates of population growth than most countries of the region can support.

TABLE 11-3 Population Growth in Latin America, 1994

Nation	Population in Millions	Birth per 1,000	Percent Increase
Central America	123	30	2.4
Belize	0.2	38	3.3
Costa Rica	3.2	26	2.3
El Salvador	5.2	33	2.7
Guatemala	10.3	39	3.1
Honduras	5.3	38	3.1
Mexico	91.8	28	2.2
Nicaragua	4.3	37	2.9
South America	311.	26	1.9
Argentina	33.9	21	1.3
Bolivia	8.2	37	2.7
Brazil	155.3	25	1.7
Chile	14.0	22	1.7
Colombia	35.6	25	2.0
Ecuador	10.6	31	2.5
Guyana	0.8	25	1.8
Paraguay	4.8	34	2.7
Suriname	0.4	23	1.6
Uruguay	3.2	18	0.8
Venezuela	21.3	30	2.6

Source: Population Reference Bureau Inc., Washington, D.C. *1994 World Population Data Sheet.*

In the face of modern technology, literacy, and communications, even the peasantry of rural Latin America is not isolated from the ideas and information of the modern world. Concepts of social justice and of the possibilities for change are replacing the older values of authoritarianism and fatalism that had been fostered by the Iberian colonizers and the more traditional Catholic Church. Liberation theologists from among the clergy, North American activists, including Peace Corps volunteers and representatives of the U.S. and other Western governments such as workers for AID, are mobilizing public opinion and beginning to organize the masses, thus breaking down what was once the isolation of the rural population. The Zapatistas' National Liberation Army, which launched an armed uprising against established authority in the southern Mexican state of Chiapas in January 1994, constitutes an example of the mobilization of the peasantry. Of course, as the populist caudillos such as Zapata and Villa showed, the peasantry was always subject to mobilization. It seems fair to say, however, that restlessness among the rural masses is much more widespread today.

Also undergoing transformation is the traditional two-tiered patron-client social structure of a privileged elite of wealthy landowners and a great mass of peasants, tenant farmers, day laborers, and even slaves, who were mostly nonwhite (Native, or "Indian," and African). Neither the "yeoman" family farmer that formed the backbone of early U.S. society nor a commercial bourgeoisie developed in traditional Latin America. Thus Latin America has had one of the most unequal distributions of income in the world.

In recent decades, however, in the context of long-term industrialization and economic growth, a middle class has been emerging, including military officers, clerks, teachers, small businesspeople, and university students. Moreover, some nations, notably Argentina and Uruguay, have from the beginning been exceptions to the two-tiered stratification system that characterized much of the rest of Latin America. Each of those nations has had a fairly strong middle class. Trade unions have also emerged with strength in a number of Latin nations, such as Argentina and Brazil, and have been effective in mobilizing the class consciousness of a growing urban working class.

The mobilized class consciousness on a pan-national basis that is familiar to some Western nations has always been impeded in Latin America by the lack of national integration. In Latin America, with the rugged Andes mountain range running the length of South America and nearly impenetrable rain forests, geographic considerations may impede national integration (although scholars are not in complete agreement as to the most important causes of such integration). Most of the population centers are close to a coast; the inland is rather sparsely inhabited. The difficulty of the terrain has also made the task of establishing consensually accepted borders between the nations more difficult, contributing, along with failure of the Spanish colonizers to establish such borders precisely, to such simmering disputes as the miniwar that erupted in 1995 between Peru and Ecuador over conflicting border claims. The border in question is on two parallel mountain ranges and difficult to determine with precision. This dispute has been simmering since the Rio Treaty ended the war between these countries in 1942, erupting in conflict in 1981 as well.

In addition to their negative impact on pan-national integration and pan-national class consciousness in some Latin American nations, geographical considerations have also limited the diversification of agriculture in the region. Thus, many nations concentrate excessively on one or two crops; hence, the use of the rather disparaging term "banana republics" to refer to some of the small nations in this situation. Coffee is a crop well suited to the mountains of parts of Latin America, and has thus become the predominant crop of Brazil, El Salvador, Guatemala, and Colombia (excluding the latter's large illegal trade in cocaine). Single-crop economies render a nation highly vulnerable to the inevitable fluctuations in the price of that commodity on the world market. Moreover, since industrial nations can and do control the importation of these goods, single-crop economies are especially vulnerable to the decisions and whims of other countries, thereby feeding the dependency perspective. To the extent that a Latin American nation's economy concentrates on one or more primary goods, as many have done, that nation would suffer a comparative disadvantage relative to the industrialized nations, because the price of manufactured goods has tended to increase relative to primary goods. Hence, even though the price of Colombian coffee or Cuban sugar might go up in absolute terms, over time it would take more coffee beans or more canes of sugar to pay for an imported vehicle or appliance from the industrial core. Yet, funds from core sources were frequently earmarked for purposes that served the needs of the North American benefactors and were not available for capital to finance economic diversification. Sometimes, this failure to industrialize and diversify was the result not of exploitation from the West but of internal policies of the Latin American nations, such as the economic nationalism pursued under early Peronism.[23]

The theme of change explored in this volume applies *par excellence* to the socioeconomic context of Latin America. Despite its history of one-crop economies, Latin American is diversifying and industrializing. The imperatives of an emerging industrial order are having far-reaching effects on the social and cultural context in which it is occurring.

A middle class is beginning to emerge because of these imperatives; hence, the old two-tiered society that for so long almost defined Latin America is becoming a thing of the past. Urbanization is generating education and literacy that are in turn generating a society that is increasing mobilized along the lines of a diverse set of interests that are pressing their respective demands. One of the results of this mobilization is an increasingly politicized and impatient youth. Latin American youth, especially among the educated, have become increasingly Marxist. This is one trend that may prove problematic in the search for stable democratic futures in the nations of the region, although Marxism is itself now competing with a new wave of neoliberalism. It is to the specific examination of three of the largest of these nations that we now turn.

MEXICO: MANAGING A STABLE, INSTITUTIONALIZED REVOLUTION

The government of Mexico projects itself as the heir and embodiment of the great social revolution that began in 1910, an image reinforced by some authorities on Latin America, who characterize Mexico as a "classic revolutionary regime."[24] The revolution of 1910 that eventually overthrew the regime of Porfirio Díaz was a genuine social revolution involving the great masses of people, as opposed to a coup d'état involving only the top ranks of the officer corps. Hundreds of thousands of people were killed. The Díaz regime, which ruled Mexico with a more or less iron hand from 1876 to 1911, catered to foreign investors more than domestic interests, and was supported by the United States and other foreign powers, making it almost a classic example of what dependency theorists mean by the "infrastructure of dependency." The chaotic conditions that prevailed when Díaz fled the country continued when his successor Francisco Madero failed to institute land reforms and thereby to win the support of the peasants under Villa and Zapata. Madero was assassinated in 1913. His successor, Victoriano Huerta, lasted only a year before being overthrown by the army of General Venustiano Carranza, who was in power only three years before he too was killed. Before his demise, Carranza did call the constitutional convention that drafted the Mexican Constitution of 1917, a document that is still officially in force. Carranza's successor, General Alvaro Obregón, served four years, but he too was murdered when he tried to run for a second term in 1928.

Hence, Mexico experienced a significant level of political violence and instability in the postindependence period to 1929, broken only by the dictatorship of Díaz. It is not difficult to understand that the values of order and stability had taken precedence for many Mexicans by the time that General Plutarco Calles, who succeeded Obregón in 1924, founded the Party of the National Revolution (PNR) in 1929, which changed its name to the oxymoronic Party of the Institutionalized Revolution during the administration of Miguel Alémon (1946–52), and which has retained power without a break since its inception. The party has maintained control through a combination of catering to those interests with sufficient power to influence the policy process and using just enough electoral fraud and repression to insure the outcomes of important elections. For example, President Avila Camacho, who succeeded General Lázaro Cárdenas in 1940, shifted the focus of policy from the peasantry and blue-collar labor to the growing middle classes following the establishment of a middle-class opposition party, the Party of National Action (PAN). Cárdenas had emphasized land reform and an expansion of the organized labor movement. His administration further catered to the ideals of the revolution and to the reaction against foreign economic holdings and control over Mexican natural resources by the expropriation and nationalization of the petroleum industry. Camacho, however, sought to make Mexico more attractive to foreign as well as domestic investment.

The PRI and its leaders tried to maintain the imagery of the revolution even while its policy sought a more stable and conservative result; hence, the seemingly oxymoronic name of the Party of the Institutional Revolution has in a way been appropriate. To varying degrees, Mexican leaders have utilized the rhetoric of the revolutionary left, especially when it could have a virtually cost-free application. Luis Echeverría Alvarez, the president from 1970 to 1976, for example, resurrected the rhetoric of dependency theory and stood with the cant of the revolutionary left in supporting the anti-Israeli resolutions at the United Nations. Such stances established the administration's revolutionary credentials without the political costs of threatening the interests of some mobilized group within the country.

Echeverría, however, tried to promote both economic growth to please the growing middle classes and "social justice"—meaning redistributing wealth and land without paying for either. By the end of his administration, deficit financing was out of control, foreign capital had fled, and the peso had to be devalued at the expense, of course, of the productive classes and their savings and capital.

José López Portillo, Echeverría's successor, borrowed heavily abroad to finance his ambitious developmental plans. His plan assumed that the price of crude petroleum would continue to rise in the 1980s, as it had in the first days of the OPEC cartel in the 1970s. However, the effectiveness of OPEC collapsed, and Mexico was saddled with a mountain of unpayable debt.

The economic woes of Mexico in the post–World War II era were exacerbated by the inverse ratio of geometrically rising population growth and declining productivity, which continued until population growth slowed in very recent years. Such an inverse relationship must necessarily deprive the nation of any domestic source of capital and of any path out of its current disastrous situation of foreign indebtedness. This ratio is depicted in Table 11-4.

More recently, government policies have been the primary factor in the economic crisis behind the collapse of the peso in December 1994, when it dropped from 3.45 pesos per dollar to over 5.5 pesos per dollar by January. The government, as it had done in other presidential election years, had overvalued the peso in order to create the appearance of prosperity for political purposes. In doing so, it ran up an imprudently large short accounts deficit of around 8 percent of the GNP. When, shortly after the inauguration of President Ernesto Zedillo, the Zapatista rebellion flared up in Chiapas, many investors pulled their capital out of Mexico.[25] In response, finance minister Jaime Serra, in violation of his pledge not to do so, devalued the peso by 13 percent, an action that frightened away many of the remaining investors. With the peso having fallen precipitously relative to the dollar, Mexico finds itself hardpressed to meet its dollar-based external debts. Meanwhile, the austerity program forced upon Mexico by the United States as the price of a $50 billion support package to slow the devaluation of the peso resulted in very high interest rates. Rising unemployment resulting from these rates and the austerity may prove a political liability for the Zedillo presidency.

Mexico's longer term financial problems stem from the borrowing that the government did in the 1970s in anticipation of oil revenues that did not fully materialize as OPEC collapsed. The borrowed money was directed to consumption rather than capital purposes. In the 1970s, the external debt of the Mexican government increased over tenfold![26] When, in 1982, Mexico was unable to meet its debt obligations, it was forced into an austerity program much like its current situation. The result was virtually no economic growth, while population in that period increased some 15 percent.

It will become apparent in the next section that the automatic hegemony of the governing elite may be weakening as its accountability is becoming more of a reality. Therefore, unless Mexico can get its fiscal house in order, the governing party will find it increasingly difficult to maintain its hold on power in the face of a changing party system, to which we now turn our attention.

Parties and Groups in Mexico

As noted, Mexico has enjoyed the stability and suffered the oppression of the unchallengeable power and control of one govern-

TABLE 11-4 Annual Percentage Growth in Population and Productivity in Mexico

Factor	1940–50	1950–60	1960–70	1970–80
Population	2.8	3.1	3.8	3.6
GDP	6.9	5.6	7.0	5.5

Source: Adapted from Marcus Ethridge and Howard Handelman, *Politics in a Changing World* (New York: St. Martin's Press, 1994), p. 480.

ing party from 1929 to the present. The Party of the Institutional Revolution (PRI) has to a significant extent managed to coopt the symbolism of the great revolution of 1910 and to become viewed as virtually coterminous with the republic that emerged from that revolution. Opposition to the PRI has been portrayed as virtual opposition to the forces that emerged victorious in the revolution. Opposition parties never were able to obtain enough support to seriously challenge the PRI's control of the government at both the national and the state level.

Given the hegemonic control of the PRI, the representation of and conflicts among the various socioeconomic forces that are inevitable in any reasonably complex society have occurred to a large extent within the dominant party rather than between parties. Thus, the PRI, lacking a coherent ideology, is split among several wings: the organized part of the Mexican work force, which is more skilled and better paid; the agricultural section of society, which is primarily the peasantry; and middle-class professional and small business interests, which have been called the "Popular Sector." Many Mexican workers are not organized and hence not represented in the party councils, and the impact of the peasantry has been weak. The party has actually become close to the model of the "catch-all party" discussed in Chapter 2—one with such a diverse base of support that it stands for little else than remaining in power.

Consequently, corruption has been rampant in the PRI, which had until recent decades been dominated by career politicians (*políticos*). This is, of course, not suprising for an organization that has not had to confront any meaningful accountability. More recently, the party leadership has come to be dominated by technocrats, scientifically or technically trained professionals with a bureaucratic background. Mexico's current president, Ernesto Zedillo, epitomizes this new style of leadership. He has been characterized as an "intelligent and austere technocrat who had never (previously) held public office."[27] This decidedly uncharismatic man fell into the role of party leader when its leading presidential candidate, Luis Donaldo Colossio, was assassinated while campaigning in March 1994, only a few months before the election.

Meanwhile, other parties have been formed and are slowly growing in support. Chief among these is the Party of National Action (PAN), representing middle-class interests such as practising Catholics and business- and professional people, and taking a general center-right orientation. PAN experienced its best finish in the 1994 presidential elections, when it received 26.8 percent of the vote, second only to the PRI, under the leadership of Diego Fernandez de Cevallos. A third party on the left, the Democratic Revolutionary Party (PRD) finished third with 17 percent.

Under pressure from Western democracies, especially the United States, to whom Mexico has become heavily indebted, the PRI has reduced the most overt fraud that has been rampant in previous elections and that has been one factor ensuring the party's continued hegemony. For example, election officials would conveniently run out of ballots in areas such as the rural parts of the country, where PRI strength was the weakest. International observers proudly pronounced that the 1994 election was "relatively free from fraud," as if only a little electoral fraud was a remarkable achievement. In this almost fair election, the PRI received its lowest share of the national vote ever, getting barely half (50.1%). The overwhelming, automatic dominance of the PRI may be weakening in the context of national and international pressures to play by the democratic rules of the game, pressures that stem in part from the wave of democratizations that have occurred in Latin America in recent years, and in part from economic and political relations with the United States. Scandals within the party councils, such as the arrest of the brother of former president Salinas in February 1995 for the contract killing of the head of the party, contribute to the declining public confidence and trust in the party. However, it is hard to imagine either of the two aforementioned opposition parties overtaking the PRI in the near future. Cuauhtémoc Cárdenas's PRD contains too many ex-Communists and former members of the Mexican Socialist Party to compete effectively for middle-class votes. Its 17 percent of the vote in the 1994 election indicates how far it needs to go to attain legitimacy as an alternative governing party. The Socialist Party has never exceeded 3 percent of the national vote. Meanwhile, on the center right, Cevallos's PAN has been unable to attract significant working-class support. Still, its support has increased steadily from 7.6 percent of the vote in 1961 to 18 percent by 1988 and then to 26.8 percent by 1994. The question is whether or at what point PAN or some other party will constitute a credible enough threat to PRI control of the government to render Zedillo or one of his successors accountable for performance in office. With government domination of the media and of organized labor and its monopoly on revolutionary legitimacy, most scholars do not expect the PRI to be voted out of national office in the near future.[28]

Political Institutions in Mexico

The constitution of 1917 set up a strong state ruled by a strong president in reaction to the chaos that dominated the revolutionary years. However, to avoid a quasi-authoritarian presidency, epitomized by the long reign of Porfirio Díaz (1876–1911), the president is limited to a single six-year term. Actual power is highly centralized in the presidency, de-

spite a formal structure that includes a bicameral Congress and a federal system. The two branches of Congress—the Senate and the Chamber of Deputies—have been overwhelmingly controlled by the PRI; hence, Congress has never been much of a serious check on the will of the presidency. A reform of the lower house provided for an additional 200 deputies (added to the 300 elected by the Anglo-American single-member district system) to be elected by proportional representation to provide greater representation of other parties. While the number of opposition deputies has in fact increased, the majority of the PRI is still secure.

Likewise, the federal structure has not been a serious check on the will of the presidency since the state governments are dependent on the federal government for revenues and since the president may have governors removed from office. The state boundaries, as in Australia but unlike Canada, do not coincide with geographically defined cultural or economic diversities; hence, the leaders of the several states do not have a clearly distinct set of interests to represent vis-à-vis the national government. The federalism of Mexico appears to be a formalistic structure rather than either creating or reflecting any genuine decentralization of power.

Prospects of the Mexican System

Despite the increased support of opposition parties, it is not likely they will be able to unseat the ruling class dominated by the PRI. The lead for democratic change will probably have to come from the new breed of PRI leaders, epitomized by Zedillo and his predecessor, Carlos Salinas de Gortari, and from the external pressure of the so-called third wave of democratization in Latin America and from the United States.

The economic crisis of early 1995, perhaps precipitated by the Zapatista uprising in Chiapas, may not be a passing phenomenon.

Rather, it appears to reflect more fundamental structural problems in the Mexican political and economic system. The overborrowing and irresponsible spending occur regularly at presidential election time as a tool to maintain the hegemonic control of the dominant party. The slowing of population growth in recent years is an encouraging sign; however, population growth is still significantly higher than in any Western democracy. The North American Free Trade Agreement may provide some help to Mexico over time, but it is not likely to overcome the financial mismanagement of the postwar era. The devaluation of the peso will cause prices to rise in Mexico. Some predict inflation will soar to 30 percent this year in contrast with the 7 percent of 1994. In fact, in July 1995 inflation did rise by 2.04% or a 27% annual rate. Meanwhile, the settlement imposed by the United States for a financial bailout included a massive rise in Mexican interest rates. While the higher rates are intended to attract foreign capital, they will, together with higher prices, flatten consumer demand and could generate a recession, a possibility which was underscored by a 10.5% drop in Mexico's GDP in the second quarter of 1995. The continued legitimacy of the regime in Mexico could depend on whether the new breed of technocrats can turn away from the policy of buying domestic political support and toward getting the nation's economic affairs in order.

Meanwhile, in the longer perspective, there are hopeful signs of progress in Mexico's aspirations with respect to both economic independence and prosperity and the evolution toward a more democratic political order. The economy has slowly been diversifying, rendering it less susceptible to fluctuations in the price of any single commodity. In Mexico's case, it was petroleum. We have noted how some of the economic difficulties originated in the drop in the price of that product, against which Mexico had borowed heavily, at the close of the 1970s. However,

the pecentage of petroleum exports fell from 24 percent in 1986 to less than 12 percent in 1993. Despite the economic crisis in 1995, Mexico has enjoyed a 3 percent annual growth rate from 1990 to 1995. This should be seen in contrast to the problems facing the Mexican economy in the 1980s. From 1981 to 1989, Mexico's gross domestic product fell by over 9 percent, and inflation averaged over 60 percent, peaking at 159 percent in 1987.[29] With the reorientation of the Salinas government toward a market economy and the servicing of foreign debt giving foreign investors confidence in the Mexican economy, the economic improvement in the early 1990s is startling. In the political realm, the hegemonic grip of the PRI, by which it always claimed over 80 percent of the votes in presidential elections, has been weakening in the 1990s. By 1995, the opposition PAN controlled 153 municipal governments and in that year won a crucial gubernatorial election in the state of Jaliso, and now controls four statehouses. While opposition parties appear to have a realistic chance for the first time in gubernatorial elections and seem close to mounting a serious challenge in presidential elections, Jorge Domínguez and James McCann find that voting in the 1988 and 1991 national elections still was not about issues.[30] Still, Mexico is clearly moving closer toward both political democracy and a modern economy. In Mexico, as in the rest of Latin America, change is the most predictable attribute of the future.

ARGENTINA: PRAETORIANISM AND INSTABILITY IN A DEVELOPED SOCIETY

Argentina provides a study in contrasts. The eighth largest nation in the world, it is also one of the most *socially* modern. That is, by most accepted criteria of social modernization—literacy, urbanization, industrialization, economic diversity, and a large middle class—Argentina qualifies as a "modernized" or "developed" society. Despite the stereotyped image of Argentina as a beef producer, less than 20 percent of the population is engaged in the primary, or agrarian (including herding), sector of the economy, and Argentina is close to having 50 percent of its workers in the tertiary, or service, sector that would qualify it as a *postindustrial society!* Buenos Aires, the nation's capital, is one of the largest and most cosmopolitan cities in the world. Moreover, Argentina's population is now overwhelmingly of European origin; the nation is not faced with the problem of significant pockets of racial and ethnic diversity that plague so many other nations discussed in this volume.

On the other hand, the political history of Argentina is characterized by substantial periods of praetorianism, numerous coups, and charismatic populist rulers—all attributes that are primarily associated with less developed *political* processes. Hence, it offers a prime example of the warning issued in Chapter 9, that social modernization is not only conceptually distinct from political development but that the former does not necessarily lead to the latter.

The first Argentine president characterized by scholars as populist was Hipólito Yrigoyen, who rode the political influence of the group that he founded, the Radical Civic Union (UCR) into the presidency in 1916.[31] Yrigoyen himself was president from 1916 to 1922, when he hand-picked his successor, another prominent UCR member, Marcelo Alvear. Yrigoyen returned to the presidency himself in 1928. The UCR was largely composed of disaffected members of Argentina's growing middle class, a group that had felt excluded from the nation's political life, as conservatives manipulated elections to maintain power. Indeed, from the founding of the group in 1890 until 1916, Yrigoyen led it in

boycotting all of the nation's elections on the grounds that were rigged by the conservatives. Yrigoyen's presidency, especially his second term, was marred by severe economic problems exacerbated by the Great Depression. Yrigoyen had tried to cut government spending, to the consternation of his middle-class supporters. Meanwhile, he further angered his middle-class base by his labor policy (*oberismo*) of peacefully integrating the labor force into the Argentine system. This involved some regulatory and social legislation favorable to labor and support for some strikes. However, Yrigoyen at the same time reverted to using the police to check labor militancy and break up other strikes.

Yrigoyen, perhaps needless to say at this point, was not a man with great political skills. His second term was marked by a personalistic style that antagonized many, not least of whom was the military. The old conservative oligarchy was alarmed by the progressive rhetoric of Yrigoyen's presidency, while his failure to implement significant economic changes discouraged potential support in the middle and working classses. Finally Yrigoyen's age had also become an issue; at age 72 he was widely suspected of verging on senility at the time of his overthrow in 1930.

The coup of 1930 brought to power the first of six military juntas to rule Argentina for 19 of the next 65 years, this time under the leadership of a cryptofascist general named José Felix Uriburu. Two years later, however, the military returned the country to the civilian rule of the conservative old cattlemen oligarchy, who ruled for the next decade through the liberal utilization of electoral fraud. The conservatives did not trust public opinion in the light of their experience with Yrigoyen and the UCR; however, the prevalent and blatant fraud weakened the legitimacy of their rule. Moreover, the pro-British orientation of the cattle baron elite was resented by many of the masses with a German, Italian, or Spanish heritage on the eve of the war in Europe. The military again assumed control with their second coup in 1943. In the post of secretary of labor in this junta was a colonel, Juan Domingo Perón, who used his post to mobilize working-class support to form new unions and expand those existing unions that were friendly to him.[32]

By 1946, Perón was ready to stand as the presidential candidate of the Argentine Labor Party. Perón was quickly evolving into a right-wing populist, as that term is discussed in Chapter 2 in reference to the emergence of such parties in Europe in the 1990s. He could, with a fair amount of legitimacy, claim to embody the aspirations and values of the working class against the competing interests of an economic and social elite. Recall from our discussion of this phenomenon in Europe that right-wing populism embodies the cooptation of the mobilized masses by a charismatic leader. This leader's support goes beyond the specific benefits that he or she obtains for the masses. Moreover, this movement of the mobilized masses is frequently in conflict with the values of pluralism and the open society—the legitimacy of the expression of different points of view and of a process of bargaining among legitimately competing interests. Thus right-wing populists often stress values of nationalism and community, emphasizing that the nation is an organic entity defined by a set of values shared by those who are truly members of that community. This denial of legitimacy to competing values and interests that is almost inherent in this type of populist movement was quickly manifested in a series of repressive moves by Perón, including strangulating freedom of the press, purging universities and the judiciary, and jailing or exiling political opponents. While, like many figures of the sociopolitical right, Perón initially sup-

ported and was supported by the Catholic Church, his impulse to control all aspects of Argentine society led him to attack it, which was one of the few remaining institutions that was still autonomous of his power. His feud with the church led to his excommunication, which, in a Catholic society, rendered him vulnerable to the next coup. The personalization of his movement is indicated by the fact that his Argentine Labor Party was soon rechristened the "Peronist Party." As with many populists of the right, Perón was a military man who ruled with the support of the military. His loss of support among the military coincided with his being deposed in 1955 by a military coup led by General Pedro Aramburu.

The Aramburu government was dedicated to the goal of eradicating Peronism. Peronism, however, by this time was more than a political preference; it was in the realm of myth and symbolism, an entrenched part of the Argentine political culture. Such cultural traits are by definition resistant to engineering. When the military turned the reigns back to a civilian president to be elected in 1958, the Peronists were able to strike a deal with the incoming president, the leader of a faction of the UCR named Arturo Frondizi, that preserved the legality of the Peronist Party. Moreover, many urban workers remained loyal to Perón throughout his exile, and the continued existence of the Peronist Party provided a focus for the survival of Peronism. Frondizi's connection to the Peronists worried the leaders of the military, who deposed him in 1962.

The chaos at the head of Argentina continued with bitter infighting in the military government over the next year, leading to the election of another civilian president, Arturo Illia. The administration of Illia, a nonaggressive and nonpolitical man from a faction of the old UCR, was characterized by three years of inaction. Illia was therefore deposed and replaced by another military man, General Juan Carlos Onganía. By 1973, however, Onganía had accomplished little, and public tolerance for the military regime had waned, leading to the reelection, after a 50-day regime of one Héctor Cámpora, of Juan Perón, triumphantly returning from 18 years in exile.

Illustrating the difficulty in placing populism on the left-right spectrum, the second Perón regime turned sharply to the right, placing neofascists in the universities and governorships, and turning against his former allies in the leftist part of the labor movement. Indeed, his followers in his first two administrations were known as *descamisados* (shirtless ones). The triumphal return was short-lived, however, as Juan died only a year into his new regime. He was succeeded by his nearly equally charismatic widow, María Estela Martínez de Perón (Isabel). However, the charisma of Isabela did not match the powerful relationship to the *descamisados* of his first wife, Evita.

Juan and Evita Perón had a charismatic power base in which their *descamisados* viewed them as their supporters against the distrusted institutions and other leaders of "the establishment." Yet, Perón's turn to the right in 1973 was hardly a bolt out of the blue. During World War II, he had incurred the enmity of most of the Argentine establishment with his support of the Axis cause, and indeed, under his regime in the late 1940s, ex-Nazis frequently found a welcome haven. Recall that it was in Argentina that the architect of the Nazi Holocaust, Adolph Eichmann, lived until he was seized by the Israelis. Yet, the adoration of the Peróns by the "shirtless ones" continued unabated through his administrations, his exile, his return, and the administration of Isabel, despite the general's turn to the right in 1973.

This phenomenon also reinforces the point about the emotional, romantic, and ir-

rational element in populism. Indeed, with her background as a second-rate actress, the politically active Evita's speeches to the *descamisados* from her balcony were increasingly infused with passion and fury. The adoration of Evita by her "shirtless ones" was so great that a labor union asked the Pope to canonize her shortly after her death from cancer in 1952.[33] The failures of the less revered Isabel's regime to control inflation and violence quickly exhausted the patience of the military, which once again seized power just two years after her inauguration.

The last junta, to this writing, to govern Argentina achieved new heights of human rights abuses, as thousands of people were subjected to arbitrary arrest, imprisonment, and torture. As far as their loved ones knew, many of them simply vanished. This, however, did not erode the public tolerance for the regime as much as did the junta's heavy-handed seizure of the British-owned Falkland Islands off the Argentine coast and the subsequent military humiliation by the British armed forces. The military gave in to pressures for a return to civilian rule, and in 1983 Argentina elected a Radical, Raúl Alfonsín, as president.

Alfonsín had the misfortune of inheriting the enormous financial debt of his military predecessors. The resultant financial woes proved fatal for the administration, and at the next election, in 1989, the Peronists once more rode into power on the back of a former governor, Carlos Menem, a nonideological populist who has engineered a constitutional change to render himself eligible to succeed himself in the election of 1995. He may succeed in doing so, having lowered the rate of inflation somewhat from the high levels associated with Alfonsín's Radical regime. One might have surmised that Menem was in political trouble with the resignation in disgrace of a member of the Argentine Assembly and director of a pension program in

April 1994 and the firing of the head of the nation's Security and Exchange Commission on charges of corruption. While Menem may not have satisfied most of the expectations of Argentines, he was able to win the May 1995 Presidential election on the basis of voters preferring "the devil you know to the devil you don't."[34]

Political Forces in Argentina

With a centralized and highly personalized presidency dominating Argentine politics, its party system is rather weak. The parties never have stood for a coherent set of principles; hence, they have not functioned to structure political debate in that country. The Peronists in particular have not stood for much beyond their fealty to one individual whose own political principles were never clear or consistent. They supported Perón in his leftist phase, when he came to power with the backing of labor and as the leader of Argentina's have-nots, and supported him again in 1973, when he turned toward the right.

Meanwhile, the Radicals have also been less than coherent and consistent. Their party, the UCR, began as essentially the opposition to the conservative economic elite that had dominated Argentine politics up to the time that the UCR was founded by Yrigoyen in 1890. Although, with its middle-class support, the UCR was clearly against the cattle baron elite, it was less specific as to what it was for. Its rhetoric used a concept of nationalism that was a vague reflection of some aspects of the dependency perspective, advocating greater control of multinational corporations, independence from control by the International Monetary Fund or World Bank, and greater foreign policy independence. However, this rhetoric did not have much of an impact on what Radical presidents actually did, except for nationalizing all

petroleum production. A second part of its rhetoric involved the term *intransigence,* which seemed to mean opposition to the compromises that electoral alliances entail. However, this insistence on preserving the ideological purity of the Radicals appeared curious in light of the fact that little ideological coherence existed to be preserved and, in practice, the entailments of this term did not always affect electoral strategy. The Radical Frondizi was elected President under this label in 1958 largely because of a deal with Perón.

Because it was so thoroughly coopted by Peronism, Argentine labor has been impeded in exercising an effective, independent influence on behalf of its workers. On the other hand, labor in Argentina, compared with other movements in the region, is a large, well financed, and politically active movement.

The military has been one of the most significant groups in Argentine society, either directly taking over the reigns of government on half a dozen occasions since 1930, or directly influencing or constraining a civilian government with the ever-present threat of a coup. Moreover, several of the elected presidents have been military men, including, of course, Perón himself, and the military exercised an effective veto over national policy in the Frondizi administration. The public acceptance of this military role in Argentine political history suggests that despite its relatively well-educated, urbanized, and in many ways Westernized population, Argentina's political culture is not conducive to Western values of liberal democracy. Not only was Peronist populism at its essence in conflict with modern liberal democracy, as populism tends to be, but his regime was curiously friendly and sympathetic to the Axis during World War II and even to the most notorious Nazi war criminals after the war. The Argentines put up with the most recent junta, which carried on one of the most notorious wars of repression against its own people ever seen in the Western Hemisphere, when, following the killing of former President Aramburu by a left-wing guerrilla group, suspected leftists were systematically eliminated without a shred of due process of law. Some 30,000 people simply disappeared during this period. Finally, the cultism epitomized by Perón and more strikingly by his wife Evita suggests cultural traits not conducive to modern liberal democracy. Thus, the traits of social modernization noted at the beginning of this section do not necessarily indicate the presence of a cultural context conducive to a political system that is either modern or democratic. As with Mexico, Argentina appears to be at a critical juncture between authoritarian populism and modern democracy. The ability of the Menem government to rise above its Peronist heritage and produce real solutions to the problems of managing a complex, modern economy will determine the future of the country for decades to come.

BRAZIL: THE STRUGGLING COLOSSUS OF THE SOUTH

When Pedro, the son of the king of Portugal, became king of Brazil in 1822, the country became an independent monarchy, thereby differentiating itself from most of the other countries in the region that had to struggle for their independence from their colonial masters. This exemption from a lengthy and divisive war of independence gave Brazil not only relative stability for a century but also enhanced the legitimacy of the regime. The relatively enlightened policies of both Pedro and Pedro II helped establish a trust in the state that allowed for a strong presidency in Brazil's periods of civilian rule. The federalism that is part of the constitution proclaimed in 1889 is more of a formalistic na-

ture; the states exercise far less independent power than do those in the United States.

The overthrow of Pedro II by the military in 1889 was the first of several military-directed or -supported coups, and set the precedent for a strong, continuing element of praetorianism in Brazil's political history. The military supported and made possible a seizure of power in 1930 by Getúlio Vargas, who governed the nation until 1945 with the combination of mass support and authoritarian suppression that is so common in Latin America. Like Perón in Argentina, Vargas instituted a number of reforms to improve the material well-being of labor, such as minimum-wage and maximum-hour laws, that may have headed off the mobilization of the working class into a strong, independent political force. Much like the case in Argentina, labor remained obsequiously devoted to their president. While handing out benefits to the working class, Vargas suppressed opposition and ruled for a quarter of a century as "a benevolent dictator and legislated by decree."[35] Nevertheless, his populist appeal to the easily mobilized masses was undamaged by his defiance of the democratic rules of the game, which do not appear to have acquired much legitimacy among Brazil's working and marginalized classes. Hence, five years after the military, rightly alarmed that his populist following would render him uncontrollable, forced Vargas from office, he was reelected to the presidency, much as Perón rode his mass base into power after a period in exile.

Vargas proved unable to deal with the complexities of managing the economy of the nation; inflation rose rapidly and corruption appeared among his closest associates, including charges that an aide was involved in an assassination attempt against an opposition journalist. Once again the military demanded his resignation. Vargas, apparently unable to cope with being forced out of office a second time, killed himself.

His successor, Juscelino Kubitschek, entered office with a promise to modernize Brazil quickly. He borrowed large sums of money to build a number of symbols of modernity, such as hydroelectric projects, universities, airports, and even a lavish new capital city, Brasilia. This is an all-too-frequent phenomenon among Third World leaders—going into debt to finance *symbols* of modernity that do not generate a proportionate growth in the gross domestic product, and that instead leave their nation with a mountain of debt and a resultant wave of uncontrollable inflation. This is what happened to Kubitschek's effort; hence, in the 1960 election, he was replaced by Jânio Quadros, who ran on a pledge to balance the budget.

Quadros, however, was beset with the personal difficulties of alcoholism and mental instability, and resigned within a year. Unfortunately for Brazil, his vice president was the man who the military had forced to resign as labor minister under Vargas, João Goulart. Goulart turned out to be a militant leftist who appointed Marxists to key posts, legalized the Communist Party, pursued agrarian reform, and promoted economic policies that produced ever higher levels of inflation. Once again, the military stepped in and saved the nation from what they saw as a disastrous electoral error. The final straw in Goulart's downfall was his challenge to the authority of the ultimately powerful military.

For the next two decades, Brazil was governed by a military junta led by a succession of officers. Political parties were abolished, and potentially critical politicians were sent into exile, especially those with a leftist orientation. Freedom of the press was suppressed. This suppression of civil liberties and democratic values seems to have been tolerated by Brazilians as long as the junta was able to engineer economic prosperity, which they did for nearly a decade. Until 1973, growth averaged 10 percent a year.

However, in 1973, OPEC drove up the price of crude petroleum geometrically and with it the price of energy. Economic crisis ensued, and the legitimacy and support for the generals began to evaporate. Much of the organized verbal attack on the regime came from the Catholic Church, many members of which, as discussed above, had begun to side with the less affluent masses under the impact of Liberation Theology.

In any event, the Brazilian military oligarchy itself took the lead in the country's transformation to democracy, according to the model outlined in Samuel Huntington's landmark treatise on democratization in the twentieth century.[36] The military itself had been divided between a more hard-line, repressive wing and the so-called Sorbonne group, which was more moderate. The latter group was in power under President Ernesto Geisel and his successor, President João Baptista de Figueiredo, resulting in the establishment of an indirectly elected civilian president, José Sarney, in 1985. A new constitution was approved in 1988. Sarney was unable to solve the nation's economic problems and his support virtually disappeared, leading to the election of a new president, Fernando Collor de Mello, in 1989. Collor's appeal was the essentially populist one frequently encountered in Latin America, with a distrust of traditional institutions and a direct, charismatic following among the masses. Such populist leaders do not come up through a party structure but rather create their own party. Such an absence of what we called in Chapter 2 "a structure of accountability" can easily lead to abuses of the authority of office. In Collor's case, widespread corruption led to his impeachment in 1992. He was replaced by his vice president, Itamar Franco, who opted to stimulate growth rather than control inflation, which hovered around 40 percent per month. In the face of such unsustainable policies, Franco was replaced in January 1995 by Fernando Enrique Cardoso. Cardoso, a Social Democrat, the third Brazilian president since the military stepped down, had to allocate political plums in his cabinet to members of the largest party, the Brazilian Democratic Movement.[37] He vowed to reduce inequalities in health care and education but at the same time to accelerate the privatization of Brazilian industries. Meanwhile, in the last six months of Franco's regime and continuing into the Cardoso regime, the rate of inflation has slowed to around 12 percent per year. Although begun in the twilight of the Franco regime, the anti-inflation plan was created by Cardoso.[38] Certainly getting the rate of inflation under control is a crucial element in avoiding another takeover by the Brazilian military, which is always lurking not far from the center of power.

Major Political Actors and Forces in Brazil

Although Brazil has only had one military junta, it lasted 21 years. Moreover, in addition to actually governing the country from 1964 to 1985, the military has been a constant threat to the tenure of civilian presidents, who ruled at the sufferance of the military. In this sense, Brazil qualifies as a praetorian state. Earlier, for instance, the military had been instrumental in driving Vargas from power.

The Brazilian party system is unlike the party systems of the West. Numerous small parties with inchoate ideological bases and weak legitimacy have sprung up for the sole purpose of supporting the political ambitions of a potential leader. Nineteen parties received seats in the legislature in the last election, and the party of the new president, Fernando Cardoso, has taken on the center-right cast of its leader, despite the leftist implications of its Social Democratic name. Frequent name changes, splitting, and consolidation of parties over the years have made

the Brazilian system difficult to follow. For example, the government party in the early 1990s was called ARENA (National Renovating Alliance), but it became first the National Democratic Union, by which name it was known when it was the main opposition to Vargas, and later the Democratic Social Party (to be distinguished from Cardoso's Social Democratic Party), with a middle-class appeal.

Clearly, the future of Brazilian democracy depends on several factors, including the strength and legitimacy of its institutions. Even its party system is poorly institutionalized as parties rise and fall, serving as the personal vehicle for whatever charismatic leader happens to arise. With Brazil not having a long history as a democratic nation, its constitution becomes an important vehicle for giving democratic legitimacy to its structures and procedures. The Brazilian constitution of 1989 is a long, unwieldy document and the seventh since independence, so the quesion of regime is far from settled. With 245 articles, the constitution is one of the world's longest. It includes details of policy that will almost certainly require modification and that will certainly displease certain interests within the population. For example, it places a ceiling on interest rates.[39] Recall that a constitution is supposed to separate what is fundamental—the essence or very nature of the kind of system it defines—from what is a policy resolution of particular circumstances, and ought to be adaptable as needs and situations change. While some interests will oppose any policy that allocates values to some interests rather than others, all parts of society ought to respect that which defines the nature of the system. By incorporating policy into the constitution, Brazil renders it unlikely that the document will be respected by all parts of the society. This failure to separate the fundamental from the circumstantial virtually guarantees that the nature of the system itself will continue to be a political question.

Problems and Prospects

In addition to the unresolved problems of constitutional instability, including the question of regime and the continuing role of the military as a political force looking over the shoulder of every Brazilian president, Brazil faces some serious social and economic problems that are likely to explode as passionately felt issues in the foreseeable future. Among the most serious of these is widespread, abject poverty. Poor Brazilians often live in incredibly poor, crime-ridden shantytowns, or *favelas,* on the edge of the cities. The inhabitants are called *marginals,* reflecting the subsistence level or below at which they live. Meanwhile, wealthy Brazilians live sumptuously.[40] Moreover, economic well-being correlates strongly with race; the rich are overwhelmingly white, while the poor are predominantly black or native. Although in 1988, Brazilians celebrated the centennial of the end of slavery, in 1990 blacks still earned 40 percent less than whites in the same professions.[41]

Meanwhile, assaults on the land and civilization of Brazil's remaining but diminishing native or Indian population have been accelerating with the attempted economic expansion into parts of the interior, such as the Amazon Valley, that had been their last refuge. Only about 200,000 Indians remain in Brazil.

The expansion into the Amazon Valley in a desperate attempt by peasants and developers to carve an economic niche for themselves is rapidly threatening the survival of one of the world's last rain forests, whose disappearance would be a worldwide ecological disaster. As predicted from Ronald Inglehart's theory of value change discussed extensively above, the wealthy may be interested in ecological issues, but the question of food predominates the concerns of Brazil's massive numbers of marginalized peoples. However, the assault on the rain forest will continue to exacerbate tensions between Brazil and nations of the West, whose people are postmaterialist and do care about such issues as the rain forest.

The poorly established legitimacy of the nation's fundamental institutions is a product of Brazil's history of regime instability, of praetorianism, and of the repeated appearance of populist leaders with a charismatic rather than a party or institutional base of legitimacy and support. Meanwhile, serious social issues born of massive inequality correlated with race loom on the horizon. It is unclear whether the fledgling and poorly legitimized institutions of Brazil's democracy can withstand the divisive impact of such conflicts when and if they explode.

CONCLUSION: THE PROSPECTS FOR DEMOCRATIZATION IN LATIN AMERICA

In the complex and variegated region called Latin America, political democracy does seem to be waxing as the wave of the future. In some places, such as Costa Rica and Uruguay, democracy seems to be well established. In others, it is struggling to find roots. The question is whether the contextual patterns in these other places are conducive to the survival of democratic institutions.

Among the common patterns found in the systems we have examined, populism appears to be prevalent. Although epitomized by Juan Perón in Argentina, numerous other leaders, such as Mexico's Luis Echeverría or Brazil's Getúlio Vargas, fit this category. Populism, based as it is on a direct charismatic linkage between the leader and the masses, is not conducive to the institutionalized structure of accountability that is at the heart of modern democracy (as discussed in Chapter 2). Charisma as a basis of legitimacy has long been held to be an attribute associated with less "developed" political systems.[42]

Parties in such systems have tended to be attached to the charismatic leader and to function as a tool for that leader to mobilize support, instead of being independent structures able to perform the functions that parties are expected to perform in the democracies of the West.[43] Compared to parties in the West, Latin American parties have less continuity in the sense of lasting through time, and their names do not carry the same ideological and programmatic entailments as do parties with the same or parallel names in the West. Cardoso's Social Democratic Party in Brazil illustrates this point.

Political institutions in Latin America in general have a weaker legitimacy than do those in the West. This weak institutional legitimacy has a reciprocal relationship to the recurring phenomenon of a charismatic leader discussed above. It is also related to the strong, ever-present influence of the military found in so many Latin nations.[44] Praetorianism—the failure to establish civilian control of the military—has become so characteristic of Latin American political history that by the end of 1977, 14 of the Latin American countries were actually under military control (in addition to those in which the military was not actually in power but exercised a disproportionate influence on the nominally civilian government).[45]

While democratic constitutions have become in vogue in Latin America, for them to function according to democratic norms, a context of democratic values is required. It is clear that Latin America varies spatially and temporally with respect to such values. However, many stereotypically Latin American cultural attributes are not very conducive to political democracy as we know it. For example, only within the past few decades has the influential Catholic Church altered its traditional authoritarian stance. Of course, Liberation Theology may be changing all that, although its long-term effect on cultural norms remains to be seen.

Meanwhile, machismo has been an almost uniquely Latin American value that constitutes a direct challenge to the democratic values of egalitarianism. Half of the citizens, women, are effectively barred from the political process and from making a contribution to the gross domestic product. Furthermore, the *macho* attitude toward women makes control of population growth more difficult, a problem that, while less acute in recent decades, has not by any means disappeared.

Thus, recent decades have seen a move away from the contextual attributes of Latin America that have until now rendered the establishment of stable, effective democracy more difficult and less probable in this area than in the nations of the West. Yet, these elements have not disappeared. It is still difficult to get a conviction for the violence and physical abuse that is routinely perpetrated upon women in Brazil, where this problem is perhaps worse than anywhere else. Overall, the status of women in Latin America is still far behind their status in the West. Population growth is much lower than it was a decade ago, but it is still much higher than in the West. Liberation Theology has attacked the authoritarian attitudes of the Catholic Church, but it has split rather than dominated the church elite. Although throughout Latin America, government has been returned to civilian control, the strength of the military in the praetorian states of the region remains intact, and rule by juntas is still far too recent to declare military takeover in Latin America a thing of the past.

Therefore, consistent with the title of this volume, Latin America is not only a variegated but a rapidly changing region. The changes that are occurring or have occurred would seem to be conducive to the success of the new wave of democratic constitutions. Whether these changes are adequate to allow these new democratic constitutions to flourish and endure is a question that can only be answered from a longer perspective. It is far too early to tell.

NOTES

1. Lawrence Graham, *The State and Policy Outcomes in Latin America* (New York and Westport, CT: Praeger and Hoover Institute Press, 1990).

2. Howard Wiarda and Henry Kline, "The Latin American Tradition and Process of Development," in Howard Wiarda and Henry Kline, eds., *Latin American Politics and Development*, 3rd ed. (Boulder, CO: Westview Press, 1990), pp. 6ff.

3. Samuel Huntington, *The Third Wave: Democratization in the Late Twentieth Century* (Norman: University of Oklahoma Press, 1991).

4. Wiarda and Kline, "Latin American Tradition," p. 2.

5. *Ibid.*, p. 24.

6. Martin Needler, *The Problem of Democracy in Latin America* (Lexington, MA: D. C. Heath Lexington Books, 1987), pp. 12–13.

7. James Petras and Morris Morley, *Latin America in the Time of Cholera: Electoral Politics, Market Economics, and Permanent Crisis* (London and New York: Routledge, 1992), see esp. chap. 3; Susan Bodenheimer, "Dependency and Imperialism: The Roots of Underdevelopment," in K. T. Fann and Donald Hodges, eds., *Readings in U.S. Imperialism* (Boston: Porter Sargeant, 1971).

8. John J. Johnson, "The Latin American Military," in John J. Johnson, ed., *The Role of the Military in Underdeveloped Countries* (Princeton: Princeton University Press, 1962), p. 92.

9. Michael Coniff, ed., *Latin American Populism in Comparative Perspective* (Albuquerque: University New Mexico Press, 1982), pp. 22–23.

10. George Blanksten, "Latin America," in Gabriel Almond and Sidney Verba, eds., *The Politics of the Developing Areas* (Princeton: Princeton University Press, 1960), p. 503.

11. Edwin Lieuwen, "Militarism and Politics in Latin America," in Johnson, ed., *Role of the Military*, pp. 131–32.

12. Peter Snow and Gary Wynia, "Argentina: Politics in a Conflict Society," in Wiarda and Kline, *Latin American Politics*, p. 129.

13. Lucien Pye, "Armies in the Process of Modernization," in Johnson, ed., *Role of the Military*, is the classic discussion of the modernizing role of the military. Cf. Samuel Huntington's discussion of modernizing regimes in Guatemala, El Salvador, and Bolivia in his *Political Order in Changing Societies* (New Haven: Yale University Press, 1968), p. 261.

14. Needler, op. cit.

15. Huntington, *The Third Wave*, pp. 22–23.

16. Gordon Richards, "Stabilization Crises and the Breakdown of Military Authoritarianism in Latin America," *Comparative Political Studies*, vol. 18, no. 4 (January 1986), pp. 449–86; Huntington, *The Third Wave*, p. 52.

17. See Population Reference Bureau, *1994 World Population Data Sheet*.

18. For a statement of Liberation Theology by one of its seminal proponents, see Gustavo Gutiérrez, *Teología de la liberación*, trans. and ed. Sister Caridad Inda and John Eagleson (Maryknoll, NY: Orbis Books, 1968 and 1973); and Gustavo Gutiérrez, "Toward a Theology of Liberation," in Alfred Hennelly, ed., *Liberation Theology: A Documentary History* (Marknoll, NY: Orbis Books, 1990), pp. 62–76. Cf. Julio de Santa Ana, *Good News to the Poor: The Challenge of the Poor in the History of the Church* (Maryknoll, NY: Orbis Books, 1979).

19. John Burdick, "The Progressive Church in Latin America; Giving Voices or Listening to Voices," *Latin American Research Review*, vol. 29, no. 1 (1994), p. 184–98.

20. Daniel Levine, *Popular Voices in Latin American Catholicism* (Princeton: Princeton University Press, 1990). See also Edward Cleary and Hannah Gambino, eds., *Conflict and Competition: The Latin Church in a Changing Environment* (Boulder, CO: Lynne Rienner, 1992); and H. E. Hewlitt, *Base Christian Communities in Brazil* (Lincoln: University of Nebraska Press, 1991).

21. Peggy Lovell, "Race Gender and Development in Brazil," *Latin American Research Review*, vol. 29, no. 3 (1994), pp. 7–35.

22. Population Reference Bureau, *1994 World Population Data Sheet*.

23. Coniff, *Latin American Populism*, pp. 40–42.

24. Needler, *Problem of Democracy*, p. 69.

25. See the discussion in *The Economist*, January 7, 1995, pp. 31–32.

26. Marcus Ethridge and Howard Handelman, *Politics in a Changing World* (New York: St. Martin's Press, 1994), p. 482.

27. *Facts on File*, 1994, p. 99.

28. See the discussion in *Newsweek*, March 6, 1995, p. 39.

29. Jorge Dominguez and James McCann, "Shaping Mexico's Electoral Arena: The Construction of Partisan Cleavages in the 1988 and 1991 National Elec-

tions," *American Political Science Review*, vol. 89, no. 1 (March 1995), p. 34.

30. Ibid., pp. 45–56.

31. David Tamarin, "Yrigoyen and Perón: The Limits of Argentine Populism," in Coniff, *Latin American Populism*, pp. 30–33.

32. Snow and Wynia, "Argentina," p. 138.

33. Marisa Navarro, "Evita's Charismatic Leadership," in Coniff, *Latin American Populism*, pp. 58–59.

34. *The Economist*, vol. 33, December 10, 1994, p. 13.

35. Donald Worcester and Wendell Schaeffer, *The Growth and Culture of Latin America* (New York: Oxford University Press, 1958), p. 860.

36. Huntington, *The Third Wave*, pp. 131–32.

37. *The Economist*, vol. 333, (November 26, 1994), pp. 73–74.

38. *The Economist*, vol. 333 (December 24, 1994), pp. 43–44.

39. Ieda Sigueira Wiarda, "Brazil: The Politics of Order and Progress," in Wiarda and Kline, eds., *Latin American Politics*, pp. 192–93.

40. This analysis of poverty in Brazil draws upon Michael Roskin, *Countries and Concepts*, 4th ed. (Englewood Cliffs, NJ: Prentice Hall, 1992), pp. 324–25.

41. See Global Studies, *Latin America* (Guilford, CT: Dushkin Publishing Co., 1994), p. 68.

42. See, e.g., Lucien Pye, "The Non-Western Political Process," *Journal of Politics*, vol. 28, no. 3 (August 1958), pp. 468–86; and Max Weber, *The Theory of Social and Economic Organization*, ed., Talcott Parsons (New York: The Free Press, 1947), p. 328.

43. For a discussion of these functions, see Lawrence Mayer, *Comparative Political Inquiry* (Homewood, IL: The Dorsey Press, 1972), pp. 240–44.

44. Samuel Huntington, *Political Order in Changing Societies* (New Haven: Yale University Press, 1968), p. 200.

45. Wiarda and Kline, *op. cit.*, "Conclusions," *op. cit.*, p. 582.

12

Conclusions: Trends and Prospects in a Changing World

The world has experienced a bewildering avalanche of change of the most fundamental nature beginning in 1989, change that has transformed the nature of the political world as we have known it. The field of comparative politics has been trying to make sense of these changes even as that field has itself been emerging from a fundamental transformation of its own. The collapse of the Iron Curtain, then of the Communist governments behind that mythical barrier, and then of the Soviet Union itself ended the bipolar superpower rivalry that had defined the entire postwar era. Leaders and structures that had become apparently permanent fixtures on the world's stage in the 1980s, people such as Margaret Thatcher and Mikhail Gorbachev, and parties such as the Communist Party of the Soviet Union, the Social Democrats of Sweden, the Christian Democrats of Italy, and the Liberal Democrats of Japan, found themselves driven from a power base on which they had seemingly acquired a hegemonic hold.

Meanwhile, a wave of democratization has swept the world. By some estimates, as much as 70 percent of the world's people now live under democratic formats, as authoritarian and praetorian regimes have been displaced by popularly elected systems. In the early 1980s, it was still possible to write that the Marxist-Leninist model of development was the most popular one among Third World elites. However, the 1980s not only saw the collapse of the Soviet Empire into a set of independent states, many of whom installed a democratic constitution, but also the rapid spread of democratic regimes among the former praetorian and authoritarian regimes of Latin America. These new democracies to a significant extent lack many of the attributes formerly identified in social science literature as requisites of democracy. This may indicate that these supposed requisites are attributes of Western society not required for democratic processes elsewhere in the world, or time may show that while democratic formats can be installed anywhere, it is quite another matter to have such formats consolidated and legitimated over time.

The changes that reshaped the world of politics as we have known it were as unexpected to the academic community as they were to the world at large. Despite the claims of the new comparative analysis to have been transformed to a predictive science, we are unaware of any scholar who predicted the aforementioned transformations of the phenomena on which they ostensibly possess expert knowledge. Thus, we have described an attempt to prescribe the explanatory and predictive methods of modern science for the field of comparative politics, and we then went on to document the transformation of the political world in a way and to an extent that the transformed field could neither predict nor even retroactively explain. This raises the question of whether the attempt to apply the methods of modern science with which we introduced this volume has been proven futile by the events that we have described. Is the "modern" systematic attempt to develop empirical, explanatory theory about politics of any use in trying to make sense of this bewilderingly transformed world of politics?

MODERN COMPARATIVE POLITICAL ANALYSIS: FACT OR FICTION?

We have discussed the attempt to transform the field in fundamental ways. The substantive material presented in the main body of this text should reflect the nature and extent of this transformation. The main elements of this transformation are as follows: the redefinition of the goals of comparative analysis from description to explanation, the search for patterns in political phenomena and events and the consequent treatment of such phenomena generically rather than idiosyncratically (as being unique), a greater effort to render truth claims accountable to sensory data and thereby to reduce the subjective component of such assertions, and the attempt to expand the field both geographically and conceptually.

The geographical expansion of the field involved abandoning the ethnocentric bias of the fixation of comparativists of the traditional school on the so-called major powers of Europe. This expansion is reflected not only by the inclusion of a discussion of the Third World but also by the frequent refer-

ences in the theory chapters to the smaller European democracies.

It is the conceptual expansion of the field that the present volume most clearly reflects. One may conveniently view modern political analysis as having three basic components—the context of politics, the structures and processes of politics, and the public policies that emanate from the first two components. What we call context refers to the setting in which human behavior and therefore politics occur. Contextual factors include the set of historical experiences that shape a political system, the structure of social and economic cleavages that group and divide individuals in any system, and the cultural setting of politics. The analysis of these factors was formerly relegated to the fields of history, sociology, and psychology. It was only with the postwar emphasis on an explanatory discipline that their causal impact on politics became obvious. The analysis of the various nations that we have presented should make it obvious that one cannot understand the operation of the constitutionally designated structures and processes of any political system without analyses of these contextual factors. The impact of Britain's lengthy history on its contemporary politics, the background and continuing impact of the Revolution on contemporary France, the tribal and colonial past of Nigeria, and the deeply rooted multicultural backgrounds in the former Soviet Union that have reasserted themselves are all examples of the profound impact of contextual factors on contemporary politics that we have studied.

We encountered in Chapter 9, however, a growing literature that rejects inferences about the causal impact of contextual factors, especially when they are typical in the West. This literature is frequently associated with the call to focus once again on the state. This position argues that political outcomes, such as the decision to install a democratic civilian regime, are the result of choices, actions, and coalition formations among political actors rather than being "determined" by contextual factors. The patterns of relationships between contextual factors and political outcomes still suggest, however, that while political behaviors result from choices by political actors, such choices are apparently constrained by the context in which they occur.

The discovery of the relevance of contextual factors led to a state of affairs in which a focus on such factors became identified with a modern, social scientific approach. The rush to analyze contextual factors resulted in a neglect of the state, the center of which presumably distinguishes political science from related social sciences. The analysis of contextual factors is not an end in itself; it is a tool to explain the political world in which we, as political scientists, are ultimately interested. Thus, after decades of focusing on these contextual factors to the near exclusion of political institutions and processes, leading comparativists have been announcing the rediscovery of the importance of the state.[1]

This does not mean that comparative political analysis has come full circle back to its traditional roots. The rediscovery of the state clearly does not mean that a concern with contextual factors has been abandoned. The study of political culture, for example, has been recently experiencing something of a renaissance of its own, as in the work of scholars like Ronald Inglehart, who once again demonstrates the impact of cultural factors on political outcomes.[2] Cultural attributes, we have shown, develop out of the experiences of each society or nation. These attributes, which constitute something like a world view or perspective through which the people of a society tend to view and interpret events, differ from one society to another and tend to be quite persistent. Our analysis of postwar Germany and of Third World systems suggests that it is difficult to engineer significant shifts in the cultural attributes of adult individuals during their own lives. Rather, as Inglehart's data suggest, cultural change is more likely to be generational in nature. That is, a new generation, growing up in a different context, may acquire cultural perspectives that differ from those of their parents or forefathers. Thus, we saw that the generation of Germans who formed the adult population of that nation through World War II continued, for a couple of decades after the fall of the Nazi regime, with public knowledge of all of its deeds, to articulate cultural orientations that were supportive of that regime. The much heralded remaking of the German culture—the widespread support for democracy and its values—began in the late 1960s to early 1970s, when the population began to be dominated by the generation raised in the postwar era. In short, it is not so much that former Nazis became democrats as that their children were more likely to be democrats. Similarly, we saw that the early stages of modernization in the Third World are characterized by a cultural dualism in which the population is divided between people with fairly modern orientations and attributes (frequently, a newer generation in the cities) and people with more traditional orientations and attributes (frequently, an older generation in the countryside).

While the impact of culture has been well established, no one factor or class of factors is sufficient in and of itself to explain complex political outcomes. Any one of the contextual factors may explain part of the variation among complex political systems. We have tried to make the case that political phenomena are in part a function of factors external to the political system—as in the exploitation explanation of underdevelopment—and in part a function of attributes intrinsic to the system—as in cultural explanations. Some political outcomes appear to be the result of unique historical experiences, such as the impact of the revolution of 1789 on subsequent French history. Yet as numerous scholars such as Crane Brinton, Theda Skocpol, and Harry Eckstein have demonstrated, it is possible to find patterns among otherwise unique revolutions. Revolutions occur in the presence of the fiscal poverty of a regime, a heightened degree of social and political awareness among the masses, and a heightened degree of intellectual freedom and activity directed largely against the system itself. Systems tend to fall victim to revolutions when political repression has been relaxed. Subsequent to these early studies, rigorous statistical analyses of a variety of indicators by the Feierabends, Nesvold, Hibbs, and Gurr identified the most significant correlates of civil violence, which were psychological, economic, and structural factors. Thus, while the events of 1989–91 in Eastern Europe and the former Soviet Union demonstrate that we cannot definitively predict the occurrence of a particular revolution at a particular time, we can stipulate the conditions under which revolution becomes significantly more likely. An analysis of the last years of the Soviet Union would reveal many of the conditions that Brinton and others delineated as associated with the likelihood of system breakdown, such as the impoverishment of the government and the desertion of the intellectuals. Thus, in retrospect, modern comparative analysis does help us explain these apparently unpredicted events. Perhaps even more clearly, the violence literature suggests conditions that help account for the instability and violence in Yugoslavia and parts of the old Soviet Empire in the post–Soviet era, such as the difficulty in establishing regime legitimacy while trying to resolve very difficult socioeconomic problems and ethnic-religious crises. It should be recalled that capitalism evolved in the West over a long period, during which severe socioeconomic disloca-

tions were encountered. It was, after all, the desperate conditions of the working poor in nineteenth-century England that nourished the ideas of Karl Marx in the first place. The hardships that may result from the sudden imposition of the market, a system that produces winners and losers, on a peasant society that has become accustomed to a guaranteed minimal if low standard of material well-being, will make the acquisition of legitimacy for any regime difficult indeed. Eastern European governments have tried both to cushion the impact of the transition to market economics with guaranteed levels of well-being and to waffle on their commitment to the privatization of the means of production. On the first point, the Hungarians, for instance, claim to have introduced a "social market economy," a term that approaches the status of an oxymoron to the extent that it connotes a market system with only winners and no losers. On the second point, Eastern European governments have tried to hold on to 85 percent or more of their assets and to dole them out as political capital.[3] The literature on violence and on modernization suggests that the tasks of modernization, which are still facing the former Soviet republics to a large extent, despite the facade of superpower military capabilities, will be very difficult to carry out without a legitimate regime capable of exercising authority and imposing hardships on individuals without generating high levels of regime or system alienation.

The point is that we have partial explanations of these phenomena; the theorizing about revolutions isolates some of the common factors—what Harry Eckstein calls the preconditions—of revolution. Such theorizing does not offer generalizations about the unique catalysts that ignite a particular revolutionary conflagration—what Eckstein calls the precipitants.[4] One cannot predict when a Lenin, a Gorbachev, a Robespierre, or another revolutionary firebrand will appear, or when an obscure, deranged sociopath will assassinate a public figure, but one can predict the kinds of contexts in which such figures are more likely to threaten a regime. Thus, the revolutionary changes in Eastern Europe and the former Soviet Union in 1989–91 can be addressed with the same kind of partial explanation that was discussed in Chapter 1.

Furthermore, the extensive literature that we examine on the social and cultural requisites of democracy in Chapters 2 through 5 still seems to provide a basis for deriving expectations about the prospects for democracy in those former Warsaw Pact nations that have recently overthrown Communist authoritarianism. While the presence and political strategies of such men as Lech Walesa in Poland, combined with the actions and incompetence of the regimes they displaced, may have been the proximate cause of the collapse of the old authoritarian orders, the choices and strategies of particular actors seem to us to be more precipitants that brought about the transition to democracy at one point in time instead of another, rather than the underlying causes that allowed that transition or that will permit a democratic regime to gain legitimacy and last over time.

In the first place, it was suggested that democracy is more likely to flourish when material essentials can be more or less taken for granted by the great preponderance of the population and when not too much is at stake in the electoral competition. In such cases, tolerance of opposition and a lack of government oppression become rational. However, the outcome of struggles for existence, such as those between the Muslim Azerbaijanis and their Christian Armenian neighbors, between the Bosnian Serbs and their Muslim neighbors in the former Yugoslavia, between the Israeli and Arab residents of the former British mandate of Palestine, between the Russian nationalists and the proponents of cultural autonomy in

Chechnya, or over the distribution of critically scarce resources of food and medicine in Russian, are not readily resolved by majority vote. In questions between zealous true believers involving conflicting conceptions of the one true religion, or in questions involving the allocation of critically scarce essential resources, the losers are unlikely to accept the outcome because of a mere vote. Hence, the heady expectations that the collapse of Communism was likely to lead directly to the establishment of the first genuine Russian democracy may turn out to be excessively optimistic. Indeed, President Yeltsin of Russia was not moving eagerly toward the establishment of a democracy, as that term is understood in the West, and indeed appears to many to be taking on the attributes of increasingly autocratic or at least incompetent rule under the pressures of the revolt in Chechnya and growing internal dissatisfaction with the deplorable state of the Russian economy.

A WORLD OF CHANGE

The momentous transformations of the postwar world constitute a challenge for modern political analysis. It was shown in Chapter 1 that explanatory analysis requires a precise definition of the concepts being examined. The analysis of the causes and impact of change in the world of politics might therefore begin with an examination of the nature of change in that world.

Change may conveniently be categorized into two broad types—progressive change, in which new patterns and structures are sought and implemented in the hope of improving the existing situation, and regressive change, in which a return to some real or apocryphal previous state of affairs is sought and in which traditional values are reasserted. Modernization would be one clear example what we mean by progressive change. Such change is not self-evidently "good." Indeed, we have stated the case that rapid modernization is likely to lead to increases in the level of domestic violence. The transition to democracy would constitute the most widespread example of what we mean by progressive change. Such change may not be permanent or "linear," that is, in one direction. Indeed, the 1930s and the 1960s were two eras in which the dominant trend was in the opposite direction, from democratic to authoritarian regimes, and some of the newly established "third wave" democracies will probably "regress" once again to authoritarian rule.

A major example of regressive change in the world today is what we have variously labeled as "cultural defense" or "the nationalities problem." By this we mean the assertion of autonomy and the preservation of distinctiveness by what had been a subcultural segment of a larger political unit. French Canadian nationalism, the cultural assertiveness of the Flemish and Walloons in Belgium, the Basque problem in Spain, and Scottish and Welsh nationalism in Great Britain have been outstanding examples of this phenomenon in the West. The electoral success of the *Bloc Québécois* in the 1993 Canadian general election attests to the undiminished alienation of the French Canadian subculture from the broader Canadian sense of community. It is in the recently collapsed Soviet Empire, however, that this phenomenon has been most strongly apparent in the 1990s. The continuing bloody conflict in the former Yugoslavia and the breakaway efforts of the Russian province of Chechnya are the latest manifestations of the strength of unresolved national irredentism in the area of the former Soviet Union. We have asserted in this volume and elsewhere that nationalism—a community's striving for autonomy and self-determination around the concept of a nation-state—may be one of the strongest ideological forces in the world today. A community connotes some shared values, ideals, and sense of some common heritage. We have suggested that self-defined communities will tend to strive for such autonomy and thereby function as a centrifugal force threatening the integrity of multi-ethnic communities. Research in progress by Ted Gurr and his associates suggests that democracies are more effective than authoritarian systems in absorbing these minority groups. This research further suggests that where the minorities constitute a distinct lower class, their grievances may not be resolved without significant costs to the dominant group; hence, the intensity of conflict over their grievances may be greater than with groups whose differences are based upon ethnicity alone. However, cultural differences usually are accompanied by the perception of unequal treatment by the dominant group, and cultural differences are inherently more difficult to compromise.

The agenda of the various subcultural groupings is another relevant factor in determining the intensity of conflict and the likelihood that the issues arising out of minority-group grievances will be successfully resolved. When the agenda envisions acceptance by the dominant group and integration into the dominant culture, the probability of realizing these goals will be greater than if the agenda envisions replacing the dominant group or culture and changing the essential nature of the system itself. The resistance to the demands of the French Canadians will be more intense to the extent that the other Canadians perceive that the French Canadian goal is to dismantle the Canadian federal system. To the extent that Israelis perceive that Palestinian elites still harbor the maximalist agenda of replacing the Jewish state with a Muslim or secular state, a resolution of the conflicts in that area is highly unlikely.

Ethnic or cultural conflicts will be more

difficult to resolve to the extent to which the dominant group does not recognize the legitimacy of the distinctive subcultural identity. The Marxian ideology of class conflict supposedly overrode all other forms of identification. With the ostensible triumph of the proletarian revolution in 1917, the Soviets created the fiction of their citizenry being psychologically and economically united under the proletarian banner. This provided the justification for the suppression of the diverse ethnicities that comprised the Soviet Empire, a suppression that could not have endured permanently. While no one predicted the demise of the Soviet Union as early and as completely as we have witnessed it, the foregoing assessment of the importance of "the nationalities problem" logically leads to the conclusion that the force of suppressed nationalism would eventually become a problem for the Soviet Empire. Not only the collapse of the Soviet Union but the continuing strife between the former component republics of that system—the struggle between the Muslim Azerbaijanis and the Christian Armenians; between the Serbs, Croats, Bosnian Serbs, Bosnian Muslims, and other formerly suppressed ethnic groupings within what was once Yugoslavia; and the rise of groups like Pamyat in the former Soviet Union, which represent a kind of Xenophobic and primordial nationalism, including traditional Slavic anti-Semitism—reinforce the conclusion about the difficulty of suppressing such diverse ethnicities over a long period. Certainly, the continuing difficulties that we have seen faced by those few who are striving to mold an integrated nation in Nigeria further reinforce these conclusions about the continuing, inescapable strength of the forces of subcultural defense and the nationalities problem. Most political leaders in that beleaguered nation are rather more interested in imposing the dominance of their particular subcultural unit over the other ethnic components of what we call Nigeria.

These conflicts raise what we think is the vital question of the importance of a sense of community for the long-term viability of a political system. The abuse of the sense of community, from the irrational "general will" of Rousseau to the "spirit of the folk" in the militant nationalism of the Nazis, has sometimes led to the too facile rejection of the concept of community altogether and to a celebration of the preservation of cultural diversity within a nation. It has become politically incorrect to favor assimilation over "multiculturalism." Yet, the experience of nations that have been unable to absorb old ethnic loyalties into some broader sense of national community, as seen in Belgium, Canada, the former Soviet Union and even its current Russian core, and Nigeria, should give pause to the strategy of abandoning the effort to establish some dominant and defining sense of national community in favor of a multiculturalism that accords all subcultural groupings equal status within a nation.

We are dealing here with old loyalties and identities that antedate the formation of the present nation-state and that compete with it for legitimacy and diffuse support. In many respects, these old ethnic and cultural loyalties entail values that are distinctly not modern. In the chapter on Germany, we learned of the characterization of the Third Reich as "a revolt against modernity," a yearning for some Dark Ages, Wagnerian utopia.[5] It is becoming obvious that the Third Reich was not the last rebellion against the rush of Western modernity. The expansionist wave of Islamic fundamentalism in the Middle East is another example of the aggressive rejection of modern values in favor of a return to a partially apocryphal and, some would say, atavistic past.

It may be that regressive change is, paradoxically, the "wave of the future." There is an apparent built-in legitimacy to the shared values of a real or imagined past that is hard to establish for some untried utopia of an imagined future. Certainly in recent years, the preponderance of radical movements for change have sought to reestablish old and lost values rather than to formulate new ones. Thus, the Serbian nationalist struggle in the former Yugoslavia is an attempt to resurrect old loyalties.

Clearly, the onrush of change poses enormous challenges for political institutions to adapt. We have seen democratic institutions that we had come to regard as immutable not only struggling to adapt to the stress and challenge of the rapidly changing world, but in fact themselves undergoing processes of fundamental change. The so-called crises of democracy posits an insolubility for many of the issues facing modern democratic states. We have seen several of the consequences of this struggle to adapt to a world of insoluble problems. This has been manifested in such trends as the decline of the impact of parties as the principles that defined their raison d'être were no longer relevant to the major issues of the postmaterialist era, a decline that has in turn been indicated by the phenomena of dealignment and realignment of voting publics. The increased vulnerability of many elites in democratic systems—indicated by such phenomena as successful votes of no confidence where no such motions had carried for nearly a century, seen in Britain, Australia, and Canada, or the fall from hegemonic control of the Scandinavian Social Democratic parties, the Italian Christian Democrats, the Japanese Liberal Democrats, and the Australian Liberal-Country coalition—may be a function of the inability of any modern government to go to its voting public and announce that it has successfully solved most of the major problems facing the country. The conventional wisdom about the advantages of incumbency may be offset by the fact that incumbents have to run to some extent on their record, which will be increasingly difficult to justify.

Meanwhile, institutions themselves have been changing to cope with the imperatives of rapid socioeconomic change. Under the pressure to govern decisively, parliamentary government evolved into cabinet government, which in Britain, under Margaret Thatcher, and in Germany, under Konrad Adenauer, evolved into prime ministerial or chancellor government. Parliamentary control of the political executive has generally been weakened throughout the Western world by the growing understanding that a parliamentary defeat on a major policy vote does not necessarily mean that the government is obligated to resign, an understanding that was reinforced in Britain by the government's acceptance of the December 6, 1994, defeat of the value added tax on fuel, an important part of the budget that once might have been assumed to present a question of confidence. Assembly-dominated parliamentary government in France became an autocratic presidency under Charles de Gaulle. The aforementioned decline in the relevance of political parties has been accompanied by what Guy Peters has called the "presidentialization" of parliamentary government, with the focus of politics being not on the party and its program but on the personality of a single leader.[6] Thus Britain was governed throughout the 1980s not so much by a Conservative government as by Thatcher. Her "un-British" autonomy, which was discussed in Chapter 3, was a function not only of her personal style but also of the imperatives of modern government that often cannot wait for a consensus to develop in a collegial style for governing. Thatcher's style in many ways approached a presidential style in the sense that the decision-making process was focused in a single leader and a few personally chosen advisers. However, "chancellor democracy" still characterizes the German system, despite the fact German chancellors since Adenauer, with the possible exception of Willy Brandt, could hardly be called charismatic figures. The French system has in fact focused on a single, powerful presidency, although none of de Gaulle's successors had his charisma. The American system continues to flounder under a decentralized check-and-balance system designed more to prevent the government from acting precipitously than to give it the capacity to respond to needs. However, the patience of the American public is waning with an ineffective government unable even to offer coherent policies that address, let alone solve, the major issues of the day. Thus, the failure of the Clinton administration to enact very much of its policy agenda, although the same party controlled the presidency and both houses of Congress for the first time in decades, led to a massive electoral rejection of that party in the congressional elections of 1994. Even this checked and balanced role of the American president has, however, become an extremely powerful one in the international arena; it is in the arena of domestic politics that the presidency is caught on a gridlock of proliferating veto groups. Thus, the pace of change in the present postindustrial era seems to create a need for centralized, effective government, a trend that appears to focus more on the personality of a single, powerful leader than on parties, programs, or ideas, and that may threaten some democratic values.

TECHNOLOGY AND CONVERGENCE

The imperatives of the pace of change and the problems and issues thereby generated in the postindustrial era are also manifested in the almost revolutionary growth in the state of technology. This growth entails an explosion in the amount of knowledge and information required to choose rationally among alternative courses of action in formulating public policy. The kinds of people who have traditionally gone into politics and who dominate the membership in national legislatures and even political executives are, for the most part, generalists. They are frequently lawyers, business leaders, occasionally academics or other intellectuals, and especially people who can make the best short, visual impression in the media. They are the kinds of people who are unlikely to understand the technical facts underlying any rational decision on the public safety—economic growth trade-offs in the formulation of environmental policy, or how to strike the optimum balance between insuring the safety of civil aviation and the costs that safety requirements generate for the consumer. The political figures who were elected on the basis of their political values, images, or promises to the electorate must defer policy choices to those who possess esoteric, specialized knowledge required for rational policy formulation in an advanced state of technology.

These people with such esoteric, specialized knowledge are frequently referred to as "technocrats." These technocrats, in effect, control the policy-making process. Since it is difficult to control and hold accountable individuals whose role is not understood, it is said that the effective power to choose among competing values and alternative courses of collective action has passed from "the people" to these technocrats; hence, instead of a democracy, it is said that we now have a *technocracy*—government by technocrats, people highly trained in a fairly narrow body of highly technical and advanced knowledge.[7]

Technocrats tend to be found in particular places in a political process—interest groups and large organizations, the form of which is called bureaucracy, including the higher levels of the public civil service. Because governments in modern and technologically advanced societies increasingly rely on these technocrats, effective decision making is increasingly being delegated by those chosen to be decision makers—such as heads of governments and legislators—to bureaucratic structures and organized interests. It has been noted that the higher civil service is playing an increasingly important role in the policy-making processes of the advanced industrial societies studied in this volume. The movement of interest groups into a cooperative role in the policy-making process through corporatist institutions is also becoming a fact of life to a greater or lesser extent in Western democracies.

These trends have also been true for the Communist-bloc countries as well. The Soviet Union developed one of the world's largest bureaucracies largely as an adaptation to the state's involvement in more and more areas. We have seen that bureaucracy works in ways characteristic of that organizational form to a large extent regardless of the setting in which the bureaucracy is found. Thus, the insulation from outside influence, the routinization, the impersonalization, and the isolated strata in the hierarchy characterized bureaucracies in Britain, France, and the old Soviet Union. We saw how the imperatives of advanced technology have involved the government in more and more aspects of public life, regardless of the nature of the political system or the ideologies underlying that system. Thus, while we noted the growth of bureaucratic involvement in public life in the Western democracies, we also noted the evolution of the Soviet system into a "bureaucratic authoritarianism" before it collapsed altogether. Thus, to the extent that bureaucracies have taken a larger role in decision-making processes, these processes will be similar in various nations, despite the differences in their constitutional formats and the values inherent in their respective cultures.

Meanwhile, we noted not only that the role of organized interests in the policy-making process tends not only to be unavoidable, even in those Western nations, such as France, that have an ideological antipathy toward them, but also that the role of interest groups grew even in the Soviet Union in its post-Stalin period.[8] This growth of interest group activity thus occurs even in settings where the culture emphasizes the value of community, a system defined by a single set of values in which the representation of particular interests is therefore less legitimate. Such group activity may therefore be one of the inexorable imperatives of an advanced industrial society.

We have therefore seen democratic theory and the structure of accountability modified in advanced industrial democracies in the West by the twin imperatives of bureaucratization and neo- or liberal corporatism in their political processes, and we have seen the phenomenon of dictatorship—government subject to the unrestrained will of a single leader (or even a small clique)—disappearing in many places into a sea of bureaucratization. It is in the smaller, simpler societies that are not beset with the imperatives of managing an economy and society at an advanced state of technology—places such as Libya, Iraq, or Iran—where dictatorship or messianic ideological leadership has not been supplanted by bureaucratization and the reliance on organized interests. It thus appears that in technologically advanced societies, the political processes are becoming similar despite constitutional and cultural differences. It is *not* clear, however, that advanced industrial systems are converging with respect to their dominant values, values that to a large extent determine the goals or policy objectives that a society sets for itself. One possible reservation to this dismissal of the idea of the convergence of values and goals is the growing popularity of the idea of democracy and perhaps of at least some of the values that the concept entails. Ultimately, however, we cannot predict the long-term impact of the convergence of processes on the values of the various systems.

In some cases, the values of a society may themselves prove to be an insurmountable obstacle to the process of modernization that is the foundation of advanced technology. These values emanated from and until recently have been endemic to what we call the West. The extent to which these values are transportable to other cultures is still unclear. The partial modernization and difficult transition to democratic and capitalist political and economic processes in the former Soviet Empire probably reflects the partial "Westernization" of that part of the world. The continuing clear and decisive rejection of Western values by the Islamic world (to a large extent irrespective of the differences within that world, as between the Sunni and Shiite Muslims) renders the adoption of Western political processes in that world highly unlikely.

A convergence—a growing similarity—in the political processes of advanced industrial societies does seem to be occurring. This convergence does not apply to the values that emanate from cultural differences. Industrial societies, therefore, despite some growing similarities in the processes by which decisions are made, will likely continue to vary with respect to the kinds of policy objectives they set for themselves. Moreover, industrialization itself will not occur uniformly in every setting. The modernization process out of which industrialization and advanced technology emanate presumes certain cultural attributes that are not present in many parts of the world. Culture tends to be a persistent factor resistant to change. In those societies that are less likely to modernize and develop advanced technology, the processes of bu-

reaucratization and the role of organized interests will not occur as they did in the West and to a lesser extent in the former Soviet Empire.

Values are not, however, immutable. Generational change is not only possible but, as we have seen, is a fact of life in many places. Moreover, we now live in what Immanuel Wallerstein has called a "world economic system,"[9] characterized by increasing levels of economic interdependence. Messianic mobilization systems such as those in Iran, Iraq, North Korea, or Maoist China cannot continue to live in isolation from the West that they may loathe. The imperatives of having to interact in that world system may have a longer range impact on the values of even these militantly anti-Western and antimodern systems. Chapter 8 showed some political and economic evolution of post-Maoist China. Forces for modernization remain active in that nation and ready to contest for succession to the present gerontocracy, despite the crackdown against the "prodemocracy" demonstrators in Beijing's Tiananmen Square in 1989. Even the mullahs in Iran have shown some interest in opening the doors to some economic interaction with the heretofore vilified West. The rigidly Communist North Koreans concluded some limited forms of cooperation in 1991 with their more Westernized neighbors in South Korea.

The broader question raised by this activity is the one of the long-term ability of these militantly anti-Western and hence antimodern (as that term is defined by Western values) systems to remain autonomous and resistant to the influence of these values while dealing in the world capitalist economic system. Thus far in such systems, the cycle has been of limited and tentative change, leading to the demand, largely by the younger generation, for faster and more fundamental change, followed by a reactionary crackdown, as in Tiananmen Square or in the attempted right-wing Soviet coup of 1990. Whether a broader convergence, including cultural values and a greater range of systems, is possible in the long run remains to be seen. Is democracy, with its attendant humane values, the wave of the future after all? Certainly, the task of comparative political analysts in ascertaining these emerging patterns and prospects is going to be more challenging than ever.

NOTES

1. For example, James Caporaso, ed., *The Elusive State* (Newbury Park, CA: Sage Publications, 1989); and Theda Skocpol, "Bringing the State Back In," *Items,* vol. 36, nos. 1–2 (June 1982). See also Theda Skocpol, *States and Social Revolutions* (Cambridge: Harvard University Press, 1979).

2. Most recently in his *Culture Shift in Advanced Industrial Democracies* (Princeton: Princeton University Press, 1990); and "The Renaissance of Political Culture," *American Political Science Review,* vol. 82, no. 4 (December 1988), pp. 1203–30.

3. See the analysis by Ivan Maiyor of the Institute of Economics of the Hungarian Academy of Sciences, "Why Eastern Europe Is Going Nowhere," *The Washington Post,* January 21, 1992, p. A21.

4. Harry Eckstein, "On the Etiology of Internal Wars," in Ivo and Rosalind Feierabend and Ted Gurr, eds., *Anger, Violence, and Politics* (Englewood Cliffs, NJ: Prentice Hall, 1972), pp. 13–15.

5. Henry Ashby Turner, "Fascism and Modernization," *World Politics,* vol. 24, no. 4 (June 1972), pp. 547–64.

6. Guy Peters, *European Politics Reconsidered* (New York: Holmes and Meier, 1991), p. 60.

7. This concept is fully developed in Daniel Bell, *The Coming of Post-Industrial Society* (New York: Basic Books, 1973).

8. For example, Andrew Janos, "Interest Groups in the Structure of Power: Critique and Comparisons," *Studies in Comparative Communisms,* vol. 12, no. 1 (Spring 1979), pp. 6–20; and Joel Schwartz and William Keech, "Group Influences and the Policy Processes in the Soviet Union," in Frederic Fleron, ed., *Communist Studies in the Social Sciences* (Chicago: Rand McNally, 1969).

9. Immanuel Wallerstein, *The Modern World System: Capitalist Agriculture and the Origins of the European World Economy in the Sixteenth Century* (New York: Academic Press, 1974).

Index

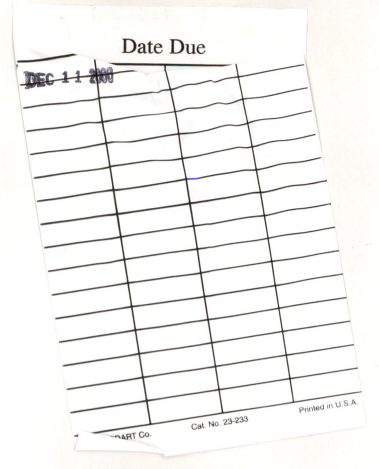

Date Due

DEC 11 2000

Printed in U.S.A.

DART Co.   Cat. No. 23-233